ST. MARY
ST. MARY

D0900263

THE LIBRARY
ST. MARY'S COLLEGE OF MARYLAND
ST. MARY'S CITY, MARYLAND

THE MOMENT AND LATE WRITINGS

KIERKEGAARD'S WRITINGS, XXIII

THE MOMENT

AND LATE WRITINGS

by Søren Kierkegaard

Edited and Translated
with Introduction and Notes by

Howard V. Hong and
Edna H. Hong

PRINCETON UNIVERSITY PRESS
PRINCETON, NEW JERSEY

Copyright © 1998 by Postscript, Inc.
Published by Princeton University Press,
41 William Street, Princeton, New Jersey 08540
In the United Kingdom: Princeton University Press, Chichester, West Sussex

All Rights Reserved

Library of Congress Cataloging-in-Publication Data

Kierkegaard, Søren, 1813–1855
[Øieblikket; Bladartikler 1854–55; Dette skal siges, saa være det da sagt;
Hvad Christus dømmer om officiel Christendom; and Guds Uforanderlighed. English]
The Moment and Late Writings / by Søren Kierkegaard;
edited and translated with introduction and notes by Howard V. Hong and Edna H. Hong.
p. cm. — (Kierkegaard's writings ; 23)
Translation of: Øieblikket; Bladartikler 1854–55; Dette skal siges, saa være det da sagt;
Hvad Christus dømmer om officiel Christendom; and Guds Uforanderlighed.
Includes bibliographical references and index.
ISBN 0-691-03226-2 (cloth)
1. Christianity and culture—Controversial literature.   2. Danske folkekirke—
Controversial literature.   3. Mynster, Jakob Peter, 1775–1854.
4. Lutheran Church—Denmark—Controversial literature.   5. Christianity and culture—
Denmark—History—19th century.   6. Denmark—Church history—19th century.
I. Hong, Howard Vincent, 1912– .   II. Hong, Edna Hatlestad, 1913– .
III. Fædrelandet.   IV. Title.   V. Series: Kierkegaard, Søren,
1813–1855. Works. English. 1978 ; 23.
BR115.C8K544   1998
270.8'1—DC21   97-27938

Production of this volume has been made possible in part by a grant from
the Division of Research Programs of the National Endowment
for the Humanities, an independent federal agency

Princeton University Press books are printed
on acid-free paper and meet the guidelines for permanence and durability
of the Committee on Production Guidelines for Book Longevity
of the Council on Library Resources

Designed by Frank Mahood

http://pup.princeton.edu

Printed in the United States of America

1 3 5 7 9 10 8 6 4 2

CONTENTS

HISTORICAL INTRODUCTION

Kierkegaard regarded *Either/Or* (1843) as the beginning of his authorship.[1] Previously he had written and published articles during his student days, *From the Papers of One Still Living* (1838), and his dissertation *The Concept of Irony with Continual Reference to Socrates* (1841). Because the articles were occasional pieces without a specific relation to the integrating aims of the authorship, they were excluded. *From the Papers* is a review of Hans Christian Andersen's *Only a Fiddler*. The dissertation was written in fulfillment of the requirements for the university degree. Therefore he looked upon *Either/Or* as the initial work in the self-initiated dual series of pseudonymous and signed works. The primary position and intrinsic continuity of *Either/Or* in the organic authorship are epitomized in the title of a piece written in draft form in the last year of his life—"My Program: Either/Or."[2]

The earlier writings did, however, touch on some themes that appeared in the authorship proper.[3] They also had a polemical tone that emerged later in three episodes of direct polemics: the *Corsair* affair in 1845–46 with editor Meïr Goldschmidt[4] on the issue of destructive anonymous journalism, in 1851 with Andreas Gottlob Rudelbach on the issue of politicizing reformation of the Church,[5] and in 1854–55 with the established ecclesiastical order on the issue that is the focus of the present volume, the acculturized, accommodated Christianity of Christendom.

In each instance the primary concern for Kierkegaard was the issue, not a person. Insofar as persons were involved, the point

---

[1] See *On My Work as an Author*, in *The Point of View*, KW XXII (*SV* XIII 494); *The Point of View for My Work as an Author*, KW XXII (*SV* XIII 517).

[2] See Supplement, pp. 476–81 (*Pap.* XI³ B 54–58).

[3] See Historical Introduction, *Early Polemical Writings*, pp. xxx, xxxiv–xxxv, KW I; Historical Introduction, *The Concept of Irony*, KW II, pp. xvi–xviii.

[4] See Historical Introduction, *The Corsair Affair and Articles Related to the Writings*, pp. vii–xxxiv, KW XIII.

[5] Ibid., pp. xxxvi–xxxviii.

was what the individual represented, not some personal antagonism. For Goldschmidt, Kierkegaard had a certain respect and high expectations. Rudelbach and Kierkegaard were acquainted through visits and conversations in the home of Michael Pedersen Kierkegaard. It was through his father that he came to know Bishop Jakob Peter Mynster's writings and later the bishop himself, for whom he had a deep appreciation that with certain changes continued throughout his life. Although Kierkegaard's eventual polemics against the empirical established ecclesiastical order centered on what Mynster symbolized in some respects, it was not until a year after the bishop's death that the direct attack began. Out of veneration for his father's pastor and appreciation of Mynster's sermons, Kierkegaard waited, and then the occasion came in the form of the Mynster memorial sermon by Hans Lassen Martensen, one of Kierkegaard's university professors and Mynster's eventual successor.

Perhaps the most adequate, yet brief, expression of the nature of Kierkegaard's authorship, and also of the context of the polemics in 1854–55, is the preface to *Two Discourses at the Communion on Fridays* (August 7, 1851),[6] the last of his published writings (along with *On My Work as an Author*, August 7, 1851, and *For Self-Examination*, September 10, 1851) before he became silent for over three years:

> An authorship that began with *Either/Or* and advanced step by step seeks here its decisive place of rest, at the foot of the altar, where the author, personally most aware of his own imperfection and guilt, certainly does not call himself a truth-witness but only a singular kind of poet and thinker who, *without authority*, has had nothing new to bring but "has wanted once again to read through, if possible in a more inward way, the original text of individual human existence-relationships, the old familiar text handed down from the fathers"—(See my postscript to *Concluding Postscript*[7]).

---

[6] *Two Discourses at the Communion on Fridays*, in *Without Authority*, pp. 165–66, *KW* XVIII (*SV* XII 267).

[7] *Concluding Unscientific Postscript to* Philosophical Fragments, pp. [629–30], *KW* XII.1 (*SV* VII [548–49]).

Turned this way, I have nothing further to add. Allow me, however, to express only this, which in a way is my life, the content of my life, its fullness, its bliss, its peace and satisfaction—this, or this view of life, which is the thought of humanity [*Menneskelighed*] and of human equality [*Menneske-Liighed*]: Christianly, every human being (the single individual), unconditionally every human being, once again, unconditionally every human being, is equally close to God—how close and equally close?—is loved by him.

Thus there is equality, infinite equality, between human beings. If there is any difference—ah, this difference, if it does exist, is like peaceableness itself. Undisturbed, the difference does not in the remotest way disturb the equality. The difference is: that one person bears in mind that he is loved—keeps it in mind perhaps day in and day out, perhaps day in and day out for seventy years, perhaps with only one longing, for eternity, so that he can really grasp this thought and go forth, employed in this blessed occupation of keeping in mind that he—alas, not because of his virtue!—is loved.

Another person perhaps does not think about his being loved, perhaps goes on year after year, day after day, without thinking about his being loved; or perhaps he is happy and grateful to be loved by his wife, his children, by his friends and contemporaries, but he does not think about his being loved by God; or he may bemoan not being loved by anyone, and he does not think about his being loved by God.

"Yet," the first person might say, "I am innocent; after all, I cannot help it if someone else ignores or disdains the love that is lavished just as richly upon him as upon me." Infinite, divine love, which makes no distinctions! Alas, human ingratitude! —What if the equality between us human beings, in which we completely resemble one another, were that none of us really thinks about his being loved!

As I turn to the other side, I would wish and would permit myself (in gratitude for the sympathy and good will that may have been shown to me) to present, as it were, and to commend these writings to the people whose language I with filial devotion and with almost feminine infatuation am proud to have the honor to write, yet also with the consolation that it will not be to their discredit that I have written it.

One of the elements in the summation above is what Kierkegaard elsewhere calls the "Archimedean point,"[8] the fulcrum outside time and finitude whereby time and finitude can be moved. For him that Archimedean point was the changeless love of God for every human being, the theme of *The Changelessness of God*, published before the last three numbers of *The Moment*. Fifteen years earlier, just after he fulfilled his father's wish by completing his university studies, he made a journey of filial piety to his father's birthplace, Sæding in Jylland. There he wrote:

His last wish for me is fulfilled—is that actually to be the sum and substance of my life? In God's name! Yet in relation to what I owed to him the task was not so insignificant. I learned from him what fatherly love is, and through this I gained a conception of divine fatherly love, the one single unshakable thing in life, the true Archimedean point.[9]

This Archimedean point, that God is changeless love, is the basis of the royal Law, "You *shall* love"; "You shall love *the neighbor*"; "*You* shall love the neighbor."[10] Christ, the prototype of essentially human perfection, calls for imitation[11] and constitutes the occasion for offense or faith.[12] Self-knowledge comes through imitating, and spiritual progress becomes retrogression in light of the ideal requirement. "In relation to God we are always in the wrong."[13] We are exceptions in need of a "tele-

---

[8] See Supplement, p. 383 (*Pap.* III A 73). See also, for example, *JP* II 2089; III 3426 (*Pap.* X³ A 430; IX A 115).

[9] See Supplement, p. 383 (*Pap.* III A 73).

[10] *Works of Love*, pp. 17, 44, 61, *KW* XVI (*SV* IX 21, 47, 63).

[11] See, for example, *Upbuilding Discourses in Various Spirits*, pp. 197, 217–29, *KW* XV (*SV* VIII 282, 305–16); *Works of Love*, p. 288, *KW* XVI (*SV* IX 275); *Practice in Christianity*, pp. 231–46, *KW* XX (*SV* XII 213–35; *For Self-Examination*, pp. 67–70, *KW* XXI (*SV* XXI 351–54); *Judge for Yourself!*, pp. 147–213, *KW* XXI (*SV* XII 423–80); *JP* II 1833–1940.

[12] See, for example, *Works of Love*, pp. 197–201, *KW* XVI (*SV* IX 188–91); *The Sickness unto Death*, pp. 83–87, 125–31 *KW* XIX (*SV* XI 194–99, 234–41).

[13] *Either/Or, a Fragment of Life*, II, p. 339, *KW* IV (*SV* II 306).

ological suspension of the ethical,"[14] in need of the paradoxical justification of forgiveness in faith,[15] and in need of grace.[16]

As a kind of poet-thinker Kierkegaard saw his special task as that of presenting the ideal, and as an ordinary individual he was to live under the claim of the ideal:

> Once again I have reached the point where I was last summer, the most intensive, the richest time I have experienced, where I understood myself to be what I must call a poet of the religious, not however that my personal life should express the opposite—no, I strive continually, but that I am a "poet" expresses that I do not confuse myself with the ideality.
>
> My task was to cast Christianity into reflection, not poetically to idealize (for the essentially Christian, after all, is itself the ideal) but with poetic fervor to present the total ideality at its most ideal—always ending with: I am not that, but I strive. If the latter does not prove correct and is not true about me, then everything is cast in intellectual form and falls short.[17]

In Kierkegaard's view, personally to fall short of the presented ideality is not only the occupational hazard of the poet but is a possible short-circuiting by everyone who reflects, because all reflection is abstracting (a casting of actuality and ideality into possibility), and therein lies also its value and power. The task of each one, then, is to translate or reduplicate the thought in one's own actuality. The pseudonymous Johannes Climacus in *Postscript* ventured the easily misunderstood theory of knowledge: "Truth is subjectivity."[18] By this it is not meant that subjectivity is the ground or source or test of truth but that what one understands is to be appropriated in one's own existence. "Spirit is the power a person's understanding exercises over his life."[19] One's understanding of the truth is the test of oneself, and therefore

---

[14] See *Fear and Trembling*, pp. 54–67, 81, *KW* VI (*SV* III 104–16, 129).

[15] Ibid., pp. 61–62 (111). See Supplement, pp. 394–95 (*Pap.* VIII^1 A 673).

[16] See Supplement, pp. 423–25 (*Pap.* X^5 A 88).

[17] *JP* VI 6511 (*Pap.* X^2 A 106).

[18] *Postscript*, p. 189, *KW* XII.1 (*SV* VII 157).

[19] *JP* IV 4340 (*Pap.* X^3 A 736). See also, for example, *JP* I 1049, 1051 (*Pap.* VIII^1 A 292; IX A 154).

subjectivity is untruth,[20] which ethically is guilt and religiously is sin. An Archimedean point is required outside the individual's actuality and abstracting ideal thought. For the ethically bankrupt individual, devoid of any temporal possibility of actualizing the ideal ethical claim, the paradox of the eternal in time, apprehended in faith and received as a gift, constitutes possibility beyond impossibility, newness despite the burden of guilt, release from the past.

At this point the imperative of the ethical as the universally human and the ultimate imperative of the imitation of Christ become transformed into the expressive or indicative ethics of gratitude. In a journal entry with the heading "The Christian emphasis," Kierkegaard writes of the ethics of gift and the ethical-religious consciousness transformed at the point of motivation:

> *Christianly* the emphasis does not fall so much upon to what extent or how far a person succeeds in meeting or fulfilling the requirement, if he actually is striving, as it is upon his getting an impression of the requirement in all its infinitude so that he rightly learns to be humbled and to rely upon grace.
>
> To pare down the requirement in order to fulfill it better (as if this were earnestness, that now it can all the more easily *appear* that one is earnest about wanting to fulfill the requirement)—to this Christianity in its deepest essence is opposed.
>
> No, infinite humiliation and grace, and then a striving born of gratitude—this is Christianity.[21]

Johannes Climacus in *Postscript* stresses a kind of Christian nonchalance on the other side of the gracious gift. The expressive indicative ethics of gratitude does not lead to inertia and social conformity.

> But if a person, existing, is supposed to bear in mind every day and hold fast to what the pastor says on Sundays and compre-

---

[20] *Philosophical Fragments, or a Fragment of Philosophy*, pp. 13–16, 28, 32, 47, 51–52, *KW* VII (*SV* IV 183–86, 196, 200, 214, 218); *Postscript*, pp. 207, 213, *KW* XII.1 (*SV* VIII 174, 179).

[21] *JP* I 993 (*Pap.* X³ A 734).

hend this as the earnestness of life, and thereby in turn comprehend all his capability and incapability as jest—does this mean that he will not undertake anything at all because all is vanity and futility? Oh no, in that case he will not have the opportunity to understand the jest, since there is no contradiction in putting it together with life's earnestness, no contradiction that everything is vanity in the eyes of a vain person. Laziness, inactivity, snobbishness about the finite are a poor jest or, more correctly, are no jest at all. But to shorten the night's sleep and buy the day's hours and not spare oneself, and then to understand that it is all a jest: yes, that is earnestness.[22]

In more traditional language, Kierkegaard agrees with Luther that works are not a meritorious substitute for faith, because such striving leads to mutinous presumption or despair;[23] but faith is a restless thing and the major premise of faith is linked to the minor premise of works,[24] witnessing to and suffering for the truth, works of love, the fruits of faith through the infinite gift.[25]

The Christian life, with its imperative vision of human existence, its radical self-knowledge, the rescuing and renewing radical gift, and the expressive, responsive ethics of gratitude, entails what Kierkegaard calls the double danger.[26] The first is the inner suffering of self-denial and the infinite humiliation preparatory to receiving the ultimate gift, a process of becoming akin to breaking the sod and disking the soil in preparation for seeding and new life. The second danger is that of the Christian's having to live in the world with its qualitatively different finite values and goals. For Kierkegaard an instance of the second danger was his action against *The Corsair:* "If I had not taken this action, I would have escaped completely the *double*-danger connected with the essentially Christian, I would have gone on thinking of

---

[22] *Postscript*, pp. 471–72, *KW* XII.1 (*SV* VII 410).

[23] See Supplement, pp. 392, 408 (*Pap.* VIII[1] A 19; X[3] A 322).

[24] See *For Self-Examination*, pp. 15–25, *KW* XXI (*SV* XII 306–14).

[25] See, for example, *Works of Love*, pp. 5–16, *KW* XVI (*SV* IX 9–20).

[26] See Supplement, p. 398 (*Pap.* IX A 414). See also, for example, *Works of Love*, pp. 192, 194–95, 204, *KW* XVI (*SV* IX 183, 185, 194); *Practice*, p. 222, *KW* XX (*SV* XII 204); *JP* I 653; VI 6548 (*Pap.* VIII[2] B 85:18; X[2] A 251).

the difficulties involved with Christianity as being purely interior to the self."[27]

In accord with this understanding of Christianity and with Holy Scriptures, especially the New Testament,[28] as highway signs and Christ as the way,[29] Kierkegaard came to distinguish between Christianity and acculturized, accommodated religion, between Christianity and Christendom, and also to have second thoughts about Mynster's presentation.

But where is the boundary between worldly wisdom and religiousness. Mynster's preaching is far from being wholly religious at all times. He gives consolation by saying that everything will perhaps turn out all right again, that better days are coming, etc., which after all is not even a genuinely religious consolation; one shrinks from going out into the current—one tries to wade as long as possible. As long as this is not definitely decided, there always remains a doubt about the importance of actuality in one's whole train of thought.[30]

Christianity is a unity of gentleness and rigorousness, in one sense infinitely rigorous, and the Christian shudders at this confounded confusion of magnanimous Christian leniency and cowardly, worldly sagacious weakness. First of all an eternity of memory, until the ethical requirement is honored (through suffering the penalty, through *restitutio in integrum* [restitution to the pristine state] where this is possible, through retraction or the like . . . and then an almost miraculous forgetfulness: this is Christianity. This is also Christianity according to Mynster's most remarkable and to me unforgettable preaching, which I have read, do read, and will read again and again to my upbuilding. But then is it not also Christianity to act accordingly? I do not think that it is Christianity to have a new sermon **about** the obligation to act according to the sermon, and then a new one **about** the danger in merely preaching **about** the obligation to act according to the sermon

---

[27] *JP* VI 6548 (*Pap.* X² A 251).
[28] See Supplement, p. 383 (*Pap.* IV A 143).
[29] See *JP* I 208 (*Pap.* VIII¹ A 50).
[30] *JP* V 5637 (*Pap.* IV A 71).

about, and then to the nth power a sermon **about**. In my opinion this constitutes a moving away from Christianity. And that simple middle-class man, "the former clothing merchant here in the city," my deceased father, who brought me up in Christianity on Mynster's sermons, was also of this opinion—is this not so?[31]

What had happened, he thought, was a confusion of categories, of customary social morality and the ethical, of the esthetic and the religious, of the finite and the infinite. "Every cause that is not served as an either/or (but as a both-and, also, etc.) is *eo ipso* not God's cause; yet it does not therefore follow that every cause served as an either/or is therefore God's cause."[32]

As I have demonstrated on all sides, all modern Christendom is a shifting of the essentially Christian back into the esthetic. Another shift is that the conception of the preparatory condition for becoming a Christian has been broadened in a completely confusing way. Thousands of people who are a long, long way from having an impression of Christianity stand on the same level as a catechumen and summarily have been made Christians. In this fashion there has been such an advance that if such people are supposed to be Christians, then a mediocre catechumen is an outstanding Christian. And this is just about the way it is in "established Christendom." Just as everywhere else, first place has been allowed to vanish; third place, which otherwise is alien here, has been promoted to an actual position, and class 2 becomes number 1. The apostles, the no. 1 Christians, the truth-witnesses, etc. become fanatics.[33]

What was needed was a "corrective,"[34] not because of doctrinal aberration but because of a lack of inward deepening, of a subjectivizing of the objectivity of doctrine, and because of an

---

[31] *JP* VI 6748 (*Pap.* X⁶ B 171, pp. 257–58).
[32] See Supplement, p. 425 (*Pap.* X⁵ A 119).
[33] *JP* VI 6466 (*Pap.* X¹ A 617).
[34] See Supplement, pp. 403–06, 410–11, 422–23, 452–53 (*Pap.* X¹ A 640, 658; X² A 193; X³ A 565; X⁴ A 596; XI¹ A 28).

avoidance of the second danger, witnessing to the implications of the doctrine.[35] Nor was the corrective needed primarily because of the state Church, the established ecclesiastical order. In his "Open Letter to Dr. Rudelbach," Kierkegaard wrote that he was "suspicious of these politically achieved free institutions" and that he had "not fought for the emancipation of the 'Church' any more than" he had "fought for the emancipation of Greenland,"[36] although he later would have welcomed disestablishment.[37] "A mismanaged established order—well, there is nothing commendable about that, but it is far preferable to a reformation devoid of character."[38]

The best form of the corrective in the interest of inward deepening and expressive action would be the application of pressure through the presentation of ideality by a poet "without authority."

The ideality involved has been lost completely. As a result, being a Christian is construed to be something everyone can be very easily. And then it becomes a matter of distinction to go further, to become a philosopher, a poet, and God knows what.

To bring this to a halt, I have affirmed ideality. At least one ought to acquire respect for what it means to be a Christian; then everyone can test or choose whether or not one wants to be a Christian.[39]

The pressure must be applied by the ideals. For example, in ideality a truth-witness is essentially higher than any actual truth-witness. Therefore from this elevation the pressure is even stronger.

The mitigation, again, lies in the fact that the whole thing happens through a "poet," who says: This I am not.[40]

---

[35] See *JP* VI 6842 (*Pap.* X^6 B 232).
[36] "Open Letter to Dr. Rudelbach," in *Corsair Affair*, p. 54, *KW* XIII (*SV* XIII 439).
[37] See pp. 98, 157–59.
[38] See Supplement, p. 412 (*Pap.* X^4 A 296).
[39] *JP* II 1798 (*Pap.* X^4 A 282).
[40] *JP* II 1796 (*Pap.* X^4 A 80).

From the beginning of the authorship with *Either/Or*, the pseudonymous writers are poets[41] (in the elemental sense of imaginative makers) of ideality and themselves are Kierkegaard's poetic productions.[42]

Essentially I am only a poet who loves what wounds: ideals; what infinitely detains: ideals; what makes a person, humanly speaking, unhappy: ideals; what "teaches to take refuge in grace": ideals; what in a higher sense makes a person indescribably happy: ideals—if he could learn to hate himself properly in the self-concern of infinity. Indescribably happy, although humbled, deeply, profoundly humbled, before the ideals, he has had to confess and must confess to himself and to others that there is the infinitely higher that he has not reached; yet he is unspeakably happy to have seen it, although it is precisely this that casts him to the earth, him, consequently the unhappy one. . . .

And in calm weather, when life seems to be tranquilized in illusions, one may think one can do without all this fantasy about ideals, think that all they do is disturb everything, and quite right—they will disturb all the illusions. But when everything is tottering, when everything is splitting up into parties, small societies, sects, etc., when, just because everyone wants to rule, ruling is practically impossible—then there is still one force left that can control people: the ideals, properly applied. For in the first place, the ideals, properly applied, do not infringe upon anyone, do not give offense to the ambitions of all, to the ambitions of anyone, which one who oneself wants to rule can so easily do; and in the next place ideals split up every crowd, seize the individual and keep control of him.[43]

---

[41] See, for example, Johannes de Silentio, who does the work of a poet and yet modestly disclaims the title, in *Fear and Trembling*, p. 90 and note 21, *KW* VI (*SV* III 138); Johannes Climacus, an outsider, a humorist who "in the isolation of the imaginary construction" asks "how do I become a Christian," in *Postscript*, pp. 15–16, 617, 619, *KW* XII.1 (*SV* VII 7, 537–38, 539).

[42] See *Postscript*, pp. 625–27, *KW* XII.1 (*SV* VII 545–47).

[43] *JP* VI 6749, pp. 400–01 (*Pap.* X⁶ B 173, pp. 275–76).

Through the series of pseudonymous works from *Either/Or* to *Postscript*, the presentation of the ideals took various forms. In *Either/Or* there are the multifaceted expositions of the esthetic life of immediacy and the ethical consciousness and the distinctions between them, with the added last word that in relation to God we are always in the wrong. *The Concept of Anxiety* is an algebraic discussion of hereditary sin. The lyrical *Fear and Trembling* poses the relation of the ethical and the religious through a consideration of Abraham and the sacrifice of Isaac. *Repetition* centers on the impossibility of esthetic repetition and intimates the possibility of a transcendent repetition. *Stages on Life's Way* gathers together the earlier themes in the theory of the potential stages of life or spheres of existence: (1) the esthetic as the life of immediacy and individual satisfaction, (2) the ethical as the universally human claim upon the individual, who is obligated to actualize the ethical ideal, and (3) the religious as the dethroning of the esthetic in its frustration and despair and of the ethical in its bankruptcy of guilt and concomitantly as the possibility of the qualitative repetition (unavailable in the other spheres) through forgiveness and grace. *Fragments* is an imaginary construction in thought about the question of how one can go beyond Socrates and presents the paradox of the eternal in time (the distinction between religiousness A and religiousness B in *Postscript*[44]) as the only way for an existing temporal being to go beyond what otherwise is the highest. In dealing with Climacus's question about how one becomes a Christian, *Postscript* clothes the algebraic thought of *Fragments* in historical costume. Alongside this series of pseudonymous works, six small signed volumes of upbuilding discourses (1843, 1844) were published, and in 1845 *Three Discourses on Imagined Occasions* (confession, wedding, burial).

The qualitative spheres of existence had already been suggested in the various means of repetition in *Repetition* (1843), although the book was written "in such a way that the heretics are unable to understand it."[45] And in the companion volume, *Fear and Trembling*, published the same day (October 13), the

---

[44] *Postscript*, pp. 555–61, *KW* XII.1 (*SV* VII 485–90).
[45] *Repetition*, p. 225, *KW* VI (*SV* III 259).

reader is told of Dutch spice merchants who sank a few cargoes "in order to jack up the price."

Do we need something similar in the world of the spirit? Are we so sure that we have achieved the highest, so that there is nothing left for us to do except piously to make ourselves think that we have not come that far, simply in order to have something to occupy our time? Is this the kind of self-deception the present generation needs? Should it be trained in a virtuosity along that line, or is it not, instead, adequately perfected in the art of deceiving itself? Or, rather, does it not need an honest earnestness that fearlessly and incorruptibly points to the tasks, an honest earnestness that lovingly maintains the tasks, that does not disquiet people into wanting to attain the highest too hastily but keeps the tasks young and beautiful and lovely to look at, inviting to all and yet also difficult and inspiring to the noble-minded (for the noble nature is inspired only by the difficult)?[46]

Of the whole series of pseudonymous works, Kierkegaard wrote in 1851:

So my idea was to give my contemporaries (whether or not they themselves would want to understand) a hint in humorous form (in order to achieve a lighter tone) that a much greater pressure was needed—but then no more; I aimed to keep my heavy burden to myself, as my cross. I have often taken exception to anyone who was a sinner in the strictest sense and then promptly got busy terrifying others. Here is where *Concluding Postscript* comes in.

Then I was horrified to see what was understood by a Christian state (this I saw especially in 1848); I saw how the ones who were supposed to rule, both in Church and state, hid themselves like cowards while barbarism boldly and brazenly raged; and I experienced how a truly unselfish and God-fearing endeavor[47] (and my endeavor as an author was that) is rewarded in the Christian state.

[46] *Fear and Trembling*, p. 121, *KW* VI (*SV* III 166).
[47] The *Corsair* affair.

That seals my fate. Now it is up to my contemporaries how they will list the cost of being a Christian, how terrifying they will make it. I surely will be given the strength for it—I almost said "unfortunately." I really do not say this in pride. I both have been and am willing to pray to God to exempt me from this terrible business; furthermore, I am human myself and love, humanly speaking, to live happily here on earth. But if what one sees all over Europe is Christendom, a Christian state, then I propose to start here in Denmark to list the price for being a Christian in such a way that the whole concept—state Church, official appointments, livelihood—bursts open.[48]

Although Kierkegaard intended to conclude (hence the title *Concluding Unscientific Postscript*) with *Postscript*, during and after the intense experience of the *Corsair* affair and the revelation of the pusillanimity of the cultural and ecclesiastical leaders who could and should have spoken up, Bishop Mynster[49] in particular, he concluded that a rigorous auditing of Christendom needed to be made.

It is neither more nor less than a matter of an auditing [*Revision*] of Christianity; it is a matter of getting rid of 1800 years as if they had never been.[50]

[48] See Supplement, pp. 401–02 (*Pap.* X[1] A 541).

[49] "It was indeed necessary at the time for that Christian Bishop, that chief literary figure, M., personally to enter in and sternly call for order. But no one would; so I, a subaltern, had to take the job, which also for that reason was undertaken with suffering. So while G. [Goldschmidt], with the largest circulation in Denmark and with privileged, free-reined unconstraint raged against me with all his talent (and he is, indeed, 'one of our most talented authors'; see Mynster, by whom he is now accredited in exactly the same sense as, for example, our talented Martensen, Paludan-Müller, myself, and such others among us), I was too pleased for words to bow 'in profound veneration' to the old gentleman, for whatever dubiousness there was in M.'s silence, or ignorance, could be concealed—and I do not matter—if I only manage to maintain M.'s reputation shining the same as before."—*JP* VI 6748 (*Pap.* X[6] B 171, p. 264), *n.d.*, 1851

[50] See Supplement, p. 395 (*Pap.* IX A 72). This is not a rejection of history or of the "historical Jesus" but a rejection of the falsification of substituting cultural accommodation and historical information for the contemporaneity

The auditing and the needed "greater pressure" came in the form of what may be called Kierkegaard's "second authorship" in a series of signed and pseudonymous works beginning with *Upbuilding Discourses in Various Spirits* (1847) and ending with *For Self-Examination* (1851) and the posthumously published *Judge for Yourself!* (written in 1851–52).

The series is marked by a heightened level of ideality in the requirement of *imitatio Christi* and in the venture into the second danger, possibly martyrdom, entailed by witnessing to the faith.[51] Part of the subtitle of *Sickness unto Death* could be used as the subtitle for the entire series: "For Upbuilding and Awakening," as could also a contemplated subtitle of *Practice*: "An Attempt to Introduce Christianity into Christendom . . . A Poetic Attempt—Without Authority."[52]

Another clue to the entire series is a pair of synonymous words: *confession* and *admission*.[53] Kierkegaard was not a reformer in the ordinary sense of one who wants to change structures and manipulate concepts and language. *Judge for Yourself!* ends with a denunciation of dabbling reformers of externals and with the call for an honest admission of having scaled down Christianity.

If, however, there is no one in this generation who ventures in character to undertake the task of "reformer," then—unless the established order, instead of making confession of the truth

---

of encounter with Christ. See *Fragments*, pp. 55–111, *KW* VII (*SV* IV 221–72).

[51] See, for example, *Discourses in Various Spirits*, pp. 217–29, 240, 245, *KW* XV (*SV* VIII 305–16, 326, 331); *Christian Discourses*, pp. 181–87, 278, *KW* XVII (*SV* X 184–89, 288); *Practice*, pp. 106, 206–09, 233, 237–57, *KW* XX (*SV* XII 101, 190–92, 213, 217–35); *For Self-Examination*, pp. 67–70, *KW* XXI (*SV* XII 351–54); *Judge for Yourself!*, pp. 136–38, 187–204, *KW* XXI (*SV* XII 413–14, 455–71).

[52] See Supplement, p. 398 (*Pap.* IX A 390).

[53] Danish: *Tilstaaelse* and *Indrømmelse*. See, for example, *Practice*, pp. 7, 227, 235, *KW* XX (*SV* XII xv, 208, 215); *For Self-Examination*, pp. 69–70, *KW* XXI (*SV* XII 353); *Judge for Yourself!*, pp. 101–02, 129, 133–43, 156, 208, 211–12, *KW* XXI (*SV* XII 384–85, 407, 410–19, 430, 473, 478–79); *On My Work*, in *Point of View*, *KW* XXII (*SV* XIII 506–07); *Point of View*, *KW* XXII (*SV* XIII 532, 592); *Armed Neutrality*, in *Point of View*, *KW* XXII (*Pap.* X⁵ B 107, pp. 292–93). See also Supplement, pp. 436–42 (*Pap.* XI³ B 15).

that Christianly it is only a toned-down approximation of Christianity, claims to be in the strict sense true Christianity according to the New Testament and thereby judges and destroys itself—then the established order should stand, be maintained. Dabblers in reforming are more corrupting than the most corrupt established order, because reforming is the highest and therefore dabbling in it is the most corrupting of all. Let the established order have faults, many of them, say what you wish—if you are not willing to walk *in the character* of being a reformer, then hold your tongue about reforming. Oh, the most horrible of all lack of character—fraudulently to want through subterfuge to look like a reformer, or to want to be a reformer through a little party alliance, through balloting, etc. etc.

No, if there is no such man among us, then let us hold to the established order; let us see the error of our ways, let each one individually confess before God how far behind we are in Christianity, but you, my God, you will surely keep me from making things even worse by fraudulently wanting to reform.

So let it be said as loudly as possible, and would that it might be heard, if possible, everywhere, and God grant that wherever it is heard it may be earnestly considered: *The evil in our time is not the established order with its many faults. No, the evil in our time is precisely: this evil penchant for reforming, this flirting with wanting to reform*, this sham of wanting to reform without being willing to suffer and to make sacrifices, this frivolous conceitedness of wanting to be able to reform without even having a conception, to say nothing of a lofty conception, of how uncommonly elevated is the idea of "to reform," this hypocrisy of avoiding the consciousness of one's own incompetence by being busy with the diversion of wanting to reform the Church, which our age is least of all competent to do. When the Church needed a reformation, no one reported for duty, there was no crowd to join up; all fled away. Only one solitary man, the reformer, was disciplined in all secrecy by fear and trembling and much spiritual trial for venturing the extraordinary in God's name. Now that all want to reform, there is an uproar as if it were in a public dance hall. This cannot be God's idea but is a foppish human device, which is why, instead of fear and trembling and much spiritual trial, there is: hurrah, bravo, applause, balloting, bumbling, hubbub, noise—and false alarm.[54]

At times during the years 1846–51, Kierkegaard delayed publishing completed writings because he was waiting and hoping. A work written in 1851–52 (*Judge for Yourself!*) was not published because he was waiting and hoping for an honest admission, in particular from the foremost representative of the established order, Bishop Mynster, whom he personally loved and to whose writings he was indebted.[55]

Kierkegaard's position with regard to Mynster was in part something personal and in part a concern for Christianity and the Church. He therefore refrained, "with only one exception,"[56] from publishing his most explicit critical thoughts of what Mynster represented. Climacus, however, toward the end in the last of the first series of pseudonymous works had already affirmed that "honesty is preferable to half measures," that confession is better than indifference.[57] After the publication of *Postscript*, Kierkegaard visited Mynster and told him, "I am in complete disagreement with you."

My thinking was: Privately I will tell him how much I am in disagreement with him—I owe that to the truth—but outwardly he is not to be diminished by an attack; on the contrary, he is to be elevated even above his actual worth; he represents what must be made known.

Bishop Mynster replied: You are the complement to me.[58]

With the publication of *Upbuilding Discourses in Various Spirits* (1847), the so-called "second authorship" began, and Bishop Mynster was irritated by Part One, "An Occasional Discourse"

[54] *Judge for Yourself!*, pp. 212–13, *KW* XXI (*SV* XII 479–80).
[55] See, for example, *For Self-Examination*, p. 21, *KW* XXI (*SV* XII 311); Supplement, pp. 397, 410–11 (*Pap.* IX A 85; X³ A 565).
[56] Presumably *Practice*. See Supplement, p. 436 (*Pap.* XI³ B 15, p. 37).
[57] *Postscript*, p. 589, *KW* XII.1 (*SV* VIII 513).
[58] See Supplement, p. 437 (*Pap.* XI³ B 15, p. 38).

("Purity of Heart Is to Will One Thing"). *"Works of Love* [1847]
offended him. —*Christian Discourses* [1848] even more."[59] Kierkegaard continued to write but did not publish—he waited,
waited for Mynster's admission. In November 1848 he wrote in
his journal:

> The question is: When should all the latest works [*Sickness unto
> Death, Practice, Armed Neutrality*] be published! I cannot thank
> God enough that I have finished them, and if I had not had
> the tension, with the addition of new pains I perhaps would
> never have completed them, because once I have come out of
> the momentum of writing, I never get into it again in the
> same way. This time I succeeded, and for me it is enough that
> they exist, finished in fair copy, containing the completion and
> the entire structure of the whole, going as far as I in fact could
> go in an attempt to introduce Christianity into Christen-
> dom—but, please note, "poetic, without authority," because,
> as I have so definitely maintained, I am no apostle or the like;
> I am a poetic-dialectical genius, personally and religiously a
> penitent.[60]

The first was finally published the next year, the second the
year following, and the third remained unpublished until 1880
(in *Efterladte Papirer* V). As the auditing was intensified in the two
volumes by Anti-Climacus (*Practice* and *Sickness unto Death*),
Mynster's negative response increased correspondingly. "And so
it mounts. *Practice in Christianity* distressed him very painfully."[61]

> What Bishop Mynster has sown I am harvesting. For Bishop
> Mynster has proclaimed true Christianity but—in an unchris-
> tian way—has derived great advantage from it, has enjoyed all
> the good things of life because of it, has gained enormous pres-
> tige, and also has ingratiated himself by making Christianity
> into "the gentle comfort" etc.

[59] See Supplement, p. 419 (*Pap.* X[4] A 511, p. 331).
[60] See Supplement, p. 400 (*Pap.* X[1] A 56).
[61] See Supplement, pp. 418–20 and also 408–10, 436–42 (*Pap.* X[4] A 511; X[3]
A 563; XI[3] B 15).

As a result he in many ways has distilled Christianity out of the country.[62]

And yet I love Bishop Mynster; it is my only wish to do everything to reinforce the esteem for him, for I have admired him and, humanly speaking, do admire him; and every time I am able to do anything for his benefit, I think of my father, whom it pleases, I believe.[63]

Having completed the writing of the two Anti-Climacus books, Kierkegaard again decided to write no more.

Just as a cabinet minister steps down and becomes a private citizen, so I cease to be an author and lay down my pen—I actually have had a portfolio

Just one word more, but no, now not one word more; now I have laid down my pen.[64]

But just as he previously had been unable to cease writing, he continued to write copiously in his journals and in 1851 wrote and published *For Self-Examination* and wrote a companion piece that was laid aside, *Judge for Yourself!* Then no more writing for publication. Kierkegaard remained silent—and waited for Mynster's admission (*Indrømmelse*) and confession (*Tilstaaelse*) of accommodating Christianity to "the demands of the times."[65] Appended to the manuscript of *Judge* was the brief statement dated March 1855, over a year after Mynster's death and a few months before Kierkegaard died:

This book is from the time when the old bishop was still living. Therefore it has been kept at a distance both because at the time I understood my relation to the established order that way and because out of respect for the old bishop I also very much wanted to understand my relation that way.

[62] See Supplement, p. 396 (*Pap.* IX A 81).
[63] See Supplement, p. 397 (*Pap.* IX A 85).
[64] See Supplement, p. 400 (*Pap.* X^1 A 45).
[65] See, for example, *Two Ages: The Age of Revolution and the Present Age. A Literary Review*, pp. 8–11, 21, *KW* XIV (*SV* VIII 8–11, 20); *Point of View, KW* XXII (*SV* XIII 557, 572–73, 590).

Now I speak much more decisively, unreservedly, truly, without, however, thereby implying that what I said earlier was untrue.[66]

Kierkegaard had seen his task to be the application of a corrective to the established order and the evocation of a cleansing admission. For over three years after his latest publication appeared on September 10, 1851, he was silent and waited for Mynster, as a representative of the established order,[67] to speak. But Mynster, too, was silent.

On January 30, 1854, Mynster died.[68] A month later Kierkegaard wrote in his journal:

Now he is dead.

If he could have been prevailed upon to conclude his life with making the confession to Christianity that what he has represented actually was not Christianity but a mitigation, it would have been exceedingly desirable, for he carried a whole age.

That is why the possibility of this confession had to be kept open to the end, yes, to the very end, in case he should make it on his death bed. That is why he must never be attacked . . . ..

Now that he has died without making that confession, everything is changed; now all that remains is that he has preached Christianity firmly into an illusion.

The relationship is altered also with regard to my melancholy devotion to my dead father's pastor, for it would indeed be too much if even after his death I were unable to speak candidly of him, although I know very well that there will always be something enticing for me in my old devotion and my esthetic admiration.

My original desire was to turn everything of mine into a triumph for Mynster. As I came to a clearer understanding later, my desire remained unchanged, but I was obliged to request this little confession, something that I did not covet for

---

[66] *Judge for Yourself!*, p. 215, *KW* XXI (*SV* XII 481).
[67] See Supplement, p. 410 (*Pap.* X³ A 565).
[68] See Supplement, pp. 434–42 (*Pap.* XI¹ A 1; XI³ B 15).

my own sake and therefore, as I thought, that could very well be done in such a way that it would become a triumph for Bishop M. . . .

. . . Something he frequently said in our conversations, although not directed at me, was very significant: It does not depend on who has the most power but on who can stick it out the longest.[69]

The occasion for Kierkegaard's renewed auditing of the established order was the declaration by Professor Hans Lassen Martensen in his memorial service sermon that Bishop Mynster was an authentic truth-witness in "the holy chain of truth-witnesses that stretches through the ages from the days of the apostles."[70] Kierkegaard's first article,[71] printed in the newspaper *Fædrelandet* on December 18, 1854, was written in February 1854 and the last, *The Moment*, 10, was written in May–September 1855.

The series of articles is marked by satire, irony, and humor, and a steadily intensified bluntness of critique that many readers found repulsive. Kierkegaard's method is an adaptation of the method of the thinker he admired most, Socrates, who thrust away, repelled, in order that the learner might be independent of him in confronting the issue.[72]

The first phase of the attack, beginning with the initial article in *Fædrelandet*, is a protest that utilizes the criterion Professor Martensen had applied: truth-witness. Under that criterion and in the light of the New Testament, Christendom and also the poet-auditor fall short. Luther had ninety-five theses and Kierkegaard has only one—New Testament Christianity does not exist.[73] An admission[74] is needed and the reception of the gracious gift of renewal, a theme that continues also toward the end

---

[69] See Supplement, pp. 434–36 (*Pap.* XI^1 A 1).

[70] Cf. p. 3 and note 2.

[71] Pp. 3–8.

[72] See Supplement, pp. 390–92, 397 (*Pap.* VII^1 A 181; IX A 343). See also, for example, *Fragments*, pp. 10–11, 23–24, *KW* VII (*SV* IV 180–81, 192–93); *The Book on Adler*, p. 42, *KW* XXIV (*Pap.* VII^2 B 235, p. 80).

[73] See p. 39.

[74] See p. 15, also, for example, pp. 28, 38.

of the series of polemical pamphlets titled *The Moment*.[75] The next phase is signaled by the pamphlet *This Must Be Said; So Let It Be Said* (May 24, 1855) and is marked by ridicule, irony, humor, and a negative appraisal in light of the New Testament. The relation of state and Church also comes under scrutiny. After the first two numbers of *The Moment* (May 24, June 4, 1855) comes another division piece, *What Christ Judges of Official Christianity* (June 16, 1855). Christ's rigorous judgment of the Scribes and Pharisees is applicable to Christendom. Kierkegaard had spoken in his own name as poet-auditor, and now Christ should speak.[76] The next division piece is *The Changelessness of God* (September 3, 1855), which is both the climactic piece and a return to the Archimedean point and to Kierkegaard's favorite text, James 1:17–21. Thereafter two numbers of *The Moment* (September 11, 24, 1855) appear with an emphasis on the contemporaneity of the Christian life in the context of the eternal and on the necessity of proclaiming ideality. The last portions are a harrowing characterization of the clergy. Number 10 of *The Moment*, including "My Task," was in final copy September 1, 1855, but did not appear until the publication of *Efterladte Papirer* (VIII, 1881).

In the meantime, the response to the articles in *Fædrelandet* and to *The Moment* was considerable and mostly negative. Bishop Martensen and J. Victor Bloch's responses are given in the Supplement (pp. 360–71). Replies to a number of the responses were given in Kierkegaard's articles. Martensen, named Mynster's successor on April 15, 1854, responded[77] to Kierkegaard's first article but made no admission and thereafter was silent. Professor Rasmus Nielsen wrote in support of Kierkegaard,[78] but with scant appreciation from him.[79] Only a brief announcement[80] of *This Must Be Said* appeared in response to the three interspersed small division pieces. Single editions of *What Christ Judges* and

[75] See p. 292.
[76] See pp. 131–32.
[77] See pp. 360–66.
[78] Rasmus Nielsen, *"En god Gjerning," Fædrelandet*, 8, January 10, 1855.
[79] See p. 343 and note 250.
[80] Anon., *"Literatur," Dagbladet*, 120, May 25, 1855.

The Changelessness of God appeared in 1855 and two printings of *This Must Be Said*. Three printings of *The Moment*, 1–4, and two of 5–9 were made in 1855.

Never particularly strong physically, Kierkegaard became progressively ill in September. At a party at Jens F. Gjødwad's (see p. 538 and note 175), he slid from the sofa to the floor, winked, and said to the friends around him, "Oh, leave it—let—the maid—sweep it up—in the morning."[81]

A few days later he collapsed on the street. After a time in his quarters at Klædeboderne 5–6, he was taken on October 2 to Frederiks Hospital, where he died November 11, 1855. He had come to the end of his money,[82] he had finished what he had to say, and for the last time he stopped writing, but he left a legacy of inestimable value, a legacy that has been rediscovered in this century.

---

[81] Reported by his former amanuensis, Israel Levin, *Hr. Cand. Israel Levins Udtalelser om S. Kierkegaard 1858 og 1869*, D. Pk. 5, Læg 31, Søren Kierkegaard Arkivet, Kongelige Biblioteket, Copenhagen.

[82] See *Efterladte Papirer*, I-VIII, ed. Hans Peter Barfod and Hermann Gottsched (Copenhagen: 1869–81), VIII, p. 598.

NEWSPAPER ARTICLES

1854–1855

I

Was Bishop Mynster[1] a "Truth-Witness," One of "the Authentic Truth-Witnesses" —Is *This the Truth?*[2]

February 1854   S. KIERKEGAARD

In the address Prof. Martensen "delivered the fifth Sunday after Epiphany, the Sunday before Bishop Dr. Mynster's funeral,"[3] a memorial address, as it perhaps can in a way also be called, since it calls to mind Prof. Martensen for the vacant bishopric—in this address Bishop Mynster is represented as a truth-witness, as one of the authentic truth-witnesses; the expressions used are as strong and decisive as possible. With the late bishop's figure, his life and career, and the outcome of his life before our eyes, we are exhorted to "imitate the faith of the true guides, of the authentic truth-witnesses"[4] (p. 5), their faith, for it was, as is explicitly said about Bishop Mynster, "not only in word and confession but in deed and truth" (p. 9). The late bishop is introduced by Prof. Martensen (p. 6) into "the holy chain of truth-witnesses that stretches through the ages from the days of the apostles" etc.

To this I must raise an objection—and now that Bishop Mynster is dead I am able and willing to speak, but very briefly here, and not at all about what made me decide to take the position that I have taken in relation to him.[5]

When *proclamation* is considered more particularly to be what is said, written, printed, the word, the sermon, one does not need to be especially sharp to be able to see, when the New Testament is placed alongside Mynster's preaching, that Bishop Mynster's proclamation of Christianity (to take just one thing) tones down, veils, suppresses, omits some of what is most decisively Christian, what is too inconvenient for us human beings, what would make our lives strenuous, prevent us from enjoying life—this about dying to the world,[6] about voluntary renunciation, about hating oneself, about suffering for the doctrine, etc.

If, however, *proclamation* is considered more particularly to be the extent to which the proclaimer's life expresses what he says (and this, note well, is Christianly decisive, and in just this way Christianity has wanted to protect itself against acquiring characterless assistant professors instead of witnesses), one in turn does not need to be especially sharp to be able to see (if by hearing or reading him one is properly acquainted at all with his preaching) that Bishop Mynster's proclamation of Christianity was not in character, that outside the quiet hours[7] he was not in character, not even in the character of his preaching, which indeed, as stated, compared with the New Testament, has considerably scaled down the essentially Christian. In 1848 and thereafter it became apparent even to blind admirers, if they were properly acquainted with his preaching so as to be able to know what this, what these quiet hours lead one to expect.

Thus, when the New Testament is placed alongside, Bishop Mynster's proclamation of Christianity was, especially for a truth-witness, a dubious proclamation of Christianity. But there was, I thought, this truth in him, that he was willing, I am fully convinced, to confess before God and to himself that he was not at all, not at all, a truth-witness—in my view, precisely this confession was the truth.[8]

But if Bishop Mynster is going to be represented and canonized in the pulpit as a truth-witness, one of the authentic truth-witnesses, then an objection must be raised. The *Berlingske Ti-*

XIV
7 *dende* (the official newspaper,[9] just as Prof. Martensen is no doubt the official preacher[10]) is, as I see, of the opinion that with this address Prof. Martensen (who with remarkable haste steals a march on the funeral and also on the monument) has from the pulpit erected a beautiful and worthy monument to the deceased;[11] I would prefer to say: a worthy monument to Prof. Martensen himself. But in any case monuments cannot be ignored; therefore an objection must be raised, which then perhaps could even contribute to making the monument (to Prof. Martensen) even more durable.

Bishop Mynster a truth-witness! You who read this, you certainly do know what is Christianly understood by a truth-witness,* but let me remind you of it, that it unconditionally requires suffering for the doctrine. And when it is said more pointedly: one of "the authentic" truth-witnesses, then the word must accordingly be taken in the strictest sense. In order to make it vivid to you, let me try in a few strokes to suggest what must be understood by this.

A truth-witness is a person whose life from first to last is unfamiliar with everything called enjoyment—ah, whether much or little is granted you, you know how much good is done by what is called enjoyment—but his life from first to last was unfamiliar with everything that is called enjoyment; on the contrary, from first to last it was initiated into everything called suffering—alas, and even if you are exempted from the prolonged, the more agonizing sufferings, you still know from personal experience how a person shrinks from what is called suffering! But from first to last his life was initiated into what is even more rarely mentioned among people because it more rarely happens—into interior struggles, into fear and trembling, into shuddering, into spiritual trials, into anxieties of soul, into torments of spirit, and then in addition was tried in all the sufferings that are more commonly talked about in the world. A truth-witness is a person who

---

*Yet this may have been consigned to oblivion through Bishop Mynster's proclamation of Christianity over many years. And a capital malpractice in his proclamation is also this—not this, that he himself was an officeholder (Christianly this subtracts), the proclamation his own brilliant career, rich in enjoyment—no, not this, but that he would authorize this kind of proclamation as the true Christian proclamation and thereby, through suppression, make the true Christian proclamation (that of the suffering truth-witnesses) into an exaggeration, instead of conversely making the confession to Christianity that the proclamation he represented is something that must be conceded to us ordinary human beings through exemption and indulgence, something that we ordinary human beings make use of because we are too selfish, too worldly, too sensate to be capable of more, something that we ordinary human beings make use of and that, understood in this way, is by no means—despite all false reformers!— to be conceitedly and pompously rejected, but rather is to be respected.

in poverty witnesses for the truth, in poverty, in lowliness and abasement,[12] is so unappreciated, hated, detested, so mocked, insulted, laughed to scorn—so poor that he perhaps has not always had daily bread, but he received the daily bread of persecution in abundance every day. For him there was never advancement and promotion except in reverse, step by step downward. A truth-witness, one of the authentic truth-witnesses, is a person who is flogged, mistreated, dragged from one prison to another, then finally—the last advancement, by which he is admitted to the first class in the *Christian* order of precedence among the authentic truth-witnesses—then finally, for this is indeed one of the authentic truth-witnesses Prof. Martensen talks about, then finally is crucified or beheaded or burned or broiled on a grill, his lifeless body thrown away by the assistant executioner into a remote place, unburied—this is how a truth-witness is buried!—or burned to ashes and cast to the winds so that every trace of this "refuse," as the apostle says he has become,[13] might be obliterated.

This is a truth-witness, his life and career, his death and burial—and, says Prof. Martensen, Bishop Mynster was one of these authentic truth-witnesses.

Is it the truth? Is talking in this way perhaps also witnessing for the truth, and by this talk has Prof. Martensen himself stepped into the character of a truth-witness, one of the authentic truth-witnesses? Truly, there is something that is more against Christianity and the essence of Christianity than any heresy, any schism, more against it than all heresies and schisms together, and it is this: to play at Christianity. But (entirely, entirely in the same sense as the child plays at being a soldier) it is playing at Christianity: to remove all the dangers (Christianly, *witness* and *danger* are equivalent), to replace them with power (to be a danger to others), goods, advantages, abundant enjoyment of even the most select refinements—and then to play the game that Bishop Mynster was a truth-witness, one of the authentic truth-witnesses, play it so frightfully earnestly that one cannot stop the game at all but plays it on into heaven, plays Bishop Mynster along into the holy chain of truth-witnesses that stretches from the days of the apostles to our times.

POSTSCRIPT

This article has, as may be seen from its date, lain ready for some time.

As long as the appointment to the bishopric of Sjælland was in question, I thought that I ought to leave Professor Martensen out of public discussion, since, whether or not he became bishop, he in any case was a candidate for this office, and no doubt desired, while it was pending, that as far as possible nothing pertaining to him would happen.

With Prof. Martensen's appointment as bishop,[14] this consideration dropped out. But since under the circumstances the article could not appear and therefore did not appear right away, I decided that, after all, there was no reason to hurry. Then, too, Bishop Martensen's appointment provoked attack on him from other sides and of a completely different kind[15]; I most definitely did not want to join in with that attack. So I waited; I thought, as stated, that there was no reason at all to hurry and nothing at all to be lost by waiting. Someone might even find that something was gained, find that such a slow emergence of the objection has a deeper significance.

Autumn 1854

*

*   *

But an objection must be raised to this, that Bishop Mynster is supposed to have been a truth-witness.

Bishop Mynster can fairly correctly be said to have carried an entire generation—therefore to bring clarity into our confused religious situation and concepts is a difficulty bordering on the impossible as long as a more truthful light does not fall on the truth of Bishop Mynster's proclamation of Christianity, which is after all also my fault, since Bishop Mynster, precisely Bishop Mynster, was in a way the distress of my life—not just that he was not a truth-witness (that matter would not have been so dangerous), but that he, in addition to all the other advantages that he derived on the greatest scale from proclaiming Christianity, also had the enjoyment, by declaiming in the quiet hours on Sunday and by worldly-sagaciously sheltering himself on Monday, of creating the appearance that he was a man of character, a man of principles, a man who stands firm when everything is tottering, a man who does not fail when all others fail etc. etc., although the truth was that to a high degree he was worldly-sagacious, but weak, self-indulgent, and great only as a declaimer—and in a way the distress of my life (which nevertheless, through the love of Governance, in a very high sense benefited me, became a blessing to me); my distress was that I, brought up by my late father on Mynster's sermons, and also out of devotion to my late father, honored this false bill of exchange instead of protesting it.

Now he is dead—God be praised that it could be put off as long as he was living! This was achieved, what toward the end I almost despaired of, but this was nevertheless achieved, what was my thought, my wish, which I also can remember once having said years ago to old Grundtvig: Bishop Mynster must first live out his life, be buried with full honors—this was achieved; he was indeed, if I dare say so, buried with full honors. And all the contributions that will come in for the monument to him have no doubt come in by now.

So the silence can no longer continue; the objection must be raised, but all the more earnestly because of its slowness, the objection to representing—from the pulpit, consequently before God—Bishop Mynster as a truth-witness, because it is untrue, but proclaimed in this way it becomes an untruth that cries to heaven.[16]

December 1854.

II

There the Matter Rests![17]

December 28*   S. KIERKEGAARD

From the pulpit to represent Bishop Mynster as a truth-witness, one of the authentic truth-witnesses, to assign him a place in the holy chain—against this an objection must be raised; there the matter rests.

[18]*This article, dated, as one will see, Dec. 28, was delivered to *Fædrelandet.* Then that same evening, to my surprise, I see from *Berlingske Tidende,* no. 302,[19] that in regard to my short articles Bishop Martensen does not have, as I was prepared to expect, an idiosyncrasy similar to the one he in the past stated that he had with regard to the whole "prolix Kierkegaardian literature,"[20] an idiosyncrasy that prevented him from making himself familiar with it. This was what I saw; what I did not see and do not see, however, is what benefit his article is supposed to have, an article that actually does not require any detailed response since it changes nothing in the matter. Bishop Martensen wants to claim that I have made "truth-witness" and "martyr" synonymous and that it is only thereby that I am right in denying that Bishop Mynster was a truth-witness. This is not so. Neither in the article, in which only at the end do I refer to the martyr (but surely the martyr also belongs to the truth-witnesses, especially to "the authentic" truth-witnesses, or what I have called "the first class in the Christian order of precedence," in which in turn there are, I may assume, many more truth-witnesses than martyrs), consequently, neither in the article nor in the *note* to the article (both can be checked) have I made *truth-witness* and *martyr* identical. In the note I have quite definitely pointed out the distinction between proclaiming Christianity in such a way that the proclaimer is "an officeholder, a person of rank, the proclamation his own brilliant career, rich in enjoyment," and a "suffering truth-witness," without in any way whatever asserting that to suffer should mean to suffer death. And this distinction is entirely adequate to substantiate that Bishop Mynster cannot be called a truth-witness, one of the authentic truth-witnesses, one of the holy chain. —As for the sundry things that Dr. Martensen, presumably in the role of duly appointed Bishop of Sjælland and somewhat in the tone of a rowdy and a pugilist, says on behalf of public morals about the offensiveness of the step I have taken, about Jesuitism etc.—this makes no impression at all on me. In part (and this is the crucial point)

To represent him in this way is really to make him ludicrous—for I can readily say the same thing in another way, coming in from another side. To represent a man who, even by proclaiming Christianity, has attained and enjoyed on the greatest scale every possible benefit and advantage, to represent him as a truth-witness, one of the holy chain, is as ludicrous as to talk about a virgin with a flock of children. But this is the situation, as Luther would say: "In this sinful world, people are acquainted with everything pertaining to lewdness; if you want to talk about that, you are promptly understood by everybody, but no one is acquainted with the Christian concepts."[21] This is why they have no understanding of and take exception to the raising of protest against a truth-witness who, from a Christian point of view, is just as ludicrous as that virgin.

XIV
17

There is much that one can be "in addition," and it is the case precisely in connection with everything unimportant that it is suitable for one to be that "in addition." One can be both this and that and in addition an amateur violinist, member of the Friendship Society,[22] captain of the popinjay trap shoot, etc. But to the degree that the important is important, it has precisely the characteristic of being to the same degree unsuitable for one to be that—and something else in addition. The qualification *truth-witness* is a very imperious and extremely unsocial qualification and scrupulously allows itself to be joined only with: being nothing otherwise. *Truth-witness* relates to Christianity's heterogeneity with this world, from which it follows that *the witness* must always be distinguishable by heterogeneity with this world, by

---

it is based, in my view, on a misunderstanding; in part Dr. Martensen is too subaltern a personality to be able to be impressive, especially since he has acquired velvet—for example, a domestic servant certainly cannot be impressive in his uniform, but he is even less impressive in the clothes of his master, the gracious count. Incidentally, I am so accustomed to enduring a blow and then after a few years to having most people agree with me—except that it is forgotten that I had to endure the blow—that I no doubt will endure this blow also, to the benefit of the clarification of Christian concepts. And the judgment about Bishop Mynster, that he was a truth-witness, one of the authentic truth-witnesses, one of the holy chain—an objection must be raised to that, and there the matter rests!

renunciation, by suffering, and from this it follows that to be this is so unsuitable to: being something else in addition. But to be willing to accept on the largest possible scale all benefits and advantages (the truth-witness is precisely what he is by renunciation and suffering) and then in addition to be a truth-witness—to that one must, Christianly scrupulous, say: That is a devil of a witness. Such a truth-witness is not only a monstrosity but an impossibility, like a bird that in addition is a fish, or an iron tool that in addition has the oddity of being made of wood.

This is the way it is; please recall that it is not I who began applying the criterion *truth-witness* to Bishop Mynster's life. No, it is a friend, Prof. Martensen, who has done the deceased this clumsy service and prompted me to say what the truth is, that seen under the light Prof. Martensen supplied Bishop Mynster was "to a high degree a worldly-sagacious man, but weak, self-indulgent, and great only as a declaimer"—this clumsy service, which nevertheless perhaps cannot be called entirely disinterested, since the possible successor to the bishopric of Sjælland, the successor at present, was indeed very well served by also being himself promoted to a truth-witness in such a convenient way.

If, therefore, there actually is so little sense of Christianity in this country that one is unable to understand with what justification I am obliged, and in the strongest terms, by the most glaring contrast, to raise an objection to this forgery, then I can readily give the objection another form. I maintain that from the pulpit to represent Bishop Mynster as a truth-witness, one of the holy chain, wrongs to the highest degree every other remarkable and well-deserving man in the country. A jurist like Privy Councilor Ørsted,[23] a poet like Heiberg,[24] a scholar like Madvig,[25] a physician like Bang,[26] actors like Nielsen,[27] Rosenkilde,[28] and Phister,[29] and so on in many contexts, all these men who while they live can by no means be said to have a more rewarding situation, to receive more of the world's benefits and enjoyments than Bishop Mynster received, on the contrary must be said to have a far less rewarding situation—all such men have altogether the same entitlement as Bishop Mynster to be buried as truth-witnesses. XIV 18

But the Protestant clergy still persist in an odd notion. Although they have become just like every one else who, within the stipulation of observing civic justice, develops what possible talent one has and thereby like all the others seeks earthly reward and enjoyment, they want *in addition* to be something more, to be truth-witnesses.

And this came out very clearly in Prof. Martensen's memorial address. Therefore an objection should be raised, and then as emphatically as possible the blood should be stirred, passion set in motion. This of course can be done only if a person does not himself fear the immediate result, that many will become enraged at him, which he ought not to fear but understand as the operating surgeon understands that the patient screams and kicks.[30] An objection should be raised, and the blow in this instance should hit the head—and when the article came out Prof. Martensen had indeed been the head for a long time.

Thus should it be; thus did it happen; there the matter rests!

*

*   *

"Also out of devotion to my late father, I have honored this false bill of exchange (the appearance that Bishop Mynster was a man of character) instead of protesting it." There the matter rests.

If the many *friends*, adherents, and admirers of the deceased, once they have calmed down a bit, do not want to understand that I—please check!—who certainly have not had benefit from my relationship to Bishop Mynster, have shown a resignation with regard to him that a younger person very rarely shows to an elder, have done and tolerated what a younger person very seldom does and tolerates in relation to an elder—if they refuse to understand that, and then in turn what it implies, that they owe me a debt of gratitude for the many years I have borne with the deceased, if they refuse to understand that—all right, then, that's their business.

I ask the *enemies* of the deceased not to jubilate or rejoice as if they had won something, which to my mind they have not done at all. According to my concepts their position is altogether unaltered, and if the occasion is presented it would not be impossible that I could once again come out in the usual way (precious recollections, how joyfully I did it!) against his enemies and do battle for Bishop Mynster, my late father's pastor.

Bishop Mynster was the only one of his kind in Denmark; there is only one single person in Denmark who is definitely in the right in relation to him, and I am that one. I have not pronounced judgment upon Bishop Mynster, no, but in the hands of Governance I became the occasion for Bishop Mynster to pronounce judgment upon himself: his sermon on Sunday he either did not recognize or dared not or would not acknowledge on Monday—because, ironically enough, I was innocently his own sermon on Mondays.[31] If on Monday Bishop Mynster had not himself worldly-sagaciously avoided taking the consequences of his Sunday sermon, if he had ventured an existence and actions that corresponded to the rhetoric of the Sunday discourse instead of availing himself of different models—his life would also have come to look entirely different.

But only an enemy will hasten to pronounce a judgment such as that as long as the man is living; the one who is devoted to him says: It must be deferred until the very end; even in the last moment he could, after all, prevent this judgment and be extraordinarily beneficial with one little word; and what resignation is capable of doing must be done, if it is possible, to move him to that.

So, then, there the matter rests: also out of devotion to my late father, I have honored this false bill of exchange instead of protesting it.

*

*   *

"I was his own sermon on Mondays," that I was. By enduring this indignation year after year, moreover, with the unaltered resignation with which I did it, I have become quite different from what I was, or it became more and more clear to me what I was: "The distress of my life became, through the love of Governance, in a very high sense a good for me, became a blessing to me." My relationship of many years to Bishop Mynster is the unity, on my part, of a profoundly planned and very carefully

XIV
20

executed purpose and, with the cooperation of Governance, my own development. Thus it is understandable that I cannot pay attention to what every anonymous person, every "Æskulap" (the signature in *Kjøbenhavnsposten*[32]) utters in a newspaper, or to what an earnest man from Nørrebro with the earnestness of *Flyveposten*[33] enlightens people about, that I lack earnestness.

As for the scream that is heard, this scream—to attack a dead person who cannot reply etc.[34]—to that must be said: It is a misunderstanding, most likely mainly female stridence. I have, after all, stated how it stands with me: "God be praised that it could be put off as long as the old man was living; toward the end I almost despaired over it." Indeed, God be praised that I escaped having to embitter on the most frightful scale an old man's last years of life by showing that, compared with the Christianity of the New Testament, the Mynsterian proclamation of Christianity and Church leadership—if he would not, and as solemnly as possible, make the confession that they were not the Christianity of the New Testament—were an illusion, and all his "earnestness and wisdom," Christianly speaking, were high treason against Christianity, which in its divine majesty disdains being served with worldly sagacity (as if it were politics, a kingdom of this world).

Moreover, seen from another point of view, I have neglected nothing that may be incumbent on me as duty to the cause I have the honor of serving. At the end of his life, I broached (but indirectly, by means of *Practice in Christianity*) to the old gentleman as proximately as possible whether he wanted to engage in battle. By what he did, I was sadly convinced of how weak he was.[35] Out of concern for him, I hid this from the contemporaries and said it personally only to him and as emphatically as possible. Yet, since this weakness of his was a fact, I had to take a little precautionary measure for the sake of the most extreme contingency

XIV
21

that could arise. That was done in *For Self-Examination* where, as one will see, I bisected him, but, it is true, so covertly that not even his enemies have seen it, so covertly that newspaper articles[36] now quote this passage[37] against me as a eulogy of him, whereas precisely there I had taken my precautionary measure for the sake of the most extreme contingency that could arise and approximately said: Your Reverence is totally out of character with your preaching. But I hid it, and why? Because, of course, I always wished to be able, if possible, to carry out my first, my so precious thought: Mynster shall live out his life and be buried with full honors. Privately I have spoken emphatically enough to Bishop Mynster. In my books I have pursued my task, and with my being and my authorship I am a continual attack on the whole Mynsterian proclamation of Christianity, yet in such a way that at any moment it was possible for Bishop Mynster by an admission to come into accord with me—then I would be his defense. But I well realize how most people read, how thoughtlessly, and that therefore if I so wished—and that I would wish for several reasons, "*also* out of veneration for my late father's pastor"—by paying him compliments I could charm people into thinking that we two were in accord; then my activity would strengthen his reputation in the eyes of most people and everything that goes by the name of unrest, revolt, catastrophe (to which the old gentleman was immensely opposed) would be avoided. Because he carefully read my books and because I talked privately with him, the old gentleman was better informed about our unity, although I am sure he never really has doubted my sincere devotion to him, even when it seemed most awkward.

Thus, God be praised, it was attained, that which was my first thought, my so precious wish, which toward the end I was close to despairing over: Mynster shall live out his life, be buried with full honors! And he did indeed live out his life undiminished; he was indeed buried with full honors; the monument will certainly also be erected—but then no further, and he must least of all go down in history as a truth-witness, one of the authentic truth-witnesses, one of the holy chain—there the matter rests!

III

A Challenge to Me from
Pastor Paludan-Müller[38]

January 11   S. KIERKEGAARD

Pastor Paludan-Müller has published a pamphlet against me that a reviewer in *Berlingske Tidende*[39] has of course promptly trumpeted as something altogether excellent, a situation reminiscent of a scene in *Figaro*, where Bartholo and Basil mime their thanks to each other for having pleaded the maiden Marceline's cause.[40] Frankly, I find it quite sensible, since I, even if I wanted to, could not possibly answer or thank all of the many who are coming out against me—I find it quite sensible of them that they are preparing, as I see, to answer and thank one another reciprocally.

So, then, a pamphlet against me by Pastor P.-M., and in it—something *Berlingske Tidende* has immediately given the greatest possible publicity—a challenge to me, assuming perhaps, who knows, that I presumably would as usual maintain silence. In my article in *Fædrelandet*, I said of Bishop Mynster's preaching, "It veils, tones down, suppresses, omits some of what is most decisively Christian." In this connection the challenge is made to me that I, with the New Testament alongside, will demonstrate this so that in some way it is worth discussing; in that case Pastor P.-M. will refute it.

"So that in some way it is worth discussing," what is this? If I were to engage in this, it perhaps would end with my running a fool's errand because I had not secured an authentic interpretation of what is supposed to be meant by: so that in some way it is worth discussing.

I shall, however, ignore this; but the reason I do not intend to engage in this is that I am afraid that there could be a trap here, so that, if I entered into it, it would very shortly turn the whole issue and the position of the issue into something altogether different from what it is. The issue is: "Was Bishop Mynster a truth-witness, one of the authentic truth-witnesses? Is this the truth?" The issue is: from my side a strongly worded protest against representing, from the pulpit, Bishop Mynster as a truth-witness, one of the authentic truth-witnesses, one of the holy chain. Now perhaps this should be forgotten, the whole thing be changed into a prolix, learned, theological investigation with quotations and quotations etc. about Mynster's preaching, an investigation in which, because of the great number and the learning of the participants, we surely would soon be in deep water up to our ears. No, thanks!*

What I have said is brief, appropriate: Bishop Mynster's preaching veils, tones down, suppresses, omits some of what is most decisively Christian. When it is said, anyone can see it, especially the simple person. For the more educated person who knows about such things, I can say: Mynster's preaching stands in relation to the Christianity of the New Testament as Epicureanism to Stoicism, or as cultivation, improvement, polish stand in relation to fundamental change, radical cure. At no point does his preaching ever lead to the essentially Christian, to what is everywhere in the New Testament, a break, the most profound, the most incurable break with this world. Just as little did Bishop Mynster's life resemble a break with this world in even the remotest way (which is easily explained by his infinite anxiety about everything radical), unless we accept the explanation: one

XIV
24

---

*I ask everyone who might want to heed my advice, provided he is of a mind to want to express himself publicly, to observe the strictest diet with regard to not becoming involved in general, broad, learned, prolix, scholarly debate with lexicon, grammar, and the enormous mass of scholarly apparatus and multitude of quotations, darkening even what is perfectly plain, because he thereby is only serving my opponent, who (as one smothers a fire with feather quilts, and as one produces oblivion by prolixity) may in this very way manage to evade the brief, clear fact, the point, what is perhaps crucial for the established order: to represent, from the pulpit, Bishop Mynster as a truth-witness, one of the authentic truth-witnesses, one of the holy chain, a point that was not made better but worse by the flippancy, ill-advised for the established order, of the same man, the head of the Church, the Honorable Right Reverend Bishop Martensen, in the face of a Christianly highly justified objection.

is a *tout-à-fait* [complete] man of the world, a man entirely of this world, and "in addition" one has unconditionally broken with this world, which is equivalent to: even by proclaiming Christianity to attain and enjoy all benefits and advantages and "in addition" to be a truth-witness, and that, as I pointed out[41] (alluding to that beautiful metaphor of heterogeneity to this world: maidenhood, virginity), is equivalent to a virgin with a flock of children.

Here I could end. Let me, however, add a few words in connection with my impression that one of his defenders has used an expression that presumably even Mynster's most zealous admirers will acknowledge as correct. "Bishop Mynster was not really a preacher of repentance." But this, especially for a truth-witness, is malpractice, since all truly Christian preaching is first and foremost the preaching of repentance. "Bishop Mynster was more a preacher of peace."[42] But this, especially for a truth-witness, is malpractice: in the capacity of a preacher of peace to proclaim the doctrine of the one who himself has said (as is well known, Jesus' own words): "I have not come to bring peace, but discord"[43]—neither did he come to the world in order to enjoy, but in order to suffer. And this is why I have said of Bishop Mynster that he, seen in the light of a truth-witness and Christianly evaluated, was self-indulgent: he loved, self-indulgently, "peace," the first condition for enjoying life, all according to Epicurus's old adage: "*nil beatum nisi quietum*" [nothing is happy unless in repose];[44] that is, the first condition for all enjoyment of life is peace.

XIV
25

Let this be enough for now. This is an exception I have made; primarily I must leave it to the many who are coming out against me to answer and thank one another reciprocally.[45]

IV

The Point at Issue with Bishop Martensen,[46] as Christianly Decisive for the, Christianly Viewed, Dubious Previously Established Ecclesiastical Order[47]

January 26   S. KIERKEGAARD

The point at issue is: from the pulpit to represent Bishop Mynster as a truth-witness, one of the authentic witnesses, one of the holy chain.

It is this that continually must be held firm, this that everyone who is involved in earnest in this matter must have impressed upon him every blessed day in order to be able to hold it firm despite the mass of confusion dished out by the press these past days.

This is the point—and it will become apparent that by canonizing Bishop Mynster in this way the new bishop will make the whole ecclesiastical established order, from the Christian point of view, into a shameless indecency.

In other words, if Bishop Mynster is a truth-witness, then—even the blindest can see this—every pastor in the country is a truth-witness, because what was esthetically remarkable and extraordinary in Bishop Mynster is not at all pertinent to the question of being or not being a truth-witness, a question that pertains to character, life, existence; and in this regard Bishop Mynster was altogether homogeneous with every other pastor in the country who does not sin against civic justice. Therefore, every pastor in the country is also a truth-witness.

But when one places the customary proclamation of Christianity in this country, the official proclamation of Christianity, carried out by royal officeholders, persons of rank, whose secular career is the proclamation, when one places this proclamation of Christianity alongside the New Testament, alongside what Jesus Christ (the poor man, the scorned man, the man mocked and spat upon) requires of *a follower of Jesus Christ* (and of course the pastor certainly should be such a one by virtue of being regarded as a truth-witness), alongside what Jesus Christ requires, to proclaim the doctrine *for nothing*,[48] to proclaim the doctrine in poverty, in abasement, in renunciation of everything, in the most unconditional heterogeneity to this world, at the greatest distance from all use or assistance of worldly power etc.—then it is all too easy to see that compared with the New Testament the official proclamation of Christianity can be defended (if it can be defended) only in the way I formerly suggested through the pseudonym Anti-Climacus.[49] In that respect, please note, the established order has heretofore not let itself be heard from, has not in even the remotest manner made a move to want to acknowledge at what distance it relates itself to the Christianity of the New Testament, and cannot truthfully be called a striving in the direction of coming closer to the Christianity of the New Testament.

As soon, however, as it is heard that the pastor is also a truth-witness, that what we call a pastor means also to be a truth-witness, at that very same moment the whole ecclesiastical established order, from the Christian point of view, is a shameless indecency. With this claim the established order can no longer be considered an extreme mitigation that still relates itself to the Christianity of the New Testament, but it is an obvious falling away from the Christianity of the New Testament, and with that claim is, from the Christian point of view, a shameless indecency, an attempt verging on making a fool of God, making a fool of him, as if we did not understand what it is he is talking about in his Word. But when in his Word he speaks about proclaiming the doctrine for nothing, we understand it in such a way that the proclamation naturally is the livelihood, the most secure way to bread and butter and with steadily advancing promotion. When in his Word he speaks about proclaiming the Word in poverty, we understand thereby a yearly salary in the thousands. When in his Word he speaks about proclaiming the Word in abasement, we understand it as making a career, becoming His Excellency. And by heterogeneity to this world we understand becoming a royal officeholder, a person of rank. By disdain for the assistance and use of worldly power we understand being safeguarded by making use of worldly power. By suffering for the doctrine we understand using the police against the others. By renunciation of everything we understand acquiring everything, the most select refinements, for which the pagan has in vain had itchy fingers— —and in addition we are truth-witnesses.

XIV
28

By representing Bishop Mynster as a truth-witness, one of the holy chain, the Honorable Right Reverend Councilor of Conference Bishop Martensen—with whomever it is that he confers—transforms the ecclesiastical established order into, from the Christian point of view, a shameless indecency. No one who considers, which Christianity teaches, that he faces a responsibility of eternity, a judgment (in which the judge is the abased one, the one mocked and spat upon, the crucified one, who taught "Follow me," "My kingdom is not of this world"[50]), an accounting in which crimes of high treason against Christianity are the very last crimes to be forgiven: no one who considers this can keep silent about Bishop Martensen's new teaching on what is to be understood by a truth-witness, one of the holy chain—no one can keep silent about that, even if (which, incidentally, makes no difference to me), even if I were to become the only one who did not keep silent; for me it is enough that it will be noticed in eternity that I did not keep silent.

*   *

*

Not mitigated but intensified, I hereby repeat my objection: I would rather gamble, booze, wench, steal, and murder than take part in making a fool of God, would rather spend my days in the bowling alley, in the billiard parlor, my nights in games of chance or at masquerades than participate in the kind of earnestness Bishop Martensen calls Christian earnestness. Indeed, I would rather make a fool of God very directly, climb to a high place or go out in the open where I am alone with him and there say outright, "You are a bad God, worth no more than for one to make a fool of you," rather than make a fool of him by way of solemnly pretending to be holy, pretending that my life is sheer ardor and zeal for Christianity, yet, please note, in such a way that it—cursed equivocation!—"in addition" is continually my temporal and earthly profit, pretending that my life first and last is enthusiasm for proclaiming the doctrine, yet, please note, in such a way that there are certain things I prefer first and last to disregard, and if they are mentioned, pretending that it is as if I did not understand them, as if I did not understand what God is speaking about, that he is speaking about suffering hunger and thirst and cold and nakedness and imprisonment and flogging[51] for the doctrine, that this is what he understands to be a truth-witness, and that if I shrink from this condition and would prefer a more pleasant way, would rather that the proclaiming of Christianity might be the same as any other work, or at least richer in enjoyment than the others, and that I, if this can be done, if in that way I can become as blessed as the truth-witness, then I shall thank my God for it and keep my damnable mouth from gossip about being in addition a truth-witness, and if ultimately I cannot hold my tongue, then I shall at least confine myself to that kind of talk over a cup of tea in the parlor with my wife and some prattling friends, but on the other hand keep watch on myself in the pulpit.

But from the pulpit, consequently before God, to represent Bishop Mynster as a truth-witness, one of the authentic truth-witnesses, one of the holy chain—before God, whose presence was indeed assured by calling on him in a prayer before the sermon to be present; to represent him (for certainly this also was done), to represent him—God in heaven!—as a prototype for the congregation, consequently, as a Christian prototype for a Christian congregation! So, then, *the Way* has now become something else, not the one in the New Testament: in abasement, hated, abandoned, persecuted, and cursed to suffer in this world—no, the Way is: admired, applauded, honored, and knighted to make a brilliant career! And just as *the Way* has become something else, indeed, the opposite, so also the interpretation of Scripture. When we read in the New Testament the passage that Bishop Martensen used in the memorial address, Hebrews 13:7: "Remember your leaders . . . and when you consider the outcome of their course of life, then imitate their faith," this is no longer to be understood to mean: Consider the outcome of their life, that is, see that their life, which was sheer renunciation and sheer suffering for the doctrine, remains faithful to itself to the end, does not regret having sacrificed everything, but also in death, perhaps in a martyr's death, retains the cheerful boldness of faith. Now it is no longer to be understood in that way, no, it is to be understood in this way, as Bishop Martensen teaches: Consider Bishop Mynster, look at the outcome of the course of his life; think of it, he advanced to the rank of Excellency; consider the outcome of his life, you yourselves of course know what preparations were made for that most pompous funeral: consider this—and then follow him; he is the Way, not Christ, who admonishingly says, "What is exalted among people is an abomination in the sight of God" (Luke 16:15).

    XIV
    30

    If I am not mistaken, a complaint has just now been made through the bishop that somewhere here in our country a church has inappropriately been used for a political meeting. Suppose that somewhere else they thought of using it for a dance—what is that compared with using the church in the name of Christian worship to make a fool of God! But of course when the bishop himself does it, one cannot complain about it *via* the bishop.

    As far as I am concerned, I do not really intend to complain to any person either; I only repeat my objection. That I will not be understood—I am understood by God and understand myself. That I will be disliked—well, that is what the New Testament predicts.[52] That I will not prevail—Christianly the victory is won only by getting the worst of it!

    But when something scandalous [*Forargelige*] has occurred, then indignation [*Forargelse*] must be aroused against it, and one must not complain that the step I have taken has unfortunately aroused such great indignation[53]—no, instead it has not yet aroused enough indignation with regard to the scandal of representing, from the pulpit, Bishop Mynster as a truth-witness, one of the authentic witnesses, one of the holy chain. "The blood should be stirred, passion set in motion";[54] if it falls on the operating surgeon, that is merely part of the operation. After more than forty years (served with great worldly sagacity) of magic charm, moreover, when the magic charmer is going to be made a truth-witness, then one cannot proceed leniently, unless one wishes oneself, together with one's objection, to be transformed into a little charming entertainment along with the old magic.

V

Two New Truth-Witnesses[55]

January 26   S. KIERKEGAARD

"There is a difference in gifts," says Bishop Martensen in *Berlingske Tidende* no. 302,[56] and rightly so. The late bishop had a very unusual gift for concealing the weak sides and frailties of the established order; the new bishop, Martensen, also a gifted man, has a rare gift for exposing, even in the least little thing he undertakes, one or another of the established order's weak sides. The late bishop had an unusual gift for sagaciously giving in, easing off, accommodating, evading; Bishop Martensen—for there is a difference in gifts—has a fateful, especially at this moment for the established order, gift for wanting obstinately to persist. Yet it could well be that the thought of Governance was possibly as follows: The established order should stand as long as the old gentleman, who was gifted also for that, was living; after his death the established order will fall, and then for that Dr. Martensen is in the bishopric, a man gifted exactly in that direction. Nor is more than Bishop Martensen really necessary; I perhaps will become entirely superfluous, or what I may eventually do will be something quite minor, I who otherwise, also in this regard, am not exactly without gifts, inasmuch as I have the gift to see—what Bishop Martensen exposes.

It was the language usage, to call *witnesses, truth-witnesses* what
we understand by pastors, deans, and bishops—it was the language usage I protested against because it is blasphemous, sacrilegious, but Bishop Martensen obstinately persists in it, as is evident in his ordination address,*[57] which he incessantly interlards with "witnessing, being a witness, truth-witness, " etc.

*The addresses given on this occasion have now been published; Diocesan Dean Tryde's introduction, a mere nothing, distinguishes itself by a footnote, as if it were something: "The author is prompted to explain that nothing has been left out—nothing changed."

In the New Testament, Christ calls the apostles and followers witnesses, requires of them that they shall *witness* for him.[58] Let us now see what is to be understood by that. They are men who in renunciation of everything, in poverty, in lowliness, then, ready for any suffering, are to go out into a world that with all its might and main expresses the contrast to what it is to be a Christian. This is what Christ calls witnessing, being a witness.

What we call pastor, dean, bishop is a livelihood just like every other livelihood in society, and, note well, in a society where, since all call themselves Christians, there is not the slightest danger connected with lecturing on Christianity, where, on the contrary, this profession must be regarded as one of the most pleasant and most honored.

Now I ask, is there the slightest similarity between these pastors, deans, and bishops and what Christ calls witnesses? Or is it not just as ludicrous to call such pastors, deans, and bishops "witnesses" in the New Testament sense of the word, just as ludicrous as to call a parade ground maneuver a war? No, if the clergy want to be called witnesses, truth-witnesses, they must also resemble what the New Testament understands by witnesses, truth-witnesses; if they are utterly unwilling to resemble what the New Testament understands by witnesses, truth-witnesses, they must not be called that either; then they may be called teachers, public officials, professors, councilors—in short, anything one wishes, but not truth-witnesses.

But Bishop Martensen untiringly insists that they are witnesses, truth-witnesses. If the clergy understand their interests, they will not hesitate to ask the bishop to discontinue this language usage, which, to put it mildly, makes the whole profession ludicrous. To be sure, I know several very respectable, competent, exceptionally competent clergymen, but I venture to claim that in the whole kingdom there is not a single one who, seen in the light of *truth-witness*, is not comical.

To make the whole profession ludicrous, to put it mildly, is really not appropriate for a bishop; nor is it appropriate for a bishop, because this language usage "witnesses, truth-witnesses" must obstinately be carried through, to change a solemn ceremony such as the consecration of a bishop into something over which one does not know whether one should laugh or cry. The ordination took place on Second Christmas Day, the martyr Stephen's day. How satirical! The bishop used the occasion to remark, among other things, that the word *truth-witness* on this day has a unique sound.[59] This is undeniable, except that this unique sound is a dissonance, because either Stephen becomes ludicrous by virtue of the "many truth-witnesses" that Dr. Martensen has available or, in the light of Stephen, they all become ludicrous in the capacity of truth-witnesses.

VI

At Bishop Mynster's Death[60]

Mark 13:2 . . . . . Do you see these great buildings?
There will not—[61]

March 31, 1854*   S. KIERKEGAARD

It certainly would have been most desirable for it to have ended
with Bishop Mynster's telling the people, directly and as solemnly as possible, that what he has represented was not the
Christianity of the New Testament, but, if you will, a pious mitigation, a toning down, in many ways shrouded in illusion.

It did not happen!

I for my part stand unchanged by my claim, except that I now
declare aloud and publicly what I privately took up with the late
bishop and concealed from his enemies—because I was fighting
against them for him—concealed from the many, who certainly
suspected nothing: official Christianity, the proclamation of official Christianity, is not in any sense the Christianity of the New
Testament. In any case this must be confessed and as loudly and
openly as possible, so that Governance, if it so pleases, can intervene and we can then find out whether it will allow such a proc-

lamation of Christianity. But without such a confession, the
proclamation of official Christianity, by passing itself off as being
the Christianity of the New Testament, is, unconsciously or
well-intentionedly—illusion. Christianity cannot be served by
calling this Christianity in the sense of being the Christianity of
the New Testament; and by this the congregation cannot be
served Christianly, because it does not become aware of what
Christianity is according to the New Testament.

*Please note the year and the date.

*   *

*

Annunciation Day

O my friend, whoever you are who chances to see this, when I
read in the New Testament the life of our Lord Jesus Christ on
earth and what he understood by what it is to be a Christian—
and I then think about our now being Christians by the millions,
just as many Christians as we are human beings, and that from
generation to generation Christians by the millions are handed
over to eternity's inspection—frightful! That this does not hang
together properly, nothing can be more sure. Say it then yourself:
But what use is it—and even if it were ever so pious and well-
intentioned—what use is it to want (lovingly?) to strengthen you
in the delusion that you are a Christian, or to want to change the
conception of being a Christian, presumably so that you are able
to enjoy this life all the more securely; what use is it, or more
correctly, must this not simply damage you, since it will help you
to allow temporality to be unused Christianly—until you stand
in eternity, where you are not a Christian if you were not one,
and where it is impossible to become one? You who read this,
say it yourself: Was I not right and am I not right, that first and
foremost everything must be done to have it definitely determined what is required in the New Testament for being a Christian, that first and foremost everything must be done so that we
are at least able to become aware?

VII

Is This Christian Worship or Is It Making a Fool of God?

(*A MATTER OF CONSCIENCE* [IN ORDER TO RELIEVE MY CONSCIENCE])[62]

May 1854   S. Kierkegaard

When at a given time the relationship is this, that one, privately aware, acts as if nothing had happened, although everything is changed:

when the *teacher* (the pastor) is committed by oath on the New Testament, is ordained, although he not only does not have a portrait-resemblance to a follower of Jesus Christ but not even a caricature-resemblance, no, is exactly the opposite, the banal contrast;

when the *doctrine*, which is proclaimed as God's Word, differs from God's Word in that it is not the same, nor the opposite, but neither the one nor the other, which is the very opposite to Christianity and God's Word;

when the *situation* in which there is speaking (and the situation is what really determines how what is said is to be understood), when the situation does not resemble the situation in the New Testament any more than a bourgeois citizen's parlor and the child's playroom resemble the most frightful decisions of the most dreadful actuality, or even less, inasmuch as one inanely still makes it look as if the two situations resembled each other;

when the relationship is this—and then one, privately aware, officially acts as if nothing had happened—is this then Christian worship or is it making a fool of God, making a fool of him by means of such official worship, perhaps in the belief that if we simply call it Christianity we probably can make him think that it is Christianity by preaching it to him every Sunday?

Ascension Day

1. About the Teacher (the Pastor), That He Is the Banal Contrast

A realistic description of the pastor is: a half-worldly, half-ecclesiastical, totally equivocal officeholder, a person of rank with a family, who (in the hope of promotion by seniority and of automatically becoming a knight—how entirely in the spirit of the New Testament!) ensures himself a livelihood, also, if necessary, with the help of the police (is this, I wonder, to carry out the apostolic admonition "not to run aimlessly?" I Corinthians 9:26*), ensures a livelihood for himself, lives on Jesus Christ's having been crucified, claiming that this profound earnestness (this "imitation of Jesus Christ"?) is the Christianity of the New Testament, sadly lamenting and bewailing that unfortunately there are only very few true Christians in the congregation—since it is quite certain that the pastor is a true Christian and is that despite his wearing long robes, something Christ does not exactly recommend when, in both Mark and Luke (Mark 12:38, Luke 20:46) he says, "Beware of those who go about in long robes."

2. About the Situation

In the New Testament the situation is this: the speaker, our Lord Jesus Christ, stands—himself unconditionally expressing the contrast—in a world that in turn unconditionally expresses the contrast to him and his doctrine. When Christ requires faith of the individual, then (and this, of course, implies the more detailed specification of what he understands by faith), then because of the situation this cannot be done without entering into a perhaps even highly dangerous relation to the surrounding world. When Christ says: Confess me before the world,[63] follow me,[64]

---

*The apostle understands it thus: "I mortify my body in order not to run aimlessly."

or when he says: Come to me[65] etc. etc., then because of the situation, which provides the more detailed understanding, the consequence will continually become an exposing of oneself to danger, perhaps even mortal danger. But where everything is Christian and all are Christians, even the atheists, the situation is this: calling oneself a Christian is the means by which one protects oneself against all sorts of trouble and inconvenience in life, and the means by which one secures for oneself earthly goods, conveniences, profit, etc. etc. But we act as if nothing had happened, we declaim ("who can do it best, our pastor can"[66]), we declaim about having faith, about confessing Christ before the world, about following him, etc. etc., and orthodoxy flourishes in the land, no heresies, no schisms, orthodoxy everywhere, the orthodoxy that is—playing at Christianity.

VIII

What Must Be Done—
It Will Happen either through Me or
through Someone Else[67]

Second Day of Pentecost 1854   S. KIERKEGAARD

First and foremost and on the greatest possible scale an end must
be put to the entire official—well-intentioned—untruth that—
well-intentioned—conjures up and sustains the appearance that
it is Christianity that is being proclaimed, the Christianity of the
New Testament. In this regard it is a matter of not being lenient.
If the "atheists" have already made a heavy attack, it must become only more forceful (unless one wants it otherwise) when
the person who is fighting this untruth does not have Satan but
has God on his side.

When that is done, the matter must be turned this way: Is not
the truth of the matter actually this, that from generation to generation everything has gone downhill for us human beings; have
not we human beings from generation to generation become
degenerated and demoralized to the degree that we have almost
become merely animal creatures, that the truth of the matter is
unfortunately that we—instead of this insolent nonsense that
Christianity is perfectible, that we are progressing, indeed, that
Christianity perhaps is not able to satisfy us anymore—that when
all is said and done we, the wretched, miserable ordinary populace, are actually unable to bear the divineness that is the Christianity of the New Testament, and that in a way we must be
satisfied with the kind of religiousness that is now the official
religiousness, after, please note, it has been made clear that it is in
no way the Christianity of the New Testament. This is how the
matter must be turned and the question must be posed: Is it perhaps the same with the human race as with the individual, that as

with him the older he becomes the worse and worse off he is (something he cannot change but must humbly be reconciled to)—is it perhaps the same with the human race, that consequently it cannot be changed, that it is not God's requirement for us to change this, but that we must reconcile ourselves to confessing humbly the wretchedness that the human race is now at the age when it literally will be true that there no longer exists or is born one single individual who is able to be Christian in the New Testament sense? This is how the matter must be turned. Away, away, away with all optical illusions, forward with the truth, say forthrightly: We are incapable of being Christians in the New Testament sense—and yet we need to dare to hope for an eternal happiness, which we therefore have to obtain on conditions completely different from those the New Testament establishes.

If the matter is turned in this way, it will become apparent whether there is some truth in this, whether it has the approval of Governance—if not, then everything must burst so that in this nightmare individuals who are able to bear New Testament Christianity might again come into existence. But an end, an end must be made to the official—well-intentioned—untruth.

IX

The Religious Situation[68]

January 1855   S. KIERKEGAARD

The religious situation in the land is:

Christianity (that is, the Christianity of the New Testament—and everything else is indeed not Christianity, least of all by calling itself that), Christianity does not exist at all, something almost everyone certainly must be able to see just as well as I do.

We have, if you please, a full staff of bishops, deans, pastors. Learned, exceptionally learned, talented, gifted, humanly well-intentioned, they all declaim—well, very well, exceptionally well, or fairly well, poorly, badly—but not one of them is in the character of the Christianity of the New Testament, any more than in the character of striving toward the Christianity of the New Testament. But if that is the case, then the existence of this Christian staff is so far from being Christianly of benefit to Christianity that instead it is much more dangerous, because it so very easily occasions an erroneous view and the erroneous conclusion that if there is such a full staff then there naturally is also Christianity. A geographer, for example, if he was convinced of the existence of this staff, would feel perfectly justified in entering in his geography: The Christian religion prevails in the land.

We have what could be called a complete inventory of churches, bells, organs, offering boxes, collection boxes, hymn boards, hearses, etc. But if Christianity does not exist, then the existence of this inventory is so far from being Christianly of benefit that instead it is much more dangerous, because it so very easily occasions an erroneous view and the erroneous conclusion that if there is such a complete Christian inventory then there naturally is also Christianity. A statistician, for example, if he had ascertained the existence of this Christian inventory, would feel perfectly justified in entering in the statistics: The Christian religion is the prevailing religion in the land.

We are, as it is called, a Christian nation—but in such a way that not a single one of us is in the character of the Christianity of the New Testament, no more than I am; I have repeated again and again and repeat once again: I am only a poet. The illusion of a Christian nation is certainly due to the power that numbers exercise over the imagination. I have no doubt at all that every individual in the nation will be honest enough to God and to himself to say in a private conversation, "If I am to be honest, I do not deny it, I am not a Christian in the New Testament sense; if I am to be honest, I do not deny it, my life cannot be called a striving toward what the New Testament calls Christianity, toward denying myself, renouncing the world, dying to the world, etc. Instead, every year I live, the worldly and the temporal become more and more important to me, and the striving of my life tends to settle me ever more firmly in the worldly and the temporal." Nor do I doubt that everyone will be able to maintain this view with regard to, for example, ten of his acquaintances, that they are not Christians in the New Testament sense any more than their lives are an effort to become that. But when it is 100,000, it becomes confusing for him.

There is an amusing story about a saloon-keeper—incidentally, one of my pseudonymous authors has told this story in passing,[69] but this ludicrous story has always seemed to me to have something profound in it, and therefore I use it again. He is said to have sold his bottled beer for a cent under the purchase price, and when someone said to him: "How does that pay? Indeed, you are losing money," he answered, "No, my friend, it is the quantity that does it"—the quantity, which indeed also in our day is omnipotent. When one has laughed at this story, one does well to heed the moral, which warns against the power that numbers exercise over the imagination. In other words, there can be no doubt that the saloon-keeper realized very well that to sell for three cents a bottle of beer that costs him four cents means a loss of one cent. Also, when it is a matter of ten bottles the saloon-keeper will be able to maintain that it is a loss. But, but 100,000 bottles—here the big number sets the imagination in motion, the round number runs away with it, the saloon-keeper is all at sea—it becomes a profit, he says, because the quantity does it.

So it is also with the reckoning that gets a Christian nation by combining the ones who are not Christians, gets it by way of "It is the quantity that does it." For true Christianity this is the most dangerous of all illusions, and of all illusions it is also the very one to which every human being is most disposed, because the number (the big number, when it gets up to 100,000, to millions) and the imagination suit each other completely. But from the Christian point of view, the reckoning is obviously wrong, and a Christian nation composed of ones who honestly confess that they are not Christians, likewise honestly confess that their lives by no means can be called a striving toward what the New Testament understands by Christianity—a Christian nation such as that is an impossibility. On the other hand, a scoundrel could wish no better hiding place than behind such phrases as "The nation is Christian," "The nation is striving Christianly," since it is almost as difficult to come to grips with such phrases as it would be if one were to say: John Doe is a Christian, John Doe is striving Christianly.

But since Christianity is spirit,[70] the sobriety of spirit and the integrity of eternity, there naturally is nothing more suspicious to its detective eye than all these imaginary magnitudes: Christian states, Christian countries, a Christian nation, a—amazing!—a Christian world. And even if there may be some truth in this talk about Christian nations and states, when, please note, all the middle terms, all the distances from the Christianity of the New Testament are honestly and straightforwardly stated and kept recognizable—it is certain that on this point, Christianly, an enormous crime lies concealed—indeed, everything the world has seen of criminal cases until now is a trifle compared with this monstrous criminal case, which, continued from generation to generation over the ages, still has not gone, as can indeed happen with human justice, beyond the control of divine justice.

This is the religious situation. And to prevent, if possible, wasting time, I shall promptly anticipate a turn that perhaps will be given to this matter. Allow me to illustrate with another

situation. Suppose there lives in some country a poet who, with
his eyes on the ideal of being in love, talked like this: "I myself
regrettably must confess that I cannot truly be said to be in love;
neither will I dissemble and say that I am striving more and more,
because regrettably the truth is that instead it is going backward.
Furthermore, my observations convince me that in the whole
country there probably is not a single person who can be said to
be truly in love." Then the inhabitants of that country might
reply and to a certain degree justifiably: "Well, my good poet,
your ideals may be just fine, but we are satisfied and are happy
with what we call being in love, and with that the matter is
decided." But this can never be the case with Christianity. Indeed, the New Testament decides what Christianity is and re-
serves eternity to judge us. After all, the pastor is bound by an
oath upon the New Testament—therefore that in which we
human beings make ourselves so comfortable by calling it Christianity cannot possibly be Christianity. As soon as one presumes
to dare to turn the matter in this way, Christianity is *eo ipso* [pre-
cisely thereby] abolished, the pastor's oath is a—but I will stop
here; I do not wish to draw conclusions before I am forced to do
it, and even then I do not wish to do it. But if one does not dare
to turn the matter in this way, then there are only two possible
alternatives: either, what I propose, honestly and straightforwardly make a confession with regard to how we relate ourselves
to the Christianity of the New Testament, or by tricks conceal
the true situation, by tricks conjure up the appearance that the
Christianity of the New Testament is the prevailing religion in
the country.

XIV
44

X

[71]A Thesis
—Just One Single One[72]

January 26, 1855   S. KIERKEGAARD

O Luther, you had 95 theses—terrible! And yet, in a deeper
sense, the more theses, the less terrible. The matter is far more
terrible—there is only one thesis.

   *   *
     *

The Christianity of the New Testament does not exist at all.
Here there is nothing to reform; it is a matter of throwing light
on a Christian crime continued over the centuries and practiced
by millions (more or less guilty), a crime whereby little by little,
in the name of the perfecting of Christianity, a sagacious attempt
has been made to trick God out of Christianity and Christianity
has been turned into exactly the opposite of what it is in the New
Testament.

   *   *
     *

In order for it to be possible to say that the ordinary, the official
Christianity here in the land even barely relates itself truly to the
Christianity of the New Testament, it must first of all as honestly,
candidly, and solemnly as possible be acknowledged at what distance it is from the Christianity of the New Testament and how
incapable it is of being truly called a striving toward coming
closer to the Christianity of the New Testament.

 As long as this is not done, as long as one either acts as if
nothing had happened, as if everything were all right and what
we call Christianity is the Christianity of the New Testament, or
one uses tricks to conceal the difference, tricks to maintain the

appearance of being the Christianity of the New Testament—as
long as the Christian crime continues, there can be no question
of reforming but of throwing light on this Christian criminal
case.

*   *
*

As for myself, I am not what the times perhaps crave, a reformer,
in no way; nor am I a profound speculative intellect, a seer, a
prophet—no, I have, if you please, to a rare degree I have a
definite detective talent. What an amazing coincidence that I
should be exactly contemporary with that period in the history
of the Church that, in the modern style, is the period of "truth-
witnesses," in which all are "saintly truth-witnesses."

XI

"Salt";
Because "Christendom" Is:
the Decay of Christianity;
"a Christian World" Is:
a Falling Away from Christianity[73]

February 1855   S. KIERKEGAARD

*

*   *

Before a person can be used as I am being used here, Governance must coerce him in a terrible way; this is also the case with me.

*

*   *

Quite simply, Protestantism is, Christianly, a falsehood, a dishonesty that falsifies the doctrine, Christianity's view of the world and of life, as soon as it is taken to be the principle of Christianity, not a necessary correction (corrective)[74] at a given time and place.

Therefore, to join the Catholic Church would be a rashness of which I shall not be guilty, but which one perhaps will expect since in these times it seems to be utterly forgotten what Christianity is, and even the people who know Christianity best are still only ordinary seamen [*Halvbefarne*].[75]

[76]No, a person can very well be alone in being a Christian. And if a person is not very strong spiritually, then for the sake of Christian precaution, the fewer the better! And in "Christendom" above all, the fewer the better! When all is said and done, the fundamental confusion, both Protestantism's and Catholicism's, lies in the very concept "Church," or it lies in the concept

"Christendom."* Christ has asked for imitators and has very exactly defined what he meant: that they should be salt, willing to be sacrificed, that to be a Christian is to be salt and the willingness to be sacrificed.[77] But to be salt and to be sacrificed are not suitable either to thousands or (even less!) to millions, or (still less!) to countries, kingdoms, states, or (unconditionally not!) to the whole world. If, on the other hand, it is a matter of profit and of mediocrity and of being blather, which is the opposite of being salt, then the possibility of it already commences with the 100,000, increases with every million, stands at its peak when the whole world has become Christian.

Therefore gaining whole nations, kingdoms, countries, a world of Christians is what interests and engages "the people"—because then being a Christian becomes something completely different from what it is in the New Testament.

This has also been achieved, and best, altogether consummately, in Protestantism, especially in Denmark, in the Danish moderate convivial mediocrity. When one sees what it means to be a Christian in Denmark, who would ever dream that it should be what Christ speaks about, a cross and agony and suffering, crucifying the flesh, hating oneself, suffering for the doctrine, being salt, being sacrificed, etc. No, in Protestantism, especially in Denmark, Christianity is sung to another tune, just as Jeppe sings, merrily, merrily, around, around, around[78]—Christianity is the enjoyment of life, reassured as neither paganism nor Judaism was, reassured by having this matter of eternity settled, settled simply in order that we should really have the desire—to enjoy this life—as well as any pagan or Jew.

Christianity does not exist at all. If the human race had risen in rebellion against God and thrown Christianity off or away, it would not have been nearly as dangerous as this skullduggery of

XIV
49

---

*You who read this, take note of the following. When Christianity entered the world, the task was to propagate the doctrine. In "Christendom," where the evil is precisely the untruthful extensiveness brought about by an untruthful propagation, the counteracting of this evil (extensiveness) must above all be careful lest it itself have the form of extensiveness—therefore the fewer the better, preferably literally a single individual, because the evil is due to extensiveness (the extensive); thus the counteraction must come from—the intensive.

having abolished Christianity by means of a false and untrue kind of propagation, of having gotten all to be Christians, and then of having given this activity the appearance of Christian fervor and zeal for the propagation of the doctrine, of having mocked God by thanking him for giving his blessing to Christianity's progress in this manner.

Christ himself has proclaimed what is to be understood by being a Christian; we are able to read it in the Gospels. —Then he left the earth, but predicted his coming again. As for his coming again, there is one prediction he made that goes like this: I wonder, when the Son of man comes again, will he find faith on earth?[79] If everything is all right with these enormous battalions of Christians, nations, kingdoms, countries, a whole world, then the prospect of the second coming is bound to be far off. Conversely viewed, one would certainly have to say: Everything is ready for the second coming.

Thank you, you silk-and-velvet[80] pastors, who in steadily increasing numbers were ready for service when it appeared that the profit was on the side of Christianity; thank you for your Christian fervor and zeal with these millions, kingdoms and countries, a world of Christians; thank you, it was Christian fervor and zeal! Is it not true that if it were to come to be as it was originally, that only a few poor, persecuted, hated people were Christians—what then would become of the velvet and silk, and the enormous incomes, and the honor and esteem and worldly enjoyment, refined as no other voluptuary's, refined by an appearance of holiness that would almost call for worship! Abominable; even humanity's most prodigal dregs still have the merit that their crimes are not hailed and honored, almost worshiped and adored as Christian virtues.

And you, you powers and princes and kings and emperors, alas that you at some moment could let yourselves be deceived by these wily people, as if God in heaven were only the supreme superlative of a human majesty, as if he had, humanly speaking, a cause, so that it would of course be infinitely more important to him that a man of power, not to mention a king, an emperor, was a Christian than that a beggar is that! O my God, my God, my God! No, if in the Christian view there is any difference for

XIV
50

God, then the beggar is infinitely more important than the king, infinitely more important, because the Gospel is preached to the poor![81] But see, to the pastors the king is infinitely more important than the beggar. "A beggar, how will he help us?" You rag of velvet, did Christianity come into the world in order to have help from human beings, or in order to help them, the poor, the beggar, since the Gospel is preached to the poor? "A beggar, how will he help us; we might even have to contribute money!" You shameless scoundrel; indeed, Christianity does mean to contribute money. "But a king, a king—this is extremely important to Christianity." No, you liar, but it is extremely important to you. If the king is a Christian, then the circle of the powerful who surround him immediately follows (and this is why, Christianly, there is something so precarious about a king who is a Christian, lest a transition is initiated to being a Christian that becomes nothing more than a change of costume). And when the king and his powerful circle have become Christians or are called that, more and more follow and at last the whole nation (this is why, Christianly, there is something so precarious about a king's being a Christian, lest the whole thing become a change that nevertheless is no change). And when the whole nation has become Christian, then—see, therefore it is so infinitely important that the king is a Christian!—then come silk and velvet and royal decorations of stars and ribbons and the most select of all refinements, and the many thousands per year. The many thousands, that blood-money! After all, it was blood-money Judas received for Christ's blood[82]—and it also was, of course, blood-money, those thousands and millions that are procured for Christ's blood, and by betraying Christianity and changing it into worldliness. But is it not true, you velvet-clad mercenary soul, that there is something almost so ridiculous about Judas that one is tempted for inner reasons to doubt the historical truth that a Jew, which Judas indeed was, that a Jew knew so little about money that for thirty pieces of silver he disposed of such an enormous cash value, if you please, as Jesus Christ, the greatest monetary object that ever appeared in the world, for whose bank account millions times quadrillions have been raised—that he disposed of it for thirty pieces of silver![83] But it goes forward;[84] the world is perfectible. Judas, after all, represents something less perfect: first, that he took only thirty pieces of silver, and next, that he did not let himself be honored and praised, almost worshiped and adored, as Christ's true follower! XIV 51

And you, you thoughtless crowd of people—but I have said enough and therefore will say no more! Alas, you are not only deceived, but you want to be deceived![85] What, then, is the use of genuine love, of all unselfishness! Not only are you deceived—then I dare say you could be helped—but you want to be deceived!

XII

What Do I Want?[86]

March 1855   S. KIERKEGAARD

Very simply—I want honesty. I am not, as some well-intentioned people—I cannot pay attention to the opinions of me
held in bitterness and rage and impotence and blather—have
wanted to represent me, I am not Christian stringency in contrast
to a given Christian leniency.[87]

Certainly not, I am neither leniency nor stringency—I am
human honesty.

I want to have the mitigation that is the current Christianity
here in this country set alongside the New Testament in order to
see how these two relate to each other.

If it proves to be so, if I or anyone else can show that it can be
maintained face to face with the Christianity of the New Testament, then I will accept it with the greatest joy.

But one thing I do not want at any price: I do not want to
create, by suppression or artifice, the appearance that the current Christianity in this country and the Christianity of the New
Testament resemble each other.

See, it is this that I do not want. And why not? Well, because
I want honesty, or, if you want me to speak in another way,
because I believe that if it is possible, if even the most extreme
mitigation of the Christianity of the New Testament can hold
good in the judgment of eternity, it cannot possibly hold good
when every artifice has been used to cover up the difference
between the Christianity of the New Testament and this mitigation. My opinion is: if someone is merciful, well, then let me
dare to ask him to forgive me all my debt; but even if his mercy
were divine mercy, this is too much to ask: that I will not ever be
truthful about how great the debt is.

This, I believe, is the untruth of which official Christianity is guilty: it does not uncompromisingly make clear the Christian requirement, perhaps because it is afraid that we would shudder to see at what distance we are living, not to mention that our lives cannot in the remotest way be called a striving in the direction of fulfilling the requirement. Or to take just one example of what is indeed present everywhere in the Christianity of the New Testament: When Christianity requires for saving one's life eternally (and this, after all, is what we believe to attain as Christians): hating one's own life[88] in this world—is there a single one of us whose life even in the remotest manner can be called even the weakest striving in this direction, whereas there are in this country perhaps "Christians" by the thousands who are not even aware of this requirement? Accordingly, we "Christians," we live and love our lives in the altogether ordinary human sense. If God by "grace" nonetheless is to assume us to be Christians, one thing must still be required, that we, by being scrupulously aware of the requirement, have a true conception of how infinitely great is the grace that is shown us. "Grace" cannot possibly stretch so far; one thing it must never be used for—it must never be used to suppress or to diminish the requirement. In that case "grace" turns all Christianity upside down.

Or to take an example of another kind. A teacher of Christianity is paid, for example, several thousands. If we now suppress the Christian criterion and assume the ordinary human criterion that it is indeed quite natural that a man should have wages for his work, wages so that he can live with his family, and respectable wages so that he can live as an officeholder in a respectable position—then several thousands a year are not very much. As soon, however, as the Christian requirement of poverty is asserted, then a family is a luxury, and several thousands are a very high salary. I do not say this in order to deduct one single shilling from such an officeholder, if I were able to do that. On the contrary, if he wanted it and I were able to do it, I would gladly have him receive double so many thousands—but I am saying that suppression of the Christian requirement changes the point of view about all his salary. Honesty toward Christianity requires that one personally bring into recollection that Christianly the requirement is poverty and that this is not some capricious whim on the part of Christianity, but it is the requirement because Christianity is well aware that only in poverty can it be served truly, and that the more thousands a teacher of Christianity has in salary, the less he can serve Christianity. On the other hand, it is not honest to suppress the requirement or to use artifices to give the appearance that this way of life and career are entirely the Christianity of the New Testament. No, let us accept the money, but for God's sake not the next, not want to cover up the Christian requirement so that by suppression or by falsification a kind of decorum is produced that is to the absolutely highest degree demoralizing and is the assassination of Christianity.

Therefore I want honesty, but hitherto the established order has not been willing of its own accord to enter into the spirit of that kind of honesty, and neither has it been willing to be influenced by me. But I do not therefore become leniency or stringency. No, I am and remain quite simply human honesty.

Let me venture the most extreme in order, if possible, to be understood with regard to what I want.

I want honesty. If this, then, is what the generation or the contemporaries want, if they want straightforwardly, honestly, candidly, openly, directly to rebel against Christianity and say to God, "We cannot, we will not submit to this power"—but, please note, this is to be done straightforwardly, honestly, candidly, openly, directly—well, then strange as it might seem, I go along with it, because I want honesty. Wherever there is honesty, I am able to go along with it; an honest rebellion against Christianity can be made only if one honestly acknowledges what Christianity is and how one relates oneself to it.

If this is what one wants: straightforwardly, openly, sincerely, as is seemly when a person speaks with his God, as everyone acts who respects himself and does not despise himself so deeply that he will be dishonest before God—thus, if one straightforwardly, sincerely, candidly makes full confession to God with regard to the actual situation with us human beings, that in the course of time the human race has permitted itself to mitigate and mitigate Christianity, until we finally have managed to get it to be the very opposite of what it is in the New Testament—and that we now wish, if it can be done, that this might be Christianity—if this is what one wants, then I go along with it.

But one thing I will not do. No, not at any price will I do it; one thing I will not do: I will not participate, even if it were merely with the last fourth of the last joint of my little finger, in what is called official Christianity, which by suppression or artifice gives the appearance of being the Christianity of the New Testament, and on bended knee I thank my God that he mercifully has kept me from entering into it too far.[89]

If the official Christianity in this country wants to take the occasion to use force against me because of what is said here, I am prepared [*rede*], because I want honesty [*Redelighed*].

For this honesty I am willing to venture. However, I am not saying that it is for Christianity I venture. Suppose, just suppose that I become quite literally a sacrifice—I would still not become a sacrifice for Christianity but because I wanted honesty.

But although I do not dare to say that I venture for Christianity, I remain fully and blissfully convinced that this, my venturing, is pleasing to God, has his approval. Indeed, I know it; it has his approval that in a world of Christians where millions and millions call themselves Christians—that there one person expresses: I do not dare to call myself a Christian; but I want honesty, and to that end I will venture.

XIII

On the Occasion of an *Anonymous* Proposal to Me in No. 79 of This Newspaper[90]

April 4, 1855   S. KIERKEGAARD

To propose that I write an exposition of the New Testament's doctrine, perhaps a big book, a dogmatics, which in turn could perhaps best be written during a scholarly journey abroad, gives me (presumably also those who follow my articles in *Fædrelandet*) the impression either of fatuousness or of a trap set for me in
order that I would be tricked out of *the moment*, would mistake my task, would enter into the prolix scholarly enterprise and possibly (which could well be the result) perish or lose myself in it. Instead of challenging me to write a new book, the anonymous author should rather (I would much prefer to have my contemporaries be challenged to read my articles in *Fædrelandet* again and again), he should rather have challenged my contemporaries to become better acquainted with my earlier writings, with *Concluding Postscript, The Sickness unto Death,* and especially with *Practice in Christianity,* which at the moment may not be available in bookstores, but that will soon be taken care of since it is being printed in a new edition.[91] These books are related precisely to the moment and provide desirable preparatory knowledge for the moment, because they are the preparatory knowledge for: the moment.

XIV

Would It Be Best Now to
"Stop Ringing the Alarm"?[92]

April 7, 1855   S. KIERKEGAARD

This has been proposed to me.[93] On this score, however, I—that
is, if I am the one who is ringing the alarm—cannot yield to
anyone; it would, indeed, be indefensible to stop ringing the
alarm as long as the fire is burning. But, strictly speaking, I am not
the one who is ringing the alarm; I am the one who, in order to
smoke out illusions and skullduggery, is starting the fire, a police
operation, and a Christian police operation, since according to
the New Testament Christianity is incendiarism—[94] Christ himself says, "I came to cast fire upon the earth."[95] And it is already
burning; indeed, it will no doubt become a spreading conflagration, best compared to a forest fire, because it is "Christendom"
that has been set afire. It is the prolixities that must go, this
enormously prolix illusion involved in the—well-intentioned or
knavish—scholarliness in the Christian sphere, the enormously
prolix delusion involved in the millions of Christians, Christian
kingdoms and countries, a world of Christians (something that
no doubt suits the princes of the Church, both for pecuniary
advantage and for the sake of material power, and something that
becomes the most select and most delicate sophistication by—
scoffing at God and the New Testament!—by passing as Christian fervor and zeal for the propagation of the doctrine). It is the
prolixities that must go, and precisely with the help of the burning issue, whose fire is not to be quenched, the burning issue of
the moment: that official Christianity is not the Christianity of
the New Testament.

No, official Christianity is not the Christianity of the New
Testament; everyone must be able to see that by merely casting

even a quick but unbiased glance at the Gospels and then looking at what we call Christianity. The reason it is not seen is that the great majority of people are prevented by all kinds of optical-illusion artifices from being able to look without bias, and the reason is that the state has installed 1000 officeholders who have much difficulty in seeing without bias, because for them the issue of Christianity also comes to stand as a pecuniary matter. Naturally they do not wish to have their eyes opened to whether what hitherto has been regarded as the most secure way to make a living, the surest of all, to whether it is not a dubious way to make a living, is Christianly perhaps even an "unjustifiable business" that people are installed by the hundreds who, instead of following Christ, are cozily and comfortably accommodated, steadily advancing, with a family (and under the name of this activity as the Christianity of the New Testament) and support themselves on the basis that others have had to suffer for the suffering truth (this indeed is Christianity)—thus the relation is completely turned around, and Christianity, which came into the world as the truth for which one dies, has now become the truth on which one ("Rejoice in life in the springtime of your days"[96]) lives with a family, steadily advancing.

Moreover, everyone must be able to see that official Christianity is not the Christianity of the New Testament, resembles it no more than the square resembles the circle, no more than enjoying resembles suffering, than loving oneself resembles hating oneself, than craving the world resembles hating the world, than being completely at home in the world resembles being a stranger and alien[97] in the world, than going shopping, dancing, and courting resemble following Christ—no, no more. The battalions of Christians that "Christendom" musters no more resemble what the New Testament understands by Christian than the recruits Falstaff has enlisted[98] resemble able-bodied, well-trained, battle-eager soldiers, cannot truthfully be said to be striving in the direction of what the New Testament understands by Christian any more than a man who at a steady pace is walking toward Vesterport can be said to be endeavoring to reach Østerport. What we call a teacher in Christianity (pastor) no more resembles what the New Testament understands by a teacher of

Christianity than a chest of drawers resembles a dancer, has no more connection with what the New Testament understands as a teacher's task than a chest of drawers has with dancing. In saying this, I do not belittle the pastor as a citizen or human being, no more than I deny that a chest of drawers can be a very useful and serviceable piece of furniture because I say what is true, that it has no connection with dancing.

POSTSCRIPT

[99]What I am writing certainly is not motivated by any hostility to the clergy. Indeed, why should I have such a hostility? To my mind, the clergy—if they are not supposed to be "truth-witnesses"—are of course as competent, respectable, and worthy a class in society as any other. The theological graduate has entered *bona fide* [in good faith] into—well, it surely is something quite wrong he is entering into, but he has entered *bona fide*. The responsibility actually lies with the state. Therefore if state and Church are separated, it becomes the direct duty of the state to take care of the pastor with whom it has contracted. What does the state want out on this thin ice! To enter 1000 livelihoods on its budget account called the suffering truth and to want to "protect" the divine—both are equally preposterous.

XV

Christianity with a Royal Certificate and Christianity without a Royal Certificate[100]

April 8, 1855   S. Kierkegaard

In State Councilor Heiberg's little masterpiece *Alferne*, it happens, as is well known, that schoolteacher Grimmermann quite unintentionally plunges 70,000 fathoms underground and even more unexpectedly, if possible, than his fall was unintentional, he finds himself surrounded by mountain trolls. "What nonsense," says Grimmermann, "Mountain trolls don't exist—and here is my certificate."[101] But, alas, to come to mountain trolls with a royal certificate is a waste of effort; what the devil do mountain trolls care about a royal certificate? Their kingdom is not of this world. For them, of course, a royal certificate = 0, at most has the value of the paper.

This scene came to my mind at one time on the occasion of Bishop Martensen's authoritative article[102] against me. It was clear to me that what he actually was pluming himself on (against me, who have only a "private Christianity") was his royal certificate, that from him one obtains Christianity with a royal certificate.

But to come—**Christianly**—to me and people like me with a royal certificate is to come just as successfully as Grimmermann did with his certificate.

A royal certificate! Please do not misunderstand me; there are few people who—civically—have such an almost unconditional respect for a royal certificate as I have. It is something I have often had to hear from my acquaintances, that politically I was a pedant who bows seven times before everything that has a royal certificate.

But Christianly I understand the matter differently. By virtue of a royal certificate—a royal certificate surely is something that pertains to a kingdom of this world—to want to have any authority whatever with regard to what involves not only a kingdom of another world but a kingdom whose passion, a matter of life and death, is not to want to be a kingdom of this world—indeed, it is even more ludicrous than Grimmermann's appealing to his royal certificate before the mountain trolls.

This is how I understand the matter: precisely this, I repeat, precisely this—note this well, because Christianly it is crucial for the whole ecclesiastical established order; I must tolerate what saying this may possibly mean for me civically and humanly—precisely this, that I have no royal certificate, is my accreditation and Christianly is, albeit negatively, a huge advantage over having a royal certificate. Grimmermann only makes himself ludicrous by appealing to his certificate, but Christianly to appeal to a *royal* certificate is actually to inform against oneself, that one is disloyal to the kingdom that at no price wants to be a kingdom of this world, or that one's Christianity is playing at Christianity.[103]

XVI

What Cruel Punishment![104]

April 25, 1855   S. KIERKEGAARD

Dean Victor Bloch introduces his article[105] against me in no. 94
of this paper by linking it to an earlier article[106] against me in the
same paper by an anonymous person, whose article Dean Bloch
(a grateful Basil[107]) in the strongest and most affable terms recognizes as what one could call "a lead [*ledende*] article"—and there
is something to that, since it was indeed a leading-astray [*vild-
ledende*] article, and accordingly it is entirely in order that it was
anonymous, which a lead article under the present circumstances
certainly could not be.

But Dean B. by no means agrees entirely with the anonymous
author; he is able to follow the anonymous author's instructive
[*vejledende*] article only a short way; the Dean has to turn off very
soon and take another path. His article now becomes what could
be called a lightning-rod [*tordenledende*] article, if one thereby
does not think of leading away [*aflede*] but of leading a thunderstorm down [*nedlede*] upon a person, on poor me.

The Dean wants—if I do not mend my ways—to have me
ecclesiastically punished. And how? Indeed, the punishment,
cruelly conceived, is so cruel that I advise women to have their
"smelling salts" handy in order not to swoon when they hear it.
If I do not mend my ways, the church door should be closed to
me. Horrible! Consequently, if I do not mend my ways, I should
be excluded, excluded from hearing on Sunday in the quiet
hours the, if not priceless, then at least invaluable eloquence of
the truth-witnesses—I, I, the silly sheep who can neither read
nor write, and who therefore, excluded in this way, must spiritually languish, die of hunger by being excluded from what truly
can be called nutritious, inasmuch as it feeds the pastor and his
family! And I should be excluded from the rest of the divine

service that the royally authorized—but their being royally authorized is, Christianly, the scandal—entrepreneurs have ecclesiastically-secularly organized! Terrible, terrible punishment, terrible Dean! Alas, where have you suddenly disappeared, you, my poet-dreams? I dreamed that I was called Victor[108]—and the truth is that it is Dean Bloch who is called Victor. Dean Bloch is capable of what even Bishop Martensen was not capable; he knows how to handle me!

Fortunately for me, however (whereas, for example, the punishment of being forced to hear several times every Sunday the, if not priceless, then at least the invaluable eloquence of the truth-witnesses would interfere disturbingly with my customary way of life), the execution of the other punishment will not change at all a way of life I have chosen for Christian reasons and to which I have been accustomed for some time now. Thus, if the punishment is carried out, I will be able to go on living without noticing it any more than I here in Copenhagen notice that a man is beating me in Aarhus. I have only one wish; if the execution of the punishment is fulfilled, it will literally not cause the slightest change in my mode of living (and this I prize highly)—this wish is: that I be permitted to go on paying the Church tax, lest the altered notice of the assessment make me notice a change.

*   *

A LITTLE POSTSCRIPT

Here I could end. But since Dean B., perhaps also feeling himself to be a representative for the whole profession, has made such a big splash, I shall use the opportunity to raise a Christianly moot point: can one be a royally authorized teacher of Christianity, can Christianity (the Christianity of the New Testament) be proclaimed by royally authorized teachers, can the sacraments be administered by them, or does this involve a self-contradiction? Through ordination the pastor properly relates himself to a kingdom that is not of this world,[109] but in addition by being royally authorized—yes, this "in addition," is it not an extremely dubious matter or are "in addition" and "either-or" just about synonymous now? "In addition"—does not a teacher of Christianity, by being royally authorized in addition, become something just as remarkable and odd as what is being complained about in *Adresseavisen*, that a Jewish rabbi, besides being a Jewish rabbi, in addition by being a Knight of the Order of the Dannebrog professes the evangelical Christian religion?[110] But if that is the case, could it perhaps turn out that the whistle would change its tune and the talk would no longer be about shutting the church door to me, but it would be the pastor who would come to close the shop or, to recall the thundering dean, the low tavern.

Allow me to continue—I see from Dean B.'s article that it becomes necessary to point out once again a Bible verse I called attention to earlier. It is Christ's own words: Will the Son of man, when he comes again, find faith upon the earth[111]? Consequently Christ sees a possibility that the situation at his second coming may be such that Christianity does not exist at all. Those words imply in addition that Christ more particularly considered that the fall from Christianity would happen with craftiness, knavishly. He does not seem to expect the situation to be such that there would be no one who called himself a Christian. After all, he does not say: Will the Son of man find no Christians? What if he had imagined it to be this way: there will be millions of Christians, Christian states, countries, a Christian world, thousands of pastors carrying on their trade—but faith (what I understand by faith), I wonder, will it be found on the earth? The falling away from Christianity will not happen openly, by everyone's renouncing Christianity, no, but cunningly, slyly, knavishly, by everyone's taking the name of being a Christian, supposing themselves in this way to be most securely secured against—Christianity, the Christianity of the New Testament, which people are uneasy about and afraid of, and therefore industrial pastors have invented, in the name of Christianity, a confection that tastes fine and that people gladly pay money for.

Finally, a word to you, you who for your own sake are reading with some genuine interest what I am writing. Let me stamp one thing upon your mind: read my articles often and in particular memorize the Bible passages so that you know them by heart.

There are not many, but it is of importance for you that you know them by heart. What I point out is precisely that which is to the pastor's interest to conceal, suppress, tone down, omit. If you have no other knowledge of what Christianity is than at most what you receive by hearing the pastor, then you can be rather sure that you will go on living kept in complete ignorance of what is not convenient for official Christianity. This is the condition in which it is intended to hand you, dying, over to eternity's accounting, where it undoubtedly will serve you as an excuse that others bear most of the guilt, but where it still remains your responsibility whether you have not taken the matter too light-mindedly by too light-mindedly believing the pastor, perhaps even because he is royally authorized.

XVII

A Result[112]

April 23, 1855   S. KIERKEGAARD

With a series of articles in this paper, I have now, as is said in military language, opened and kept up a brisk fire against official Christianity and thereby against the clergy here in this country.

And from their side what have the clergy done? They have—indeed, even if I did not want to, I am compelled to be so polite, because it is true—they have observed a significant silence. Strangely enough, if they had responded, no doubt something very insignificant would have emerged; perhaps the whole thing would have become insignificant. But now how significant the whole thing has become because of this significant silence!

What does this significant silence mean? It means that what occupies the clergy is making a living. In any case it means that the clergy are not truth-witnesses; otherwise it would be unthinkable that all the clergy—especially after their leader, the Honorable Right Reverend Bishop Martensen, had made such an unfortunate attempt to speak—could want to maintain silence while it so obviously was made perceptible that official Christianity is, esthetically and intellectually, a ludicrousness, an indecency, Christianly a scandal.

If, however, it is assumed that making a living is what occupies the clergy, then the silence is quite in order. I have not taken aim at their making a living in the finite sense, and, knowing me as they do, the clergy know very well that such a thing would not readily occur to me, know that I not only am not a politician but that I hate politics, indeed, that I would perhaps even be inclined to fight for the clergy if in the finite sense the livelihoods are attacked.

That total silence, then, for this reason: my attack actually has not concerned the clergy at all, that is, it has no connection with what occupies them. Take an example from—I almost misspoke and said "another world"—so take an example from the same world: from the world of the merchant. If it was possible to attack a merchant in such a way that one showed that his goods were bad but this still did not have the slightest influence on his customary sales of goods, he would presumably say, "Such an attack is of no importance to me at all, because whether the goods are good or bad does not in itself concern me. After all, I am a merchant, and what concerns me is the sales. Indeed, I am to such a degree a merchant that if it could be shown not only that the coffee I sell is damaged, spoiled, but that what I am selling under the name of coffee is not coffee at all—if only I am assured that this attack has no influence whatever on the sales, such an attack is of no importance to me at all. Why should I care about what people guzzle under the name of coffee; I care only about the sales."

On this point the merchant *qua* merchant is indeed right—and likewise the clergy in their silence—if one considers the clergy as a merchant class.

But what was it that I protested against at the time? Have I protested against the clergy's being regarded as a merchant class? No, I have protested against their wanting to be regarded as truth-witnesses. By claiming to be truth-witnesses, the clergy are the very furthest from being truth-witnesses; of all the social classes they are the least truth-witnesses.

A German author has said that the most honest social class is the merchants, since they say outright that profit is their object.[113] I would propose a somewhat more comprehensive scale: the moneylenders are the most honest social class, since they say outright: There is cheating here. Next comes the merchant; and last would come the fantasy by Bishop Martensen: truth-witnesses. It was against Bishop Martensen's fantasies that I protested. I did not turn the matter this way: The clergy must be pledged to be truth-witnesses. No, I turned it this way: They must take down that sign. After all, to take an example, it would cause great confusion and disorder, indeed, in many a case probably harm, if a number of people hit upon the idea of placing over their door "Practicing Physician" and hanging out a red

XIV
72

light.[114] The social order would have to demand that all those signs be removed. It is the same with hanging up the sign "Practicing Truth-Witnesses." This seems calculated to prevent the introduction of even the slightest bit of truth into this world. "Where there are 1000 truth-witnesses, it certainly must be a world of truth"; quite right, if those very 1000 signs were not the most dangerous untruth in—the world of truth. Have them take down that sign. For the clergy to have a sign out is of course quite in order, but not as truth-witnesses.

And that they are not truth-witnesses has now through the impression of a current circumstance become plain to everyone who wants to see. If it is assumed that what I say is true—the clergy would not have kept silent but would have declared themselves for this truth if they had been truth-witnesses. If it is assumed that what I say is untrue—the clergy would not have kept silent but would have declared themselves against this untruth if they had been truth-witnesses. If they had been truth-witnesses, they would not have done the one thing that they have done, they would not have tried through silence to sneak away from something true—if it is assumed that what I say is true. Neither would they in silence have allowed something untrue to remain in force—if it is assumed that what I say is untrue.

POSTSCRIPT

May 6

In order to make my contemporaries take notice, and in order to cut off from the clergy the escape that this was something no one would read, I have used a widely circulated political journal.

In covenant with God as I am, unselfish as all my effort was—humble before God, in proud self-respect, I dare to have the greatest conception of the cause that I have the honor to serve, of its significance, of its progress, although I certainly must also have the greatest conception of its difficulty. Indeed, what would be more difficult, more to despair over, than to have to bring to bear the ideals in a generation ruined by sagacity and lack of character, in which therefore also the pastors—how deplorable to earn money in this way—live off the delusion that all are Christians. On looking more closely, one might rather say that what they live off is this—the most deplorable way to earn money!—that the majority do not want the inconvenience or are unwilling to expose themselves to the civic troubles associated with acknowledging that they neither are nor imagine themselves to be Christians. XIV 73

By now the point has probably been reached that people are aware of the protest against official Christianity as being the Christianity of the New Testament, and of the objection against regarding "the pastor" as "a truth-witness," since what occupies him is: the sales.

This should be made generally known in such a way that no one would dare to venture to say, "This is something no one has read"—this is why I used a widely circulated political journal.

XVIII

A Monologue[115]

Studenstrup is, of course, obviously correct in saying that the city hall and courthouse is a most prestigious building and, for the pittance for which these "worthy men" want to dispose of it, certainly the most brilliant business deal possible; his paternal uncle in Thy, everyone in Salling, and all sagacious people here and there must admit that.[116]

What escapes Studenstrup is whether these worthy men's position with regard to the city hall and courthouse is such that they are able to dispose of it. If not, then if it were only four marks and eight shillings, this is much too high—for the city hall and courthouse. Indeed, a low price is not to be recommended unconditionally, has its limitations; if one does not obtain what one buys at the unprecedented low price—then the price is not low but very high.

It is the same with Christianity. That an eternal happiness is a priceless good, something far more important than the city hall and courthouse, that buying it for the pittance for which the pastors are disposing of it must be regarded as a far, far more brilliant business deal than Studenstrup's for the city hall and courthouse—that I am willing to admit.

The only misgiving I have is whether the relation of the pastors to eternal happiness is such that they are able to dispose of it. If not, then a mere four marks and eight shillings would be an enormous price.

The New Testament stipulates the condition of eternal happiness. Compared with the New Testament price—truly, words fail me to describe the extent to which the pastor's price, by comparison, is cheap, is a steal. But, as stated, is the pastor's position with regard to eternal happiness such that he is able to dispose of it and you are able to buy it from him?

If the pastor's position with regard to eternal happiness is such that he is able to dispose of it, which he of course cannot do since he is not our Lord, and if the pastor's Christianity does not resemble the Christianity of the New Testament any more than the square resembles the circle—of what use to me, then, are all his bargain prices? As for gaining an eternal happiness, I do not come the least bit closer by buying from him; therefore the most I achieve by buying from him is to perform, if you will, a kind of good deed by contributing my mite, too, so that 1000 learned men can live with families.

May 6   S. Kierkegaard

XIX

Concerning a Fatuous Pompousness in Regard to Me and the Conception of Christianity to Which I Am Calling Attention[117]

Although I consider this pompousness so fatuous that it ought to be ignored, yet, for the sake of many people, it perhaps is proper for me to say a few words about it.

That I (a theological graduate like others, and also a seasoned author for some time, so I presumably can be regarded as ranking with pastors) would not be just as knowledgeable as any pastor or professor here in our land about what is usually said in defense of the established order and its Christianity is really a fatuous assumption.

Meanwhile, in the books by me or by pseudonymous authors, I have thoroughly, as I always work, expressed and described the different stages before reaching where I am at present. Thus one will find, especially in the pseudonymous Johannes Climacus,[118] what approximately may be said in defense of the kind of Christianity that is closest to that of the established order, and will find it described in such a way that I would like to see whether any of my contemporaries here in the country can do it better.

How fatuous, then, vis-à-vis me and what I am now saying, to lecture in didactic tones and with great pompousness about what
I have finished and put behind me in order to advance further in the direction of, if I dare to say so, discovering the Christianity of the New Testament! Do not misunderstand me. I do not find it fatuous for someone to have the view of Christianity that I, after making it known, have put behind me; but I find it fatuous that someone in didactic tones and with great pompousness wants to lecture about it vis-à-vis me, wants to talk about my lack of the

discernment to see, to see—what in my books one will surely find always presented just as discerningly as the person speaking against me is capable of doing.

To name one representative of this fatuous pompousness, I will mention Dr. Zeuthen.[119] He has, so it seems, expressed himself in *Evangelisk Ugeskrift* and now on occasion lectures didactically and with great pompousness about what he could have read, for example, in *Concluding Postscript*. Yet this is lectured didactically to me by Dr. Z., who thus has the discernment that I, according to him, lack—a modest pleasure, even though in another sense it perhaps is neither modest nor humble, something that Dr. Z. himself must know best, he who in the role of author has, as is well-known, devoted himself mainly to the subjects of modesty and humility,[120] yet of course without becoming guilty of any "one-sidedness," such as, for example, that theory and practice should be in agreement.

This is what I wanted to say. One may read my books. If one does not want to do that, one may leave them alone. But I do not really intend to go through the lesson from the beginning with everyone who even wants to lecture didactically about what I have discussed.

Just one thing more, since I have pen in hand. That one can, by means of the kind of Christianity Bishop Mynster and now Bishop Martensen represent, charmingly deceive oneself and make a brilliant career in this world, whose invention it is, I have never doubted. Now, if anyone can provide me with news from the other world—if it says that this kind of Christianity is also recognized to be the Christianity of the New Testament, then I am fencing with a phantom and am a fool. But then there still remains one I take along with me,[121] God in heaven, whose Word, after all, is the New Testament; in that case God, the God of truth, is the biggest liar of us all.

April 1855

*   *

*

I wrote these lines at the end of April. But, I thought, there is no hurry about having them printed; perhaps there may come an additional occasion.

XIV
78

This did not fail to come. I see now that Dr. Bartholo (Zeuthen) of *Evangelisk Ugeskrift* has found his grateful Basil,[122] an anonymous person in *Kjøbenhavnsposten*,[123] who wants to disarm me with Zeuthen's miscellaneous casual remarks in various articles, to which I have been silent. As in everything untrue, there is something true there, and what is true is that I have passed over Dr. Z.'s casual remarks in silence. This truth and the circumstance that Dr. Z.'s comments are found in a weekly that presumably is read only by theologians are then utilized to produce a fantastic effect, as if what Dr. Z. lectures about is something very significant; perhaps also in this way someone can be successfully fooled.

I shall not, however, involve myself further with the anonymous writer in *Kjøbenhavnsposten*, but allow me to use the occasion to call attention to the true connection between me and my appearance in a newspaper. I am not a totally unknown person who writes a newspaper article and now ought to submit to discussing with every anonymous pen-pusher on a totally equal footing. No, what is being talked about here is an issue that in one sense was finished in a whole literature of significant books, to which books of mine I must refer those who actually are interested. It was for religious reasons that I decided to use a widely circulated political paper: in order to make people aware. This I have religiously understood as my duty, indeed do it gladly, even though I dislike it very much. But, humble before God and with proud self-respect, which I dare and which I ought to have, I will surely be on guard lest there come to be all too much comradery with everyone who feels like writing in a newspaper.

May 13, 1855   S. KIERKEGAARD

XX

For the New Edition of *Practice in Christianity*[124]

Because I regard this book as a historical document, I have had it come out in a totally *unaltered* edition.

If it were to come out now, now when both pious consideration for the late bishop has lapsed and I have convinced myself, also by having this book come out the first time, that Christianly the established order is indefensible, it would be altered as follows: it would not be by a pseudonym but by me, and the thrice-repeated preface[125] would be dropped and, of course, the Moral to No. 1,[126] where the pseudonym turns the matter in a way I personally agreed to in the preface.

My earlier thought was: if the established order can be defended, this is the only way to do it: by poetically (therefore by a pseudonym) passing judgment on it; then by drawing on *grace* in the second power, Christianity would come not only to find forgiveness for the past by *grace*, but by grace a kind of indulgence from the actual imitation of Christ and the actual strenuousness of being Christian. In this way truth still manages to come into the established order; it defends itself by judging itself; it acknowledges the Christian requirement, confesses its own distance, yet without being able to be called a striving in the direction of coming closer to the requirement, but resorts to grace "also in relation to the use one makes of grace."[127]

In my opinion this was the only way Christianly to defend the established order; and, lest I in any way incur the guilt of setting to work too fast, I dared to give the matter this turn in order to see what the old bishop would do about it. If there was power in him, he would have to do one of two things: *either* decisively declare himself for the book, venture to go along with it, let it be the defense that wards off what the book poetically contains, the charge against the whole official Christianity that it is an optical illusion "not worth a pickled herring," *or* as decisively as possible throw himself against it, stamp it as a blasphemous and profane attempt, and declare the official Christianity to be the true Christianity. He did neither of the two, he did nothing; he only wounded himself on the book; and to me it became clear that he was powerless.[128]

Now, however, I have completely made up my mind on two things: both that the established order is Christianly indefensible, that every day it lasts it is Christianly a crime; and that in this way one does not have the right to draw on grace.

Thus, take away the pseudonymity, take away the thrice-repeated preface and the Moral to No. 1: then *Practice in Christianity* is, Christianly, an attack upon the established order; but out of pious consideration for the old bishop and out of cautious slowness it [the attack] was concealed in the form of: the final defense of the established order.

Incidentally, I am well aware that the old bishop saw the attack in this book; but, to repeat, he powerlessly chose to do nothing more than condemn it in the living room, but not once in private conversation with me, despite my asking him to do it after I was told, with his consent, of his verdict in the living room.[129]

April [30,] 1855   S. KIERKEGAARD

THIS MUST BE SAID;
SO LET IT BE SAID

By S. Kierkegaard

"But at midnight there was a cry."[130]
Matthew 25:6

December 1854

This must be said; I place no one under obligation to act accordingly—for that I do not have authority. But by having heard it you are made responsible and must now act on your own responsibility as you think you can justify it before God. Perhaps one person will hear in such a way that he does what I say, another in such a way that he understands it as acceptable to God and thinks he renders God a service by participating in raising a cry against me: neither one concerns me; my only concern is that it must be said.

This must be said; so let it be said:

Whoever you are, whatever your life is otherwise, my friend—by ceasing to participate (if you usually do participate) in the public divine service as it now is (professing to be the Christianity of the New Testament), you always have one and a great guilt less—you are not participating in making a fool of God by calling something New Testament Christianity that is not New Testament Christianity.

*   *

With this—yes, may your will be done, O God, infinite love!—with this I have spoken. If an equivocal sagacity, which is best aware of the facts of the matter, should find it most sagacious to act, if possible, as if nothing had happened—at least I have spoken—and perhaps the established order has nevertheless lost, because one can also lose by keeping silent, especially when the situation is as it is, that not a few people know more or less clearly what I know, except that no one will say it; if that is the case, only one person is needed, one sacrifice, one person to say it—and now it has been said!

*   *

May 1855

Yes, this is the way it is, the official divine worship (professing to be the Christianity of the New Testament) is, Christianly speaking, a forgery, a falsification.

But you, you ordinary Christian, you, on the average, probably suspect nothing; you are entirely *bona fide* [in good faith] credulous in the conviction that everything is quite in order, is the Christianity of the New Testament. This falsification is so entrenched that there may even be pastors who entirely *bona fide* go on living in the delusion that everything is quite in order, is the Christianity of the New Testament. This falsification is really forgery brought about over the centuries, whereby Christianity has gradually become just the opposite of what it is in the New Testament.

So I repeat, this must be said: by ceasing to participate (if you usually do participate) in the public divine worship as it now is, you always have one and a great guilt less—you are not participating in making a fool of God.

The road on which you are going toward eternity's accounting is a road full of dangers—"the pastor" says somewhat the same thing. But there is one danger he forgets to speak about and to warn against, the danger that you are letting yourself be trapped or that you are trapped in the enormous illusion that the state and the pastor have brought about, making people think that this is Christianity. Wake up, take care that you do not think that you are securing the eternal for yourself by taking part in what is only a new sin. Wake up, watch out; whoever you are, this much you can perceive, that the person who is speaking here is not speaking in order to make money, since instead it has cost him money, or to gain honor and esteem, since he has voluntarily exposed himself to the opposite. But if this is the case, you are also able to understand that this means that you ought to become aware.

ADDENDUM

April 9, 1855

XIV
89

Just as carefully as it has been hitherto concealed what my task could become, just as circumspectly as I have remained in impenetrable incognizance—just as decisively shall I now, when the moment has arrived, make it known.

The question about what Christianity is, including in turn the question about the state Church, the people's Church, which they now want to call it, the amalgamation or alliance of Church and state, must be brought to the most extreme decision. It cannot and must not go on as it did year after year under the old bishop ("It will no doubt last as long as I live"), nor as the new one seems to want by understanding our age as a great interim age, which said in another way is again: It will no doubt last as long as I live.

To be strained in this way, as I am and must be, is certainly not something that, humanly speaking, can be called desirable, even though in a much higher sense I must thank Governance for it as for the greatest benefaction. To become strained as the contemporaries must become if this matter is to be taken decisively is, I well understand, something that, humanly speaking, one cannot desire, something one would wish at almost any price to avoid unless one learns to be uplifted by the thought that in a much higher sense what is decisive is still the most beneficial. I am fully convinced that it could be avoided, that the decision could be passed over for another generation if the late bishop had not been as he was, if his whole relation to me had not been a more shocking untruth with each year. My opinion is that it perhaps could be avoided and the decision passed over for another generation if the present bungler—in the work I am doing, one uses words as accurately as a descriptive natural scientist; compliments do not belong here—had not made such a splash that with the necessity of contradiction I must take the matter to the limit. In any XIV
90

case, it is now decided; the matter, the issue, will be carried to the ultimate decision.

The only thing I could wish to find out as soon as possible is whether the government has the view that Christianity (or what calls itself Christianity, and, *in parenthesi* [parenthetically], if Christianity wants any such help it thereby informs on itself as not being the Christianity of the New Testament) ought to be defended by the use of judicial power or not.

Do not misunderstand me as if I intended to shut my mouth and duck down another street if this is the view of the government. Certainly not. For a person in my state of health and for someone who because of an unfortunate physical weakness needs exercise in a very special way, the thought of being arrested etc. can indeed be a serious matter, something to avoid. But I dare not retreat; I am constrained by a higher power, who provides the strength, it is true, but always wants to be unconditionally obeyed, unconditionally, blindly, as the soldier obeys the command, if possible with the involuntary precision with which the cavalry horse obeys the signal.

But also do not misunderstand me as if I intended in any way, if from the side of the government such measures are taken against me, to counter-demonstrate if possible by means of a popular movement—certainly not. I am so far from this that I understand it as my task to avert such things as much as possible, I who have nothing at all to do with popular movements but, if possible, purer than the purest virgin in Denmark, am kept pure in the separateness of singleness.

But I would wish only to find out whether my task will be to arm myself with patience and peace of mind with regard to legal action, arrest, etc., or whether the government has the view that Christianity must defend itself and that 1000 pastors with families in opposition to literally one single person can be considered as being of adequate physical strength, an almost inhuman proportion, so that the state should instead—even when I am speaking about the greatest decision of my life I cannot be unmindful of the jest—furnish me with some police for assistance against these 1000 pastors, prevent them from acting against me *en masse*, arrest some of the worst blatherers when they are guilty for the third time of having to be charged with blather, and in some other way make a contribution so that the question about what spirit is (and Christianity is indeed spirit) would be decided as far as possible by spirit.

The sound eye of the minister of ecclesiastical affairs and education[131] cannot help but see that I do not in the remotest manner clash disturbingly with any civic arrangement whatever, and of course one single person can never literally become a physical power. I pay the Church rates as everyone else does; I admonish everyone for whom my word has significance to conduct himself as I do; and I am firmly resolved not to involve myself with anyone I know to have made the least civic trouble for the pastor. In a Christian sense, we live in a world of gibberish, but this is not something contemporary pastors have caused; no, it goes far back in time. Yet, fundamentally all of us are guilty, and to that extent all of us also deserve punishment; but it actually would be a very merciful punishment to get by with supporting the factually given crew of pastors.

XIV
91

April 11, 1855

IN AGONIES such as a human being has rarely experienced, in mental strain that in a week would probably drive another out of his mind, I am, it is true, also a power, undeniably a seductive consciousness for a poor human being if the agony and strain were not dominant to the degree that often my wish is for death, my longing for the grave, and my desire that my wish and my longing might soon be fulfilled. Yes, O God, if you were not the Omnipotent One, who omnipotently could compel, and if you were not love, who irresistibly can move—on no other condition, at no other price, could it at any second occur to me to choose the life that is mine, embittered in turn by what is unavoidable for me, the impression I am obliged to have of people, and not least of their misunderstanding admiration. Every creature feels best in its own element, can really live only there. The fish cannot live in the air, the bird cannot live in the water—and for spirit to have to live in an environment devoid of spirit means to die, agonizingly to die slowly so that death is a blessed relief. Yet your love, O God, moves me; the thought of daring to love you inspires me—in the possibility of being omnipotently compelled—joyful and grateful, to want to be what is the consequence of being loved by you and of loving you: a sacrifice, sacrificed to a generation for whom ideals are tomfoolery, a nothing, a generation for whom the earthly and the temporal are earnestness, a generation whom worldly sagacity in the form of teachers of Christianity has, in the Christian sense, shamefully demoralized.

XXI

That Bishop Martensen's Silence Is (1) Christianly Indefensible; (2) Ludicrous; (3) Obtuse-Sagacious; (4) in More Than One Regard Contemptible[132]

1. That it, Christianly, is indefensible. It is, as an apostle also emphasizes, a Christian's duty always to be willing to make a defense for the hope that is in him,[133] that is, for his Christianity. And how very much in order that is; a Christian, this lover and follower of truth, should he not always be willing to answer for himself and his view, always be ready to witness for the truth and against untruth, and most of all detest sneaking into something or from something through silence!

And now a Christian bishop, and the country's highest bishop! The country's highest bishop—it is to him that the congregation looks, from him that it expects guidance, upon him that it puts its trust that he will witness against untruth and declare himself for the truth.

And how does this highest bishop of the country conduct himself? Somewhat like boys on New Year's Eve, who, when they see their chance, use the occasion to toss a pot at people's door and then take off by another street lest the police get hold of them. Similarly in the big hullabaloo on the occasion of my article about Bishop Mynster,[134] Bishop Martensen saw his chance[135] and threw a garbage can of insults and abusive remarks over me—and then took off. From that moment he observed the
deepest silence, although the matter really commenced to be earnest after that time, inasmuch as with each subsequent article in *Fædrelandet* the matter really became much more earnest than the issue of whether I actually had treated a dead man unfairly.

But Bishop Martensen observes the deepest silence, although he has been challenged to express himself.[136] He did not reply to this challenge either, while on the other hand there appeared an anonymous article in the *Berlingske Tidende* advising Bishop Martensen not to reply to that challenge.[137]

And this (reminiscent of Leporello and his line: I answer not, no matter who it is[138])—this is supposed to be defensible for a truth-witness, a Christian bishop, the country's highest, upon whom the congregation can depend! No, a silence such as this is Christianly indefensible, and Christianly such lamentable behavior is far worse than if the bishop had become addicted to drink.

2. It is ludicrous. Wherever there is the ludicrous, so declares one of my pseudonyms, there is also a contradiction.[139] It is the same with silence. A silence can have many different characteristics tending toward good or evil, but silence is ludicrous when it has the exasperating characteristic—that it speaks. This is very ludicrous: a silence that speaks, speaks very loudly, and says what it is concealing so that everyone can hear it, says precisely what one wishes to hide with the help of silence. Just as when Countess Orsini says to Marinelli, "I want to whisper something to you"[140] and then shouts very loudly what she wants to say—so also this silence shouts very loudly what it is hiding. Just like making oneself invisible by putting a white stick in one's mouth,[141] whereby all that is achieved is that one additional thing is seen, that one has a white stick in one's mouth—so also this silence shouts more loudly than the most solemn declaration by the bishop: I am in hot water. It shouts it so clearly that not only the better informed can hear it but the people, the common man, can understand it, and shouts it so loudly that it can be heard in a neighboring country.[142]

3. It is obtuse-sagacious. It is not simply obtuse, no, it is obtuse in wanting to be sagacious, obtuse-sagacious. It is just as when there is something a teacher does not know—which of course can very well happen—and he does not directly say, "I do not know it" but sagaciously pretends as if he knew it, and then from it the pupils privately draw conclusions that subtract from his reputation. This silence is presumably very sagacious, but it is still an obtuseness, since with every day Bishop Martensen remains silent there is privately a subtracting from his reputation. Even if

a silence does not have the damaging characteristic that it betrays what it hides, in order to be able to hold out it requires,
unless the opponent is an altogether unimportant person, a reputation gained and maintained over many years. And here it is a
beginner in the bishopric, and a beginner who began as unfortunately as Bishop Martensen did with his discourse in *Berlingske
Tidende*; and the other party is at least on a fully equal footing
with him, intellectually and literarily, except that I do not have,
Christianly speaking, the ludicrous characteristic of being a
councilor of conference with a salary in the thousands.

No, this silence is obtuse-sagacious. Even those who do not
have the true criterion for what this silence means can see this.

Bishop Martensen and I are not, as they say, entirely unac-
quainted with each other. For many years there has been, literarily, an unsettled account between us.[143] But as long as the old
bishop, who for better or for worse was such a friend of calmness,
was living (*also* out of devotion to my late father), I took care
from my side that it could go on quietly. Things went on very
quietly with regard to the system, in which Bishop Martensen
did not draw the longest straw. I refused to attack him by
name—and Bishop Martensen maintained silence. Even when
the person who for Bishop Martensen certainly must be regarded
as the most dangerous person to say it, even when Prof. Nielsen
in print gave him to understand that my pseudonym had disposed of him,[144] which then for him the most dangerous person
(next to Prof. Nielsen) to say it, Dr. Stilling, again in print gave
him to understand,[145] and which later was quite bluntly said to
him in print[146]—Bishop Martensen maintained silence.

Then he believed that I had blundered by speaking about
Bishop Mynster, that the mood was against me, and from his
article it was apparent how he would like to drench me with
abusive remarks, consequently how he would like to speak if
only he believed that he could have the advantage.

And so he again wants to maintain silence! Indeed, as obtuse-
sagacious silence, this silence deserves to be called Martensenian
silence, different from the silence of a Brutus,[147] of an Orange.[148]

4. In more than one regard, it is contemptible. I will single out
only two points. If one is a man, it is contemptible not to behave

like a man, not to look danger in the eye manfully, not to win or lose decisively but to sneak away from it. And it is doubly contemptible if one allows oneself to be paid by the state to take a leading position, and perhaps in other ways to play the leader.

And this silence is contemptible because it seems to be calculated to be able to signify different things, all in relation to the outcome.

Worldly sagacity teaches, "Never become involved with a phenomenon."* And I suppose I am to be classified under the category of phenomenon. I, of course, am one of the incongruities who have not made their efforts commensurate with a government position and the like.

So one is silent. If it turns out that the phenomenon prevails— oh, good heavens, of course one has said nothing, one's silence was respect, or perhaps "Christian resignation"—which Prof. Nielsen unfortunately played into Martensen's hands[151] without even taking the precaution of at least having Bishop Martensen take back his abusive remarks. Otherwise the Christian resignation that maintains silence after having poured out all those abusive remarks is odd; resignation of that sort is somewhat like repentance for having stolen and then keeping the stolen goods. —But if it turns out that the phenomenon does not prevail— well, then one's silence was superiority, which, as long as the outcome is critical, one tries the best one can to make it out to be in order to weaken the phenomenon.

How contemptible is this silence, which instead of acting wants to wait for the outcome in order to obtain fraudulently what one's silence has signified!

S. Kierkegaard

POSTSCRIPT

This is, religiously, the matter I must pursue; therefore I must do what I am doing, whether it personally goes against the grain or not.

*This one can read in *Practice in Christianity*,[149] which opportunely is now in its second edition.[150]

I am well aware that when someone as young as Bishop Martensen[152] has been so fortunate (!)—indeed, when I think of the
New Testament and the oath, it is quite satirical!—as to make   XIV
such a brilliant (!) career (!), I am well aware that one can then   98
wish for tranquillity [Ro] (but the Christianity of the New Testament is precisely restlessness [Uro]) in order to enjoy (but the
Christianity of the New Testament is to suffer) these worldly
things: the ample income, the high esteem in society, the pleas-
antness of having influence on the welfare of many people. I am
also well aware (and in one sense this of course does not diminish
Bishop Martensen) that Bishop Martensen could not wish to be
so bold as to declare publicly under his name and as bishop that
the official Christianity is the Christianity of the New Testament
or even a striving in that direction, and that thus far he was
obliged (he did indeed at first make an attempt, extremely unfortunate for silence, to speak) to arrive at the conclusion that for
him silence was the only way out or escape. But from this it does
not follow that I dare to be silent to this silence or to what it, even
though impotently, yet perhaps unashamedly, points to, that a
person who was especially chosen very early by Governance and
slowly brought up for a special task (and this is the case with me),
a person who, with an unselfishness, strenuousness, and diligence
that in our setting are almost unique, has willed only one thing,
that such a person (perhaps also as a reward for his having honestly renounced aspiring to what, Christianly speaking, is ques-
tionable: profit, rank, title, decorations, etc.) should come to be
regarded as a kind of loudmouth whom the high ecclesiastics did
not consider worthy of a reply, so that the common man, trusting the high ecclesiastics, could feel justified in concluding that
what this loudmouth says (surely what he says is Christianly perhaps the most justifiable objection ever raised!) is blather. An
attempt to bring this about has already been made. It was in
Dagbladet,[153] an anonymous person—very likely a spiritual counselor! Even if he was so kind as to concede "great capabilities" to
me, he nevertheless managed to say that to the common man
what I say appears to be blather! Honorable, honest spiritual
counsel: say that the common man says it—in order to get him
to say it!

I am, however, of a different opinion, I who perhaps am also acquainted with the common man. Is it not true, you common man, that you can understand it very well—I mean that you are the very one who can understand it much more easily and much better than demoralized pastors and a corrupted upper class—is it not true that you are well able to understand this, that it is one thing to be persecuted, mistreated, flogged, crucified, beheaded, etc. and that it is something else, comfortably situated, with a family, steadily advancing, to live off describing how someone else was flogged etc.—but this is also a difference between the Christianity of the New Testament and the official Christianity.

If now, prompted by Prof. R. Nielsen's articles, there should again begin to appear in *Berlingske Tidende*, perhaps even from Norway,[154] anonymous articles that advise Bishop Martensen not to become involved, then the people will no doubt gradually understand what such a thing means and be obliged to Bishop Martensen for the contribution he makes to public entertainment by way of the anonymous articles advising him not to become involved. Or if Bishop Martensen should choose (as I hear is the case with individual pastors here in the city) to say something or other in a church—then it is not my fault if it probably ends up with someone's laughing in church, since, viewed comically, this method is a very valuable contribution to illuminating what "truth-witnesses" understand by "witnessing."

*

*   *

Do not misunderstand me, as if the intention with what I am writing here were to prompt Bishop Martensen to a discussion, thinking that we would then come to know something very important and instructive. Certainly not. As far as that goes, I am essentially finished with Bishop Martensen; I know very well what is in play here. No, but Bishop Martensen is, after all, the Church's ranking ecclesiastic; it is due to him that I succeeded in getting at this matter of "truth-witnesses"—and, as I have said, this is, religiously, the matter I must pursue. Therefore it is my duty also to utilize what happens in order to make it visible so that everyone who wants to see can see: (1) what the situation actually is with these "truth-witnesses," that what occupies them is not truth but producing or maintaining an appearance; (2) what paltry means are used, for which reason it will no doubt end with being a failure; (3) that the issue of the established eccle- siastical order is not a religious but a financial issue, that what keeps the establishment going is the 1000 royally authorized teachers, who maintain the established order in the capacity of stockholders, who quite properly are silent about what I speak of, because I, of course, have no power to deprive them of their incomes; (4) whether the one who in the matter of eternal happiness relies on "truth-witnesses" has perfect reason and right to be calm and unconcerned.

XIV
100

Finally, what was desirable for the cause (and so desirable that I despaired of it, because I was fully prepared for Bishop Martensen to maintain silence from the beginning) has been achieved. The point was to get Bishop Martensen to speak just one single time so that whoever wants to see could have a criterion for what powers he has when it comes down to brass tacks. That happened. Then the point was to force him, if possible, back into silence. That happened. Let him now play the sagacious one through silence. When one knows what his speaking signifies, one knows also what his silence signifies. By his silence he may have managed, yet just barely, to fool himself, but not anyone who is willing to see—something he has fairly earned.[155]

THE MOMENT[1]

No. 1–2

THE MOMENT

No. 1

CONTENTS

May 24, 1855   S. KIERKEGAARD

Exordium[2]

Plato, as is well-known, states somewhere in his *Republic* that the
state will not amount to anything until it has rulers who have no
desire to rule.[3] He presumably means that, given the presupposition that there is competence, the disinclination to rule is an
excellent guarantee that the ruling will be true and competent,
whereas the power-seeker too easily becomes one who misuses
his power in order to tyrannize, or one whom the desire to rule
brings into a concealed relation of dependency on those whom
he is supposed to rule, so that his ruling actually becomes an
optical illusion.

This observation can also be applied to other relations where
the situation calls for something to become downright earnest:
given the presupposition that there is competence, it is best that
the persons involved not have the desire. It certainly is the case,
as the proverb says, that willing hands make light work; but true
earnestness does not actually emerge until a person of competence is compelled against his desire by something higher to
undertake the work, that is, a person of competence against his
desire.

Understood in this way, I can say that I have the proper relation to the task: to work in the moment—God knows there is
nothing I dislike more.

To be an author—well, yes, this appeals to me. If I am to be
honest, I must indeed say that I have been in love with being
productive—but, please note, in the way I want it. And what I
have loved is exactly the opposite of working in the moment;
what I have loved is precisely the distance from the moment, the
distance in which I, like a lover, can tag after the thoughts and,
just like an artist in love with his instrument, I can converse with
the language, draw forth the expressions just as the thought requires them—blissful pastime!—throughout an eternity I could
not become weary of this occupation!

To contend with people—well, yes, this appeals to me in a certain sense. By nature I am so polemical[4] that I really feel in my element only when surrounded by human mediocrity and scurviness. But on one condition: that I be permitted silently to disdain, to satisfy the passion that is in my soul, disdain—for which my life as an author has richly provided an occasion.

Thus I am a person of whom it may truthfully be said that he has not the least desire to work in the moment—most likely that is just why I was selected for it.

If I am to work in the moment, then I must, alas, take leave of you, you beloved distance, where there was nothing urgent to be done, where there was always plenty of time, where I could wait for hours, days, weeks to find the expression exactly as I wanted it, whereas now a break must be made with all such considerations of tender love. And if I am obliged to work in the moment, there will be some people to whom I owe it, at least at times, to take into consideration all the trivialities that mediocrity with great pompousness didactically recites, all the gibberish that they, by bringing it along themselves, get out of what I write, all the lies and slander to which a person is exposed, against whom the two great powers in society, envy and obtuseness, must with a certain necessity conspire.

Why, then, am I willing to work in the moment? I am willing to do it because I would eternally regret not doing it, and eternally regret it if I let myself be put off because the contemporary generation will perhaps at the very most only be able to find a true presentation of Christianity interesting and odd, in order for it to remain quite calmly where it is, in the delusion of being Christians and that the pastors' play-Christianity is Christianity.

Addition *to* This Must Be Said, or *How Is Something Decisive to Be Introduced?*[5]

The objection I have raised against the established order is decisive. Now, if someone says—and I am prepared for even the person most kindly disposed to me to speak this way—"The objection is so frightfully decisive," then to that I could answer: It cannot be otherwise. Or I could answer with a line by one of my pseudonyms: When the castle gate of inwardness has been closed for a long time and finally is opened, it does not move noiselessly like an inside door that operates with springs.[6]

But I can also explain myself more fully. To introduce something decisive—and this is the task—cannot be done in the same manner as everything else; and therefore now, especially when the disaster of the time is precisely this "to a certain degree," to enter into everything to a certain degree, when precisely this is the sickness, every care must be taken so that as far as possible it does not happen that one also enters into this task to a certain degree, whereby everything is lost. No, something decisive is introduced differently from anything else. Like the leap of the wild beast upon its prey, like the strike of the plunging eagle, something decisive is introduced—suddenly and concentrated in one sortie (intensively). And just as the wild beast combines cunning and strength—at first cunningly keeps perfectly quiet (no tame animal can be that quiet) and then totally pulls itself together into one single leap or strike (no tame animal can pull itself together or rise in a leap that way)—in the same way something decisive is introduced. At first quiet—the weather on a still day is never so quiet; only before the thunderstorm is it this quiet—and then the storm breaks.

This is how something decisive is introduced. Believe me, I am all too well acquainted with the defect of the age, that it is lack of character, everything to a certain degree. But just as "a mirror-bright shield of polished steel," so bright "that when the sun's rays fall it reflects the sun with double brilliance,"[7] just as such a shield fears most of all even the least little spot, since even with the least little spot it is no longer itself—just so does something decisive fear every contact by and with this "to a certain degree." I understand that, and why should I not understand it, I who am known even to children on the street by the name of Either/Or.[8]

What is Either/Or, if I, who presumably must know it, must tell you? Either/Or is the word before which the folding doors spring open and the ideals appear—blissful sight! Either/Or is the symbol that gives admittance to the unconditional—God be praised! Indeed, Either/Or is the key to heaven! On the other hand, what is, was, and remains a human being's disaster? This "to a certain degree" of Satan or of pettiness or of cowardly sagacity, which, applied to Christianity, transforms it—a miracle in reverse, or a miraculous reversal—transforms it into blather! No—Either/Or! And just as it is so that however tenderly the actor and actress embrace and caress each other on the stage, it still always remains only a theatrical connivance, a theater-marriage—in the same way everything "to a certain degree" is theatrical in relation to the unconditional, grasps a delusion; only Either/Or is the embrace that grasps the unconditional. And just as (in order to speak of something about which it could never occur to me to speak in this way here except for the sake of contrast to what follows, in order to speak of life's jest)—just as every officer who belongs to the king's personal entourage bears a symbol (distinction) by which this is recognized, just so all those who have served Christianity in truth were marked "Either/Or," the expression of majesty or the expression of having a relation to the divine majesty. Everything that is only to a certain degree has not served Christianity but perhaps itself and at most can never honestly request any other mark than (as on a letter): royal service, since the mark of what is God's service is: Either/Or.[9]

The question itself certainly needs no explanation in order to be answered. Surely everyone must say to himself that it cannot be defensible.

What does need to be explained, then, is that what the state has done and is doing amounts to making, if possible, Christianity impossible; and this can be explained very easily and very briefly, because the factual situation in the country is actually this, that Christianity, the Christianity of the New Testament, not only does not exist but, if possible, is made impossible.

Suppose that the state employed 1000 officials who, along with their families, lived on, and therefore were financially interested in, hindering Christianity—it would certainly be an attempt aimed at making, if possible, Christianity impossible.

And yet this attempt (which of course has this obviousness about it, that it obviously is for the purpose of hindering Christianity) would not be as dangerous as what is factually happening, that the state employs 1000 officials who—in the name of proclaiming Christianity (exactly here is the greater danger compared with very obviously wanting to hinder Christianity) are financially interested in *(a)* having people call themselves Christians—the larger the flock of sheep the better—take the name "Christians," and in *(b)* letting the matter rest there, so that they do not come to know what Christianity in truth is.

But it is the case with the existence of these 1000 officials that if one holds the New Testament alongside it is easy to see that, Christianly, their whole existence is malpractice. Whereas, then, if people did not assume the name "Christians," the pastor would have nothing on which to live; to be obliged to proclaim what Christianity in truth is would of course be the same as opening people's eyes to the fact that the pastor's own existence is malpractice, that even if the teacher of Christianity receives something to live on, being a pastor cannot become a royal appointment, a career, and steady promotion.

And this, this activity, does not take place in the name of hindering Christianity; that is not why 1000 officials with families are paid. No, it takes place in the name of proclaiming Christianity, of propagating Christianity, of working for Christianity. Between too little and too much, which of course spoils everything, between this too little (that people would not assume the name "Christians") and this too much (that they would learn what Christianity in truth is and really become Christians) lies, with equilibristic earnestness, the Christianity of "Christendom," the official state Church and people's Church Christianity, which, compared with the Christianity of the New Testament, does indeed look amazing numerically, Christians by the millions, all of the same quality.

Is not this just about the most dangerous thing one can come up with in order to make, if possible, Christianity impossible? "The pastor" has a pecuniary interest in having people call themselves Christians, since every such person is of course (through the state as commission agent) a contributing member and also contributes to giving the whole profession visible power—but nothing is more dangerous for true Christianity, nothing is more against its nature, than getting people light-mindedly to assume the name "Christians," to teach them to have a low opinion of being a Christian, as if it were something that is so very easy. And "the pastor" has a pecuniary interest in having it rest there, so that by assuming the name "Christians" people do not come to know what Christianity in truth is, since otherwise the whole machinery of 1000 royal offices and class power would come to naught—but nothing is more dangerous for true Christianity, nothing is more contrary to its nature, than (this abortion) causing it to rest there, so that people assume the name "Christians."

And this is supposed to be working for, propagating, promoting Christianity!

There is to me something so revolting and shocking in the mere thought of this kind of worship, to worship God by making a fool of him, that I will strive with all my power and to the best of my ability to make a contribution so that this does not happen and so that people's eyes are opened to how things hang together and thereby prevent them from becoming guilty of a crime in which the state and the pastors have actually implicated them— because however light-minded and sensate the great majority of people may be, there is still too much good in them to want to worship God in that way.

XIV
111

So let there be light on this matter, let it become clear to people what the New Testament understands by being a Christian, so that everyone can choose whether he wants to be a Christian or whether he honestly, plainly, forthrightly does not want to be that. Let it be said aloud to the whole nation: It is infinitely dearer to God that you plainly acknowledge—the condition for your possibly becoming a Christian—that you are not and do not want to be a Christian, infinitely dearer than this foulness that to worship God is to make a fool of him.

Yes, this is how it must be done; light must be shed in the darkness in which this state Church and people's Church issue is being kept. Instead of facing, with unconditional respect for what the New Testament understands by being a Christian, the question: How many Christians are there really in the land, the relation is reversed in this way: There are a million people in the land, ergo a million Christians—and 1000 officials are employed to live on this. And then one more step, then the statement is reversed and the conclusion is: If there are 1000 officials who are to live on Christianity—and we have them now—then there also must be a million Christians. We must strictly hold to that; otherwise we certainly cannot secure the livelihood for all these officials.

So there are 1000 officials who along with their families are to live on this; ergo there must be a million Christians. Thus the proclamation of Christianity corresponds to this (to this very awkward kind of predicament into which we have brought ourselves): to work for Christianity becomes, as was said, getting people to assume the name "Christians" and also bringing about the result that the matter rests there, and this is what I call: making, if possible, Christianity impossible, thereby in turn (to repeat) making the human mass guilty of a crime they otherwise would be innocent of, namely, in the name of worshiping God to make a fool of him, something I—who surely have hitherto experienced little gratitude for the love I have for people—still want in every way to prevent.

If the issue is to be taken in the way I am indicating, I realize very well that a very serious, in the earthly and temporal sense, question is bound to arise about the livelihood of these officials (just as people talk about mansions on the moon, just so do they become partners in a chimera: a million Christians). And in this

XIV
112

regard I am the most accommodating and willing person, am as far as possible from wanting to participate in any chicanery to which they may be subjected, perhaps from the side of certain politicians. It was precisely in order to be able to get to the issue that I had to try to get blown away, if possible, what Bishop Martensen began to serve up about being truth-witnesses. Above all, this nauseating drivel had to go. Then—let us be agreeable people!—then there can be reasonable discussion about a very serious issue in a plain human sense. And in this way I believe that it will serve us all. The kind of pastors we have now best hold their own by not playing along the line of wanting to be regarded as truth-witnesses; if they do, well, then the difficult problem is solved with infinite ease: immediately suspend their entire salary and save every pension—truth-witnesses must indeed put up with such things. And the notion about truth-witnesses, that pastors are truth-witnesses, would be a very witty notion—if it had not come from a bishop and in such a way that it became obtuse and offensive—if, for example, it had come from a sagacious statesman, a minister of ecclesiastical affairs and education who wished to be rid of the clergy in a deft way.

No doubt there are some people upon whom my articles in *Fædrelandet* have made an impression. Then perhaps their situation is something like this: they have become aware, or at least they have begun to think about whether the whole religious situation is in an extremely wretched condition. But, on the other hand, there is so much that makes them disinclined to devote themselves to such thoughts; they love the usual order of things, which they relinquish very reluctantly.

Therefore their condition is somewhat like that of a person who walks around with a bad taste in his mouth, a coated tongue, and the shivers—and so the physician says to him: Take an emetic.

Likewise I, too, say: Take an emetic. Come out of this vacillating condition.

First of all, think for a moment about what Christianity is, what it requires of a person, what sacrifices it calls for, what sacrifices have in fact been brought to it. Thus (as one reads in stories) even "tender maidens" (who unlike our Christian maidens did not fill their time and their thoughts wondering whether they should wear the light blue or the poppy red to the theater) did not shrink back but, commending their souls to God, bravely surrendered their "delicate limbs" to the cruelty of the executioners. Think about that first for a moment. And make this so very clear, entirely clear and present to yourself (swallow it, however disagreeable it is): to live in such a way that this is supposed to be *Christian* worship, that in a quiet hour[10] a dramatically costumed man comes forward and with dismay in his demeanor proclaims with choking sobs that there is an accounting of eternity, that we are advancing toward an accounting of eternity—and that we then live in such a way that, outside the quiet hour, even merely to have to set aside some conventional consideration, quite apart from consideration for one's promotion, one's earthly advantage, the favors of the elite, etc., is regarded as something that no one could think of, obviously not the declaimer either, or if someone does it, it is punished by being declared a kind of lunacy—think about living in this way, that this is supposed to be **Christian** worship—now, is the emetic not working?

Well, then take one more dose! Make it perfectly clear and present to yourself how nauseating it is to live in this way, that this is supposed to be *Christian* worship: that then when the declaimer dies a new costumed declaimer comes forward and in a quiet hour from the pulpit represents the deceased as a truth-witness, one of the authentic truth-witnesses, one of the holy chain—is it not working?

Well, then take another dose! Make it perfectly clear and present to yourself that to live in such a way that if someone says, "No, surely the late declaimer could not be called a truth-witness"—then it is supposed to be *Christian* zeal, continually repeated and publicized as widely as possible, to express the opinion that this man defiles—just listen!—he defiles the memory of an honorable man, he violates the peace of the grave—just listen!—he violates the peace of the grave etc. etc.

It is working, isn't it? Then you will see that you will be all right, the bad taste will disappear—that is, it will become clear to you that the whole thing is putrid, a loathsomeness that nonetheless could begin really to work as it should only when Bishop Martensen applied the word "truth-witness."

So let it do its work; and next to God thank Bishop Martensen for this extremely beneficial emetic.

[11]In my work I have now come so close to the present time, to the moment, that I cannot do without an organ by which I can instantaneously address my [12]contemporaries, and I have called this:

THE MOMENT[13]

If anyone interested in this matter should wish to be sure of receiving what may come out, he can, for the sake of his own convenience, arrange a subscription with the publisher. But I reserve for myself in *every* regard the *most unconditional* freedom; otherwise I cannot do it.

I call it: The Moment. Yet what I want is not something ephemeral, any more than it is something ephemeral I have wanted; no, it was and is something eternal: by means of the ideals, against the illusions. But in one sense I must say of all my earlier work that its time has not yet come. I have been at a distance from the present age, even very distant, and close only insofar as this distance was well calculated and full of purpose. Now, however, I must in any case make sure of a possibility of being able to use the moment.

I do not urge anyone to subscribe; I rather ask everyone at least to think twice before he does it. Eternally he will not regret heeding my words, but it is quite possible that he could regret it temporally. He himself is then to consider whether it is the eternal he wants or the temporal. I, who am called Either/Or,[14] cannot serve anyone with: both-and.

I have in my possession a book that probably is almost unknown here in our country, and therefore I will give the precise title: *The New Testament of our Lord and Savior Jesus Christ*. Although I have a completely free relation to this book and am not, for example, bound to it by an oath, it nevertheless exercises great power over me, instills in me an indescribable horror for both-and.

THE MOMENT

No. 2

CONTENTS

June 4, 1855   S. KIERKEGAARD

To *My Reader!*

XIV
117

You whom I have called *my reader*,[15] to you I would like to say a few words.

When a person ventures out as decisively as I have done, furthermore, in a matter that so profoundly bears on everything as religion does, it is natural to expect that everything will be done to oppose him by distorting and falsifying what he says, also that his character will in every way be thrown to the wolves and he will be regarded as someone to whom one has no obligations but against whom everything is permitted.

As things generally go in this world, the one attacked ordinarily gets busy at once to pay attention to every accusation, every falsification, every dishonesty, is in this way on the move early and late to refute the attack—I do not intend to do this.

It is about this that I want to say a few words to you, my reader, in order very earnestly to impress something upon you. That the one attacked is so terribly busy defending himself—just consider, could that not most often be connected in a sheer egotistical sense with his being interested in guarding himself, fearing that the falsification of what he says, the bad personal comments about him, will harm him in the worldly and temporal sense? And—just consider!—do you not think that this very point, that when all is said and done most people who step forward in public have worldly and temporal goals and for that reason are so busy justifying themselves against every accusation—do you not think that this universal busyness is also harmful in that it coddles people into not caring to grasp an issue for themselves and to be able to judge, into being unwilling to be inconvenienced themselves, to have any strain, because today in all circumstances there no longer are teachers—but waiters?

XIV
118

In any case, I intend to take up the matter differently. I intend to consider much more slowly the refutation of all this falsifying and distorting, all these lies and slander, all this babbling and balderdash. For one thing, I learn from the New Testament that encountering such things is the sign that one is on the right road; thus I should, of course, not exactly hasten to remove them, lest I wish to get on the wrong road as soon as possible. For another, I learn from the New Testament that what may temporally be called an affliction, and what according to temporality's conception one must seek to dispose of the sooner the better, has eternal worth.[16] So I should, of course, not exactly hasten to escape, unless I want to fool myself with regard to the eternal.

This is how I understand it, and now I come to what will be the consequences for you. If you have ever actually had an idea that I am serving something true—well, then I for my part will on occasion do something, but only what is exactly necessary, so that you, if you will make the effort and take care, will be able to withstand the falsification and distortion of what I say and all the attacks upon my character—but your comfortableness, no, my dear reader, that I will not promote. If you imagine that I am a waiter, then you have never been my reader; if you actually are my reader, then you will understand that I can even regard it as my duty to you that you be strained a little if you do not want the falsification and distortion, the lies and the slander, to wrest from you the idea you have had about my serving something true.

When Christianity entered the world, the task was to proclaim Christianity directly. The same is the case wherever Christianity is introduced into a country in which the religion is not Christianity.

In "Christendom" the relation is different, since the state of things (situation) is different. What is found there is not Christianity but an enormous illusion, and people are not pagans but are made blissfully happy in the delusion that they are Christians.

If Christianity is to be introduced here, then first and foremost the illusion must be removed. But since this illusion, this delusion, is that they are Christians, then it of course seems as if the introduction of Christianity would deprive people of Christianity. Yet this is the first thing that must be done; the illusion must go.

This is the task; but this task has a double direction.

It is directed to what can be done to clear up people's concepts, to instruct them, to stir them by means of the ideals, through pathos to bring them into an impassioned state, to rouse them up with the gadfly sting[17] of irony, scorn, sarcasm, etc. etc.

The task would not be something else if this illusion, that people imagine that they are Christians, if this illusion did not hang together with an enormously huge illusion that has a purely external aspect, the illusion that Christianity and the state have been fused together, that the state installs 1000 officeholders, whose interest, with the instinct of self-preservation, is that people do not find out what Christianity is and that they are not Christians. That is, the personal existence of these pastors is, Christianly, an untruth. Thoroughly secularized and in the service of the state (royal officeholders, personages of rank, career makers, etc.), they naturally are not in a position to tell the congregations what Christianity is, since to tell that would mean resigning one's state office.

Now, this illusion is different from that first one, which was related to people's conceptions, individuals' entrapment in the delusion that they are Christians. With regard to this latter illusion, the work must be done in a different way; the state, after all, has the power to remove it. Thus the second aspect of the task is to work along the lines of getting the state to remove this illusion.

If I were to compare this task to something, I would say: It resembles the medical treatment of a mentally ill patient. The treatment must be psychical, says the physician, but that does not mean that there may not also be something physical to do.

*   *

*

In consequence of what has been presented here, may I urge something on my reader—and I hope that he will excuse my speaking in another way than, unfortunately, is ordinary: to bow and scrape before the reader because one wants his money and regards his opinion to be the verdict.

What I would like to urge upon my reader is this, that he not limit himself to reading each number of *The Moment* through once, but, inasmuch as the number contains several articles, that he acquaint himself with the contents in a first reading and then later read each separate article by itself.

It is these two things—one could almost be tempted to ask what the devil these two things have to do with each other—yet it is these two things that official Christianity or the state with the help of official Christianity has managed to lump together, and with the same equanimity as that of someone who, in order to include all at a party, combines toasts to many in one toast.

It seems that the state's process of thinking must have been this. Among the many different things that people need in a cultured mode of life and that the state tries to provide for its citizens as cheaply and comfortably as possible, among these many different things, such as public security, water, lighting, roads, pavement, etc. etc., there is in addition—an eternal happiness in the life to come, a necessity that the state likewise ought to satisfy— how generous!—and in as inexpensive and comfortable a way as possible. Naturally it will cost money, since without money one gets nothing in this world, not even a certificate for becoming eternally happy in the next world. No, without money one gets nothing in this world. But what nevertheless makes the state the greatest blessing to individuals is that it procures this more cheaply than if the individuals were to make private arrangements, also more securely, and finally, as comfortably as only the grandiose can do it.

First, then, in order to introduce Christianity, a comprehensive census is arranged, whereupon the whole country is entered on the tax rolls—just exactly as happened when Christianity entered the world[18]—and then 1000 royal officials are installed. "My dear subjects, you shall"—this undoubtedly must be the state's thinking—"you shall also in regard to the great and priceless boon, an eternal happiness, have everything as convenient, as comfortable and as inexpensive as possible. Having water on tap on every floor instead of the old-fashioned laborious toil of lugging it up the steps cannot be more convenient than what you will have with regard to an eternal happiness in the life to come (for which, in the uncultured ages of ignorance, one ran to the ends of the earth and on one's knees). Just whistle, and it will be at your service, yes, even before you whistle. Neither do you need to go up the steps or down the steps, God forbid; it is delivered to you—just like beer these days—by the royal licensed dispensers, who will surely be enterprising and alert, since it is their livelihood. Yet the price is so low that this inexpensiveness completely exposes Catholicism's exorbitance."

Far be it from me to speak disparagingly of comfort! But let it be used, wherever it can be used, only in relation to everything that is something in such a way that this something is indifferent to the way in which it is had, so that one can have it both in one way and in another, because when this is the case, the convenient and comfortable way is undeniably preferable. For example, water. Water is something that can be obtained in the hard way by fetching it from the pump, but it also can be obtained in the convenient way by high pressure; naturally I prefer the convenient way.

But the eternal is not something like that, indifferent to the way in which it is obtained; no, the eternal really is not a something but is—the way in which it is obtained. The eternal is obtained in only one way—and it is precisely in this that the eternal is different from everything else, that it can be obtained in only one way. That which can be obtained in only one way is the eternal—it is obtained in only one way, in eternity's hard way, to which Christ points with the words: The way is narrow and the gate is strait that leads to life, and few there are who find it.[19]

That was a severe *nota bene*; the comfortable—precisely that in which our age excels—cannot be brought into any relation at all to an eternal happiness. If, for example, walking is what is required, it is utterly useless to make the most amazing inventions for the production of the most comfortable carriages and to want to convey yourself in them when walking is the task assigned to you. And if the eternal is the way in which it is obtained, it does not help admirably to want to change the way in the direction of comfort, because the eternal is obtained only in the difficult way, is not obtained indifferently, both in an easy and in a difficult way, but is the way in which it is obtained, and this way is the difficult way.

So, thanks, you government administrators, you councilors of chancery, of justice, of state, and of privy councils, thanks for the prodigious scribbling you have had to do to arrange for all his majesty's subjects, each one individually, an eternal happiness in an inexpensive and comfortable way. Thank you, you 1000 ec- clesiastical councilors. It is true that you have not done it for nothing; you have, of course, had your percentage, but yet it is not more than fair that you are also formally thanked. Thank you, all of you—if only it now is certain that they are saved and if it is not rather the case that a testimonial from "the state" is the worst recommendation in the life to come, where the judgment is whether you have belonged to the kingdom that does not want at any price to be a kingdom of this world.[20] ·

The Human Protects (Protegerer[21]) the Divine!

That it is abracadabra, that the human protects the divine, is easy enough to understand. How in the world, then, could something like that occur to such a rational entity as the state?

Well, it is a long story, but it is mainly connected to Christianity's being served over the years less and less in the character of what it is: the divine.

Imagine a statesman contemporary with Christianity's entry into the world and say to him: *Quid tibi videtur* [What is your opinion];[22] do you not think that this would be a religion for the state? In all probability he would consider you lunatic, would scarcely deign to reply.

But served in craven fear of people, in mediocrity, in temporal interest, well, then it looks somewhat different, then it actually can seem that Christianity (which by that service gradually became spavined and chest-foundered and lame and a wretched "critter") might be very happy to be protected by the state and in this way achieve honor.

Seen from this point of view, the responsibility lies with the clergy, who in a way have, as we say, taken the state by the nose, led it to think that here was something for the state to do, which sooner or later is bound to end with the state's paying dearly because it has become too high-flown. Even if it is sure that it is not at all too high-flown for the state to protect what has been palmed off as Christianity—as soon as it is recognized what Christianity is, then the state has become fatuously high-flown and on its own behalf must desire to come down to earth, the sooner the better.

The situation of Christianity protected by the state is like that in a fairy tale or story. A king, dressed in the clothes of an ordinary man, lives in a provincial town, and the mayor is so kind as to want to protect this citizen—then suddenly an emissary arrives, who with a deep bow and finally a bended knee addresses this ordinary citizen: Your Majesty. If the mayor is a reasonable man, he sees that he, well-intentioned, has been a little too high-flown in protecting this citizen.

Imagine—not what has been talked about so frequently that it has become almost banal, that Christ returned to earth—no, imagine that one of the apostles returned; he would shudder to see Christianity protected by the state. Imagine him approaching the Christianity degraded in this way and bowing before it. There is no statesman in our day so narrow-minded but that he sees it was a mistake for him to want to protect Christianity, that it is a shocking *quid pro quo* [one thing for another] to confuse the pastors' need for the protection of the state with Christianity's need for it—Christianity, which if it had any need needs only to be rid of such pastors, who do not know how to bow to Christianity, since one bows to it by a willingness to bring sacrifices, to suffer for the doctrine, but know only how to bow to the king, to bow to one's having acquired rank equal to that of Councilor of State, having been made a Knight of the Dannebrog, which is faithlessness on the part of the one who in the capacity of a teacher of Christianity is bound by an oath on the New Testament, faithlessness to the New Testament. Christianity teaches: "You shall fear God, honor the king"[23]; a Christian is to be, if possible, His Majesty's best subject. But, *Christianly*, the king is not the authority; he is not and cannot and shall not and will not be the authority in relation to a kingdom that at no price wants to be of this world, at all costs does not want to be of this world.[24] Faithfulness to the oath on the New Testament would therefore help a person to prevent what one, precisely if one loves the king, must want to prevent—the placing of His Royal Majesty in a wrong light. In its exalted divine earnestness, Christianity has always allowed the king's existence its earnestness. It is only the detestable play-Christianity, traitorous to the New Testament, that was traitorous also to the king and placed him in a light that was confusing for the dignity and earnestness of his royal existence.

xiv
126

Therefore the moment will certainly come when a king suddenly stands up and says: "Now I see it. These scoundrel pastors, so it was to this that I have been brought, to what I have least of all deserved to become, to be made ludicrous. By our royal honor I know, if anyone does, what the king's majesty signifies. I also know what I have in my power, gold and property and rank and dignity and all the symbols of prestige; yes, I can give away kingdoms and countries, I who, above other kings, even have crowns to bestow. But what, then, is Christianity? Christianity is renunciation of all this. Christianity is not only not to covet such things, no, it is at no price to be willing to accept them even if they are offered, to shun them more apprehensively than the earthly mind shuns misery and suffering, to shun them more passionately than the earthly mind hankers after them. How in all the world did I get into this folly: to protect with gold and property, with titles and dignities and stars and badges of honor—that which shuns all such things more than the plague! I am indeed ludicrous! And who is to blame for this, who but these scoundrel pastors who have made Christianity into the very opposite of what it is in the New Testament and thereby have led me to think that I could protect Christianity. I am a fool, because what is it that I have protected, certainly not Christianity—in all its lowliness and suffering it is superior to me—but some scoundrels who in this very way have least of all deserved my protection."

In the New Testament, the Savior of the world, our Lord Jesus Christ, presents the matter thus: The way that leads to life is narrow, the gate is strait—and few are they who find it[25] — —now, however, to stay only with Denmark, we are all Christians; the way is as broad as possible, the broadest in Denmark, since it is the one we are all walking on, moreover, easy and comfortable in every way, and the gate as wide as possible— indeed, no gate can be wider than one through which all are walking *en masse*:

ergo the New Testament is no longer the truth.

All honor to the human race! You, however, you Savior of the world, you have held too lowly an opinion of the human race, so that you did not foresee the elevation that it, perfectible as it is, can reach through steady, continuous striving!

Consequently to this degree the New Testament is no longer the truth: the way is the broadest, the gate is the widest, and we are all Christians. Yes, I venture to go a step further (this inspires me, since it is indeed a eulogy in praise of the human race), I venture to maintain that the average Jews living among us are to a certain degree Christians, Christians like all the rest of us—to the degree to which we are all Christians, to that degree the New Testament is no longer the truth.

Since the point is to see what serves to the glorification of the human race, while care ought to be taken so as not to come out with some falsehood, care also ought to be taken so that nothing, nothing at all, escapes one that is evidential in this regard or merely suggestive. Therefore I venture to go a step further, yet without expressing any definite opinion, in view of my lack of knowledge in this regard, and therefore I ask the experts, the professionals, whether among domestic animals, the nobler ones, the horse, the dog, and the cow, there would appear a sign of something Christian? It is not improbable. Consider what it means to live in a Christian state, in a Christian nation, where everything is Christian and all are Christians, where one sees, wherever one turns, nothing but Christians and Christianity, truth and truth-witnesses—it is not improbable that this is bound to have an influence upon the nobler domestic animals and thereby, in turn, upon what, according to the judgment of both the veterinarians and the pastors, is always the important thing: the offspring. Jacob's trick is well known, that in order to obtain striped and spotted lambs he laid striped and spotted sticks in the water troughs so the ewes saw only what was motley and therefore gave birth to striped and spotted lambs.[26] It is not improbable—although I do not presume to have a definite opinion, since this is not my profession, but prefer to refer it to a committee composed, for example, of pastors and veterinarians—it is not improbable that eventually it will turn out that domestic animals in "Christendom" bring Christian offspring into the world. I become almost dizzy at the thought. But then, on the greatest possible scale—all honor to the human race—the New Testament will not be the truth anymore.

Savior of the world, when in concern you said, "When I come again, will I find faith upon the earth?"[27] and when you bowed your head in death,[28] you surely did not have the slightest idea that your expectations would be exceeded on such a scale, that the human race would make the New Testament untruth in such a beautiful and moving way and your significance almost doubtful—such rare creatures, can they truthfully be said to need or to have ever needed a Savior!

That we all are Christians is something so generally known and taken for granted that it requires no demonstration but is surely even starting to work its way up from being a historical truth to becoming an axiom, one of the eternal principles with which a child is now born; thus it may be said that with Christianity a change has come about in human beings so that "in Christendom" a child is born with one principle more than a human being outside Christendom: the principle that we all are Christians.

But of course it can never do any harm to make it clear to oneself again and again to what degree it is certain that we all are Christians.

Here is my attempt, and I flatter myself that it actually does make clear to what degree it is true that we all are Christians. We are that to such a degree that if there lived among us an atheist who in the strongest terms declared all Christianity to be a lie, moreover, in the strongest terms declared he was not a Christian—it is futile, he is a Christian; according to law he can be punished—that is another matter, but he is a Christian. "What nonsense," says the state, "what would this lead to; as soon as we allowed someone to declare that he is not a Christian, it would soon end with everyone's denying that he is a Christian. No, no, *principiis obsta* [resist beginnings][29] and stand firm on the principles. We now have well-tabulated statistics, everything classified, everything accurate, always on the presupposition that we all are Christians—ergo, he also is a Christian. A conceitedness such as that, which merely wants to be eccentric, must not be indulged; he is a Christian, and there the matter rests."

XIV
130

If he dies—and he leaves so much that the man of God, the pastor, as well as the undertaker and several others are each able to get what is coming to him, all his protests are futile: he is, he is a Christian, and he is buried as a Christian—to that degree is it certain that we all are Christians. If he leaves nothing (a little makes no difference; the pastor, who is Christianly contented, is always contented with little when there is not more), if he leaves literally nothing—that is bound to be the only case in which attention might be paid to his protests, since by being dead he would also be prevented from corporally paying with physical labor the costs of being Christianly buried—to that extent is it certain that we all are Christians. In "Christendom" it stands firm, as firm as the principle of contradiction outside Christendom, it stands firm, this eternal principle that no doubt is able to shake: we all are Christians.

In the New Testament, all relations, all dimensions are structured on a large scale.

The true is presented ideally; on the other hand, errors and aberrations are in turn on a large scale; there are warnings against hypocrisy,[31] against all sorts of false doctrine,[32] against the presumptuousness of works[33] etc. etc.

But, strangely enough, the New Testament pays no attention at all to that of which there is, unfortunately, much too much in this world, indeed, which is the substance of this world: blather, wretchedness, mediocrity, prattle, chatter, playing at Christianity, changing everything into platitudes etc.

From this arises the difficulty that it is almost impossible with the help of the New Testament to strike a blow at actual life, the actual world in which we live, where for every one qualified hypocrite there are 100,000 blatherers, for every one qualified heretic there are 100,000 pedants.

The New Testament seems to foster high conceptions of what it means to be a human being. On the one hand it points to the ideal; on the other, where it describes what is wrong, one sees that it nevertheless has a high conception of what it means to be a human being—but the blow continually overlooks the blather, pedantry, and mediocrity.

From time immemorial blather has made use of this to set itself up as the true Christian orthodoxy—with these incalculable battalions of millions of Christians as the result. This orthodoxy, strong in numbers if not in spirit, makes use of one's inability truthfully to accuse it of hypocrisy, false doctrine, etc.—which one cannot really do—ergo, it is the true Christian orthodoxy.

And this is done very easily. That is, in every relation the highest and the lowest have a certain fleeting resemblance to each other in not being lower than the high or in not being in the middle between the high and the low. Thus in being above all criticism and being beneath all criticism, these two qualifications have a certain fleeting resemblance to each other. So it is with that orthodoxy of the masses and of the pastors living off them en masse—it resembles the truly Christian inasmuch as it undeniably is not false doctrine, heresy.

Otherwise it resembles the truly Christian even less than any heresy and false doctrine whatever. The relation is this: blather lies just as far below heresies and false doctrines and errors as the truly Christian stands above all heresies and false doctrines and errors. But, as stated, the difficulty with the New Testament is that, while requiring the ideal[34] and contending with spirits,[35] it has not taken aim at all at this enormous corpus that in "Christendom" continually provides the true Christian orthodoxy, the Christian earnestness of which finds its expression in "truth-witnesses" who make a career and are a success in this world—what a satirical self-contradiction!—by describing on Sunday how the truth must suffer in this world.

Close attention must be paid to this. And if one does pay close attention to it, one will see that the New Testament nevertheless proves to be right, that things do go as the New Testament has predicted. In the midst of this enormous population of "Christians," in this swarm of "Christians," there now and then live some individuals, an individual. For him the way is hard[36]—see the New Testament; he comes to be hated by all[37]—see the New Testament; to put him to death is regarded as service to God[38]—see the New Testament. This is indeed a curious book, the New Testament; it proves to be right after all, because this individual, these individuals—yes, those were the Christians.

Suppose that it is not so, that what we understand by being a Christian is a delusion, this whole machinery of the state Church and 1000 ecclesiastical-worldly councilors etc. an enormous optical illusion that will not be the least help to us in eternity, on the contrary will be used as an indictment against us—suppose it is not so, because in that case let us (for eternity's sake!) get rid of it, the sooner the better— —

— —suppose that it is not so, suppose that what we understand by being a Christian actually is what it means to be a Christian—what then is God in heaven?

He is the most ludicrous being that has ever lived, his Word the most ludicrous book that has ever come to light: to set heaven and earth in motion (as he indeed does in his Word), to threaten with hell,[39] with eternal punishment—in order to attain to what we understand by being a Christian (and, after all, we are true Christians)—no, something that ludicrous has never happened! Imagine that a man confronted a person with a loaded pistol and said to him, "I am going to shoot you down," or suppose something still more dreadful, that he said, "I am going to seize you and torture you to death in the most horrible way if you do not (pay attention now, here it comes!), if you do not make your life here on earth as profitable and enjoyable as you possibly can"—this certainly is the most ridiculous talk, because to bring this about one really does not need to threaten with a loaded pistol and the most agonizing death penalty; perhaps neither the loaded pistol nor the most agonizing death penalty would be able to prevent it. And so it is also, to want, through a fear of eternal punishment (fearful threat!), through the hope of eternal happiness, to bring about—yes, to bring about what we are (for what we call Christian is, after all, what it means to be a Christian), that is, to want to bring about what we are: that we live just as we please—since to abstain from civil crimes is, of course, merely ordinary sagacity.

*   *

*

What "Christendom" is guilty of is the most dreadful kind of blasphemy: to transform the God of spirit[40] into—ludicrous blather. And the most spiritless kind of worship, more spiritless than anything that is or was found in paganism, more spiritless than worshiping a stone, an ox, an insect as God, more spiritless than everything, is: to worship under the name of God—a blatherpate!

If We Actually Are Christians, If Everything Is in Order with "Christendom," "a Christian World," Then the New Testament Is eo ipso No Longer Guidance for the Christian, Cannot Be That

On the given assumptions, the New Testament neither is nor can be guidance for the Christian—because the Way has been changed, is entirely different from that in the New Testament.

On these assumptions, the New Testament, considered as guidance for the Christian, becomes a historical curiosity, somewhat like a handbook for travelers in a particular country when everything in that same country is completely changed. Such a handbook is not to be taken seriously by travelers in that country, but it has great value as entertaining reading. While one is comfortably riding along in the train, one reads in the handbook, "Here is the frightful Wolf Ravine, where one plunges 70,000 fathoms down under the earth"; while one is sitting and smoking a cigar in the cozy dining car, one reads in the handbook, "Here is the hideout of a robber band that attacks and beats up travelers"—here it is, that is, here it was, since now (how amusing to imagine how it was), now it is not the Wolf Ravine but a railroad, and not a robber band but a cozy dining car.

If we actually are Christians, if, Christianly, all is in order with "Christendom" and a Christian world, then I will shout, if possible so loudly that it could be heard in heaven: You Infinite One, even if you have otherwise shown yourself to be love, it was truly unloving of you not to let us know that the New Testament is no longer the guide (handbook) for Christians! How cruel, when everything is changed to the very opposite, and yet it is true that we are Christians, then to alarm the weak by still not having revoked or changed your Word!

Yet I cannot assume that God could be like that, and therefore I am compelled to attempt another explanation, one that I also much prefer: this whole matter of "Christendom" and "a Christian world" is a piece of human skulduggery; that we actually are Christians is a delusion by way of a piece of skulduggery. On the contrary, the New Testament is the completely unchanged handbook for Christians, for whom things will continually go in this world as it says in the New Testament, and who should not let themselves be disturbed by things going differently for the knave-Christians in this world, this world of skulduggery.

Imagine that a society was formed for the purpose of discouraging the drinking of wine.

To that end, the director of the society considers it appropriate to appoint some men who as representatives, speakers, and pastors could travel around the country and work to win people to join the society.

"But," says the director of the society at the meeting in which the matter was decided, "to scrimp on the pastors is damned impractical; to require them not to drink wine is futile—in that case we simply get this watered-down and fasting sort of thing that doesn't inspire anyone to join our organization. No, there must be no scrimping on the pastor; he must have his bottle of wine every day and a bonus in proportion to his zeal so that he can have his heart in his work, can sweep people off their feet with warmth, vigor, and conviction so that they join our society in great numbers."

Suppose that everyone became—not members of this society, but pastors in the service of this society!

It is the same with Christianity and the state. Christianity, the doctrine of renunciation, of suffering, of heterogeneity to this world, the doctrine that issues no checks except on another world—the state wants to have this doctrine introduced. "But," says the state, "to scrimp on the pastors is really impractical; then we get nothing but this fasting and watered-down sort of thing that wins nobody for this doctrine but instead frightens everyone away. No, the pastor must be rewarded in such a way and his life be organized in such a way that from proclaiming this doctrine he can have pleasure both for himself and with his family. Then there can be hope of winning people to the renunciation of the earthly, because then the pastor will be disposed, with warmth, vigor, and the full power of conviction, to depict to people how blessed this renunciation and suffering are, how blessed it is to

receive checks drawn only on another world, that it is—listen to
him!—blessed, blessed, blessed!"

How fortunate that not all of us are pastors!

*   *
*

God in heaven acts differently when he wants to introduce
Christianity. He makes sure that there shall in any case be one
Christian: the teacher of Christianity. And now winning people
for this doctrine gets started. Well, it scarcely amounts to anything, and to the same degree as it is certain that the teacher is a
Christian, it probably ends with the teacher's being put to death,
and it all would remain one: the teacher.

But God in heaven is also totally lacking in sagacity, especially
high statecraft. He is a poor wretch of the old school, so simple
as actually to think that when one wants to sew one must knot
the thread.[41] He has no intimation of what the secret of statecraft
is, how much faster it goes when one gives up such tomfoolery
and then earnestly gets busy so that there are millions of Christians in a jiffy with the help of teachers who are not Christians.

O human nonsense! And this has come to be called earnestness! Centuries have been wasted on this costly tomfoolery,
which has been paid for with money at an exorbitant price, and
paid for even more exorbitantly—by having forfeited eternity!

WHAT CHRIST JUDGES
OF OFFICIAL CHRISTIANITY

By S. Kierkegaard

June 1855[42]

What Christ Judges of Official Christianity

It might seem strange that only now do I come forward with this, since Christ's judgment is certainly decisive, however unwelcome it is to the ecclesiastical guild of swindlers that has seized possession of the firm "Jesus Christ" and in the name of Christianity has done splendid business.

It is, however, surely not without reason that only now do I present what is so decisive, and anyone who has carefully followed my entire work as an author is bound to have seen that there is a certain method in the way I go about it, that it carries the mark *both* of what I say, that the whole matter of "Christendom" is a criminal case corresponding to what is usually known as forgery and swindling, except that here it is religion that is used in this way—*and* of my actually having, as I say it, a detective talent.

Just think about this so that you can follow the progress of the case. I began by passing myself off as a poet, subtly aiming at what I thought was the truth about official Christianity, that the difference between the atheist and official Christianity is that the atheist is an honest man who directly *teaches* that Christianity is fiction, poetry[43]; official Christianity is a falsification that solemnly assures that Christianity is something else entirely, solemnly declaims against atheism, and by means of this covers up that it is itself *making* Christianity into poetry and abolishing the imitation of Christ [*Efterfølgelse*], so that one relates oneself to the prototype [*Forbillede*] only through the imagination but oneself lives in totally other categories, which amounts to relating oneself poetically to Christianity or to changing it into poetry, no more binding than poetry is. Finally one discards the prototype altogether and lets what one is, mediocrity, be regarded more or less as the ideal.

In the name of being a poet, I advanced some ideals, presented what—yes, what 1000 royal functionaries are bound to by oath.

And these good men did not notice anything at all, they were perfectly safe; to such a degree everything was, Christianly, spiritlessness and worldliness. These good men did not suspect at all that something was hiding behind this poet—that the method was that of a detective in order to make those in question feel safe—a method police use precisely in order to gain an opportunity to look more deeply into a case.

Time went on this way. I was even on very good terms with these oath-bound men—and I quietly both introduced the ideals and became acquainted with the people with whom I was dealing.

But finally even these good men became impatient with this poet; he became too offensive to them. This came about by way of the article against Bishop Martensen with regard to Bishop Mynster. Perfectly safe as they were, they now made a big splash (this will be recalled from that time) about its being "a much too high criterion that has been applied here"[44] etc.—feeling perfectly safe.

Then this poet suddenly changed; he—if I may say it this way, threw away his guitar and—took out a book called *The New Testament of Our Lord and Savior Jesus Christ*, and with—yes, indeed, it was with the eye of a detective—he put it to these good oath-bound teachers, "truth-witnesses": Is it not this book to which they were bound by oath, this book whose criterion is a great deal higher than the one he had used?

From that moment, as is known, silence began. So quick they were, so clever to declaim as long as they thought they could not only escape but could also be self-important in this way: It is a poet we have before us, his ideals are exaggerated, the criterion is far too high—then they became silent the moment this book and the oath entered into the game. This is just like what happens in police cases. First of all one makes the person in question feel safe; and even if a police detective otherwise has all the other gifts, if he is not a virtuoso in the art of being able to make suspects feel safe, he does not have a "definite detective talent." In that condition, the adversary switches around the entire relation; he, it is precisely he who is the honest man, and it looks very much as if it were the police detective who was in a predicament.

But when the latter has learned what he wants to know by making the adversary feel safe, he changes his method and goes about the job directly—and then the adversary suddenly becomes silent, bites his lips, and no doubt thinks: This is a confounded business.

So, then, I took out the New Testament and most respectfully took the liberty of calling to mind that these esteemed truth-witnesses are bound by oath to the New Testament—and then the silence set in. Was this not strange?

I considered it best, however, to keep them yet a while, if possible, uncertain about how well informed I am and to what extent I have the New Testament on my side, something I did succeed in doing, but it never occurred to me to pride myself on it.

Then I spoke in my own name, ever more decisively, it is true, since I of course perceived that they continually scorned my first attempt to represent the case for the adversary as favorably as it was possible for me to do it; and finally I took it upon myself, in my own name, to say that it is a guilt, a great guilt, to participate in public worship as it is at present.[45] This was in my own name; now, of course, it certainly was no longer possible to escape me in that way, that I am a poet and thus it is indeed the others who represent the truth. But yet it is always somewhat reassuring that I am speaking in my own name, and then, in view of this reassurance, by making the adversary feel a little safe I succeeded in getting opportunity to know them better, to know whether they intended to stiffen themselves against the charge, for these oath-bound men certainly must have been smitten in their consciences to hear these words that changed everything: It is a guilt, a great guilt to participate in the public worship as it is at present, because this is as far as possible from being worship.

But as stated, what was reassuring was that I spoke in my own name. Even if it is so that I know with God that I have spoken truthfully and spoken as I ought to speak, and even if what I have said is true and should be said, and even if there were no words from Christ himself, it is still always good that we know from the New Testament how Christ judges official Christianity.

And this we know from the New Testament; his judgment is

found there—but of course I am fully convinced that, whoever you are, if you know nothing else about what Christianity is than what you know from the Sunday sermons of the "truth-witnesses," then you can attend three churches every Sunday year after year, can hear, ordinarily, any of the royal function-aries whatever—and you will never have heard the words from Christ to which I refer. The truth-witnesses presumably think like this: The proverb says, "Do not mention rope in the house of a hanged man"; it likewise will be lunacy to call attention in churches to the words in God's Word that deafeningly witness against all the pastor's mummery. Indeed, I could be tempted to make the following demand, which, reasonable and modest as it is, yet is the only punishment of the pastors that I want: Take certain passages from the New Testament and require the pastors to read them aloud before the congregation. Naturally I would have to make one reservation, that after having read such a pas-sage from the New Testament the pastor does not, as is custom-ary, lay aside the New Testament to "interpret" what was read. No thanks! No, what I could be tempted to propose is the fol-lowing divine worship service: the congregation is assembled, a prayer is prayed at the church door, a hymn is sung, then the pastor ascends the pulpit, picks up the New Testament, pro-nounces God's name, and then reads before the congregation the specified passage loudly and clearly—after that he must be silent and remain standing silent in the pulpit for five minutes, and then he may go. This I would regard as extremely beneficial. It does not enter my mind to make the pastor blush. It is not easy to get the one to blush who, conscious of wanting to understand by Christianity what he understands by Christianity, has been able to take an oath upon the New Testament without blushing. And presumably it may be said to be part and parcel of really being able to be an official pastor that first and foremost one has weaned oneself from the puerilities of youth and innocence: to blush etc. But I assume that the congregation would begin to blush on the pastor's behalf.

*   *

*

And now to the words of Christ of which I speak. XIV
145
They are found in Matthew 23:29–33; Luke 11:47–48, and
read as follows:

> MATTHEW 23:29–33. (29) Woe to you, scribes and Pharisees,
> you hypocrites! that you build the tombs of the prophets and
> adorn the graves of the righteous and say: (30) If we had lived
> in the days of our fathers, we would not have taken part with
> them in the blood of the prophets. (31) Thus you bear witness
> against yourselves, that you are sons of those who murdered
> the prophets. (32) Fill up, then, the measure of your fathers.
> (33) You serpents! You brood of vipers! How are you able to
> escape the sentence of hell?

> LUKE 11:47–48. (47) Woe to you! that you build the tombs of
> the prophets, but your fathers killed them. (48) So you are
> witnesses and consent to the deeds of your fathers; for they
> killed them, and you build their tombs.

But what, then, is "Christendom"? Is not Christendom the
greatest possible attempt to worship God by "building the tombs
of the prophets and adorning the graves of the righteous, and
saying: If we had lived in the days of our fathers, we would
not have taken part with them in the blood of the prophets"—
instead of, as Christ has required, following him and suffering for
the doctrine?

It is of this kind of worship that I have used the expression:
Compared with the Christianity of the New Testament, it is
playing at Christianity. The statement is entirely true and perfectly descriptive. When one considers how the words must be
understood in this connection, what does it mean to play? It
means to counterfeit, to mimic a danger where there is no danger, and in such a way that the more art one applies to it the more
deceptively one can pretend as if there were danger. This is the
way soldiers play at war on the parade grounds; there is no danger, but one pretends as if there were, and the art consists of
making everything deceptive, just as if it were a matter of life and
death. And this is the way Christianity is played in "Christendom." Dramatically costumed, the artists make their appearance

in artistic buildings—there truly is no danger at all, anything but; the teacher is a royal officeholder, advancing steadily, making a career—and now he dramatically plays at Christianity, in short, he is performing comedy. He discourses on renunciation, but he himself is steadily advancing. He teaches the scorning of worldly titles and rank, but he himself is making a career. He describes the glorious ones ("the prophets") who were put to death, and the continual refrain is: If we had lived in the days of our fathers, we would not have taken part with them in the blood of the prophets—we who, after all, are building their tombs and adorning their graves. Thus they will not even at least be so honest (as I continually, urgently, imploringly have proposed) as to confess that they are no better at all than those who killed the prophets—no, this circumstance, that they are indeed not contemporary with them, they want to utilize to feign to be much, much better than those who put them to death, to be creatures altogether different from those monsters—indeed, they are building the tombs of those unrighteously put to death and adorning their graves.

Nevertheless, to play at Christianity—however descriptive this phrase may be, the authority cannot use such a phrase; he speaks differently about it.

Christ calls it—oh, pay attention!—he calls it: hypocrisy. And not only this, he says—shudder!—he says that this guilt of hypocrisy is just as great, just exactly as great a crime as putting the prophets to death, therefore blood-guilt. Indeed, if one could ask him, he would perhaps reply that this guilt of hypocrisy, precisely because it is so subtly concealed and slowly continued through a whole lifetime, is a greater guilt than the guilt of those who in flaming rage killed the prophets.

This, then, is the judgment, Christ's judgment on Christendom, on the Sunday worship service, on official Christianity. Shudder, for otherwise you are caught in it. It is so deceptive: are we not good people, true Christians, we who build the tombs of the prophets and adorn the graves of the righteous; are we not good people, and especially compared with the monsters who put them to death? Moreover, what are we supposed to do; after all, we cannot do more than to be willing to contribute money for building churches etc., not to scrimp on the pastor, and then to listen to him ourselves. The New Testament replies: What you are to do is this, you are to follow Christ[46] and suffer,[47] suffer for the doctrine. The worship service you want to hold is hypocrisy and equal to blood-guilt. What the pastor, along with his family, is living on is that you are a hypocrite, or on making you into a hypocrite and keeping you a hypocrite.

"Your fathers killed them, and you build their tombs: so you are witnesses and consent to the deeds of your fathers." Luke 11:48.

Yes, Sunday Christianity and the enormous guild of business-operating pastors must indeed become furious at such talk, which with one single word shuts all their shops, cashiers the entire royally authorized livelihood, and not only that, but also admonishes against such church worship as against blood-guilt. XIV 147

Yet this is Christ who is speaking. Hypocrisy coheres so deeply with what it is to be human that just when the natural man feels his very best, has managed to arrange a church worship just to his taste, Christ's judgment is pronounced: This is hypocrisy, is blood-guilt. It is not the case that, although your life on weekdays is worldliness, there still is this good in you, that on Sunday you go to church in the company of official Christianity—no, no, official Christianity is much worse than all your worldliness on weekdays, is hypocrisy, is blood-guilt.

At the root of "Christendom" is the truth: the human being is a born hypocrite. The Christianity of the New Testament was the truth. But people sagaciously and knavishly invented a new kind of Christianity, one that builds the tombs of the prophets and adorns the graves of the righteous and says: If we had lived in the days of our fathers. And this is what Christ calls blood-guilt.

What Christianity wants is: imitation. What the human being does not want is to suffer, least of all the kind of suffering that is authentically Christian, to suffer at the hands of people. So he discards imitation and thereby suffering, the distinctly Christian suffering. Then he builds the tombs of the prophets—that is one thing. And then he lies to God, to himself, to others, and says that he is better than those who put the prophets to death—that is the next. Hypocrisy first and hypocrisy last—and according to Christ's judgment: blood-guilt.

*   *

*

Imagine people assembled in a church in Christendom—that then Christ suddenly entered into this assembly—what do you think he would do?

Well, you can read in the New Testament what he would do.

He would address the *teachers*—because he presumably would judge the *congregation* as formerly: They are misled[48]—he would address those "in long robes,"[49] the merchants, the mummers, who have turned God's house, if not into a den of robbers,[50] then into a shop or into a booth, and would say, "You hypocrites, you serpents, you generation of vipers"[51]; and he would no doubt as of old make a whip of cords to drive them out of the temple.[52]

You who read this—I am fully prepared for this—if you know nothing else about Christianity than from Sunday babble, you will be shocked at me; it will seem to you as if I were guilty of the most atrocious blasphemy in representing Christ in this way, "putting words in his mouth such as: serpents, generation of vipers; it is dreadful—they certainly are words one never hears in the mouth of a cultured person; and to have him repeat them several times—it is so terribly vulgar, and to make Christ into a person who uses force!"

My friend, you can, of course, check in the New Testament. But if a comfortable, pleasurable life is to be achieved by proclaiming and teaching Christianity, then the Christ-picture must be changed somewhat. Adornment, no, there will be no sparing of gold and diamonds and rubies etc.; no, pastors find that very acceptable and make people think that this is Christianity. But rigorousness, the rigorousness that is inseparable from the earnestness of eternity, that must go. So Christ becomes a sentimental figure, pure Mr. Goodman[53]—this is connected with passing the plate during the sermon and the congregation's feeling inclined to pay out something and fork out generously in the

XIV
148

collection box. Above all it is connected with wanting, out of fear of people, to be on good terms with people, whereas the Christianity of the New Testament is: in fear of God to suffer for the doctrine at the hands of people.

But "woe to you for building the tombs of the prophets" (teaching people that this is the Christianity of the New Testament) and "adorning the graves of the righteous" (continually joining money and Christianity) and saying "if we"—yes, if you had lived as a contemporary with the prophets, you would have put them to death, that is, you would, as did indeed happen, have secretly had the people do it and bear the guilt.[54] But in vain do you hide yourselves in "Christendom"; what is hidden there will indeed be disclosed[55] when truth judges: "So you are witnesses and consent to the deeds of your fathers; for they killed them, and you build their tombs." In vain do you make a show of sanctity; in vain do you think that just by building the tombs of the righteous you are showing how different you are from the ungodly people who killed them. Oh, the powerlessness of hypocrisy to hide itself. You are seen through; precisely this, to build the tombs of the righteous and to say, "If we—" precisely this is to kill them, is to be the true children of the ungodly people, is to do the same as they, is to certify the deeds of the fathers, to consent to them, is "to fill the measure of the fathers," that is, to do what is even worse.

XIV
149

THE MOMENT

No. 3–7

THE MOMENT

No. 3

CONTENTS

June 27, 1855   S. KIERKEGAARD

"State" is related directly to number (the numerical); therefore, when a state dwindles, the number can gradually become so small that the state has ended, the concept has dropped out.

Christianity is related to number in another way: one single true Christian is enough for it to be true that Christianity exists. Yes, Christianity is related inversely to number—when all have become Christians, the concept "Christian" has dropped out. Because the concept "Christian" is a polemical concept, one can be a Christian only in contradistinction or by way of contrast. So it is also in the New Testament with regard to God's wanting to be loved, and it is a relation of contradistinction precisely in order to intensify love; thus the Christian, who loves God, in contradistinction to other persons comes to suffer because of their hatred and persecution. As soon as the contradistinction is taken away, being a Christian is blather—as it is in "Christendom," which has cunningly abolished Christianity by means of: We all are Christians.

So, then, the concept *Christian* is related inversely to number—*state* is related directly to number—and then Christianity and state have been merged— —to the advantage of blather and pastors. To place state and Christianity together in this way makes just as much sense as talking about a yard of butter, or there is, if possible, even less sense in it, since butter and the yard measure are nevertheless simply entities that have nothing to do with each other, whereas state and Christianity are inversely related to or, indeed more correctly, away from each other.

But this becomes difficult to understand in "Christendom," where one quite naturally has no intimation of what Christianity is, and where one could least of all hit upon the idea or, if it is stated, get it into one's head that Christianity has been *abolished* by *propagation*, by these millions of Christians in name only, the number of which presumably is supposed to cover up that there is no Christian, that Christianity does not exist at all. Just as one speaks of talking oneself out of something by way of lengthy chitchat, so has the human race, the individual in it, wanted to chatter and sneak out of being a Christian by way of this swarm of Christians in name only, a Christian state, a Christian world, on the assumption that God will become so dizzy in his head over these millions that he will not discover that he is being fooled, that there is not a single—Christian.

To *entice*, this word is used particularly in relation to the feminine. One speaks of enticing a young girl and associates it with opening to the poor child, at an age when the mind's craving is for the earthly and the vainglorious, a way that leads her to all that is desired, but alas, at the cost of her innocence. One finds it very indefensible to entice a young girl simply because at her age the craving for life's pleasure and vanity is so strong in her own inner being that what she particularly needs is to be externally influenced in the opposite direction. As the saying goes, it is easy to inveigle someone who is a born sucker, and for that very reason it is very indefensible to exploit this.

In exactly the same way the state may Christianly be said to be guilty in relation to young theological students. In other words, Christianity's view of life is so high that what is customarily called innocence and purity is far from adequate to match its requirement.

According to the Christianity of the New Testament, to be a Christian, to say nothing of being a teacher of Christianity, is sheer renunciation and suffering, and for the natural man the situation of the teacher is the least attractive of all situations.[56]

But at the very moment when the youth's craving for the things of this world[57] is only all too powerful, at the very moment when he would really need the strongest influence in the opposite direction, so that he will either be scared away from wanting to take this road or, if he actually has a call, will set foot on it as one matured—the state uses that very moment to spread its net XIV for him, to capture him, to "entice" him, so that to the youth in 156 the erroneous judgment of enticement it looks as if being a teacher of Christianity is exactly the way that will lead him to all that he desires, to an ample, secure, and in the course of the years increasing reward for his work, to a cozy domestic life in the bosom of his family, perhaps to make a career, perhaps even a brilliant career—to be sure, alas, to be sure, at the cost,

Christianly, of his innocence, because there is indeed an oath he must take on the New Testament, an oath that then opens up to him, the one enticed, the door to what he desires, but which takes its revenge later.

*   *

*

Christianly the demand would have to be presented in this way: Would not the state deign to announce as soon as possible that after a certain date it can no longer assume the responsibility for appointing as teachers of Christianity those who have sworn an oath on the New Testament. The state has contracted with the present clergy; in my opinion, it has contracted even with all the present theological students—let it therefore declare a specific year after which it can no longer engage in appointing such teachers.

Is It Defensible for the State to Accept an Oath That Not Only Cannot Be Kept But That in Being Taken Is a Self-Contradiction?

If one has eyes for such things and has used them, one need not be very old to have convinced oneself that people have a decided predilection for optical illusion, are most comfortable in optical illusion.

If there is some issue important to society, people ordinarily concentrate their energy on having a committee established. Once it is established, they are reassured, do not concern themselves very much about the committee's doing anything, and finally forget the whole thing.

Likewise, when something is to be really in earnest, people think: There must also be an oath, an oath that guarantees that it is in earnest and remains in earnest. Thus the taking of the oath is true earnestness—whether it is kept or not is of less concern.

Indeed, out of sheer earnestness one at times does not notice that the very taking of an oath contains a self-contradiction.

This is the case with the pastor's oath on the New Testament, which the state nevertheless accepts. If it should so happen that the oath is not kept, it would still be less dubious, but the truth is that the taking of it contains a self-contradiction. Yet probably neither society nor individuals would be able to be reassured with regard to something as earnest as being a teacher of Christianity if the earnestness is not guaranteed by—an oath that in being taken certainly contains a self-contradiction; thus one reassured by this oath is reassured by: an optical illusion.

Christianity relates itself to the kingdom that is not of this world[58]—and then the state accepts from the teacher of Christianity an oath, an oath that signifies that he is swearing loyalty to what is the very opposite of the state. An oath such as that is a self-contradiction, similar to having a man swear by placing his hand on the New Testament, where it says: You shall not swear.[59]

If the pastor is in any way a disciple of Christ, his life an imitation of Christ, something to which the oath on the New Testament commits him, then his engagement as a royal officeholder is the greatest hindrance. In the very moment he is to move in the direction to which his oath on the New Testament commits him, he must dump his position as a royal officeholder. Consequently, by his oath as a royal officeholder, he is bound in such a way that if he is to keep the oath one has him take on the New Testament he must dump the first oath. What a self-contradiction! And what a strange kind of earnestness, that an oath is taken (how solemn!), an oath that in being taken is a self-contradiction! And how demoralizing both for the state and for Christianity.

*   *

*

The Christian request to the state must be: Would not the state deign, the sooner the better, to release all the clergy from their oath on the New Testament, give the oath back to them, thereby expressing that the state has become involved in something it cannot engage in? It will thereby also be expressed, what is true, that God, if I may say so, is making a break with the whole present crew of pastors and gives their oath back to them.

If we take the merely human and omit consideration of the divine (Christianity), the relation is this: the state is the highest human authority, is humanly the highest.

Thus the nation and the individual in the nation live in such a way that everything that carries a particular mark of being certified, sanctioned, or authorized by the state is in a monarchical state labeled "royal," is regarded as being more than the same thing without this adjective that provides, by way of the middle term of the state, a safeguard (guarantee) that here is something on which one can depend, something one is to respect.

This is how a nation lives and it is desirable that it does live this way, because this is connected with being a quiet and calm subject who reposes trustingly in the state. But this is how a nation lives—from morning until night the individual in the nation has a continual impression of this; his whole way of thinking has coalesced with this notion of what is royal, what is authorized by the state. This attitude penetrates even the most minor relations. The tradesman, the professional, etc. think that by obtaining permission to apply the word *royal* they are worth more than the person who does not have this adjective.

Let us now turn to Christianity. It is the divine, and *the* divine that, precisely because it is in truth the divine, wants at no price to be a kingdom of this world, on the contrary wants the Christian to risk life and blood to prevent its becoming a kingdom of this world.

And yet the state undertakes to appoint, under the name of   XIV
teachers of Christianity, 1000 royal officeholders!   160

Christianly, how misleading! As stated, people live and breathe in the view that what is royally authorized is something more, more than what is not royally authorized. As a result, people apply this here also, have more respect for a royally authorized teacher of Christianity than for someone who is not, and in turn, with regard to the royally authorized ones, have more respect to the same degree as they are recognized by the state, have higher rank, more decorations, larger salaries.

What fundamental confusion. It is (as one speaks of murdering a language) murdering Christianity, or turning it upside down, turning it around completely, or in a refined manner smuggling it out—under the appearance of Christianity one lives paganism!

No, since Christianity is the very antithesis of the kingdoms of this world, is heterogeneity, not to be royally authorized is the more true. To be royally authorized can be—a convenience, a coziness, a comfort for the pastor—*das ist was anders* [that is another matter]. But Christianly it is—a disrecommendation, and is that to the same degree as one, according to the state's ranking, draws the longer straw, has more decorations, a larger income.

The test is very simple: have the state (and this is the only true Christian requirement, just as it is also the only reasonable one) make all the proclamation of Christianity a private practice—

—and it will soon be evident whether there are one and a half million Christians in this country, and likewise whether there is use in this country for 1000 pastors with families.

The truth will no doubt prove to be that there perhaps is no real use for 100 pastors, and that perhaps not a single one of all these bishops, deans, and pastors is capable of undertaking a private practice.

Just as when the mother tongue replaced Latin in examinations, this proved to be an intensification, because now the examinee had no excuse, that it was the language that prevented him from manifesting all his knowledge—likewise private practice in the sphere of religion is something earnest in a way altogether different from this fatuousness with royal officeholders, in which ultimately it is not necessary even to have a religion, but merely to lecture *qua* officeholder, paid by the state, protected by the state, guaranteed esteem *qua*—royal officeholder.

What sustains the illusion of a Christian nation is in part the universal human laziness and love of comfort that prefer to remain in the old routine—but it is mainly these 1000 interested parties, among whom there is not a single one who does not have a pecuniary interest in maintaining the illusion. If the illusion is taken away, 900 will very likely be altogether without an occupation, and the 100 who are able to undertake private practice will realize only too well that this is something completely different from the present service in uniform with state-guaranteed steady promotion that can end up even in many thousands. That a person needs medical help is something so palpably understandable that the state does not need to help people to understand it. But when people are made free religiously, one can have plenty of trouble in making their spiritual need clear to them. It

is here that the state helps—but, it is true, very unchristianly—
"What, you feel no need for Christianity—perhaps you want to
go to prison?" "What, you feel no need for Christianity—then
perhaps you feel a great need to become nobody, because unless
you are a Christian, all the roads in society are barred to you!"
Ah! That helped the pastor's practice—and on that the pastor for
the most part lives, on that (to recollect a passage in *Peder Paars*)
he "lives Christianly."[60]

It is no good; we must get rid of all disguises and mystifications
and solemnities in order to come to the issue: that the question
of the continued existence of the established ecclesiastical order
is a financial question, that the clergy's solemn silence has a very
simple explanation, corresponds to what takes place in commer-
cial dealings, that when someone is requested to pay he at first
attempts to escape by pretending that he did not hear. Therefore
the clergy should much rather openly admit the truth of the matter; this kind of silence only makes the matter worse and worse.
When a man with sedately [*gravitetisk*] measured steps walks sedately down the street, one is prompted to think: There is something unusual here. But if one happens to learn that the explanation for this sedateness is that the man is a little tipsy, that this is
why (a counteractive measure lest he spontaneously gravitate
[*gravitere*] toward the curb) he has to hold himself with such sedateness, it might be much better for him simply to stagger a
little. Perhaps one would smile, perhaps, perhaps not even notice
his condition at all, whereas he arouses interest because of his
sedateness, does not escape teasing, which becomes more merci-
less in proportion to his effort to walk more and more sedately.
It is the same with the clergy's silence—an open, candid, direct
word would have been infinitely more serviceable than this silence that with solemnity, highly, highly elevated solemnity,
covers up—that it is a financial question, because now the gibes
gain interest; by this solemn and pretentious silence the circumstances of the clergy become so very interesting.

As long as there are in Denmark 1000 royal livelihoods for teachers of Christianity, the best thing possible is being done to hinder Christianity.

As long as there are 1000 royal livelihoods, there will continually be a corresponding number of people who intend to earn their livelihood in this manner.

Among these there may be a few who perhaps have discovered a call to proclaim Christianity. But at the very moment when they should really do this in earnest by taking the responsibility of acting as teachers at their own risk and trusting only in God—then the state offers them the comfort of accepting a royal post, whereby these few are, Christianly, spoiled.

The far greater number will have no call whatever to proclaim Christianity but will regard it simply as a livelihood.

In this way the state manages to fill the whole land with corrupted Christianity, the greatest difficulty of all for the introduction of true Christianity, much greater than downright paganism.

Take an example. If the state was inclined to hinder all true poetry, it would need only—and poetry is still not as heterogeneous to this world as Christianity is—it would need only to establish 1000 livelihoods for royal poet officeholders; then it would soon be achieved, and the country would continuously be flooded with bad poetry to such a degree that true poetry would be just about impossible. At just the critical moment, the few who actually had a call to become poets would back away from the hard effort, which venturing out at their own risk would mean, and into the indolence of a royal post; but that hard effort is precisely the condition for their poet-call to amount to something. Most of them will merely see a livelihood in being a poet, a livelihood that is secured by enduring the pain of cramming for the examination.

THE MOMENT

No. 4

CONTENTS

July 7, 1855   S. KIERKEGAARD

1.

That a proper diagnosis (the opinion about the illness) is more than half the job, every physician will admit, and likewise that all other competence, all solicitude and care, do not help if the diagnosis is wrong.

So also with regard to the religious.

People have allowed and want to allow to stand as valid this point about "Christendom," that we all are Christians; and so they have directed attention and perhaps want to direct more attention now to one and now to another aspect of doctrine.

But the truth is: not only are we not Christians, no, we are not even pagans, to whom the Christian doctrine could be proclaimed without hesitation, but by means of an illusion, an enormous illusion ("Christendom," a Christian state, a Christian country, a Christian world), we are even hindered in becoming that.

And then people want the illusion to be left undisturbed, to remain in force unchanged, and on the other hand want to provide a new exposition of the Christian doctrine.[61]

This is what people want, and in a certain sense this is quite in order. Precisely because they are ensnared in the illusion (to say nothing of even being an interested party in the illusion), for that very reason they may want what is bound to nourish the illness (something that is very common), so that what is most pleasing to the sick person is the very thing that nourishes the illness.

2.

Imagine a hospital. The patients are dying like flies. The treatment is changed in one way and another—it does not help. To what, then, is it due? It is due to the building; there is toxin in the whole building. That the patients are listed as dead, the one from this sickness, the other from another, is actually not true, because they are all dead from the toxin that is in the building.

It is the same in the religious sphere. That the religious condition is wretched, that people are in a pitiable condition religiously is undeniable. So one person thinks that it would help if we had a new hymnbook,[62] another a new altar book, a third a musical worship service,[63] etc. etc.

It is futile—because it is due to the building. This whole junk heap of a state Church, where from time immemorial there has been, in the spiritual sense, no airing out—the air confined in this old junk heap has become toxic. Therefore the religious life is sick or has expired, because, alas, precisely what worldliness regards as health is, Christianly, sickness, just as, inversely, Christian health is regarded by worldliness as sickness.

Let this junk heap tumble down, get rid of it; close all these boutiques and booths, the only ones that the strict Sunday Observance Act exempted; make this official equivocation impossible; put them out of business and provide for them, all the quacks. If it is the case that the royally authorized physician is the legitimate physician and the unauthorized one the quack, Christianly it is the opposite, precisely the royally authorized teacher is the quack, is that by being royally authorized—and let us once again worship God in simplicity instead of making a fool of him in magnificent buildings. Let it again become earnestness and cease to be play—because a Christianity proclaimed by royal officeholders, salaried and protected by the state, using police against the others, a Christianity such as that has as much connection with the Christianity of the New Testament as swimming with a life jacket or water wings has with swimming—it is playing.

Yes, let it happen. What Christianity needs is not the suffocating protection of the state; no, it needs fresh air, persecution, and—God's protection. The state only does harm; it averts persecution, and it is not the medium through which God's protection can be conducted. Above all, rescue Christianity from the state; with its protection it smothers Christianity just as when a woman smothers her baby with her body, and it teaches Christianity the most loathsome bad habits: in the name of Christianity to use police force.

3.

A person is becoming thinner and thinner day by day, is wasting away. What can be the matter—he certainly is not in want. "No, definitely not," says the physician, "it is not due to that; it is due simply to his eating, to his eating at the wrong times, to his eating without being hungry, to his using stimulants to create a little appetite, and in that way he is destroying his digestion and declining as if he were in want."

So it is religiously. The most corrupting of all is to satisfy what is not yet a need. So one does not wait until the need is there but anticipates it, may also seek to produce with stimulants something that is supposed to be a need and then is satisfied. How shocking! Yet this is what is done in the religious sphere; people are thereby cheated out of what is the meaning of life and are assisted in wasting their lives.

This is the purpose of the whole machinery of a state Church and 1000 royal officeholders, who in the guise of the care of people's souls cheat them out of the highest in life—the coming into existence of self-concern within them, the need that would then truly find a teacher, a pastor after one's own heart—but now, instead, the need (and the coming into existence of this very need is life's highest meaning) does not come into existence at all, but by being satisfied long before it has come into existence is hindered in coming into existence. And this is supposed to be carrying on the work that the Savior of the human race completed, this, this botching of the human race—and why? Because now there are ever so many royal officeholders who along with their families will live on this in the name of—the care of souls!

That the Christianity of the New Testament is what we human beings are most opposed to (to the Jews an offense, to the Greeks foolishness[64]), that it seems to such a degree to be calculated to incite us human beings against itself that as soon as it is heard it is the signal for the most passionate hatred and the cruelest persecution—the New Testament by no means makes a secret of this, on the contrary states it as definitely and decisively as possible. It is continually heard when Christ speaks with the apostles[65] so that they might not be offended. It is emphasized again and again that they must be prepared for what faced them, and the apostles' words[66] sufficiently testify that they were bound to experience what had been foretold.

Therefore, it could never occur to anyone who understands himself Christianly to be angry at a person if he became the object of that person's hatred and indignation by telling him what Christianity actually is; not at all, he must, if he understands himself Christianly, find it quite in order.

But even the person most indignant with him will perhaps still agree with him and understand that he finds it shocking that from generation to generation there goes on living a whole family of parasites who (called teachers of Christianity and bound by oath on the New Testament) make a living by, in the name of Christianity, foisting on people something to their own liking—the utterly decisive evidence that it is not the Christianity of the New Testament—make a living, in the name of Christianity, by proclaiming what is the very opposite of the Christianity of the New Testament, priding themselves on the royal commission, which Christianly is just as ludicrous as wanting to trump with an ordinary card in a card game, or wanting to identify oneself *qua* shepherd by a certificate from the wolf.

This is what is shocking. But there is perhaps no analogy in history that a religion has been abolished in this way—by flourishing—but please note that what is understood as Christianity is the opposite of what the New Testament understands as Christianity; the religion of suffering has become the religion of zest for life but has kept the name unchanged.

This is what is shocking—that for Christianity the situation at present is, if possible, twice as difficult as that when it entered the world, because now it does not confront pagans and Jews, whose utter indignation it is bound to arouse, but *Christians*, whose indignation it is bound to arouse in the very same sense as in the past it aroused the indignation of pagans and Jews, *Christians*, whom the ecclesiastical guild of swindlers has led to believe that they are Christians, and that Christianity is sung to the tune of a drinking song, even more zestful than such songs, which are always accompanied by the sadness that it is soon over and in 100 years everything will be forgotten,[67] whereas the zest-for-life Christian drinking song, the pastors assure us, "lasts an eternity."[68]

As is well known, Heiberg's Councilor Herr Zierlich is so sensitive to propriety that he even finds it improper for women's and men's clothing to hang together in a wardrobe.[69]

We will leave that to Herr Zierlich. But, on the other hand, what in our characterless age must of necessity be practiced is the separation, the distinction between the infinite and the finite, between a striving for the infinite and for the finite, between living for something and living on something that our age—very improperly—has gotten put together in the wardrobe, has gotten blended or made the same, and that, on the contrary, Christianity with the passion of eternity, with the most appalling Either/Or, holds apart from each other, separated by a chasmic abyss.

Christianity, which is indeed well acquainted with human beings and knows what fine fellows they are, how easy it is to get them to accept anything and to swear to anything whatever if only one shows that it is the way to make a living, the way to make a career, to be able to find a wife, etc., Christianity has therefore exercised as much police precaution as possible and put up a barricade to prevent a merging: Christianity and a livelihood, Christianity and a career, Christianity and becoming engaged, etc.

The state is different; it has made Christianity and a livelihood, a theological degree and becoming engaged, etc. etc. synonymous. Therefore it has also obtained a completely different kind of Christianity from the moment the state picked it up. Instead of that bagatelle, the winning of a few Christians, which is all that Christ's work in particular and also that of the apostles amounted to, it now went into the millions: millions of Christians and 100,000 livelihoods—Christianity has completely triumphed.

Yes, or a monstrous skulduggery, in the name of Christianity, has triumphed; this whole business with Christendom is just like that inscription "This must be Troy"[70] instead of Troy, and like the title on the spine of an empty volume. In this way any religion whatever can be introduced successfully into the world. Unfortunately, Christianity introduced in this way is the very opposite of Christianity. Or in our sagacious times would there be found even some young person who does not readily understand that if the state got the idea of wanting to introduce, for example, the religion that the moon is made of green cheese and to that end established 1000 livelihoods, with steady advancement, for a man with family, the result of this would be—if the state just held firmly to its idea unchanged—that after some generations a statistician would be able to testify that the religion (the moon is made of green cheese) is the prevailing religion in the country.

A livelihood—oh, those demonstrations of the truth of Christianity that are propounded, those devilishly learned and profound and completely convincing demonstrations that have filled folios and on which Christendom prides itself just as the state prides itself on its military, of what good are they all compared with—a livelihood, and a position where one can make a career to boot!

A livelihood—and then Juliane, that Fredrik and Juliane can unite—oh, those demonstrations of the truth of Christianity that are propounded, those devilishly learned and profound and completely convincing demonstrations, of what good are they all compared with: Juliane, and that Juliane and Fredrik can then unite! If at some time Fredrik should struggle with the thought· "But I myself do not actually believe in this doctrine, and then to have to proclaim it to others"; if Fredrik should struggle with such thoughts—go to Juliane; she can drive such thoughts away. "Dear Fredrik," she says, "let us just see about getting united; why do you want to go and trouble yourself with such thoughts; after all, there are 1000 other pastors just like you; short and sweet, you are a pastor just like the others."

Yes, Juliane plays a large role in procuring clergy for the state. Therefore one should have been cautious about bringing in Juliane, as well as about establishing the livelihoods. It is possible, as Don Juan says to Zerline, that true happiness resides only in the tender arms of a blameless wife;[71] and possibly it is true, as both poets and prose writers have asserted, that in these tender arms one forgets the troubles and vexations of the world; but the question is whether there might not be something else one all too easily forgets in those tender arms: what Christianity is. And the older I become, the clearer it becomes to me that the blather into which Christianity has sunk, especially in Protestantism, and especially in Denmark, is largely connected with the way those tender arms have come to intervene a little too much, so that one might on behalf of Christianity request that the respective owners of those tender arms withdraw a little.

In order to get to know some truth about Christianity in this country, it would be of great importance if one could put aside the livelihoods and Juliane in order to be able to see. It is highly desirable that the state would understand it in such a way that it would announce that it felt committed to pay the pastors with whom it has once contracted in the event that they felt that they had to resign from office! No doubt there are many upright and respectable, humanly speaking, men who would feel their consciences greatly eased—and it actually is the state, after all, that bears the responsibility, the state that has seductively beckoned and shown young, inexperienced theological graduates and their fiancées something that Christianly cannot be upheld. Later (as soon as one has become paterfamilias etc.), later, yes, then it is too late, then one lacks the strength to break with this wrong thing that one has innocently gotten into, but remains in it— with a troubled conscience.

Christianity's interest, what it wants is: true Christians.

The *clergy's* egotism, for the sake of financial advantage as well as of power, is connected with: many Christians.

"And that is very easily done; there is nothing to it. Get hold of the children, drop a little water on each child's head—then he is a Christian. If a number of them do not even receive their drops, it makes no difference if they just imagine that they did and along with that, in turn, imagine that they are Christians. Then in a very short time we have more Christians than there are herring in the herring season, Christians by the millions, and then, through the power of money, we are also the greatest power the world has ever seen. This matter of eternity is and remains the most ingenious of all inventions, if it gets into the right hands, practical hands, since the founder, impractical, was mistaken about what Christianity really is."

No, let us instead stick to what by comparison is almost angel-purity, but what the state punishes with the house of correction—enriching oneself by counterfeiting customs stamps or forging the labels of famous factories! But to become a power and to gain the things of this world by falsely stamping what was served in suffering to the last and to the utmost, to being abandoned by God,[72] by falsely stamping what the one dying on the cross entrusted to human honesty in imitation, consequently to do this, unmoved by the fact that it was love that suffered, and love that, dying, entrusted its cause to human honesty, and unmoved by the fact that it was millions who were in this way cheated out of the highest and the holiest, cheated by leading them to think that they were Christians—no, this is dreadful. Ordinarily it is indeed the case that the magnitude of a crime, its meanness, its extended ramifications inflame the police detective and increase his zeal. But there is a limit, and, if the crime exceeds that, it could very well happen that he, like someone swooning, must grasp for something to rest on, wishing to escape and find in tears a relief from what otherwise had never happened to him before.

So there were the millions of Christians, the Christian states, kingdoms, countries, the Christian world. But that is only the first half of the Christian criminal case; we now come to the sophistication. The sophistication is unique in its kind, utterly without analogy; the people who enrich themselves by counterfeiting the stamps of customhouses or the labels of famous factories do not insist upon being honored and respected as true friends of the customhouse or of those factories. This is reserved for the Christian counterfeiters. That zeal, egotism's zeal, zeal for procuring many Christians in the very way that is repugnant to Christianity in its innermost heart, that zeal was prinked up to be true Christian fervor and zeal for the propagation of the doctrine, as if it were Christianity one was serving in this way instead of its being Christianity that one, serving oneself, was betraying. Yet this zeal on the part of egotism was falsely stamped as Christian fervor and zeal, and these forgers insisted upon being regarded as true friends of Christianity. And those unfortunate millions who were cheated out of their money and misused as a tangible power while in return they were cheated out of the eternal by having some gibberish palmed off on them—those millions who idolized and adored the Christian forgers as the true servants of Christianity.

A child, a boy makes mistakes that are punished by "a box on the ear," and it would be certifiable lunacy if the father or the teacher insisted that for such a mistake the child should be punished by a workhouse sentence for life. On the other hand, it would be certifiable lunacy to think that the crimes that the state reasonably punishes with the workhouse for life could be compensated by a box on the ear. But what we in our day, in these Christian states and countries, where all the pastors are truth-witnesses, never hear mentioned is that there are crimes (for quite another reason than in the case of the child) for which punishment with the workhouse for life would be a kind of lunacy, because here again the punishment would have no relation to the crime. The longer I live, the clearer it becomes to me that the real crimes are not punished in this world; the child's mistakes are punished, but they, after all, are not real crimes. The state punishes crimes, but the real crimes, in comparison with which the crimes the state punishes can hardly be called crimes, are not punished—within time.

In "Christendom" All Are Christians; If All Are Christians, eo ipso the Christianity of the New Testament Does Not Exist at All; Indeed, It Is Impossible

The Christianity of the New Testament is based on the thought that one is a Christian in a *relation of contrast*, that to be a Christian is to believe, to love God in a relation of contrast. While the Christian according to the Christianity of the New Testament has all the strenuousness, struggle, and anguish associated with what is required, to die to the world,[73] to hate oneself,[74] etc., it also has suffering because of the relation of contrast to other people, something the Christianity of the New Testament repeatedly mentions: to be hated by others, to be persecuted, to suffer for the doctrine, etc.[75]

In "Christendom" we all are Christians—the relation of contrast has consequently disappeared. In a meaningless sense all have been made Christians and everything Christian—and thus we are living a life of paganism (under the name of Christianity). We have not in defiance dared to rebel overtly against Christianity; no, we have hypocritically and knavishly abolished it by falsifying the definition of what it is to be a Christian.

It is about this that I say: (1) this is a Christian criminal case, (2) this is playing at Christianity, (3) this is making a fool of God.

Every hour that this order of things stands, the crime is continued; every Sunday divine worship service is conducted in this
way, Christianity is made a game and a fool is made of God. Everyone who participates is participating in playing at Christianity and in making a fool of God, is involved in the Christian criminal case.

Yes, O God, if there were no eternity, then you, God of truth, would have said the most untrue words ever spoken in the world: Be not deceived; God does not let himself be mocked.[76]

That the official Christianity, what we call Christianity, is not the Christianity of the New Testament, is not a striving toward it, has not the slightest resemblance to it—nothing is easier to see; and I would regard making this clear to people a small matter if it did not involve a very singular difficulty.

If it is assumed that what the New Testament understands as Christianity and as being a Christian is something really to a human being's liking, something that is really bound to be pleasing and appealing to the natural man, almost as if it were his own invention, as if spoken out of his own heart—well, then we would soon have everything in order.

But, but, but right here is the difficulty. What the New Testament understands as Christianity and as being a Christian (something of which the New Testament by no means makes a secret but emphasizes as decisively as possible) is precisely what the natural man is most opposed to, is to him an offense, is what he either in wild passion and defiance must rebel against or what he slyly must try to get rid of at any price, for example, by means of skulduggery, calling the very opposite Christianity, and then thanking God for Christianity and for the great and priceless good that one is a Christian.

When I now want to make it clear that what we call Christianity, that the official Christianity is not at all the Christianity of the New Testament, and with that in mind show what the New Testament understands as Christianity and being a Christian, that this is sheer anguish, misery, and wretchedness (but then, it is true, eternity is also assured), whereas what we call Christianity is pleasant and enjoyable (but then, it is true, there is no other assurance of eternity than the pastor's)—when I do that, it will be unavoidable that most people come to confuse these two things: that what I am pointing out to be the Christianity of the New Testament does not please them, and that whether it pleases or displeases them makes no difference either way concerning the question of what the Christianity of the New Testament is, indeed, that its being displeasing must be considered an indication that what I call the Christianity of the New Testament is the Christianity of the New Testament, since the New Testament itself repeatedly says that it displeases the human being, is an offense to him.[77]

It is really not without cause that I call this matter of "Christendom" a criminal case. As could be expected, the proclamation by the official Christianity has naturally not missed the opportunity but, falsifying, has started from the ground up—to win people is, of course, the important matter to it, Christianity the less important. Then the procedure is this: the human passions are aroused, and what appeals to them is called Christianity; this is made to be Christianity—and thus people are won for Christianity.

The Christianity of the New Testament, however, is what to the highest degree displeases and shocks people. Christianity proclaimed in this way wins neither Christians by the millions nor earthly rewards and benefits. Rare in any generation is a person who exercises the power over himself to be able to *will* what does not please him, so that he is able to hold firmly to the truth that does not please him, to hold firmly to its being the truth although it does not please him, to hold firmly to its being the truth just because it does not please him, and then, although it does not please him, is able to will to become involved with it. For most people this is immediately confusing, consciously or unconsciously; what they engage in must be something that appears to please them, to appeal to them.

This is what the counterfeiters of Christianity aim at. In explaining to people what Christianity is, they continually twist the matter in this way: You can be sure that this and that is Christianity because it appeals to you; conversely, you can easily make sure that this and that would not be Christianity because it must shock you in your innermost being.

The clerical company that speculates in human numbers has in this way won people, has led them to think that they are Christians by duping them into something under the name of Christianity, something that appeals to them. Millions have then been very gratified to be, in addition, Christians in such a cheap and appealing way, in one half hour and with the turn of a hand to have the whole matter of eternity arranged in order then rightly to be able to enjoy this life.

Here, you see, is the difficulty. It is not at all a matter of making clear that the official Christianity is not the Christianity of the New Testament, but it is that the Christianity of the New Testament and what the New Testament understands by Christianity is anything but pleasing to a human being.

And now think of what it means to have to get people who are demoralized by this knavish proclamation of Christianity, spoiled by the notion that the mark of the essentially Christian is that it appeals to them, to have to get them to be willing to see what the New Testament understands as Christianity, to get them to see this while the thousand "shepherds of souls [*Sjelesørgere*]" presumably want to set everything in motion so as not to lose sheep, continually want to arouse all the emotions in the sheep in this way—you can easily make sure that this and that cannot possibly be Christianity; after all, you feel how it shocks you.

Indeed, you shepherds of souls, you have peopled heaven— how empty it would be had you not existed. And these millions, who by your soul care have been transported—into heaven— how they will thank and bless you someday in the next world! In civil life a phrase is used that, strictly speaking, is metaphorical; it is the word *Seelenverkoperie* [soul-selling].[78] Strictly speaking, it is metaphorical, since actually it is only bodies that are sold: the real soul-selling is reserved for soul-shepherding—indeed, it fits better. This real soul-selling is not punished in this world but is esteemed and honored! The magnitude of a crime is related also to the length of time. The real crimes cannot even be punished within time, because they use all of temporality in order to come into existence, and if they were punished within time, they would be prevented from becoming the real crimes—only eternity punishes them!

You who are reading this, imagine the following incident. You are visited by someone who, quiet and earnest, yet deeply shaken (without in any way conveying to you any idea of being demented), says to you: "Pray for me, oh, pray for me"—is it not true that this would make an almost terrifying impression on you? Why? Because you yourself personally received the impression of a human personality who in all likelihood must be engaged in the severest struggle with a personal God, since it could occur to him to say to another person: Pray for me, pray for me.

When, however, you read, for example, in a "pastoral letter": Brothers, include us in your intercessory prayers, just as we unceasingly pray for you night and day and include you in our intercessory prayers[79]—why does this very likely make no impression at all on you? I wonder if it is not because you involuntarily have the suspicion that this is formula, rigmarole, something official, from a handbook or from a music box. Alas! One cannot say of something official that it has a bad taste. No, what is repugnant about something official is that one thereby or as a consequence of it becomes so exceedingly indifferent because it has no taste, because it, to use an old saying, tastes like sticking one's tongue out the window and getting spanked for it.

And now when the man whom the state has recently engaged as a shepherd to walk in velvet in order to proclaim that Jesus Christ lived in poverty and taught "Follow me,"[80] when Bishop Martensen presumably has decided to fight with all his might—for what is official—against sects and heresies etc., [81]and, moreover, when there are hundreds in the service of what is official—then it may certainly be made necessary that there be at least one person who concerns himself with what is official. In this regard I dare not expect any appointment from the side of the state, perhaps instead—just between us—from the side of our Lord. Believe me, there is nothing so repugnant to God, no heresy, no sin, nothing so repugnant to him as what is official. You can easily understand that. Since God is a personal being, you can surely comprehend how repugnant it is to him that one wants to wipe his mouth with formulas, wants to wait upon him with official solemnity, official platitudes, etc. [82]Indeed, just because God in the most eminent sense is personality, sheer personality, for that very reason what is official is infinitely more repugnant to him than it is for a woman to discover that a proposal is made to her according to—a book of formulas.

THE MOMENT

No. 5

CONTENTS

July 27, 1855   S. Kierkegaard

Let me illustrate this with reference to just one single point.

When Christianity requires that one shall love one's enemy,[83] it could in a certain sense be said that it has good reason to require this, because God does want to be loved, and, to speak merely humanly, God is indeed a human being's most appalling enemy, your mortal enemy. Indeed, he wants you to die, to die to the world; he hates specifically that in which you naturally have your life, to which you cling with all your zest for life.

The people who do not become involved at all with God enjoy—appalling irony!—the benefit that God does not torment them in this life. No, it is only those he loves, those who become involved with him, whose mortal enemy, to speak merely humanly, he must be said to be—yet out of love [*Kjerlighed*].

But he is your mortal enemy; he, love, he out of love wants to be loved by you, and this means that you must die, die to the world; otherwise you cannot love him.

So he, omnipresent and omniscient as he is, watches you, knows even the slightest little thing taking place within you—he knows that, your mortal enemy! Beware of wishing for something, beware of fearing something, because what you wish for will not be fulfilled, but instead the opposite, and what you fear, and the more you fear it, will happen to you instead. He loves you and he wants to be loved by you, both out of love; but as soon as there is something you wish for, then you are not thinking of him, just as when there is something you fear. Or if you bring him into connection with your wish and your fear, then you are not thinking of him in and for himself—that is, you are not loving him—and he wants to be loved, wants it out of love.

XIV
190

Take an example. A prophet—first of all think of what it means to be a prophet, how strenuous and sacrificial such a man's life is with its renunciation of just about everything that we human beings ordinarily value. Think of the prophet Jonah![84] Such a man, strained and tormented in the service of God, has the modest wish to rest a while under the shade of a tree. He finds this tree, the shade, the rest in this shade under the tree; it makes him feel so good that he very likely *wished* that he might retain this refreshment, *feared* that it would be taken away from him—it happened, God the Omnipotent promptly fixes his attention upon this tree; a worm is ordered to sap its roots.

So terrible, to speak merely humanly, is God in his love, so terrible, to speak merely humanly, is it to be loved by God and to love God. The minor premise in the statement "God is love" is: he is your mortal enemy

— — —and then we play the game that we all are Christians, all love God, whereas people today interpret "God is love" and "to love God" as nothing but the syrupy sweets stocked by truth-witnesses of the lie.

*   *
*

If it is assumed that there is no God, no eternity, no accounting, the official Christianity is a very charming and pleasant invention aimed in a reasonable way at making this life as pleasurable as possible, more pleasurable than the pagan could have it. What continually tormented the indulgent pagan was, as is well known, this matter of eternity; but the official Christianity has given this matter of eternity such a turn that eternity is precisely for the purpose of properly giving us taste and zest for being gladdened by this life and for enjoying it.

Just as if one of the composers who compose variations had used one or two strains from a funeral march to compose with poetic license a vigorous galop, just so has the official Christianity used some sentences in the New Testament (this doctrine about the cross and agony and terror and trembling before eternity etc.) to compose with poetic license a lovely idyll with procreation and waltzing, where everything is so merry, so merry, so merry,[85] where the pastor (a kind of pious municipal musician) for a fee has Christianity—this doctrine about dying to the world— provide music at weddings and christening parties, in short, where everything is delight and merriment in this, according to Christianity's doctrine, vale of tears and prison[86]—this glorious world that still is only, yes, according to the New Testament is the time of testing[87] related to an accounting and judgment[88]—a foretaste of the even more enjoyable eternity that the pastor guarantees to families who by their relation to him have shown a sense for the eternal.

That not everyone is a genius is no doubt something everyone will admit. But that a Christian is even more rare than a genius—this has knavishly been totally consigned to oblivion.

The difference between a genius and a Christian is that the genius is nature's extraordinary; no human being can make himself into one. A Christian is freedom's extraordinary or, more precisely, freedom's ordinary, except that this is found extraordinarily seldom, is what every one of us should be. Therefore God wants Christianity to be proclaimed unconditionally to all, therefore the apostles are very simple, ordinary people, therefore the prototype [*Forbillede*] is in the lowly form of a servant,[90] all this in order to indicate that this extraordinary is the ordinary, is open to all—but a Christian is nevertheless something even more rare than a genius.

But let us not be fooled by the circumstance that it is open to all, possible for all, as if from that it followed that it is something rather easy, and that there are many Christians. No, it must be possible for all; otherwise it would not be freedom's extraordinary; but a Christian still becomes even more rare than a genius.

If it is assumed that it is all in order with these battalions and millions times millions of Christians, an objection arises here that really has significance: that the situation of Christianity is then completely without analogy in the rest of existence. Ordinarily we see everywhere the enormous proportions found in existence: the possibility of millions of plants is blown away as pollen, millions of possibilities of living entities are wasted, etc. etc.; there are probably thousands times thousands of people to one genius etc.—always this enormous waste. Only with Christianity is it different: in relation to what is more rare than a genius, it so happens that everyone who is born is a Christian.

Similarly, if this matter of millions of Christians is supposed to be the truth, a second objection also acquires great significance. This earth is only a little point in the universe—and yet Christianity is supposed to be reserved for it, and at such a bargain price that anyone and everyone who is born is a Christian.

The matter looks different when it is perceived that to be a Christian is such an ideality that instead of the rubbish about Christianity and Christianity's eighteen-hundred-year history, and about Christianity's being perfectible, the thesis may well be posited: Christianity has not actually entered the world; it never went any further than the prototype and at most the apostles. But these were already proclaiming it so powerfully along the lines of propagation that already here the dubiousness begins. It is one thing to work for propagation in such a way that one uninterruptedly, early and late, proclaims the doctrine to all; it is something else to be too hasty in allowing people by the hundreds and thousands to take the name of Christian and pass as followers of Jesus Christ. The prototype's proclamation was different, because just as unconditionally as he proclaimed the doctrine to all, living only for that, just as unconditionally did he hold back with regard to becoming a follower, to receiving permission to call oneself that. [91]If a crowd had been gripped by Christ's discourse, he would not therefore have immediately allowed these thousands to call themselves followers of Christ. No, he held back more strongly. Thus in three and a half years[92] he won only eleven, whereas one apostle in one day, I dare say in one hour, wins three thousand followers of Christ.[93] Either the follower is here greater than the Master,[94] or the truth is that the apostle is a bit too hasty in striking a bargain, a bit too hasty about propagation; thus the dubiousness already begins here.

Only divine authority could impress the human race in such a way that unconditionally willing the eternal would become unconditional earnestness. Only the God-man can unite these: unconditionally working for propagation and unconditionally just as strongly holding back with regard to what being a follower is supposed to mean. Only the God-man would be able to endure (if one can imagine this) working unconditionally for a thousand years and then another thousand for the propagation of the doctrine by proclaiming it, even if he did not gain one single follower, if he could win them only by changing the conditions. The apostle still has some selfish urge for the alleviation, acquiring adherents, becoming many, something the God-man does not have. He does not selfishly crave adherents and therefore has only the price of eternity, no market price.

It so happened that when Christ proclaimed Christianity the human race was unconditionally impressed.

But *naturam furca expellas* [if you expel nature with a pitchfork],[95] it still comes back again. The human tendency is to turn the relation upside down. Just as a dog that is forced to walk on two legs continually has a tendency to begin to walk on all fours again and does it immediately just as soon as it sees its chance, and waits only to see its chance, just so all Christendom is the human race's striving to get to walk on all fours again, to be rid of Christianity, knavishly in the name of its being Christianity and with the claim that this is the perfecting of Christianity.

First of all, they turned around the other side of *the prototype*; the prototype was no longer the prototype but the Redeemer. Instead of looking at him with respect to imitation, they dwelt on his good works and wished to be in the place of those to whom they were shown, which is just as upside down as to hear someone described as a prototype of generosity and then refuse to look at him with the intention of imitating his generosity but with the idea of wishing to be in the place of those to whom he showed generosity.

So the prototype dropped out. Then the apostle was also abolished as prototype. Then after that, the first Christian age as prototype. In this way the goal was finally achieved—walking on all fours again, and that, precisely that, was true Christianity. By means of dogmas, they protected themselves against anything that with any semblance of truth could Christianly be called a prototype, and then under full sail went in the direction of—perfectibility.

When I in this way place one Christianity opposite another, it
surely could not occur to anyone to misinterpret this, as if I had
now come to agree with veterinarian Pastor Fog that there are
two kinds of Christianity.[98] No, I place them opposite each other
in the unaltered opinion that the Christianity of the New Testament is Christianity, the second a piece of skulduggery; they
resemble each other no more than a square resembles a circle.
But the reason I place them opposite each other is to clarify in a
few words what I said in an article in *Fædrelandet*[99]: Whether we
human beings, the human race, have not so degenerated that no
longer are human beings born who are able to bear the divine,
which is the Christianity of the New Testament; and if that is the
case, a stop is put in the simplest way to all the oath-sworn pastors' demonstration that the official Christianity is the Christianity of the New Testament and that Christianity exists.

There are two differences in particular between the spiritual
person and us human beings, to which I want to draw atten-   XIV
tion and thereby in turn to clarify the difference between the   196
Christianity of the New Testament and the Christianity of
"Christendom."

1. The spiritual person is different from us human beings in
that he is, if I may put it this way, so solidly built that he can bear
a redoubling [*Fordoblelse*][100] within himself. By comparison, we
human beings are like a half-timbered structure compared with
a foundation wall—so loosely and weakly built that we are unable to bear a redoubling. But the Christianity of the New Testament relates specifically to a redoubling.

The spiritual person is able to bear a redoubling within himself; with his understanding he can maintain that something is
against the understanding and then will it nevertheless; with his
understanding he can maintain that something is an offense and
then will it nevertheless; that something, humanly speaking,
makes him unhappy and then will it nevertheless, etc. But that is

precisely the way the Christianity of the New Testament is constituted. We human beings, however, are unable to endure or
bear a redoubling within ourselves; our will changes our understanding. Thus our Christianity ("Christendom's") is also designed for this; it removes from the essentially Christian the offense, the paradox, etc. and replaces it with: probability, the direct. That is, it changes Christianity into something completely
different from what it is in the New Testament, indeed, into the
very opposite; and this is the Christianity of "Christendom" (of
us human beings).

2. The spiritual person is different from us human beings in
that he is able to endure isolation, ranks as a spiritual person in
proportion to how strongly he can endure isolation, whereas we
human beings continually need "the others," the crowd; we die,
despair, if we are not safeguarded by being in the crowd, are not
of the same opinion as the crowd, etc.

But the Christianity of the New Testament is precisely designed for relating itself to this isolation of the spiritual person.
Christianity in the New Testament is to love God in hatred of
humankind, in hatred of oneself and thereby of all other people,
hating father, mother, one's own child, wife,[101] etc., the most
powerful expression for the most agonizing isolation. And it is
about this I say: Such human beings, of that quality and caliber,
are not born anymore.

The Christianity of us human beings is: to love God in accordance with loving other human beings and being loved by them,
always the others, including the crowd.

Let me take an example. In "Christendom" this is Christianity. A man with a woman on his arm steps up to the altar,
where an elegant, silken-clad pastor, half educated in the poets,
half in the New Testament, delivers an address, half-erotic, half-
Christian, conducts a marriage ceremony—this is Christianity in
"Christendom." The Christianity of the New Testament would
be: if that man actually could love in such a way that with the
passion of his whole soul the girl truly was the one and only
beloved—but already people like that do not appear anymore—
then, hating himself and the beloved, to let the girl go in order
to love God. —And this is why I say: Such human beings, of that
quality and caliber, are not born anymore.

XIV
197

Christianity's idea was: to want to change everything.

The result, "Christendom's" Christianity is: that everything, unconditionally everything, has remained as it was, only that everything has taken the name of "Christian"— and so (strike up, musicians!) we are living paganism, so merrily, so merrily, around, around, around;[102] or more accurately, we are living paganism refined by means of eternity and by means of having the whole thing be, after all, Christianity.

Test it, take whatever you want, and you will see that it does fit, is as I say.

Was it this that Christianity wanted: chastity[103]—away with brothels. The change is this, that brothels have remained the same as in paganism, dissoluteness proportionately the same, but they have become "Christian" brothels. The brothel keeper is a "Christian" brothel keeper; he is a Christian just like the rest of us. To exclude him from the means of grace—"Heaven forbid," the pastor will say, "what would it come to if we began to exclude one single paying member?" He dies and, all in proportion to what he pays, he has a decent eulogy at his grave. And after earning his money in a way that, Christianly, is base and ignoble—since, Christianly, the pastor might rather have stolen it— the pastor goes home; he is in a hurry, he is going to church to—declaim or, as Bishop Martensen says: to witness.

Was it this that Christianity wanted: honesty and integrity, away with cheating[104]—the change that was brought about is this: the cheating remained altogether the same as in paganism. "Everyone" (the Christian!) "is a thief in his job"; but the cheating took the title "Christian," it became "Christian" cheating— and "the pastor" pronounces a blessing on this Christian society, this Christian state, where one cheats as in paganism, and also by paying "the pastor"; thus the biggest cheater cheatingly makes out that this is Christianity.

Was it this that Christianity wanted: earnestness in life, and away with the glories and honors of vanity[105]—everything remained as it was; the change was that it took the title "Christian": the dingledangles of knightly orders, titles, rank, etc. became Christian—and the pastor (of all equivocations the most indecently equivocal, of all ludicrousness the most ludicrous hodgepodge!) is pleased as Punch about himself—to be decorated with "the cross." The cross! Yes, in "Christendom's" Christianity the cross has become something like the child's hobbyhorse and trumpet.

And so it is with everything. If the natural man has any instinct almost as strong as the instinct for self-preservation, it is the instinct for propagation of the race, which Christianity therefore tries to cool down, teaching that it is better not to marry, but if worst comes to worst, then it is better to marry than to burn.[106] But in Christendom the propagation of the race has become the earnestness of life along with Christianity; and the pastor—this essence of nonsense mantled in long gowns!—the pastor, the teacher of Christianity, the Christianity of the New Testament, has even had his salary set in proportion to the human activity of propagating the race and receives a fixed sum for each child!

As stated, test it and in everything you will find that it is as I say it is: the change from paganism is this, that everything has remained unchanged but has taken the title: "Christian."

This is, when it is pointed out, very easy to perceive, and once perceived it is unforgettable.

Any term that applies to all cannot have a bearing on existence itself but must either underlie existence or lie outside as insignificant.

Take the term *human being.* We all are human beings. This term, therefore, has no bearing whatever on human existence, because the presupposition of the whole is that we all are human beings. In the sense of underlying—we all are human beings— this term lies before the beginning, and now it begins.

This is an example of a term that applies to all and is fundamental. The other point was that a term that applies to all, or by applying to all, lies before the beginning, lies outside as insignificant.

Assume—and let us not babble about its being an odd assumption; we must indeed get this matter cleared up—assume that we all are thieves, what police call frequent offenders. If we all are that, this term will *eo ipso* have no influence whatever on the whole. We will go on living just as we are living; everyone will be regarded as he is now regarded. Some—frequent offenders— would be labeled as thieves and robbers, consequently within the definition that we all are frequent offenders; others—frequent offenders—would be ranked high etc. In short, everything down to the merest trifle will be as it is, because we all are frequent offenders. Thus this concept is canceled; if we all are that, to be that = nothing. Not only does it not mean anything to be a frequent offender if we all are that—no, it says nothing whatever.

It is exactly the same with the concept that all are Christians. If we all are Christians, then the concept is canceled. To be a Christian is something that lies before the beginning, outside— and now it begins; we then live the merely human life, just as in paganism. The term *Christian* cannot have any bearing at all, because, since we all are that, it is simply set outside.

God's idea with Christianity was, if I may put it this way, to get really tough with us human beings. To that end, he put "individual" and "race," the single individual and the many, together inversely, set them at odds, introduced the category of discord, because, according to his thought, to be a Christian was precisely the category of discord, the discord of "the single individual" with "the race," with millions, with family, with father and mother, etc.

God did it this way *partly* out of love [*Kjerlighed*], because he, the God of love, wanted to be loved but is too great a judge of what love is to have anything to do with the rascality of being loved by battalions or by whole nations, which *ein, zwei, drei* are ordered to the church parade. No, the formula continues to be: the single individual in contrast to the others. And he did it *partly* as the Sovereign, in order in this way to hold human beings well in hand and bring them up. This was his thought, even though in one sense we human beings must, if we dared, say that it was the most mischievous whim God could have—to put us together in this way, or in this way to deter us from (what we animal-creatures regard as the true state of well-being) running with the herd, the one always "like the others."

God succeeded; he really impressed human beings.

The human race, however, gradually came to itself and, sagacious as it is, perceived that Christianity could not be thrown out by power—so let us do it by slyness: we all are Christians; then Christianity *eo ipso* is abolished.

And that is where we are now. The whole thing is skulduggery; Christianly, these 2000 churches, or whatever the number, are skulduggery; likewise these 1000 pastors in velvet, silk, broadcloth, and bombazine are skulduggery—because it all depends upon the knavish assumption that we all are Christians, which is simply the knavish abolishing of Christianity. Thus it is also an odd euphemism that we reassure ourselves with "We all will be saved" or "I will be saved just like the others," since with that label one is not received into heaven; one arrives there no more than one reaches Australia by land.

That the human being is a defiant creature is well known, but that he is to a high degree a sagacious creature—as soon as it is a matter of flesh and blood and earthly well-being—is not always perceived. Yet this is the case, although the lament over human obtuseness may well be true also.

When there is something that does not please the human being, he sagaciously looks to see whether the power that is in command is weaker than the opposing power that he can command. If he is convinced of that, the rebellion is made in defiance.

But if the power that commands what does not please the human being is so superior to him that he unconditionally despairs of rebelling in defiance—then he resorts to hypocrisy.

This is the case with Christianity. That the fall from Christianity happened long ago has not been noticed because the fall happened, the rebellion was carried out—in hypocrisy. Christendom itself is the fall from Christianity.

In the New Testament, according to Christ's own teaching, to be a Christian is, to speak merely humanly, sheer agony, an agony compared with which all other human sufferings are almost only childish pranks. What Christ is speaking about—he makes no secret of it—is about crucifying the flesh,[107] hating oneself,[108] suffering for the doctrine,[109] about weeping and wailing while the world rejoices,[110] about the most heartrending sufferings caused by hating father, mother, wife, one's own child,[111] about being what Scripture says of the prototype—and being a Christian, after all, surely ought to correspond to the prototype—a worm, not a human being.[112] Hence these continual admonitions about not being offended,[113] not being offended because that which in the highest, in the divine sense, is the salvation, the help, will be, humanly speaking, so dreadful.

This is what it is to be a Christian. See, this is not something for us human beings; we would prefer to plead to be excused from something like that. Indeed, if any human power had hit upon something like that, humankind would promptly have rebelled in defiance.

But unfortunately God is a power against whom one cannot rebel in defiance.

Then "humankind" resorted to hypocrisy. People did not even have the courage and honesty and truth to say directly to God, "I cannot accept that" but resorted to hypocrisy and felt perfectly secure.

People resorted to hypocrisy and falsified the concept of what it is to be a Christian. To be a Christian, so it was said, is sheer happiness. "What would I be, oh, what would I be if I were not a Christian; oh, what a priceless good to be a Christian. Indeed, to be a Christian is the only thing that really gives meaning to life, savor to joys, and relief to sufferings."

That is the way we all became Christians. And now everything went splendidly with big words and grandiose phrases and heavenly glances and torrents of tears, all by artists paid to do that, artists who could not find expressions to thank God adequately for the great good that we are Christians etc.—and the secret was: we have falsified the concept of being a Christian but hope by means of knavish, hypocritical flattery and sweet words, thanking and again thanking, that we—are the opposite of what he understands by being a Christian—we thereby hope, fooling ourselves, to make a fool of him; and thus, by thanking him *inbrünstigt* [fervently][114] that we are that, we hope to avoid becoming that.

This is why a church is the most dubious place. No doubt there are other places called dubious places, but they are not actually that; they are indeed unequivocally what they are. By being called "dubious," they are prevented from actually being

dubious. A church, however, yes, that is a dubious place; a royally authorized church in "Christendom" is the most dubious thing that has ever existed.

To make a fool of God is not dubious, but to do it under the name of worshiping him is dubious; to want to abolish Christianity is not dubious, but it is dubious to abolish Christianity under the name of propagating it; to contribute money to work against Christianity is not dubious, but it is dubious to accept money to work against it under the name of working for it.

Let me relate a little incident, psychologically noteworthy, from the criminal world.

It was in a case in which one can, as it is said, "clear oneself" with an oath—that is, clear oneself temporally in return for eternally binding oneself with a false oath. The person involved was a frequent offender, sufficiently well known to an authority; the authority did not have the power to prevent the oath but was altogether convinced morally that it was a false oath—then he administered the oath.

At the conclusion of the case, the official visited the person in jail, spoke with him privately and said, "Do you dare to give me your hand on it that what you swore was the truth?" "No," he answered, "no, Your Honor, that I refuse to do."

See, here is an example of the difference between the official and the personal. For someone who essentially belongs to the criminal world to clear himself by taking an oath is something official, something he does not for a moment hesitate to do, or the defensibility of which he does not doubt at all, since it is something he knows all about from long-standing practice. For him it is settled; one does such a thing officially, impersonally. The art consists in skillfully turning a matter in such a way that one can clear oneself with an oath; the taking of an oath is saying "God bless you!" to someone who sneezes, or writing S. T. [*salvo titulo*, with a reservation regarding the title] on a letter. The oath and the solemnity of taking an oath futilely seek to make an impression on him precisely with regard to the personal— futilely, he himself (this is a business matter!) is official, officially armed against every attempt, which he knows in advance, that will be made to impress him. So he takes the oath officially; the whole thing, as he understands it, *is ex officio.*

But personally, no, personally he could not make up his mind solemnly to confirm a lie. "Do you dare to give me your hand on it?" "No, Your Honor, that I refuse to do."

*　　　　*

*

Anyone who has the slightest experience will no doubt admit that it is correct to say (shifting now to a completely different world) that not infrequently in a private conversation with a pastor, especially if one is able to touch him personally, one can get him to admit to a conviction different from the one he *ex officio* recites or about which he perhaps personally has some doubts but *ex officio* recites "with full conviction." And yet the pastor is indeed bound by an oath; he has taken an oath that should assure that what he recites is his conviction! But, alas, in the world of the clergy this taking of an oath now belongs to the official—so it must be if one wishes to get a position. One takes the oath officially, recites officially that to which one is bound by oath. "But tell me honestly, dear Pastor P., will you give me your hand on it that this is your conviction, or will you affirm it on the memory of your late wife—because to me, for the sake of possibly putting an end to my doubting, it is very urgent to get to know your true opinion?" "No, my friend, no, that I cannot do, that you must not ask of me."

The taking of an oath—it should, of course, really assure that the matter is personal! Yet the oath, the oath, the condition for getting a job etc.—O God, lead us not into temptation!—the oath is perhaps taken officially. "But is what you are teaching actually your conviction; I beseech you by the memory of your late wife to help me by telling me your honest opinion!" "No, my friend, that I cannot do!"

Once upon a time, in a long, long ago vanished age, the matter was understood this way: it was required of the person who wanted to be a teacher of Christianity that his life provided the guarantee for what he taught.

That was abandoned long ago; the world has become more sagacious, more earnest, has learned to scorn all this narrow-mindedness and morbidity about the personal, has learned to desire only the objective—now the requirement is that the teacher's life provide the guarantee that what he says is pleasantry, dramatic festivity, *divertissement*, purely objective.

Some examples. If what you wish to speak about is that Christianity, the Christianity of the New Testament, has a preference for the single state[116]—and you yourself are unmarried—My dear fellow, that is not anything for you to speak about. Indeed, the congregation might think that it was in earnest, might become uneasy, or it could resent that you so inappropriately mix your own person into it in this way. No, it will be a long time before you can become competent to speak in earnest about that in such a way that you truly satisfy the congregation. Wait until you have buried your first wife and are well along with the second—then the time has come for you, then you step forward before the congregation, teach and "witness" that Christianity has a preference for the single state—and you will satisfy it completely, for your life provides the guarantee that it is dalliance, pleasantry, or that what you are saying is—interesting. Indeed, how interesting! Just as the husband must be unfaithful to the wife and the wife to the husband if a marriage is to be safeguarded against boredom, is to be interesting, so also the truth does not become interesting, enormously interesting, until one allows oneself to be gripped in mood, to be carried away, enchanted by it—but of course does exactly the opposite and is subtly protected by letting it end there.

If the aspect of Christianity you wish to speak about is that
Christianity teaches contempt for titles and knightly orders and
all the tomfoolery of honors—and you yourself are neither a person of rank nor anything resembling that—my dear fellow, that
is not anything for you to speak about. Indeed, the congregation
might think it is in earnest or resent the lack of good manners in
thrusting your person into it this way. No, wait until you yourself
have acquired a bunch of decorations, the more the better; wait
until you yourself drag a long string of titles along with you, so
many titles that you yourself scarcely know what you are
called—then the time has come, then you step forward, preach
and "witness"—and without a doubt you will satisfy the congregation, because your life will provide the guarantee that it is dramatic amusement, an interesting forenoon entertainment.

If it is this you wish to speak about, proclaiming Christianity
in poverty, that this is the true Christian proclamation—and you
yourself literally are a poor devil—my dear fellow, that is not
anything for you to talk about. Indeed, the congregation might
think it is in earnest, could become anxious and afraid, could be
completely put off and be most uncomfortably disturbed to have
poverty brought so close to life. No, first of all secure for yourself
a fat livelihood, and then when you have had it so long that you
will soon advance to an even fatter one—this, then, is the oppor-
tune time, then you step forward before the congregation,
preach and "witness"—and you will give complete satisfaction,
because your life will provide the guarantee that the whole thing
ends in a joke, which earnest men now and then crave in the
theater or in church, a refreshment in order to gather new energy
for—earning money.

[117]And this is the way God is worshiped in churches! And then
these velvet-and-silk orators weep, they sob, the voice fails,
choked in tears! Ah, if it is so (and so it is, after all, since God
himself says it) that he counts the sufferer's tears and keeps them
in a bottle,[118] then woe to these speakers if God has also counted
their Sunday tears and kept them in a bottle! Yes, woe to us all
if God actually pays attention to these Sunday tears, especially the
speakers', but also the listeners'! A Sunday orator would be right

in what he said, and it would, oratorically, appear brilliant, especially if supported by tears and choked sobs—but he would be
right when he said to the listeners: I will collect all the futile tears
you have shed in church and with them will step forward on
judgment day and accuse you—he is right, but do not forget that
the speaker's own dramatic tears still are far more terrible than
the listeners' thoughtless tears.

(MARK 12:38; LUKE 20:46)

June 15, 1855

Since the "truth-witnesses," as proper "truth-witnesses, " most likely prefer, instead of publicly warning against me, to be all the more active in secrecy, I shall take their business upon myself and shall loudly, loudly *witness* before the whole nation: Beware of the pastors!

Above all, beware of the pastors! It belongs to being a Christian (if one is to be that in such a way that it can pass on judgment day, and otherwise what is the use of one's being a Christian!): to have suffered for the doctrine. And believe me, as sure as my name is Søren Kierkegaard, you will get no official pastor to say that—which is natural, since to do so would be suicide for him. At the same moment it is said that to have suffered for the doctrine is required even for being an ordinary Christian, at the same moment the whole machinery with its 1000 livelihoods and officials is disturbed, all these 1000 livelihoods are exposed. That is why you will get no official pastor to say it. On the contrary, you can be completely sure that he with all his might will declaim the opposite, prevent you from thinking those thoughts so that you can be kept in the condition he considers to be Christian: a good sheep for shearing, a harmless mediocrity, to whom eternity is closed.

Do believe me; I offer my life as the security you may demand, because I do not involve myself with you in a finite sense at all, do not seek to draw you to me in order to form a party etc. No, I am only religiously doing my duty, and in a certain sense it is for me, if only I do it, indifferent, altogether indifferent whether you follow what I say or not.

*   *

*

Beware of those who go about in long robes. It is unnecessary to say that Christ does not mean these words to be a criticism of their clothing. No, it certainly is not a comment about robes; this is not what Christ is against, that they are long. If the professional apparel for pastors had been short robes, then Christ would have said: Beware of those in short robes. And if you want me to carry this to the extreme in order to show that it is not a criticism of the clothing—if the professional attire for pastors had been to go without clothing, Christ would have said: Beware of those who go without clothing. It is at the profession, which he characterizes by its special costume (for he has a completely different understanding of what it is to be a teacher), that he wants to strike.

Beware of those who *like* to go about in long robes. A wishy-washy exegesis will immediately pounce on the word *like* and explain that Christ was aiming only at individuals in the profession, those who place a conceited honor in the long robes etc. No, my good long-robed man, perhaps from the pulpit and with great solemnity you can make women and children believe this; it also fits exactly the Christ-picture that is presented in the Sunday service. But you cannot make me believe it, and the Christ of the New Testament does not speak in this way. He always speaks about the whole profession, does not come with the meaningless chitchat that there are a few of them who are corrupted, something that applies in all ages to all ranks and classes, so that nothing at all is said thereby. No, he views the profession as a whole, says that the profession as a whole is corrupted, that the profession as a whole also has the corruption of liking to go about in long robes, namely, because being a pastor in the official sense is just the opposite of what Christ understands by being a teacher, which means to suffer, while the former means to enjoy the things of this earth, refined by the glory of being God's representative. Thus it is no wonder that they like to go about in long robes, because all other positions in life are rewarded only with the earthly, but the official clergy include a little of the heavenly for refinement.

*   *

*

Thus in itself it is totally unimportant whether professional apparel is long robes or short robes. On the contrary, what is crucial
is: as soon as the teacher acquires "vestments," a special costume,
professional apparel, then you have official worship—and that is
what Christ does not want. Long robes, splendid church buildings, etc., all this hangs together, and it is the human falsification
of the Christianity of the New Testament, a falsification that
shamefully makes use, unfortunately, of the fact that a great many
people are all too easily deceived by sense impressions and therefore (completely counter to the New Testament) are inclined to
identify true [*sand*] Christianity by sense[*Sandse*]-impressions. It
is the human falsification of the Christianity of the New Testament; and with the clerical profession it is not as with other pro-
fessions, that in itself there is nothing evil in the profession—no,
the clerical profession in itself is, Christianly, of evil, is a corruption, a human selfishness that makes Christianity the very opposite of what Christ made it.

But since long robes have now become the professional apparel for pastors, one can also be sure that this implies something,
and I think that by paying attention to what it implies one can
interpret very characteristically the nature or odious practice of
official Christianity.

Long robes involuntarily prompt the thought that there is
something to hide; when one has something to hide, long robes
are very appropriate—and official Christianity has a great deal to
hide, because from start to finish it is an untruth, which therefore
is best hidden—in long robes.

And long robes—that, after all, is feminine attire. The thought
is therefore prompted of something that is also characteristic of
official Christianity: the unmanliness, the use of slyness, untruth,
and lies as its power. This is in turn very characteristic of official
Christianity, which, itself an untruth, expends an enormous mass
of untruth both to hide what the truth is and to hide that it is itself
untruth.

This femininity is characteristic of official Christianity in yet
another way. The feminine trait of being willing and yet reluctant; this coquetry, in woman unconscious, finds its unpardon-
able parallel in official Christianity, which wants the earthly and

the temporal so very much but yet for the sake of decency must pretend that one does not want it, carefully sees to attaining it but secretly, since one must pretend, of course, one must swoon, faint when one must accept the high and fat positions to which one is so decidedly opposed that only out of a sense of duty, simply and solely out of a sense of duty, has one been able to decide to accept such a position, and only after one has on bended knee groaned to God and pleaded, alas, in vain, that he take away this cross, this bitter cup[119]— —and yet one would perhaps be in a confounded predicament if the government were ironic enough to release one.

Finally, there is something dubious about men in women's apparel. One could almost be tempted to say that it conflicts with the police ordinance that forbids males from going about in women's apparel and vice versa. But in any case it is something dubious—and dubiousness is exactly the most descriptive term for what official Christianity is, descriptive of the change that in the course of time has taken place with Christianity, that from being what it is in the New Testament: simplicity, the unequivocal, it has—probably with the help of perfectibility!—become something more: the dubious.

*   *

*

Therefore beware of those who like to go about in long robes! According to Christ (who surely must be best informed about the way, since he is the Way[120]) the gate is narrow and the way is hard—and few are they who find it.[121] And perhaps the greatest cause of all for the smallness of the number, proportionately smaller with every century, is the enormous illusion that official Christianity has conjured up. Persecution, cruelty, bloodshed have certainly not done this kind of damage. No, they have been beneficial, incalculably beneficial, compared with the fundamental damage: official Christianity, calculated to serve human indolence, mediocrity, by leading people to think that indolence and mediocrity and pleasure are—Christianity. Do away with official Christianity, let persecution come—at the same moment Christianity exists again.

THE MOMENT

No. 6

CONTENTS

August 23, 1855   S. KIERKEGAARD

1.

Christianity can be perfected (is perfectible); it advances; now it has attained perfection. The ideal that was aspired to but that even the first age only approximately attained, that the Christians are a people of priests,[123] that has now been perfectly attained, especially in Protestantism, especially in Denmark.

If, namely, what it is to be a priest is what we call a pastor—indeed, then we all are pastors!

2.

In the splendid cathedral the Honorable Right Reverend *Geheime General-Ober-Hof-Prædikant* [Private Chief Royal Chaplain][124] comes forward, the chosen favorite of the elite world; he comes forward before a chosen circle of the chosen ones and, deeply *moved*, preaches on the text he has himself chosen, "God has chosen the lowly and the despised in the world"[125]—and there is no one who laughs.

3.

When a man has a toothache, the world says, "Poor man"; when a man's wife is unfaithful to him, the world says, "Poor man"; when a man is financially embarrassed, the world says, "Poor man." —When it pleases God in the form of a lowly servant[126] to suffer in this world, the world says, "Poor human being"; when an apostle with a divine commission has the honor to suffer for the truth,[127] the world says, "Poor human being"—poor world!

4.

"Did the Apostle Paul have any official position?" No, Paul had no official position. "Did he, then, earn a lot of money in another way?" No, he did not earn money in any way. "Was he, then, at least married?" No, he was not married.[128] "But then Paul is certainly not an earnest man!" No, Paul is not an earnest man.

5.

A Swedish pastor, shaken by the sight of the effect his discourse had on the listeners, who were swimming in tears, is reported to have said reassuringly: Do not weep, children, it may all be a lie.

Why does the pastor no longer say that? It is unnecessary, we know that—we are all pastors.[129]

But we can very well weep, since both his and our tears are not at all hypocritical but well meant, genuine—just as in the theater.

6.

When paganism was disintegrating, there were some priests called augurs. It is reported that one augur could not look at another without grinning.[130]

In "Christendom" it may soon be the case that no one will be able to look at a pastor or one person at another without grinning—but we are, of course, all pastors!

7.

Is this the same teaching, when Christ says to the rich young man: Sell all that you have and give it to the poor,[131] and when the pastor says: Sell all that you have and give it to me?

8.

Geniuses are like a thunderstorm [*Tordenveir*]: they go against the wind, terrify people, clear the air.

The established order has invented various lightning rods [*Tordenafledere*].

And it succeeded. Yes, it certainly did succeed; it succeeded in making the *next* thunderstorm all the more serious.

9.

One cannot live on nothing. One hears this so often, especially from pastors.

And the pastors are the very ones who perform this feat: Christianity does not exist at all—yet they live on it.

The Measure of Distance and Thereby in Turn the Actual Difficulty with Which I Have to Contend

My dear reader! In order to make you aware of where, Christianly, we are, in order that you may have an opportunity to measure the distance from the Christianity of the New Testament and the earliest Christianity, allow me with that in mind to use two men who are regarded individually as representatives of true Christianity, but in different ways, and who are generally known.

First of all take Bishop Mynster; he was regarded by almost the entire population as being true Christian earnestness and wisdom.

Yet this is how it was with Bishop Mynster: all his earnestness reached no further than the thought: in a human, permissible, and honest or indeed also in a human, honorable way, to go happily and comfortably through this life.

But this life-view is not at all the Christianity of the New Testament, is not the life-view of original Christianity. Original Christianity relates itself so militantly to this world that its view is: not to want to slip happily and comfortably through this world but to take care to collide in dead earnest with this world so that after having fought and suffered in this way one might be able to pass in the judgment, in which the judge (whom, according to
the New Testament, one can love only by hating this world and one's own life in this world[132]) will judge whether one has fully done his will.

Thus there is a world of difference, a heaven of difference between the Mynsterian life-view (which actually is Epicurean, one of the enjoyment of life, of zest for life, belonging to this world) and the Christian view, which is one of suffering, of enthusiasm for death, belonging to another world. Indeed, there is such a difference between these two life-views that to Bishop Mynster the latter must look (if it should be carried out in earnest and not at the very most be delivered on a rare occasion in a quiet hour) like a kind of lunacy.

Now measure, and you will see that what you under the name of Mynster are accustomed to designate as Christian earnestness and wisdom is, measured Christianly, lukewarmness, indifferentism. The difference must be designated as the difference between wanting to contend in a life and death struggle with this world, at no price wanting to have friendship with this world (Christianly the requirement) and wanting to slip happily and comfortably through this world, at the very most contending a little, if this could contribute to one's slipping happily and comfortably through this world.

Consider, then, Pastor Grundtvig.[133] Grundtvig, of course, is regarded as "a kind of apostle,"[134] representing enthusiasm, the courage of faith that fights for a conviction.

Let us now take a closer look. The highest he has fought for is to receive permission, for himself and for those who want to join him, to express what he understands by Christianity. This is why he wanted the yoke removed that the state Church laid upon him;[135] it shocked him that they wanted to use police power to prevent him from, religiously, having his freedom.

Fine. But if G. had attained for himself and his own what he wanted, then it was his idea to let stand the whole enormous illusion that the state passes itself off as being Christian, that the people imagine themselves to be Christians—in short, that every single day a gross affront is committed, high treason against God by falsifying what Christianity is. To fight in that direction has certainly never occurred to G. No, freedom for himself and those in agreement with him, freedom to express what he and they along with him understand by Christianity, that is the most he has wanted—and then he would conduct himself calmly, at ease in this life, belong to his family, and otherwise live like those who are essentially at home in this world, and perhaps call his tranquillity tolerance toward the others, the other—Christians.

XIV
222

Now think of the passion that was in original Christianity and without which it never would have entered into the world; submit to one of those personages the question: Does a Christian dare to set his mind at ease in this way? "Abominable," he would answer, "dreadful, that a Christian, if only he could receive permission for himself to live as he wanted to, should calmly be silent about God's being insulted every day by people in the millions falsely passing as Christians, worshiping him by making a fool of him; that he should keep silent about it and not immediately—to the glory of God—venture out, suffering, among these millions, gladly suffering for the doctrine!" Let us not forget that Christianity, although in one sense it certainly is the most tolerant of all religions inasmuch as it abhors most of all using physical force, in another sense is the most intolerant of all religions, inasmuch as its true followers know no limit when it comes to sufferingly constraining others, constraining them by suffering their mistreatment and persecution.

Measured by this measure, it is easily seen that G. actually can never be said to have fought for Christianity; he actually has fought only for something earthly, civil freedom for himself and his adherents; and he has never fought with Christian passion. No, compared with the passion of original Christianity, Grundtvig's enthusiasm is lukewarmness, indifferentism.

What is deceptive about both Mynster and Grundtvig is that by living in an age that does not have the slightest idea of original Christianity they have come by way of comparison to be regarded respectively as earnestness and wisdom, and as enthusiasm and the courage of faith.

But if it is the case that at a given time the two most eminent representatives of Christianity, who are regarded as earnestness and wisdom, enthusiasm and the courage of faith, measured with the measure of original Christianity, must be said to be lukewarmness and indifferentism, then one gains thereby an idea of the entire age and of the difficulty with which I actually have to contend.

The difficulty is that the entire age has sunk into the deepest indifferentism, has no religion at all, is not even in the condition of being able to have religion.

What is misleading is that they call themselves Christians and that they are unaware of what indifferentism actually is, or of the most corrupt form of indifferentism.

By indifferentism is meant actually having no religion at all. But decisively, resolutely, definitely to have no religion, this is already something passionate and thus not the most dangerous kind of indifferentism. This is why it also seldom makes its appearance.

No, the most dangerous kind of indifferentism, and the very common kind, is to have a specific religion, but this religion is diluted and botched into sheer blather; therefore one can have the religion in an entirely passionless way. It is the most dangerous kind of indifferentism, because, simply by having this trumpery under the name of religion, one is, so one thinks, safeguarded against, made immune to every charge that one has no religion.

All religion involves passion, having passion. Therefore it would be the case with every religion, especially in ages of rationalism, that it has very few true followers. On the other hand, there are thousands who in a way take a little of the religion, dilute and botch it, and thereupon passionlessly (that is, irreligiously, that is, indifferently) have—the religion, that is, by having the religion, they, altogether indifferent, are safeguarded against the charge of having no religion.

This constitutes the difficulty with which I have to contend, a difficulty akin to floating a grounded ship by means of cables fastened to pilings when the surrounding ground is a bog, so that every piling that is driven down gives way and fails.

What I confront is indifferentism, the deepest, the most corrupt, and the most dangerous kind of indifferentism. It is a society about which an apostle would say, "Christians, they are Christians! They have no religion at all, are not even in the condition of being able to have religion!" A society about which Socrates would say, "They are not human beings but are dehumanized to being the public or by being the public."

They all are: the public. This humanness, to ask whether an opinion is in itself true, no one cares about; what they care about is: how many have this opinion. Aha! The number decides whether an opinion has physical power, and this is what they care about all the way through: the single individual in the nation—well, there is no individual, every individual is the public.

Thus it eventually becomes a kind of pleasure, corresponding to the pleasure it must have been to be a spectator at the baiting of wild beasts; in the capacity of the public, to witness this battle becomes a kind of pleasure—one single human being, who has nothing but spiritual power and at no price wants any other, fighting for the religion that is the religion of sacrifice and against this gigantic body of 1000 tradesmen pastors, who decline spirit with thanks, but heartily thank the government for salary, title, knighthood cross, and the congregation—for the offering.

And because the condition on the whole is this, the deepest indifferentism, it is in turn made only all too easy for the individual who is a bit more advanced to become self-important, as if he were the earnest one, a character, etc. —A young man, he is indignant over this universal lukewarmness and indifference; he, who is enthusiastic, also wants to express his enthusiasm, ventures—anonymously to express it. Well intentioned as he no doubt is, and that is indeed gratifying, he perhaps fails to notice that this is somewhat weak, and he perhaps allows himself to be fooled by this, that by way of comparison with the ordinary it seems to be something. —A citizen, an earnest man, he is upset by the lukewarmness and indifference that many show who prefer to hear nothing at all about religion. He, however, reads; he promptly obtains what is published, talks about it, talks excitedly—in the living room. He perhaps fails to notice that the earnestness, Christianly, is nevertheless not really earnestness, that it is earnestness only by way of comparison with what should never be used for comparison if one wants to advance, since the striving becomes possible only by comparison with what lies ahead, the more advanced.

"Yes, O God, if you were not the Omnipotent One, who omnipotently could compel, and if you were not love, who irresistibly can move! . . . . . But your love moves me, the thought of daring to love you inspires me, joyful and grateful, to accept the condition, to be a sacrifice, sacrificed to a generation" etc. See *This Must Be Said.*[136]

This, as is well known, is Socrates' thesis; he feared most of all to be in error.[137]

Christianity, which certainly in one sense does not teach people to fear, not even those who are able to put one to death, nevertheless teaches in another sense a still greater fear than that Socratic fear, teaches to fear the one who can destroy both soul and body in hell.[138]

But first to the first thing, to become aware of the Christianity of the New Testament; and for that purpose that Socratic fear, to fear most of all to be in error, will assist you.

If you do not have this fear, or (in order not to strike too high a note) if this is not the case with you, if this is not what you want, if you do not want to gain the courage "to fear most of all to be under a delusion"—then never become involved with me. No, then stay with the pastors, then let them convince you, the sooner the better, that what I say is a kind of lunacy (that it is in the New Testament is, after all, utterly unimportant; when the pastor is bound by an oath on the New Testament, you are of course perfectly assured that nothing that is in the New Testament is suppressed). Stay with the pastors; strive to the best of your ability to establish firmly for yourself that Bishop Mynster was a truth-witness, one of the authentic witnesses, one of the holy chain, Bishop Martensen ditto, ditto, every pastor likewise, and the official Christianity is the saving truth; that Christ in the most dreadful tortures, even abandoned by God,[139] expired on the cross, in order that we should have the pleasure of spending our time and diligence and energy on sagaciously and tastefully enjoying this life; that his purpose in coming to this world actually was to encourage the procreation of children, which is why it is also "inappropriate for anyone who is not married to be a pastor"; and that the unforgettable significance of his life is (like a true benefactor!) to have made possible by his death (one person's death, another's bread!) a new way of making a living, the pastors', a way of making a living that must be regarded as one of the most advantageous, just as it also engages the greatest number of tradesmen, shippers, and shipowners, whose *Geschäft* [business] is to ship people for an unbelievably cheap remuneration (in relation to the importance and length of the journey, the gloriousness of the place of destination, the length of the stay) to the blessedness of eternity, a *Geschäft*, the only one of its kind, that has, compared with all shipping to America, Australia, etc., the inestimable advantage of insuring the shipper against even the possibility of getting a bad name because no news whatever is received from those transported.

But if you do have the courage to want to have the courage that fears most to be in error, then you can also get to know the truth about becoming a Christian. The truth is: to become a Christian is to become, humanly speaking, unhappy for this life; the proportion is: the more you involve yourself with God and the more he loves you, the more you will become, humanly speaking, unhappy for this life, the more you will come to suffer in this life.

This thought, which certainly throws a somewhat disturbing light on (what is supposed to be the Christianity of the New Testament!) all the brisk traffic of the cheerful, child-begetting, career-making preacher-guild, and like a lightning flash[140] trans-illuminates this fantastic mirage, masquerade, parlor game, tomfoolery with (the abode of all illusions!) "Christendom," Christian states, countries, a Christian world—this is a frightful, death-dealing, almost superhumanly exhausting thought for a poor human being. This I know from experience in two ways. I know it partly from this, that I actually cannot endure the thought and therefore merely investigatingly scrutinize this true Christian definition of being a Christian,* while I for my part

---

*Therefore I do not yet call myself a Christian; no, I am still far behind. But I have one advantage over all the official Christianity (which moreover is bound by oath upon the New Testament!); I report truthfully what Christianity is. Consequently I do not permit myself to change what Christianity is, and I report truthfully how I relate to what Christianity is; consequently I do not participate in changing what Christianity is in order thereby to obtain millions of Christians.

help myself to bear the sufferings with a much easier thought, a
Jewish idea, not in a highest sense Christian: that I am suffering because of my sins; and partly from this, that through the circumstances of life I was bound to be led in a very special way to become aware of it, and otherwise I would never have become aware and would have been even less capable of bearing the pressure of this thought, but, as stated, I was helped by the circumstances of my own life.

The circumstances of my own life were my preparatory instruction; with their help I became, accordingly as I developed over the years, more and more aware of Christianity and of the definition: of becoming a Christian. In other words, what does it mean, according to the New Testament, to become a Christian, why the repeated admonition against being offended,[141] and why the frightful collisions (to hate father, mother, wife, child,[142] etc.), in which the New Testament breathes? I wonder if both are not because Christianity knows very well that to become a Christian is to become, humanly speaking, unhappy in this life, yet blessedly awaiting an eternal happiness. According to the New Testament, what does it mean to become loved by God? It is to become, humanly speaking, unhappy in this life, yet blessedly expecting an eternal happiness—according to the New Testament, God, who is spirit, cannot love a human being in another way. He makes you unhappy, but he does it out of love; blessed is the one who is not offended! According to the New Testament, what does it mean to love God? It is to be *willing* to become, humanly speaking, unhappy in this life, yet blessedly expecting an eternal happiness—a person cannot love God, who is spirit, in another way. And solely by the help of this you can see that the Christianity of the New Testament does not exist at all, that the fragment of religiousness found in the land is at most Judaism.[143]

That We, That "Christendom," Cannot Appropriate Christ's Promises at All, Because We, "Christendom," Are Not Where Christ and the New Testament Require One to Be in Order to Be a Christian

Imagine that there was a mighty spirit who had promised a few people his protection, but on the condition that they should present themselves at a specific place that involved danger to reach—suppose now that these people failed to appear at this specific place but went around in their living rooms at home and spoke enthusiastically with each other about how the spirit had promised them his powerful protection; hence no one would be able to harm them—is this not ludicrous?

It is the same with Christianity. Christ and the New Testament understand something very specific by having faith; to have faith is to venture out as decisively as possible for a human being, breaking with everything, with what a human being naturally loves, breaking, in order to save his life, with that in which he naturally has his life.[144] But to those who have *faith*, to them is also promised assistance against all dangers.[145]

But in "Christendom" we play at having faith, play at being Christians. As far removed as possible from any break with what the natural human being loves, we remain at home in the living room, in the routines of finiteness—and then we go and blather to each other or let ourselves be prattled to at length by the pastors about all the promises that are found in the New Testament, that no one shall be able to harm us, the gates of hell shall not have power over us, over the Church,[146] etc.

"That the gates of hell shall not have power over his Church,"
these words by Christ have recently been recalled against me again and again, against my claim that Christianity does not exist at all.[147]

My reply is this. That promise does not help us at all, because the blather in which we live as if this were being a Christian is by no means what Christ and the New Testament understand by being a Christian.

Venture out so decisively that you break with all temporality and finiteness, with everything a human being ordinarily lives for and in, venture out decisively in this way in order to become a Christian—then (this is Christianity's doctrine) then you will, this is the first, thereby come into conflict with devils and the powers of hell (something that fusspot "Christendom" indeed avoids). But then, too, God the Omnipotent will not abandon you, and you may be sure that the gates of hell will never have power over Christ's Church.

But "Christendom" is by no means Christ's Church; neither do I say that the gates of hell have gained power over Christ's Church, certainly not. No, I say that "Christendom" is a pack of blather that has fastened itself to Christianity like a cobweb on fruit and that now is so good as to want to confuse itself with Christianity, just as when the cobweb considers itself to be the fruit because it, although rather less choice, is something that clings to the fruit. The kind of existences manifested by the millions in Christendom has absolutely no relation to the New Testament, is an unreality that has no claim to Christ's promise concerning the believers; yes, an unreality, since true reality is present only when a person has ventured decisively in this way, as Christ requires—and then the promises immediately pertain to him. But "Christendom" is this nauseating dalliance, to want to remain completely and totally in finiteness and then—to make off with the promises of Christianity.

If inspection were not so easy, these legions of Christians, or the preacher-prattle delivered to them, would probably claim that the Christians are able to perform miracles, since Christ has indeed promised this to the believers. He left the earth with the very words (Mark 16:17–18) that these signs would follow those who believe: "In my name they will cast out demons; they will speak in new tongues; they will pick up serpents, and if they drink anything poisonous, it will not harm them; they will lay their hands on the sick, and they will be healed." But it is also exactly the same with the promise that the gates of hell shall not have power over Christ's Church; both promises pertain only to what the New Testament understands by believer, not to the preacher-cheating with these battalions of Christians who, by

XIV
230

analogy to the distinction between Sunday hunters and real hunters, can be called Sunday Christians. But such beings Satan does not even try to capture. After all, he perceives very well that the blather has caught them; thus it is even ludicrous that it is in trust in Christ's promises that they think themselves safeguarded against the gates of hell.

When a person has in any sense what is called a cause, has something he earnestly wants—and then there are others who take upon themselves the task of opposing, preventing, and doing harm—everyone immediately realizes that he is obliged to take measures against these his enemies. But not everyone realizes that there is, if you please, a good-natured well-meaning that perhaps is far more dangerous and that will most likely prevent the cause from truly becoming earnestness.

When a person suddenly becomes ill, well-meaning persons rush to help, and one recommends this, another that. If they all received permission to advise, the patient's death would indeed be certain; the individual's well-intentioned advice may already be sufficiently dubious. Even if none of this happens, and neither the advice of all the well-meaning ones nor of the individual is followed, their bustling, nervous presence may still be harmful insofar as they stand in the way of the physician.

It is the same at a fire. Scarcely is the fire alarm heard before a human mob storms to the place—nice, kind, sympathetic, helpful people; the one has a pail, the other a slop basin, the third a spray pump, etc., all nice, kind, sympathetic, helpful people eager to help put out the fire.

But what does the fire chief say? The fire chief, he says—well, usually the fire chief is a very affable and cultured man; but at a fire he is what one calls coarse-mouthed—he says, or rather he bellows, "Hey! Get the hell out of here with your pails and spray pumps." And when the well-meaning people perhaps become offended, find it extremely indecent to be treated this way, and insist on at least being treated with respect, what does the fire chief say? Well, usually the fire chief is a very affable and cultured man, who knows how to show everyone the respect due him, but at a fire he is something else—he says, "Where in hell are the police!" And if some policemen arrive, he says to them, "Get rid of these damned people with their pails and spray pumps; and if they won't go with kindness, then tan their hides so that we can get rid of them—and get going."

At a fire, then, the whole point of view is entirely different from the one in quiet everyday life; what makes one well-liked in quiet everyday life—kind, worthy, good intentions—is saluted at a fire with abusive language and finally with some hide-tanning.

And this is quite as it should be. A fire is a serious matter, and wherever there is really something serious these worthy, good intentions are utterly inadequate. No, seriousness introduces a completely different law: either/or—either you are the person who can do something in earnest here and have something to do in earnest here, or, if that is not the case with you, then the earnestness is simply that you take off. If you refuse to understand this, then let the fire chief have the police knock it into you, something that can be especially beneficial to you and perhaps can contribute to making you a little earnest, in accord with the seriousness of the fire.

It is just the same in the world of the spirit as at a fire. Wherever there is a cause to be advanced, an enterprise to be carried through, an idea to be applied—one can always be sure that when the person who is the man, the right one, the person who in the higher sense has and should have command, he who has earnestness and can give the cause the seriousness it truly has— one can always be sure that when he arrives on the scene, if I may put it this way, he will find a congenial company of blatherers who, in the name of earnestness, dabble in wanting to serve this cause, to advance this enterprise, to apply this idea, a company of blatherers who naturally regard unwillingness to make common cause with them (which is earnestness) as clear evidence that the person in question lacks earnestness. I say, when the right one comes, he will find this. I can also turn the matter this way: whether he is the right one is properly decided by how he understands himself in relation to this company of blatherers. If he thinks that it is they who are going to assist and that he will strengthen himself by joining them—he is *eo ipso* not the right one. Like the fire chief, the right one promptly sees that this company of blatherers must go, that its presence and actions are

XIV
233

the most dangerous assistance the fire could have. But in the world of the spirit it is not as at a fire, where the fire chief merely needs to say to the police: Get rid of these people.

Just as it is in the whole world of the spirit, so it is also in the religious sphere. History has often been compared to what the chemists call a process. The metaphor can be very appropriate if, note well, it is rightly understood. There is what is called a filtering process. Water is filtered, and in this process the impure components are removed. History is a process in an entirely opposite sense. The idea is applied—and now enters into the process of history. But this, unfortunately, does not consist in—ludicrous assumption!—the purifying of the idea, which never is purer than at the beginning. No, it consists, at a steadily increasing rate, in botching, babbling, and prattling the idea, in vitiating the idea, in—the opposite of filtering—putting in the impure components originally lacking, until eventually, by way of the enthusiastic and mutually approving collaboration of a series of generations, the point is reached where the idea is completely destroyed, the opposite of the idea has become what is now called the idea and this, it is claimed, has been achieved by the historical process, in which the idea is purified and ennobled.

When the right one finally comes, he who in the highest sense has the task, perhaps chosen early for it and slowly brought up for this operation, which is to shed light onto the matter, to get a fire set to this tangle, the abode of all the blather, of all the illusions, of all the skulduggery—when he comes, he will always find a company of blatherers, who in convivial heartiness have some sort of idea that something is wrong and that something must be done, or who are prepared to chatter about the fact that something is terribly wrong, to become self-important by chattering about it. If at any moment he, the right one, is mistaken and thinks that it is this company that is going to help—he is *eo ipso* not the right one. If he makes a mistake and becomes involved with this company—Governance immediately lets him go as unfit for use. But the right one sees with half an eye what the fire chief sees, that the company that with good intentions wants to help put out the fire with a pail or spray pump, that this same company, here where it is not a matter of putting out a fire but of just getting a fire started, that with good intentions wants to assist with a wooden match without the sulphur or with a damp candle-lighter—that this company must go, that he must not have the least thing to do with this company, that he must be as coarse-mouthed with them as possible, he who perhaps otherwise is anything but that. But everything depends upon getting rid of the company, because its effect in the form of hearty sympathy is to enfeeble the genuine earnestness of the cause. Naturally the company will be infuriated with him, with this frightful arrogance,[148] and the like. This must not make any difference to him. Wherever there is truly to be earnestness, the law is: either/or; either I am the one who is involved with this cause in earnest, is called to it and is unconditionally willing to venture decisively or, if this is not the case, then the earnestness is: have nothing at all to do with it. Nothing is more abhorrent, more villainous, betraying and causing a deeper demoralization, than this: to want to be involved a little in what should be *aut—aut, aut Caesar aut nihil* [either—or, either Caesar or nothing],[149] to want to be a little involved, so heartily dabbling, to babble about it, and then with this babbling to want falsely to credit themselves with being better than those who are not at all involved with the whole enterprise—credit themselves with being better and make the cause more difficult for the one who actually has the task.

1.
MEDIOCRITY'S BIBLE INTERPRETATION

interprets and interprets Christ's words until it gets its own, the spiritless (banal) out of them—and now, after having removed all the difficulties, is reassured, and appeals to Christ's words!

It totally escapes mediocrity that thereby a new difficulty is produced, certainly about the most ludicrous it is possible to imagine: the difficulty that God should let himself be *born*, that *the truth* should have entered into the world—in order to make banal remarks; and likewise a new difficulty, the difficulty of explaining that Christ then could be crucified, inasmuch as in this world of banality the death sentence is ordinarily not passed on the making of banal remarks. Thus Christ's crucifixion becomes both inexplicable and ludicrous, since it is ludicrous to be crucified because one has made banal remarks.

2.
THE THEATER/THE CHURCH

[150]The difference between the theater and the church is essentially this: the theater honorably and honestly acknowledges being what it is; the church, however, is a theater that in every way dishonestly seeks to conceal what it is.

An example. On the theater poster it always states plainly: money will not be returned. The church, this solemn holiness, would shrink from the offensiveness, the scandalousness, of placing this directly over the church door, or having it printed under the list of preachers on Sundays. Yet the church does not shudder at insisting, even more stringently than the theater, that money will not be returned.

Therefore it is fortunate that the church has the theater alongside,[151] because the theater is a rogue, actually a kind of truth-witness, who betrays the secret: what the theater says openly, the church does covertly.

3.

GOD/THE WORLD

If two people are eating nuts together, and the one likes only the shell, the other only the kernel, they must be said to be well matched. In the same way God and the world also match each other. What the world rejects, throws away, scorns—the sacrificed ones, the kernels—God places an infinite price precisely on that, gathers it more zealously than the world gathers what it loves most passionately.

THE MOMENT

No. 7

CONTENTS

August 30, 1855   S. KIERKEGAARD

Why Do "People" Love "the Poet" above All? and Why, in a Godly Sense, Is Precisely "the Poet" the Most Dangerous of All?

Reply: The poet is, in a godly sense, the most dangerous of all just because people love the poet above all.

People love the poet above all because he is to them the most dangerous of all. It is the nature of a sickness to crave most vehemently, to love most, precisely that which is most harmful to the one who is sick. But, spiritually understood, the human being in his natural state is sick, he is in error, in a self-deception. Therefore he craves most of all to be deceived; then he is allowed not only to remain in error but to feel really at home in the self-deception. And a deceiver capable of this is precisely the poet; that is why people love him above all.

The poet relates himself only to the imagination; he depicts the good, the beautiful, the noble, the true, the exalted, the unselfish, the magnanimous, etc. in a mood at the distance of imagination from actuality. And at this distance how lovely it is indeed: the noble, the unselfish, the magnanimous, etc.! If, however, it is brought so close to me that it would almost compel me to make it an actuality because the one who depicted it was no poet, but a character, a truth-witness, who himself made it an actuality—frightful, that would be unendurable!

In every generation there are very few so callous and corrupt that they would have the good, the noble, etc. entirely eradicated; but in every generation there are also very few so earnest and honest that they truly want to make the good, the noble, etc. actual.

"Humankind" does not wish the good as far away as those first few, but neither as close as those latter few.

Here "the poet" is situated, the human heart's beloved favorite. He is that, and no wonder! Among other characteristics, this human heart has one that is, to be sure, seldom mentioned—yet this in turn is presumably an effect of this same characteristic—the characteristic of subtle hypocrisy. And the poet—he can play the hypocrite with people.

Something that will become the most terrible suffering if it is made into actuality, the poet deftly changes into the most subtle pleasure. Actually to renounce this world is no jest. But to revel in mood in a "quiet hour" with the poet, secure by possessing this world, is a subtle, very subtle pleasure.

—— —and it is by this kind of worship that we have accomplished the feat that we all are Christians. That is, all this about Christendom, Christian states, countries, a Christian world, a state Church, a national Church, etc. is at a distance of the imagination from actuality, is a delusion and, Christianly, such a corrupt delusion that the proverb "Delusion is worse than pestilence" applies here.

Christianity is renunciation of this world. The professor lectures on this and then makes lecturing on this his career, without ever admitting that this actually is not Christianity—if this is Christianity, where then is the renunciation of this world? No, this is not Christianity; it is a poet-relation. —The pastor preaches, he "witnesses" (well, thanks for that!) that Christianity is renunciation, and then makes preaching this his livelihood, his career; he does not himself ever admit that this actually is not Christianity—but where then is the renunciation? Is this then not also a poet-relation?

But the poet plays the hypocrite with people—and the pastor is a poet, as we have now seen—consequently official worship becomes hypocrisy; and it is in order to attain this great good that the state naturally does not hesitate to provide money.

If the hypocrisy is to be prevented, this is the mildest way for it to happen: the "pastor" makes the admission that this actually is not Christianity—otherwise we have hypocrisy.

Thus the title to this piece is not altogether true, that the poet, in a godly sense, is the most dangerous of all. The poet claims only to be a poet. *What is much more dangerous is that the person who is only a poet, by being, as it is called, a pastor, passes himself off as being something much more earnest and true than the poet, and yet is only a poet. This is hypocrisy to the second power.* Therefore a detective talent was needed, someone who simply by mentioning the word, by claiming to be only a poet, could get behind all this disguise.

[152]They are Christ's own words: "Follow me, and I will make you fishers of people." Matthew 4:19.

So the apostles went out.

"But what would come of it with those few people, who also probably understood Christ's words in this way, that it was they who should be sacrificed in order to catch people. It is easy to see that if it was done in this manner nothing would have come of it. It was God's idea, beautiful perhaps, but—well, every practical person must admit that God is not practical. Or can anything more preposterous be imagined than this kind of fishing, in which to fish is to become sacrificed; consequently it is not the fisherman who eats the fish, but the fish who eat the fisherman; and that this is to be called fishing is almost as mad as Hamlet's saying that Polonius is at supper, yet is not there where he eats, but there where he is eaten."[153]

Then humankind took over God's cause.

"Fishing for people! What Christ meant is something much different from what those simple apostles accomplished, defying all language usage and language analogies, because in no language does one understand fishing to mean that. What he meant and intended is plainly the beginning of a new industry: fishing for people, to proclaim Christianity in such a way that fishing in this fishery will really amount to something."

Watch now and see how it comes to amount to something!

Yes, upon my word, it did come to amount to something—it came to amount to "the established Christendom" with millions and millions and millions of Christians.

The arrangement was quite simple. Just as a company is formed that speculates in herring fishing, another in cod fishing, or in whaling etc., so a fishery for people was formed by a company that mutually guaranteed one another a clear profit of such and such percentage.

And what was the result of that? Ah, if you have not done it otherwise, use this opportunity to admire human nature! The result was that they caught an enormous amount of herring, I mean human beings, Christians, and of course the company was very profitable. Indeed, it turned out that the most prosperous herring company did not in the remotest manner profit in the way the fishery for people profited. And then one more thing, yet another profit, or at least a piquant spice added to the profit— no herring company dares to claim to have Scriptural backing when they send the boats out fishing.

But the fishery for people is a godly enterprise; the stockholders in this company dare to claim to have Scriptural backing, because Christ himself did indeed say, "I will make you fishers of people." They calmly approach the judgment seat, saying, "We have fulfilled your Word; we have fished for people."

FIRST PICTURE

It is a young man—let us think of it this way; actuality provides abundant examples—it is a young man with even more than ordinary capacities, knowledge, involved in public events, a politician, himself playing a role as such.

As far as religion is concerned, his religion is: he has none at all. It never occurs to him to think of God; it is the same with going to church, and it certainly is not for religious reasons that he abstains; and he would almost be afraid that to read God's Word at home would make him ludicrous. When it one day happens that a situation in his life, involving some danger, prompts him to express himself about religion, he chooses the expedient of saying what the truth is: I have no opinion at all about religion; such a thing has never concerned me.

The same young man, who feels no need for religion, does, however, feel a need to become—a father. He marries; now he has a child; he is—the alleged father—and what happens?

Well, our young man is, as they say, in hot water with this child; in the role of the alleged father, he is compelled to have a religion. And it turns out that he has the Evangelical Lutheran religion.

How pitiable to have a religion in this way. As an adult one has no religion; when merely having an opinion about religion could involve some danger, one has no religion: but in the role of an alleged father one has (*risum teneatis* [refrain from laughing]![154]) the Christian religion, which specifically recommends the single state.

Then a message is sent to the pastor; the midwife comes with the baby; a young lady coquettishly holds the baby's bonnet; some young men, who also have no religion, as godparents show the alleged father the courtesy of having the Evangelical Christian religion and of taking on the commitment of the child's Christian upbringing; a silk-clad pastor gracefully sprinkles water over the sweet little baby three times, gracefully dries his hands with a towel—

—and one dares to offer this to God in the name of: Christian Baptism. Baptism; it was by this holy ceremony that the Savior of the world was consecrated to his life's task,[155] and after him the disciples, men who long ago had reached maturity and the age of discretion and who now, dead to this life (this is why they were immersed three times, signifying being baptized into the communion of Christ's death[156]), promised to live as sacrificed ones in this world of lies and evil.

Yet the pastors, these holy men, do indeed understand their job, and likewise, that if it were to be, as Christianity unconditionally must require and every reasonable person, that not until one has reached maturity and the age of discretion does one receive permission to decide what religion one will have—the pastors understand very well that then their livelihood would never really amount to much. And therefore these holy truth-witnesses invade the nurseries and make use of the sensitive moment when the mother is weak after coming through the suffering, and the father is—in hot water. And then one dares in the name of Christian Baptism to offer to God an act as described, into which a little bit of truth could be brought if the young lady, instead of sentimentally holding the bonnet over the baby's head, satirically held a nightcap over the alleged father. To have religion in that way is, spiritually speaking, a comic pitifulness. One has no religion, but because of the circumstances [*Omstændigheder*]—because first the mother got in a family way [*Omstændigheder*] and then as a result of that the father in turn got in a family way, one has, because of the circumstances involving this sweet little darling—the Evangelical Lutheran religion.

SECOND PICTURE

It is a tradesman. His principle is: Everyone is a thief in his trade. "It is impossible," he says, "to be able to get through this world if one is not just like the other tradesmen, all of whom hold to the principle: Everyone is a thief in his trade."

As far as religion is concerned—well, his religion is actually this: Everyone is a thief in his trade. He also has a religion in other respects, and in his opinion every tradesman ought to have one. "A tradesman," says he, "should, even if he has no religion, never allow it to be noticed, because this can easily become harmful by possibly throwing suspicion on his honesty; and a tradesman should preferably have the prevailing religion in the land." As for the latter, he accounts for that by the fact that the Jews always have a reputation for cheating more than the Christians, which he claims is by no means the case. He claims that the Christians cheat just as much as the Jews, but what harms the Jews is that they do not have the religion that prevails in the land. As for the former, the advantage that having a religion provides with regard to favoring one in cheating, he refers to what one learns from the clergy. He claims that what helps the clergy to be able to cheat more than any other social class is simply that they are so close to religion; if such a thing could be done, he would gladly pay a handsome sum to obtain ordination, because it would pay for itself splendidly.

Two or four times a year this man dresses up in his best clothes and goes to Communion. There a pastor makes his appearance, a pastor who (like those figures that jump out of a snuffbox when the spring is touched) jumps as soon as he sees "a blue bank-note."[157] And then the holy ceremony is celebrated, from which the tradesman, or rather both of the tradesmen (both the pastor and the citizen) return home to their ordinary way of life, except that one of them (the pastor) cannot be said to return home to his ordinary way of life—after all, he had not left it, has been much more engaged as a tradesman!

And one dares to offer this to God in the name of the Sacrament of the Altar, the Communion of Christ's body and blood!

The Sacrament of the Altar! It was at the Communion table that Christ, himself consecrated from eternity to be the sacrifice, for the last time before his death was together with his disciples and consecrated them also to death, or to the possibility of death if they truly followed him. Therefore, in all its solemnity, what is said about his body and blood is so dreadfully true, this blood-covenant that has united the sacrifice with his few faithful blood-witnesses, which they surely would become.

And now the solemnity is this: to live before and after in a completely worldly way—and then a ceremony. Yet to instruct people about what the New Testament understands by the Lord's Supper and its commitment—for good reasons the pastors guard against that. That others have been sacrificed, to *live on* this is the basis of their whole livelihood; their Christianity is *to receive the sacrifice*. To suggest to them that they themselves be sacrificed would be regarded by them as *eine sonderbare und höchst unchristliche Zumuthung* [a strange and highly unchristian presumption], totally in conflict with the New Testament's *sound* doctrine,[158] which they presumably would demonstrate with such colossal learning that no individual's lifetime would suffice to study this thoroughly.

The theological graduate Ludvig From[160]—he is seeking. When one hears that a "theological" graduate is seeking, one does not need a lively imagination to understand what it is that he is seeking—naturally, the kingdom of God, which, of course, one is to seek *first*.

But no, it is not that; what he is seeking is a royal livelihood as a pastor, and very much, which I shall indicate by a few episodes, happened *first* before he attained that.

First he attended high school, from which he graduated to the university. Thereupon he *first* passed two examinations, and after four years of study he *first* passed the degree examination.

So then he is a theological graduate, and one would perhaps think that after having *first* put all that behind him, he finally can get a chance to work for Christianity. Yes, one would think so. No, *first* he must attend the pastoral seminary for a half year; and when that is finished, nothing can be said about having been able to seek during the first eight years, which had to be put behind him *first*.

And now we stand at the beginning of the story: the eight years are over, he is seeking.

His life, which until now cannot be said to have any relation to the unconditioned, suddenly assumes such a relation. He is seeking unconditionally everything; he fills one sheet of officially stamped paper after the other with writing; he runs from Herod to Pilate; he recommends himself both to the minister [of ecclesiastical affairs] and to the janitor—in short, he is totally in the service of the unconditioned. Indeed, one of his acquaintances, who has not seen him the last few years, is amazed to discover that he has become smaller; perhaps the explanation is that the same thing happened to him that happened to Münchhausen's dog, which was a greyhound but because of much running became a dachshund.[161]

Three years go by in this way. After such enormously strenuous activity, our theological graduate really needs a rest, needs to have a respite from activity or to come to rest in an official position and be looked after a little by his future wife—for in the meantime he has *first* become engaged.

Finally, as Pernille says to Magdelone, the hour of his "deliverance" arrives,[162] so with the full power of conviction and from his personal experience he will be able to "witness" before the congregation that in Christianity there is salvation and deliverance—he obtains an official position.

What happens? By obtaining even more exact information about the income of the call than he had, he discovers that it is 150 rix-dollars less than he had believed. That did it! The unhappy man almost despairs. He has already bought official stamped paper in order to apply to the minister for permission to be considered as if he had not been called—and in order then to begin again from the beginning—but one of his acquaintances persuades him to give up this idea. So it ends with his retaining the call.

He is ordained—and the Sunday arrives when he is to be presented to the congregation. The dean, by whom this is done, is a more than ordinary man. He not only has (something most pastors have, and most often in proportion to their rank) an impartial eye for earthly gain, but also a speculative eye on world history, something he cannot keep for himself but lets the congregation share to its benefit. By a stroke of genius he has chosen as his text the words by the Apostle Peter, "Lo, we have left everything and followed you,"[163] and now explains to the congregation that precisely in times such as ours there must be such men as teachers, and in that connection he recommends this young man, who he knows was close to withdrawing because of the 150 rix-dollars.

Now the young man himself mounts the pulpit—and the Gospel for the day[164] (strangely enough!) is: Seek **first** the kingdom of God.

He delivers his sermon. "A very good sermon," says the bishop, who himself was present, "a very good sermon; and it made the proper impression, the whole part about 'first' the kingdom of God, the manner in which he emphasized this *first*."

"But, your Reverence, do you believe that there was here the desirable agreement between the discourse and the life? On me this *first* made almost a satirical impression."

"How absurd! He is called, after all, to proclaim the doctrine, the sound unadulterated doctrine about seeking first the kingdom of God, and he did it very well."

*   *

*

This is the kind of worship one dares—under oath—to offer to God, the most horrible insult.

Whoever you are, just think of this Word of God, "first the kingdom of God," and then think about this story, which is so true, so true, so true, and you will not need more to make you realize that the whole official Christendom is an abyss of untruth and optical illusion, something so profane that the only true thing that can be said about it is: By ceasing to participate (if you usually do participate in the public divine service) in it as it now is, you always have one and a great guilt less, that of not participating in making a fool of God (see *This Must Be Said; So Let It Be Said*).[165]

God's Word says "First the kingdom of God," and the interpretation, perhaps even "the perfecting" of it (since one does not want to do it shabbily) is: first everything else and *last* the kingdom of God; at long last the things of this earth are obtained *first*, and then finally last of all a sermon about—first seeking God's kingdom. In this way one becomes a pastor, and the pastor's entire practice thus becomes a continual carrying out of this: first the things of this earth and then—the kingdom of God; first the consideration for the things of this earth, whether it pleases the government or the majority, or whether there is at least a group—that is: first a consideration for what fear of people bids or forbids, and then God's kingdom; first the things of this earth, first money, and then you can have your child baptized; first money, and then earth will be thrown on your coffin and there will be a funeral oration according to the fixed rate; first money, and then I will make the sick call; first money, and then: *virtus post nummos* [virtue after money];[166] first money, and then virtue, then the kingdom of God, and the latter finally comes last to such a degree that it does not come at all, and the whole thing remains with the first: money—only in that case one does not feel the urge "to go further."[167]

This is how in everything and at every point official Christianity is related to the Christianity of the New Testament. And this is what is not even acknowledged to be wretchedness; no, it is brazenly insisted that Christianity is perfectible, that one cannot stay with the first Christianity, that it is only an element, etc.

Therefore there is nothing to which God is so opposed as official Christianity and participation therein with the claim to be worshiping him. If you believe, and that you surely do, that God is opposed to stealing, robbing, plundering, whoring, slandering, gluttonizing, etc.—the official Christianity and its worship are infinitely more loathsome to him. To think that a human being can be sunken in such brutish obtuseness and lack of spirit that he dares to offer God such worship, in which everything is thoughtlessness, spiritlessness, lethargy, and that people then brazenly dare to regard this as a forward step in Christianity!

This it is *my* duty to say, this, "Whoever you are, whatever your life is otherwise—by ceasing to participate (if you usually do participate) in the public divine service as it now is, you always have one and a great guilt less."[168] You yourself, then, bear and have to bear the responsibility for how you act, but you have been made aware!

That "Christendom" from Generation to Generation Is a Society of Non-Christians, and the Formula for the Way This Happens

XIV
252

The formula is this: when the individual has arrived at the age when there could be any question of becoming a Christian in the sense of New Testament Christianity, he thinks that he still cannot really make a decision on that. On the other hand, he has a real desire—to marry. Ah! He then indulges in the following observation, "I actually am already too old to become a Christian" (Christendom's basic lie, a lie because according to the New Testament one must be an adult in order to be able to become a Christian). "No, one must become Christian as a child; it must be commenced in childhood. So I will now get married, have children—and they, they will become Christians."

Excellent! And when each of these children has arrived at the age when there could be any question of becoming a Christian in accordance with the New Testament, each one of them reasons *S. T.* [*salvo titulo*, with reservation of the title], as their Mr. Father and Mrs. Mother did, "I actually am already too old to become a Christian. No, it must be commenced in childhood; at present I must" (just as Trop says that it is on behalf of Pryssing that he is lying out in Deer Park[169]) "on behalf of Christianity climb into the marriage bed and my children, they will become Christians."

Abracadabra; amen, amen, forevermore amen; honor be to the pastors!

This is "Christendom's" secret, an incomparable insolence smacking of wanting to put a wax nose on God, an insolence that nevertheless is blessed, in the name of being true Christianity, by the clergy, those oath-bound teachers, that dubious company (as everyone who has any experience must know is the case without everyone's knowing the Christianity of the New Testament well enough really to be nauseated by them) that seeks especially to stand in well with the midwives. Look closely and you will see that it is as I say. There is a secret understanding between every

pastor and the midwives; they mutually understand that how
the pastor stands with the midwives is extremely important to
him, and they mutually understand that they share a common
livelihood—and the pastor is bound by an oath on the New
Testament, which recommends celibacy.[170] But of course the
Christianity of "Christendom" is indeed the very opposite of
the Christianity of the New Testament, and therefore these
petticoated people (I do not mean the midwives, but the pastors), officious as matchmakers, are about their business in the
nurseries.

For the Christianity of "Christendom" everything depends on
firmly establishing that one becomes a Christian as a child; if one
is really going to become a Christian, one becomes that as a child,
from childhood on. This is the basic lie; if it prevails, then
goodnight to the Christianity of the New Testament! Then
"Christendom" has won the game, a victory that is most fittingly
celebrated by a real eating and drinking club, a wild club with
bacchants and bacchantes (pastors and midwives) at the head of
the hilarity.

The truth is: one cannot become a Christian as a child; it is just
as impossible as it is impossible for a child to beget children. To
become a Christian presupposes (according to the New Testament) a full human life, what in a natural sense could be called
maturity—in order now to become a Christian by breaking with
everything to which one is immediately attached. To become a
Christian presupposes (according to the New Testament) a personal consciousness of sin and of oneself as a sinner. Thus one
easily sees that this whole business of becoming a Christian as a
child, indeed, that one must become that precisely as a child, is
neither more nor less than dalliance, which dallying pastors, presumably by virtue of their oath on the New Testament, put into
people's heads in order that "the pastor's" livelihood and career
can be arranged.

Let us return to the beginning. The individual said, "I actually
am already too old to become a Christian; but I will get married,
and my children will" etc. If this individual actually had been
earnest about becoming a Christian, he would have said, "I am
now at the age when I can become a Christian. Obviously, then,

it could of course never occur to me to want to marry. Even if it were not the case that Christianity recommends the single state, something the prototype expresses, although 'the apostle,' clearly against his will, sees himself compelled to give in a little to the eager-for-matrimony crowd and, like someone weary of hearing an everlasting fussing about the same thing, gives in a little, so that if worst comes to worst it is better to marry than to burn[171]— even if this were not the case, it still could never occur to me to marry. The task of becoming a Christian is so enormous; why, then, would it occur to me to become involved in this procrastination, however much people, especially at a certain age, describe it and regard it as the greatest bliss! I honestly do not comprehend how it has occurred to anyone to want to link being a Christian with being married. This does not mean, please note, that I thereby am thinking, for example, of someone who is already married and has a family and now just at this age becomes a Christian—no, my thought is: How can someone who is unmarried and says he has become a Christian, how can it occur to him to marry?

"A Savior comes to the world to save—whom? The lost.[172] There certainly are plenty of those, for they all are lost, and by being born everyone who is born is a lost soul. The Savior then says to each individual: Do you want to be saved? Even if the Savior said nothing now about the single state, it seems to me to follow as a matter of course that it is unnecessary to say that a Christian does not marry; it would actually be the least that one could ask of someone who himself became saved, and so dearly bought[173] that it came about by another's agonizing life and death; the least that one could ask of him would be that he not occupy himself with producing more lost souls by begetting children, since there certainly are enough of them. By means of propagation of the race, lost souls are poured out as through a cornucopia—and should the person who is saved, grateful for his salvation, then make his contribution also to the lost souls by propagation of the race?"

Consequently the individual who wanted to be earnest about becoming a Christian stopped with himself—and right there, Christianly, is the earnestness; he stopped with himself and

understood that the task was: that he become a Christian. He
stopped with himself to the extent that it could not occur to him
at all to marry. He expressed the opposite of what every human
being naturally must be said to express, a possibility, perhaps for
many years, of a line descending from him. He expressed the
opposite: to terminate; he related himself inversely (therefore
Christianly, properly) to the mass of lost souls, did not engage in
adding to it, but related himself negatively to it. In "Christendom's" Christianity it is different; battalions of fertile men and
women are brought together, whereby millions of children are
produced—and this, claim the pastors (who, after all, must
know, since they have sworn an oath on the New Testament),
this, claim the pastors (but what will pastors, even more than the
Germans, not do for money[174]), this, claim the pastors, is Christianity, pastors, these holy men, of whom it cannot be said, as
otherwise about everyone, that he is a thief in his trade; the pastor
is an exception—he is a liar in his trade.

"One must become a Christian as a child, it must be commenced in childhood"; that is, the parents want to be exempt
from becoming Christians, but then want to have a mask, and
therefore this: to bring their children up to be true Christians.
The pastors understand the secret very well, and thus there is
frequently talk about the Christian upbringing of children, about
this earnestness—by which parents want to be exempt from the
true earnestness. The relation of the parents to the children
comes to resemble the relation of the pastors to their congregations. The pastors are not exactly desirous of becoming Christians themselves either—but their congregations, they are to
become true Christians. The hoax is always to get rid of the
earnestness (of becoming a Christian oneself) and to introduce
instead the profound earnestness (!) of wanting to make others
Christians.

So one brings up one's children to be Christians, as they say—
that is, one swills into the child some childish confection that is
not at all the Christianity of the New Testament. This childish
confection, which does not resemble the doctrine about the cross
and anguish, about dying to the world, hating oneself, any more
than jam resembles cream of tartar—of this childish confection

the parents themselves lick a little and then become sentimental over the thought that they themselves, unfortunately, are no longer the Christians they were as children, because only as a child can one really be a Christian.

To all this gibberish "the pastor" naturally agrees—yes, naturally! Only one thing is important to the pastor, in every way (by virtue of his oath on the New Testament) to do exactly the opposite of what the New Testament does, in every way to preserve, protect, and encourage in human beings the desire to propagate the race so that battalions of Christians can continually be supplied, something that is definitely a life-necessity if thousands of very prolific pastors are to be able to live with their families on this. Furthermore, "the pastor" also knows very well what every politically sagacious government knows (something the lovers discover only afterward), that people are trivialized by marriage, that therefore the point is to promote—by means of cattle shows, by prizes for those who can beget the most children, and in other ways, for example, by making this into Christianity—the propagation of the race, which, after all, is what most strongly calls to mind humankind's kinship with God. Finally, "the pastor" thereby avoids all precarious conflicts with the human throng. Christianity's whole view of life is lofty and therefore is easily an offense to the human throng. If, however, true Christianity actually comes to consist in begetting children, it then becomes as popular and understandable as possible. And, as the pastor says, people should not be scared away from religion; they ought to be won for it—for example, by making the satisfaction of their desires into religion. In this way one also wins them in large numbers, and then in turn gains (profits) by the winning of people for religion in this way—but one does not thereby win heaven.

*   *

*

"Christendom," from generation to generation, is a society of non-Christians; and the formula for the way this happens is this: the individual himself is unwilling to be a Christian, but takes it upon himself to beget children, who are to become Christians;

XIV
256

and these children in turn conduct themselves in the same way. God sits in heaven—made to look like a fool. But his oathbound servants on earth, the pastors, delight in life and in this comedy; hand in hand with the midwives they assist in the propagation of the race—the true Christian earnestness!

Conscience (insofar as there can be any question of it in this connection), conscience seems to have pricked "Christendom" into the realization that it was really too bad that it could not continue this sheerly bestial nonsense that one becomes a Christian by receiving from a royal officeholder a sprinkling of water on one's head as a child and that on the occasion the family arranges a party, a feast, where one celebrates this ceremony.

This cannot go on, "Christendom" thought; that the one baptized *personally* takes upon oneself the Baptismal promise must also find expression.

Thus confirmation, a glorious invention if one assumes two things: that the effect of worship is to make a fool of God, and that it is primarily intended to give an occasion for family festivities, parties, a convivial evening, a feast, different from other feasts in that this one—how refined!—is "also" of religious significance.

"The baby," says Christendom, "cannot, of course, personally take upon itself the Baptismal promise; that requires an actual person." So the age of approximately fourteen or fifteen years, the age of boyhood, has been chosen—is this a stroke of genius or of ingenuity? This actual person—there is no hindrance here; he is man enough personally to take upon himself the Baptismal promise made on the baby's behalf.

A boy fifteen years old! If it were a matter of ten rix-dollars, the father would say: No, my boy, you can't be allowed to have that at your disposal; you are too damp behind the ears for that. But when it is a matter of his eternal salvation and, as an actual personality, of adding the earnestness of personality to what still could not in a deeper sense be called earnestness, that a baby is bound by a promise—the age of fifteen years is most appropriate.

XIV
258

The most appropriate—ah, yes, if, as was noted earlier, divine worship is taken to have a double purpose: in a refined way (can it be called that?) to make a fool of God, and to occasion pleasant

family festivities. Then it is splendidly appropriate, as is everything on this occasion, also the assigned Gospel text of the day,[175]
which, as is known, begins this way, "When the doors were
shut"—and it is particularly appropriate for a confirmation Sunday; it is with true upbuilding that one hears a pastor read it aloud
on confirmation Sunday.

It is easy to see, then, that confirmation is far more extreme
nonsense than infant Baptism, simply because confirmation
claims to supply what was lacking in infant Baptism: an actual
personality who is able consciously to take over a promise pertaining to the decision of an eternal happiness. In another sense,
however, this nonsense is ingenious enough, serving the clergy's
egotism, which realizes very well that if the decision with regard
to religion is postponed until maturity (the only Christian and
the only sensible thing), many would perhaps have the character
not to pretend to want to be Christians. Therefore "the pastor"
seeks to take hold of people in the young, tender years, so that in
their mature years they would have the difficulty of having to
break a "sacred" commitment, dating from childhood, to be
sure, but still something against which perhaps many have a su-
perstition. Therefore the clergy take hold of the child, the boy,
receive sacred promises from him, etc. And what God's man,
"the pastor," does is, after all, a godly enterprise. Otherwise by
analogy it could perhaps be required that, just as there is a police
ban that forbids cafés to serve liquor to boys, a ban would be
published against receiving solemn promises pertaining to an
eternal happiness from—boys, a ban in order to prevent the pastors, because they themselves are perjurers, from being allowed
to work (for their own consolation) toward the greatest possible
commune naufragium [common shipwreck], prevent the whole
community from becoming perjurers, and it seems as if having
fifteen-year-old boys pledge themselves by a sacred promise pertaining to the decision of an eternal happiness is designed for that
purpose.

Consequently confirmation in itself is far more extreme nonsense than infant Baptism. But in order not to neglect anything
that in any way could contribute to making confirmation the

very opposite of what it purports to mean, this act has been connected with everything finite and civic possible; thus the actual meaning of confirmation becomes: the certificate the pastor issues, without which certificate the boy or girl concerned cannot succeed in this life at all.

It is all a comedy—and in that regard perhaps something could be done to bring more dramatic illusion into this ceremony, as, for example, issuing a ban against confirming anyone wearing a jacket, which is inappropriate for an actual personality, likewise a regulation that male confirmands should wear a beard when being confirmed, which naturally could be removed at the family festivity in the evening or perhaps be used for fun and practical jokes.

But I do not attack the congregation in what I write; it is led astray and cannot be blamed (it is human) if, left to itself, deceived by the pastor's having taken an oath upon the New Testament, it likes this kind of worship. But woe to the pastors, woe to them, those oath-bound liars! I know full well that there have been mockers of religion; they would have given—yes, what would they not have given to be able to do what I am able to do, but they failed, because God was not with them. Not so with me; originally as well-intentioned toward the pastors as anyone has seldom been, I simply wanted to help them—they themselves have brought the opposite upon themselves. And the Omnipotent One is with me; and he knows best how the blows should be struck so that they are felt, that laughter, used in fear and trembling, must be the scourge—this is why I am used.

THE WEDDING

True worship quite simply consists in doing God's will.

But that kind of worship was never to people's liking. What occupies people in every age, what gives rise to scholarship, becomes many, many branches of scholarship, spreads to immeasurable prolixity, what thousands of pastors and professors live on and for, what is the content of the history of Christendom, the study of which shapes the prospective pastor and professor—is to

XIV
260

arrange another kind of worship that consists of doing their own will, but in such a way that God's name, calling upon God, is connected with it, whereby people think themselves protected against being ungodly—alas, although precisely this is the most definite kind of ungodliness.

Example. A man intends to support himself by killing people. He of course sees from God's Word that this is not permitted, that God's will is: You shall not kill.[176] That may well be, he says, but that kind of worship is of no use to me—but I do not want to be an ungodly person either. So what does he do? He gets hold of a pastor who in God's name blesses the dagger. *Ja, das ist was anders* [Yes, that is another matter]!

In God's Word celibacy is recommended.[177] "But," says the man, "that kind of worship is really of no use to me—and I certainly am not an ungodly person either. Such an important step as marriage" (which, please note, God advises against; thus *he* thinks that the important thing is to refrain from taking "this important step")—"should I do this without securing for myself God's blessing." Bravo! "This, after all, is what God's man, the pastor, is for; he blesses this important step" (the importance of which is that one refrains from it) "and then it is pleasing to God"—and I have my way; and my will becomes worship; and the pastor has his way, gets ten rix-dollars, not earned in a simple way, such as, for example, by brushing people's clothes or by serving beer and brandy. No, he was of course working on God's behalf; earning ten rix-dollars in that way is worship. Bravissimo!

What depth of nonsense and abomination! When something is displeasing to God, does it become pleasing to him by—indeed, it makes the evil worse!—having a pastor come who—indeed, it makes the evil worse!—receives ten rix-dollars for pronouncing it to be pleasing to God?

Let us continue with the wedding! In his Word, God recommends celibacy. Now there is a couple who want to marry. Since they call themselves Christians, this couple really ought to be informed about what Christianity is, but let that be as it may. The lovers turn to the pastor—and the pastor, of course, is bound by an oath on the New Testament, which recommends celibacy.

Unless he is a liar and perjurer, who in the basest manner earns shabby money, he must conduct himself accordingly. With human sympathy for this human situation of being in love, he can at most say to them, "Little children, I am the last person to whom you should turn; to turn to me on this occasion is really just as strange as if someone would go to the police chief to ask him how he should go about stealing. My duty is to use every means to hold you back; and at most I can say with the apostle (for it is not the Master's words): Well, if it finally is to be and you cannot control your lust, then see to coming together; 'It is better to marry than to burn.'[178] And I know very well that you will shudder when I speak this way about what you consider to be the most beautiful thing in life, but I must do my duty. And that is why I said that I was the last person to whom you should turn."

It is different in "Christendom." The pastor—of course, as long as there are some to hitch together. If the persons involved were to turn to a midwife, there they perhaps would never be so assured of being strengthened in the belief that what they are doing is well pleasing to God.

So they are married—that is, the "human being" gets his way, but getting his way is refined into also being worship, because God's name is brought into connection with it. They are married—by the pastor! Ah, that the pastor is present, that is the reassuring thing; this man, who is bound by an oath on the New Testament, and then for ten rix-dollars is the most agreeable person with whom one can have anything to do—this man guarantees that this act is true worship.

Christianly, it must be said that the very circumstance that a pastor takes part is the worst thing of all. If you want to marry, then it is preferable to be married by a blacksmith,[179] because then, if one may speak this way, it perhaps could still escape God's attention; but if a pastor takes part, it cannot possibly escape God's attention. Precisely this, that the pastor takes part, makes it as criminal as possible. Remember what was said to someone who called upon the gods in a storm: Just don't let the gods notice that you are present.[180] In the same way one must say: Just see to it that there is no pastor present. The others, the

XIV
261

blacksmith and the lovers, have not taken an oath on the New
Testament; therefore, if one may speak this way, it is more acceptable than when the pastor comes with his—holy presence.

*   *

*

All religion in which there is any truth, certainly Christianity,
aims at a person's total transformation and wants, through renunciation and self-denial, to wrest away from him all that, precisely
that, to which he immediately clings, in which he immediately
has his life. For that kind of religion, as he understands it, the
"human being" has no use. Therefore, as the story goes, from
generation to generation there lives a highly respected (how dubious!) social class: the pastors. Their trade is to turn the whole
relation around so that what people desire becomes the religion,
but in exchange for calling on God's name and paying a certain
sum to the pastors. The rest of society, if one looks at the matter
more closely, is egotistically interested in maintaining the concept of the pastor—otherwise the forgery cannot be carried out.

To become a Christian in the New Testament sense is such a
radical change that, from a purely human point of view, one
must say it is the heaviest sorrow for a family if one of its members
becomes a Christian. In such a Christian the God-relationship
becomes so preponderant that he is not "as if" lost; no, in a far
more decisive sense than by dying he is lost to everything that is
called family. It is of this that Christ continually speaks, both
when he says about himself that to be his disciple is to be his
mother, brother, sister, that in another sense he does not have a
mother, brothers, sisters,[181] and when he continually talks about
the collision of hating father and mother, one's own child,[182] etc.
To become a Christian in the New Testament sense is designed
to work the individual loose (as the dentist speaks of working the
gum loose) from the context to which he clings in immediate
passion, and which clings in immediate passion to him.

This kind of Christianity was never to the human being's liking, as little now, unconditionally as little now, as in the year 30,
but is deadly repugnant to him in his innermost heart. Therefore,
as the story goes, from generation to generation there lives a

highly respected social class whose trade is to make Christianity into the very opposite.

The Christianity of "the pastors" is this: with the help of religion (which unfortunately is intended to bring about the very opposite) to glue families together more and more egotistically and to arrange family festivities, beautiful, glorious family festivities—for example, Baptism and confirmation, which festivities, compared with, for example, picnics and other family delights, have their own special charm—that they are "also" religious.

"Woe to you," Christ says to those learned in the law (the scribes), "you have taken the key of knowledge; you yourselves do not enter in (namely, into the kingdom of heaven; see Matthew 23:13) and you forbid those who would enter in" (Luke 11:52).

This is the highly respected activity of the pastor, a livelihood that prevents people from entering into God's kingdom. In return, "the pastor" does his best by way of performances (for which producer Carstensen[183] has a decided talent in grand style), beautiful, glorious festivities with—just as a little wine tastes good in lemonade—a little religion added, something Carstensen cannot do . . . . . but perhaps he could be ordained.

That the Christian Family's Christian Upbringing of Children, So Highly Praised, Especially in Protestantism, Is, Christianly, Based on a Falsehood, a Downright Falsehood

Life in "Christendom" is ordinarily such that parents do not concern themselves at all with being Christians except in name and actually have no religion. The child's upbringing thus consists of a kind of training, of teaching a number of things, but on the other hand one does not become involved in providing the child with any religious, much less Christian, view of life or in speaking to it of God, much less according to the concepts and ideas of God characteristic of Christianity.

It is different in the families that ordinarily feel very self-important by being earnest Christians and who know how to talk much about Christian family life and about the importance of a Christian upbringing of children. Here there is chattering about bringing up the child in Christianity from earliest childhood, as it is called, and an importance is attached to it.

The truth, however, is that this (the pride of Protestantism!), this Christian family life's Christian upbringing of children is, Christianly, based on a falsehood, a downright falsehood.

And this is very easy to show.

In the first place. How the child's coming into existence is *Christianly* to be understood—about this the parents cannot, Christianly, speak truthfully to the child. The parents are sufficiently egotistical—and in the name of Christianity!—to bring the child up in the view that it is an extraordinary good deed on the part of the parents that the child exists, that it was especially pleasing to God, this masterwork on the part of the parents by which the child came into existence. In other words, in the name
of a Christian upbringing of children, Christianity is turned completely upside down and its life-view is made into the exact opposite of what it is. *Christianly* it is anything but the greatest good deed to give a child life (this is paganism). *Christianly* it is anything but pleasing to God that one engages in begetting children,

whereby one makes oneself attractive in his eyes (such an idea of God is paganism and even a lower form of paganism, or it is the kind of Judaism that Christianity would explicitly omit). *Christianly* it is the highest degree of egotism that because a man and a woman cannot control their lust another being must therefore sigh in this vale of tears and prison for perhaps seventy years and perhaps be eternally lost.

In the second place. That the world into which the parents are so good as to bring the child by their great good deed is, *Christianly*, a sinful, ungodly, wicked world; that misery, agony, and wretchedness await everyone who is born if he is among those who are saved; and that eternal damnation awaits those for whom it goes the opposite way in this world—this the parents cannot say to the child. For one thing, the child cannot understand it; the child is by nature too happy to be able to understand such things. For another, the parents for their own sakes cannot very well say this to the child. Every child in its naïveté is more or less a genius. Suppose that the child in its naïveté said to the parents, "But if it is that kind of world, and if that is what awaits me, then it certainly is not good that I came into this world." Bravo, my little friend, you hit the mark! It is an extremely calamitous situation for the parents! No, there can be no dabbling in Christianity!

In the third place. The parents cannot give the child the true *Christian* idea of God and are egotistically interested in not doing it. That to God this world is a lost world and everyone who is born is lost by being born, that what God wants—out of love—is that a person shall die to the world, and that, if God is so gracious as to turn his love toward him, that what God then does—out of love—is to torment him in all the agonies designed to take life away from him, because it is this that God wants—yet out of love—he wants to have the life of the one who is born, wants him transformed into one who has died, someone who lives as one who is dead—this the child cannot grasp, even if the child is told this, and the parents for egotistical reasons guard themselves well against saying it. So what do they do? In the name of "Christian" upbringing of children, they indiscriminately talk a lot of nonsense out of the barrel of paganism on a level with the above:

It is an extraordinary benefaction that you came into existence, it is a nice world you came into, and God is a nice fellow; just stay with him, he very likely will not fulfill all your wishes, but he certainly does help. A downright falsehood.

Consequently the very highly extolled Christian upbringing of children consists of filling the child full of—downright falsehood. The much extolled Christian family life is itself, Christianly, a falsehood; Christianly there is no family life, least of all in the sense that this is supposed to be the truest form of Christianity, and it can at most be indulgently tolerated. Itself based on a falsehood, Christian family life fills the child full of falsehood, then itself develops a taste for this kind of childish Christianity (which is not so strange, since it is paganism) and becomes sentimental at the thought that only as a child is one a true Christian.

And what is the result of this extolled Christian upbringing of children? The result is: either that the child fools around in the same blather throughout his whole life as an adult, father, and old man, or that there inevitably comes a moment in this life when the child will be tested in the most dreadful agony about whether God is a base wretch who lets a poor child believe that he (God) is altogether different from what he actually is, or his parents are liars.

Then when this agony has been surmounted, when he has understood that with regard to God everything is all right, that God, after all, has no part in what people hit upon to say about him, and that in any case the parents were well-meaning in their human love—then he still may need a long, long time and the most painful cure to get everything out of him that has been poured into him in the name of the Christian upbringing of children.

See, this is the result of the very highly extolled Christian upbringing of children; based upon a falsehood, it is a downright falsehood. But the pastors, they praise it. Well, that is understandable. One person is enough to give a whole city cholera, and 1000 perjurers are more than enough to give scabies to a whole society; so what is lived in the name of Christianity is, *Christianly,* a downright falsehood.

Just as a statistician who is competent in this area, when he is informed of the population of a large city, must be able to give the proportionate number of public prostitutes such a city uses; just as a statistician who is competent in this area, when he is informed of the size of an army, must be able to determine the proportionate number of physicians an army of that size needs in order to be well served—just so a statistician who deals in this sort of thing, when informed of the population in a country, must also be able to determine the proportionate number of perjurers (pastors) such a country needs to be completely protected, in the name of Christianity, against Christianity, or completely safe-guarded, so that, in the guise of having Christianity, it is able to live—a life of paganism, even tranquilized and refined by its being Christianity.

From this viewpoint, the truth of "the pastor's" importance for society is apparent, or how it all hangs together with his importance.

In its view of human existence, Christianity has as its presupposition that the human race is a lost race, that everyone who is born, by being born, by thus belonging to the race, is a lost soul. Christianity then wants to save every individual, but it by no means makes a secret of the fact that if there is to be earnestness herewith this life becomes unconditionally the very opposite of what is to a human being's taste and disposition, becomes sheer suffering, agony, wretchedness.

This, of course, is unacceptable to the human being; there perhaps is not one single person in millions who is sufficiently honest and honorable to accept this. Thus the task for "the human being," for "the human race," for "society," is with all its might to guard itself against Christianity, which must be regarded as humankind's mortal enemy.

But openly to break with Christianity—"No," says the human being, sagacious as he is, "no, that is injudicious; it is even uncircumspect and in no way adequately safe. Such an enormous power as Christianity is—if face to face with it one is so honest, becomes so much involved with it that one rejects it outright, then one runs the risk that at the end of the game this power will get its fingers on one in punishment for one's injudiciously becoming involved with it, because rejecting it honestly is nevertheless becoming involved with it in a way."

No, totally different means are needed here; here this sagacious fellow, "the human being," must be on his guard in a totally different way.

And now the comedy begins. For a population of such and such a size, says the statistician, such and such a large number of perjurers is needed. These are engaged. That what they proclaim, that what their lives express is not the Christianity of the New Testament, they themselves perceive very well. But, they say: This is our livelihood; for us it is a matter of keeping our wits about us and not letting ourselves be intimidated.

That was the perjurers. Society perhaps has some notion that not all is well with this oath on the New Testament. Yet, society thinks, naturally the task for us is to keep our wits about us and pretend that everything is all right. "We," says society, "we are only lay people; we cannot occupy ourselves with religion in this way; we calmly rest in confidence in the pastor, who, after all, is bound by oath on the New Testament."

Now the comedy is complete. All are Christians and everything is Christian, and the pastors—and everything express the very opposite of the Christianity of the New Testament. But it seems impossible to catch hold of the end of this very slyly complicated affair; it seems impossible to get behind appearances. How would it occur to anyone to doubt that Christianity exists? Indeed, that is just as impossible as for someone to get the idea that the pastor is a tradesman (after all, he is bound by oath to renounce this world; so the trade, *Geschäften*[184] [the business], therefore goes under the heading "renunciation of this world"), just as confusing as it would be if someone upon arriving says "good-bye." How would it occur to anyone on hearing the word *good-bye* to think that someone is arriving, and how would it occur to anyone—indeed, it did not occur to anyone, or if I had not said it myself, no one would have known whom I am talking about under the name *perjurers*, known that it is "the pastor," "the pastor" who is indeed: the truth-witness.

This is "the pastor's" importance for society, which from generation to generation uses a "necessary" number of perjurers in order, in the name of Christianity, to be completely protected against Christianity and, completely protected, to be able to live paganism, safeguarded, even refined, by its being Christianity.

There is, of course, not one honest person in the entire clergy. Yes, I am well aware that people who otherwise are not disinclined to agree with me in what I say nevertheless think that I should make exceptions, that there nevertheless are a few. No, thank you. To begin discussing that would mean to become embroiled in blather. The result probably would be that the entire profession and the whole society would admit that I am right in everything I say, since each one would naturally think that he is the exception. But there is quite literally no exception; there is quite literally not one honest pastor. Just have the police look a little more closely at this presumably honest person, this rare and extraordinary honest person—and the one who wants to see will soon see that he is not excepted either, because there is quite literally not a single honest one.

In the first place, he certainly cannot be so obtuse that he is unable to perceive that the way in which he is remunerated is, Christianly, altogether inadmissible, is diametrically opposite to Christ's decree;[185] also that his entire life as a synthesis of state employee and follower of Christ is, Christianly, altogether inadmissible, diametrically opposite to Christ's decree, an equivocation, so that one (even though for a reason entirely different from that for which it is used against criminals—since "the pastor" is not likely to run away; one need not be afraid of that) could insist that his uniform be in two colors in order to express: partly-partly, both-and.

In the second place, by being a member of the profession, he shares in the guilt of the entire profession. When an entire profession is corrupted, honesty can be expressed only by one's terminating membership in the profession; otherwise the only effect (supposing we for a moment would acknowledge his honesty) would be that the profession, by having him as member, has someone to refer to, which is precisely what it should not have. It is similar to the situation at a riot where the police have given people to understand that they must disperse—then no good citizen remains. To remain is the very sign that one is not a good citizen, because this is expressed by being unwilling to associate with those who remain despite the police ban. But let us just suppose for a moment that this man who remains is a highly respected, a good citizen; let us disregard that by remaining he invalidates this—by remaining he does great harm in another sense. The riot now has someone to refer to, and the result may be that the police cannot proceed as energetically as necessary simply because this "good citizen" is present.

In the third place, this presumably honest man may be so far from being an exception that he, only in a more refined way, is even worse than the others. Among the blind, as is known, the one-eyed man rules. If one aims to pass as something extraordinary at a cheap price, it is a sagacious scheme to enter into partnership with mediocrity, wretchedness, and dishonesty. By contrast, here one's little bit of honesty looks splendid—ah, yes, unless this sagacious use of elucidation is a far more profound kind of dishonesty than the outright dishonesty of the others.

No, quite literally, there is not one honest pastor. On the other hand, through "the pastor's" existence, the entire society is, Christianly, a baseness in a way that would not be the case if the "pastor" were not along.

From morning until night these thousands or millions of society express the life-view that is diametrically opposed to Christianity's, as opposed as living is to dying. This cannot be called villainous; it is human. But now comes the villainy: that there are 1000 men bound by oath on the New Testament who themselves, just like the rest of society, express the life-view that is diametrically opposite to Christianity's, but *also* reassure society that this is Christianity. Now the society is a villainy.

To be a Christian in the New Testament sense is, in an upward direction, just as different from being human as being human in a downward direction is different from being animal. Although he stands, suffering, in the middle of the actuality of this life, a

Christian in the New Testament sense is completely alienated from this life. He is, as it says in Scripture, also in the collects (which—scathing satire!—are still read aloud by the kind of pastors we now have, and before the kind of Christians now living)—a stranger and an alien[186]—just think of the late Bishop Mynster, for example, chanting: We are strangers and aliens in this world. A Christian in the New Testament sense is literally a stranger and alien: he feels himself a stranger, and everyone feels instinctively that he is a stranger to him.

Let me take an example. To live in such a way that one works more strenuously than any forced laborer (and in the process puts out money), then to become a nobody, to be laughed to scorn, etc.—to most people that way of living must seem to be a kind of lunacy; in any case, many will feel alienated and will not understand such a life. But the truth is that such a life relates itself to the Christianity of the New Testament. Now, imagine that someone who lives this way lives in a Christian society where there is a whole crew of teachers bound by an oath on the New Testament—then comes the villainy. These oath-bound teachers—indeed, most people do not feel alien to them and their way of life; they are familiar with this, indeed, they are all for it: three cheers for profit, for work in a job that pays in both one way and another. But these teachers are indeed pastors—consequently, as bound by oath on the New Testament, they certainly must know what Christianity is; consequently they provide the multitude with the guarantee that this profiteering and the like are true Christianity. When most people, taught in this way, feel alienated from the kind of life described and are inclined to regard it as madness (which still is not villainous but human), they think they are *Christianly* justified in judging that such a way of living is a kind of lunacy. This is villainous, and this villainy is due to—"the pastor's" existence.

At one time my conversation with the late Bishop Mynster went as follows. I told him that pastors could just as well stop preaching, that all their preaching had no effect at all because the congregation secretly thought: Well, that's his livelihood. Surprisingly enough, Bishop Mynster replied: There is something to that. I had not really expected this response. To be sure, it was said in a private conversation, but as a rule Bishop Mynster was accustomed to being circumspection itself on this point. With regard to that remark of mine, I have changed only to the extent having become clear that in one sense the pastor does produce an enormous effect, because his existence changes, Christianly, all society into a villainy.

In one way this interest is sufficiently great. What I write is circulated, in one sense almost more than I ask, although in another sense (of course without wanting to use even the least thing that could in the remotest way resemble the familiar tricks of politicians and hawkers and catchpenny writers) I must want the widest circulation. People read what I write; many read it with interest, with great interest—that I know.

But for many that is perhaps all it amounts to. Next Sunday one goes to church as usual. One says: What K. writes is basically true, and it is extremely interesting to read what he points out, that the whole official divine worship makes a fool of God, is blasphemy—but, when all is said and done, we are now accustomed to this; we cannot extricate ourselves from it; such powers we do not have. But one thing is sure, we shall read with enjoyment what he writes; one can really be very impatient to go and get a new number and learn more about this undeniably enormously interesting criminal case.

Yet the interest is not really gratifying but instead is saddening, is one more sorrowful demonstration that Christianity not only does not exist but that people in our day are not even in what I would call the condition of religion but are strangers to, unfamiliar with, the kind of passion that every religion must require, without which one cannot have any religion at all, least of all Christianity.

Allow me to use an illustration for what I say. In one sense I use it very reluctantly, because I do not like to speak of such things. Yet I choose and use it advisedly; yes, I consider it indefensible not to use it, since the seriousness of the matter demands that everything be used to make whoever needs it really nauseated by his condition, really disgusted with himself.

XIV
274

There is a man whose wife is unfaithful to him, but he does not know it. Then one of his friends enlightens him about it—a dubious act of friendship, many will perhaps say. The man replies: It is with intense interest that I have listened to you speak; I admire the keenness with which you have known how to track down such carefully concealed unfaithfulness, of which I have really had no inkling. But that I should therefore, now that I know it is so, divorce her—no, that I cannot decide to do. After all, I am accustomed to this domestic routine; I cannot do without it. Moreover, she has money; I cannot do without that either. On the other hand, I do not deny that I will listen with the most intense interest to what you can tell me further about this affair, because—I do not say this to pay you a compliment—but because it is extremely interesting.

There is something frightful about having a sense for the interesting in that way. Similarly, there is also something frightful in this: to be aware in the form of interesting information that one's worship is blasphemy and then to continue in it because, after all, one is accustomed to it. Basically this is not so much to hold God in contempt as to hold oneself in contempt. It is considered contemptible to pass for a husband and yet not be that—something that through no fault of one's own can be occasioned by a wife's unfaithfulness; it is considered pitiable to be willing to put up with this situation, to remain in it. But for a person to have religion in such a way (something that cannot possibly happen to anyone without its being his own fault) that he himself knows that his worship is blasphemy, and yet still be willing to continue to let it stand that he has the religion—this is to hold oneself most profoundly in contempt.

Oh, there is still something even more sorrowful than what people are inclined to consider the most sorrowful thing that can happen to a person, namely, to lose one's mind; there is something that is more sorrowful! There is an apathy about the obligation to have strength of character, a stupidity of characterlessness that is more dreadful than stupidity of mind, perhaps more incurable. And perhaps the most sorrowful thing that can be said about a person is: He cannot be lifted up, his own knowledge cannot lift him up. Like the child who lets his kite go skyward, he lets his knowledge ascend; he finds it interesting, enormously interesting, to watch it, to follow it with his eyes but—it does not lift him up; he remains in the mud, more and more desperately craving the interesting.

Therefore, whoever you are, if this in any way is the case with you; shame on you, shame on you, shame on you!

THE CHANGELESSNESS OF GOD

A DISCOURSE

By S. Kierkegaard

DEDICATED TO THE MEMORY OF

MY LATE FATHER

MICHAEL PEDERSEN KIERKEGAARD[187]

FORMERLY A CLOTHING MERCHANT HERE IN THE CITY

AUGUST 1855

This discourse was delivered in the Citadel Church on May 18, 1851. The text is the first one I have used;[188] later it was used on several occasions;[189] now I return to it again.[190]

May 5, 1854   S. K.

You Changeless One, whom nothing changes! You who are changeless in love, who just for our own good do not let yourself change—would that we also might will our own well-being, let ourselves be brought up, in unconditional obedience, by your changelessness to find rest and to rest in your changelessness! You are not like a human being. If he is to maintain a mere measure of changelessness, he must not have too much that can move him and must not let himself be moved too much. But everything moves you, and in infinite love. Even what we human beings call a trifle and unmoved pass by, the sparrow's need, that moves you; what we so often scarcely pay attention to, a human sigh, that moves you, Infinite Love. But nothing changes you, you Changeless One! O you who in infinite love let yourself be moved, may this our prayer also move you to bless it so that the prayer may change the one who is praying into conformity with your changeless will, you Changeless One!

JAMES 1:17–21

Every good gift and every perfect gift is from above and comes down from the Father of lights, with whom there is no change or shadow of variation. According to his own counsel, he brought us forth by the word of truth, that we should be a first fruit of his creation. Therefore, my beloved brethren, let every
person be quick to hear, slow to speak, slow to anger, because a person's anger does not work what is righteous before God. Therefore put away all filthiness and all remnants of wickedness and receive with

meekness the word that is implanted in you and that

is powerful for making your souls blessed.

My listener, you have heard the text read. How natural now to think of the opposite: the temporal, the changefulness of earthly things, and the changefulness of human beings! How depressing, how exhausting, that all is corruptibility, that human beings are changefulness, you, my listener, and I! How sorrowful that so often the change is for the worse! What poor human consolation, but yet a consolation, that there is yet one more change in the changeful: that it has an end!

Yet if we were to speak this way, especially in this spirit of gloom, thus not in the way corruptibility and "human instability" are earnestly discussed, we not only would not stick to the text, no, we would abandon it, indeed we would change it. The text speaks about the opposite, about the changelessness of God. The text is sheer joy and gladness; as from the mountain peaks, where silence lives, even so the apostle's words are lifted above all the changefulness of earthly life; he speaks of the changelessness of God, not about anything else. About a "Father of lights," who lives up there where there is no variation, not even the shadow of it. About "good and perfect gifts" that come down from above, from this Father who, as the Father "of lights" or the light's Father, perpetually knows how to make sure that what comes from him is truly good and perfect, and as *Father* wants nothing else, thinks of nothing else than, unchanged, to send good and perfect gifts. Therefore, my beloved brethren, let everyone be "quick to hear," that is, not listen to fast and loose talk, but listen upward, because from *above* there is always only good news; "slow to speak," since the talk we human beings can offer, especially about the here and now and in all haste, most often can only make the good and perfect gifts less good and perfect; "slow to anger," lest when the gifts do not seem to be good and perfect we become angry and by our own guilt cause to turn into corruption what was good and perfect and intended for our good—this is what a man's anger can do, and "a man's anger does not work the righteousness of God." "Therefore put

XIV
285

away all filthiness and remnants of wickedness"—just as one cleans and decorates one's house and sits all dressed up, festively awaiting the visit: so that in this way we may worthily receive the good and perfect gifts. "And receive with meekness the Word that is implanted in you and that is powerful for making your souls blessed!" With meekness! Truly, if it were not the apostle who was speaking, and if we did not swiftly comply with the command "to be slow to speak, slow to anger," we might well say: That was a strange way to talk. Are we then such fools that we need to be admonished to meekness in relation to him who only wants our good? Indeed, using the word *meekness* in this way seems to mock us. See, if someone were to strike me unjustly and a bystander said admonishingly: Put up with it meekly—this is straight talk. But imagine the friendliest of beings, love itself. He has selected a gift intended for me, and the gift is good and perfect, yes, as love itself; he comes and wants to present me with this gift—then a bystander says admonishingly to me: Now let me see that you put up with this meekly. And yet that is the way we human beings are. A pagan, and just a human being, that simple wise man of old, laments having often experienced that when he wanted to take one or another fatuity away from someone in order to impart to him a better knowledge, that is, to do him good, the other person could become so enraged that he, as the simple one jestingly says in earnest, wanted to bite him.[191]

Alas, what has God not had to experience these 6000 years,[192] what does he not experience every day from morning until night with every single one of these millions of human beings; we sometimes become most angry when he wants to do us the most good. Indeed, if we human beings truly knew our own good and in the deepest sense truly wanted our own good, then no admonishing to meekness would be needed about this. But in our relationship to God we human beings (and who has not personally experienced this!) are still like children. This is why the admonition about meekness with regard to receiving the good and the perfect is necessary—so convinced is the apostle that only good and perfect gifts come down from him, the eternally Changeless One.

What different points of view! The merely human point of view (as is indeed apparent in paganism) speaks less about God and has a predominant tendency to want to speak sorrowfully only about the changefulness of human things. The apostle wants to speak only about the changelessness of God. So it is with the apostle. For him the thought of the changelessness of God is simply and solely sheer consolation, peace, joy, blessedness. And this is indeed eternally true. But let us not forget that for the apostle its being so is due to the apostle's being the apostle, that he had already long since submitted in unconditional obedience to God's changelessness, that he was not standing at the beginning but rather at the end of the way, the hard[193] but also the good way, which he, renouncing everything, had chosen, and, unchanged, followed without looking back,[194] at a more and more rapid pace, hastening toward eternity. We, however, who are still only beginners under instruction, we must also see the changelessness of God from another side; and if we forget this, we easily run into the danger of taking the apostle's exaltation in vain.

So, then, we shall speak, if possible both in terror and for reassurance, *about you, you Changeless One, or about your changelessness.*

God is changeless. Omnipotent, he created this visible world— and made himself invisible.[195] He put on the visible world as a garment; he changes it as one changes a garment—himself unchanged.[196] So it is in the sensate world. In the world of events, he is everywhere present at every moment. In a truer sense than the most watchful human justice is said to be everywhere, he, never seen by any mortal being, is omnipresent, everywhere present, at the least and at the greatest, at what can only figuratively be called an event and at what is the unique event, when a sparrow dies[197] and when the Savior of the human race is born. At every moment he holds all actuality as possibility in his omnipotent hand, at every moment has everything in readiness, changes everything in an instant, the opinions of people, judgments, human loftiness and lowliness[198]; he changes everything—himself unchanged. When to all appearances everything

XIV
286

is unchangingness (it is only in appearances that the external is for a certain time unchanged; it is always being changed), in the upheaval of everything, he remains just as unchanged; no variation touches him, not even the shadow of variation; in unchanged clarity, he, the Father of lights, is eternally unchanged. In unchanged clarity—indeed, that is precisely why he is unchanged, because he is pure clarity, a clarity that has no darkness in it,[199] and to which no darkness can come close. This is not the way it is with us human beings. We are not clarity in this way, and that is why we are changeful—at times something becomes clearer in us, and at times darker, and we are changed. Now change takes place around us, and the shadow of variation slides changingly over us; now the changing light from the surrounding world falls upon us, while we ourselves in all this are in turn changed within ourselves. But God is changeless.

XIV
287

This thought is *terrifying, sheer fear and trembling.* Ordinarily this is perhaps less emphasized. One complains about the changefulness of humanity, about the changefulness of everything temporal, but God is changeless; that is the consolation, sheer consolation, so says even light-mindedness. Yes, indeed, God is changeless.

But first and foremost, are you also on good terms with God, are you considering this quite earnestly, are you honestly trying to understand—and this is God's eternal changeless will for you as for every human being, that one should strive for this—are you honestly striving to understand what God's will for you can be? Or do you go on living in such a way that this does not occur to you? How terrible, then, that he is the eternally Changeless One! Yet you must at some time, sooner or later, come in conflict with this changeless will, this changeless will that wanted you to consider this because it wanted your good, this changeless will that must crush you if you in any other way come into conflict with it.

In the second place, you who are still on good terms with God, are you indeed on good terms with him; is your will, is it, and unconditionally, his will; are your wishes, every wish of yours, his command, your thoughts, the first and the last, his thoughts—if not, how terrible that God is changeless, eternally,

eternally changeless! How terrible just to disagree with a human being! Yet perhaps you are the stronger and say about the other: Yes, well, he will change all right. But now suppose that he is the stronger; yet you may think you are able to stick it out longer. But now suppose that it is a whole contemporary generation; yet you perhaps say: Seventy years is not eternity. But the eternally Changeless One—suppose you are in disagreement with him—it is indeed an eternity: terrible!

Imagine a traveler; he is brought to a stop at the foot of an enormous, an impassable mountain. It is this that he . . . . . no, he shall not cross, but it is this that he wants to cross, because his wishes, his longings, his cravings—his soul (which has an easier kind of transportation) is already over on the other side, and what is lacking is only that he follow after. Imagine that he became seventy years old, but the mountain stands unchanged, impassable. Let him live yet again seventy years, but the mountain stands unchanged in his way, unchanged, impassable. During all this he perhaps has been changed; he dies to his longings, his wishes, his cravings; he scarcely recognizes himself any longer. Now a new generation finds him sitting, changed, at the foot of the mountain, which stands unchanged, impassable. Suppose it was 1000 years ago. He, the changed, has long since been dead; there is only a legend about him, it is the only thing that remains—yes, and then the mountain, which stands unchanged, impassable. And now the eternally Changeless One, for whom 1000 years are as a day.[200] Alas, even this says too much; they are for him as an instant, indeed, for him they actually are as if they were not—if you want even in the remotest manner to go another way than he wants you to go: terrible!

True enough, if your will, if my will, if the will of these thousands upon thousands is not wholly in agreement with God's will, things nevertheless go on the best they can out there in the busyness of the so-called real world. God does not actually show any sign of noticing. It is more likely that if a righteous person (if there were such a one!) looked at this world, a world that Scripture says lies in the power of evil,[201] he is bound to become discouraged over God's not showing any sign of noticing. But do you therefore think that God has changed, or is his not showing

XIV
288

any signs of noticing the lesser terror when it nevertheless is certain that he is eternally changeless? I do not think so. But consider this, and then tell which is the more terrible: either this, the infinitely strong one who, weary of allowing himself to be mocked, rises up in his power and crushes the rebels—this is terrible, and this is indeed how it is pictured when it is told that God does not let himself be mocked[202] and reference is made to the times when his punishment devastated the generation. But is this actually the most terrible? Or is this not even more terrible: the infinitely strong one who—eternally changeless!—remains absolutely still and looks, without a change of countenance, almost as if he did not exist, while nevertheless, so the righteous person certainly must lament, falsehood is progressing, has the power, violence and wrong are victorious, and in such a way that even a better person is tempted to think that he has to use a little of the same means if there is to be any hope of accomplishing something for the good; so it seems as if he is mocked, he the infinitely strong one, the eternally Changeless One, who lets himself be neither mocked nor changed—is this not the most terrible?

Indeed, why do you think he is so quiet? Because he is serenely aware that he is eternally changeless. Someone who was not eternally sure of himself, sure that he is the changeless, could not remain quiet in that way; he would rise up in his power; but only the eternally Changeless One can be that quiet. He takes his time, and that he can of course do. He has eternity, and eternally he is changeless. He takes his time, he does it deliberately. Then comes the accounting of eternity, in which nothing is forgotten, not one single idle word that was spoken,[203] and eternally he is changeless. That he takes time in this way can, however, also be mercy, time for turning around and reformation. But how terrible if this time is not used that way, because then the foolishness and light-mindedness in us must instead wish that he would be promptly on hand with the punishment rather than that he takes time in this way, ignores it and yet is eternally changeless.

Ask a pedagogue (in the relation to God we are all indeed more or less children!), ask the person who has been involved with people who have gone astray (and everyone of us has gone astray at least once, goes astray for a longer or shorter time, with longer or shorter intervals), and you will hear him verify that it is a great help to light-mindedness, or rather in the prevention of light-mindedness (and who dares claim to be entirely free of light-mindedness!), to have, if possible, the suffering of the punishment follow the transgression immediately, so that the memory of the light-minded one becomes accustomed to remembering the punishment simultaneously with the guilt.

Yes, if transgression and punishment were related to each other in such a way that if one, just as with a double-barreled gun, pressed one spring and at the instant one snatched the forbidden pleasure or committed the transgression, at that very same instant the punishment would come—I think that light-mindedness would then be on guard. But the longer the time between the guilt and the punishment (which truly understood expresses the criterion for the seriousness of the case), the more tempting it is to light-mindedness, as if the whole thing could perhaps be forgotten, or justice itself could perhaps change and have completely different concepts at that time, or as if at least it would be so long since it happened that it would be impossible to present the case unchanged. Then light-mindedness changes, and not for the better. Then light-mindedness becomes secure, and when light-mindedness has become secure it becomes bolder. And so it goes year after year—the punishment fails to come and forgetfulness supervenes, and again punishment fails to come, but new transgression does not fail to come, and the old transgression has now become more malignant. Then it is over; then death ends everything—and to all this (it was only light-mindedness!) an eternally changeless one was witness, and it is with him you will have to make an accounting. At the moment, when temporality's pointer, the minute hand, pointed to seventy years[204] and the man died, during that time eternity's pointer had scarcely moved a trifle—to that degree everything is present for eternity and for him, the Changeless One!

Therefore, whoever you are, remember—something I say to myself—that for God nothing is significant and nothing is insignificant, that in one sense for him the significant is insignificant, and in another sense for him even the least insignificance is

XIV
290

something infinitely significant. If, then, your will is not in accord with his, consider this: you will never escape him. Thank
him if he through gentleness or severity teaches you to bring
your will into accord with his—how frightful it is if he does not
show any sign of noticing anything, how frightful it is if a person
goes so far as almost to boast that God either does not exist or that
he has changed, or even just that he is too great to notice what
we call trivialities, inasmuch as he both exists and he is eternally
changeless, and his infinite greatness is precisely that he sees even
the least little thing, remembers even the least little thing, yes,
and if you do not will as he wills, he remembers it unchanged for
an eternity!

Consequently, for us light-minded and unstable human beings
there is sheer fear and trembling in this thought of God's changelessness. Oh, do consider this well, whether he shows any sign of
noticing anything or not—he is eternally changeless! He is eternally changeless, do consider this well if you have, as they say, an
account to settle with him—he is changeless. Perhaps you have
promised him something, have committed yourself by a holy
promise . . . . . but in the course of time you have changed. Now
you think about God less often (have you perhaps as an older
person found more important things to think about?), or perhaps
you think differently about God, that he does not bother about
the trivialities of your life, that such faith is childishness. In any
case, you have in a way forgotten what you promised him, then
after that have forgotten that you promised it to him, and then
finally have forgotten, forgotten—yes, forgotten that he forgets
nothing, he the eternally Changeless One, that it is simply the
reverse childishness of old age to think that something is insignificant for God and that God forgets something, he the eternally
Changeless One!

In human relationships there is frequent complaint about
changefulness; one person complains that the other one has
changed. But even in human relationships someone's unchangingness can at times be a torment. Perhaps someone has told
another person about himself. Perhaps he talked, excusably,
somewhat childishly. But perhaps the matter was actually more
serious—the vain and foolish heart was tempted to speak in high

tones of its enthusiasm, of its emotional stability, of its will in this world. The other one listened to it calmly, did not smile or interrupt him; he let him talk, he listened silently, only promised, as he was asked to do, not to forget what was said. Time passed, and the first person had long since forgotten all this, but the other one had not forgotten. Indeed, let us imagine something even stranger. He had let himself be moved by the thoughts that the first person in an emotional moment had expressed and, alas, had handed over, as it were; by honest effort he had shaped his life in accord with these thoughts—what torment in the unchangingness of his memory, he who all too clearly manifested that he remembered to the last detail what was said at that moment!

And now the eternal Changeless One—and this human heart! Ah, this human heart, what do you not hide in your secret inclosures, unknown to others—that would not be the worst—but at times almost unknown to the person himself! It is almost, as soon as a person is a few years old, it is almost like a grave, this human heart! There lie buried, buried in forgetfulness, the promises, the intentions, the resolutions, complete plans and fragments of plans, and God knows what—yes, that is how we human beings talk, for we seldom think about what we say; we say: There lies God knows what. And this we say half light-mindedly, half in weariness of life—and then it is so frightfully true that God knows what. He knows down to the least detail what you have forgotten, knows what has changed in your remembering; he knows it unchanged. He does not recollect it as if it were something in the past; no, he knows it as if it were today, and he knows if something with regard to these wishes, intentions, and resolutions was said, as it were, to him—and he is eternally unchanged and eternally changeless. If another person's memory may become a burden—well, it is still never completely trustworthy, and in any case it cannot last an eternity. I will still become free from this other person and his memory, but an Omniscient One, and an eternally changeless memory from which you cannot escape, least of all in eternity—frightful! No, eternally changeless, everything is for him eternally present, eternally equally present, no shifting shadow either of morning or evening, of youth or of old age, of forgetfulness or of excuse, no shifting shadow shifts him—no, for him there is no shadow. If we are, as it is said, shadows, he is eternal clarity in his eternal changelessness; if we are shadows that hasten away—my soul, take heed, because whether you will or not, you are hastening to eternity, to him, and he is eternal clarity! Therefore he does not only hold an accounting, he is the accounting. It is said that we human beings must make an accounting, as if it were a long time away, and then perhaps an overwhelming mass of prolixities in order to get the accounting arranged. O my soul, it is being done every moment, because his unchanging clarity is the accounting, completely ready down to the least detail and kept by him, the eternal Changeless One, who has forgotten nothing of what I have forgotten; neither does he do as I do, remember something different from what it actually was.

Thus there is sheer fear and trembling in this thought about the changelessness of God. It is almost as if it were far, far beyond human powers to have to be involved with a changelessness such as that; indeed, it seems as if this thought must plunge a person into anxiety and unrest to the point of despair.

But then it is also the case *that there is reassurance and blessedness in this thought.* It is really so that when you, weary from all this human, all this temporal and earthly changefulness and alteration, weary of your own instability, could wish for a place where you could rest your weary head, your weary thoughts, your weary mind, in order to rest, to have a good rest—ah, in God's changelessness there is rest! If for that reason you allow his changelessness to serve you as he wills, for your good, your eternal good, if you allow yourself to be brought up so that your self-will (and this, even more than external factors, accounts for changefulness) expires, the sooner the better—it does not help you; you must be either with the good or with the evil. Imagine the futility of wanting to be at odds with an eternal changelessness; be like the child when it really profoundly senses that it is in the position of being face-to-face with a will where only one thing helps, to obey. When you allow yourself to be brought up by his changelessness so that you renounce instability and changefulness and caprice and willfulness—then you rest ever more blessedly in this changelessness of God. That the thought of

God's changelessness is blessed, indeed, who doubts that; just see to it that you become like that so that you can blessedly rest in this changelessness! Ah, such a person speaks as someone who has a happy home: My home is eternally safeguarded; I rest in God's changelessness. No one but you yourself can disturb this rest. If you could become completely obedient in unchanged obedience, you would at every moment freely rest in God with the same necessity as a heavy body sinks to the earth, or with the same necessity as something that is light rises toward heaven. XIV 293

Then let everything else change, as it does. If the stage of your activity is large, you will experience the changefulness of everything on a larger scale; but on a small stage, the smallest, you will still experience the same thing, perhaps just as painfully. You will experience how people change, how you yourself change; at times it will also seem as if God changed, which is part of the upbringing. On that subject, the changefulness of everything, an older person will be better able to speak than I, whereas what I could say perhaps could seem to the very young to be something new. We shall not, however, develop this further but leave the complexity of life to unfold for each individual as it is defined for him so that he can come to experience what all others before him have experienced. At times the change will be such that you will be reminded of the saying: Change is pleasing[205]—yes, unspeakably! There will also come times when you will personally invent a saying that the language has concealed, and you say: Change is not pleasing—how could I say that change is pleasing? When that happens, you will be especially prompted to seek him (something you will surely not forget in the first case either), the Changeless One.

My listener, this hour is now soon over, and the discourse. If you yourself do not want it otherwise, this hour will soon also be forgotten, and the discourse. And if you yourself want it otherwise, this thought about the changelessness of God will also be soon forgotten in changefulness. Yet this fault is not due to him, the Changeless One! But if you do not make yourself guilty of forgetting it, then you will be sustained in this thought for your lifetime, for an eternity.

Imagine a solitary in the desert; almost scorched by the heat of the sun, dying of thirst, he finds a spring. Ah, delicious coolness! Now I am provided for, God be praised, he says—and yet he found only a spring. How must the one speak who found God!—and yet he also must say, "God be praised," I found God!—now I am, God be praised, provided for. Your faithful coolness, O beloved spring, is not subject to change. In the cold of winter, if it were to reach here, you do not become colder but keep exactly the same coolness; the water of a spring does not freeze! In the noonday heat of summer you keep exactly your unchanged coolness; the water of a spring does not become tepid! There is nothing false in what he says (he who in my opinion did not choose an unrewarding subject for a eulogy, a spring, something everyone better understands the better he knows what it means: the desert and solitude); there is no false exaggeration in his eulogy. His life, however, took a turn completely different from what he had thought. At one time he strayed away, was pulled out into the wide world. Many years after, he came back. His first thought was the spring—it was not there, it had dried up. For a moment he stood silent in sorrow; then he collected himself and said: No, I will not take back a word of what I said in your praise, it was all truth. And if I praised your delicious coolness while you were, O beloved spring, then let me also praise it now when you have vanished so that it may be true that there is unchangingness in a human breast. Nor can I say that you deceived me; no, if I had found you, I am convinced that your coolness would be unchanged—and more you had not promised.

But you, O God, you Changeless One, you, unchanged, are always to be found and are always to be found unchanged. No one, either in life or in death, travels so far away that you are not to be found, that you are not there; you are indeed everywhere—this is not the way springs are on this earth, springs are only in special places. Moreover—what overwhelming security!—you do not remain on the spot like a spring; you travel along. No one strays so far away that he cannot find his way back to you, you who are not only like a spring that lets itself be found—what a poor description of your being!—you who are

XIV
294

like a spring that even searches for the thirsting, the straying, something unheard of about any spring. Thus are you unchanged and everywhere to be found. And whenever a person comes to you, at whatever age, at whatever time of day, in whatever condition—if he comes honestly, he will always find (like the spring's unchanged coolness) your love just as warm, you Changeless One! Amen.[206]

THE MOMENT

No. 8–9

THE MOMENT

No. 8

CONTENTS

September 11, 1855   S. KIERKEGAARD

"Whoever receives a prophet because he is a prophet will receive a prophet's reward, and whoever receives a righteous person because he is a righteous person will receive a righteous person's reward. And whoever gives to one of these lowly ones just a cup of cold water to drink because he is a follower, truly, I say to you, he will not lose his reward," says our Lord Jesus Christ (Matthew 10:41–42).

Truly, more than both royal and imperial openhandedness, only the divine is this openhanded!

Yet look a little more closely. The discourse here is about what one does for a contemporary, what one as a contemporary does for the prophet, for the follower. "Whoever gives to one of these lowly ones just a cup of cold water"—yes, but the emphasis cannot be on that. No! The emphasis is on: because he is a follower, a prophet. Consequently, if a contemporary were to say, "I certainly am a long way from regarding the person as a prophet, a follower; I am, however, very willing to offer him a cup of wine"; or if someone who perhaps secretly regarded this person as a follower, a prophet, but was too cowardly to have the courage to acknowledge his conviction, or despicably utilized the contemporary disregard of the prophet, the follower, to make himself look better than others by showing honesty to the follower, the prophet, yet at a cheaper price, if he said, "I certainly do not regard this person as a prophet, but he is nevertheless a remarkable man, and it will give me great pleasure to offer him a cup of wine"—in both cases, the reply will be: No, my good fellow—let him just keep his cup of wine; that is not what Scripture is speaking about.

XIV
298

*This article is from 1853, except that here and there I have inserted a few lines or changed a word; but the article itself is from 1853. My judgment about its conclusion the reader will learn from my article in *Fædrelandet:* "For the new edition of *Practice in Christianity.*"[207]

It speaks about giving him only a cup of water—but *because* he is a follower, a prophet, thus fully and totally in acknowledgment of him for what he truly is. What Christ is pointing to is: acknowledgment of the follower, the prophet, and in contemporaneity. Whether the acknowledgment is expressed by giving him a glass of cold water or by giving him a kingdom is utterly unimportant; it depends on contemporaneity's acknowledging "because." So it is not as the money-minded pastors for the sake of the pastoral dollar fool people into thinking that, since ten rix-dollars is more than a glass of cold water, it makes the one who gives ten rix-dollars to a prophet, a follower—but not *because* he is a prophet, a follower—far more perfect than the one who gives him a glass of cold water *because* he is a prophet, a follower. No, that the gift is *because*, consequently expressing that one acknowledges the man for what he truly is, that is what it depends upon.

And this is not easy in contemporaneity. For this it presumably is not required to be a prophet oneself, a follower, but nevertheless to have two-thirds of a follower's, a prophet's character (something, incidentally, do not forget, everyone can have if he honestly wants it). In contemporaneity this cup of water or, more correctly, this "because" can come to be costly for one. In other words, in contemporaneity or in one's lifetime, the prophet, the follower, is scorned, laughed at, hated, cursed, detested, persecuted in every way—and you can be sure that at least a punishment is imposed on offering him a cup of water "because he is a follower," the punishment the New Testament speaks about, of being excluded from the synagogue,[208] a punishment imposed upon being involved with Christ in contemporaneity, something that the preacher-lie naturally "tones down, veils, suppresses, omits";[209] on the other hand it languishes, with hiccoughing, belching, and agonized sobbing expresses its unspeakable longing to have been contemporary with Christ in order—to be excluded from the synagogue, which is naturally the deepest and most fervent longing of livelihood-men and titled persons.

Consequently the one who gives a follower only a cup of cold water because he is a follower will by no means lose his reward; he will receive a prophet's reward—and on the other hand the one who, when the prophet, the follower, is dead, builds his tomb and says, "If . . . . . "²¹⁰—he is, according to Jesus Christ's judgment, a hypocrite; his guilt is blood-guilt.

He is a hypocrite. Indeed, *partly* because contemporary with the one who builds the tomb of the dead prophet there perhaps again lives a prophet—whom he together with others persecutes, or if there is not a prophet, there is perhaps a righteous person who is suffering for the truth—whom the one who builds the tomb of the dead prophet persecutes just as the others are doing; *partly* because, if no contemporary such as that is living, it is your task, in order to avoid hypocrisy, to make present the life of the departed glorious one in such a way that you thereby would come to suffer as you would have suffered in contemporaneity if you had acknowledged a prophet to be a prophet.

Oh, if you are in any way eternally concerned for your soul, are thinking with fear and trembling about judgment and eternity, or, on the other hand, if you in any way are uplifted and desire to be even more so by the thought of what it is to be a human being, and that you, too, are a human being and belong to the same race as the glorious ones, the authentic ones, whose worth therefore is not known by the inauthentic, by profit, stars, titles, but by the authentic, by poverty, abasement, mistreatment, persecution, suffering—if this is the case, then pay attention to this matter of contemporaneity so that either, if in contemporaneity there lives such a person who is suffering for the truth, you suffer for acknowledging him for what he is, or, if there is no such contemporary, you make present the life of the departed glorious one in such a way that you come to suffer as you would have suffered in contemporaneity by acknowledging him for what he is. Pay sharp attention to this matter of contemporaneity, because the crucial point is not the fuss you make over a dead person, no, but what you do in contemporaneity or that you make the past so present that you come to suffer as if you were contemporary with it—this decides what kind of a person you are. But to make a fuss over a dead person—well, that of course also shows what kind of a person you are—namely, that according to Christ you are a hypocrite, indeed, a murderer, more detestable to the dead person than those who put him to death.

XIV
300

Pay sharp attention to this matter of contemporaneity! To that end do not fail to become acquainted, if you have not already done so, with a book I published in 1850, *Practice in Christianity*, since the emphasis there is particularly on this. The book, as it is put out into the world, is in all its contentiousness a quiet book. I shall accurately describe to you how it relates to the established order, to the official proclamation of Christianity, or to the official representative for the proclamation of official Christianity, Bishop Mynster's proclamation of Christianity. If Bishop Mynster directly says of it: This is truly Christianity, this is how I myself secretly understand Christianity—then the book makes clear Bishop Mynster's proclamation of Christianity—to me an infinitely precious thought! But if Bishop Mynster even so much as blinks an eye at this book, to say nothing of flying into a temper against it—then read it, and you will perceive that it illuminates Bishop Mynster's whole proclamation of Christianity in such a way that it shows itself to be an extraordinarily, extraordinarily, extraordinarily artistic and masterly—optical illusion. But that is not the fault of the book. And in any case this does not involve you. However, if you wish it, the book can help you to become aware of this matter of contemporaneity.

And this is the decisive point! This thought is for me my life's thought. I also dare truthfully say that I have had the honor to suffer in order to set forth this thought. Therefore I die joyful, infinitely grateful to Governance that it was granted me to become aware of this thought and to draw attention to it in this way. Not that I have invented it, God forbid that I become guilty of such presumption—no, it is an old invention, it is the New Testament's. However, it was granted to me, in suffering, to bring this thought once again into recollection, this thought that, like rat poison for rats, is poison for "assistant professors,"* those vermin who actually have demolished Christianity, the assistant

*See *Fear and Trembling*, where for the first time I took aim at assistant professors, those blackguards about whom it also says that (page 65) "no manacled robber of churches is so despicable a criminal as the one who plunders holiness in this way, and Judas, who sold his Lord for thirty pieces of silver, is not more contemptible than someone who peddles greatness in this way."[211]

professors, those noble men who build the tombs of the prophets, **objectively** recite their teachings, turn the suffering and death of the glorious ones into a profit—most likely objectively and most likely proud of the objective, since the subjective is sickliness, affectation—but keep themselves, naturally with the aid of the much-praised objectivity, on the outside, far away from everything that even in the remotest manner could resemble suffering like the glorious ones, or suffering as one would inevitably suffer in contemporaneity if one had acknowledged the glorious ones for what they were.

Contemporaneity is the decisive point. Imagine a truth-witness, that is, one of the derivative prototypes. For a long time he endures all kinds of mistreatment and persecution; finally he is put to death. The manner of his death is cruelly determined: to be burned alive. With deliberate cruelty it is more specifically stipulated: to be broiled on a grill over a slow fire.[212]

Imagine this! Earnestness and Christianity is that you make this present in such a way that you come to suffer as you would have come to suffer if in contemporaneity you had acknowledged the man for what he is.

This is earnestness and Christianity. Bestiality, to which the pastors do not object, is of course something else. Thus one does not care a fig for the truth-witness together with all his sufferings—and yet, no, this is still not actually bestiality. No, one says: We will not forget this glorious one. Therefore we decide that December 17, which was the day of his death, shall be celebrated in his memory. And in order to maintain the impression of his life, and in order that our lives, too, can acquire "some likeness" to his, as "a striving," be it solemnly ordained that on that day every household shall eat a broiled fish, which is, please note—mind the point!—broiled on a grill; and the pastor shall have the choicest part. That is, the worship of God by suffering for truth, yes, by suffering death, is changed into the worship of God by eating and drinking, and the pastor gets the best piece—as the true (official) Christianity, in which the pastor, like the broiled fish in its way, in a similar manner, for example, by a splendid discourse, contributes to enhance the day's festivity, and thereby guarantees an increasing salary over the years, perhaps makes a career, perhaps one so brilliant that he is dressed in silk and velvet[213] and decorated with stars and ribbons.

This is only an example. Indeed, I admit that none of the derived prototypes unconditionally places everyone under obligation—but then not to bestiality either. If the derived prototypes do not unconditionally place unconditionally everyone under obligation, *the prototype*, Jesus Christ, however, does unconditionally place, and unconditionally everyone, under obligation. If there is no one in your time who suffers for truth so that you, too, would come to suffer if you acknowledged him for what he in truth is—and this is Christianly indeed your duty, is Christianly the requirement—then you must make *the prototype* present in such a way that you come to suffer as if you in contemporaneity had acknowledged him for what he is. All the fuss that is made afterward, all the fuss with building his tomb etc. etc. etc. etc. etc. is, according to the judgment of Jesus Christ, hypocrisy and the same blood-guilt as theirs who put him to death.

This is the Christian requirement. The lenient, the most lenient form of this is undoubtedly that which I used in *Practice in Christianity*, namely, that you admit that this is the requirement, and then have recourse to grace. But not only not wanting to honor the requirement, no, wanting to have the requirement suppressed—and then, on the other hand, wanting to give something for grave monuments, something the pastor for good reasons calls being an earnest Christian—this is what our Lord Jesus Christ surely sought to prevent most of all.

This saying is frequently heard in the world. "One lives only once; therefore I could wish to see Paris before I die, or to make a fortune as soon as possible, or at least to become something great in this world—because one lives only once."

It rarely happens, but nevertheless it does happen, that a person appears who has only one wish, very definitely only one wish. "This," he says, "this I could wish; oh, that this, my wish, might be fulfilled, because, alas, one lives only once!"

Imagine such a person on his deathbed. The wish was not fulfilled, but his soul, unchanged, clings to this wish—and now, now it is no longer possible. Then he rises up on his bed; with the passion of despair he once again states his wish, "Oh, what despair, it is not fulfilled; what despair, one lives only once!"

It seems terrible, and it truly is, but not as he thinks; what is terrible is not that the wish was unfulfilled, what is terrible is the passion with which he clings to it. His life is not wasted because his wish was not fulfilled, not at all; if his life is wasted it is because he refused to give up his wish, refused to learn anything higher from life than this matter of his only wish, as if its fulfillment or nonfulfillment would decide everything.

Therefore, what is truly terrible is something else entirely: for example, if a person on his deathbed discovers, or if on his deathbed he clearly perceives, something that he had dimly understood throughout his life but never wanted to understand, that to have suffered for the truth in this world belongs to being able to become eternally happy—and one lives only once, the once that for him is now over! And he did, after all, have it in his power; and eternity does not change, the eternity toward which, simply in dying, he then advances as his future!

We human beings are by nature inclined to view life as follows: we regard suffering as an evil that we strive in every way to avoid. And if we succeed, we then one day on our deathbed think we have good reason to be able to thank God that we were

spared suffering. We human beings think that the point is merely
to be able to slip happily and well through this world; and Christianity thinks that all terrors actually come from the other world,
that the terrors of this world are childish compared with the terrors of eternity, and that the point is therefore not to slip happily
and well through this life, but rightly to relate oneself to eternity
through suffering.

One lives only once. If when death comes your life has been
used well—that is, used so it rightly relates itself to eternity—
God be eternally praised. If not, it is eternally irreparable—one
lives only once!

One lives only once; this is the way it is here on earth. And
while you are now living this once, the temporal extent of which
dwindles with each dwindling hour, the God of love is in heaven
fondly loving also you. Yes, loving; that is why he would like
you finally to will what he for the sake of eternity wills for you:
that you might resolve to will to suffer, that is, that you might
resolve to will to love him, because you can love him only in
suffering, or if you love him as he wills to be loved you will come
to suffer. Remember, one lives only once; if it is neglected, if you
do not come to suffer, if you avoid it—it is eternally irreparable.
Compel you, no, the God of love will not do that at any price;
he would then obtain something completely different from what
he wills. Indeed, how could it occur to the God of love to will
to compel to be loved! But he is love and out of love he wills that
you should will as he wills. In love he suffers as only infinite and
omnipotent love can suffer, which no human being is capable of
comprehending; therefore he suffers when you do not will as he
wills.

God is love. No human being was ever born whom this
thought does not overwhelm in indescribable blessedness, especially when it comes close to him in such a way that "God is
love" means "you are loved." In the next moment, when the
understanding comes, "This means beginning to suffer"—how
frightful! "Yes, but it is out of love that God wills it; it is because
he wants to be loved; and that he wants to be loved by you is his
love for you"—well, then! —In the next moment, as soon as the
suffering is in earnest—how frightful! "Yes, but it is out of love.

You have no inkling of how he is suffering, because he knows very well that it is painful to suffer, but he nevertheless cannot be changed, because then he would become something other than love"—well, then! —In the next moment, as soon as the suffering is in earnest!—how frightful!

Yet be careful, take care that time does not go by unused, perhaps in useless suffering; remember, one lives only once. If it can be of help to you, look at the matter this way: be assured that in love God suffers more than you are suffering, but he cannot be changed by that. Yet above all remember: one lives only once. There is a loss that is eternally irreparable; thus eternity—even more frightful—far from wiping out the recollection of what is lost, is an eternal recollection of what is lost!

Permit me to tell a story.[214] I have not read it in any devotional book but in what could be called light reading. I have no misgiving about using it and say this only lest someone should be disturbed if by chance he recognizes it or eventually discovers my source—lest he be disturbed by my having failed to disclose it.

Somewhere in the East there lived a poor old couple, a husband and wife. They had, it was said, only poverty, and worry for the future increased, of course, along with the thought of old age. They certainly did not besiege heaven with their prayers, they were too God-fearing for that; yet they did again and again implore heaven for help.

It happened one morning that as the wife came out to the fireplace she found lying on the hearth a very large precious stone, which she promptly took in and showed to her husband, who, well-informed about such things, easily perceived that now they had assistance for their lifetime.

A bright future for these old people—what joy! Yet frugal and God-fearing as they were, they decided, since they still had enough to live on for another day, that they would not sell the precious stone on that day. But tomorrow it should be sold, and from tomorrow a new life would begin.

The night before the next day or before tomorrow, the wife dreamed that she was carried away to paradise. An angel showed her around in all the glory that an oriental imagination can invent. Then the angel also took her into a large room where long rows of armchairs stood completely embellished with precious stones and pearls, which the angel explained were intended for the pious. Finally he also showed her one—intended for her. As she looked more closely at it, she saw that a very large precious stone was lacking in the back of the chair. She asked the angel how that could have happened. He

— —oh, now pay sharp attention, now comes the story! The angel answered: That was the precious stone you found on the hearth; you received that in advance, and it cannot be replaced.

In the morning the wife told her husband the dream, and she was of the opinion that it would then indeed be better to endure the few years they could have of life rather than lack the precious stone throughout all eternity. And her pious husband agreed.

So that evening they laid the precious stone on the hearth again; that evening they prayed to God that he would take it back. Sure enough, the next morning it was gone. What had become of it the old people of course knew; it was now in its right place.

*　　　　　*

*

This husband was truly happily married, his wife a sensible wife. But if it were indeed true, as is said so often, that it is the wives who make the men forget the eternal, even if all were unmarried, everyone still has within himself a something that, more slyly and more insistently and more incessantly than a woman can, will make a person forget the eternal, make him measure wrongly, as if a few years, or ten years or forty years, were such an enormously long time that even eternity becomes something quite brief in comparison with it, instead of the reverse, that these years are very short and eternity is enormously long.

Remember this well! You perhaps can sagaciously avoid what it has pleased God to unite with being a Christian, suffering and adversity. By sagaciously dodging, you perhaps can, to your own corruption, achieve the opposite, achieve what God has eternally separated from being a Christian: enjoyment and all earthly goods. Fooled by your sagacity, you perhaps can finally be totally lost in the delusion that you are on exactly the right road because you are gaining the things of this world—and then: an eternity for repenting. An eternity for repenting, namely, for repenting that you did not use the time for what can be eternally recollected: truly to love God, the result of which is that in this life you come to suffer from people. ^{XIV 308}

Therefore do not deceive yourself; of all deceivers, fear most yourself! Even if it were possible for a person in relation to the eternal to take something in advance, you would deceive yourself by: something in advance—and then an eternity for repenting!

Only one thing: to have suffered for the truth. If you want to take care for your eternal future, see to it that you come to suffer for the truth.

There *is*, of course, at every second the opportunity, the opportunity to suffer for the truth; how could it be otherwise in this world of lies and deception and skulduggery and mediocrity! But you are not lunatic enough to utilize this opportunity, are you? You are much more sagacious—you employ all your keenness to avoid clashing with this nice world in such a way that you would come to suffer. Moreover, you perhaps play the hypocrite to yourself a little and say that you are willing enough to suffer if there were the opportunity. O my friend, you are only deceiving yourself, eternity never. The result will be that you have nothing to recollect eternally, consequently that you will be eternally tortured by this emptiness and by the painful thought that your life was wasted, filled with what cannot be recollected eternally!

Perhaps you are contemporary with *a righteous person* who suffers for the truth—here, then, is the opportunity: acknowledge him for what he is and you will come to suffer like him! But you, you presumably think that you are acting very sagaciously, that you not only do not acknowledge this person openly, publicly for what he is but you shun him in every way; or you may even think that you are acting very nobly, that you are not like the others, because you acknowledge him for what he is—but in secret, so there is no danger, whereas you do not acknowledge him when danger is involved. O, my friend, you are deceiving yourself; you foolishly did not use the opportunity that was offered, whereby you would have come to suffer for truth—the only thing that can be recollected eternally.

Yes, the only thing that can be recollected eternally; take what you will, of everything else it holds true that it cannot be recollected eternally. If you have loved the most beautiful girl, have lived a whole life happily with her, the most lovable wife—it cannot be recollected eternally; it is formed from what is more fragile than the eternal. The greatest achievements in the external world, to have conquered kingdoms and countries, the most interesting and most thrilling enterprises, to have been the idea in them, the greatest discoveries in the world of nature, to have been the discoverer etc.—they cannot be recollected eternally. Perhaps they can be preserved from generation to generation through all subsequent generations, but you yourself will not be able to recollect them eternally; neither are they the eternal truth, nor do they belong to you eternally. Only one thing remains, only one thing is to be recollected eternally—to have suffered for the truth.

Here in the world the truth walks in lowliness and abasement, has nowhere to lay its head,[215] must give thanks if someone will give it a glass of water—but if he does it openly, publicly acknowledging it for what it is, then this lowly figure, the poor, insulted, laughed-to-scorn, persecuted wretch, "the truth," has, if I may say it this way, a pen in its hand; it writes on a little slip of paper "for eternity," which it hands to this person who, suffering for the truth, has contemporaneously acknowledged it for what it is. His name is written in heaven;[216] his life was used for the only thing (for which, to be sure, a human being is most reluctant to want to use it) that can be recollected eternally.

Whoever you are, consider this! Avoid above all the guidance of the pastors. Indeed, you no doubt can well understand that from tradespeople you do not learn to know anything true about the suffering truth—that is, about Christianity. Avoid them; they trick you out of the eternal simply by leading you to think that you can receive the eternal on some condition other than that of the sufferings. Be yourself watchful, because the earnestness of existence is precisely this, that you are placed in a world where the voice that calls you to the right way speaks very softly, while thousands of voices outside and inside you speak ever so loudly about exactly the opposite—precisely this is the earnestness: that this voice speaks softly because it wants to test you to see if you will obey even its faintest whisper. Consider, it is not eternity that needs you and then for its own sake raises its voice when the other voices become strident; no, it is you who need eternity, and it wants to test—what earnestness!—your attentiveness, and therefore it becomes softer to the same degree that the others become louder—something that cannot happen except through your fault. Nothing is easier than to shout down the voice of eternity, which speaks about suffering for the truth, that it is the only thing that can be recollected eternally; for that the pastors are not needed, but by their help it naturally becomes the easiest thing in the world—how terrible, to deceive oneself eternally! And even more terrible, that it is done so frightfully easily, that eternity is so earnest that one must say it is made easiest of all for a human being—to deceive oneself eternally!

Take the pupils in a class—which one is the most admired by his comrades? Is it the laziest? No, that is definitely out of the question. Is it the hardest worker? Not that one either. Is it the one with the greatest mental capacity? Not that one either. But if there is one who has the sagacity to know how to cajole the teachers and do it so subtly that he always gets by with it, always gets good grades, is always at the top of the class, is always praised and singled out—he is the admired one, and why? Because his comrades realize very well that he has a double advantage. He has the advantage, which the lazy pupil also has, that he does not actually work; he has lots of time to play and entertain himself—the lazy pupil, to be sure, also has this advantage, but he of course is punished for it. Then in addition he has the advantage that the diligent pupil has. He is the admired one, and his comrades say admiringly of him: That Ludvigsen, that Ludvigsen, he's a dickens of a fellow. "But Fredricksen is still more diligent." What's the good of that? L. always gets just as good grades; so Fredricksen has only one thing more—the bother. "Yes, but Olsen is still a lot smarter." Aw, forget it! That doesn't help him much anyway; he just has a lot of trouble from it. No, Ludvigsen, Ludvigsen, he's a dickens of a fellow.

That was a picture of life; I now go on to a picture from life.

Which one is the most admired teacher of Christianity in this world? Is it the brash worldling, who *sans phrase* [without circumlocution] and without cover-up acknowledges that he aspires only to things of this world, to money, power, etc. and has the good luck to gain it? No, that is definitely out of the question. Is it, then, the truly pious individual, who is earnest about Christianity and therefore actually misses out on the benefits and enjoyments of this life, so his life becomes an interpretation of the apostle's words, "If we hoped only for this life, we would be the most pitiable of all"?[217] No, not that one either.

But if there is someone who has this sagacity, that he knows subtly, subtly, how to cajole God and in such a way that he always gets by with it and wins, perhaps even more assuredly than the brash worldling, all the earthly benefits and enjoyments, while he still is always the pious, the God-fearing, the man of God, earnestness itself—he is the admired one, and why? Because he wins double advantage: the benefits—and then *in addition* the glory, the appearance of a saint, the appropriate high honor, and esteem.

And if he is able to do this so very subtly that no one, no one can with surety see through it—that does it; this is the genuine *non plus ultra* [unsurpassable], the matchless, in a class by itself—especially for women, but also for men. But especially for women, because it cannot be denied that the woman is such that if she is really to appreciate something, to say nothing of being at the peak of admiration, adoring admiration, there must be a little anxiety involved. And in this situation there is a little bit of that. In the midst of the most blissful exaltation, in the midst of the most heavenly rapture over this admired one, there is in the distance—but it is still there—an anxiety, what if? . . . . . and yet, no, it is impossible! And this combination produces: adoring admiration.

There is nothing to which *God* is so much opposed as hypocrisy—according to God's stipulation, it is precisely life's task to be transformed, since every human being is by nature a born hypocrite.

There is nothing *the world* admires as much as the more subtle and the most subtle forms of hypocrisy.

The more subtle and the most subtle forms of hypocrisy! It must be noted here that at times these can appear in such a way that, viewed morally, in the person in question they are not always the most blameworthy. Take great talents, extraordinary sagacity, weak character—this combination will produce one of the most subtle of all forms of hypocrisy, whereas from the moral point of view the person in question is perhaps not very blame-worthy, before God not very blameworthy. On the other hand, it is quite certain that for the others this very form is the most dangerous of all; for the others, that is, for those who have a learner's, a recipient's relation to such a teacher.

If you have ever paid attention to how things go in this world, then it has very likely happened with you, as with others before you, that in despondency you have turned away from the whole thing and complainingly said to yourself: Is this a just Governance? Where indeed is divine justice? Trespassing on the property of others, theft, deception, everything connected with money (this world's idol) is punished, is severely punished in this world. Even what can scarcely be called a crime, that a poor person even with just a look beseeches a passerby is punished severely—that is how severely things go in this—just world! But the dreadful crimes, that a person takes the holy, takes the truth in vain,[218] and that in this way his life every single day is a continuous lie—in connection with them no punishing justice intrudes disturbingly; on the contrary, he receives permission to expand unhindered, to embrace a greater or lesser circle of people, perhaps a whole society, which, admiring and adoring, rewards him with all earthly goods! Where, then, is divine justice?

The answer to this must be: it is precisely divine justice that in its frightful severity allows things to go this way. It is present, nothing but eyes, but it conceals itself and, precisely in order to be able properly to disclose itself for what it is, does not want to be seen prematurely, whereas when it reveals itself it is obvious that it was there, present in even the slightest. In other words, if divine justice, punishing, quickly intervened, the really capital crimes could not completely come into existence. The one who out of weakness, beguiled by his desire, carried away by his sensate passions, but yet out of weakness took a wrong path, the path of sin—upon him divine justice takes pity and allows the punishment to fall, the sooner the better. But the genuinely capital criminal—remember what you complained about, that it seemed as if justice was very lenient or nonexistent!—Governance dazzles [*forblinde*] him so that to his eyes it illusively looks as if his life pleased God, so he certainly must have succeeded in hoodwinking [*blende*] God—how frightful you are, you Divine Justice!

Let no one, therefore, be troubled anymore about this objection against divine justice. Precisely in order to be justice, it must first allow the crime to come into existence in its full guilt; but the genuine capital crime needs—note this well!—a whole lifetime in order to come into existence, is specifically the genuine capital crime by being continued a whole lifetime. But of course no crime can be punished before it comes into existence. Therefore this objection collapses. The objection actually ends up saying that God should punish so quickly that he (it amounts to the same thing) should punish the thief before he steals. But if the crime must have come into existence before it is punished, and if the capital crime (the very one that upsets you) needs a whole lifetime to come into existence, then it cannot be punished in this life; to punish it in this life would not be to punish it but to prevent it, just as it would not be a punishing of the theft if one punished the thief before he stole but would be a preventing of the theft and of his becoming a thief.

Therefore never complain when you see the success of something terrible that will rouse your indignation against God; do not complain—no, tremble and say: God in heaven, so he is one of the capital criminals whose crime needs all of temporal life to come into existence and is not punished until eternity.

Therefore it is precisely severity that brings it about that the capital crime is not punished in this world. Moreover, it may also at times be solicitude for the rest of us. People do, after all, differ; one person can be very superior to another. But to be able to be the capital criminal is also a superiority. So Governance lets him be unpunished also because it might completely confuse our conceptions if we were to perceive that he was a criminal. As you can see, it can be even worse than you pictured it to yourself when you complained. You complained that God did not punish what you could see was a crime. At times there has perhaps lived a criminal on such a scale that no one, not one, has suspected it, indeed, that God would have been unable, as it were, to make himself understandable to the people among whom this criminal lived if he punished him, that by wanting to punish him within time (also apart from the result that this would of course prevent the crime) God must have almost confused the people among whom he lived, something his love and solicitude for them did not have the heart to do. So he went unpunished within time: frightful!

Yes, tremble, that there are crimes that need all of time in order to come into existence, that occasionally, perhaps out of consideration for the rest of us, cannot be punished in this life. Tremble, but do not accuse God's justice; no, tremble at the thought of this (how frightful it sounds when said this way!) dreadful advantage of being able to be punished only in eternity! To be able to be punished only in eternity—merciful God! Every criminal, every sinner who still can be punished in this world can also be saved, saved for eternity! But the criminal whose distinction was that he cannot be punished in this world consequently cannot be saved; by not being able to be punished within time, he cannot be saved for eternity. No, he can—this, indeed, was his advantage!—be punished only in eternity. Do you think, then, that there is reason to complain about God's justice?

Ordinarily when such things are talked about (but speaking of
trembling will soon become obsolete), the subject is given this
turn: Tremble, because it is impossible to deceive God, the Omniscient, the Omnipresent One. And such is indeed the case. I do
not, however, think that one achieves the intended effect by
continually turning the subject this way.

No, tremble—because in one sense it is so infinitely easy to
fool God! O my friend, he is something so infinitely sublime, and
you, on the other hand, are so infinitely nothing in relation to
him that a whole lifetime of sleepless exertion in mortal anxiety
to please him and to heed his every beck and call is still infinitely
too little to be able worthily to beg for a single moment of his
attention. And him you want to cheat—O man, it is all too easily
done! Therefore tremble, that is, keep watch, keep watch! He
has a punishment that he himself regards as the most frightful—
indeed, he is also the only one who has a true conception of the
infinite that he is! This punishment is: not to will to be aware
(which in one sense, in accord with his sublimity, he is not) of the
nothing that you are. For an omnipotent being it must, if one
may speak this way, be an immense effort to be obliged to look
after a nothing, to be aware of a nothing, to be concerned about
a nothing.[220] And then this nothing wants to fool him—O man,
shudder, it is done so infinitely easily.

Let me illustrate this thought for you. Take a townsman—
who supposedly would be most difficult for this townsman to
fool? Would it not be precisely his peer? This peer of his is absorbed in watching out lest he be fooled. "I really could not bear
to have him fool me" etc. It will rather occur to the townsman
that a very distinguished man would be easier to fool, because it
does not much concern the very distinguished man, the king
even easier, because it does not concern His Majesty at all. Do
not misunderstand me. I do not think, of course, that the very
distinguished man, that the king, if it could concern him, would

be unable to see that the good townsman is fooling him, but this townsman is of no concern to him at all. Remember the story of the fly and the deer. You recall that the fly, which was sitting on one of its horns, said to the deer, "I hope I am not troubling you." "I did not know that you even existed."[221] The townsman's task obviously must be to get His Majesty to take notice of him because of his honesty, his integrity; on the other hand, it is so infinitely obtuse and inane to want to fool the one who is too sublime to be able to be concerned with him—it is done so infinitely easily!

Think, now, about how infinitely sublime God is, and about the nothing that you are—and tremble at the thought of how infinitely easy it is for you to fool God! Because you say "du"[222] to God, because you have been acquainted with him from childhood, because you are accustomed to mix his name lightmindedly into all sorts of talk, you perhaps believe that God is your comrade, that you associate with him as one tavern keeper with another, that he consequently will promptly give the alarm when he detects that you want to fool him, falsify his Word, pretend that you did not understand it, etc., and that when he does not do that it is evidence that you succeeded in fooling him. O man, shudder—you succeeded!

Yes, in his sublimity God himself turns the relation in such a way that it is as easy as possible for a human being, if he so wishes, to fool God. That is, he arranges it in such a way that the few he loves and who love him must suffer dreadfully in this world, so everyone can see that they are abandoned by God. The deceivers, on the other hand, make a brilliant career, so everyone can see that God is with them, in which view they themselves are strengthened more and more.

So distinguished is God, so far removed is he from making it difficult, so infinitely easy is it to deceive him, that he even himself offers a prize to the one who does it, rewards him with all the things of this earth—O man, tremble!

THE MOMENT

No. 9

CONTENTS

September 24, 1855   S. KIERKEGAARD

May 31, 1855

The one party is a person who by his many years of activity as an author and by his whole life as a public personality gives the assurance (the guarantee) of being entitled (as not many are, perhaps as no other person in the country is) to join in the discussion about what Christianity is.

The other party is the clergy, who at first were sufficiently verbose as long as it was this easy matter of utilizing the circumstance that a dead man must be discussed, of exciting women and children with funeral orations, but who, when the matter became earnest, observed the profoundest silence in print, but—with the courage of truth-witnesses!—are perhaps secretly all the more garrulous.

The attack upon me—for the benefit of "the truth-witnesses," whose silence, deservedly, is thereby properly displayed—is carried out by *Kjøbenhavnsposten*[223] and *Flyveposten*;[224] and the death-dealing tip (point) in this attack is that I am called: Søren.[225]

Only one thing is lacking, that truth-witness Bishop Martensen also—if there should be a new hubbub, then the Bishop, "like the boys on New Year's Eve,[226] might think he sees his chance"—to write an article against me in which the point is that I am named Søren. In that case I would have to droop, succumb under the power of this truth that I would futilely seek to oppose, for it is true, my name is Søren.

My beloved deceased father, to think that you should become my misfortune in this way! Seen from the point of view of the idea, I have been as victorious as anyone has seldom been;[227] I have deserved it—but my name is Søren.

Yet I will certainly put up with it—indeed, O God, "joyful and grateful!"[228]—put up with the ill-temper of impotence. But it is quite another matter whether the Danish people are served by this effort to make it ludicrous as a people, ludicrous in the eyes of every other nation that becomes aware that it is a people among whom the only argument used against spirit is that the man is called Søren.

*   *
*

So I repeat, "This must be said: by ceasing to participate (if you usually do participate) in the public divine service as it now is, you always have one and a great guilt less."[229] Whoever you are, watch out, you will not enter rightly into eternity if you do not take the matter of religion more earnestly than to allow an optical illusion to be your divine worship and to participate in making a fool of God. One certainly does not have religion for the sake of this life, in order to get through this life happy and well, but for the sake of the other life; in this other world lies the earnestness of religion. And from this other world God's Word says to you as to me, "Do not be deceived; God is not mocked."[230] No, he is not mocked; eternally he does not tolerate what he will not omnipotently keep from possibly happening within time, that in the name of divine worship one understands the very opposite of what Christianity is in the New Testament. And that this has happened, slowly, insidiously over the centuries may excuse you but does not help you. Above all, do not let yourself be deceived by the pastors. Believe me, or just look for a moment without bias into the New Testament, and you will see that Christianity did not enter into the world in order to reassure you in your natural condition (thus assuring the pastor a thriving and pleasant livelihood), but that it, renouncing all things, entered into the world in order, with the terrors of eternity, to wrest you out of the peace in which you naturally are.

*   *
*

In what has happened so far, there is only one thing that makes me shudder, and I shudder again as I reflect on what I know, that when I speak of it I will not even be understood.

What makes me shudder is this. While my life, although weak in comparison with the lives of the glorious ones who have lived, nevertheless expresses fighting for eternity in concern for the salvation of my soul, I stand surrounded by contemporaries who at most are interested in this matter in the capacity of the public. In a fleeting mood one is perhaps gripped by what I say; in the next moment one judges it esthetically; in the next moment one reads what is written against me; then one is inquisitive about the outcome etc. etc.: in short, one is—the public. And it occurs to no one, no one, that by being human beings they are indeed subject to the same conditions as I am, that the accounting of eternity awaits them also, and that one thing is certain, that eternity is closed to everything that in this life wanted only to be the public, "just like the others." It makes me shudder that these people live in the notion that I am the one who is in danger, whereas after all, eternally understood, I am in far less danger than they, inasmuch as I am fighting for eternity. And I shudder again when I reflect on the fact that this is happening in Christendom, that these contemporaries are a society of Christians who have 1000 teachers who have taken an oath upon the New Testament—and that then the truth is that these people have no intimation of what Christianity is. This is appalling; to me it is appalling to be to such a degree right in what I say, in what I am speaking about, that Christianity does not exist at all, and in what I am saying about how this is connected with the "truth-witnesses'" proclamation of Christianity.

Take another situation. There is an adage that says: It is a poor soldier who does not hope to become a general.

So ought it to be. If there is to be any life and enthusiasm in an army, these words ought to animate everyone: a poor soldier who does not hope to become a general.

As experience teaches from generation to generation, it is another matter that only a few of the enormous mass of soldiers become even merely noncommissioned officers, that very few become lieutenants, that exceptionally few individuals become staff officers, that very seldom even as an exception does one person become—a general.

Reverse the situation. One proceeds from what experience teaches, from what is experienced as truth from generation to generation, and then speaks this way, "It is fatuous for a soldier to fancy that he will become a general; be satisfied with being what you are, just as the rest of us are satisfied with what experience teaches, that the thousands always get only that far." Does this not demoralize the army?

So it is also in connection with Christianity. Instead of proclaiming the ideals, only what experience teaches is introduced, what the experience of all the centuries teaches, that millions attain only mediocrity.

Then Christianity is introduced: **reassuringly**.

A villainous preacher-lie, but one that pays, to introduce Christianity as *reassuring*, instead of its being radically *awakening*, *unsettling*! It is introduced as reassuring: "To strive after ideals is a fatuity, a foolishness, a lunacy, is arrogance, conceit" (that is, something God is against); "the middle way is the true wisdom. Be calm, you are exactly like the millions, and the experience of all the centuries teaches that one does not get further! Be calm, you are like the others, be happy just like the others"—a euphemism for: You are going to hell just like all the others; but this true statement would not provide pastors with money; the former pays superbly.

If there is an individual who is unwilling to be satisfied, to be reassured by this kind of happiness, then the whole mass, commanded by the perjurers, turns against him, declares him to be an egotist, a dreadful egotist, for refusing to be like the others.

The New Testament, however, always proves to be right; this individual really gets into the true Christian collisions: to be hated by people because he wants—to be a Christian—except that these people are costumed and addressed as Christians, and are led by teachers (what solemnity!) who have taken an oath upon the New Testament.

In this way they have demoralized Christianity by doing exactly the opposite of proclaiming the ideals.

But what good is it, what good is it to have this life, assisted by the preacher-lie, made easy and cozy? Eternity is not fooled. And just as rigidly as the human race stands on its right to punish, even with death, this not wanting to be like the others, so inflexibly does eternity hold to its right to punish with eternal damnation this reassuring of oneself by being just like the others.

Just as the human being—naturally—desires what can nourish and enliven zest for life, in the same way the one who is to live for the eternal continually needs a dose of life-weariness in order not to become infatuated with this world[232] but instead really needs to learn to be nauseated by, weary of, and disgusted with the folly and lies of this wretched world. Here is such a dose.

The God-man is betrayed, mocked, abandoned by all, all, all; not a single person, literally not one single one, remains faithful to him[233]—and then afterward, afterward, afterward there are millions who on their knees have made pilgrimages to the places where many hundreds of years ago his foot may have left a trace; afterward, afterward, afterward millions have worshiped a splinter of the cross on which he was crucified!

And so it always is, proportionately, in contemporaneity; but afterward, afterward, afterward!

Must one not, then, be nauseated by being a human being!

Once again, must one not be nauseated by being a human being! These millions who on their knees made pilgrimages to his grave, this human crowd that no power was able to disperse—only one thing is needed, that Christ would come again—and all these millions would promptly find feet to walk upon in order to take to their heels; the whole crowd would be as if blown away, or it would, as a mob, in upright position, rush at Christ in order to kill him.

*   *

*

The only thing that Christ, the apostle, every truth-witness desire is: imitation—the only thing the human race has no pleasure in or taste for.

No, take away the dangers—so that we can begin to play. Then the battalions of the human race perform (how nauseating!) amazing feats of mimicry. Instead of the imitation of

Christ, then come the holy monkey tricks (how nauseating!), under the guidance and command of (how nauseating!) oath-bound pastors, who serve as sergeants, lieutenants, etc., ordained men, who therefore have the special assistance of a Holy Spirit for this earnestness.

Be a Blatherskite—and You Will See, All Difficulties Vanish!

If my intention with this advice were to instruct the race about what it has to do in the future, I certainly might correctly be said to come too late, terribly late, because what is done has been practiced for centuries with decided success and triumphant progress.

While every higher conception of life (for example, even the best in paganism, not to speak of Christianity) sees the issue in this way, that the task for a human being is to strive to be in relationship with the deity,[234] and that this striving makes life difficult, proportionately more difficult as the striving is more earnest, more energetic, more strenuous—in the course of time the human race has had other thoughts about the meaning of life and the task. Sagacious as the human race is, it has spied out the secret of life, has got wind of the secret that if one wants to have life made easy (and this is just what people want), then this is easily done. One merely needs more and more to trivialize oneself, what it means to be a human being—then life becomes easier and easier. Be a blatherskite—and you will see, all difficulties vanish.

There was a time when "the woman" related herself to herself in her conception of her feelings. One sorrow was sufficient to decide her life for a whole lifetime; the beloved's death or his unfaithfulness was enough. She understood it as her task to be lost to this life, which when it is consistently carried out makes for long, long inner battles and spiritual trials, occasions many a painful collision with the surrounding world—in short, makes life difficult. Therefore, to what end all these difficulties—be a blatherskite, and you will see, all difficulties vanish! Then the beloved's death or his unfaithfulness becomes at most a little pause, something like sitting out a dance at a ball; half an hour later you are dancing with a new partner—indeed, it would be boring to dance all night with one partner. And as far as eternity is concerned, it is really advantageous to know that several partners are waiting for one there. So, you see, all difficulties vanish; life becomes enjoyable, cheerful, jolly, easy—in short, it is a glorious world in which to live if one just knows how to conduct oneself properly in it—by being a blatherskite.

There was a time when "the man" related himself to himself in a great conception of what it is to be a person of character. A man had principles, principles that he did not betray or relinquish at any price—indeed, he would rather lose his life, expose himself his whole lifetime to every mistreatment rather than to give in the slightest on his principles, because he understood that to give in the slightest with regard to principles is to give them up, and to give up one's principles is to give up oneself. Thereby life naturally would become sheer difficulty. Therefore, to what end all these difficulties—be a blatherskite, and you will see, all difficulties vanish! Be a blatherskite, have one viewpoint today, tomorrow another, then the one you had yesterday again, and then in turn a new one on Friday. Be a blatherskite, make yourself into several persons, or parcel out yourself, have one viewpoint anonymously, another in one's name, one orally, another in writing, one as a public official, one as a private individual, one as your wife's husband, another at the club—and you will see, all difficulties vanish. You will see, you will find out that this world is a glorious world, just as if designed for you (whereas all persons of character have found out and witnessed to—and proportionately more as they were more persons of character—the fact that this world is a mediocre, a wretched, a miserable, a corrupted, an evil world, designed only for scoundrels or for blatherskites).

There was a time when the "human being" related himself to himself in an infinite conception of what it means to be a Christian; then he was in earnest about dying to the world, hating oneself, suffering for the doctrine, and now found life so difficult, yes, so agonizing, that even the toughest ones almost drooped under these difficulties, writhed like worms,[235] and even the most humble ones were not far from despairing. Therefore, to what end all these difficulties—be a blatherskite, and you will see, all difficulties vanish! Be a blatherskite, and then be either a pastor, dean, bishop, who—by virtue of a sacred oath upon the New Testament—once a week for three quarters of an hour

babbles something elevated but otherwise does not care a fig for
everything higher, or be a layman, who for three quarters of an
hour is uplifted by the elevated things the pastor babbles for three
quarters of an hour, but otherwise does not care a fig for everything higher—and you will see, all difficulties vanish! Then fundamentally falsify God's or Christianity's view of this life; let its
being easy[236] (directly contrary to God's Word) be the sign to
you that the way is the right way, the way pleasing to God—and
you will see, all difficulties vanish, this world becomes a glorious
world, more glorious and pleasant and easier with each century
it is lived in this way. And be altogether unconstrained. Believe
me, there is no one before whom you need to blush with shame;
the whole lot is of the same quality, and therefore the eulogy is
prepared for you, the eulogy on your sagacity, the eulogy by the
others, who by delivering a eulogy on you (how sagaciously
planned!) eulogize themselves, and who therefore would only
condemn you if you were not—like the others.

What is meant by cannibals everyone certainly knows; indeed, the word [*Menneske-Ædere*, man-eaters] says it. One shudders to read or hear about this horrible practice, that there are savages who kill their enemies in order to eat them. One shudders, one is inclined to deny kinship with that sort of creature, to deny that they are human beings.

I shall now show that the pastors are cannibals and in a much more abominable way.

What is the Christianity of the New Testament? It is the suffering truth. In this mediocre, wretched, sinful, evil, ungodly world the truth must suffer—this is Christianity's doctrine—Christianity is the suffering truth because it is the truth and is in this world.

For this its founder therefore suffered not only death upon the cross, but his whole life from first to last was suffering; for this the apostle suffered, for this the truth-witness. Only one thing did the Savior require; the same thing the apostle in turn after him and the truth-witness required as the one and only thing: imitation.

But what does "the pastor" do? This university-educated man is not lunatic. "To follow them, what a proposal to make to a sagacious man. A change would have to take place in a sagacious man; he would have to become lunatic before it could ever occur to him to become involved in such a thing. No, but cannot the sufferings of these glorious ones be depicted, their teaching be proclaimed as doctrine? Cannot this be done and in such a way that it would yield enough so that a man who wishes to enjoy life could live on it, marry on it, beget children who are fed on it?" In other words, is it not possible to turn the glorious ones into money, or to eat them, to live with wife and children by eating them?

See, there you have it: cannibals, that the pastors are cannibals! You departed glorious ones, that is what in the animal world, *a parte potiori* [according to its more distinctive part], the world of human beings is called; that is your fate in life and after death—to be eaten. While you are living, you are eaten by the vermin of your contemporaries; finally you are put to death. And when you are dead, then the real cannibals take hold, the pastors, who live by eating you! Just as provisions for the winter are salted down in households at slaughtering time, so "the pastor" similarly has in salt-meat barrels the glorious ones who had to suffer for the truth. Futilely the dead one cries: Follow me, follow me! "Fine talk," replies the pastor, "no, just keep quiet and stay where you are. What nonsense—to require that I should follow you, I who, after all, must live by eating you, and not I alone, but my wife and my children—to require that I should follow you, perhaps become a sacrifice instead of, by living off you or eating you, making the most brilliant career, rolling in money for myself and my wife and children, who are thriving (you should just see this) so that it is a pleasure to see them."

This is cannibalism, and it is cannibalism in its most abominable form, which I shall now show.

1. The cannibal is a savage; "the pastor" is a cultured, university-educated man, which makes the abomination much more shocking.

2. The cannibal eats his enemies. Not so "the pastor." He gives the appearance of being exceptionally devoted to those whom he eats. The pastor, specifically the pastor, is the most devoted friend of those glorious ones. "Just listen to him, listen to how he can describe their sufferings, expound their teaching. Does he not deserve a silver cruet-stand, a knight's cross, a complete set of embroidered armchairs, a few thousands more a year, he, this glorious man who, himself moved to tears, can describe the sufferings of the glorious ones in this way?" The cannibal, you see, is not like that. He openly acknowledges that he is a cannibal, and he does not call the person he eats his friend but calls him his enemy and himself the other's enemy. The pastor, however, hides as carefully as possible that he is a cannibal (like the crocodile when it piteously weeps,[237] hides it by giving the appearance of being most devoted to the very one he eats. "The pastor" binds himself by an oath on the New Testament, that is,

to imitation, to follow the Savior of the world—and then does not care a fig for imitation, but along with his family lives (eating him) by describing his sufferings, expounding his teaching as doctrine, and gives the appearance of being the true, devoted disciple of the Crucified One. "You should hear him on Sundays; that man is a true disciple of Christ, the way he can describe Christ's suffering and witness . . . . . does he not deserve velvet panels on the front of his gown and stars and thousands a year?"

3. The cannibal makes it brief and to the point: he ferociously jumps to his feet, overpowers his enemy, kills him, eats a little of him. Then it is over. Then he lives again on his customary food, until once again ferocity against his enemies comes over him.

"The pastor" is a different sort of cannibal. His cannibalism is well considered, ingeniously arranged, based on the assumption of not having anything else to live on for a whole lifetime and that what one has to live on will be able to support a man with a family and will increase year after year. The pastor is cozily situated in his rural residence, and the prospect of promotion also beckons. His wife is plumpness personified, and his children no less so. And all this is owing to: the sufferings of the glorious ones, to the Savior, the apostle, the truth-witness. It is on this that the pastor lives, this that he eats, this with which he, with joyful zest for life, feeds his wife and children. He has these glorious ones in salt-meat barrels. Their cry: Follow me, follow me! is futile. For a time he perhaps must guard himself against this cry lest it—in connection with the oath he has taken!—begin to have a disturbing effect on his whole *negotie* [business]. As the years pass, he becomes so hardened against the cry that he no longer hears it. At the beginning, it is perhaps with a certain embarrassment that he hears himself called a true disciple of Christ; as the years pass, he becomes so accustomed to hearing it that he himself believes he is that. As such he dies, as basically corrupted as it is possible for a human being to become, and then he is buried as a "truth-witness."

The Pastor Not Only Demonstrates the
Truth of Christianity, but He Simultaneously Refutes It

There is only one relation to revealed truth: to have faith.

That one has faith can be demonstrated in only one way: by being willing to suffer for one's faith; and the degree of one's faith is demonstrated only by the degree of one's willingness to suffer for one's faith.

That is the way Christianity entered into the world, served by witnesses who were willing unconditionally to suffer everything for their faith, and actually did come to suffer, to sacrifice life and blood for the faith.

The courage of their faith then makes its impression on the human race, which is prompted to the following conclusion: that which is able to inspire the human being to sacrifice everything in this way, to risk life and blood, that must be the truth.

This is the demonstration that is made for the truth of Christianity.

Now, however, the pastor is so kind as to want to make it into a livelihood (but a livelihood that is just the opposite of suffering, being sacrificed, which constitutes the demonstration)—to demonstrate the truth of Christianity by pointing out that people have lived who have sacrificed everything, have risked life and blood for Christianity.

Therefore demonstration and refutation at the same time! The demonstration of the truth of Christianity, that one has risked everything for it, is refuted, or certainly made dubious, because the pastor who presents this demonstration does the very opposite. By seeing the glorious ones, the truth-witnesses, risk everything for Christianity, one is led to the conclusion: Christianity must be the truth. By observing the pastor, one is led to the conclusion: Christianity probably is not the truth, but the profit is the truth.

No, the demonstration that something is the truth that consists in the willingness to suffer for it can be made only by the one who is himself willing to suffer for it. The pastor's demonstration:

to demonstrate the truth of Christianity by his accepting money for, having profit from, living on, steadily promoted, living on with his family—the fact that others have suffered—is a self-contradiction, Christianly is cheating.

Therefore, Christianly, "the pastor" must be stopped, as one in civic life speaks of stopping a thief. And just as "Hep"[238] is shouted at a Jew, so must "Stop, thief! Stop him, he is stealing what belongs to the glorious ones!" be shouted until there is no pastor to be seen. What they had earned by their noble unselfishness but, rewarded with ingratitude, persecuted, put to death, did not receive, this the pastor steals by making capital of their lives, by describing their sufferings, by demonstrating the truth of Christianity by the willingness of those glorious ones to suffer for it. That is how the pastor steals from the glorious ones; and thus he deceives the simple person, the masses of people who do not have the capacity to see through the pastor's trafficking, that he is demonstrating the truth of Christianity and at the same time refuting it.

No wonder, then, that Christianity does not exist at all, that this whole business of Christendom is gibberish, when those who are Christians are that on the basis of trust in the pastor's demonstration and assume that Christianity is the truth on the basis of trust in the pastor's demonstration—that something is the truth because a person is willing to profit from it and perhaps sophisticatedly even adds to the profit by giving assurances that he is willing to suffer. To assume the truth of Christianity on the basis of trust in this demonstration is as meaningless as for a person to regard himself as a man of means because much money that does not belong to him passes through his hands, or because he owns a lot of banknotes issued by a bank that has no assets.

No. 10²³⁹

CONTENTS

d.   S. K.

[*On draft:* August 25]

This consists in something that looks as if it served something higher, the infinite, the idea, God, yet on closer inspection proves to serve the finite, the low, the profits. And it was this that Bishop Mynster practiced with masterly virtuosity.

As an example, let me recall something that still cannot be forgotten and that illustrates what I mean, and in which the two bishops, the one deceased and the present one, Mynster and Martensen, are the characters.

When Martensen had been a professor for several years, there was a rumor in Copenhagen that Professor Martensen felt a need, in addition to his activity at the University, also to proclaim the Word to a congregation.[240]

Beautiful! Martensen is a professor, has been successful, humanly speaking—well, then, this need also to proclaim the Word to the congregation—he wants to keep it pure, free from every qualification of the finite, of temporal reward and the like, because it is a real religious need in him. And the matter is, of course, easily taken care of; when he feels the need, he simply asks one of the pastors in the city to make his pulpit available to him: every pastor will be pleased to do that.

If Martensen had done it that way, then, as sure as my name is Søren Kierkegaard, it would not have found favor in Bishop Mynster's eyes. With his sensitive nose, Bishop Mynster would have immediately smelled: a person who has a need in this sense is not one of my people, and as a church administrator I am deeply opposed to this kind of need; it is impossible to calculate how far such a need can lead a person. Bishop Mynster was like that, and no one knows that better than I, who know it from the fact that Bishop Mynster no doubt considered that he was showing me a great favor (his enemies were inclined to understand it as fear) even by just tolerating me, not to mention—something altogether extraordinary!—by liking me a little. My whole existence was very objectionable to him, completely indeclinable according to the only Christian paradigm actually acknowledged by him on Mondays, the perfected paradigm of Christianity that every striving for the infinite is measurable by finite rewards and advantages, something a power-seeking man is indeed absolutely right in acknowledging as the only paradigm, because what is declined according to that is very easy, only all too easy to manage and dominate.

But back to Prof. Martensen's need. What if this need is satisfied by becoming the royal court chaplain? *Das ist was Anders* [That is another matter]! It is four hundred rix-dollars for twelve sermons, and thereby also the prospect of the bishopric is made more probable, which otherwise would remain very doubtful. Moreover, in this position there of course can be no more question of gathering a congregation around him than if he *qua* professor had chosen a specific church and occupied the pulpit every sixth Sunday (which would have been very easy to accomplish).

So, then—royal court chaplain, four hundred rix-dollars for twelve sermons, the possibility of the bishopric—now that was to Bishop Mynster's liking; now he could in every way understand and appreciate and sympathize with this need, find beautiful the need Martensen also feels to proclaim the Word to a congregation. That evening the power-seeking church administrator calmly played his lively game of *L'Hombre*,[241] was elation itself, because there was no reason to fear any movement from a need such as this Martensenian need; on the contrary, it was precisely the right thing to quench the spirit.

So, then, in the text: a religious need; and the note: royal court chaplain, four hundred rix-dollars, the prospect of a bishopric. Yet the good-natured population notices nothing, is touched by this religious need: "How beautiful that Martensen feels such a religious need, what confidence one must have in a man who feels so deep a need to proclaim the Word." This is an optical illusion.

And Bishop Mynster's whole administration of the Church was based on an optical illusion; his virtuosity in equivocation became his second nature.

Over a series of years, with admirable virtuosity he led his generation by the nose, Christianly speaking, a generation so grateful that it wants to erect a monument to him,[242] presumably in the capacity Martensen has had him promoted to: a truth-witness, one of the authentic witnesses, one of the holy chain— Martensen, who knows just as well as I that Bishop Mynster's secret was the same as the Epicurean's, the hedonist's, "the plea-sure-seeker's": *après nous le déluge* [after us the deluge][243]— indeed, he knows that just as well as I; if he should want to deny it, I shall come to the aid of his memory.

XIV
345

How Can You Believe, You Who Receive Glory
from One Another?

(JOHN 5:44)

[*On draft:* July 15, 1855]

Here, again, is the death sentence on all official Christianity!

This enormous castle in the air: a Christian world, Christian states, kingdoms, countries; this game with millions of Christians, who mutually acknowledge one another in mediocrity, but all nevertheless are believers—this whole thing is resting on a foundation that according to Christ's own words makes it impossible to believe.

The Christianity of the New Testament is to love God in a relation of opposition to people, to *suffer* for one's *faith* at the hands of people, to suffer for the doctrine at the hands of people. Only that is believing; *to receive glory* from one another makes it impossible to believe.

As I say: Christianity does not exist at all. The kind of passion that belongs to being involved with God alone in the most complete separation, in a situation of opposition to people (and only that does Christ understand as believing, which is why, in contrast to "receiving glory from people," v. 41, or receiving glory from one another, he speaks of "seeking the glory that comes from the only God" v. 44)—that kind of passion does not appear at all anymore. The kind of people now living are altogether incapable of bearing anything as strong as the Christianity of the New Testament (they would perish as a result of it or lose their minds), in the very same sense as children cannot tolerate strong drink, which is why a little lemonade is prepared for them—and the official Christianity is lemonade-blather for the kind of creatures that are now called human beings, is the strongest they are able to bear; and in their language they call this blather Christianity, just as children call their lemonade wine.

Christianity in "Christendom," what it is to be a Christian, goes according to this paradigm: So-and-so is an excellent man, a true man of faith; he ought to be a Knight . . . . . ah, that is not enough for such a remarkable man of faith—he ought to be a Commander etc. etc. And the New Testament, where it says "How can you believe, you who receive glory from one another?" is continually made the basis for the so-rich-in-blessing operations of the Knight, the Commander, the Councilor of the Consistory, the Councilor of Conference. That is, from generation to generation, from century to century, Christendom performs the feat of declining *mensa* according to *domus*.[244]

Therefore, rather than participating in official Christianity with the thousandth part of the nail of my little finger, I infinitely prefer to participate in the following solemnity. One buys a flag in a hardware store; it is unfurled; one steps up to it with great ceremony, extends three fingers, and swears to the flag. Costumed in a three-cornered hat, a cartridge belt, and sword (all from the hardware store), I thereupon mount a hobbyhorse in order, joined with the others, to make an attack upon the enemy, contemptuous of the mortal danger into which I am seemingly hurling myself with the earnestness of someone who knows what it means to have sworn to the flag. Honestly speaking, I am no friend of participating in that kind of solemnity; but if worst comes to worst I shall infinitely prefer this to participating in the solemnity of official Christianity, of Sunday worship, of the oath-bound. The former only makes a fool of himself; the latter makes a fool of God.

[*On draft:* July 9]

Folios upon folios are written to show again and again how one
is to recognize what true Christianity is.

This can be done in a much simpler way.

Existence [*Tilværelse*] is acoustic. Just pay attention to what the
rejoinder replies and you will immediately know which is
which.

When someone proclaims Christianity in this world in such a
way that the rejoinder replies, "Glorious, profound, earnest
Christian, you ought to be elevated to the princely rank etc."—
then know that this signifies that his proclamation of Christianity
is, Christianly, a low-down lie. It is not unconditionally certain
that someone who walks with shackled feet is a criminal, since
there are cases of the civic authorities' having condemned an
innocent person. But it is eternally certain that the one who—by
proclaiming Christianity!—wins all things earthly is a liar, a deceiver. On one point or another, he has falsified the doctrine that
is designed by God in such a way, in such a militant relation to
this world, that it is impossible, eternally impossible, to proclaim
truthfully what Christianity truly is without coming to suffer in
this world, without being cast off by it, hated, cursed.

When someone proclaims Christianity in such a way that the
rejoinder replies, "He is lunatic"—then know that this signifies
that there are considerable elements of true Christianity in his
proclamation, yet without its being the Christianity of the New
Testament. He may have hit the mark, but probably neither his
verbal proclamation nor the proclamation by his life presses
strongly enough; thus he, Christianly, slides over too lightly,
and his proclamation is still not the Christianity of the New
Testament.

But when someone proclaims Christianity in such a way that
the rejoinder replies, "Remove this person from the earth; he

does not deserve to live"—then know that this is the Christianity of the New Testament.

Completely unchanged, as in the time of our Lord Jesus Christ, there is a death penalty for proclaiming what Christianity truly is, that it is: hating oneself, to love God; hating oneself, to hate everything in which a person has his life, everything that for him is life, hating that for the sake of which he selfishly wants to make use of God in attaining it or in being comforted if he does not attain it or loses it—the death penalty for proclaiming Christianity in character remains unchanged. To proclaim it in character, because if the proclaimer plays the objective game, something that in our day is considered to be far superior, then his life expresses exactly the opposite, then we get forms of the interesting, which never prompts persecution; on the contrary, any lack of character pleases this world.

But "Christendom's" merit is: by means of the doctrine that Christianity is perfectible, to have made Christianity over into worldliness. Persecution thereby naturally disappears, because it is indeed unthinkable that worldliness would persecute worldliness. This was the first lie: to make Christianity over into worldliness. The second lie then is: that the world has now become tolerant, has made a forward step, that persecution no longer takes place—that is, there is not anything to persecute.

XIV
348

Yes, Christianity is perfectible! And it is continually advancing! Christianity entered into the world and found it lost in worldliness and worldly craving and striving. So Christianity taught: renunciation. But, says Christendom, Christianity is perfectible, we hereby cannot stand still. Renunciation is an element; we must go further—to: Hurrah for profits! How sophisticated! Paganism was worldliness prior to renunciation; the worldliness of Christianity claims to be superior to renunciation, which is a one-sidedness.

[*On draft:* August 24]

A man dies and in his will designates someone as the heir to his entire fortune—but there is a condition, something that is required of the heir, and this does not please the heir. What does he do then? He takes possession of the fortune left to him—because, as he says, he is indeed the heir—and says good-bye to the responsibility.

This, as everyone knows, is dishonesty. It is a lie that he is summarily the heir to the fortune; he is that only on the condition that he assumes the responsibility; otherwise he is no more the heir than anyone else.

It is the same with "Christendom." Christianity is a gift, if you will, stipulated for humanity according to the testament of the Savior of the world. But there is a responsibility; with regard to Christianity, the relation is this: the gift and the responsibility correspond to each other altogether equally; to the same degree that Christianity is a gift it is also a responsibility.

"Christendom's" skulduggery is to accept the gift and say good-bye to the responsibility, to want to be the heir to the gift but without accepting the responsibility, to want to make it appear as if humanity is indeed the heir whom the Savior of the world himself has in his will designated as the heir, whereas the truth is that only with the observance of the responsibility is humanity or, more correctly (since, precisely because it is a responsibility, an abstraction such as "humanity" can at most be called the heir only figuratively), each individual within humanity the heir.

Yet hypocritical as is everything involving "Christendom," it has been made to appear that Christendom also maintained that Christianity is a responsibility—one must be baptized. Ah! If anything, that makes the responsibility confoundedly brief! A sprinkle of water on the infant's head in the name of the Triune God: that is responsibility!

No, the responsibility is: the imitation of Jesus Christ.

Yet, if this is to be included, and if the gift and the responsibility are equal to each other, equally as much responsibility as gift—then "humanity" declines Christianity, saying: Thanks for nothing; then there is nothing else to do but resort to forgery—and so you have "Christendom," whose crime is wanting to appropriate an inheritance unjustifiably.

When Is "the Moment"?

[*On draft:* May 29, 1855]

The moment is when the man is there, the right man, the man of the moment.

This is a secret that will forever be hidden from all worldly sagacity, from everything that is only to a certain degree.

Worldly sagacity stares and stares at events and circumstances, calculates and calculates, thinking that it should be able to distil the moment out of the circumstances and then become itself a power with the aid of the moment, this breakthrough of the eternal, and be rejuvenated, something it greatly needs, with the aid of the new.

But it is futile; sagacity does not succeed and will never in all eternity succeed with this substitute, any more than all the arts of the dressing table can produce natural beauty.

No, only when the man is there, and when he ventures as it must be ventured (which is exactly what worldly sagacity and mediocrity want to avoid)—then is the moment—and then the circumstances obey the man of the moment. If nothing but worldly sagacity and mediocrity are involved, the moment never arrives. It can continue one hundred thousand and millions of years, continually the same, and it may at times look as if it will come soon, but as long as it is only worldly sagacity and mediocrity and the like, the moment does not come any more than a sterile person begets children.

But when the right man comes, yes, then is the moment. The moment is precisely this (which is not due to circumstances), the new thing, the woof of eternity—but at the same instant it manages the circumstances to such a degree that it illusively (calculated to make a fool of worldly sagacity and mediocrity) looks as if the moment emerged from the circumstances.

There is nothing for which worldly sagacity is so feverishly eager as the moment; what would it not give to be able to calcu-

late correctly! Yet there is nothing more certain of being excluded from ever seizing the moment than worldly sagacity. The
moment is heaven's gift to—as a pagan would say: to the fortunate and the bold—but a Christian says: to the believer. Indeed,
to have faith, which is held in such profound contempt by
worldly sagacity or at best is a Sunday ceremony all prinked up
with borrowed platitudes—to have faith, this and only this relates itself as possibility to the moment. Worldly sagacity is forever excluded, disdained, and detested, as it is in heaven, more
than all vices and crimes, since by nature it of all things belongs
to this wretched world, it of all things is furthest removed from
having anything to do with heaven and eternity!

[*On draft:* September 1, 1855]

"I do not call myself a Christian; I do not speak of myself as a Christian." It is this that I must continually repeat; anyone who wants to understand my very special task must concentrate on being able to hold this firm.

Yes, I well know that it almost sounds like a kind of lunacy in this Christian world—where each and every one is a Christian, where being a Christian is something that everyone naturally is—that there is someone who says of himself, "I do not call myself a Christian," and someone whom Christianity occupies to the degree to which it occupies me.

But it cannot be otherwise. In this world of blather, what is true must always appear to be a kind of lunacy; and that it is a world of blather in which I live and that among other things it is also by this very blather that everyone is summarily a Christian—that is certain enough.

Yet I neither can, nor will, nor dare change my statement: otherwise perhaps another change would intervene—that the power, an omnipotence that especially uses my powerlessness, would wash his hands of me and let me go my own way. No, I neither can, nor will, nor dare change my statement. I cannot serve these legions of huckstering knaves, I mean the pastors, who by falsifying the definition of Christian have, for the sake of the business, gained millions and millions of Christians. I am not a Christian—and unfortunately I am able to make it manifest that the others are not either—indeed, even less than I, since they fancy themselves to be that, or they falsely ascribe to themselves that they are that, or they (like the pastors) make others think that they are that, whereby the pastor-business flourishes.

The point of view I have set forth and do set forth is of such a distinctive nature that I quite literally have no analogy to cite, nothing corresponding in eighteen hundred years of Christianity. In this way, too—facing eighteen hundred years—I stand quite literally alone.*

The only analogy I have before me is Socrates; my task is a Socratic task, to audit the definition of what it is to be a Christian—I do not call myself a Christian (keeping the ideal free), but I can make it manifest that the others are that even less.

You, antiquity's noble simple soul, you, the only *human being* I admiringly acknowledge as a thinker: there is only a little preserved about you, of all people the only true martyr of intellectuality, just as great *qua* character as *qua* thinker; but how exceedingly much this little is! Even though over the centuries there have lived in Christendom a few isolated significant thinkers—how I long to be able to speak with you for only a half hour, far away from these battalions of thinkers that "Christendom" places in the field under the name of Christian thinkers!

"Christendom" lies in an abyss of sophistry that is even much, much worse than when the Sophists flourished in Greece. Those legions of pastors and Christian assistant professors are all sophists, supporting themselves—here, of course, in accord with antiquity's characterization of the Sophist[247]—by making those who understand nothing believe something and then making this human number the authority for what the truth is, for what Christianity is.

But I do not call myself a Christian. That this is very awkward for the sophists I understand very well, and I understand very

*Note. Inasmuch as I have made a critical comment with regard to "the apostle,"[246] please note the following. 1. I am perfectly right, because the apostle is only a human being. My task requires its being pressed to the limit. If in the apostle's proclamation there is even the slightest thing that could pertain to what has become the sophistry corruptive of all true Christianity, then I must raise an outcry lest the sophists summarily cite the apostle. 2. If it is of great importance, to Protestantism in particular, to correct the enormous confusion Luther caused by inverting the relation and actually criticizing Christ by means of Paul, the Master by means of the follower. I, on the contrary, have not criticized the apostle, as if I myself were something, I who am not even a Christian; what I have done is to hold Christ's proclamation alongside the apostle's. 3. It is one thing to be able intellectually to make a dialectically true comment; it is something else to want to disparage, to weaken the apostle, something I am as far from doing as anyone.

XIV
352

XIV
352

well that they would much rather see that with kettledrums and
trumpets I would proclaim myself to be the only true Christian,
and I also understand very well that an attempt is being made to
represent my conduct falsely in this way. But they do not fool
me! In a certain sense I am very easy to fool; I have almost been
fooled in every relationship I have been in—but that has been
because I myself wanted it. If I do not want it, there is not one of
my contemporaries who fools me, a definite detective talent such
as I am.

Consequently, I am not fooled; I do not call myself a Christian. In a certain sense it seems easy enough to get rid of me; the
others are indeed such completely different fellows, they are true
Christians. Yes, indeed, so it seems. But it is not so; just because
I do not call myself a Christian, it is impossible to get rid of me,
having as I do the confounded capacity of being able, also by
means of not calling myself a Christian, to make it manifest that
the others are even less so.

O Socrates! If with kettledrums and trumpets you had proclaimed yourself to be the one who knew the most, the Sophists
would soon have been finished with you. No, you were the
ignorant one; but you also had the confounded capacity of being
able (also by means of being yourself the ignorant one) to make
it manifest that the others knew even less than you—they did not
even know that they were ignorant.

But the same thing has happened to me that happened to you
(according to what you say in your "defense," as you ironically
enough have called the cruelest satire on a contemporary
age[248])—namely, that you thereby made many enemies for yourself by making it manifest that they were ignorant and, as im-
puted to you, that you yourself must be what you could show
that the others were not, and therefore in envy they had a grudge
against you. It has provoked rage against me that I am able to
make it manifest that the others are even less Christian than I am,
who nevertheless relate myself to Christianity so much that I
truly perceive and acknowledge that I am not a Christian. Some
want to foist on me that my saying that I am not a Christian is
only a hidden form of pride, that I presumably must be what I
can show the others are not. But this is a misunderstanding. It is

XIV
353

altogether true: I am not a Christian; and it is rash to conclude
that because I can show that the others are not Christians, then
I myself must be one, just as rash as to conclude, for example, that
someone who is one-fourth of a foot taller than others is, ergo,
twelve feet tall.

*   *

My task is to audit the definition: Christian. There is only one
single person who is qualified to give a true critique of my work,
and that is I myself. Thus there was some truth in what the
present Dean, Kofoed-Hansen,[249] said to me as early as a few
years ago on the occasion of having considered doing a review
of *Concluding Postscript*, namely, that on reading in *Concluding* XIV
Postscript my view of my earlier works he gave up wanting to 354
review something of which the author was the only one who
could do a true review. No, there is not one single contemporary
who is qualified to review my work. The only one who on occasion has said more or less true words about my significance is
Prof. R. Nielsen;[250] but this truth he has heard from me in private
conversations.

When such competent authorities as, for example, Messrs. Israel Levin,[251] Davidsen,[252] and Siesby,[253] or such unbefuddled
thinkers as Grüne,[254] or such open characters as Anonymous et
al.—when all such persons now are going to judge such a singularity, and before such a well-informed court as the public, it
follows as a matter of course that it must end up becoming—
well, what it has become, what only pains me on behalf of this
little nation, which by such a situation is actually made ridiculous
qua nation.

But even if someone considerably better informed takes it
upon himself to want to say something about me and my task, it
actually does not amount to anything more than that he, after a
superficial glance at my work, quickly finds some earlier something or other that he declares to be comparable.

In this way it still does not amount to anything. Something on
which a person with my leisure, my diligence, my talents, my
education (something to which Bishop Mynster has indeed at-
tested in print[255]) has spent not only fourteen years but essentially

his entire life, the only thing for which he has lived and breathed—then that some pastor, at most a professor, would not need more than a superficial glance at it in order to evaluate it is really a fatuity. And that something that has been so singularly characterized that it was at the outset stamped "the single individual—I am not a Christian," something that certainly has not appeared in Christendom's eighteen hundred years, where everything is stamped "community, society—I am a true Christian"—then that some pastor, at most a professor, would promptly find an analogy to it is also a fatuity; by a more careful inspection he would discover precisely that it is an impossibility. But this is what one does not find worth the trouble; one prefers a superficial glance at my work and an equally superficial glance at something earlier, and then one promptly has plenty of analogies to my work—this the public can promptly understand.

XIV
355

Indeed, it is as I say: In Christendom's eighteen hundred years there is absolutely nothing comparable, no analogy to my task; it is the first time in "Christendom."

This I know, and I also know what it has cost, what I have suffered, which can be expressed by a single line: I was never like the others. Ah, of all the torments in youthful days, the most dreadful, the most intense: not to be like the others, never to live any day without painfully being reminded that one is not like the others, never to be able to run with the crowd, the desire and the joy of youth, never free to be able to abandon oneself, always, as soon as one would risk it, to be painfully reminded of the chain, the segregation of singularity that, to the point of despair, painfully separates a person from everything that is called human life and cheerfulness and gladness. It is true that one can by means of the most frightful effort strive to hide what one at that age understands as one's disgrace, that one is not like the others. Perhaps one can succeed to a certain degree, but the agony is still in the heart—yet it is only to a certain degree, and therefore a single lack of caution can bring its frightful revenge.

With the years, this pain does decrease more and more, because, accordingly as one more and more becomes spirit, it does not pain that one is not like the others. Spirit is precisely: not to be like the others.

And then perhaps the moment finally comes when the power that has almost mistreated one—yes, so it seems at times—explains itself and says, "Do you have anything to complain about; does it seem to you that I, in comparison with what is done for others, have treated you unfairly, even though I—out of love—have had to embitter your childhood for you, both your earlier and later youth; does it seem to you that I have let you down with what you received instead?" To that there can be only one answer: "No, no, Infinite Love," although surely most people would very definitely decline with "Thanks for nothing" what I in such an agonizing way have become.

In other words, in agonies such as mine a person is brought up to be able to endure being a sacrifice, and the infinite grace that was shown and is shown to me is to be singled out to be a sacrifice, to be singled out for that—yes, and then one thing more, under the cooperative influence of omnipotence and love to be developed to be able to hold firm that this is the highest degree of grace that the God of love can show anyone, and thus only toward the loved ones. XIV
356

My dear reader, you do see that this does not lead straight to profits; that will not be the case until after my death, when the oath-bound tradesmen will also appropriate my life for the salt-meat barrel.

Christianity is so high that what it understands by grace is what all the profane (*procul, o procul este profani*[256] [away, away, O unhallowed ones]) will of all things most decline with "Thanks for nothing." The pastors or lie-pastors get grace changed into indulgence. Grace consists, quite plainly, of a person's having benefits from God, and the pastor has benefits from the people whom he makes believe this, inviting them with Christ's words "Come here, all of you,"[257] the true meaning of which is that the invitation is undeniably to all, but when it comes down to brass tacks and it must be certain what it is that Christ invites them to (in imitation to become a sacrifice), and this is not turned into something that pleases everybody—then it will be manifest, just as in contemporaneity with Christ, that all will most decidedly decline this with "Thanks for nothing" and that only exceptionally does a very rare individual follow the invitation, and of these individuals in turn only a rare individual follows the invitation in such a way that he holds firm that it is an infinite, an indescribable grace that is shown him: to be sacrificed. An indescribable grace, for it is the only way in which God can love a human being and be loved by a human being, but it is indeed an indescribable grace that God wills to do this and wills to allow it. So never mind that, as a precaution and in order to remove everything profane, a middle term is introduced: to become sacrificed. It would indeed be almost nauseating, stifling, oppressive, embarrassing that to be loved by God and to dare to love him should spiritlessly and idiotically be saddled with having the idea that one would have profit from it!

You common man! The Christianity of the New Testament is something infinitely high, but please note that it is not high in such a way that it pertains to differences among people with regard to talents etc. No, it is for all. Everyone, unconditionally everyone—if he will unconditionally, will unconditionally hate himself, will unconditionally put up with everything, suffer everything (and everyone can indeed do that if he will)—then this something infinitely high is accessible to him.

XIV
357

You common man! I have not segregated my life from yours, you know that; I have lived on the street, am known by all.[258] Furthermore, I have not become somebody, do not belong to any class-egotism. So if I belong to anyone, I must belong to you, you common man, you who nevertheless at one time, enticed by someone who, making money on you, gave the appearance of desiring your welfare,[259] have been willing enough to consider me and my life ludicrous, you who least of all have reason to be impatient over or should be unappreciative of my belonging to you, something the more elite have rather had reason to be because I definitely have not joined them but have kept only a loose relation to them.

You common man! I do not keep it a secret from you that, according to my concepts, to be a Christian is something so infinitely high that there are always only few who attain it (which both Christ's life affirms if one pays attention to his contemporaries and his proclamation suggests if one takes it strictly)—yet it is possible for all. But one thing I beseech you for God in heaven's sake and by all that is holy: avoid the pastors, avoid them, those abominations whose job is to hinder you in even becoming aware of what true Christianity is and thereby to turn you, muddled by gibberish and illusion, into what they understand by a true Christian, a contributing member of the state Church, the national Church, and the like. Avoid them; only see to it that you willingly and promptly pay them the money they are to have. One must at no price have money differences with someone one scorns, lest it be said that one was avoiding them in order to get out of paying. No, pay them double so that your disagreement with them can become obvious: that what concerns them does not concern you at all, money, and that, on the contrary, what does not concern them concerns you infinitely, Christianity.

[*On draft:* August 2]

1

THE PASTORS' DIVINE WORSHIP

Let us construct an altogether arbitrary example in order to perceive the truth more clearly!

Let us assume that it is God's will that we human beings must not go to Deer Park.[260]

Naturally "humankind" would not accept this. What would happen then? What would happen is that "the pastors" would make out that when, for example, one blessed the four-seated Holstein carriage and made the sign of the cross over the horses, then going to Deer Park would become well-pleasing to God. The result would therefore be that there would be no change at all and people would go to Deer Park just as much as now, except that it would become a little more expensive, would perhaps cost five rix-dollars more for persons of rank, five rix-dollars for the pastor, and four shillings[261] for the poor. But then trips to Deer Park would have the added charm of also being divine worship.

Perhaps it would occur to the pastors to run the business themselves as renters of horses and carriages. So if it is to be really well-pleasing to God to go to Deer Park, the carriage must be rented from the pastors; perhaps a pastor would ride along, perhaps even—then it would be especially well pleasing to God—a pastor would be the coachman, perhaps even—then it would be most exceptionally well pleasing to God—a bishop would be the coachman. But to achieve this, the supreme maximum of God-pleasingness, would be so expensive that such a divine worship could be reserved only for those who according to the perfected Christianity (the New Testament has, as is well known, another interpretation) are the only ones who have the financial means to please God perfectly: millionaires.

2

THE PASTOR/THE ACTOR

The actor is an honest man who says outright: I am an actor.

Never for any price, never for any price would one get a pastor to say that.

No, "the pastor" is just the opposite of an actor; indeed, al-   xiv
together disinterestedly (since he knows that it does not pertain   359
to him) he raises and answers the question whether an actor may
be buried in Christian ground. It never crosses his mind at all (a
masterpiece of theatrical art, if it is not obtusity) that he does
indeed have a co-interest in the settlement of this question—yes,
that even if it is decided in favor of the actor, it still could remain
doubtful whether it is defensible that the pastor be buried in—
Christian ground.

3

"THE PASTOR" AS A FOLDING SCREEN

Just as in the world of business one has a silent partner, almost a
fictitious quantity, a pure form—but when there is a question of
acting perhaps a little disinterestedly, a little leniently, of not
being too egotistical, well, then it sounds like this, "My good
man, rest assured that I for my part would be happy to oblige
you; I have a soft heart, but my partner, to persuade him is utterly
unthinkable." The whole thing is, of course, skulduggery, con-
trived to be as small-minded, as mercenary as possible, and yet to
give the appearance of being something else . . . . . if only one
did not have the partner.

Just as in practical life one has a wife—and when there arises
an occasion in which it befits a person to act somewhat courageously, resolutely, one then says, "Indeed, my friends, rest assured that as far as I am concerned my heart is in the right place,
I would be willing enough, but my wife—it is utterly useless for
me to want to think of such a thing." Of course, the whole thing
is skulduggery, whereby one simultaneously manages to be a
coward and enjoy the benefits of that in life and also to be a
courageous fellow, if only one were not so unfortunate as to have
the wife.

In this way "the pastor's" existence has importance for safe-guarding the hypocrisy of society. "We have no responsibility, we are ordinary people; we stand with the pastor, who, after all, has taken an oath." Or, "We dare not judge the pastor; we have to keep to what he says, he, the man of God who has taken an oath on the New Testament." Or, "We would be willing enough to forsake everything if this is required; but even if it is required, we dare not take it upon ourselves to decide. We are only lay people, and the pastor is the authority, which we dare not evade, and he says it is an exaggeration etc."

All of "humankind's" sagacity aims at one thing: to be able to live without responsibility. The pastor's importance for society ought to be to do everything to make every human being eter-nally responsible for every hour he lives, even for the least thing he undertakes, because this is Christianity. But his importance for society is: to safeguard hypocrisy, while society shoves the re-sponsibility away from itself and upon "the pastor."

XIV
360

4

PAGANISM—THE CHRISTIANITY OF
"CHRISTENDOM"

The difference is like that between the schnapps a drunkard drinks as a matter of course and the one he drinks—as a reward for abstinence; the latter is infinitely worse than the former, be-cause it is sophistication; the former is, frankly, intemperance; the latter is, in a sophisticated way, *also* abstinence.

5

FRIGHTFUL PROPORTION!

The proportion is not this, that for every person who in truth has willed the truth (as a result of which he became a sacrifice) there live one hundred thousand sensate, worldly-minded, mediocre persons. No, the proportion is this: for every person who in truth has willed the truth, there live—shudder!—there live one thou-sand pastors, who with families support themselves by hindering the sensate, the light-minded, the worldly-minded, the enormous crowd of mediocre people from receiving a truer impression of that one who in truth willed the truth.

6

HEARTINESS/HEARTLESSNESS

People who have their hearts in their mouths, on their lips, on their sleeves, in short, any place but in the right place, are quite naturally guilty of charging with heartlessness the very person who has his heart in the right place.

XIV
361

That is, after they have futilely sought his heart in every one of the places for the heart known to them, they are convinced that he has no heart; as a matter of fact, he has it in the right place, and it does not occur to them to seek it there.

7

SOPHISTICATED VILLAINY

is in a certain sense not seen in the world; precisely this belongs as its crowning achievement—that it looks like the very opposite.

What is seen in the world and seen stamped as abominable, villainous can be frightful enough; but it does not amount to much compared with the sophisticated kind that—sophisticated—passes for the very opposite of villainous. It is the same with it as with what is called a crying-to-heaven sin; the most crying-to-heaven sin is precisely the one that sophisticated— knows how to give the appearance of holiness, so that it least of all can be said to cry to heaven, which it nevertheless does in another sense simply by the muteness of the hypocrisy, more crying-to-heaven than the crying-to-heaven sin.

Let me illustrate.

In a town there lives a stranger; he possesses only one banknote, but one that is of a very large denomination. But no one in the town recognizes the banknote; to them it = 0, and of course no one will give him anything for the paper note.

Then a man comes along, a stranger, for example, who recognizes the banknote very well and says to him one day, "I am your friend, and, as befits a friend, I will help you out of your predicament, I offer you"—and then he offers him half its value. See, this is sophisticated! It is calculated to look like friendship and devotedness, which must be admired and praised by the inhabitants of that town, and at the same time to cheat out of fifty percent. But this is not seen, the inhabitants of that town are unable to see it; on the contrary, they see very unusual magnanimity etc.

As in money matters, so in matters of the spirit.

Someone can be so situated in an age that among his many contemporaries not one has any idea of who he is, of his worth, of his significance. That the people regard everything about him as *Nul und Nichts* [null and void] is, of course, nothing to take exception to.

Then a man comes to him who knows his actual worth and says to him, "I am your friend, and I will give evidence for you"—and thereupon he publicly gives him only half of the acknowledgment he knows is due him. This is sophisticated, calculated to be regarded by his contemporaries as rare, rare sacrificial unselfishness, rare courage and enthusiasm, which give the unappreciated person the justice due him, and yet by risking himself as little as possible he does the unappreciated one the greatest possible harm in that he makes for him a new, an even greater difficulty than to be completely misunderstood—namely, a half acknowledgment. But this is not seen; the contemporaries are unable to see anything but the sophisticated person's noble, disinterested, courageous enthusiasm.

8

[*On draft of no. 8–10:* July 7, 1855]
"IT IS FOR THE SAKE OF THE SUCCESSOR"

But perhaps I am doing the pastors an injustice. To be sure, when one sees how determinedly they stand upon their rights, demand every penny due them, and, like lawyers, take scarcely a step without being paid—one is tempted to say good-bye to their assurances that things of this earth are of no concern to them at all.

But perhaps I am the one who is at fault, I who, impractical as I am, have overlooked something that completely changes the matter. When, for example, Bishop Martensen petitions for six hundred bushels of barley instead of three hundred,[262] then it perhaps is I who have overlooked something—namely, that this is not in any way because such an earthly thing concerns such a holy man, but that His Holiness is doing it—for the sake of his successor, because His Holiness is duty bound to his successor, who in turn does the same thing—for the sake of His Holiness who will be his successor. Indeed, that is something else! So, after all, it is even a noble act—for the sake of the successor!

Now I understand Bishop Martensen and find his petition in agreement with what I know from his own lips—thus it is certain—and something I do not hesitate to share with others since it serves to his glorification: that it was simply and solely a sense of duty that made him able to accept election as bishop. Truly, it was just that sort of man we needed for the bishopric of Sjælland—that is certain.

XIV
363

Therefore, it is for the sake of the successor, simply and solely for the sake of the successor, from a sense of duty to the successor. Thus, for example, if Bishop Martensen were to be faced with the change that there would no longer be a successor, he would immediately withdraw his petition, or, if it was already granted, he would immediately renounce the three hundred bushels of barley—because of course it was not for his own sake that he petitioned for it, not at all; it was for the sake of the successor. Or if there was a minister of ecclesiastical affairs and education who, in consideration of the fact that it was simply and solely for the sake of the successor, decided that the six hundred bushels of barley be granted, but in such a way that three hundred bushels would be saved for the successor (since it was, after all, for the sake of the successor), or that the increase (300 bushels) would not begin until the successor's accession—then Bishop Martensen would thank this minister of ecclesiastical affairs and education who helped remove from the bishop every possible suspicion that it might perhaps be "also" for his own sake, indeed, that he was very delighted, provided that he would receive the six hundred bushels, no matter what happened to the successor later.

9

CONVENT[ION] BEER[263]

It was one of the points on which I was happy to agree perfectly—to me a precious recollection!—with the late Bishop Mynster. He, too, regarded the convention [*Convent*] performances as thin beer.

Therefore it is with a certain satisfaction that not very long ago I accidentally saw in a book something I actually had not known before, that thin beer is called convent beer. If Bishop Mynster had not happened to know it, he would have rejoiced to hear it.

10

XIV
364

THE HIGHER WISDOM IN THERE BEING A PREDECESSOR
AND A SUCCESSOR

Everything that is wrong—is the fault of the prede

cessor. All coveting of the things of this earth—is for

the sake of the successor.

In this way, with the aid of having a predecessor and a successor, one goes through life pleasantly and is in addition a truth-witness. God help the one who has no predecessor and no successor; for him life truly becomes what it, according to the will of Christianity, is supposed to be: an examination in which there can be no cheating.

SUPPLEMENT

KEY TO REFERENCES

Marginal references alongside the text are to volume and page [XIV 100] in *Søren Kierkegaards samlede Værker*, I-XIV, edited by A. B. Drachmann, J. L. Heiberg, and H. O. Lange (1 ed., Copenhagen: Gyldendal, 1901–06). The same marginal references are used in Søren Kierkegaard, *Gesammelte Werke*, Abt. 1–36 (Düsseldorf, Cologne: Diederichs, 1952–69).

References to Kierkegaard's works in English are to this edition, *Kierkegaard's Writings* [*KW*], I-XXVI (Princeton: Princeton University Press, 1978-). Specific references to the *Writings* are given by English title and the standard Danish pagination referred to above [*Either/Or*, I, p. 109, *KW* III (*SV* I 100)].

References to the *Papirer* [*Pap.* I A 100; note the differentiating letter A, B, or C, used only in references to the *Papirer*] are to *Søren Kierkegaards Papirer*, I-XI³, edited by P. A. Heiberg, V. Kuhr, and E. Torsting (1 ed., Copenhagen: Gyldendal, 1909–48), and 2 ed., photo-offset with two supplemental volumes XII-XIII, edited by Niels Thulstrup (Copenhagen: Gyldendal, 1968–70), and with index, XIV-XVI (1975–78), edited by N. J. Cappelørn. References to the *Papirer* in English [*JP* I 100], occasionally amended, are to the volume and serial entry number in *Søren Kierkegaard's Journals and Papers*, I-VI, edited and translated by Howard V. Hong and Edna H. Hong, assisted by Gregor Malantschuk, and with index, VII, by Nathaniel J. Hong and Charles Barker (Bloomington: Indiana University Press, 1967–78).

References to correspondence are to the serial numbers in *Breve og Aktstykker vedrørende Søren Kierkegaard*, I-II, edited by Niels Thulstrup (Copenhagen: Munksgaard, 1953–54), and to the corresponding serial numbers in *Kierkegaard: Letters and Documents*, translated by Henrik Rosenmeier, *Kierkegaard's Writings*, XXV [Letters, Letter 100, *KW* XXV].

References to books in Kierkegaard's own library [*ASKB* 100] are based on the serial numbering system of *Auktionsprotokol over*

Søren Kierkegaards Bogsamling [Auction-catalog of Søren Kierkegaard's Book-collection], edited by H. P. Rohde (Copenhagen:
Royal Library, 1967).

In the Supplement, references to page and lines in the text are
given as: 100:1–10.

In the notes, internal references to the present work are given
as: p. 100.

Three spaced periods indicate an omission by the editors; five
spaced periods indicate a hiatus or fragmentariness in the text.

BACKGROUND MATERIAL PERTAINING TO
FÆDRELANDET [NEWSPAPER] ARTICLES

Hans Lassen Martensen, "Sermon Delivered in Christiansborg Castle Church on the Fifth Sunday after Epiphany, February 5, 1854, the Sunday before Bishop Dr. Mynster's Funeral":[1]

So let us now imitate his faith, seek the consolation to which he himself always led us, so that his memory among us may in truth be for upbuilding! Let us admonish ourselves, saying: Imitate the faith of the true guides, of the authentic truth-witnesses.

Imitate the faith of the true witnesses! From the man whose precious memory fills our hearts, our thoughts are led back to the whole succession of truth-witnesses that like a holy chain stretches through the ages from the days of the Apostles to our own day. But they all harmonize in the witness: Times change and shift, but Jesus Christ is the same yesterday and today and for all eternity; this world's wisdom and this world's kingdoms change and grow old, but the wisdom of Christ and the Kingdom of Christ remain eternally. Our departed teacher and ministering link was also in this holy chain of truth-witnesses to the glory of God and Father; and the witness to the faith, how he carried it on among us in a demonstration of spirit and power!

But when we look back to the glorious ones who in various ways have been our teachers, prototypes, guides, let us above all lay this upon our hearts: Remember your guides who have proclaimed *God's Word* to you, which remains eternally when all human glory fades like flowers in the field; consider the outcome of their course of life and imitate their faith! So let us also imitate this man's faith. For surely, whatever the new times might bring, his faith and his preaching of Jesus Christ, the same yesterday and today, will never become out of date. Let us imitate his faith, for it was not only in word and confession but in deed and in truth, was in the love of the good shepherd, who did not flee like a hireling when the wolves came but was always ready to sacrifice himself for the congregations, concerned for their weal and woe in the dangers both spiritual and temporal. And if we cannot be like him in the great, the extraordinary talents, then let us still be like him in faithfulness, in steadfastness. For surely he was not like those who begin in the spirit but end in the flesh, not like those who begin with zeal and burning ardor and then end in luke-warmness and worldliness. No, in his life there was a growth, indeed quiet but sustained, in wisdom and grace; ever more in-wardly, ever more closely he became united with his Lord and Savior, whose shepherd Gospel fused more and more with his nature, with the Savior, who has said: I know my own and I am known by my own! And therefore his extreme old age was also illuminated by the incorruptible youthfulness and power of eter-nal life, and the prophetic words are applicable to him: The youths shall become weary and faint, but they who expect the Lord shall gain new strength; yes, they shall mount up with wings like eagles. This faith, my friends, would that we might imitate it!

XIV   *Bishop Hans Lassen Martensen, "On the Occasion of Dr. S. Kierke-*
11   *gaard's Article in* Fædrelandet, *no. 295":*[2]

In the cited article, which has rightly attracted much attention, Herr Dr. S. Kierkegaard has made a loud objection to my having, in a sermon I delivered a few days after Bishop Mynster's death, called Bishop Mynster a Christian truth-witness, a man whose faith was not only in word and confession but in deed and truth. A truth-witness, according to S. K.'s interpretation, is a person who in poverty witnesses to the truth, in lowliness and abase-ment, a man who finally is crucified and beheaded, his lifeless body slung by the assistant executioner into a remote place, un-buried, etc., consequently, as far as I understand Herr Doctor's opinion, one of the men who in the historical sense are called martyrs. By classing Bishop Mynster with the Christian truth-witnesses, I therefore am supposed to have made myself guilty before God and the congregation of having spoken a crying-to-heaven untruth in the holy place—indeed, I am supposed to have "played" with Christianity in the most dreadful way. —On this occasion I feel it incumbent on me to give a testimony.

If it had to be conceded to Dr. S. Kierkegaard that the appellation "truth-witness" was limited only to martyrs, then I surely would have made myself guilty, if not of a crying-to-heaven untruth and other offenses against the sacred, which Dr. S. K. on this occasion also takes in vain, then at least of an erroneous use of words. But whatever can it be that justifies his restricting the concept in such an arbitrary way, contrary to all ecclesiastical usage, a restriction according to which the apostle John—who, as has already been noted against him, was neither beheaded nor crucified, nor after death slung aside by the assistant executioner, but buried by his congregation—must be excluded from the number of truth-witnesses. And then what can it be that justifies his casting a false light upon my statement that there stretches from the days of the apostles until our day a chain of truth-witnesses, as if I thereby had said that the Christian truth-witnesses in our day should as a matter of course be compared to those in the apostolic age, although I have expressly added what he fraudulently omits—that while the Lord and the Spirit are the same,[3] there is a difference in the times, the gifts, and the instruments, something sufficiently obvious to everyone who does not want to misunderstand—and I have distinguished between the ordinary and the extraordinary in the development of the Church, a distinction that is familiar to my listeners. But it assuredly will not do to forget, because of the great difference in the various developmental stages of the Church, what must be the same in all ages, unless we want to give up the article in our catechism: I believe in one holy universal Church. Those who believe this article know also that there is in the Church from generation to generation a propagating truth-witness, and that there also are those in every age and in every generation, both in the congregation and among the teachers, who bear this witness, who vitally and personally testify to the great fact of Christianity. If this had not been the case, the unity of the Church would have been broken over the years. Of course, it is useless to make

XIV
12

such observations to Dr. S. Kierkegaard, whose Christianity is
without Church and without history, and who seeks Christ only
in the "desert" and in "private rooms." But it is contrary to all
congregational consciousness to maintain that the truth should
be witnessed to only in extraordinary times and under extraordinary trials and with extraordinary powers and gifts of grace, since
"the service of the Word" in the congregation is instituted precisely so that in every age and in every generation there shall be
witnessing to the truth, while the Church at no time ceases to be
militant.

   Next, with regard to Dr. S. Kierkegaard's claim that the only
authentic mark of a truth-witness is suffering, it must be herewith
pointed out that many zealots and fanatics have also undergone
great sufferings without therefore being truth-witnesses. Furthermore, what justifies his overlooking the fact that there are
sufferings other than tangible persecution? For example, cannot
an age's spiritual death, cannot people's indifference to eternal
life be a source of deep suffering for those who work with the
doctrine? Or are not words—attacking, persecuting words—a
weapon like a sword, and cannot a truth-witness be stoned in a
way other than by the actual casting of stones? And is there any
age in which lies and slander do not send out their poisoned
arrows? Dr. S. Kierkegaard must either be so obsessed by a *fixed*
idea that he has eventually lost the simplest presence of mind, or
against his better judgment he must have defined the concept of
a truth-witness in this exorbitant way because now once again a
sensation should be created with "playing at Christianity." But in
that case this bold game ought to be arranged somewhat more
subtly. It is indeed rather mediocre for such a practiced sophist as
Dr. S. Kierkegaard to offer us, without any further addition, that
presupposition, the baselessness and arbitrariness of which is so
crude and obvious that it becomes almost banal to refute it, and
it must be feared that his thinking has now begun to pass from the
much too fluid to the much too firm, or that his ideas have now
actually begun to become fixed.

   The next question, then, is whether, on the presupposition
that the true Church is in fact to be found among us, Bishop

Mynster has a place among the Christian truth-witnesses in our fatherland. I truly believed it when I said it to the grieving assembly of the congregation just a few days after his death, and I still believe it, and I do not assume that I will ever in my life change my mind. Of course, from Dr. S. Kierkegaard we hear that Bishop Mynster's proclamation of Christianity has suppressed some of what is most decisively Christian, namely, the doctrine of dying to the world and hating oneself. It is easy to dash off claims of that sort. But what must first and foremost be said at Bishop Mynster's grave is that he was not silent but opened his mouth to speak at a time when most were silent and when the few voices raised for the Gospel were drowned out by the voices of unbelief and denial. Or does not precisely this belong to Bishop Mynster's undying praise that at the beginning of the century he stood up against unbelief, defended our Lutheran divine worship service when it was in danger of being distorted,[4] and prepared the way for the Lord in many souls? And has he not through the many years he has served in our Church continued to preach Jesus Christ and him crucified,[5] which certainly belongs to some of what is most decisively Christian and includes that doctrine of dying to the world, even if not in Dr. S. Kierkegaard's way? And can what I have said about him be contradicted, that over the years his witness became more full-bodied and more full-toned and, what I wish to add at this time, that there are few preachers in whom such a progressive development can be pointed out? Moreover, in the sermon Dr. S. Kierkegaard attacked there was no mention of what he wants to insinuate, of "canonizing" or idolizing, but only of remembering in love and gratitude. But when Dr. S. Kierkegaard dashes off accusations of having suppressed the truth, he ought also to have taken into consideration that a servant of the Lord must not only guard against suppressing anything of what he is sent to say to people but likewise must guard against saying *more* than he is sent to say, which includes also that he must guard against saying more than *he* in particular is sent to say according to the specific gift of the Spirit that is placed in his soul. Bishop Mynster has always observed this golden rule, and if it were more generally followed, much untruthful and exorbitant talk about the heights and depths of the Christian life, for example, about dying to the world, about which the speaker had information only through fantasizing, would be avoided; indeed, many upbuilding discourses and books would be unwritten. Moreover, there is certainly no need to discuss at length that mention can and must be made of the various developmental stages in the Christian truth-witnesses, both with regard to the power and the completeness of the witness and the fact that the character of their witness cannot help but be conditioned, partly by the time in which they appeared, partly by their given individuality. But to pass judgment on a man who is publicly known to have built upon the ground of faith,[6] to pronounce the verdict that what Bishop Mynster, who has been a teacher not only for a small circle but for his nation, has built up through more than half a century of activity, that this, even though in other respects it must be respected, in the Christian sense is false and unauthentic—that calls not only for something else and more than Dr. S. Kierkegaard's slovenly article in *Fædrelandet* but for something else and more than the entire prolix Kierkegaard literature—also because the scrutiny and judgment of such things call for a criterion totally different from that which Dr. S. K. possesses, he whose Christianity is not at all the faith of a community but solely and simply a private religion, a Christianity in which the Christian Church and the work of the Holy Spirit in the Christian Church are left out, and along with that much else of "what is most decisively Christian."

But it is not only Bishop Mynster's proclamation of Christianity that Dr. S. Kierkegaard attacks, but also the man's life and character. Bishop Mynster, namely by declaiming on Sunday and by worldly-sagaciously sheltering himself on Monday, is supposed to have created the appearance that he was a man of character, a man of principles, a man who stands firm when everything is tottering etc., whereas "the truth was that to a high degree he was worldly-sagacious, but weak, self-indulgent, and great only as a declaimer." From this amazing communication we learn among other things that one of the hardest-working men in Denmark is now to be classed among the "self-indulgent." From this communication it is apparent that to the best of his ability Dr. S. Kierkegaard wants to see to it that Bishop Mynster, at least after his death, can gain not merely a good but also a bad reputation.[7] But as I see him hurling invectives against one of our fatherland's noblest men, against a man he himself formerly acknowledged as his teacher, his spiritual benefactor, as I see him like a Thersites at the hero's grave,[8] I concede that by his graveside conduct he will most certainly achieve his aim—namely, to offend many. But please note that not only heavenly truth and love can offend people, but also conscienceless untruth and injustice, also the unclean and undisciplined spirit, also the flippancy that plays with the venerable, plays with a man's own better feeling.

So Bishop Mynster was great only as a declaimer, but in other respects without principles and character; so he was only a man who had the appearance of godliness but denied its power. This is the view to which Dr. S. Kierkegaard has come after having liberated himself from the filial relation of devotion to his father, who "to the distress of his life" brought him up on Mynster's sermons. This is the view he repressed for many years while he outwardly continued to show Bishop Mynster the accustomed veneration. This veneration was only a mask, which he now, after Bishop Mynster is buried "with full honors," lets fall in order to bring "clarity into our confused religious situation"!—truly, this discarded mask in *Fædrelandet* will surely be long preserved in the history of our public morality and will increase S. Kierkegaard's renown. But the following observation seems probable: might it not come about that among us Dr. S. Kierkegaard himself will eventually become an itinerant masker who wants to clarify our confused religious situation by something far worse than religious confusion! Or does Dr. S. Kierkegaard actually believe that we would still assume that this is his *earnestness* about what he continually pontificates, namely, that the truth must be expressed in "existence"? Or may he find it paradoxical if we are led to the opinion that the truth, Christian and moral, as well as the intellectual gifts with which he is equipped (but far from equipped on the scale he himself "to the distress of his life" fancies), that all this may serve him only to the "refine-

XIV
14

ments" of vanity and of other more select pleasures. I do not know how he will justify this masquerade to himself, since a knight of faith[9]—and Dr. S. Kierkegaard has often given the appearance of being such a one—in his relation with people, living or dead, surely ought to strive for knightly behavior. I have, however, no doubt at all that he will know how to justify to his own conscience his conduct by some other higher morality of genius, perhaps even by some other higher religious requirement that orders every other consideration to retreat and gives him a criterion for his conduct far elevated above the ordinary. But I cannot avoid thinking of Jacobi's words: "*Mir fallen gleich Maulschellen ein, wenn ich Leute mit erhabenen Gesinnungen herankommen sehe, die nicht einmal nur* rechtschaffene *Gesinnungen beweisen* [I immediately think of boxing ears when I see people come along with sublime dispositions who do not even demonstrate *upright and honest* dispositions]"[10]—words that are by no means striking enough to describe S. K.'s behavior, since in those moral pseudo-existences Jacobi is complaining only of the inner lack of integrity, but not of the *falseness* and masked character that justify the immoral means by an imaginary religious motive, all of which belongs to the character we as Christians are obliged to repudiate.[11] This much is certain: Dr. S. Kierkegaard, who once wrote a discourse about "the work of love in recollecting one who is dead"[12] (see S. Kierkegaard's *Works of Love*), has brought himself to remembrance, at least by this, his most recent discourse about one who is dead, in a way that will safeguard him for a long time against the danger, to the averting of which he does not seem to spare any sacrifice whatever: the danger of being forgotten.

N-n, "A Proposal to Hr. Dr. S. Kierkegaard":[13]

. . . It is now almost a half year since Herr Dr. Kierkegaard first stepped forth as the rigorous preacher in the desert. . . . From the beginning it seemed that the prophetic repentance address moved in a rather limited circle; it was the late Bishop and his *parentator* [funeral orator] against whom it was actually turned. But now the design is broadened. Now "the official Christianity" is the cue phrase. Everything that is taught and preached by the appointed servants of Christianity is lumped together and stamped as Anti-Christianity. And yet the boundary is not here. *Christendom in its totality, Christianity in its whole existence is included*—except that it is not possible to grasp whether the Christian world in general is to be understood, or the Protestant Church, or only the Church in Denmark. . . .

I venture, therefore, to ask Herr Dr. Kierkegaard *whether he should not find that the time has come for him to move a step further . . . . Let him place a guide in the hands of his countrymen. Let him give his countrymen a clear, definite outline of the New Testament's doctrine in such a way that, according to him, "it will be justified to bear the name of New Testament." . . .*

J. Victor Bloch, "*On the Occasion of the 'Proposal' to Dr. S. Kierkegaard*":[14]

XIV 62

With great satisfaction I read in *Fædrelandet*, no. 79, 1855, a "Proposal to Herr Dr. S. Kierkegaard," without, however, as I shall explain in more detail below, being able to subscribe to the proposal itself. This contribution is written with much sobermindedness, discretion, and competence and deserves to be called "a lead article," but only until one comes to the proposal, where it seems to become misleading. With proper limitations, it acknowledges the justification and merit of Dr. Kierkegaard's action in the last half year, namely, as it manifested itself in the beginning, when he spoke earnest, arousing words against an alliance between God's kingdom and the world, a veiling, a toning down, and a suppressing of the essential in Christianity; but it also clearly and definitely points out how he has been more and more carried away without taking the matter a step further. But then when the request is put to Dr. K. "whether he should not find that the time has come for him to move a step further," and this request later emerges as the definite proposal that "he place a guide in the hands of his countrymen: an exposition in clear, definite outline of the New Testament's doctrine in such a way that it, according to him, will be justified to bear the name of New Testament"—then I can no longer follow the honored

XIV 63

propounder of the proposal, partly because Dr. K. by his most recent conduct has made impossible every discussion with him about Christianity, partly because the matter now demands, not a *theological* discussion with respect to such an explanation, but an *ecclesiastical* decision.

Dr. K., who in the beginning seemed to act as a truth-witness within the Christian Church, has recently roved about and has been carried away to the point where he has gone completely *outside*, so that he forthrightly admits that he himself not only is not a truth-witness, not a reformer, but not even a Christian in the sense of the New Testament; he is only a "poet,"[15] or, as he recently has expressed it, one with "a definite detective talent."[16] But as amazing as this explanation sounds after, indeed, even during "the prophetic penitential discourse," it loses all meaning and sinks down into the most superficial triviality when one hears him cry in the same breath that Christianity no longer exists,[17] that Christianity has become extinct, that there are no Christians, no truth-witnesses anymore, etc.* But if what he has written on this matter is not to be regarded as extreme "*licentia poetica* [poetic license]" or as a coarse practical joke with a police club, then in this extra-churchly stance he becomes involved in the obvious *self-contradiction* that he, who is not a Christian, wants to decide what Christianity is and what it is not, that he, who says that Christianity does not exist anymore, preaches against a veiling and distortion of Christianity. The honored propounder of the proposal has not overlooked this self-contradiction but has assumed—as he had to assume in order to be able to make his proposal—that it could be canceled if Dr. K. would revoke or at least essentially limit his strong words that Christianity does not exist anymore, and if he himself relates to the so-called Christendom only as one with a definite detective talent. Most assuredly if he would make such an admission, make such a confession, then with his stepping back the matter could move a good step forward. But just as I do not think that a renewed study of the New Testament will lead Dr. K. to such a desirable stepping

---

*What Dr. K. has said more specifically about the Danish national Church, he no doubt wants to have extended to all Christendom.

back, neither do I believe that he, if he in any way gained the Christian perception and ecclesiastical orientation necessary for this, would seek to have the pending issue decided by complying with the challenge directed to him. In other words the issue, as already noted, needs an ecclesiastical decision. Dr. K. has contradicted not only himself, but he has contradicted the *Lord*, who has promised his Church an eternal life with victory over the forces of darkness.[18] As a preacher of penitence he has castigated not only lukewarm Christendom, but he has rejected the anointed-by-the-Lord eternal truth-witness, has denied his "Holy Universal *Church*." But then he will have to put up with it when the Lord's congregation allows his loud outcry to go unheeded on the outside and only shuts the church door to him when he becomes all too impertinent and strident, while it, however, cheerfully continues to sing its hymns, to pray its Lord's prayer, to read its Bible, to listen to the preaching of God's Word, and to live on its Lord's sacraments, without involving itself in demonstrating its existence, a demonstration that only the *Holy Spirit* can give with the clarity and power of truth and life, just as he—God be praised—has given it hitherto and gives it anew every Church year.

Dr. K. stands outside the Church of Christ at the foot of the rock[19] and reads the New Testament until he loses his sight. Then he begins to prate that the Church has vanished, since he does not see it anymore. And people out there and down there who would wish it to be true stream in to listen avidly, yet nourish a secret fear that this eccentric man with the singular gestures and the dark discourses, who, although he is delivering a funeral sermon over Christendom, yet in no way wants to make common cause with the world, may devote himself to giving lectures on the downfallen Church and get it to rise again. What is feared by these people is hoped for by others who until now have looked with favor on the Church and, although they have been unwilling to enter, yet are reluctant to see it crumble to ruin. But while all this is being read and prated and feared and hoped on the outside, *the Lord's Church stands firm on the rock—a fact*, that again and again will be made manifest by the Church's living testimony (whereby, as said previously, Holy Scripture also

XIV
64

receives its seal) but that is never demonstrated by theological research. And *his congregation lives* within on his sacraments under the care and discipline of his Spirit and is enlivened every year by Christmas, Easter, and Pentecost joy, indeed, lives eternally, when the whole great Church year ends in eternity in and with him who has said, "I live, and you shall live."[20] But that "many are called but few are chosen,"[21] that "the Lord knows his own,"[22] that the name alone does not make anyone a Christian, the clerical gown does not make anyone a truth-witness—this certainly needs to be emphasized again and again, but it is not, after all, something new that we are now to learn from Dr. K.

Such is the life of the Church that Dr. K. has had the audacity to put in question, indeed, has finally directly disowned, has *forever decided*, and presumably it is hereby also decided what is to be believed and done for salvation, what is the authentic—"New Testament" and Church—Christianity, the Christianity that the Lord's congregation confesses by its Baptism and Lord's Supper, its prayers and preaching. Since I, as stated, abide by this ecclesiastical decision, I have no proposal to Dr. Kierkegaard on this issue and have nothing to do with him as long as he stands where he stands and fights the way he fights. If, however, he could and would use the New Testament with the mirror image of the apostolic Church to chastise and punish both clergy and laity, he would be doing a good deed; but he can do this only with the faith that the Lord's Church is standing where he has built it, that his Church is alive, no matter how Dr. K. and others handle the New Testament and personally go in through the church door in order to have discussion with the congregation. I fear, however, that it will appear to him much too difficult to give up his eccentricity, his solitary position, and sign the universal Church marriage contract. But I also fear that he will be more and more forgotten in the wedding house,[23] and specifically by those very people whom he earlier has helped on the way to it and who at that time had no doubt but that he himself wanted to be included. "Human honesty"[24] is all right, but it certainly will not do when it comes in conflict with *divine* honesty; then it makes the Lord's yes into no. Honest humility or humble honesty that for a time makes a person not dare to call himself a Christian is all right, but it truly will not do if it continues to prevent a Christian baptized as an infant from being a child of God through his Baptism and faith and with gratitude and worship admitting that the Lord is in the right when he always "loves first"[25] and gives what he requires.[26]

Lønborg parsonage, April 10, 1855   J. VICTOR BLOCH.

Var Biskop Mynster et „Sandheds-vidne", et af „de rette Sandhedsvidner" — er dette Sandhed?

i Febr. 1854.   S. Kierkegaard.

I den Tale, Prof. Martensen har „holdt 5te Søndag efter hellig tre Konger, Søndagen før Biskop Dr. Mynsters Jordefærd", en Erindringstale, hvad den maaskee ogsaa forsaavidt kan kaldes, som den bringer Prof. Martensen i Erindring til den ledige Bispestol — i denne Tale stilles Biskop Mynster frem som et Sandhedsvidne, som et af de rette Sandhedsvidner; der tales i saa stærke og af-gjørende Udtryk som vel muligt. Med den afdøde Bi-skops Skikkelse, hans Liv og Levnet, Udgangen af hans Vandel for Øie formanes vi til at „efterligne de sande Veilederes, de rette Sandhedsvidners Tro" (p. 5), deres Tro, thi den var, hvad der udtrykkeligt siges om Bi-skop Mynster „ikke blot i Ord og Bekjendelse, men i Gjerning og Sandhed" (p. 9); den afdøde Biskop indføres af Prof. Martensen i (p. 6) „den hellige Kjæde af Sandhedsvidner, som strækker sig gjennem Tiderne fra Apostlernes Dage" osv.

Dette maa jeg gjøre Indsigelse mod — og nu da Biskop Mynster er død, kan jeg ville tale, her dog meget kort, og da slet ikke om, hvad der bestemte mig til at indtage det Forhold til ham, som jeg indtog.

[Nb: The essay was written in February 1854 and published December 18, 1854.]

Was Bishop Mynster a "Truth-Witness," One of "the Authentic Truth-Witnesses" —*Is This the Truth?*

_____

February 1854.   S. Kierkegaard.

In the address Prof. Martensen "delivered the fifth Sunday after Epiphany, the Sunday before Bishop Dr. Mynster's funeral," a memorial address, as it perhaps can in a way also be called, since it calls to mind Prof. Martensen for the vacant bishopric—in this address Bishop Mynster is represented as a truth-witness, as one of the authentic truth-witnesses; the expressions used are as strong and decisive as possible. With the late bishop's figure, his life and career, and the outcome of his life before our eyes, we are exhorted to "imitate the faith of the true guides, of the authentic truth-witnesses" (p. 5), their faith, for it was, as is explicitly said about Bishop Mynster, "not only in word and confession, but in deed and truth" (p. 9). The late bishop is introduced by Prof. Martensen (p. 6) into "the holy chain of truth-witnesses that stretches through the ages from the days of the apostles" etc.

_____

To this I must raise an objection—and now that Bishop Mynster is dead I am able and willing to speak, but very briefly here, and not at all about what made me decide to take the position that I have taken in relation to him.

Dette skal siges; saa være det da sagt.

Af

S. Kierkegaard.

———————————————

Kjøbenhavn.

Forlagt af C. A. Reitzels Bo og Arvinger.

Bianco Lunos Bogtrykkeri.

1855.

This Must Be Said; So Let It Be Said.

By

S. Kierkegaard.

———————

Copenhagen.

Published by C. A. Reitzel's Estate and Heirs.

Bianco Luno's Press.

1855.

Øieblikket.

Nr. 1.

Indhold:

1) Stemning.
2) Til „dette skal siges"; eller hvorledes anbringes et Afgjørende?
3) Er det forsvarligt af Staten — den christelige Stat! — om muligt at umuliggjøre Christendom?
4) „Tag et Bræk-Middel!"

24 Mai 1855.   S. Kierkegaard.

Kjøbenhavn.

Forlagt af C. A. Reitzels Bo og Arvinger.
Bianco Lunos Bogtrykkeri.

The Moment.

No. 1.

———————

Contents:

May 24, 1855.   S. Kierkegaard.

———————

Copenhagen.

Published by C. A. Reitzel's Estate and Heirs.
Bianco Luno's Press.

Hvad Christus dømmer

om

officiel Christendom.

Af

S. Kierkegaard.

Kjøbenhavn.

Forlagt af C. A. Reitzels Bo og Arvinger.

Bianco Lunos Bogtrykkeri.

1855.

What Christ Judges

of

Official Christianity.

By

S. Kierkegaard.

———————

Copenhagen.

Published by C. A. Reitzel's Estate and Heirs.

Bianco Luno's Press.

1855.

Guds Uforanderlighed.

En Tale.

Af

S. Kierkegaard.

Kjøbenhavn.

Forlagt af C. A. Reitzels Bo og Arvinger.

Bianco Lunos Bogtrykkeri.

1855.

The Changelessness of God.

A Discourse.

———

By

S. Kierkegaard.

———

Copenhagen.

Published by C. A. Reitzel's Estate and Heirs.

Bianco Luno's Press.

1855.

SELECTED ENTRIES FROM
KIERKEGAARD'S JOURNALS AND PAPERS
PERTAINING TO *THE MOMENT*
AND LATE WRITINGS

See 263:1–281:7:

I sit here all alone (I have frequently been just as alone many times, but I have never been so aware of it) and count the hours until I shall see Sæding.[27] I cannot recall any change in my father, and now I am about to see the places where as a poor boy he tended sheep, the places for which, because of his descriptions, I have been so homesick. What if I were to get sick and be buried in the Sæding churchyard![28] What a strange idea! His last wish[29] for me is fulfilled—is that actually to be the sum and substance of my life? In God's name! Yet in relation to what I owed to him the task was not so insignificant. I learned from him what fatherly love is, and through this I gained a conception of divine fatherly love, the one single unshakable thing in life, the true Archimedean point.—*JP* V 5468 (*Pap.* III A 73) *n.d.*, 1840

III
A 73
35

III
A 73
36

It is not easy to have both the Old and the New Testament, since the O.T. contains altogether different categories. What, indeed, would the N.T. say about a faith that believes that it is going to be well off in the world, in temporality, instead of giving this up in order to grasp the eternal. Hence the instability of clerical discourse, depending on whether it is the Old or New Testament that is transparent in it.—*JP* I 206 (*Pap.* IV A 143) *n.d.* 1843

Fragment of a Letter[30]

. . . . . However strange it seems, it is nevertheless true that in a parsonage fixed ideas can be superbly developed. If one may

VII¹
B 195
373

even say of life in the big city that it actually stifles the highest in
a person, then it also has the good side that it contains a constant
corrective that prevents extravagances. One becomes so accustomed to hearing all this about the age as an age of movement,
that the times demand one thing today, tomorrow the opposite,
that a brand new system is imminent—one becomes so accustomed to hearing this that it makes no more impression on one
than cursing makes an impression on a sailor. One becomes as
accustomed to the vortex of the newspapers as to evening
prayers—to be sure, one would think that it could not be good
to read something so shocking and stimulating at night that it
could easily make a person sleepless—but one becomes so accustomed to it that one falls asleep reading it. This is how it is in the
capital city. It is different, however, when a theological graduate,
full of the superficiality of the city, becomes like a new bottling
sent out to a parsonage: then it can easily and quietly become
earnest fantasy, and he, precisely because he lacks a corrective
and a criterion, becomes a very earnest visionary. Wonderful!
Ordinarily just to mention the phrase "a rural pastor" makes one
spontaneously think of a modest but calm and contented life out
there in a quiet landscape where the mill goes klip klap klip
klap,[31] where the stork stands on the roof the long summer day,
where in the evening the pastor sits "paternally happy [*Fader-
glad*]" in the arbor with his wife, happy with his life, happy in his
modest but meaningful work. When the one who is employed at
the big theater in the capital city, where energies are lavishly
squandered, sometimes wishes for a little recreation, he spontaneously thinks of visiting a rural pastor. Out there, so he thinks,
where the lily does not spin and yet is lovely, out there is rest;
there is no prying, thoughtless crowd, there is no bravo-shouting
and noise, there one hears no cannonade—from the amusement
parks;[32] out there everything is quiet yet so smiling, there everything is very small and yet very beneficent, there meals are very
plain and yet very tasty, there work is to be done and yet such a
blessing, there everyone tends to his own business and yet there
is harmony, there the pastor's wife is a domestic sage for the
parish and the pastor a spiritual counselor for the congregation.
Alas, but sometimes it is otherwise. There is now, for example,

Pastor Damkiær;[33] he is in a village parsonage—and thinks that there is an enormous stirring in the Danish state Church; indeed, "in 70 years there has not been such stirring in the Danish state Church."[34] One notices at once that it is no "man from the country" who is speaking; one must rather say that it is a man from the capital city who is doing the opposite of rusticating in the country—without, however, exactly doing anything wise. Just as the shadow at times caricatures the likeness of the object, so also the hectic life of the capital city is caricatured by being enacted by a solitary pastor out in the country—*von einem bösem Geist in Kreis herumgeführt, und rings umher liegt schöne grüne Weide* [encircled by an evil spirit, and round about lies a beautiful green pasture].[35]

The pastor, who sits out there in the parsonage or on "the wonder stool"[36] in the parsonage, thinks that it is the hymnbook affair that is producing this enormous movement. What enormous movement? Why, of course, that which is in the state Church, "the like of which there has not been in 70 years." But is it indeed absolutely certain that there is such an enormous movement in the Danish state Church? In any case, it nevertheless seems most fitting to make sure of this fact before one proceeds comparatively to determine its degree, before one goes ahead and explains its basis, lest the whole thing become like someone's explaining the reason for an enormous fire, the like of which there had not been since the great fire—a fire that had never occurred at all. Such a manner of proceeding only makes every somewhat sensible person feel strange. I recollect from an earlier time that I frequently heard mention that there was something that Pastor Grundtvig with his [*in margin:* matchless] "falcon eye"[37] is supposed to have predicted with regard to Denmark's and the North's matchless future. I also recollect that I did not succeed in understanding what it was that he predicted. In later years the matter changed; now it is said that what he predicted has even been fulfilled—so I am deucedly sure that one can find out what it is. And yet, despite honest effort, I at least have come just as far and remained just as sagacious, despite my question. That is, when I ask: What is it that Pastor Grundtvig predicted, the answer is: Oh, it is, of course, what has been

VII¹
B 195
375

fulfilled. And when I ask: But what is it that has been fulfilled, the answer is: Oh, it is, of course, what he predicted. Grundtvig unconditionally holds the honor (of that there is absolutely no doubt) both of having predicted, thus the honor as a prophet, and the honor of its having been fulfilled, which rarely happens and could easily seem to be a precarious situation for a prophet—to become contemporary with the fulfillment—but what it is, that which was predicted and which was fulfilled, well, that one cannot find out.

Is there actually such an enormous movement in the Danish state Church? It is one against one, consequently my word against Pastor Damkiær's;* so I would say: At the moment there is no movement in the Danish state Church worth mentioning, but there certainly are a few journalists to whose interest, in the same sense as it is to the interest of attorneys that there are cases, it is to publicize it—in order that if possible there could come to be a little stirring; and thus there are a few gullible people who, like the soapmaker in *Egmont*,[38] spread the rumor further saying, "There is something, there is definitely something"—which one can unconditionally say at any time and in every situation. Generally one must, insofar as one wishes to form the correct opinion concerning the movement in an age, use considerable caution with regard to the press. The press is often guilty of a *petitio principii* [begging of the question] in its tactics; it pretends to be *reporting* a *factual* state and *aims* to *produce* it. There is something the journalist wants to promote, and perhaps there is no one at all who thinks about it or cares about it; what does the journalist do then? In lofty tones he writes, and in the name of many (since every journalist is like Maren Amme,[39] who could speak in several voices), an article about its being a need deeply felt by everyone etc. (see any newspaper anywhere). His newspaper perhaps has wide circulation, and now we have the game underway. That is, the article is read, discussed; another paper perhaps proceeds to write against it; there are polemics, a sensation is cre-

*Note. That he perhaps speaks in the name of the century and of the public makes no difference; the main point, after all, is that it is he who is speaking, and he is only one; the other is an empty and superfluous and meaningless ceremony, with which I do not even care to comply.

ated—"I have found it; I see Aarhus,"[40]—that is, I have found it; now the stirring is there, *quod erat demonstrandum* [that which was to be demonstrated]. Of course, there certainly was *quod erat demonstrandum* at the time when he wrote the first article; now, however, every dialectician must call his behavior a *petitio principii*: he demonstrates that this or that is factual—by his making it factual. If someone at the time of evening when the watchmen are on the street were to run about shouting "Fire" and calling for the watchmen to whistle, thereby causing the watchmen to whistle, and then an hour later one were to argue with him about there not having been a fire alarm that evening—well, then one would lose. As a precautionary measure one must introduce a little determination of time in the question whether there was a fire alarm when he began. Yet a fire alarm is an even more definite thing than those flimsy concepts: stirring, movement, about which our age battles in the air or in the newspapers. The mortality figure in a city is something definite that can be definitely established; the sanitary conditions can also be determined by the aid of factual information about the number of diseases; but if someone were to start a discussion about indisposition, would this then not be arguing about the emperor's beard? Yet indisposition, even if it is as flimsy a concept as movement and stirring, is not dialectical in the same way, because indisposition can still not be produced by being written about. But in connection with movement and stirring, a *generatio aequivoca* [spontaneous generation] has the validity that was earlier attributed to it in nature—it is produced *eo ipso* by being much discussed. It is already sufficient that it has been in the newspaper. One sees how it is easily in every person's power to make merry as much as he wishes with regard to movement and stirring if he only chooses to be a journalist: he gets it into the newspaper and then argues from its having been in the newspaper. He says with emphasis: It has been said officially in print; it is read by the whole nation.

In civil life, as far as I know, it is forbidden under penalty of the law to raise an untruthful hue and cry; in literature we are thrown to the wolves, all we poor wretches who do not publish a newspaper every evening. We live as if under a bushel compared with a journalist, whose whistle is not heard, like the watchman's, in

VII^1
B 195
377

a few streets but over the whole country, not one single evening but every evening. Speaking is indeed the universally human, and then in turn there is little difference if one person has a somewhat stronger voice than another—but a journalist has a suprahuman voice by which he drowns out all others, and he does this every evening. Previously the world has seen despot tyranny, money tyranny, mental tyranny—but yelling tyranny is the most

recent; it is journalism's. Yelling* tyranny, one could also call it begging tyranny. Just as a beggar by running after a man up and down the street finally extorts a shilling, in the same way journalism extracts a little concession by daily sticking to the same story. It must, therefore, if equality is to be established, end up with this, that everyone publishes a newspaper—or that what is said in a newspaper diminishes to being nothing. The most obtuse journalist, provided he only has a little brashness, has *eo ipso* absolute predominance over the wisest if the latter does not want to publish a newspaper. When everything is lost on the day of battle, the journalist quite correctly says to his heart, "It makes no difference; now with that business over, if I begin and continue every single evening, then what I want will no doubt establish itself firmly in the public. If Jacob with the aid of the motley-colored sticks could get the ewes to bear as he wished,[42] should I not then

be able to do the same with the public merely by daily holding

In margin: Note. Anyone who occupies himself with more difficult subjects cannot become involved with a journalist at all and must thank God if the journalist is so gracious as not to attack him. If he merely says one word with the idea that it is addressed to the few who are able to concern themselves with such things, the journalist yells it to the whole country.[a] All the citizens, assistant butchers, and schoolboys and market town geniuses[b] etc. become immediately interested in the matter. Thus by a journalist's virtuosity[c] the question about Madvig's Latin grammar[41] has been debated by innkeepers and barber apprentices and whatever authorities for whom the journalist makes a living by writing and at the head of which he proudly boasts of being—the crowd, the most mediocre of all categories, which even antiquity so superbly understood, so that one would be mutilated if one merely dared to print what Plato and particularly Aristotle in a few passages say about it.

[a](and then a journalist cannot talk softly and cannot address himself to a few; his idea is to yell—to all)

[b]mistresses of the house

[c]communistic

my story up before them? No devil, not the greatest genius who has lived, is a match for me, unless he becomes a journalist—and in that case I will give the matter a new turn and scoff at him because he will stoop to being a journalist."

As for the hymnbook affair, the whole movement is purely simulated. A committee is established [*hensat*], not to mention set up [*nedsat*]; it has met, now it meets no more.* One appeal after the other has been received—indeed, it reminds one of the wonders of antiquity, where thousands of people were used to drag together masses of stone for the pyramids: in the same way these appellants harness themselves to drag the committee ahead. But despite all this, despite the many teams, the committee gets nowhere; the whole thing ends up in a little bit of a pamphlet. Of course the many appeals, although factually real, are indeed a fiction. It is a party that wants to have a new hymnbook. Now, the party could have agreed to submit one appeal—and this would not have signified much, or rather, nothing at all; it would have been like a demonstration of the correctness of a hypothesis that needs no demonstration. When a party wants to have a new hymnbook and the appeals are to demonstrate some sympathy for the cause, then the appeals certainly must come from others instead of from the party. This has not happened; on the contrary, some of the appellants have been honorable enough to admit, something that is always commendable, that they have tried to acquire the signatures of others but obtained none. This potentiated non-fact (that no signatures were acquired despite the effort to do so) is especially strong evidence of the lack of universal sympathy, especially in our age, in which people usually are enticed easily enough if only they get to sign their names to something. Thus the appeals are from the party and yet there

VII¹
B 195
380

---

*Note. On the whole our age is remarkably superstitious about getting a committee set up; if only that has been done, everything is quiet again. Perhaps it is thought that the setting up of a committee is like clabbering milk—if the milk is merely set aside, one need do nothing more; it becomes sour by itself. The *most* glorious powers are set in motion in order to get a committee set up; as soon as it is done, no one cares about the matter anymore. Strange that the government does not want to take advantage of this; the whole demand for a constitution would very likely be quieted if only a committee were set up.

is not a single petition; no, they have divided into five and six batches or packs: thus about five and six appeals are received—the same can at least be said in a baseless report, just like a baseless truth. Five or six appeals—and each appeal is, like Gideon's troops, armed with torch and trumpet—other weapons are not used. Five or six appeals, that means something; that means much more than if the whole party had submitted one appeal—which according to the foregoing would have meant nothing at all. The many appeals mean something; in a village parsonage it may very well look like an enormous stirring in the Danish state Church, and the little morsel of a first pamphlet seems like a prodigious, gigantic work, the equal of which the Danish state Church has never seen. It depends so much on the place from which one sees something—from a basement entrance, for example, a low little house looks like a tower. No, only one man is needed; he writes the new hymnbook in three months without a committee and an appeal. Descartes correctly says somewhere that nothing great ever came out of an association.[43] And why did it not amount to anything with the hymnbook? It was the committee. In our age if only a committee is set up, one can be sure that nothing more happens with the matter. There is something so extraordinarily reassuring in the most satisfying consciousness that a committee was set up, something so inviting to inaction that it would be a sin and a shame if the laborer is not granted peace.—*JP* III 2815 (*Pap.* VII¹ B 195) *n.d.*, 1845–46

See 78:8–15; 210:26–31; 345:12–19:

VII¹
A 181
116

The whole question of the relation of God's omnipotence and goodness to evil (instead of the differentiation that God accomplishes the good and merely permits the evil) is resolved quite simply in the following way. The greatest good, after all, that can be done for a being, greater than anything else that one can do for it, is to make it free. In order to do just that, omnipotence is required. This seems strange, since it is precisely omnipotence that supposedly would make [a being] dependent. But if one will reflect on omnipotence, one will see that it also must contain the unique qualification of being able to withdraw itself again in a manifestation of omnipotence in such a way that precisely for this reason that which has been originated through omnipotence can be independent. This is why one human being cannot make another person wholly free, because the one who has power is himself captive in having it and therefore continually has a wrong relationship to the one whom he wants to make free. Moreover, there is a finite self-love in all finite power (talent etc.). Only omnipotence can withdraw itself at the same time it gives itself away, and this relationship is the very independence of the receiver. God's omnipotence is therefore his goodness. For goodness is to give oneself away completely, but in such a way that by omnipotently taking oneself back one makes the recipient independent. All finite power makes [a being] dependent; only omnipotence can make [a being] independent, can form from nothing something that has its continuity in itself through the continuous withdrawing of omnipotence. Omnipotence is not ensconced in a relationship to another, for there is no other to which it is comparable—no, it can give without giving up the least of its power, that is, it can make [a being] independent. It is incomprehensible that omnipotence is able not only to create the most impressive of all things—the whole visible world—but is able to create the most fragile of all things—a being independent of that very omnipotence. Omnipotence, which can handle the world so toughly and with such a heavy hand, can also make itself so light that what it has brought into existence receives independence. Only a wretched and worldly conception of the dialectic of power holds that it is greater and greater in proportion to its ability to compel and to make dependent. No, Socrates had a sounder understanding; he knew that the art of power lies precisely in making another free. But in the relationship between individuals this can never be done, even though it needs to be emphasized again and again that this is the highest; only omnipotence can truly succeed in this. Therefore if a human being had the slightest independent existence over against God (with regard to *materia* [substance]), then God could not make him free. Creation out of nothing is once again the Omnipotent One's expression for being able to make [a being] independent. He to whom I owe absolutely everything, although he still absolutely

VII¹
A 181
117

controls everything, has in fact made me independent. If in creating man God himself lost a little of his power, then precisely what
he could not do would be to make a human being independent.—*JP* II 1251 (*Pap.* VII[1] A 181) *n.d.*, 1846

Concerning the Relationship between
Good Works and Faith

Good works in the sense of meritoriousness are naturally an
abomination to God. Yet good works are required of a human
being. But they shall be and yet shall not be; they shall be and yet
one ought humbly be ignorant of their being significant or that
they are supposed to be of any significance. Good works are
something like a dish which is that particular dish because of the
way in which it is served—likewise good works should be served
in humility, in faith. Or it is like a child's giving his parents a
present, purchased, however, with what the child has received
from his parents; all the pretentiousness that otherwise is associated with giving a present disappears when the child received
from the parents the gift that he gives to the parents.—*JP* II 1121
(*Pap.* VIII[1] A 19) *n.d.*, 1847

    Right away the first time I talked with him and several times
later I said to Bishop Mynster, and as solemnly as possible, that
what I expressed was the opposite of what he expressed and that
it was for that very reason (besides my veneration of him) that he
was of importance to me. And to that he replied very graciously;
he solemnly acknowledged in the conversation that he understood me. At one point he said that we were complements to
each other, which, however, I did not enter into, since it was
more courteous than I expected, but merely reiterated very
firmly my dissimilarity. I have said to him that frequently there
was something I knew must displease him, but that I certainly
kept him in mind and have kept him particularly in mind—
without, however changing it.
    So I know that my relationship to him is as pure as possible.
                    —*JP* V 6058 (*Pap.* VIII[1] A 332) *n.d.*, 1847

According to Mynster's view, Christianity is related to the natural man in the same way as horsemanship is related to the horse, as the trained horse to the untrained horse, where it is not a matter of taking away its nature but of improving it. That is, Christianity is a culture; being a Christian is approximately what the natural man in his most blissfully happy moment could wish to be at his best: poised, harmonious perfection in itself and in himself consummately prepared virtuosity. But such talk is 100,000 miles removed from the Redeemer who must suffer in the world and who requires the crucifixion of the flesh, all that agony as the birth pangs of salvation, because under the circumstances there is in fact an infinite, a qualitative difference between God and man,[44] and the terror of Christianity is also its blessedness: that God wants to be the teacher and wants the pupil to resemble him. If God is to be the teacher, then the instruction must begin with disrupting the learner (the human being). For the sake of quality it cannot be otherwise. There is not much use in speaking of God as the teacher and then have the instruction be only a purely human improvement program.

In many ways Mynster himself is the inventor of this confusion of Christianity and culture. But in another sense he has done an extraordinary service and has certainly demonstrated the deep impression made from his former days.[45] If there is not to be any conflict between Christianity and the world, if the insignia of battle are not to be carried, if there is to be peace of that sort, then it is really something great to have a figure such as Mynster. He has resolved a most difficult problem. If a debate starts that brings the very concept of "state Church" under discussion, then Mynster's position is dubious—if the concept of state Church is accepted, then Mynster is the master, and it must always be remembered that in judging a man it is an outrageous wrong unceremoniously to delete all the very presuppositions within which a man is to be judged.

Let us pay tribute to Bishop Mynster. I have admired no one, no living person, except Bishop Mynster, and it is always a joy to me to be reminded of my father. His position is such that I see the irregularities very well, more clearly than anyone who has attacked him. But the nature of what I have to say is such that it can

VIII¹
A 415
180

VIII¹
A 415
181

very well be said without affecting him at all—*if only he himself does not make a mistake.* There is an ambivalence in his life that cannot be avoided, because the "state Church" is an ambivalence. But now it is very possible to ascribe to him the whole element of awakening within the established order[46]—and then he would once again stand high. If he makes a mistake, if instead of calmly sitting in lofty eminence and, holding his scepter and letting a second lieutenant decide things, he makes the mistake of believing that he should start a battle, then no one can guarantee the results. My corps is just the reinforcement he needs. If he makes a mistake, he will have lost not only my auxiliary-corps— that is of least importance—but he will also have lost his own position.—*JP* V 6076 (*Pap.* VIII¹ A 415) *n.d.,* 1847

VIII¹
A 415
182

See 296:2–297:9:

There are many excellent stories in the fourth volume of *A Thousand and One Nights*—for example, nights 759, 760, 763– 765.[*][47] About the poor couple who prayed to God for a little help, and he let a ruby fall down. They rejoiced greatly. But that night the wife dreamed that she was in paradise and saw the countless pulpits and thrones. When she asked for whom they were, she was told that they were for the prophets, for the righteous and the pious. She asked if there was one for her husband. It was shown to her—but she noticed a chink on one side, and it was explained to her that this chink signified the ruby that had fallen down to them. Then she became despondent, implored her husband to pray God to take the ruby back. "It is better to endure poverty these few days than to have to sit among the glorious ones on a throne that has a defect."
[*]*In margin:* All of these stories are excellent and ought to be remembered.—*JP* IV 4615 (*Pap.* VIII¹ A 631) *n.d.,* 1848

VIII¹
A 673
321

Something about the Forgiveness of Sins

To believe the forgiveness of one's sins is the decisive crisis whereby a human being becomes spirit; one who does not believe this is not spirit. Maturity of the spirit means that immediacy is completely lost, that a person is not only capable of nothing by himself but is capable only of injury to himself. But how many in truth come in a wholly personal way to understand of themselves that one is brought to this extremity. (Here lies the absurd, offense, the paradox, forgiveness of sins.)

Most people never become spirit, never experience becoming spirit. The stages—child, youth, adult, oldster—they pass, to their shame, through these with no credit to themselves; it is none of their doing, for it is a vegetative or vegetative-animal process. But they never experience becoming spirit.

The forgiveness of sins is not a matter of particulars—as if on the whole one were good (this is childish, the child always begs forgiveness for some particular thing that he did yesterday and forgets today etc.; it could never occur to a child, in fact, the child could not even get it into his head, that he is actually evil); no, it is just the opposite—it pertains not so much to particulars as to the totality; it pertains to one's whole self, which is sinful and corrupts everything as soon as it comes in slightest contact with it.

The one who in truth has experienced and experiences what it is to believe the forgiveness of one's sins has indeed become another person. Everything is forgotten—but still it is not with him as with the child who, after having received pardon, becomes essentially the same child again. No, he has become an eternity older, for he has now become spirit. All immediacy and its selfishness, its selfish attachment to the world and to himself, have been lost. Now he is, humanly speaking, old, very old, but eternally he is young.—*JP* I 67 (*Pap.* VIII¹ A 673) *n.d.*, 1848

VIII¹
A 673
322

It is neither more nor less than a matter of an auditing [*Revision*] of Christianity; it is a matter of getting rid of 1800 years as if they had never been. I believe fully and firmly that I shall succeed; the whole thing is as clear as day to me. Yet I note all the more soberly that if there is the very slightest impatience and self-assertiveness, then I shall not be able to do it, then my thought will be confused.

IX
A 72
40

IX
A 72
41

I get up in the morning and thank God—then I begin to work. At a definite time in the evening I break off, thank God—and then I sleep. This is the way I live, although not without assaults of depression and sadness, yet essentially in the most blissful enchantment day in and day out. Alas, and so I live in Copenhagen—and in Copenhagen am the only one who is not serious, the only one who bestows no benefits and accomplishes nothing, a half-lunatic eccentric. That is how the crowd judges me, and the few who see a bit more deeply really have nothing against this being the general estimate of me.—*JP* VI 6168 (*Pap.* IX A 72) *n.d.*, 1848

What Bishop Mynster has sown I am harvesting. For Bishop Mynster has proclaimed true Christianity but—in an unchristian way—has derived great advantage from it, has enjoyed all the good things of life because of it, has gained enormous prestige, and also has ingratiated himself by making Christianity into "the gentle comfort" etc.

As a result he in many ways has distilled Christianity out of the country. Then when the one who is supposed to move forward with the task and the specific orders to observe the way, that is: to reflect doubly, then it becomes outright martyrdom. And Bishop Mynster is responsible for this. Such a person would always have opposition, but it would not have needed to become a martyrdom if Mynster had not gone in advance.

This being the case, I have worked against myself by strengthening Bishop Mynster, but Governance certainly is aware of why I did it and will also know how to show me why it was good. If I had not done it, I perhaps would have gotten away with a good bargain.—*JP* VI 6171 (*Pap.* IX A 81) *n.d.*, 1848

Bishop Mynster's service to Christianity is essentially that, through his outstanding personality, his culture, his superiority in distinguished and most distinguished circles, he has created the fashion or more solemn way of regarding Christianity as something no deep and earnest person (how flattering to the persons concerned) could do without.

However, this service, eternally and Christianly understood, is dubious, for Christianity is something much too distinguished to need patronage.

And yet in his earnestness there is something of a mélange—so touched, so profoundly moved by the thought of those glorious ones—and so sensitive when it comes to the part where this should be made earnest by minimizing oneself just a little bit. —*JP* VI 6172 (*Pap.* IX A 83) *n.d.*, 1848

And yet I love Bishop Mynster; it is my only wish to do everything to reinforce the esteem for him, for I have admired him and, humanly speaking, do admire him; and every time I am able to do anything for his benefit, I think of my father, whom it pleases, I believe.—*JP* VI 6173 (*Pap.* IX A 85) *n.d.*, 1848

Counsel, guidance I almost never find. The few outstanding religious individualities usually are rooted in immediacy. A person like that is spontaneously enthusiastic; he is convinced that he will soon be victorious, so (—spontaneously—*) convinced of the rightness of his cause that he has the fixed idea that if he merely gets it publicized it will be accepted with open arms. In this kind of enthusiasm he talks to the others, he sweeps them off their feet, since spontaneous enthusiasm always charms. So they storm ahead—and now comes the opposition. Perhaps the leader does weather the battle gallantly, but from him I learn nothing of what occupies me—the beginning.

In reflection everything looks different. In reflection a person understands in advance that the danger must come, knows its consequences exactly. He sees it every moment and step by step. On the other hand, he cannot sweep anyone off his feet, for if anyone wants to attach himself to the reflective person, he must above all make that one aware of the danger, thus warn, repel—rather than charm him.

In margin: *Note. In reflection he can also be convinced of the rightness of his cause without necessarily being ignorant of the nature of the world or lacking an essential view of life—and truth.—*JP* VI 6265 (*Pap.* IX A 343) *n.d.*, 1848

N.B.

Perhaps it would be best to publish all the last four books ("The Sickness unto Death," "Come Here," "Blessed Is He Who Is Not Offended," "Armed Neutrality") in one volume under the title

Collected Works of Completion [*Fuldendelse*] [*]

with "The Sickness unto Death" as Part I. The second part would be called "An Attempt to Introduce Christianity into Christendom" and below: Poetic—Without Authority. "Come Here" and "Blessed Is He Who Is Not Offended" would be entered as subdivisions. Perhaps there could also be a third part, which I am now writing,** but in that case Discourse No. 1 would be a kind of introduction that is not counted.

And then it should be concluded.

[*]*In margin:* Perhaps rather: "Collected Works of Consummation[*Fuldbringelse*]" and the volume should be quarto.

**"From on High He Will Draw All to Himself." The three: "Come Here," "Blessed Is He Who Is Not Offended," and "From on High," would then have a separate title-page: An Attempt to Introduce Christianity into Christendom, but at the bottom of the title page: A Poetic Attempt—Without Authority.—*JP* VI 6271 (*Pap.* IX A 390) *n.d.*, 1848

N.B.   N.B.

To be a Christian involves a double danger.

First, all the intense internal suffering involved in becoming a Christian, this losing human reason and being crucified on the paradox. —This is the issue *Concluding Postscript* presents as ideally as possible.

Then the danger of the Christian's having to live in the world of secularity and there express that he is a Christian. Here belongs all the later productivity, which will culminate in what I have ready at present and which could be published under the title: *Collected Works of Completion* (see this journal, p. 21 [*Pap.* IX A 390]).

When this has been done, the question bursts forth as with elemental power: But how can it occur to a human being to want to subject himself to all this, why should he be a Christian when it is so demanding? The first answer might be: Hold your tongue; Christianity is the absolute, you shall. But another answer may also be given: Because the consciousness of sin within him allows him no rest anywhere; its grief strengthens him to endure everything else if he can only find reconciliation.

This means that the grief of sin must be very deep within a person, and therefore Christianity must be presented as the difficult thing it is, so that it may become entirely clear that Christianity is related solely to the consciousness of sin. To want to be involved in becoming a Christian for any other reason is literally foolishness—and so it must be.—*JP* I 493 (*Pap.* IX A 414) *n.d.*, 1848

IX
A 414
243

See 213:29–32:

Here we see the striking contrast between Judaism and Christianity. Jewish piety always clings firmly to the worldly and construes essentially according to the ratio: the more pious a person is, the better it goes for him on earth, the longer he lives, etc. A proverbial metaphor of how Jewish piety describes impiety is found in the saying: He shoots up like a mighty tree—but in a flash it is all over.

And so I ask: Humanly understood (if we do not lie on the basis of subsequent knowledge), is this not a description of Christ's life—a man who in three years shoots up so high that they want to proclaim him king, and then he is crucified like a criminal.

Judaism postulates a unity of the divine and this life—Christianity postulates a cleft. The life of the true Christian, therefore, is to be fashioned according to the paradigm that for the Jews is the very paradigm of the ungodly.—*JP* II 2217 (*Pap.* IX A 424) *n.d.*, 1848

For
Collected Works of Consummation
there could be a very brief preface.

Just as a cabinet minister steps down and becomes a private citizen, so I cease to be an author and lay down my pen—I actually have had a portfolio.

Just one word more, but no, now not one word more; now I have laid down my pen.—*JP* VI 6312 (*Pap.* X^1 A 45) *n.d.*, 1849

X^1
A 56
42

N.B.   N.B.

The question is: When should all the latest works be published! I cannot thank God enough that I have finished them, and if I had not had the tension, with the addition of new pains, I perhaps would never have completed them, because once I have come out of the momentum of writing, I never get into it again in the same way. This time I succeeded, and for me it is enough that they exist, finished in fair copy, containing the completion and the entire structure of the whole, going as far as I in fact could go in an attempt to introduce Christianity into Christendom—but, please note, "poetic, without authority," because, as I have always so definitely maintained, I am no apostle or the like; I am a poetic-dialectical genius, personally and religiously a penitent.

X^1
A 56
43

But when shall they be published? If I publish them while I am still in the position of heterogeneity maintained up till now—that is, independent, free, unrestricted, floating—if I publish them while still maintaining this mode of life, all the extremely exact dialectical categories in the books will be of little help in guarding against the unhappy confusion, and I will still be confused with such a one.

But if I had first of all gotten myself a position in the established order, then my life would be a hindrance to that misunderstanding. But if I had taken such a position, I would not have been able to write the books; of that I am sincerely convinced, and it is really easy to understand. But now it is done and the delay is simply a matter of publishing.

By being situated this way, I, like everyone else, will myself be placed under "the judgment," if you please, the judgment on Christendom contained in these books. Precisely this will prevent my being confused with an apostle or someone like that.

The books are poetical, as if they were by an apostle, but I have stepped aside—no, I am not the apostle, anything but, I am the poet and a penitent.

I have always kept my eyes open for that reef, being confused with an apostle. If that enters in, then I have spoiled my work and am guilty of disloyalty. x¹
A 56
44

Without a doubt Governance has supported me beyond telling; that I myself knew best of all, but not in such an extraordinary way as if I had a special relationship to God.

The influence of this whole "*monumentum aere perennius* [monument more enduring than bronze]" will be purely ideal. It is like a judgment, but I am not "the judge"; I submit myself to the judgment.—*JP* VI 6317 (*Pap.* X¹ A 56) *n.d.*, 1849

De se ipso [About oneself] x¹
A 541
344

Actually, something else will happen than what I originally had in mind.

When I began as the author of *Either/Or*, I no doubt had a far more profound impression of the *terror* of Christianity than any clergyman in the country. I had a fear and trembling such as perhaps no one else had. Not that I therefore wanted to relinquish Christianity. No, I had another interpretation of it. For one thing I had in fact learned very early that there are men who seem to be selected for suffering, and, for another thing, I was conscious of having sinned much and therefore supposed that Christianity had to appear to me in the form of this terror. But how cruel and false of you, I thought, if you use it to terrify others, perhaps upset ever so many happy, loving lives that may very well be truly Christian. It was as alien as it could possibly be to my nature to want to terrify others, and therefore I both sadly and perhaps also a bit proudly found my joy in comforting others and in being gentleness itself to them—hiding the terror in my own interior being. x¹
A 541
345

So my idea was to give my contemporaries (whether or not they themselves would want to understand) a hint in humorous form (in order to achieve a lighter tone) that a much greater pressure was needed[48]—but then no more; I aimed to keep my heavy burden to myself, as my cross. I have often taken exception to anyone who was a sinner in the strictest sense and then promptly got busy terrifying others. Here is where *Concluding Postscript* comes in.

Then I was horrified to see what was understood by a Christian state (this I saw especially in 1848[49]); I saw how the ones who were supposed to rule, both in Church and state, hid themselves like cowards while barbarism boldly and brazenly raged; and I experienced how a truly unselfish and God-fearing endeavor (and my endeavor as an author was that) is rewarded in the Christian state.

That seals my fate. Now it is up to my contemporaries how they will list the cost of being a Christian, how terrifying they will make it. I surely will be given the strength for it—I almost said "unfortunately." I really do not say this in pride. I both have been and am willing to pray to God to exempt me from this terrible business; furthermore, I am human myself and love, humanly speaking, to live happily here on earth. But if what one sees all over Europe is Christendom, a Christian state, then I propose to start here in Denmark to list the price for being a Christian in such a way that the whole concept—state Church, official appointments, livelihood—bursts open.

I dare not do otherwise, for I am a penitent from whom God can demand everything. I also write under a pseudonym because I am a penitent. Nevertheless, I will be persecuted, but I am secure against any honor and esteem that from another side could fall to me.

For some years now I have been so inured to bearing the treachery and ingratitude of a little country, the envy of the elite and the insults of the rabble, that I perhaps—for want of anything better—am qualified to proclaim Christianity. Bishop Mynster can keep his velvet robe and Grand Cross.[50]—*JP* VI 6444 (*Pap.* X[1] A 541) *n.d.*, 1849

X[1]
A 541
346

[*In margin:* Martensen]

Martensen can lecture on anything. In his *Dogmatics*,[51] p. 456 mid.: "The more fervently and powerfully faith is proclaimed in the world, the more it becomes the signal for opposition, and the world is constrained to manifest its enmity to the truth, which becomes effective by means of this very opposition." That is all very well and good for rote-reading—but now take Martensen's life: he is in collusion with speculation, floridly courts the favors of philosophy, makes accommodations, etc., etc.—and this he himself alludes to as wisdom in contrast to the paradox. But faith cannot be proclaimed powerfully without the paradox, and the paradox is precisely what tenses the world in torment, so that deliberately or against its will it must disclose itself.

This, you see, may be called a professor—well, yes, in contrast to a thinker.—*JP* VI 6465 (*Pap.* X^1 A 616) *n.d.*, 1849

My Writings Considered as a "Corrective" to the Established Order

The designation "corrective" is a category of reflection just as: here/there, right/left.

The person who is to provide the "corrective" must study the weak sides of the established order scrupulously and pene-tratingly and then one-sidedly present the opposite—with expert one-sidedness. Precisely in this consists the corrective, and in this also the resignation in the one who is going to do it. In a certain sense the corrective is expended on the established order.

If this is done properly, then a presumably sharp head can come along and object that "the corrective" is one-sided and get the public to believe there is something in it. Ye gods! Nothing is easier for the one providing the corrective than to add the other side; but then it ceases to be precisely the corrective and itself becomes an established order.

Therefore an objection of this nature comes from a person utterly lacking the resignation required to provide "the correc-tive" and without even the patience to comprehend this.—*JP* VI 6467 (*Pap.* X^1 A 640) *n.d.*, 1849

[*In margin:* To supply the corrective.]

To supply the corrective is essentially a task of resignation.

At first, when one begins, the dominating misconception abroad in the world looks haughtily down on the poor correc-tive: "It is antiquated, obsolete," etc.

When the corrective, through its slow but quiet and deeper influence, by its threatening stance, gradually has taken the courage out of this misconception, people surreptitiously utilize the corrective and pretend as if they themselves had said it. Or they circumspectly allow a certain amount of time to elapse, as long—so to speak—as the corrective's operation lasts. During that time there is official silence; that is, they do not write. If they detect that the corrective has power, they advance and covertly utilize the corrective—and then appropriate to themselves the honor of exemplifying this moderation. If this is successful, they go a step further. Since they take only part of the corrective and, on the other hand, the corrective in order to be effective has to move forward by means of the incitement of the paradox—they abandon the corrective as an exaggeration.

Cowardly sneaking—that is what Martensen is capable of. . . .

—*JP* I 707 (*Pap.* X¹ A 658, p. 411) *n.d.*, 1849

See 221:18–222:2:

A martyr who gesticulates with his daily existence cannot concentrate in the moment the way these delicate speakers can who are coddled all week long until they dress up and make protestations for one hour on Sunday. A martyr who gesticulates with his daily existence cannot sensuously draw esthetic attention to his melodious voice and his mighty gestures, for inasmuch as all his gesticulating is basically a translating into action it escapes that fleeting attention of the moment.

Merely to understand this takes patience. But of course the impostors, who stick to the sensuous in the human being, naturally have absolute dominance.

This difference alone: what I have to say requires quiet almost like that of an individual in the confessional—what the others say seems better the more thousands there are to hear.

The actor is really an honest man: he advertises in advance by poster that tonight, between 7 o'clock and 10, he will play the noble father, the chief forester, the suffering truth-witness, the glorified hero, etc.; he is honest, he prompts no one into the fatal confusion that he himself is what is represented.

X²
A 143
107

There has been a lot of comment about placing the theater under the minister of culture; to me it would seem better for the minister of culture to have the theater and Church under him, but to take the title of theater-director.

From the standpoint of Christianity, I really do not see how there can be any objection to the theater with respect to truth; the simple truth is that the actor acknowledges that he is an actor.

Nothing disturbs me more than a man who misuses his imagination and eloquence to depict suffering truth when his life expresses just the opposite—and then he himself fraudulently becomes the object of admiration, affection, sympathy, whereas the actual truth-witness suffers derision and mistreatment.

What is an actual seducer compared with a seducer like that? He infatuates a girl, heightens her desires, to be sure, but in the deepest sense he does not actually confuse her concepts as does that other seducer, whose forgery is instrumental in hardening our hearts still more against the true truth-witness, because his existence only becomes still more incongruous in comparison with that delusive image.—*JP* IV 4965 (*Pap.* X^2 A 143) *n.d.*, 1849

X^2
A 143
108

About Myself

X^2
A 193
151

The thought of publishing all the writings in one swoop under my name and thereby with the greatest possible impetus, and then leaping back without really even knowing where, without regard for the consequences I would invite by such a step, other than wanting to live in retirement: this was sheer, desperate impatience.

X^2
A 193
152

My task has never been to bring down the established order but continually to infuse inwardness into it.

Already from the beginning I perceived the wrongness of it, but it momentarily tempted my imagination and was related to a poet-impatience.

My task has always been difficult. With regard to a brash scientific scholarship, a brash culture, etc., which wants to go even further than Christianity, I jack up the requirements of ideality so high—and at the same time I also have a great responsibility, since I have the most intense sympathy for the common man, women, etc., and I do not want to make them anxious.

On the whole, the woman is and ought to be a corrective in proclaiming the ethical-religious. One must not make it rigorous for men and have something different for women, but in making it rigorous one ought to respect the woman as an authority also and temper it through assistance from that source. And for the sake of the cause, a woman perhaps can lift the burden just as well as a man precisely because she has fewer ideas and also fewer half-ideas than the man, and thus more feeling, imagination, and passion.—*JP* VI 6531 (*Pap.* X² A 193) *n.d.*, 1849

[*In margin:* The Formations of the World]

X²
A 265
194

The Formations of the World

Governance is becoming more and more thrifty; less and less is to be squandered. In old times there lived only an individual; the mass, the thousands, were squandered on him. Then came the idea of representation. Those who really lived were again only individuals, but the mass nevertheless saw themselves in them, even participated in their life. The last formation is: the single individual, understood in such a way that the single individual is not in contrast to the mass, but each one is equally an individual.

X²
A 265
195

But the task becomes more and more rigorous for the missionaries who should prepare for this. Formerly the teacher was an individual, but then he had followers. For the humanness in him there was something consoling in this; he had a kind of human probability that all his striving would not be without a trace, since, indeed, he had followers, and in this way he expanded in finitude. [*In margin:* and the teacher also had the opportunity to make himself comfortable with the help of the followers, had relief with the help of the relative criterion.]

But when the last formation begins, the teacher will become the single individual who wants or dares to have no followers. What frightful rigorousness! How can one possibly avoid dizziness! In the midst of this vortex of millions, where everything is usually alliances and parties, such a single individual stands utterly helpless. He makes himself helpless, because he does not want to have followers. How easy for the wave of time to wash over him and erase all his effort as a nothing! What faith it takes to persevere in this life day after day, what faith it takes to believe that his life is noticed by God, that this is enough! And how squandered such a person is in the service of God! But the greater the squandering in regard to the teacher, the greater the thrift in regard to the generation. Formerly the teacher was spared and the many were spent; now the teacher is spent precisely in order that there be upbringing in the category: the single individual.—*JP* II 2019 (*Pap.* X² A 265) *n.d*, 1849

The question in relation to Christianity is always to what extent a person must be transformed in the direction of becoming spirit so that he dares to appropriate grace. X²
A 445
317

The situation at present is too lunatic; actually it is nothing but refined paganism. A person remains within all the qualifications of sensuousness and worldliness, has his life in them, willingly acknowledges that he is far behind (this is called repentance) but stays on the same spot, and then introduces "grace" as—as the new patch on the old garment.

On the other hand, if a person must be decisively developed to be *spirit* so as to dare to appropriate *grace*, then God knows how many there will be in each generation who actually feel any need for or have any use for Christianity. If I must actually die to my dearest desires, renounce everything that makes an earthly human being happy, then I do indeed, humanly speaking, become as unhappy as possible—and then the question is whether I am *spirit* enough so that I actually have use for Christianity.

There is a shameful abuse fostered by the division: the Law terrifies—the Gospel reassures. No, the Gospel itself is and must be terrifying at first. If this had not been the case, why in the world did it go with Christ as it did when he said: Come to me[52]—and they all went away, they fled from him.

It becomes more and more clear to me that only an apostle can in the stricter sense proclaim Christianity, because only he has the authority to be rigorous in this way. A human being does not X²
A 445
318

have this authority and therefore must compromise. Only a person who in the more rigorous sense is himself transformed to *spirit*, only he can no longer understand, does not want to understand the confounded blather, the infirmity in which the rest of us are trapped, with the result that we coddle ourselves much too much and *rest* in grace too soon, and in it rest from striving instead of resting in it to be renewed for renewed striving.—*JP* IV ·
4333 (*Pap.* X² A 445) *n.d.*, 1850

X³
A 322
233

Faith—A Striving

Luther is completely right in saying that if a human being had to acquire his salvation by his own striving, it would end either in presumption or in despair, and therefore it is faith that saves.

But yet not in such a way that striving vanishes completely. Faith should make striving possible, because the very fact that I

X³
A 322
234

am saved by faith, that, inasmuch as nothing at all is needed from my side, should in itself make it possible that I can begin to strive, that I do not collapse under impossibility but am encouraged and refreshed, because it has been decided that I am saved, that I am God's child by virtue of faith.

This is how faith must relate itself to striving, both in its beginning and during its progress, but it cannot mean that striving is to vanish entirely.—*JP* II 1139 (*Pap.* X³ A 322) *n.d.*, 1850

X³
A 563
368

My Conversation with Bishop Mynster October 22, 1850, after he had read *Practice in Christianity*

The day before I had spoken with Paulli,[53] who told me the following: The bishop is very angry; the minute he came into the living room that first day he said, "The book has made me very indignant; it is playing a profane game with holy things." And when Paulli obligingly asked him if he should report that to me since he probably would be talking with me, Mynster answered: "Yes, and he no doubt will come to see me sometime and I will say it to him myself."

Perhaps, who knows, those last words were fabricated by Paulli to keep me, if possible, from going to the bishop.

But in any case I interpreted the matter another way. When Mynster talks like that: "The next time he visits me I shall tell him so myself," he has essentially given the book a permit and me along with it.

My decision was made at once.

The following morning I went to him. Acquainted as I am with his virtuosity in stateliness (recalling the time I once visited him and as I made my entrance he asked most formally and ceremoniously: Is there something in particular? —To which I answered: No, I see you have no time today, so I would just as soon go. And then when he said he did have time, I stuck to what I had said and parted from him *in bona caritate* [in good friendship] etc.), I began at once: "Today I do have an errand of sorts. Pastor Paulli told me yesterday that you intend as soon as you see me to reprimand me for my latest book. I beg you to regard it as a new expression of the respect I always have shown you that, immediately upon hearing of it, I come at once."

X³
A 563
369

In my opinion this was a happy notion. The situation was all in order; there could be no vehemence or stiff sarcasm, which I deemed unworthy of us both in this case. No, his role was delineated for him as one of venerableness and mine of piety.

He answered, "No, I have no right to reprimand. That is, as I have said to you before, I do not mind at all that each bird must sing with its own beak." Then he added: "Indeed, people may also say what they want to about me." This he said mildly and with a smile. But his added remark led me to fear a little sarcasm, and I tried at once to save the situation. I answered that such was not my intention and I would beseech him to tell me if I had distressed him in any way by publishing such a book. Then he replied: Well, I certainly do not believe that it will prove beneficial. I was pleased with this answer; it was friendly and personal.

Then we went on talking just as we are accustomed to doing. He pointed out that however much one twisted and turned, there had to be observation. I did not pursue this further, fearing to get into the existential, but I explained what I meant with a few ordinary examples.

The rest of the conversation was not noteworthy. Except that in the very beginning he said: Yes, half of the book is an attack on Martensen, the other half on me. And later we discussed the passage on "observations,"[54] which he thought was directed at him.

Otherwise the conversation was just as usual.

I explained this and that about my method, also informed him that now we were over the worst; at least this was the way it looked to me at the moment—but I was a young man and therefore dared to say no more than that this was the way it seemed to me at the moment: that now we were over the worst.

As stated, the rest of the conversation was just as usual.

God be praised. Oh, what have I not suffered. I considered it my duty to maintain the cause in such a manner that I might let the established order determine to what extent it would force me to go further by taking steps against me.

Nothing has happened yet, all are silent—and Mynster talked this way.

Perhaps what Paulli said is true—but that, after all, was the first day. Maybe Mynster, having given up the intention of doing something officially, actually thought of doing something privately but later gave that up.

Still, a little nip may well come out in a sermon.—*JP* VI 6691 (*Pap.* X³ A 563) *n.d.*, 1850

Mynster's Significance for All My Work as an Author

My task has been to apply a corrective to the established order, not to introduce something new that might nullify or supplant it.

Now if I had envisioned this completely from the beginning and there had been no Mynster, then first of all I would have had to create someone to represent the established order and firmly bolster him up.

But since I did not understand my task that clearly in the beginning, I very well could have failed to notice this and the whole thing would have turned out differently, perhaps gone wrong.

But, as it was, Mynster stood there as a representative of the established order; this came as a free gift, and it was inevitable that I venerated Mynster and did everything to express it.

That is how I found my proper position. Here again my good

fortune is apparent. Purely personally my veneration for Mynster was indispensable to me—and not until later did I see that this was very important for my task and for enabling me to get positioned properly.—*JP* VI 6693 (*Pap.* X³ A 565) *n.d.*, 1850

My Task

is continually to provide the existential-corrective by poetically presenting the ideals, inciting with regard to the established order, with which I have an understanding, criticizing all the false reformers and the opposition, who simply are evil—and whom only the ideals can halt.—*JP* I 708 (*Pap.* X⁴ A 15) *n.d.*, 1851

My Reckoning

There is hardly a person hereabouts who is as cognizant as I of all the objections that can be leveled from a Christian point of view against a state Church, a people's Church, an established Christian Church, and the like, also that in the strictly Christian sense the requirement is: separation—this is ideality's maximum requirement.

But I maintain that undertaking this separation is such a qualitatively religious operation that only a qualitatively distinguished religious character can accomplish it. Strictly speaking, it requires an apostle, at least a truth-witness. And it has to be done in character. There must be no characterless confabulating about this. Getting a characterless rattlebrain to venture such a thing is far more lunatic than to put a butcher in command of a brigade or to have an apprentice barber do a difficult surgical operation.

Now, I have not found one single person on our scene who bears any likeness to such a distinguished religious character. There are, however, some who want to dabble blindly in trying to organize this operation in a characterless manner and in an inadmissible form.

This is absolutely corrupting [*in margin:* according to the phrase: *corruptio optimi pessima* (corruption of the best is the

X⁴
A 296
161

X⁴
A 296
162

worst)]. A mismanaged established order—well, there is nothing commendable about that, but it is far preferable to a reformation devoid of character.

This is how I go about it. If I were to pass myself off as a truth-witness or something similar, I would be a nonentity. But I do not do that. For that very reason I am sufficiently authentic to be able to cope with these characterless, immoral reformations.

In this way I safeguard the established order.

But to do this, I demand what I demand of myself: admissions. Just as when a regiment has disgraced itself and has been totally reduced in rank, so I believe that we—if we will not and dare not venture out any further than the people's Church and the like—must tolerate being totally reduced in rank, that we must confess that in the more rigorous sense we are not Christians.

And how do I operate in this respect? Do I step forward as the one who on God's behalf, so to speak, has orders to reduce Christendom in rank? Oh, no, I am without authority. Stirred by the ideal myself, I find a joy in being reduced in rank myself, and I strive "without authority" to stir others to the same.

The mistake in the Mynsterian approach is: (1) he has been hesitant, as if there were truth and meaning in it, that all of us thousands and millions are Christians, (2) second, he has become set in opposition to me.

X⁴
A 296
163

Thus the whole established order can continue. A Christian in the rigorous sense is so rare that there hardly is one to be found in each generation.

A Christian in the volatilized sense, a Christian such as we are, is one who accepts the doctrines, rests in grace, but does not in the more rigorous sense enter into *imitation*. To such a Christian Christ is the Savior, the Redeemer, but not in the stricter sense *the prototype*, unless in the direction of humiliation unto inward deepening.

See, *imitation* in the more rigorous sense is precisely what Mynster has abolished, completely omitted. His malpractice consists precisely in pretending that nothing is wrong, for it has to be said, the truth about where we are has to come out—otherwise everything is secularized.—*JP* VI 6761 (*Pap.* X⁴ A 296) *n.d.,* 1851

See 281:7:

God's Faithfulness

X⁴
A 297
163

This was actually written as a conclusion to the sermon on God's changelessness,⁵⁵ but it is more appropriate to the theme of God's faithfulness.

. . . . . But have you personally experienced God's changelessness, does it perhaps seem as if you have experienced rather the opposite? When you were a child, did you not have a conception of God different from the one you have now as an adult? Has not your experience with God been the same as with a human being—on closer contact you find him to be different from what you had pictured to yourself and in the course of years you find him changed?

Let us talk quite humanly about it. The changelessness of God is sometimes talked about so positively that the positiveness itself is a kind of swindle. In every situation it seems to be true that what the inexperienced say is likely to have a dubious positiveness and assurance, while at first glance what the experienced say appears to be less positive, but it is more durable.

So God's changelessness and faithfulness are spoken about. Even one word suggesting that he would be able to change or at times even want virtually to deceive a person—oh, the very thought of saying anything like that makes one shudder. But what about Luther—he certainly was a man of experience! He says: If I am to be deceived, I would rather be deceived by God than by human beings.⁵⁶ There is a pious man—and not merely a pious man, but a blood-witness—and he says in a sermon: You deceived me, O God, etc. (It is Savonarola, the quotation is found on page 18 in this journal [*Pap.* X⁴ A 264]).

X⁴
A 297
164

So it is with every human being who truly gets involved with God; there come moments when he must say: You deceived me, O God—and he is unable to say right away—but for my own good; you deceived me, O God—but into the truth.

That God is obliged to use deception does not mean he is not faithful or has changed—no, he is eternal, unchanged, educating love. But it is inherent in us to be very reluctant to venture out. We want very much to put God off by assuring him that we really do want to recognize the truth; at the same time we assure him that if only we understood the right thing to do, we would surely do it. This is the swindle. This is why God, like any other pedagogue, has to use cunning.

And you deceived me in the same way, O God! You showed me those lovely pictures. You did not say to me: Just watch out, be sagacious, use the intelligence with which I have so richly endowed you, never get involved in anything like this. No, you beckoned to me, so to speak. I cannot say that I followed recklessly, because early in life fear and trembling were a part of my nature. So I followed. Sometimes it was as if you frightened me back: then I gave up everything. But there were beckonings again and I followed. Oh, it is horrible to be deceived, to be deceived by God—frightful! As the fainting person grabs at something to hang onto and, not finding it, collapses, so it is with the one who is deceived. The thing that in possibility looks so very inviting is extremely forbidding in actuality. And yet even if one were deceived, there would still be nothing to regret; to become deceived in having ventured out in order to seek the eternal is still always preferable to being worldly sagacious. Oh, but you only deceive one into the truth. And this pain of seeming to have been deceived is part of it all before the eternal is reached—alas, but soon it will again be necessary for you to deceive me, for otherwise I will doze off into worldly security.

But who glorifies you more truly, consequently better: the one who merely cries out for your faithfulness—and perhaps does not say a thing, or the one who says: You faithful one, you deceived me—into the truth. You were too loving and faithful not to deceive me; then I would have gone on living with an imaginary notion of your faithfulness but without ever becoming involved with you.—*JP* IV 4890 (*Pap.* X⁴ A 297) *n.d.*, 1851

X⁴
A 297
165

X⁴
A 305
173

New Themes for Sermons on
the Changelessness of God.

Everything Moves Him—Nothing Changes Him

Your sigh, your prayer, etc. are heard. Oh, in grace they have touched him, moved him deeply, him who is infinite love. But it does not follow from this that your desire is fulfilled. He has so infinitely much to take care of, and one thought is to be maintained throughout the whole, and thus it may well be that he must deny you this. But it touches and moves him, both your prayer and that he must deny it—for nothing changes him.

X⁴
A 305
174

*   *

God is changeless—could you wish it otherwise.
—JP IV 4891 (Pap. X⁴ A 305) n.d., 1851

The Changelessness of God

It is unbelievable how recklessly we human beings speak of the consolation in the thought that God is changeless. Yes, of course God is changeless, but what good is it to me, am I really capable of having anything to do with a changeless being? For a poor, unsteady human being this is the greatest possible strain; the pain I have to go through is far greater than everything I can suffer because of another person's changeableness.

This is how serious the matter is. But then it must be said that we nevertheless *must* follow through, and that then the blessedness is there as well. But this sentimental flirtation, this brashness with which we generally speak of the consolation in the thought of God's changelessness, is an illusion.—*JP* II 1428 (*Pap.* X⁴ A 311) *n.d.*, 1851

See 203:1–205:9:

[*In penciled brackets:*
Ein, Zwei, Drei /
    or
Three Aphorisms.]

X⁶
B 253
419

[*In pencil:* Reflections.]

respectfully dedicated to a most esteemed public by the author, who requests a lenient judgment of this his first attempt, the imperfection of which no one—except, of course, a highly esteemed public, which knows

everything—knows better than
the author.

1.

Geniuses are like a thunderstorm: they go against the wind,
terrify people, clear the air.

The "established order" has invented various lightning rods to
counteract or divert geniuses; they are successful—so much the
worse for the established order, for if they are successful once,
twice, thrice—"the next thunderstorm" will be all the more
terrible.

There are two kinds of geniuses. The first is characterized by
a lot of thunder, whereas the lightning is slight and rarely strikes.
The other kind has a category of reflection by which they con-
strain themselves or hold back the thunder. But the lightning is
all the more intense; with the speed and sureness of lightning
certain selected points are hit—and lethally.

2.

"Did the apostle Paul have any official position?" No, Paul did
not have any official position. "Did he, then, have a livelihood?"
No, he did not have any livelihood. "Did he, then, earn a lot of
money in another way?" No, he did not earn money in any way.
"Was he not, then, at least married?" No, he was not married.
"But then Paul certainly was not an earnest man!" No, Paul was
not an earnest man [*deleted:* (particularly every tradesman will
easily understand this)].

X⁶
B 253
420

3.

When a man has a toothache, the world says: Poor man!
When a man is financially embarrassed, the world says: Poor
man! When a man's wife is unfaithful to him, the world says:
Poor man! —When God lets himself be born, becomes man, and
suffers, the world says: Poor man! When an apostle with a divine
commission has the honor to suffer for the truth, the world says:
Poor man! —Poor world!!!

4.

In the splendid cathedral a handsome Royal Chaplain, the cultured public's chosen one, appears before a chosen circle of the chosen, and preaches movingly [*rørt*]—I say "movingly," I do not say "dryly" [*tørt*]—no, he preaches movingly on the apostle's words: God has chosen the lowly and the despised in the world—and no one laughs!

5.

It is one thing to profit (*profiteri*) an art, a science, a faith—it is another thing to have profit from it.

6.

When someone asks a man "Do you know this and that" and he *promptly* answers Yes or No, then this answer is a *popular* answer and shows that he is a simpleton, a teachers' college student, etc. But if it takes ten years before the answer comes, if it comes in the form of a detailed dissertation that scrupulously, as Holophernes says, maintains the strict tempo of "*Ein, Zwei, Drei,*"[57] and at the end of the detailed dissertation it is *not exactly clear* whether he knows it or not—this is an authentic speculative answer and demonstrates that the one who was asked is a professor in speculation, or at least so cunning [*udspekuleret*] that he ought to be.

X⁶
B 253
121

7.

The reflection found under no. 1 of the reflections on a loose sheet in the high desk is about a poet who wants to be mistaken for a truth-witness.

———————

Respectfully,

[*In brackets:* Victorin Victorius Victor   Respectfully,
                                              Johannes de Silentio]
            —*JP* VI 6787 (*Pap.* X⁶ B 253) *n.d.*, 1851

See 203:1–205:9:

> Ein, Zwei, Drei
> or
> Three and a Half Aphorisms

No. 1. The one about geniuses and thunderstorms
  perhaps under the title: A Meteorological
  Observation
No. 2. The one that ends: ergo, Paul was not an earnest man
  perhaps under the title: A Flower Respectfully
  Planted on
   the Grave of "Established Christendom."
No. 3. The one ending with: Poor world.
  perhaps under the title: For the Jew's-harp.[58]
No. 4. The most dreadful punishment, according to their own
  view, with which the prophets threatened the Jewish
  people is this: Boys shall rule over you[59]— — — —this
  is only half an aphorism; the consequent clause is lacking.
       —*JP* VI 6788 (*Pap.* X[6] B 254) *n.d.*, 1851

X[4]
A 511
330

The Possible Collision with Mynster

From the very beginning what Mynster has fought for in opposition to me—often in rather ordinary ways—has been to maintain this view: My proclamation, the Mynsterian approach, is earnestness and wisdom; the Kierkegaardian an odd, perhaps remarkable, but an odd exaggeration.

My position is: I represent a more authentic conception of Christianity than Mynster.

X[4]
A 511
331

But I desire nothing less than to attack Mynster, to weaken him. No, just the opposite. A little admission from his side, and everything will be as advantageous as possible for him; no one will see how it all hangs together, something I always have concealed by bowing so deeply to him.

From the very beginning I actually have been an alien figure to Mynster (in fact, I myself said to him the first day: We are completely at variance, something he no doubt instinctively perceived even better than I). I have a kind of passion for the truth and ideas that is utterly foreign to him. In this way I am opposed to him. —Things were still all right with *Concluding Unscientific Postscript*, partly because in the conclusion[60] I personally emphasized him so strongly, partly because Johannes Climacus is a humorist, and thus it was easier for Mynster to maintain that this was only poetic exaggeration, humor, but that his own approach was authentic earnestness and wisdom.

The first part of *Upbuilding Discourses in Various Spirits*[61] irritated him more; but perhaps in appreciation of the postscript to *Concluding Postscript* he let the judgment be: This is an excellent book—especially the last two parts. *Works of Love* offended him. —*Christian Discourses* even more. —And so it mounts. *Practice in Christianity* distressed him very painfully.

Am I out to get Mynster? No, no, I am attached to him with a hypochondriacal passion, the extent of which he has never suspected. But here there is something else that puts pressure on me. I can no longer afford to maintain the battle for the idea that I have represented. Therefore I must make haste. If my future were economically secure so that I knew I was completely able to give myself to the idea, I certainly would bide my time and let Mynster live out his life—oh, it pains me so deeply to have to draw my sword on him. But the economic situation forces me to hurry. Only when I accept an official position can Mynster more easily make his interpretation prevail. He knows that I have financial worries, has known it for several years; I myself told him. Now he is waiting and watching for this to force me to cut back, perhaps even to throw myself into his arms so that he can exploit me and have further proof that his way is the way of wisdom and earnestness.

x⁴
A 511
332

The line about Goldschmidt[62] was fateful. (1) It gives a sad insight into the bad side of Mynster. (2) It provides me with the circumstantial datum against Mynster that I had to have if I were to attack. That everything about him is rather close to the worldly mentality I have perceived for a long time, and therefore I made a division and took his *Sermons*.[63] But this plain fact betrays everything. And it has happened here as generally happens, that I first of all induce someone to provide me with the circumstantial datum I need. (3) It shows that in the sphere of the idea

Mynster considers himself impotent. But he has been in an emotional state.

For me the possibility of this collision means that in order to survive I must take a still higher view of Christianity. This is a very serious matter; I have very much to learn and to suffer. —But on the other hand the possibility of this collision signifies that there is a power that works against Mynster. The collision, if it occurs, will occur against my will; it is my economic situation that pressures me to hurry, and Mynster has had it in his power to buy at the most advantageous price what can become extremely dangerous to him if there must be a collision.

He was an old man. Something truer was offered by someone who "in profound veneration"[64] was willing to introduce it in such a way that it appeared to be Mynsterian. He would not have it. True enough, after having enjoyed life as he has, it could be a bitter experience to find out at the end of his life what kind of Christianity it actually was.—*JP* VI 6795 (*Pap.* X⁴ A 511) *n.d.*, 1852

X⁴
A 531
348

"The Monastery"

The error of the medieval monastic movement was this. Asceticism, renunciation, and the like were still an expression of an infinite passion and of Christianity's heterogeneity to the world. Therefore it all should have been done very simply; it should have explained to the monastic candidate that this was simply the requirement.

But instead something else occurred. The monastic candidate nevertheless made himself homogeneous with the world, for he allowed himself and his way to be regarded as the extraordinary, which was directly honored with the admiration of his contemporaries. This meant that the monastic candidate shared in the general scaling down of the Christian requirement. He did not make asceticism the requirement but made the way others lived into the requirement and thus reaped admiration for doing the extraordinary. But such extraordinariness was made homogeneous with everything else worldly.

X⁴
A 531
349

In a similar manner the monastic candidate avoided persecution, suffering for the doctrine, etc. It is easy to see that asceticism and the like, existentially presented simply as the requirement required of everyone, would have made people furious. But when the ascetic is willing to accept the admiration of others and to let the others be exempt because of their admiration of him, then one can get involved even with asceticism.

The sign that Christianity had been reduced is precisely the emergence of the rank of extraordinary Christian. That helped! Instead of there being, Christianly, only one requirement for all of us, there was a progression: the Christian who was directly honored by admiration came to be the extraordinary, and the ordinary Christians became plain worldliness.

Christianity received its first blow when the emperor became a Christian. The second, and far more dangerous blow, came when the category of the directly recognizable extraordinary Christian emerged. The error lay, as stated, not in entering the monastery but in the title of extraordinary Christian, which was directly honored with admiration by the contemporaries.—*JP* III 2760 (*Pap.* X^4 A 531) *n.d.*, 1852

See 195:30–196:7:

Remarks by Bishop Mynster

X^4
A 566
384

In one of his "observations" (probably the one on God's Word or on hearing the Word or one similar, anyway it is in his *Betragtninger*[65]), he has some moving words to say about the futility of tears. He says that he will collect all those hypocritical tears wept by people listening to his sermons; afterward, however, it has become evident that they have not acted accordingly at all. He will step forward on judgment day with these tears and say, "I have done my part." — —Strange to say, I have just been thinking of collecting the tears Mynster himself has shed in the pulpit; afterward, however, it has become evident that he does not act accordingly at all. This hangs together with something Mynster said to me the first time we talked together—"We are

X^4
A 566
385

complements"[66]—I complete his collection of hypocritical tears with the collection of his tears.—*JP* VI 6806 (*Pap.* X⁴ A 566) *n.d.*, 1852

"The Sacrificed Ones," the Correctives

Just as a skilled cook says of a dish that already has a good many ingredients mixed into it, "It still has to have a little dash of cinnamon" (the rest of us probably would scarcely be able to taste that this little dash of cinnamon was added, but she knows for sure why and how it tastefully blends in with the whole mixture); just as the artist says of the color-tone of the whole painting, which is composed of many, many colors, "A little bit of red has to be introduced here and there, at this little point" (and the rest of us probably would scarcely be able to discover the red, since the artist has shaded it so well, although he knows exactly why it should be introduced)—just as with the cook and the artist, so also with Governance.

The governance of the world is an enormous household, an immense painting. Yet it is the same for him, the Master, God in heaven, as it is for the cook and the artist. He says, "There must be a little dash of cinnamon now; a little bit of red must be introduced." We have no idea why; we can hardly detect it since the little smidgen vanishes in the whole, but God knows why.

A little dash of cinnamon! This means: here a person must be sacrificed; he must be added to give the rest a specific taste.

These are the correctives. It is an unhappy mistake if the one who is to be used to introduce the corrective becomes impatient and wants to make the corrective normative for the others, an attempt that will confuse everything.

A little dash of cinnamon! Humanly speaking, how painful to be sacrificed in this manner—to be the little dash of cinnamon! But on the other hand God knows very well whom he chooses to be used in this manner, and he knows with the most intimate understanding how to make it blessed for him to be sacrificed so that among the thousands of heterogeneous voices, each of which in its own way expresses the same thing, his voice also is heard, and perhaps his in particular is truly heard *de profundis* [out of the depths]—that God is love. The bird on the twig, the lily in the field, the deer in the forest, the fish in the sea, countless crowds of happy humans jubilate: God is love. But underneath, supporting, as it were, all these sopranos as the bass part does, sounds the *de profundis* from the sacrificed ones: God is love.

—*JP* I 709 (*Pap.* X⁴ A 596) *n.d.*, 1852

Christ as Prototype—the Apostle as Prototype—Grace—
the Christian Requirement Must Still Be Proclaimed

X⁵
A 88
100

Christ is the prototype. This is true, and surely this is what must be particularly stressed in our time. But he still is not altogether literally the prototype, because he is, of course, heterogeneous to an ordinary human being by a full quality—and still he is the prototype. What does this mean? It means that in being the prototype he is also intended to teach us how greatly we need *grace*. Basically it is this change or the successive steps in this change that is the movement in the history of Christianity. To the degree that a person becomes more and more aware of how infinitely ideal the prototype is, yes, that he is heterogeneous by a full quality, to the same degree grace must be more and more affirmed; whereas in the beginning and naively in the Middle Ages people went all out for imitation [*Efterfølgelse*] and for copying the prototype. —Luther then came to a halt. I am now in the position that I think grace must be put in first place, as I call it. What I do take a little exception to in Luther's position is that he did not more clearly and definitely indicate that thereby the New Testament's, particularly the Gospel's, requirement for being a Christian was reduced. I am not objecting so much to the reduction, because this may be the case inasmuch as every advance toward the ideal is a step backward, but then this should be indicated and *grace* all the more emphatically applied—that is, not in empty forms of speech but in an accurate accounting.

Not even *the apostle* is a wholly direct prototype, that is, neither I nor anyone can summarily order his life in likeness to him. Generally speaking, no prototype may be that, for then human life would not sufficiently have the rigor of personal responsibility, and then one guilt could never come into existence—that of

X⁵
A 88
101

presumptuously wanting to copy the prototype. No, the very fact that the prototypes are irregular is part and parcel of the paradox—and yet it seems that to be a prototype means that others should decline their lives accordingly. And so it indeed is, and yet the prototype is also irregular, the prototype does what no human being has the right to do; yes, humanly speaking, it is quite in order if we place *the apostle* in the defense box, since no human being has the right to act in that way. The apostle therefore has no other defense than this: I have a direct relationship with God.

So it goes generally. God empowers a particular human being, makes him his instrument. He has, then, an immediate relationship with God and, aided by this, turns all human concepts upside down. Now, if a person without this immediate relationship with God (and someone who himself has an immediate relationship with God is himself an apostle and consequently does not need the other as prototype) wants to copy him directly, this is an offense. In a certain sense the apostle must humanly shudder at what he is doing as an apostle, but he has nothing more to say than: God drives me to it.

Yet *the apostle* is the prototype. But the fact that the prototype is an irregularity has been wisely arranged this way by God, both in order to tighten human beings properly in the tension of rigorous imitation [*Efterfølgelse*] and humility and also in order to test and to judge the presumptuousness that wants to copy the prototype summarily.

No, the prototypes cannot be copied summarily. Generally the older the world and humanity become, the more it is developed intellectually. But the more it is developed intellectually, the more ideal become the concepts of God and the God-man, but the more ideal these become, the more difficult imitation becomes, and the greater the emphasis that must be placed in the direction of relying upon grace.

Let each one test oneself. I wonder if there is a single human being alive in our time who in a beautiful and true way is naive enough to be able to call God "his friend." To be a friend of God! No! Or to call Christ his brother! No! No, I can call God Father—even a little child does this—but the little child is not a

X⁵
A 88
102

friend of his father. I can call Christ my Savior, my Lord, my Redeemer, my benefactor, perhaps even my friend, but, please note, not in the sense that I dare call myself his friend—but "my brother" is inappropriate for me. Is this because I am such a worm compared with the millions who talk about being friends of God and brothers of Christ? I do not think so; but, no matter, the rising intellectuality has made ideality so high that the prototype does not have the effect of emphasizing imitating as much as it emphasizes relying upon grace.

But one of the components ought to be: either/or. The mistake Mynster and the whole official clan make is that they know neither how to apply the prototype to *imitation* nor how to use this effectually with regard to relying upon grace.

This last is what I wanted and now want: I want to apply the Christian requirement, imitation, in all its infinitude, in order to place the emphasis in the direction of grace.—*JP* II 1922 (*Pap.* X⁵ A 88) *n.d.*, 1853

X⁵
A 88
103

Either/Or

Every cause that is not served as an either/or (but as a both-and, also, etc.) is *eo ipso* not God's cause; yet it does not therefore follow that every cause served as an either/or is therefore God's cause.

Either/Or, that is, that the cause is served as an Either/Or, is an endorsement similar to "in the royal service."

The symbol for the merely human, for mediocrity, the secular mentality, dearth of spirit, is: both-and, also.

And this is the way Mynster actually has proclaimed Christianity, that is, if consideration is given to his own personal life.
—*JP* VI 6841 (*Pap.* X⁵ A 119) *n.d.*, 1853

My Christian Position

1853   S. K.

X⁶
B 232
371

[*Deleted:* First a friendly word to the readers. It is not customary, least of all in journals, to speak in the manner in which I intend to speak and must speak here. Forgive me, then, bear with me, and put the best construction upon it. I cannot speak in any other way, and I must speak, and at this moment precisely in a journal. I do not need to make this excuse to my reader and, indeed, to anyone who is religiously more mature; he will understand that this may and must be said just this way.

*   *

Although I fully realize that as an author I have not had finite, earthly, temporal goals, which explains why I have come to stand curiously alien, not to speak of appearing ridiculous, in our sagacious age in which practically everyone knows all too well what finite, earthly, temporal goals he is striving for, I do, however, as an author have something on my conscience in the strictest sense of the word. Let me quite accurately describe how I feel about it. There is something very specific that I have to say, and it so weighs on my conscience that I dare not die without getting it said. In the moment I die and leave this world, I will then (as I understand it) in the very second (so frightfully fast does it happen!), in the very second I will be infinitely far from here at another place where even in that very same second (what frightful speed!) the question will be put to me: Have you carried out the [*changed from:* your] errand, have you *very specifically* said the specific thing you were to say! And if I have not done it, what then! [*In margin:* But in one sense it has not been this way from the beginning. On the contrary, there was a period in the beginning when I hoped to be released by death from *very specifically* saying this specific thing, even if I eventually would say it, inasmuch as I would leave it said *very specifically* in writing. Then came a period when it looked like this to me: You will see, you will not die young; instead you will become an old man, and in any case you will live so long that finally you will have to say this specific thing in your lifetime; you will have to say it *very specifically*. Then came the latest period, which has already lasted for some time now, during which with every month that passes it more and more insistently confronts me thus: I dare not die without having said the specific thing very specifically.]

X⁶
B 232
372

Imagine a [*deleted:* royal] servant. He is sent somewhere on a specific errand; there is something very specific he has to say and to a specific man. But he is extremely reluctant to say what he has to say, because it is not a happy message, and he is so extremely reluctant to say it to this particular man. So he makes the journey and arrives at the place; he is at the place—alas, he lets time go by. He puts it off and puts it off; like a child playing truant from school, so he plays truant from the task, but continually anxious, because he has no idea at all of how much time he is going to be given, but he does know and is positively certain that if his recall came, for example, today and he would have to return home and would not have taken care of his errand—then, yes, as we say, he is in for trouble.

[*Deleted:* So it is with me.] There is something very specific I have to say. But to be truthful, I am not eager to say it; on the contrary, I would very much like to see that another would say it, which, however, would not help me since, after all, as I understand it, it was and is my task to say it. But I am not eager [*deleted:* to say it]; just the opposite, I have wished, craved, at times almost hoped that I perhaps might get out of saying it. For it is not a happy message, this specific thing, and there are various persons dear to me who I am positive will be sorry to have it said. Above all [*deleted:* there is among us a most worthy old man] there is one consideration that has constantly held me back, re-strained my tongue or my pen, a consideration for this highest clergyman[67] of this Church, a man to whom I—also in remem-brance of a deceased father—feel drawn in an inexplicable, al-most melancholy love [*deleted:*—and I must believe that he, he in particular, would be very sorry to have it said].

How have I conducted myself then? Let me relate the past briefly but in the historical present, consequently as something close at hand.

This is how I conduct myself. I make clear to myself the spe-cific thing I have to say. Then—well, whether it is keen discern-ment, whether it is more or less keen discernment, let others be the judge of that—but what I personally dare to say and as truth-fully as possible is this: With extremely *troubled* discernment I seek to find the mildest, gentlest form in which it can be said—and then I send it out into the world. Simultaneously I move

X⁶
B 232
373

over to the other side. I myself do everything to draw attention away from it, and internally I shout and cry (yes, or sigh): Grant, O God, that it all may go off quietly. It is done in such a way, I know, that very few are able to grasp the true situation. Now, if these few are only sagacious enough to keep absolutely calm and not throw themselves at me to pressure me (since that is what I unavoidably find most abhorrent), the successful outcome would be that I have saved my conscience, that I have said the specific thing, and [*deleted:* that I have saved my love for the old gentleman.] that I have avoided a collision with Bishop M.; yes, in the eyes of most people I even seem to have strengthened his regime, something that in one sense I quite literally am doing.

And so it goes, everything goes off very quietly. Then I am happy; I say to my soul: Be happy, for now you dare to be happy and you have reason to be happy.

But conscience, this, as the poet says, blushing, bashful spirit that brings a person nothing but unrest, conscience is something wonderful and marvelously designed for the individual. While there certainly are various people of whom it might be said that they have a far more sagacious conscience than I have, because in fact they are far more sagacious than I, and while, on the other hand, there also are various ones of whom it might be said that they have a far more sagacious conscience than I, because they are far more sagacious than I—the single individual's conscience (what an ingenious divine invention the conscience is, so incomparably designed for the individual) is precisely, just exactly, as sagacious as he is; therefore his conscience will always be just sagacious enough to be able to see through his most sagacious invention.

I have experienced the truth of this. After some time had passed, there came a day when conscience called to me and said: But, my good friend, how about this specific thing that you have to say; do you dare to say that you have said it! After all, I know just as well as you do how cunningly you are behaving—.

See, this is another story. Now it is no longer: Rejoice my soul, and be happy. No, I start over again. I make altogether clear to myself that specific thing—and I must say that it becomes more and more clear each time. Then I am ready. I sit down and

X⁶
B 232
374

do nothing else from morning until evening with—well, whether it is keen discernment, whether it is more or less keen discernment, let others be the judge of that—I dare truthfully to say that it is with an *extremely troubled* keen discernment that I seek to find the mildest form in which it can be said. Then I send it out into the world. Simultaneously I move to the other side—I do everything to draw attention away from it; internally I shout and cry or sigh etc. etc.

But conscience, this, as the poet says, blushing, bashful spirit that causes a person nothing but unrest, conscience is something wonderful etc. etc.

Step by step I could point this out through my whole authorship. I believe that I was successful in saying the specific thing I have to say, but yet in such a way that it can go off very quietly—I myself help it along. It does go off very quietly—"Now I, too, will he happy"—but conscience is wonderfully designed for the individual etc.

But I do not intend to go through the whole authorship in this manner. I will take only the last part.

In 1850 a book titled *Practice in Christianity* came out. There the specific thing I have to say is actually said.

But, but. In the first place, it came to be a big book, and I know very well that few people read books, especially the bigger ones. In the second place, a pseudonym was used, which almost poetically distances from actuality what was said. In the third place, in a thrice-repeated preface,[68] I let the book recoil upon myself and thereby deflected the attack so that it does not really drive home to actuality. In the fourth place, when the book came out, I did manage to lead attention away from it—and those few I mention were, as I secretly wished, quite properly sagacious enough to keep completely calm—it turned out all right, everything went off very quietly.

"Now I will be happy, rejoice in life as I have reason to, because what I thought to be very, very difficult and to require rare good luck from the other side turned out all right; I have saved my conscience, I have spoken, have said it—and I have avoided a collision with Bishop M. [*changed from:* saved my love]; nothing actually has happened."

x⁶
B 232
375

[*Deleted:* But conscience—yes, it is wonderfully designed for the individual! And this time it has also found something new.] But conscience . . . . . yet, no, it did not operate this time just as before. After a short time something else happened. In a little book ([69]) Bishop M. found opportunity in a quick turn to place me as an author on a level together with Goldschmidt of *The Corsair.* What is this, I said to myself; is this the old gentleman, the, to say no more, distinguished, brilliant His Excellency, Bishop M.? In the meantime I surveyed the situation and I finally was of the opinion that it could be regarded as if nothing had happened—what is a line when one is as attached to a man as I am to Bishop M. Time passed, then conscience spoke up. It said something like this: Do you dare to deny that you understand very well what that line signifies, that you can read this hieroglyph only all too well, that it means Bishop M. has ascended the scale of wrath very high since he descends so low as to use such means, that, while his worldly sagacity perhaps told him there really is nothing to do or it is not prudent to do anything against Magister K., he nevertheless has been so provoked that he—no doubt a rare instance—still has been unable to control his anger and it has to come out in one way or another—have you not understood this, and do you dare to let this pass without settling the matter, since it is now clear how at odds he must he with you? —I pondered this. —Time passed, again conscience began wanting to engage me in conversation and about the same matter, also gave the matter a new turn. Assume, it said to me, that the old gentleman was dead; then do you think it easier to come out with it and to get said very specifically, briefly and to the point, the specific something you have to say? You assume that it is devotedness to the old gentleman—and this I will not completely deny—that holds you back. But watch out, could not this also be a little selfishness, that you want to protect yourself, that you think the matter cannot be either as serious or as painfully exhausting for you as soon as he is gone? Oh, but think of the accounting! [*Deleted:* Suppose you dared to answer yes to the question, "Have you taken care of the errand?" but] Suppose the question is [*changed from:* Suppose, then, that the examination began]: Why did you let the moment go unused when you knew

X[6]
B 232
376

that the matter would have become most earnest the moment when that old gentleman, who represents the opposite, stood at the peak of his power, supported by the tradition of his whole life, possessing all the advantages of being an old man, yet still young and energetic? Or did you not realize that you had to see to it that the matter would become as earnest as it is? But this you dodged! [*Deleted:* Consequently you cannot truthfully answer yes to the question: "Have you taken care of the errand?" but you must be silent.] [*In margin:* Consequently in answer to this question you must be silent—and as a reward for not using the time to speak, you can have an eternity in which to be silent, yes, or to sit in despair, brooding over your not speaking.]

[*Deleted:* Well, so it must be said, briefly and to the point. And all this business [*changed from:* all this—as Luther would say—all this gossip] with the big books must have an end. *It must be said briefly, specifically—and my hesitation is not due to inability, for I can do it all right, oh, but I will do it so very reluctantly and I would so very much like to be free.]

[*In margin:* *What I chiefly have to say must be brief and specific. If Prof. M.[70] has found me to be too prolix—may I only not be too brief for him now; if Bishop M.—otherwise kindly—has taunted me about using too many devices—may I only not charge him too directly now.]]

My Christian position is: **Christianity**—I speak of Denmark and, of course, within the limits [*changed from:* relativity] of what is humanly [*changed from:* officially] possible to know—**does not exist at all**.

Christianity does not exist at all; but through having the objective doctrine, we [*deleted:* human beings] are more or less captivated in the delusion, trapped in the illusion, that we are Christians.

O Luther! And yet in one sense a [*deleted:* more] fortunate situation—at that time there were ninety-five theses and controversy over doctrine—now there is only one thesis: that Christianity does not exist at all.

X⁶
B 232
378   It is not doctrinal heresy, not a schism; no, it is the most dangerous of all, the most sly invention of natural human cunning. It may be [*changed from:* is] the *Fall* [*changed from:* a *fall*] from Christianity. It is a mirage, inasmuch as behind this objectivity that is boasted about and undauntedly appealed to, this objectivity that we have the objective doctrine and, *objectively*, pastors and churches, attention is diverted from what is crucial, the subjective, that we are not Christians. . . .—JP VI 6842 (Pap. X⁶ B 232) n.d., 1853

XI²
A 263
264   *Crisis*

How does a crisis come about in the relationship of the spirit? Quite simply—by leaving out some intermediate links, by producing a conclusion and not giving the premises, by drawing a XI²
A 263
265 conclusion without first showing that of which it is the consequence, etc.—then the collision of the person acting in this way and the contemporaries can become a crisis.

For example, let the one who actually is a bearer of whatever idea there is in the age, let him work silently for a few years. During all this time he will himself be developed more and more, will thereby become more and more alienated from his contemporaries; let him then take the very latest stage and with the most intense brevity begin with that—then it can become a crisis. On the other hand, it would not have become a crisis if he had successively communicated the earlier stages, and neither will it become a crisis if he begins with the earliest.

It has happened frequently that an individual has collided with his contemporaries to the point where it became a crisis. But this has been spontaneous. The individual involved has actually had no idea of how far his contemporaries were from being able to understand him, to what extent they lacked the intermediate links, and the premises.

This is the crisis collision of geniuses.

The conscious arranger of a crisis is altogether different—to be so clear that one can measure with the eyes that the distance must now be so great that it must become a crisis collision, consciously to lay out the whole thing. This consciousness, however, is really only the Christian consciousness, the really Christian concept of being sacrificed, a voluntary sacrifice.

But here I stop again and am tempted to ask: Does a human being have the right to this? Is it not harshness toward others?

It is futile to seek enlightenment in Christendom. As far as the New Testament is concerned, this after all is the God-man, and the God-man is qualitatively different from every human being.

On the other hand, it is not possible to put an end to lack of character, sophistry, and the nonsense of reflection without a crisis. A crisis is the real μετάβασις εἰς ἄλλο γένος [shifting from one genus to another]; what the sign of the cross is for the devil, the crisis is for reflection.

But to begin with the conclusion, to leave out the premises and the like—and then to say one does it to bring on the crisis is, again, to prevent the crisis, because in this explanation there is again a rapprochement that reduces the contemporaries' distance, and then the collision does not become a crisis.—*JP* I 615 (*Pap.* XI² A 263) *n.d.*, 1854

XI²
A 263
266

Playing at Christianity

XI²
A 289
290

We all know what it is to play at war, that it is to *simulate* as convincingly as possible everything that happens in war: the troops line up, they take the field, everyone looks serious but also full of courage and enthusiasm, the orderlies dash back and forth fearlessly, the officers' voices are heard, the signals, the battle cries, the musket volleys, the thunder of cannon . . . . . everything, everything just as in war; only one thing is lacking—the dangers.

So it is also with playing at Christianity—it is to simulate the Christian proclamation in such a way that everything, everything, everything is included as convincingly as possible, but one thing is omitted—the dangers.

In the proclamation as it is in the New Testament the whole emphasis falls on the personal—this accounts for the dangers; when we play at Christianity, the thing to do (but carefully, convincingly) is to draw attention away from the personal—so the dangers are also absent.

The proclaimer, then, is—a public official! Aha, so perhaps it is not his personal conviction that he proclaims, but it is a function of his office! —The proclamation is his means of making a living for himself and family, his career! Aha, so what he says is perhaps nothing more nor less than a special jargon—like the lawyer's, physician's, etc. —And the doctrine is proclaimed not on the street[71] but in a church, an artistic building where everything is set up to provide artistic tranquillity and enjoyment and

XI²
A 289
291

the kind of illusion the theater insists upon. Aha, so perhaps we are actually in a theater when we are in church. —And the discourse does not personally address those present, no, no, that would be lack of culture—it keeps a seemly distance from them, talks quite generally about, about, etc. Otherwise everything belonging to the proclamation of Christianity is as convincing as possible—the upraised glance to call upon God, the hands lifted in prayer, the voice almost choked with tears, the loud voice defying the opposition of the whole world . . . . . taratatata, taratatata! And outside the quiet hours it would be most inappropriate, a lack of culture to remind "the pastor" of what he said in the quiet hours; it would be just as fatuous as if an actor, after the curtain had fallen, [*deleted:* drew his sword] wanted to continue to be what he was in the play.

This is called playing at Christianity. Every human being naturally pursues the things of the world. Christianity wants to lift people to a higher life. To that end the state pays 1000 clergymen, each one of whom—exactly like the rest of worldliness—is in pursuit of earthly things. This is how Christianity was successfully introduced into the nations: it is not so much Christianity that has been introduced as a new way of making a living—being a pastor.—*JP* III 3541 (*Pap.* XI² A 289) *n.d.*, 1853–54

March 1, 1854

XI¹
A 1
5

Bishop Mynster

Now he is dead.

If he could have been prevailed upon to conclude his life with making the confession to Christianity that what he has represented actually was not Christianity but a mitigation, it would have been exceedingly desirable, for he carried a whole age.

That is why the possibility of this confession had to be kept open to the end, yes, to the very end, in case he should make it on his death bed. That is why he must never be attacked; that is why I had to submit to everything, even when he did such a desperate thing as that matter with Goldschmidt,[72] because, after all, no one could know whether this might not be the thing that perhaps could influence him so that, moved, he would still come forth with that confession.

Now that he has died without making that confession, everything is changed; now all that remains is that he has preached Christianity firmly into an illusion.

The relationship is altered also with regard to my melancholy devotion to my dead father's pastor, for it would indeed be too much if even after his death I were unable to speak candidly of him, although I know very well that there will always be something enticing for me in my old devotion and my esthetic admiration.

XI¹
A 1
6

My original desire was to turn everything of mine into a triumph for Mynster. As I came to a clearer understanding later, my desire remained unchanged, but I was obliged to request this little confession, something that I did not covet for my own sake and therefore, as I thought, that could very well be done in such a way that it would become a triumph for Bishop M.

According to our secret misunderstanding, I hoped that I at least could avoid attacking him during his lifetime; I also considered it possible that I myself might die.

And yet I came very close to thinking that I would have to attack him. I have heard all his sermons except the last,[73] but it was not sickness that prevented me, for I was in church where Kolthoff[74] preached. I took this to mean: now it must come, you must break the tradition received from Father. It was the last time M. preached. God be praised, is it not like guidance?

If Bishop Mynster could have yielded (something that could, after all, have been concealed from all, for whom it would have become his triumph), my external situation would also have been much more free from care than it was, inasmuch as Bishop

Mynster, who secretly did indeed make concession enough to
me in the intellectual sphere, in his worldly sagacity counted on
its ending with my yielding to him in one way or another because financially I would be unable to keep on opposing him.
Something he frequently said in our conversations, although not
directed at me, was very significant: It does not depend on who
has the most power but on who can stick it out the longest.

—*JP* VI 6853 (*Pap.* XI^1 A 1) March 1, 1854

XI^3
B 15
37

My Relationship to Bishop Mynster
in the Shortest Possible Resumé

March 1854   S. Kierkegaard

Lest at some time I come to stand in a much too curious light,
from a Christian point of view, in the verdict of history because
of the fuss I made about Bishop M., it probably is quite in order
for me to give an explanation, something I owe both to Christianity and the circumstances and to my own striving, which in
its Christian intent is related to Bishop Mynster's proclamation of
Christianity. Now that he is dead, I can do this. It was my desire,
for me a very special desire, to hold it in abeyance as long as he
lived—I thank Governance that it was granted. Only I know
how difficult it was for me toward the end, how close I nevertheless was to having to deny myself the fulfillment of my desire.

What led me to take the position I took toward Bishop M. was
in part something purely personal and in part a Christian concern, and that is why I refrained from saying what I Christianly
thought of his proclamation of Christianity, with only one exception and then guardedly and very briefly.[75]

When one considers that Bishop M. reached seventy-eight years
of age, one must wonder very much how it came about that this
man's proclamation of Christianity never was the object of any
attack. Whether it ought to have happened earlier, I leave open,

XI^3
B 15
38

but in any case from the very beginning I was, if I may put it this way, his natural opposition.

But I did not express this. On the contrary, I gave expression to something else. When I had completed the esthetic part of my writing, when on the largest possible scale I had made room for Bishop M. (in a postscript to *Concluding Postscript*), made room for him as the one and only in Denmark, I went to him. I said: I am in complete disagreement with you, in disagreement as much as is possible. To tackle the matter in that way was personally very satisfying to me. My thinking was: Privately I will tell him how much I am in disagreement with him—I owe that to the truth—but outwardly he is not to be diminished by an attack; on the contrary, he is to be elevated even above his actual worth; he represents what must be made known [*deleted:* , even if one works indirectly].

Bishop Mynster replied: You are the complement to me.

I will not dwell further on whether it is not really a strange division that the one, rewarded with all the worldly goods and advantages, takes Christianity in such a way that it provides every possible enjoyment, and that the other, certainly more intensely engaged than any pastor in Denmark, rewarded with ingratitude, even condemned, at his own expense must proclaim Christianity, and then the first one does not even put in a word for the second but limits himself to saying it privately to him in his living room. This I will not dwell upon further; I did not ask to have it otherwise. It was completely satisfying to me; it satisfied my depression; it satisfied my devotion to the old man, my late father's pastor; it satisfied my esthetic admiration for all the exceptional qualities in Sjælland's admired bishop.

But there is another difficulty involved in this matter of the complement. If it were the case that Mynster's proclamation of Christianity truly, in his own words, relates itself to a complement, then, whether or not this complement exists, one would have to be able to detect it in his proclamation; it would, so to speak, have to be manifest that it relates itself to a complement. But such was not the case. On the contrary, Bishop M. had, as they say of a draftsman, rounded off, finalized, his proclamation of Christianity; it was Christianity lock, stock, and barrel, capped

XI³
B 15
39

and crowned, the true Christianity. —Only when someone comes along who in profound veneration completely disagrees with him—only then does Bishop M. have his eyes opened and says: It is the complement to me. This is dubious.

And there is something else dubious about this idea of the complement. If my activity is really a complement to his proclamation, then this certainly must be mentioned officially. It is not good enough to say: Officially Bishop Mynster's proclamation of Christianity is true Christianity; privately Magister Kierkegaard is the complement. I do not say this on my own behalf; I require no change. To me it is good just as it is. It satisfies me personally, and whatever Christian motive I may have had could not have anything against it.

Time went on; I was quite at ease in providing the complement.

But it cannot have been long before Bishop M. became wary and said to himself: Despite all this man's honest devotion to me, there is something almost fatal about this complement; at times it seems as if it all must end with the complement's pushing my proclamation aside and rendering it false. As far as I am concerned, that was not my aim at all, and if it happens I am innocent. If it happens, it has to be the result of the dubiousness of privately having a complement that one does not have officially—otherwise it can never happen.

Time passed, and now we are in the year 1848.[76] It was a crisis. In a crisis like that, the Christianity Bishop Mynster's proclamation represents is utterly untenable. If in the opposition there is one single person of character, then everything is lost—here I am looking at it from Mynster's side—because what Bishop Mynster represents is not Christianity. From a Christian point of view it is a characterless mitigating and a toning down that can be harmonized with Christianity only by means of a confession. Up to a point Bishop M. has surely seen this, but he probably has thought: There is not one single person of character in the opposition—ergo, we do not need to do anything at all.

That was not my view. I believed that Christianly this was not allowed, that Christianity is indeed the truth, and thus one does not dare avail oneself of the accidental circumstance that at the

XI³
B 15
40

moment there is not a person of character in the opposition. No, one must perceive what truth there may or could be in the opposition and then make the admission. I was perhaps as much in disagreement with Bishop Mynster on how the established order should be defended as I was in agreement with him that it had to be defended as vigorously as possible. I believed it should be defended Christianly; he perhaps thought: I will manage with my worldly sagacity.

I then turned my attention to the official proclamation of Christianity locally, to Bishop M., to see if he intended to do anything. No, Bishop M. stays put (good-natured journalists have—what cruel satire!—portrayed this as admirable); while the old world to which he belongs is falling, he stays put, "he is suitable."

Well, then the complement must do its best. Here lies one of my books, called *Practice in Christianity*. In a time of crisis such as 1848 and later, with an official proclamation of Christianity like the Mynsterian, this is Christianly the only possible defense for the established order. [*Deleted:* It defends it by making a confession to Christianity, not by concealing or veiling.]

Before sending the book into the world, I had tried out of Christian concern to influence the old gentleman in various ways, somewhat like this: "You are an old man now, Bishop M. You have enjoyed life as very, very few people have done; in all human probability you have only a few years to live—then dedicate these last ones solely to the service of Christianity—put on all your dignity, use all the oratorical power you have, come before the people, but do not address your words to the listeners, no, address them to God in heaven, dare to use them yourself [*changed from:* to accuse yourself] and then say: The confusion of these times has taught me that I have been too mild in proclaiming Christianity; I have scaled it down. I do not owe it to you listeners to say this, but I owe it to you, O God! Do that, do it, and you will see the enormous effect it will have. Do it; you cannot ever rule as long as you have not made this confession to God. But do it—and then take up the reins."

So I sent the book out. It is a defense of the established order, not by concealing and covering up, note well, but by making a

XI³
B 15
41

confession to Christianity. Properly understood, Christianly understood, this was the only possible defense for the established order as well as the most fatal blow to the opposition. However much I wanted to, I did not dare directly advise or ask Bishop M. to declare himself in favor of the book, for then I would have fallen out of my character, because, although it is true that I have provided the complement, it is also true that if there is falsehood in the Mynsterian proclamation, I must become the judgment or the very work I am doing must make it manifest.

Bishop M. proved unable to make a decision, to dare boldly to declare himself in favor of this view.

Now then, when he could not do that, there was only one thing left for him to do if he was to continue to be of significance—he could rise up in all his strength, turn against the complement, curse this book to hell as an appalling abomination, "a profane playing with the sacred"—in his drawing room one no doubt would have detected symptoms of something like this. As far as I was concerned, I was prepared; I had wished it for Mynster's sake if he would not accept the complement. But I was forced to say to myself: M. is too old and too overtaxed by your work for that.

XI³
B 15
42 Since he could not decide either to go along with the complement or to cast his weight against it, the complement naturally began to be an affliction to him. In the inconsequential meaning of the word, he became passionate—alas, perhaps I, even though well-intentioned, was responsible for that! He wrote a line—also in thanks for the article against Rudelbach[77]—in which he, even though with his customary caution, put me on a level together with Goldschmidt.[78]

If anyone were to ask me if I gave up on Bishop M. from that moment, I would answer, "Yes," and thereupon would answer, "No, I almost began to hope, but in a new way; when a man has flared up passionately, he sometimes, if not goaded further, becomes conciliatory afterward, is moved—this was indeed possible." In any case Bishop M. is so important that if he can be brought to make this confession—that what he has represented is not Christianity but a mitigation—then for Christianity this is the most desirable turn possible in Denmark, because Bishop M.

is a representation that carries a country. That is why he must not be diminished (so he does not become less as a representation), must not be attacked (for this makes it impossible for him to be that); that is why there must be a waiting period, to the end if possible, which also completely satisfies my devotedness to him.

But he dies without this confession; hence in the interest of Christianity this proclamation must be protested as quickly as possible—and moreover I also owe it to myself—so that we do not remain stuck in it, do not get a flat continuation of it, which may even make the Mynsterian proclamation the true proclamation, true Christianity. Even if it were ten times and, if you will, ever so honestly, a pious fraud (*pia fraus*) on Bishop M.'s part to mitigate and tone down Christianity this way for the very purpose of winning people to it, and even if every minute of his life Bishop M. had been inwardly willing to make the confession to God—something I could never doubt—if such a proclamation of Christianity is to be Christianly tenable in any way, it must in one way or another end with making the confession also to us people. This must—*Christianly*—be required. Christianly it makes no difference at all whether his proclamation was artistically matchless, unique, his "countenance beautifully modeled, his use of language hitherto unattained."[79]

If Bishop M. could have been prevailed upon, what could not have been achieved, what an awakening! And also how beautifully it could have been achieved, how solemnly, with what an elevating effect, without any commotion, which now perhaps can hardly be avoided, although it still may be only a misunderstanding. And how gently, how peacefully, how reconcilingly, whereas now there perhaps must be a battle and only God knows how violent. How many tears could have been spared that now perhaps will flow even though in secret; how many a sigh could have been prevented, how many a cry of terror that now perhaps will be heard even though against the will of the apprehensive! It is possible, even though everything may come only through a misunderstanding, but now it is possible. Is it so hard when a man has come to be seventy years old, when a man has enjoyed life and all its advantages on such a scale as Bishop M. but still at times must have had misgivings about whether achieving all this by proclaiming Christianity can hang together, and with that kind of Christian proclamation—is it so hard then in the seventieth year or the seventy-second year or the seventy-sixth year or the day before one dies to make a confession to Christianity—can it be so hard? It must have been, since even this man, to whom I steadily remain attached in melancholy admiration and devotion, could not bring himself to it. But if it can be that hard, then I can scarcely envision how hard is that which those glorious ones consummated, who with a whole life before them proclaimed Christianity, the foolishness of the Gospel, in self-renunciation, twenty, thirty, forty years, perhaps, in self-renunciation, and who were rewarded with hatred, curses, mistreatment, a martyr's death.—*JP* VI 6854 (*Pap.* XI^3 B 15) March 1854

Bishop Mynster's
Proclamation of Christianity

What I am doing here I do with sorrow. Yet it must be done; of that I have made up my mind. I will not have peace before it is done. I regard it as a mitigation by providence that I was exempt from doing it while he lived. But even after his death, how willingly I would keep silence. Let no one [*deleted:* be angry] reproach me for doing it, or if someone does—well, I certainly resign myself to it; for me the pain is that I have had to do it, because, to tell the truth, when all is said and done there certainly are not many, more correctly, perhaps only very few, perhaps no one, who has been more sincerely devoted to Bishop M. and has had more joy from admiring the, humanly speaking, excellence in him than I, who also on behalf of my late father felt myself bound to him.—*Pap.* XI^3 B 27 *n.d.*, 1854

XI^3
B 28
58

You who are dead, while you lived you had enough who bowed before you—in order to attain something; I attained

nothing, yet no one bowed more deeply before you. — —God
be praised that it could last as long as you lived. You knew it; I
never concealed it from you. Thank you for what love and sympathy you have shown by kindly being willing to understand it.
Forgive (something I did not forget to say while you were living), forgive me if I almost plagued you by repeating continually
that what occupied me chiefly (for "despite my admiration I am
in complete disagreement with Your Grace") was the memory
of a late citizen of the city whom you also recalled in print[80] long
after his death, your old listener, your grateful reader, my father!

You who are dead, at your grave there has been sufficient
trumpeting. And as you once jestingly (and who could forget
your jesting, no more than one could forget everything else that
was soundly and truly remarkable about you), as you jestingly
said to me, "There must be a little trumpeting," so presumably
must it be as you said—but is it not true that a little truth must
also be heard, a little truth—and without trumpets.—*JP* VI 6855
(*Pap.* XI³ B 28) *n.d.*, 1854

XI³
B 28
59

[*Deleted:* **My Proposal.** *Changed to:*
To My Contemporaries
A proposal—and yet not a proposal]

XI³
B 32
63

[*Deleted:* March 1854]

So let it then in God's name be said, that for which all my
earlier work is a preparation [*changed from:* so that in God's name
I can come to begin; the earlier work was only a preparation], to
which it is related and for which it waited [*changed from:* waits]—
thus in one sense I now stand at the end, in another sense precisely now at the beginning.

When one takes the New Testament and holds it alongside
[*deleted:* what with us is ordinarily proclaimed as Christianity,
everyone certainly must be able to see that the difference is this,
that what with us is officially proclaimed as Christianity] what
here in this country is the ordinary "proclamation" (this word
taken both in the one sense and in the other) of Christianity,
everyone certainly must be able to see that the difference is this,

XI³
B 32
64

that with us the official proclamation (this word taken both in the one sense and in the other) of Christianity is exactly the opposite of what the New Testament calls Christianity.

I doubt that there would be any pastor so dense that he himself cannot to a certain degree see this and therefore privately knows that there is something wrong. Even less do I doubt that there would be any pastor whom I would be unable to convince in private conversation so that he—in this private conversation—would say: Yes, what you say is basically true; Christianity does actually not exist.

But as little as I doubt this, just as little do I hide from myself that these same persons perhaps will mount the greatest possible opposition to me if I say it publicly—"This is preposterous; this is becoming all too frightfully earnest." In what way all too frightfully earnest; I thought that precisely this was the frightful earnestness, to allow everything to remain as it is and thereby to change the public worship of God into a kind of blasphemy of God, whereby every Sunday one makes a fool of God, since it is making a fool of God to know privately that there is something wrong while officially everything remains the same. Therefore the earnestness, the frightful earnestness the pastor is thinking of must be something else—the consequences in the earthly, in the temporal, in the civic sense.

Do not misunderstand me. It is my most sincere desire, both for my own sake—since I am not the strong one—and for the sake of others, among whom (in order not to speak too generally and thereby to say less) are this one and that one whom I love just as highly as I love myself—thus it is my most sincere desire that everything may remain as lenient and quiet and peaceful as possible, and therefore it is again my wish that for that purpose the matter will simply be left to me, undisturbed. Precisely this—let us be honest!—precisely this that is feared most, the earthly, temporal, and civic consequences, I do not fear at all. My idea is that everything—if no one intervenes disturbingly—in this respect can remain completely unchanged. It was with regard to such changes that I was so decidedly in harmony with the late bishop. How often did I not repeat to him: I am—in this respect—so

XI³
B 32
65

conservative that if I might have my way, not so much as one button will be changed on the assistant gravedigger's frock, even if the opposition ever so zealously insists upon it.

What I am aiming at is something else; and I think that if I—let us imagine it—prevail as I could wish, I think that thereby the gain will be:

putting an end to the practice of wanting to conceal, to veil the true situation;

getting the more truthful to cast light on the situation;

making it possible to be able in the future to work Christianly for Christianity, which is indeed impossible as long as even the slightest artifice is used to conceal the true condition, to say nothing of when, as during the administration of the late bishop, all possible artifices are used on the greatest possible scale to conceal, to cover up—and why? for what purpose? Well, I do not comprehend, because I do not perceive what use there is in concealing, in veiling in a matter concerning which one goes to meet an eternity's accounting.

I think this can be achieved if I am allowed to prevail, and then one thing more might be achieved, which I will develop a little further simply because I know very well that we human beings are so far from being spirit in such a way that—let us be honest, to what end are artifices in a matter in which one goes to meet an eternity's accounting!—that the earthly, the temporal, is not what occupies us the most. What I think will be achieved is that the pastor will be pleased about it, that more than one will say: It gave relief, it relieved my conscience.

Let me now speak of something that is so very human. He is 25 years old, a theological graduate, he is engaged to be married; the clerical career is the one for which he has prepared himself, and he otherwise does not know any career in which he could earn a living—nobody has made him aware that there might be something suspicious here—then he becomes a pastor; happy in the thought of now being able to marry and to start to work, he takes the position. A few years go by, he is already supporting a family—then at some time there awakens a doubt, a suspicion. But now, now it would take almost a hero's power for some-

XI³
B 32
66

one with a wife and children and everything belonging to that
to make a break with what he once—alas, joyful and happy—
entered into, perhaps without knowing much more about it than
that one did it "of course just like all the others." The result of
this becomes something that is rarely discussed, especially in our
age, and that nevertheless is perhaps found more frequently in
our day: a burdened conscience. This is seldom discussed, and
precisely because of that the situation becomes worse; and the
fact that it is seldom discussed is indirect evidence that a burdened conscience may be even more common in our day, and
for that very reason there is this silent agreement: Let us never
touch on this point; let us mutually guard each other against this
by condemning touching on it as a lack of culture.

A burdened conscience! Thus a person becomes a dual personality: privately, personally, he is one thing; officially he is
something else. And the more he is tormented by it, the more
important it is for him—alas, this is the way he understands it!—
to put a bold face on it and not to let himself worry, to be able
to guard against any personal contact pertaining to this matter,
with which he is involved only officially and professionally. Thus
religion becomes—this certainly is the safest way!—objectively
served; the doctrine is objectively proclaimed—personally?
"You must excuse me; it is a lack of culture to ask me about my
personal opinion." Objectively the pastor is a public official;
everything is objective, and this must also be the most reliable of
all. I am of another opinion. I see in this precisely what is in-
excusable, direct evidence that there is uncertainty, uncertainty,
something one is concealing, something one does not want
exposed.

XI³
B 32
67
I will not—then I would have to speak differently, and in any
case it can happen only very rarely—I will not speak about
whether, unfortunately, a person can over the years succeed in so
perfecting himself in the art of being objective that finally he
himself is not aware of the burdened conscience at all. I do not
speak about this rarity; I speak about what is very human: a
young man, humanly innocent, has entered into something—
and now he is situated in it, is a public official, breadwinner, a
family man, perhaps has already known plenty of troubles, and

then in addition has a burdened conscience, does not harden himself against it, is too honest for that, but neither does he have the courage to venture everything in order to struggle out of it, and so the matter rests there.

Let no one misunderstand me. If someone should incidentally be aware of my personal life, I ask him not to misunderstand it, as if in any way it were by hostile intention that I am unmarried, without an official position, etc. No, this has an altogether special reason, and therefore—I do not conceal it—therefore it is certainly also in order that I, if things are made much too hot for me, can justify myself and withdraw sufficiently. But if this is not done, then there is in the country no pastor more interested, by being a pastor, in fighting for the pastor than I am voluntarily. I simply would like to see to it that the pastor's conscience is eased—since I am both sufficiently courteous and devoted to him to assume that he honestly has a burdened conscience, that he is not among those great artists who have perfected themselves in transforming the heaviest load a human being can carry, a burdened conscience, into the lightest thing a human being can have: no conscience.

To put it briefly and to the point, there must be confession with regard to how we relate ourselves to the New Testament; we must submit to an exposure of the condition—lest a better condition not be gained in the future and the pastor not gain a lighter conscience either.

By means of a confession, by getting the condition exposed in relation to the New Testament, we are still in harmony with Christianity—this is what I am aiming at. Now that I am saying it, I almost fear that it is too little, that I perhaps am also aiming at something else, to spare myself. Therefore I must add: this is how I understand it now, but I cannot know whether it must be moved further out.

XI³
B 32
68

But it is my most sincere desire for my own sake—I am not the strong one—and for the sake of others, that the matter can rest there. And if that does not happen—in the way I now understand it—the opposition to me must be due to a misunderstanding, or it must be a punishment upon us for the whole Church administration of the late bishop. Everything that is said and written about his being irreplaceable is, *Christianly*, most preposterous. No, his whole Church administration—and even if it were ten times as well-intentioned—was, *Christianly*, an abomination, a loathsomeness to Christianity, since it was a concealing, veiling, gilding, plating, and a blinding of the eyes, all perhaps well-intentioned—but Christianity is truth, and the truth that discloses. As a result, he therefore also leaves an enormous illusion, because during the many years he lived he had influence, and he was active—this cannot be denied. But when a man is to go out to Amagerport, it of course is utterly useless for him, an excellent walker, to hurry with praiseworthy doggedness and in a forced pace out to Nørreport. Christianity wants to be served Christianly. If someone possesses all possible gifts and abilities, admirable for optical illusions, and is willing to serve Christianity with them—Christianity is not only indifferent to all such things but is in its innermost heart opposed—thus it was quite possible that we would be punished because of a Church administration that, Christianly, was high treason, since Christianity is infinitely, if you please, too distinguished to be served diplomatically. On the other hand, when Christianity has for a long, long time been served in this way, people will perhaps be so ensnared in the illusion that the most lenient of all, the proposal of a confession, will find the most violent opposition and occasion the most vio-

XI³
B 32
69

lent battle. Relative to that, the proposal may again be changed, but since it is the most lenient, it cannot, of course, become more lenient.

> My proposal, then, was and is:
> that we see to getting the true condition assessed and submit to this exposure;
> after that make a confession to Christianity,
> and then take the consequences of what we, Christianly, have found out about ourselves;
> and finally, that we, in order not to oppose this, in the meantime refrain from everything that could strengthen the opposite, from everything, for example, that is called wanting to reform the Church, because, if there is to be meaning in this, it must be assumed that it is correct that we are Christians, but

the truth, which the exposure will show, is simply that we are not Christians, nor is our life a striving in that direction but is a distancing from it—that is, if the New Testament decides what Christianity is. Let us not then—in order to divert!—convene synods or—in order to gain postponement!—appoint commissions. No, if something like this is to be done, then let a universal day of repentance and prayer be prescribed. One cannot get into difficulty about the text [*Text*], nor about someone who can choose the text; the difficulty will perhaps be to find the one who really could, as they say, call one (us) to account [*læse en (os) Texten*].

Let me repeat: it is my most sincere desire, both for my own sake (I am not the strong one) and for the sake of others, that everything may proceed as quietly, as peaceably, as leniently, as desirably as possible—and I am hoping for that.

But if it is to be otherwise, if there is going to be a battle—all right, my life seems to qualify me to go into battle. I am a solitary person, have neither wife nor children nor that kind of cares, worries, and considerations. I am a nobody; I will not need to take off any clerical gown, since I have never worn any; I do not belong to any profession that is especially, selfishly, or sympathetically interested in my fate. Known by many, I nevertheless am to all of them like a stranger, even to the closest ones, who in various ways understand: This is a person one must let go his own skewed way. The crowd finds my existence ludicrous [*in margin:* (to some extent according to my order, insofar as it is according to the order of the naughty child in literature, who did indeed receive permission from me[81])]; a few find it moving but all in one way or another odd, which I actually do not find odd. In this way I am solitary. Indeed, so solitary that my life, tried in much sadness, is also tried in this sadness: not to be able to thank the two people to whom I—again sadness!—sadly owe the most. Namely, the two people to whom I owe what I would become as an author are two departed ones: an old man, his melancholy love's mistake, a very young girl, almost only a child, her lovable

XI[3]
B 32
70

imprudent tears. You who read this, grant me space for a little address to these two; this belongs to the cause. You superb man, you no doubt made me as unhappy as I could become, but you did it out of love—and you became the beloved. You lovable child, I no doubt made you as unhappy as you could become, but I did it out of love—you were the beloved! This became my preparatory knowledge whereby I, as I was developed in the course of years, became aware of Christianity. According to the New Testament, what is Christianity, from whence the dreadful collisions in which the New Testament breathes, and for what purpose the continual admonition about not being offended? Are not both due to Christianity's knowing that to become a Christian is to become, humanly speaking, unhappy for this life, yet in blessed expectancy of an eternal blessedness? According to the New Testament, what is it to be loved by God? Is it not to become, humanly speaking, unhappy for this life, yet in blessed expectancy of an eternal blessedness? According to the New Testament, God, who is spirit, cannot love a human being in a different way. He must make you unhappy; yet it is out of love— blessed is the one who is not offended. And according to the New Testament, what is it to love God? It is to be *willing* to become, humanly speaking, unhappy for this life, yet in blessed expectancy of an eternal blessedness. According to the New Testament, a human being cannot love God, who is spirit, in a different way. And only from this point of view will it be evident that Christianity actually does not exist, that the bit of religiousness found in this country is, in one way or another, Judaism.

—*Pap.* XI³ B 32 *n.d.*, 1854

XI³
B 32
71

Addition to Pap. XI³ B 32:

Postscript

To anonymous objections I do not intend to pay attention, for the very simple reason that in a matter of conscience it is nonsense to be anonymous.

But as a matter of fact I do indeed have a special reason. Fairness seems to demand that I should at least be protected against

any pastor's writing anonymously against me. Let us see why. A
pastor writes an article against me; it is well written, warmly eloquent, etc., but it is anonymous. By this an injustice is done to
me, because this element must and should be taken into consideration, that what he is fighting for is his livelihood, that he is in
an egotistical sense interested in what he is fighting for. I do not
say therefore that it is his livelihood that inspires him or that he
preaches only for his bread and butter, far from it, and to me it
seems that what I have said above is as polite and well disposed
as possible toward the pastor, but I do say that this element must
be taken into consideration, and that it therefore must exist for us
others and not be hidden or taken away by anonymity. If I were
to champion gas-lighting, I think fairness would demand that I
would be protected against allowing all those to write anonymously who are financially interested in whale-oil lamps. I do
not say that it is the financial that determines the writer, no, but
I do say that the possible vigor, warmth, eloquence, and persua-
sive power of such an article are nevertheless changed somewhat
when the article, by being anonymous, occasions the assumption
that the determining factor is simply and solely the pure enthusiasm for whale-oil lamps.

And since I cannot assure myself of this, I choose, also for this
special reason, not to pay attention to any anonymous objection.
—*Pap.* XI³ B 33 *n.d.*, 1854

See 41:24–42:11:

According to the New Testament, to Be a Christian Is to Be Sacrificed   XI¹
A 7
Yet this is presented in such a way that it does not always mean   11
becoming a martyr to people but to become sacrificed in the
context of and in connection with relating oneself to the unconditioned, since Christianity is the unconditioned, and to relate
oneself unconditionally to the unconditioned means *eo ipso* that
the conditioned is to be sacrificed.

I refer here to Mark 9:42–50, which presents the uncondi-   XI¹
A 7
tional requirement in terms of *unconditionally* avoiding offense.   12
And then it reads (consequently with reference to those who

unconditionally avoid offense): "For everyone will be salted with
fire, and every sacrifice will be salted with salt." Therefore this
unconditioned means to be sacrificed, to become a sacrifice.
Then it reads further, "Have salt within yourselves," so that even
without becoming a sacrifice for others the Christian becomes a
sacrifice by being sacrificed in the unconditional relation to the
unconditioned.

That he is a sacrifice is expressed by the metaphor that Christ
continually uses and is here repeated: to be salt. To be salt means
not to exist for oneself but to exist for others, that is, to be sacrificed. *Salt* has no being in itself but is purely teleological, and to
be qualified wholly in a teleological way means to be sacrificed.

Yes, as mentioned, Christ presents sacrifice here in such a way
that unconditionally relating oneself to the unconditioned also
means to be sacrificed; therefore not only the martyr is a sacrifice
but also the one who unconditionally relates himself to the unconditioned, even though he is not persecuted.

Understood in this way, there is no objection to the Middle
Ages' unconditional renunciation. The fault, as I have pointed
out elsewhere (in the journals [*Pap.* X^4 A 531]), lay in conform-
ing to the world by wanting to enjoy prestige as the extraordinary instead of simply expressing that it was only the simple
requirement. In this way the unconditional relation to the unconditioned was further hindered, since a finitizing middle term
of this sort was interpolated.—*JP* IV 4906 (*Pap.* XI^1 A 7) *n.d.*,
1854

XI^1
A 28
23
Lutheranism

Lutheranism is a corrective—but a corrective made into the normative, into the sum total, is *eo ipso* [precisely thereby] confusing
XI^1
A 28
24 in the following generation (where that for which it was a corrective does not exist). And with every generation that goes by
in this way, it must become worse, until the end result is that this
corrective, which has independently established itself, produces
the very opposite of its original intention.

And this has been the case. The Lutheran corrective, when it

independently is supposed to be the sum total of Christianity, produces the most refined kind of worldliness and paganism.
—*JP* I 711 (*Pap.* XI^1 A 28) *n.d.*, 1854

See 307:1–308:34:

Hypocrisy

People usually are much inclined to ridicule someone who religiously pioneers a new way because they understand that such a person does not get a chance to enjoy life, to accumulate money, and so on and on.

What people want in fact is the most convenient religion possible, a kind of accompaniment to all finite striving.

This slackness and spiritlessness is hypocritically prinked up (especially by hypocritical clergymen) into the solemnity of holding firmly to the faith of our fathers.

But take a closer look and you will see, however, that it is as I have said. If someone were to lose sight of all the finite by holding firmly to the faith of our fathers, people would regard it as ridiculous. You see, what people want is that religion should be approximately nothing or a divine confirmation of the pursuit of the finite.

The reason there is so much talk about God's majesty is that we understand it in such a way that he is so extremely elevated—that he willingly puts up with our making a fool of him.

Incidentally, there is considerable truth in this, but in quite another sense. It is much easier to fool God than my neighbor. Why? Because my neighbor is insignificant enough to keep a sharp eye on me. But, but, but that God is easiest to fool means: God punishes—how genuinely majestic—by ignoring.

But here is the sting. In times past God has punished frightfully—this meant that he still found something that pleased him so that he did not give human beings up entirely. Now the most horrible punishment of all has come upon us, the truly majestic punishment upon "Christendom," whose guilt is high treason [*Majestæts-Forbrydelse*, crime against His Majesty] itself—God ignores us entirely. And therefore—what dreadful punishment!—

worldly life goes on splendidly for us and humankind makes
great strides in physical discoveries etc.—but God ignores us!
—*JP* III 2563 (*Pap.* XI^1 A 37) *n.d.*, 1854

A Modern Clergyman

When I think, for example, of what in my father's childhood was
understood by a store clerk, a clumsy, uncouth Jutlander—and
what is understood by a store clerk today: an adroit, active person, a gentleman, etc.—this is indeed a kind of progress.

A modern clergyman is just about the same. He is an active,
adroit, quick person who, in beautiful language, with an attractive presence, etc., knows how very lightly to introduce a little
Christianity, but very lightly, as lightly as possible. In the New
Testament Christianity is the deepest wound that can be dealt to
a person, is designed to collide with everything on the most appalling scale—and now the clergyman is perfectly trained to introduce Christianity in such a way that it means nothing; and
when he can do it perfectly, he is the model [*Mynsteret*^{82}]. How
disgusting! It would be fine if a barber could become so perfect
that he could shave off beards so lightly that one would not notice it—but with respect to what is explicitly designed to deal a
wound, to become so skilled in introducing it that it is as far as
possible unnoticeable—this is nauseating.—*JP* VI 6860 (*Pap.* XI^1
A 69) *n.d.*, 1854

See 119:1–120:27:

> A Difficulty with the New Testament, That in
> One Sense It Seems Useless in Actual Life

The dimensions in the New Testament are all on a large scale.
From this it follows that the dimensions of error, corruption, etc.
are also on a large scale, are structured ideally.

Yet the result of this is the misfortune that the greatest, greatest, and most widespread error and misunderstanding, the most
triumphant in every age, are barely warned against in the New
Testament; it is as if the New Testament were so ideal that it

neither could nor would give any thought to the idea that people could sink so deep, become something so lamentable.

The New Testament denounces false doctrine, hypocrisy, works-righteousness, etc.— —but there is really not a passage in the New Testament against the orthodoxy that is blather, mediocrity, prattle, chatter, playing at Christianity, living in platitudes, etc. It is almost as if the New Testament regarded thinking about such things as beneath its dignity.

But, alas, such is the true Christianity and orthodoxy of millions and millions and of the official preachers. And then we exploit the fact that the New Testament does not speak of such things in order to make ourselves out to be the true Church.

The New Testament contains the divine truth. Just as high as this is above all errors, extravagances, etc., so low are mediocrity, chatter, pettiness, and blather beneath every one-sidedness. But since blather nevertheless has the characteristic of not being one-sided, it capitalizes on this by passing itself off as the truly divine, which stands high above all one-sidedness.

This is the way history marches on—millions and millions of Christians. Yet the New Testament is a strange book; it is always right, even if the opposite seems to be the case. When one considers "Christendom," these millions of Christians, and then reads in the New Testament: The way is hard and those who find it are few; you will be hated by all; whoever kills you will think he is offering service to God—it certainly seems that the New Testament is wrong and has been proved untrue. O my friend, be at ease, for the New Testament is all too right. In the course of time there will have lived among these millions a single individual, some single individuals—the way was hard and they came to be hated by all and killing them was regarded as Christian service to God—yes, these single individuals were the Christians—see the New Testament.—*JP* III 2903 (*Pap.* XI[1] A 107) *n.d.*, 1854

My Task

is new in such a way that there literally is no one in Christendom's 1800 years from whom I can learn how to go about it.

XI[1]
A 107
75

All who up until now have been extraordinary ones have worked in the direction of propagating Christianity, and my task is aimed at putting a stop to a mendacious propagation, also at getting Christianity to shake off a whole mass of nominal Christians.

Thus none of the extraordinary ones has so literally stood alone as I, even less has understood it to be his task to ward off in order to remain alone, because if there is to be a halt, it is easy to see that the fewer the personnel used for bringing about a halt, the better the task will be done.

Well, well, this will be something for the assistant professors once I am dead. Those infamous rascals! And yet it is futile, even if this, too, is printed and read again and again, it is still futile. —The assistant professors will still make something profitable out of me, will teach directly, perhaps adding: The singular character of this is that it cannot be taught directly.—*JP* VI 6872 (*Pap.* XI¹ A 136) *n.d.*, 1854

See 181:19–182:3:

XI¹
A 189
149

An Alarming Nota Bene

Those three thousand who were added *en masse* to the congregation on Pentecost—is there not something dubious here at the very beginning? Should the apostles not have had misgivings about the appropriateness of Christian conversions by the thousands *auf einmal* [all at once]? Has not something human happened to the apostles, so that, remembering all too vividly their despair over Christ's death when everything was as lost, and now overwhelmed with joy over the effect they have brought about, they forgot what Christianity really is, forgot that if true imitation [*Efterfølgelse*] is Christianity, such an enormous conquest as three thousand at one time will not do?

It is very difficult, because there is a curious meeting of two thoughts, something like the meeting of two persons in a bottleneck where they cannot pass each other. In Christ Christianity has the orientation of intensity, that is, it is the pure intensity.

XI¹
A 189
150

The apostles' task seems to be oriented toward extensity, the more extensity the better. But, but to the degree that I accentuate intensity, I stop intensity and—yet it surely was true Christianity the apostles were to propagate.

In Christ Christianity is the single individual [*den Enkelte*]; here is the one and only single individual. In the apostle there is at once—community. But in this way Christianity is transposed into an entirely different conceptual sphere. It is also this concept that has become the ruination of Christendom. This concept is responsible for the confusion that whole states, countries, nations, kingdoms are Christian.—*JP* II 2056 (*Pap.* XI¹ A 189) *n.d.*, 1854

Christianity as a Regulating Weight

XI¹
A 252
203

Christianity has been abolished somewhat as follows. People have entrenched themselves more and more firmly in the fixed idea that Christianity's meaning should be in a banal sense to make life easier and easier, the temporal easier and easier, something that again is consistent with the fact that the preaching of Christianity has for a long time been, in a banal sense, an occupation, so these rascally preachers, for the sake of profit, have administered Christianity just as shopkeepers or journalists—higher things cannot be bought and sold for money—and therefore the meaning of Christianity becomes in the banal sense: to make life easier.

Thereby they have succeeded in completely abolishing Christianity, for Christianity is not some physical externality that remains even though untrue affirmations are made about it; no, Christianity is an inwardness that is transformed by the affirmations.

And since Christianity has been abolished this way, the whole realm of the temporal has also come to be muddled, with the result that it is no longer a question of a revolution once in a while, but everything rests on a revolution that can break out at any moment.

XI¹
A 252
204

And this is consistent with the fact that we have abolished Christianity as the regulating weight, as weight, of course, but as a regulating weight.

It certainly is true, as I have pointed out elsewhere, that the more meaningless we make life, the easier it is, and therefore that

life in one sense has actually become easier, not, as the pastors
falsify, by means of Christianity, but by means of abolishing
Christianity. But, on the other hand, this still has its difficulty
when a person or when a generation is to live in and for merely
finite ends; life becomes a vortex, meaninglessness, and either a
despairing arrogance or a despairing disconsolateness.

There must be weight—just as the clock or the clock's mecha-
nism needs a heavy weight in order to run properly, and the ship
needs ballast.

Christianity would furnish this weight, this regulating weight,
by making it every individual's life-meaning that whether he
becomes eternally saved is decided for him in this life. Consequently Christianity puts eternity at stake. Into the middle of all
these finite goals, which merely confuse when they are supposed
to be everything, Christianity introduced the weight, and this
weight was intended to regulate temporal life, both its good days
and its bad days etc.

And because the weight has vanished—the clock cannot run,
the ship steers wildly—and therefore human life is a vortex.

—JP I 1003 (Pap. XI¹ A 252) n.d., 1854

See 92:2–4:

XI¹
A 275
220

The Extraordinary

In one sense it is dreadful, almost fatal, to be the extraordinary
under the polemical conditions of the Christian extraordinary.
Not merely that it is the greatest possible, an almost superhuman,
strain, but this relation of contrast to others and the dimensions
of that contrast are almost fatal to all merely human sympathy.

That is why I have steadfastly—sympathy is my passion—
desired only to point out the extraordinary.

I recall the words of the dying Poul Møller,[83] which he often
said to me while he lived and which, if I remember correctly, he
enjoined Sibbern[84] to repeat to me (and in addition the words:
Tell the little Kierkegaard that he should be careful not to lay out
too big a plan of study, for that has been very detrimental to me):
XI¹
A 275
221
You are so thoroughly polemical that it is quite appalling.

Although I am so thoroughly polemical and was so even in my youth, still Christianity is almost too polemical for me.—*JP* VI 6888 (*Pap.* XI[1] A 275) *n.d.*, 1854

The Divine—The Human

relate to each other as polemically as possible, according to Christian doctrine.

When Peter, with every good intention, *humanly* wants to hold Christ back, Christ says as categorically as possible: You perceive only what is human; this is Satan's impulse. Get behind me, Satan.[85]

On the other hand, when Christ talks to the Jews about God and himself (for example, John 8[86]), the Jews cry: He is possessed by Satan, the devil; he is a Samaritan. And Christ declares the Jews to be the children of the devil.

The human as such is the relative, the mediocre, this bliss-bestowing "to a certain degree." Seen from this point of view, the unconditional is the devil, because the unconditional is a real plague for this human mediocrity, which egotistically wants an easy life of sensate enjoyment and does not want to have anything to do with the unconditional—the unconditional is indeed sheer restlessness and strenuousness and anguish.

That the unconditional should be the divine, that what occasions so much torment and trouble should be the divine, cannot be grasped by a human being before he has surrendered to it and learned from the unconditional itself that it is the divine. If a human being continues with this purely human outlook, then the unconditional is the devil, or God is the evil, as modern French philosophy maintains,[87] that is, God is the evil in the sense that he is guilty of all human unhappiness; if we could only eliminate the unconditional, knock all ideals out of our heads, everything would go well—but God makes us unhappy, he is the evil.

On the other hand, from God's point of view it is this very mediocrity, which seeks a life of sensate enjoyment, that is demonic possession, is of the devil. From God's point of view the worst we say of the wildest sins—that they are devil-inspired—is very likely more true of mediocrity's sensate enjoyment of life, because, ideally, this mediocrity is much further from the higher than the greatest sins. Where there is restlessness—and this is present where there are great sins—there is still a possibility of a higher life, but this rest is as far as possible from *spirit*.

Mediocrity is the principle that forms the human race's *compact mass*. And what the unconditional and thus also God must require as the first condition for entering into relation with people is that they be split apart. This, again, is why great crimes make the relation more possible than mediocrity does, because great crimes isolate.

Instinctively *the human being* has a tactic (just as the cuttlefish stirs up mud and the skunk spreads a stench and the porcupine raises quills) that he uses against *spirit*: Let us form a crowd; this is the human being's tactic, his mode of defense.* Just as one puts on many coats in order to keep out the cold, so the "crowd" keeps away idea and spirit. Just as the ostrich sticks its head into the ground and thinks it is invisible, so the human being forms a crowd and thinks no one can see him. We speak of not being able to see the forest for the trees; by his tactic the human being hopes that one cannot see the trees for the forest. Just as a person says he is not at home to visitors, the human being is not at home by becoming a third person—that is, in the crowd—instead of being an *I*.

XI¹
A 516
393 As a crowd, the human being is physical power; he carries on *en masse* as an animal-creature and is very happy and pleased to be protected as a crowd against God, the unconditional, idea, spirit, the ideals. What lamentable well-being, because whatever is a crowd is always that which goes to waste in every generation, and is itself to blame for it.—*JP* IV 4911 (*Pap.* XI¹ A 516) *n.d.*, 1854

In margin of Pap. XI¹ A 516:

*It is done cunningly in this way: Let us join together, form a crowd, *in order to* strive toward the ideals—because to form crowds is precisely the way to get rid of ideals.—*JP* IV 4912 (*Pap.* XI¹ A 517) *n.d.*, 1854

A Tactical Precaution

XI¹
A 526
400

When the unconditional is to be introduced—and since the contemporary age excels on the most dreadful scale in characterlessly agreeing to everything, everything to a certain degree—then caution invites one not to do what one otherwise would prefer doing both for one's own sake and the sake of others: before making the crucial charge, to go and speak to the powers that be to see if this possibly could lead them to yield a little bit. No, this one does not dare to do, because—yes, the misfortune is simply the certainty that however strongly one expressed oneself, they would go along with it to a certain degree—and thus one would simply have defeated one's purpose: to introduce the unconditional [*in margin:* the heterogeneity of the unconditional would promptly or soon be made unrecognizable in the homogeneity of characterlessness]. No, especially in the face of this characterless "to a certain degree," the unconditional is introduced with something of the beast of prey's lunging leap and the bird of prey's plunging blow.

It is this that has been long overlooked in Christendom. Christianity is the unconditional—millions have been persuaded to enter into it from generation to generation, but it has not been observed that they went along with it only to a certain degree, whereby in the course of time what is now called Christianity has come to be something unconditional in only one sense—namely, it is unconditionally the opposite of New Testament Christianity.—*JP* IV 4913 (*Pap.* XI¹ A 526) *n.d.*, 1854

XI¹
A 526
401

Making Distinctions

XI¹
A 568
431

Basically, all *upbringing* is a matter of making distinctions, learning to make distinctions. The child is continually admonished: You must make distinctions. The farm boy who becomes a soldier has it pounded into him: You must make distinctions! The person from the country offends continually in the metropolis because he does not know how to make distinctions. It is the same in more serious situations. A stupid prank by an adolescent is counted as nothing, but if it is an older person, they say: He should know how to make distinctions.

Now from this point of view, consider Christendom, particularly Protestantism, particularly in Denmark, and you will see that it can be quite simply understood as a lack of upbringing, a churlish attitude toward the divine. This wanting to have an eternal happiness and—**also**—the lack of upbringing lies in this "also"; it is obvious that one who talks this way has not been brought up, lacks upbringing, has not learned to make distinctions. There are many things in relation to which it is suitable, very suitable, to say that one wants them and also; yes, actually it holds for all things—with one exception, the unconditional, but the unconditional is precisely what Christianity is. To want to have an eternal happiness and—also—is just like the behavior of a country bumpkin who, having just arrived by cattleboat from Jylland, goes up to the full-uniformed general in the barracks and says: Listen here, my good man. But the corporal will no doubt teach him something else, teach him to make distinctions.

Christendom has removed from Christianity the expression of respect, the expression of respect that is related to divine majesty—Christendom needs upbringing. The time of the prophets, both major and minor, is long past; our age no longer believes in prophets: thus there is only one kind of prophet left—the cudgel-prophets, who have always known how to make sure they are believed, since even the worst infidel has never doubted a good thrashing that he gets.

Christendom is badly brought up. It does not help much that magnificent houses have been built to God, that both his Word and his priests have been bound in velvet; this is of no interest whatever to God, but this *also* has to go. God has a particular language for addressing him—it is action, the transformation of the mind, the expression in one's life; it is no good for us to bow and scrape before him in words and phrases and in such activities as building churches and binding Bibles in velvet.

How epigrammatic: if any man has had any pretensions of being a cultured, cultivated person and been very satisfied that he is that—it is Bishop Mynster. And yet I maintain that from a Christian point of view he was as ill-bred a churl as any bumpkin from the country.—*JP* IV 4914 (*Pap.* XI¹ A 568) *n.d.*, 1854

XI¹
A 568
432

Christian Auditing

XI²
A 36
37

What money is in the finite world, concepts are in the world of spirit. All transactions are conducted with them.

When it so happens that generation after generation everyone takes over the concepts he got from the previous generation—and then devotes his days and his time to enjoying this life, works for finite goals, etc.—the all too ready result is that the concepts are gradually distorted, become entirely different from what they were originally, come to mean something entirely different, come to be like counterfeit money. Meanwhile all transactions nevertheless continue to be conducted smoothly with them, which, incidentally, does not disturb people's egotistical interests (which is not the case when counterfeit money appears), especially if the concept-counterfeiting is oriented precisely toward human egotism; thus the one who is actually fooled, if I dare say so, is the other partner in the affairs of Christianity: God in heaven.

Yet no one likes the business of auditing the concepts. Everyone understands more or less clearly that to be employed in such a way in this business is practically the same as being sacrificed, means that a person's life becomes so impounded that he cannot follow his natural inclination to occupy himself with finite goals. No, the human way is: to treat the concepts as superficially as possible and to plunge into the concrete details of life the sooner the better, or in any case not be particularly scrupulous about the concepts, not so scrupulous that one cannot move full speed into the concrete details of life.

XI²
A 36
38

Nevertheless the auditing is needed, and more and more with each decade.

Therefore Governance must take possession of an individual who is to be used for this purpose.

Such an auditor, of course, is nothing at all like the whole chattering company of preachers and professors—yet he is not an apostle either, but rather just the opposite.

What the auditor needs is just what the apostle does not really need—intellectuality, superior intellectuality—moreover, he must be extremely familiar with all possible kinds of skulduggery and counterfeiting, almost as if he personally were the trickiest of all knaves—in fact, his business is to *know* the counterfeits.

Since all this knowledge is so very equivocal that it could occasion the greatest possible confusion, the auditor is not treated as the apostle. Alas, no, the apostle is a trusted man; the auditor is put under the strictest supervision. I continually have only one metaphor, but it is very suggestive. Imagine that the Bank of London became aware that counterfeit notes were in circulation—so well counterfeited that the bank despaired of identifying them with certainty and of protecting itself against future copying. Despite all the talented bank and police personnel, there was only one with absolute talent in precisely this area— but he was a criminal, one of the condemned. So he has to be used, but he is not used as a trusted man. He is placed under the most terrifying supervision: with death hanging over his head, he must sit and handle all that mass of money; each time he is given a body search etc.

It is the same with the Christian auditor. If the apostle has the task of proclaiming the truth, the auditor has the task of discovering counterfeits, of identifying them and thereby rendering them impossible. If the apostle's personal attribute is a noble and pure simplicity (which is the condition for being the instrument of the Holy Spirit), the auditor's is this equivocal knowledge. If the apostle is entirely in the power of Governance in a univocal and only good sense, the auditor is completely in the power of Governance in an equivocal sense. If with all his efforts and work the apostle still has no merit before God, the auditor has even less and could not possibly gain any (if it were otherwise possible), since he has a negative service to fulfill and thus is essentially a penitent—but essentially both of them are sacrificed and both are chosen in grace by Governance, for it is not in disgrace that the one is chosen as auditor. And just as it begins with the apostle, the auditor of course can come only toward the end, since he has the dissemination as a presupposition. And if the apostle has his name from being sent out because he proceeds from God outwards, the examiner's task is to penetrate the counterfeits, to lead back to God.

Apostles can never come again; otherwise Christ also must be able to come again in a way different from his second coming.

XI²
A 36
39

Christ's life on earth is Christianity. The apostle signifies: Now Christianity has been introduced; from now on you people have to take it over yourselves, but with responsibility.

So humankind took it over. And even though it is an everlasting lie that Christianity is perfectible, humankind certainly displayed a mounting perfectibility—in counterfeiting Christianity.

Confronted with this counterfeiting, God—even if he wanted to and even if there were no other hindrance—cannot use an apostle, because through its counterfeiting Christendom has set itself at such a distance from God that a trusting appeal to humankind, if I dare put it this way, is out of the question. No, since Christendom is the counterfeit, and since sin nowadays is primarily sagacity, on the side of Governance—from whom people with their counterfeiting have distanced themselves—all is distrust. Joyous emissaries no longer come from God, any more than we hail the police as such; no, only experts in fraudulence come, and even these, since they in fact essentially belong to the general fraudulence, are treated by providence as equivocal characters.

Christendom nowadays is happy and satisfied. Not infrequently we are given the impression that a new epoch is coming, new apostles are coming—because Christendom, which of course has done an excellent job, has so perfectly practiced and appropriated what the apostles introduced that now we must go further. The truth is that Christendom has done the shabbiest, trickiest job possible, and to expect new apostles (if there were any truth to this idea at all) is the most confounded insolence.

—*JP* VI 6921 (*Pap.* XI² A 36) *n.d.*, 1854

XI²
A 36
40

See 51:5–29:

"I came to cast fire upon the earth"

XI²
A 41
45

————

How fearfully true are Christianity's metaphors. To cast fire upon the earth. Yes, what is a Christian? A Christian is a person who has caught on fire.

On Pentecost this comes again—spirit is fire; tongues of fire settled upon them.

Spirit is fire. This is in accord with language usage. An example from a completely different world, which for that very reason illuminates ordinary language usage. In Kruse's adaptation of *Don Juan*, Don Juan says of Elvira, "In her eyes there flames a *fire* that seems to be from another world," and this is why "his heart pounds at the sight of her."[88]

Spirit is fire. Therefore the expression: to burn out to spirit (in Baggesen: "burned out to spirit"[89]). Alas, but in the fire Christianity wishes to light not all are burned out to spirit; some are burned out to ashes—that is, they do not become spirit in the fire.

Spirit is fire, Christianity is fire-setting. And by nature a person shrinks more from this fire than from any other. Therefore even if someone were a victim of fire ten times, if only his zest for life does not die out, he perhaps can still get to be a prosperous person and enjoy life. But the fire Christianity wants to light is not intended to burn up a few houses but to burn up the zest for life—burn it out to spirit.

Spirit is fire. From this comes the frequent expression: As gold is purified in fire, in the same way the Christian is purified. But fire must not be regarded merely as the fire of "tribulations"— that is, something coming from the outside. No, a fire is kindled in the Christian, and by means of this or in this burning comes the purification. Thus there was a diabolical ingenuity in the most horribly shocking atrocity perpetrated on some of the first Christians—burning them as torches along the road. One can almost hear those inhuman emperors scornfully say: After all, Christ wanted to cast fire upon the earth, so let the Christians serve as torches.—*JP* IV 4355 (*Pap.* XI² A 41) *n.d.*, 1854

See 64:2–65:10:

Eternity's Price (Buying and Selling)

. . . . . Studenstrup is perfectly correct in saying that the city hall and courthouse is a very impressive building and at the pittance for which these worthy men would sell it is about the most brilliant business deal possible. The only thing Studenstrup has over-looked is whether these worthy men's position with regard to the city hall and courthouse is such that they are able to sell it—it may in fact be the case that only ten dollars is also too much.

So also with Christianity and eternal happiness. That an eternal happiness is an indescribable, priceless good is indeed certain—and for the price at which the pastor will dispose of it: well, there is absolutely no doubt that this is a still more brilliant business deal than Studenstrup's would be.

But what makes me suspicious is whether the relation of "the pastor" to eternal happiness is such that he is able to dispose of it, or whether his relation resembles that of the two *Gaudiebe* [knaves] to the city hall and courthouse—for then ten dollars is much too much.

Probably it is better, then, not to let oneself be fooled by the pastor's ridiculous price but to apply to him who actually owns and controls eternal happiness—but who certainly does not have a clearance sale.—*JP* VI 6926 (*Pap.* XI² A 75) *n.d.*, 1854

See 55:20:

Playing at Christianity

XI²
A 102
109

The more I look at it, the clearer it becomes to me that the guilt of Christendom is actually this—that instead of what the New Testament understands by Christianity, Christendom, of course as bold and inexhaustible as the human imagination can be, has hit upon—playing at Christianity.

All playing at Christianity is recognizable by the partitioning of life so that in practical life, in the actual world, one lets life go the way it is going—and then one is a Christian.

What God wanted through Christianity was a transformation of the world, but a transformation of the actual, the practical world.

To that end he had his will proclaimed, and as much as said: Begin now; I am sitting and waiting, willing to be involved with you.

Everyone who is a Christian in such a way that he says: In hidden inwardness or on Sunday in church I evoke these exalted

XI²
A 102
110

thoughts, but in practical life I know very well things don't go that way, and so in practical life I do just as the practical world does—he plays at Christianity, and he makes a fool of God. For it is making a fool of God to let him sit and wait, willing to join in—when, please note, the Christian actually ventures out.

When it sometimes is said of a child that he continues too long with this playing—it is probably a matter of a year or two at most, and the child is, to be sure, only one child—but that this can go on in such a fashion for hundreds of years with millions of people playing at Christianity—this is frightful! The proportions of existence [*Tilværelse*] are so frightening that one becomes dizzy—fortunately the individual, in the Christian sense, has only to take care of himself.—*JP* I 561 (*Pap.* XI² A 102) *n.d.*, 1854

See 55:20:

XI²
A 103
110

Playing at Christianity

The medium in which you are a Christian has decisive significance for the Christian life.

To be a Christian in the medium of imagination (hidden inwardness—the artistic pomp and ceremony on Sunday etc.) is playing at Christianity.

To be a Christian in the world, which Christianity calls the evil, sinful world, this actual world—that is what is meant by being a Christian according to the New Testament.

The consequence of this, prophesies the New Testament, will be suffering. But on the other hand, according to the New Testament, God is willing to enter in, to help, admittedly according to the enormous yardstick he always uses, which makes it so strenuous for us human beings.

But God will not be made a fool of, and the last thing he wants is that making a fool of him should be called Christianity. God, XI²
A 103
111 who is himself actuality [*Virkelighed*], wants this actual [*Virkelige*] world to be the setting for being a Christian.

An illustration: when the swimming instructor himself leaps into the deep water and then says to the beginner that he will help him, that there is nothing to be afraid of—the teacher expects one thing—that the beginner will leap out into the deep water. If the beginner gets the notion of walking out in the shallows and playing at swimming—that makes a fool of the swimming instructor, who is ready and waiting out in the deep water.—*JP* III 2359 (*Pap.* XI² A 103) *n.d.*, 1854

The Way Things Stand with Bishop M.

XI²
A 312
338

In character he was a weak man; moreover, he had a great sense and fondness for enjoying life, and not the simpler pleasures but the more refined, yes, the most refined of all, precisely this: being honored, esteemed, and respected as a man of earnestness, character, and principles, a man who stands firm when everything is tottering etc.

He was in fact a very gifted man intellectually, an exceptional orator, and definitely was brilliantly [*changed from:* enormously] sagacious.

This combination is Bishop M., and this combination has managed to confuse a whole generation with regard to Christianity. His weakness of character is never seen, since it is covered up by his brilliant sagacity; his desire for pleasure is never seen, it is accepted as—a new refinement!—devout freedom of spirit in contrast to pietistic anxiety.

How dangerous it is to be as brilliantly sagacious as he was, something that is demonstrated in every one of his sermons. Yes, there perhaps is not one man in each generation with such an indisputable Christian detective eye that he can definitely see and show the dubiousness of this. It is so deceptive, the pure doctrine, well-intentioned—and perhaps not one of his points is in some way without sagacity—yet it is that which has altered Christianity a little bit or the way of speaking about Christianity, so that when all is said and done it is not really Christianity. It is well-intentioned, of that I have no doubt; it is well-intentioned—namely, to win us people to Christianity—but on the other hand it also serves to conceal. One is concealed better behind this proclamation than behind a Christianly correct proclamation, with which it is so enormously dangerous to get involved, both because it sheds light on the speaker himself (as if in hate toward

XI²
A 312
339

him) and because it so readily provokes people against the speaker.

Such was his proclamation in the sense of word and speech, but with regard to the other side of the proclamation, the speaker's life, his brilliant sagacity was again of assistance to him. There was a chasmic abyss between his personal life and "the quiet devotional hours" (when he was the speaker, the orator, and here boldly ventured much). He knew how to use all his brilliant sagacity to deflect objectively any contact, to eliminate if possible everything, any situation, any event, etc. that might prompt disclosure of just how much he actually was the man of earnestness, the elevated man of character such as the quiet devotional hours led one respectfully to regard him. And he was a virtuoso in this respect—I could write a whole book and yet fail to mention and describe all the modes and means he had at his command, and always with unquestionable virtuosity.

Such was Bishop M. I make no secret of my feelings: I have been infatuated with the man—alas, that is the way we human beings are. On the other hand, my opinion has been essentially the same from the beginning as it is now. But it was my fate to become unusually aware and, in all my striving, to be open in my relation to Bishop M., with whom I—for I make no secret of my feelings—have always been infatuated and basically still am.

—*JP* VI 6848 (*Pap.* XI² A 312) *n.d.*, 1854

XI²
A 346
357

How I Understand the Future

Certainly there must be reforming, and it will be a frightful reformation—by comparison the Lutheran Reformation will almost be a jest—a frightful reformation [*in margin:* a frightful reformation that will have as its watchword "Will faith be found on earth," and it will be identified by this, that people will "fall away" from Christianity by the millions, a frightful reformation], because the point is that Christianity actually does not exist at all, and it will be dreadful when a generation pampered by a childish Christianity, enthralled in the delusion of being Christian, once again gets the deathblow from what it is to become a Christian, to be a Christian.

The pagan was right in understanding Christianity to be hatred of humankind—so frightful it was to become a Christian. But it is more dreadful—when one has been pampered and made soft by the lollipop that is called Christianity, enthralled in the delusion of being a Christian—to have to learn it all over again.

If this were to be brought to bear suddenly upon an individual, a generation, it would no doubt be beyond human limits, and it would also be beyond human limits if a person dared to speak this way, too rigorously, of the divine, since, good heavens, that poor pampered wretch cannot be blamed totally for what generations have been guilty of for a long time.

Therefore, as I understand it, since God is forbearing, he sizes it all up, does not throw out the whole generation, nor does he set them a task that would have to be their ruin.

But it does not follow that everything is to go on as before. No, there must be a beginning: we must thoroughly, completely, and truthfully draw up a balance sheet—and this is my task, this is how I see it.

In the New Testament salvation is bound up with being a Christian—and in the New Testament interpretation of it not a single one of us is a Christian, not one. In the meantime—while we go on living carefree lives—God sits serene in heaven, with eternity's accounting in mind; and remember clearly that he is not impressed by the millions he has to dismiss, because by the millions we are not Christians, although we call ourselves that. See, what are we going to do about that? Furthermore, if the requirement were to be applied at this moment, the requirement as it stands in the New Testament, there is not one of us, not a single one, who would not be crushed, annihilated, simply because we all are (and this is far more dangerous than to be a pagan or a Jew) pampered, softened, demoralized—and most dangerous of all, demoralized by means of Christianity—but God, remember this!—God is not impressed by millions.

Is it not forbearance, indescribable forbearance—oh, that it may be true, but I dare to believe it is—that he allows us to be regarded as Christians, but nevertheless at least one thing is required, that truth must be brought into it, that a balance sheet

XI^2
A 346
358

must be made, that we should not try to find, if possible, an even greater artist than the late bishop, an even greater artist in the art of concealing, veiling, covering with the aid of illusions, but that we should be honest enough to be willing to endure having the true situation uncovered.—*JP* III 3737 (*Pap.* XI² A 346) *n.d.*, 1854

XI³
B 49
94

Church Administration
(Mynster—Martensen)
and
Christianity

The late Bishop Mynster, everyone must concede, was a master with regard to optical illusion, and what he used and excelled in was principally: dignity, distinguished bearing, artistic performance, esthetic bravura, etc. By drawing his contemporaries' attention to and fixing their attention upon these qualities that Christianly are completely irrelevant, he was successful in thoroughly diverting attention from what Christianly is more important or, more correctly, is the real issue: that Christianity simply does not exist at all.

Prof. Martensen became his successor, a change, a change so discernible that anyone who has glanced at just the little that has happened will promptly be able to see the change, in which new way we now shall have—optical illusion. Bishop Martensen seems to have understood correctly that what Bishop Mynster used can no longer be used, and this is altogether true. For one thing, it is always the case in connection with an optical illusion that a repetition is extremely dubious, and furthermore the late bishop was such a master in his own way that even if Bishop Martensen, the late bishop's maladroit right-hand man, were a good deal less maladroit in all these aspects than he is, it would still be very risky to have such a recollection as the criterion.

So Bishop Martensen has chosen something new. What he has chosen—and entirely up-to-date—is optical illusion along the lines of what could be called journalistic officiousness, journalistic self-importance and hustle. Now comes a pastoral letter, now a communication to the pastors, now to the deans, now to the parish clerks, now to the congregational councils, all printed, all calculated to interest an esteemed and estimably cultured public, to convince this esteemed public of what a busy church administration we have, how it is keeping an eye on orthodoxy in our country, how it is doing everything to satisfy the demands of the times—since what is called for is the creation of official excitement, so that there is something official on the move all the time, something to talk about, something to do. [*In margin:* somewhat as the French government, when fearing a crisis, plans its own diversionary *émeute* (disturbance).]

XI³
B 49
95

Thus by continually and resourcefully manufacturing new disturbances (incitements) that perpetually draw his contemporaries' attention to what Christianly is completely unimportant, Bishop Martensen perhaps will succeed in drawing all attention away from what Christianly is more important or, more correctly, is the real issue: that Christianity does not exist at all.

And then when Bishop Martensen is dead, the same thing will happen to him as happened to Bishop Mynster: there will be one, a possible successor, who will step into the pulpit and in the strongest terms will represent Bishop Martensen as a truth-witness, one of the authentic truth-witnesses, a link in the holy chain of truth-witnesses that stretches from the days of the apostles through the ages—that is what Martensen did with Mynster.[90] And then perhaps this eulogizer will become Martensen's successor (just as Martensen became Mynster's successor)—and by means of an optical illusion in a new model [*Mynster*[91]] will lead his contemporaries' attention entirely away from what Christianly is the more important or, more correctly, what is the crucial issue: Christianity does not exist at all.

Perhaps it will go this way, for who indeed is capable of halting Bishop Martensen on his journey [*Fart*], which actually began at the "funeral [*Jordefærd*]," that is, with Bishop Martensen's discourse "the Sunday before Bishop Mynster's funeral," where everyone with a nose for such things promptly smells a rat [*Fært*].

—*JP* VI 6875 (*Pap.* XI³ B 49) *n.d.*, 1854

(Who I Am and) What I Want

XI³
B 53
100

Now that the old bishop is dead [January 30, 1854], and that consideration is removed together with much else that made me keep indefinite (who I really am) what I want, I now can and must and will speak as directly as possible.

I understand it as my very particular task assigned by Governance, for which I was selected very early and was educated very slowly, and in which I am only now fully in compliance, also because I have always understood that this really would be about the same as having to be a sacrifice—I understand it as my task [*deleted:* to undertake a complete auditing of all the Christian concepts,] to extricate the Christian concepts from the illusions in which we have entangled them, and in so doing work toward an awakening [*in margin:* that is urgently needed in Denmark, since for more than a generation an artistically perfect and worldly sagacious, skillful proclamation of Christianity has hexed us into a kind of esthetic spell] with all the power the Omnipotent One [*changed from:* Governance] may have granted me and with the willingness to suffer that he may have loved forth in my soul both by severity and by leniency.

XI³
B 53
101

But first of all I consider it my responsibility to the established order—an expression of how I acknowledge an established order as an authority—to state my view and opinion of the established order as definitely and candidly as possible, and thereby in every way enable the established order, if it regards this as justified, to take measures against me with the power and authority it has. [*In margin:* therefore after great effort over the years to keep from being at the head of a party etc., taking care only to be a solitary (which, after all, is in harmony with my having in the highest sense this very special task)]

My judgment is: compared with the situation when Luther put in his appearance, what at first glance seems to be horrible, that there were ninety-five theses, on closer inspection seems to be an alleviation—for now there is only one thesis: Christianity, the Christianity of the New Testament, does not exist at all.

The point has been reached, especially in Protestantism, especially in Denmark, of having the very opposite of what the New Testament understands by Christianity to be Christianity.

Here in this country the official "proclamation" (taking this word in its double meaning), if placed alongside the New Testament, is, in my opinion, a perhaps well-intentioned attempt to make a fool of God—if one does not want to avoid this by confessing that this is not the Christianity of the N.T. (and in that case the whole proclamation of Christianity used today must be done over completely; everything must be done, not to maintain, perhaps with good intentions, the appearance that what we have is the Christianity of the N.T., but, just the reverse, everything must be done to get us to see how in truth we do relate to the Christianity of the N.T.).

Of course, I consider it a guilt to take part in an official divine worship of that kind, and the kind of guilt that is the last to be forgiven in eternity, because it is high treason. Therefore I do not take part any longer in the official divine worship and have not done so for some time.

XI³
B 53
102

Now it is up to the established order to act.

If I am not disturbed [*in margin:* if I am not perhaps prosecuted, arrested, perhaps even executed], I will begin my task: to work toward stripping the costumes and disguises of illusions from the Christian ideas and concepts [*changed from:* to audit the Christian ideas and concepts, to strip the disguises of illusions from them].

I will also work toward an awakening, and the power I will use (as I understand it from Governance) is—yes, people will be amazed, but so it is—it is laughter. Governance will no doubt find it appropriate. The situation in the Church is not that the clergy are sunk in dissoluteness and wild debauchery, by no means; no, they are sunk in spiritlessness, in banal philistinism, and they have dragged the congregation down into this flat spiritlessness and mediocrity. Here only one power can be used—the power of laughter. But, please note, divinely dedicated, as it is when I make use of it—and, see, this is why it pleased Governance that I, doted upon by profane grinning mockery, should voluntarily expose myself to become—if you please—a martyr to grinning mockery, in this way consecrated and dedicated with the highest approval of divine Governance to becoming a vexing *gadfly*, a quickening whip on all this spiritlessness, which in secularized mediocrity has blathered Christianity down into a triviality, into being spiritless impotence, suffocated in illusion.—*JP* VI 6943 (*Pap.* XI³ B 53) *n.d.*, 1854

My Program:
Either/Or
By
S. Kierkegaard
—*JP* VI 6944 (*Pap.* XI³ B 54) *n.d.*, 1854

Addition to Pap. XI³ B 54:

It is laughter that must be used—therefore the lines in the last diapsalm in *Either/Or*.[92]

But the laughter must first of all be divinely consecrated and devoutly dedicated. This was done on the greatest possible scale. Socrates.

An example. From a Christian point of view, Mynster was comical—like someone about to run a race who then puts on three coats—intending to proclaim him who was mocked and spit upon, to proclaim renunciation and self-denial, and then pompously appearing in silk and velvet and in possession of all earthly advantages and goods. But on the other hand, the comic of this sort is Christianly something to weep over, for it is something to weep over that this has been regarded as Christian earnestness and wisdom.

And this is how the comic must be used. The laughter must not prevail; it must not end with laughter either—no, it is merely a power that is to throw some light on the trumpery and the illusions so that I might succeed, if possible, "in moving by means of the ideals."[93]—*JP* VI 6945 (*Pap.* XI³ B 55) *n.d.*, 1854

Addition to Pap. XI³ B 54:

Either/Or! We must examine the implications of the Christian requirement, that whole side of Christianity that is suppressed these days.

We must examine this, and then we must—either/or—*either* our lives must express the requirement and we are then justified in calling ourselves Christians, *or*, if our lives express something quite different, we must give up being called Christians, we must be satisfied with being an approximation of what it is to be a Christian, etc.

The latter is my aim (at least for the time being). But there must be truth in this whole affair—this shirking and suppressing and concealing and toning down must go—divine worship must not be: making a fool of God.—*JP* VI 6946 (*Pap.* XI³ B 56) *n.d.*, 1854

Addition to Pap. XI³ B 54:

. . . So then let it be (the article against Prof. Martensen on Bishop M.[94] was "the occasion"), so then let it be said; it should and must be said yet again!

It can by no means be denied that the whole official proclamation of Christianity here in this country, when one regards what is said as well as what the teacher's (the pastor's) life expresses, is [*deleted:* completely] different from what is found in the N.T. It can by no means be denied that the whole official proclamation, to take just one aspect, as a matter of course suppresses and omits a whole side of Christianity, of which the pastor's life is not a reminder either—of dying to the world, of voluntary renunciation, of crucifying the flesh, of suffering for the doctrine. How can we ourselves accept this: is not the public divine service, in which every Sunday a book called God's Word is brought out, on which the sermon is based, as they say, and to which appeal is made—is it not changed from a divine worship service into mockery when this Word of God is treated in such an arbitrary way that one leaves out what is not convenient for one, whereas (and is this not again mockery!) the teacher is nevertheless committed by a sacred oath to the N.T., furthermore is ordained, which then presumably means that the Holy Spirit is imparted to him in a special way—how can we ourselves accept this?

Recall what I have repeated again and again, "I am without authority, only a poet,[95] belonging to the average of humankind." I do not claim to be better than others, only that I am not bound by a pledge to the New Testament and am not an ordained man either. No, in no way do I pretend to be better than

XI³
B 57
104

others; I only want it made known that this is the way we carry
XI³
B 57
105
on—I want truth in this, want it said loudly and clearly. But I do
not pretend to be better than others. Therefore what the old
bishop once said to me is not true—namely, that I spoke as if
the others were going to hell. No, if I can be said to speak at
all of going to hell, then I say something like this: If the others are
going to hell, then I am going along with them. But I do not
believe that; on the contrary, I believe that we will all be saved,
I, too, and this awakens my deepest wonder.

But, to repeat, clarity must be brought into this matter, we
must have it said—this shirking is abominable. We must—to
take just one aspect—bring forward again that whole side of
Christianity in order to see things in the context of the Christian
requirement, see whether one can be a Christian without complying with it. But not this scurvy business of suppressing it.

Bishop M. died at the right time. God be praised that things
could go on as long as the old bishop lived.

He had actually placed Christianity in the category: "both-
and," or "also," both the temporal and the eternal, the eternal and also the temporal. [*In margin:* This is what his life expressed, and it is really the life, after all, that preaches; what the
mouth says is insufficient, especially when one never uses the
mouth again and again to make the confession, "My life expresses something entirely different."] In order to examine
how things are, Christianity must be brought under the rubric:
Either/Or.

I am without authority, only a poet—but oddly enough
around here, even on the street, I go by the name "Either/Or."[96]

The illuminating light is "Either/Or." Under this illuminat-
XI³
B 57
106
ing light there must be an examination of the doctrine of the
imitation of Christ, the doctrine of grace (whether it can give
indulgence for the future, scale down the requirement for the
future, or only forgive the past), the doctrine of the Church,
whether a relaxed Christianity, established Christianity, is not
Judaism.

[*In penciled parentheses:* O Luther, you had ninety-five theses;
in our present situation there is only one thesis: Christianity does
not exist at all.]

Some suggestions by way of a few questions. Can one be a Christian at all without being a follower, can one as a teacher be committed by a sacred oath to the New Testament and be ordained without being a follower—can this be done? (See the enclosed [*Pap.* XI³ B 58].) Can Christianity, which in the New Testament, especially in the Gospels, is sheer commitment (and this is also the conception in the early Church; recall only that therefore even Baptism was delayed until the deathbed), be changed; can Christianity be changed so that it is purely and simply a gift, donation, present, "Be so kind as to accept this"—if this can be done, can one in this way be a Christian? —Can Christianity, which in the New Testament, especially in the Gospels, is about how God wants to be loved, wants to be loved by us, can it be changed in such a way that it is simply and solely about how God loves us, so that in order to give total protection against being obliged to love God, which undeniably may strike us human beings as very inconvenient, it is even made presumptuous to want to love God—can one change Christianity in this way and then be a Christian? —Can Christianity, which came into the world to strengthen and inspire human beings morally, be changed in such a way that it demoralizes them with the help of *grace*—can one be a Christian in that way? —Is it all right to take away the possibility of offense that is present in everything essentially Christian, because Christianity realizes that to make a person eternally happy it has to make him temporally unhappy (and precisely here is the possibility of offense), is it all right to take away this possibility of offense so that Christianity becomes very directly supportive of the enjoyment of this life—is it all right to be a Christian in this way? —Is it all right to take from Judaism, which, just because it had no eternal salvation to point to, had promises for this life, is it all right to take from Judaism promises for this life and to take the promises of eternity from Christianity, which just because it requires renunciation of this life has the promises of eternity, and then to mix these together so it gets to be really (two times) bonbon—is it all right to call this Christianity and to be a Christian in this way? Christianly speaking, can this and this etc. etc. be done? And if by virtue of *grace* it can be done, must not one thing at least be required, that we

XI³
B 57
107

realize clearly what we have done and how heavily we are drawing upon *grace?*

It must not be forgotten that "I am without authority, only a
poet," yes, "only a poet who wishes, if possible, to move by
means of the ideals."[97]

But it was precisely the ideals that the old bishop with his great
sagacity—a dangerous power, far more dangerous than riches,
which nevertheless are supposed to be so dangerous that it is
easier for a camel to go through a needle's eye than for a rich man
to enter into the Kingdom of God—it was precisely the ideals
that the old bishop with his great sagacity was in the process of
abolishing, although he still had sufficient truth in him, I am
sure, to be willing to confess that he was not any truth-witness.
Professor Martensen "goes further"—that is to be expected of
Prof. M.—he goes further in abolishing the ideals and from the
pulpit proclaims Bishop M. to be a truth-witness, one of the
authentic truth-witnesses. Alas, just as in housekeeping sterling
silver has been discontinued and silver plate is used—it was not
thus in the old days, when one either had silver and it was sterling
silver or one did not have it at all, but one did not have something that was supposed to be silver—so now worldliness and
ambitious enterprise aim to abolish the ideals and introduce
plated ideals, and then we get "both-and," one gets all the
earthly advantages and is also a truth-witness, one of the authentic truth-witnesses.—*JP* VI 6947 (*Pap.* XI³ B 57) *n.d.*, 1854

XI³
B 57
108

Addition to Pap. XI³ B 57:

Will not true Christianity or Christianity in character produce
the same effect in every age, the effect that is foretold in the New
Testament: persecution—is this not the view of the N.T.? When
nowadays there is no mention or thought at all of persecution,
can this not be explained by the fact that none of us is in the
character of being Christian, that nowadays by a true and earnest
Christian, as the pastor calls us churchgoers, must be understood
a characterless, spineless person, a milksop—and such persons are
not persecuted in this world (nor does it say that in the N.T.)—or
a worldly-sagacious sly fox—and such persons are not persecuted

in the world (nor does it say that in the N.T.)—or a good-natured fellow, or someone just like all the rest of us and like the pastor, who in turn is just like all the rest of us etc. [*deleted:*—and such persons are not persecuted in this world (nor does it say that in the N.T. etc.)]. Consequently, by not being Christians in character, we all, together with the pastor etc., escape, we quite properly escape persecution; yes, what is more, we laity have various conveniences in being Christians, and the pastor along with many others even has advantage [*changed from:* profit] from it— —but can this be done, can one be a true, earnest Christian, as the pastor calls us, can one be a true, earnest teacher of Christianity, as we in return call the pastor, can one be that without being in the character of being Christian; can this be done?

—Pap. XI³ B 58 n.d., 1854

From draft; see 3:1–6:38:

XI³
B 201
337

Was Bishop Mynster "a Truth-Witness," One of "the Authentic Truth-Witnesses"— Is This the Truth?

———————

[*Essentially the same as 3:6–19.*]

Is this the truth? And is talking this way about Bishop M. perhaps also witnessing to the truth, and by this mitigating talk has Prof. M. himself stepped into the character of a truth-witness, one of the authentic truth-witnesses? Is this the truth—and is this divine service? That a man who is bound by an oath on the New Testament—and that you indeed are, Prof. Martensen!—that in a building called God's house—thus *before God*—he takes out a book called God's Word, in a prayer addresses God—so that we may rightly sense his presence—thereupon reads a few lines from this Word of God—and then begins to talk this way about Bishop M.—if this is divine service, what is it then to make a fool of God? If this is being a teacher for the people, what is it then to deceive them? If this is what it is to lead, then what is it to mislead?

Bishop M. a truth-witness! Unspeakably much, I had almost said, can be said in praise, commendation, and celebration of Bishop M.; I for my part do not conceal (moreover, something I shall not, Christianly, boast about) that I have been sadly infatuated with this man; I am honor-bound to write whole books in his praise. But if I am assigned the task of presenting Bishop M. as a truth-witness, then I must be brief: no, that he was not; there is nothing more to say about that, he was not that.

XI³
B 201
338

A truth-witness! You who read this, you indeed know what is understood Christianly by a truth-witness, and now, as Prof. M. strongly declares, one of the authentic truth-witnesses. But let me nevertheless make it vivid to you. [*Essentially the same as 5:11–6:21.*]

Thus Prof. M. I am fully convinced that Bishop M. was of a different opinion. In my view the good thing about Bishop M., of this I am fully convinced, was that in inwardness before God he willingly confessed that he was by no means a truth-witness. [*Bracketed:* I do not deny how desirable it would have been if he had ended with making this confession also to us people.

But it did not happen; no, unfortunately it did not happen! You departed one, from having enjoyed life over a long period of years, something that is only exceptionally granted to a person, from having enjoyed life on a scale and to a degree that a person rarely, rarely does, you have now come to the accounting and judgment—with a great responsibility! By a little confession you no doubt could have made it easier for yourself. True, when one presumably even piously believes that in order to serve Christianity one must use illusions, since otherwise one gets no one at all to embrace Christianity; true, when someone as experienced and worldly-sagacious as you were and to that degree informed about how things go in practical life and the actual world and therefore presumably even devoutly is of the opinion that there must be a little scaling down, since otherwise all will recoil from Christianity; true, when someone, a master to the degree you were in being able to use illusions; true, when someone has grown so old in the use of them as you, and when in addition one is the powerful one, the distinguished one, the most influential one in an age—true, then it is hard to make such a confession. But if it is done, it in turn makes eternity's accounting easier; thus

XI³
B 201
339

what comes easily for a person usually ends with becoming hard, and what begins with being hard usually ends with being made easy.]

You departed one, whom I—incidentally, something only very few know, possibly no one—whom I perhaps more than once or whom I, more correctly, for a long time have continually caused anxiety and concern, while you also more than once have certainly done me no little wrong, you departed one, this I must say [*changed from:* I could not speak otherwise] at your grave! While you were living, you had plenty who bowed before you—in order to obtain something; I have obtained nothing, and yet no one has bowed more deeply before you. Now at your grave there has been sufficient trumpet blowing, and as you yourself once jestingly said—who could forget your jesting any more than everything else that was remarkable about you!—as you jestingly said, "There may be a little trumpet blowing." As you said, so it must surely be. Ah, but is it not true that there also must be a little truth heard at the grave, a little truth—and without trumpets, indeed, without trumpets, because ordinary trumpets are not for the truth [*changed from:* are too worldly] and the trumpets of the judgment [*deleted:* too superhuman (*changed from:* divine)] not for human beings.—*Pap.* XI³ B 201 *n.d.*, 1854

Addition to Pap. XI³ B 201; *see 5:3–6:38:*

Bishop Mynster a truth-witness, no, he in truth was not that, although on the other hand whole books could certainly be written, and with truth, about this remarkable, highly deserving, and in a rare way illustrious man, artistically appraised, [*deleted:* but a truth-witness, no!] who also became appreciated, although truly not beyond his merits, whereas he cannot be said to have suffered for the doctrine—a truth-witness, no, that he was not. The intrinsically unimportant position in which he began he immediately changed by his personality into an important one, and from that moment he was a powerful man, not only favorably looked upon everywhere, but esteemed, looked upon with admiration, not only listened to everywhere, but listened to with the attention of submission, not only influential everywhere, but almost decisively influential, throughout his life appreciated, acclaimed,

XI³
B 202
340

honored by men, possessing the goods of this world, also sharing in fullest measure women's almost adoring admiration, not wasted [*changed from:* (not wasted, because the object was indeed worthy)]—a truth-witness, no, he was not that.

As the country's foremost clergyman, Bishop of the royal orders, Grand Cross of the Dannebrog, he became Your Excellency (which previously was not used for the Bishop of Sjælland). This made me extraordinarily happy; indeed, I still recollect quite clearly that the deceased almost gave me a little rebuke because I was too childishly happy over it—to that degree did it make me happy. So he became Your Excellency. In my view, adequate appreciation of his merits was still not shown by that; he ought also to have been Knight of the Elephant. And if I (oh, forgive me a poetic freedom!) were the man who decides such things, then he would have been ennobled, then raised to the princely rank—certainly on the basis of his merits, but also for my own sake in order to give myself joy, in order really to be gladdened by the sight of this most justifiably admired, if you please, princely figure—but a truth-witness, no, he was not that.

He died, he was buried, and, according to what I hear, the burial was as his life deserved: a watch was kept at his coffin, a guard of honor—yes, for you who had the honor to keep watch at his coffin, where the sign of honor, which rested on it, really was honored. Innumerable crowds gathered from city and country to show him the last honor—yes, and yet no, place a punctuation mark after "him" and then read, is it not yet so true, even though sadly, that he himself was almost the last honor, perhaps Denmark's last honor for a long, long time—but among the truth-witnesses he was neither the first nor the last, since a truth-witness he was not.

People are now considering erecting a monument to him; I naturally find that entirely appropriate, also if it will be made magnificent. But if on this monument, even only in a more concealed place, there should be placed a little curlicue or the like that is supposed to signify a fraction of the first letter with which the word *truth-witness* begins, and all this is supposed to signify that Bishop M. was nevertheless that much of a truth-witness—then I would protest. I certainly would not have the power to

XI³
B 202
341

prevent it, but on the other hand nobody can prevent me from protesting. The one who placed Bishop M. under the light: a truth-witness, or into the company of "the holy chain of truth-witnesses that stretched from the days of the apostles to our time," did not truly do him a service. The severest judgment on Bishop M. will become the one who uses "the truth-witness" as the criterion; but now, since Prof. M. has officially established it, people will be prompted to use it.

February 1854.   S. Kierkegaard.

Deleted from margin: My opinion is that one person does not have the right to require of another that he shall be a truth-witness; Bishop M. did not give himself out to be a truth-witness—so I was happy in my admiration of what was admirable in him. Then along comes Prof. M. and is going to make it so extraordinarily good and (to use here an appropriate although a bit vulgar expression) lay it on with a trowel, make him into a truth-witness, one of the authentic truth-witnesses—against that I must protest. If the deceased had been living, if Prof. M. had shown him the talk, I am thoroughly convinced that Bishop M. would have said: Do not use that word; Magister K. will raise an objection. He bows in veneration of me as deeply as anyone; that he does, I must allow him that. But if you say of me that I am a truth-witness, then he will raise an objection.

To that I can only reply: Quite right, that he does. You departed one, you once jestingly said to me—who could forget your jesting any more than everything else that soundly and truly was remarkable in you!—you jestingly said: "There may be a little trumpet blowing"; but to present you as a truth-witness, that is too much.—*Pap.* XI³ B 202 February 1854

See 71–72:

The Objection

[*Changed to:* **In the name of Christianity!**]
[*Changed to:*   The Cry.]
[*Changed to:* **"But ('when all had fallen asleep') at midnight there was a cry."**]
                              —*Pap.* XI³ B 78 *n.d.*, 1854

See 72:

[*Deleted:* **"But ('when all had fallen asleep') at midnight there was a cry."** Matthew 25:6]
"But ('when all had fallen asleep') **at midnight there was a cry."**
(Matthew 25:6)

By
S. Kierkegaard.

With the help of the ideals—against illusions:
for eternity!
—*Pap.* XI³ B 59 *n.d.*, 1854

Addition to Pap. XI³ B 59:

In the smallest possible brevier.
A couple of supplementary pages.
—*Pap.* XI³ B 61 *n.d.*, 1854

Addition to Pap. XI³ B 61; *see 93:30–32:*

How is something decisive introduced?

. . . And believe me, I [*deleted:* to be sure, only a kind of poet and thinker without authority, I] know only all too well the defect of the age, that it is characterlessness, everything to a certain degree. . . .—*Pap.* XI³ B 64 *n.d.*, 1854

Addition to Pap. XI³ B 64; *see 94:32:*

XI³
B 66
115

But within me, within my silent inwardness, the genesis of the objection[98] has a history. For a long time now I have kept silent. During all that time I have not been exactly inactive. Indeed, in a step-by-step escalation, I have gone through minor decisive forms in which I could say what I have to say. Each such form I have made ready. Then I have deliberated whether I could want to send it out in the world. But, no, my soul would not consent. Finally I found the form that the objection has; it is decisive, and see, my soul rested entirely in it. To that extent now, when the step is made, the matter will for a time perhaps appear less decisive, inasmuch as I perhaps will first publish some earlier piece, but a beginning is made with the most decisive.

[*Deleted:* And now, my dear reader, farewell. If you will still follow along, (*deleted:* it will be somewhat strenuous, but if you will), I say, "Fine!" If you do not, God be with you!

XI³
B 66
116

*   *   N.B.

But you, Infinite Love, you who indeed follow along, what shall I say to you! Yes, if people could find out how you—oh, that I must talk this way—how you mistreat me, in what torments I have lived and do live, how my life's day goes on and it never becomes day—I am convinced, although sympathy for me is usually not great, that nevertheless people, just as it sometimes happens with a child mistreated by parents, would make an attempt to wrench me out of your omnipotent hands, Infinite Love!]—*Pap.* XI³ B 66 n.d, 1854

Deleted addition to Pap. XI³ B 66:

Not to be used.
[*Deleted: Postscript.*]

XI³
B 67
116

I do not dare at any price to betray my task. The step I have to take should be taken and now is taken in such a way that everything is possible. If the established order wants to see in me a dedicated and well-intentioned person, it would please me. I truly am that as I dare to be that. If it wants to see in me a dangerous person, an enemy, or in any case wants to look hostilely at me, from my side the step is taken in such a way that it is made possible for the established order to take every, unconditionally every measure [*changed from:* to insist, if so be it, on my being punished by death]. I have not—something I at no price dared to do; in a far higher sense it is a matter of life and death to betray in this way—I have not raised an objection to the established order to a certain degree; no, the objection is unconditional. This is how it must be done; this way it is truth and truth in me—now it is up to the established order. I have—loving

truth and respecting what is spirit—in a steady ascent purposely
shaped my life in such a way that in one sense it is infinitely easy
for the established order to get rid of me: a solitary human being
who has himself voluntarily asked to become and did become a
caricature. We shall now see whether in another sense it is so easy
to get rid of me, whether in one sense I am an infinitely light
thing, something one could imagine an established order could
blow away like a piece of fluff, whether in another sense this
piece of fluff has its own kind of weight in itself. [*Deleted:* But
God knows it; my wish is to be on good terms with the established order. And while I see everything darkly, as perhaps no
one in the established order sees it, I perhaps also see the way out
where no one in the established order sees it—if the established
order so wills it.]

You Omnipotent One, you truly know how to tighten a bow!
The recently deceased bishop—sad remembrance!—left me
with the explanation that the bow was far, far too tightly
stretched—then it was stretched much, much tighter! Frightful
torture to have to be the bow in this way [*deleted:* a bow that took
not only all power but the Omnipotent One to tighten]; frightful
torture, poor, poor man—that you know best, ẏou Omnipotent
One! [*Deleted:* But nevertheless how blessed, what infinite light-
ness to be the arrow.] But yet blessed, blessed, blessed, wonderful
reward for sins, aberrations, errors, mistakes, lapses—Infinite
Love! Shove me away, cast me out, forget me, if this were possible for love—just to be involved with you so much that you cast
me out is of infinitely much more worth than everything the
world and humankind have to offer, worth so much that it will
be able to be recollected eternally, that not even an eternity
could consign it to oblivion or put it out of mind—and in this
way, yes, alas, in this way you do not get rid of me, Infinite Love!

But whoever you are, you who read this, do not forget this:
whatever your life is otherwise—by ceasing to participate in the

XI³
B 67
117

XI³
B 67
118

public divine worship as it now is, you always have one and a great guilt less, that of not participating in making a fool of God. I for my part do not set my foot in any church. On the other hand, I of course pay up the church tax as I usually do, and I advise anyone who could wish a suggestion from me to sign for an even higher church tax in the future in order to keep it as clear as possible what the struggle is about. But, as stated, I will not go to church before I have gotten the established order to consider the question: how do we with our Christianity relate ourselves to the Christianity of the New Testament?

In margin: See the enclosed [*Pap.* XI³ B 68].

—*Pap.* XI³ B 67 *n.d.*, 1854

Deleted addition to Pap. XI³ B 67:

Not to be used

Just one word about myself [*changed from:* one thing more]— and it is so infinitely important to me to be completely understood—I am of anything but what is called a deep religious nature; I am of an extremely sensate nature. I am anything but what is called a saintly person; I am just the opposite. Neither can I really be said to show courage, since it is only quite figuratively that the soldier can be called courageous who courageously advances against the enemy because behind him stands a man with a loaded gun who shoots him down if he does not—courageously advance against the enemy. Thus I have, divinely weighed, absolutely no worth, and, in consideration of what I personally may have deserved (for that very reason I have tried to keep my work as an author all the more pure and unselfish as a sacrifice), I am best compared to one of the kind of people, spies they are called, who because of their past life are *unconditionally* in the power of the police, who use them specifically in the most complicated and for society the most dangerous cases. Such am I, because I am frightfully well-informed, and I have eyes rare for a human being—and I am, alas, not because of my virtue, unconditionally in the power of Governance. [*Deleted:* The difference is only that the police cannot exactly be called love—which,

XI³
B 68
118

XI³
B 68
119

however, you are, Infinite Love, you who in rescuing mercy use such a person, use him simply in order to save him.]

But if I resemble a spy, the police do not resemble you at all, are so different from you that they infinitely lack any resemblance to you—Infinite Love!—*Pap.* XI³ B 68 *n.d.*, 1854

Sincerely,
To My Reader

*   *

[*Deleted:* Whoever you are who reads this, have the courage most of all to fear to be under a delusion, so you can really get to know the truth] You whom I have called my reader, have you not thought about this, which has not escaped me, that we now may possibly be separated; in any case—I beseech you—consider very earnestly whether in the future you are able to choose to follow me or not; I do not persuade, I rather caution [*deleted:* see the enclosed[99]]. But if you will, then I say: Fine; if you will not: Farewell, God be with you. . . .—*Pap.* XI³ B 70 *n. d.*, 1854

See Pap. XI³ B 67, 68:

N.B. Perhaps best to drop the postscript, so
     that only the ending, which begins "Just one thing
     more" etc.
     becomes the postscript.
                                        —*Pap.* XI³ B 75 *n.d.*, 1854

Deleted addition to Pap. XI³ B 75:

Perhaps the title will best be:

In the Name of Christianity!

by

S. Kierkegaard
          —*Pap.* XI³ B 76 December 1854

Deleted addition to Pap. XI³ B 76; see 72:

The title probably would be better a bit more complete:
The Cry at Midnight.
Or simply in the words of the Gospel [*Matthew 25:6*]:
But at Midnight There Was a Cry.
—*Pap.* XI³ B 77 *n.d.,* 1854

Draft of unpublished response to Martensen's reply; see Supplement, pp. 360–66:

Bishop M's. Reply in the *Berlingske Tidende*[100]

XI³
B 82
124

Bishop M. has surprised me with a reply [*deleted:* in *B. T.*]. He has surprised me. Since, namely, as is well-known, Bishop M. in the past stated that his personal inclination did not permit him to acquaint himself with my prolix literature,[101] I was, at the time I published my little article in *Fædrelandet,*[102] entirely prepared for the information that Bishop M. had a corresponding inclination to take notice of very short articles. Furthermore, my acquaintance of Bishop M. is from neither yesterday nor last year; therefore I know very well that he is of the kind of truth-witnesses who prefer to be silent, to remain uninformed as long as it is in any way possible. His motto is Leporello's phrase: I do not reply; no matter who it is, I do not reply.[103] Therefore I was surprised. Then I read the article and was surprised again, because—well, why should I not say it if it is true—it is more trivial than I had expected if Bishop M. would answer.* It is almost as if my little article had made Bishop M. a totally different person: he replies—how changed! something very trivial—also a change! He is exceedingly coarse—likewise a change!

XI³
B 82
125

[*Deleted:* The article is trivial. The circumstance that it is by Bishop M., that he, with the rank of Councilor of Conference,

---

*Note. And since, as far as the late Bishop Mynster is concerned, it is of utmost importance to me not to do the man the least wrong, or, if I do, not to escape suffering for it—so I ask one or another of the excellent men who were his friends, if it is made necessary, to bring a charge against me, because, in my opinion, Bishop Martensen will not do for that.

clad in velvet, has a salary in the thousands for proclaiming Christianity—this circumstance does not make the article more significant in my eyes; since Christianly, according to the N.T., everything is the opposite of what the order is in the secular world, and the proclamation of Christianity Bishop M. represents is precisely the lowest of all.]

A reply was not actually needed [*changed from:* A reply was not actually needed, since what he has to say about the issue is nothing, and the accompanying personal insults are, of course, not worth answering]. But I shall [*changed from:* As far as that goes, I could wish to leave the article unanswered but shall] nevertheless, [*deleted:* with joy] for the sake of them [*changed from:* the many] in whose eyes Bishop M. is perhaps even something extraordinary, under several points shed light on his article [*changed from:* what his article seeks to confuse!].

XI³
B 82
126

1. The issue is: Was Bishop Mynster a t.-w. [truth-witness], one of the authentic, one of the holy chain? Bishop Martensen now puts the issue this way: I am supposed to have said that every t.-w. is also a blood-witness, and that if this is true, I am right, Martensen is wrong, but that this is not true.

Quite right, Reverend Sir, but neither is it true that I have said that. In order to show that Bishop Mynster was not a t.-w., I used on an ascending scale a description of what is Christianly understood by a t.-w., showed first what it is to be a t.-w., without implying therein that it was to be a blood-witness; and then, utilizing Bishop M.'s heightening of the expression t.-w. by adding "one of the authentic" t.-w., I ended by describing a blood-witness. But I have by no means said that every t.-w. is a blood-witness. And what becomes the main point there, in a note to the article I set forth the actual issue by pointing out the difference between two kinds of proclamation of Christianity—being a public official, a person of rank, one's proclamation a brilliant secular career—and being a suffering truth-witness, without even in a single word identifying a suffering t.-w. with a blood-witness.

2. Using the claim, now shown to be wrong, that I am supposed to have made a t.-w. identical with a blood-witness, Bishop M. then raises an objection against me, which is also sup-

posed to have been made somewhere else, that in that way not even the Apostle John is a truth-witness. The reply to that is contained in the previous remarks. In the article I have not made a t.-w. identical with a blood-w.; therefore there is nothing in what I have said to prevent the Apostle John's being called a t.-w. On the contrary, I look forward—and with a certain excitement, since if it should succeed, I have certainly lost—I look forward to seeing whether Bishop M. manages to make clear that the Apostle John was a royal official, a person of rank, the proclamation his own brilliant worldly career. And, see, it is that about which I have spoken and am speaking, stating: either/or, either the proclaimer of Christianity must give up that kind of existence or he must renounce the title: t.-w. If not, all Christian concepts are fundamentally confused, and the result is that the proclamation of Christianity is not only just as worldly a thing as everything else worldly but is even more worldly than the worldly because the refinement is to be also a t.-w.

3. In my article I have, Christianly correctly, placed suffering and t.-w. together and have, Christianly correctly, understood by suffering: to suffer for the doctrine, and have, thus understood, denied that Bishop Mynster can be called a truth-w., one of the authentic t.-w., one of the holy chain.

Bishop Martensen seeks to invalidate this by several vitiating remarks about what is to be understood by suffering, that there are indeed also sufferings other than tangible persecutions. Quite right, Right Reverend Sir, but it does not change the matter in the least. Christianity is, as everywhere, so very clear also on this point. [*Deleted:* It is one thing to suffer for the doctrine, it is the mark of the t.-w.; it is something else to have every possible earthly advantage and profit from proclaiming the doctrine. And it is of this I speak and say: either/or. If one wants to have every possible advantage, then one must renounce the title t.-w., one of the authentic t.-w., one of the holy chain.] According to Christianity, the world and Christianity are two heterogeneous entities, and that is the reason that the true proclamation relates to suffering. And it is one thing to suffer for the doctrine, the mark of the t.-w., to suffer for the doctrine by, for example, proclaiming it in poverty and lowliness (which, after all, is

XI[3]
B 82
127

suffering other than "tangible persecution") and is something else to have every possible earthly advantage and enjoyment on the greatest possible scale from proclaiming Christianity: and it is of this I have spoken and am speaking, saying: either/or, one of the parts, not both parts [*Del*], every advantage [*Fordeel*] and enjoyment and in addition the title of t.-w., one of the authentic t.-w., one of the holy chain.

[*Deleted:* 4. I have said that the truth was that Bishop Mynster was self-indulgent. In connection with that, Bishop Martensen is very severe.]

4. I have said that Bishop Mynster's preaching tones down, veils, suppresses, omits some of what is most decisively Christian. Bishop Martensen wants to invalidate this by explaining that gifts are different, and that a servant of the Lord must watch out lest he say more than *he* in particular is sent to say. Excellent! As a result of this, it is not firmly fixed what Christianity is; one leaves out the most decisive and defends oneself by saying: Gifts are different. Ah! Then one person perhaps has the gift to proclaim Christianity as "Long live profits," another the gift in renunciation to proclaim Christianity as renunciation—but both are true Christianity, except that the gifts are different.

5. I have said that the truth is that Bishop Mynster was self-indulgent. In that connection Bishop Martensen was very severe, to talk that way about the most industrious man in Denmark. And Bishop Martensen is right in what he says. Mynster was one of the most industrious men in Denmark, in my opinion *non plus ultra* [unsurpassable] as a public official, but this does not change the correctness of my judgment. With all his excellence as a public official, Mynster was an Epicurean [*deleted:* enjoying life with intelligence, with good taste]. His life's motto was the old Epicurean adage: *nil beatum nisi quietum*[104]; we must have repose, because otherwise one cannot enjoy life. Therefore he was by nature so radically different from what Christianity actually is, since Christianity is precisely—restlessness.[105]

6. Bishop Martensen says that the view of Bishop Mynster that I have arrived at has come "after having liberated myself from the filial relation of devotion to my father." This is a shameless untruth. I have said that it became the distress of my life that out

XI³
B 82
128

XI³
B 82
129

of devotion to my deceased father, by whom I was brought up on Mynster's preaching, I have honored the appearance that Bishop M. was a man of character instead of protesting it. What shamelessness to want from that to demonstrate that I have liberated myself from the filial relation of devotion to my deceased father. It is indeed out of filial devotion to my deceased father that I endured what I have endured in the relationship with Bishop Mynster. But it is really demented to demand that this should also continue after Bishop Mynster's death, so that in regard to Bishop Mynster I must never say what the truth is because I, as long as he lived, "also out of filial devotion to my deceased father," have not said it, must not say it, not even when Bishop Martensen from a pulpit, thus insulting the sanctuary in which he is speaking, offending the God whose presence he has secured by the prayer before the sermon, confusing all Christian concepts, presents Bishop Mynster as a t.-w., one of the authentic t.-w., one of the holy chain!

Inasmuch as Bishop Martensen alludes to my having written a discourse titled "The Work of Love in Recollecting One Who Is Dead"[106]—and presumably thereby aims to make the turn that it must be a contradiction that I, who speak lovingly about recollecting one who is dead, can speak in this way, that is, truthfully, about the late Bishop Mynster—then the matter is indeed very simple. I have actually not only spoken about but also practiced the work of love in recollecting one who is dead—him, my late father. My life has been almost absorbed in being his son, in recollecting him; not a day has passed without my recollecting him; I have recollected him today also, as I will also do tomorrow and thus until the end. I have indeed recollected him; also out of filial devotion to him I have endured everything in the relation to Bishop Mynster as long as he lived, and it is the truth, which no doubt will come to light someday, that Bishop M. misused my depression, availed himself of my being willing to put up with just about everything because of this relation to my father.

And now to the matter of public morality, of my article in *Fædrelandet* as a breach of public morality.

7. What Bishop Martensen, most likely as the duly appointed Bishop of Sjælland, finds himself prompted to speak about in the

XI³
B 82
130

name of public morality, the scandalousness of my action, makes no impression on me. For one thing (which is the main thing), it is a misunderstanding; for another, Bishop Martensen is such a subaltern personality that he actually cannot be impressive, least of all in velvet, just as a servant does not impress in his livery, but even less when he is wearing the count's clothes.

And inasmuch as he finally has embarked (something that no doubt also belongs under the rubric: public morality) on the not-thankless theme of talking about the odiousness that all my devotion for the deceased Bishop Mynster has been a mask that I have now thrown off, consequently that I am a kind of Jesuit (one who perhaps claims a higher morality of genius)—then I am afraid that our virtuous Bishop of Sjælland [*in margin:* that the one who, while Bishop Mynster was living, had all the advantages from the relation to Bishop Mynster, while I certainly had not the least advantage but only harmed myself by this relation, I am afraid that he, the present Bishop of Sjælland, Dr. Martensen] has here entered into an area extremely dangerous for him, because I really cannot doubt that he, through Pastor Paulli,[107] for example, and others, must have some idea that with the one deceased I have actually not worn a mask; there probably is no one else who has spoken so unreservedly to Bishop Mynster as I. On the contrary, yes, I confess it, I have, *also* out of filial devotion to a deceased father, committed the horrible crime of upholding a greater conception of him than I actually had. [*In margin:* also in the past in relation to Prof. Martensen, since he, at the head of the system, in order to make a career, wanted to diminish Bishop Mynster (*changed from:* the old man) as someone who had not kept up with the times.] This surely cannot be called a crime against the deceased. If it should be a crime against anyone, it would have to be against the contemporaries, and I would say: Well, yes, I have committed the crime, also out of filial devotion to my late father, of being fonder of Bishop Mynster than of the others, when I, without exactly becoming guilty of a lie, could contribute to what I knew gave the old man so much joy, to uphold the greatest possible idea of him. If I could do that, I would acquiesce—*Pap.* XI³ B 82 *n.d.*, 1854

XI³
B 82
131

Addition to Pap. XI³ B 82:

Note. Although the expression is sufficiently clear, I would like to explain myself a bit more fully. On Mondays I am Mynster's own preaching; that is, I am, ironically enough, the innocent consequence of Mynster's preaching. In other words, I have been brought up on Mynster's preaching—but not by Bishop Mynster; then in the living room I certainly would have received a hint that this is not how things go in practical life on Mondays, and that in practical life one conforms to how things go in practical life. No, I have been brought up on Mynster's preaching by a simple citizen, a man of prodigious will, and in the living room I in no way learned that in practical life things do not go this way and that one must conform to how things go in practical life. With the impression of Mynster's preaching about fundamentals, about character-action etc., with this I was sent out into the world by my father; "It is to this that you are to conform." Therefore what Bishop Mynster's life lacks from one end to the other, what there is not a trace of in his whole life, because on Mondays he managed with worldly sagacity: character-action—that my life has. Therefore my life, which nevertheless is Mynster's preaching, in most people's eyes looks like a kind of lunacy, which in a certain sense is quite in order. In a quiet hour to describe a character-action does not look like lunacy—Bishop Mynster knew that very well; but on Mondays to insert a Christian character-action into this world of mediocrity—that looks like lunacy—and that is why he certainly was on his guard against it.

What stern nemesis by divine Governance—to have his own preaching, in the form of the most honest and most sincere devotion of a depressed person, come so close to himself, at his side, and then not to dare to say aloud, publicly: The man is right; his life relates to my preaching quite differently from the way my own does. And on the other hand not dare to say aloud, publicly: The man is wrong—because in that case the reply perhaps would have been: After all, it is your own preaching!—*Pap.* XI³ B 83 *n.d.*, 1854

XI³
B 83
131

XI³
B 83
132

See Supplement 360–66:

Martensen in the Bishopric

Although it was by way of an injustice to an older colleague[108] that Martensen became bishop, it nevertheless appears more and more clear that I could not possibly wish anyone else in the bishopric but precisely him. The man [*deleted:* (I see it more and more clearly)] has the gift (gifts are different, as he himself says in *Berlingske Tidende*, no. 302[109]), he has the gift of promptly exposing, in the least little thing he undertakes, the weak sides of the established order. Thus we two completely suit each other; no more is actually needed than he and I—he, moreover with the officiality of being the primate of the Church—he to provide the exposure, and I (who am not entirely without gifts either) I—to see it.

Everyone who is the least bit acquainted with my writings knows what great efforts I have made to throw light on this point of being a truth-witness; therefore these continual and perpetual repetitions: I am not—although my proclamation of Christianity is considerably closer to the Christianity of the New Testament than that of royal officials and persons of rank whose career is the proclamation—"I am not any truth-witness."[110]

The issue, I have very clearly seen, is this: is there not something very dubious here, that Christianity is proclaimed in this way and that we never get a more specific explanation of how this is to be understood, although this kind of proclamation does not at all resemble the Christianity of the New Testament. Furthermore, is it not something dubious again that although these proclaimers in this way do not resemble what the New Testament understands by proclaimers of Christianity, yet they do make some small claim to be also truth-witnesses.

But I have said to myself: To say the latter directly cannot be done. The whole profession will immediately stand up as one man and declare this to be an untruth. And since I, strictly speaking, do not have any fact to hold on to (although I still may very well be completely right), the result will be that I will eventually stand as someone who has said something untrue, whereby I would have scarcely benefited the cause I have the honor to serve.

So infinitely important is this point for me.

Then Bishop Mynster dies. Now is the moment, thinks Prof. Martensen. For him it was naturally of the utmost importance to strengthen himself by acquiring the appearance that he was the one who inherited Mynster's tradition; thus the choice of him would acquire and did acquire (what an acquaintance of mine rather wittily remarked) a certain resemblance to what frequently happens in civic life, that when a man dies the widow then continues the profession under the direction of a competent foreman.

Then he delivered a memorial address.[111] You who read this, have you seen a fisherman sit perhaps many hours and wait—the moment before as relaxed as one can become by sitting and waiting this way—but now, now, what a change: there is a bite! Have you seen a detective who perhaps for years has been tracing a criminal case but waited in vain, waited for a fact so that he would dare to set to work directly—five minutes before so tired, almost indifferent, and now, now, what a change now—here is a fact, rewarding the many years of toil and waiting.

It was the memorial address on Bishop Mynster—I received the fact. What I with great effort over many years had only managed to suggest weakly, indirectly, I officially received through a gift from Prof. M.

Now all that remained for him was to come into the bishopric. If he had not become bishop, very likely no wrong would have been done him, yet there would have been for me something depressing in attacking him. Moreover, in that case his words would not have acquired the importance either. No, he becomes the primate; then everything is completely as I wish it. It is the Church's primate who has canonized the predecessor; in addition it is (just as if the Danish king ennobled the citizens of Copenhagen) a compliment to the whole profession, who by the new bishop's accession have been officially declared to be also truth-witnesses, which certainly is not a salary increase (something—to bring to mind Bishop Mynster's classification—that

XI³
B 89
137

would be preferred by some preacher interested in cattle or *L'Hombre*), but still an amenity, and moreover something so light, as is said of a coat, that one does not notice at all that one has it on, something even lighter than one of the fancy coats (what this existence could usually be best compared to) offered for sale in the summer but which still weighed 1¼ ounces, whereas this fancy coat ("also truth-witnesses") weighs nothing at all [*deleted:* , like the clothing a Roman satirist, characterizing the looseness of Roman women, charges them with wearing; he says: They are clothed in a wind[112]]. Just as in Catholicism the new prelate perhaps gives the Church a costly adornment as a gift, similarly the new primate gave the whole profession, each one individually, a fancy coat.

There is, however, a deep irony in existence. No doubt it was of the greatest concern to Martensen to inherit Mynster's tradition, and it was hidden from his eyes that there was someone present who, allowing the old man to live out his years, a long time ago understood it as his task to confiscate the Mynsterian tradition and could only wish (to refer to an earlier well-known police case, which I nevertheless cannot develop, however extraordinarily it fits)—for someone who could only wish to get Martensen "in the frock coat" in order to halt this tradition.

XI³
B 89
138

* *

It was the memorial address. On that occasion I raised an objection,[113] and Bishop Martensen replied in the *Berlingske Tidende*,[114] and see, another present and gift of utmost importance for the cause I have the honor to serve.

How often have I not circled around this point, like a bird of prey its booty and like a detective the suspect: Is not all the Christianity we have here in the country actually official Christianity?

My reader, you certainly know what is understood by this, but let me say just two words.

All Christianity, just like all religion, is and should be a personal matter: speaking should be by personality to personality. All religion does this and especially when the religion of spirit makes an even more specific requirement than, for example, erotic love [*Elskov*] makes upon the personality, erotic love, which indeed has an anxiety about the official and everything that resembles the official, because this throws suspicion on the personal, makes it ambiguous whether one is loved personally or only officially.

But now when a religion is proclaimed by officeholders, does not something most dangerous for all true religion readily emerge here: that the proclaimer can personally hold himself apart by his speaking in an official capacity (perhaps, for example, as a lawyer who in an official capacity conducts a case), and for the listener it is kept ambiguous whether it is the speaker's personal conviction or it is official, in an official capacity. In any case, one must then wish for an understanding as to how this kind of proclamation relates to the Christianity of the New Testament, which has an altogether different kind of proclamation, whether it is an advance (perhaps with the help of Christianity's perfectibility) or something that can be conceded by indulgence—in short, how it is to be understood in relation to the New Testament.

See, this is a very important point to have illuminated, how we are —with the New Testament alongside—in agreement that the proclaimers are differentiated in this way from what the New Testament understands by proclaimers of Christianity.

This is how the matter stands; then comes the reply from the primate of the Church in the *Berlingske Tidende*, no. 302. Stately mantled in velvet, which, esthetically viewed, the old man undeniably wore as impressively as anyone has scarcely ever worn velvet, the head-journeyman, or what he perhaps resembles better, the pawned peasant boy (also betraying who he actually is, if not by blowing his nose in his fingers,[115] then by talking about boxing ears[116] etc.)—wants to show off. The article itself is a triviality, which I therefore have dismissed.

On the other hand, there is a phrase in it that perhaps in one minute gives me completely what I could wish.

With authority the primate of the Church speaks disparagingly about me and says that I "have only a Christianity without Church and without history"[117]—fine, I would reply, if only I do not have a Christianity without the New Testament. The

Yet the prize has still not come, but now it comes. The

XI³
B 89
139

primate continues, that I seek Christ in the deserts and in private rooms.[118]

"In private rooms"—that about the desert, after all, does not fit our climate, so I will let it drop—in private rooms, then. In private rooms, what does that mean? It practically says: "You, S. Kierkegaard, you poor, wretched, mediocre man, you have only a private Christianity, you have a private religion; you have"—I beg Your Reverence, "Finish what you have to say; be not ashamed of it"[119] . . . . . so, out with it; is it not true that I have no official Christianity, no royally privileged Christianity, that I am a nonunion Christian?

XI³
B 89
140
Most assuredly (this I know all too well) the late bishop long ago became firmly fixed in an illusion, so that in the end he took it into his head that true Christianity can be proclaimed only by royal officeholders and persons of rank whose career is proclamation; most assuredly, as long as he, carefully concealed, could manage with no actual danger, he would at no price tolerate that Christianity be proclaimed by anyone other than royal officeholders and career-makers; most assuredly there is only one for whom he made an exception, and so he, although I was not in uniform, still wished to preserve good understanding with me— for many reasons—but it was not possible to get him to say this officially. Read his sermons, which I know by heart, and you will see that "his preaching" relates precisely to a "Christ in private rooms." The dubiousness about him was just this, that he himself (without ever explaining how we understand this to hold together with the New Testament) was the royal officeholder, a person of rank, proclamation his own brilliant career, rich in enjoyment, and thus the dubiousness was that he on Mondays undeniably (hidden behind the royal Danish chancellery) administered along the lines of official Christianity. But to say it in this way, only a Christ in private rooms—no, for that the old man was too sagacious; for that, already at a very young age, he was— too old.

Consequently a Christianity, which otherwise is not charged with being untrue, a Christ in private rooms, a private religion— it is this that should be warned against, it is this that with authority should be disparaged before people. Official Christianity, on the other hand, that is true Christianity, not something that face-to-face with the New Testament can be admitted only by indulgence. To that I can only reply: Happy New Year, Bishop Martensen.

Indeed, it is truly a New Year that we are entering—and God in heaven, you know how I have needed change! I almost shudder when I consider what I have endured because of what I, "also out of filial devotion to my late father," had depressingly bewitched myself into. The old man shall not and must not be diminished; everything that he does shall be regarded as wisdom, everything shall be tolerated and at most be told to him privately in the most serious way. Indeed, not only shall I tolerate everything (and remarkable things will come to light if I ever want to explain this in more detail), but as long as I am able, it must be known that one crosses me by doing, saying, undertaking anything that could lead to the old man's being diminished.

Yet these years are far from wasted; in them I have managed to get my whole "prolix literature" situated in literature until its time comes, and what I have suffered is truly not in vain either. No, Governance knows best how a person ought to be brought up in relation to the special task for which he is to be used. And the one who is to be used as indignation over all worldly sagacity and optical illusion, he is brought up by—suffering indignation, yet in such a way (which indeed is also my case) that he is anything but an out-and-out sufferer but is rather someone who has himself continually *voluntarily* endured sticking it out, which only gives indignation more resiliency.—*Pap.* XI³ B 89 *n.d.*, 1855

XI³
B 89
141

At Bishop Mynster's Grave

January [1855]   S. Kierkegaard

XI³
B 95
150

Since, according to what I see [*changed from:* Since, according to what I see in the newspapers], it seems to be the fashion this season for one pastor after the other to step forward in print [*changed from:* in a newspaper] to Mynster's grave, alarming the crowd of people, women and children, to say just about the same thing as the other (fearing that if he does not say it, it will not be said), altogether superfluously, since this same thing is in turn just

XI³
B 95
151

about the same as what the whole crowd, on the occasion of some untrue words, says about the ghastly crime of saying some true words about a deceased person—so I, too, who it is true lack the (Christian?) earnestness to be a royal officeholder, person of rank, career-maker, I will, understanding it as my duty, precisely because what Christianity really is has been concealed for more than a generation by a proclamation of Christianity that has been very accomplished artistically and subtly aided by a rare worldly sagacity—I, too, will say a few words at Mynster's grave, and say:

Now he is dead. From titles and dignities, from the rich incomes, from the head place at the banquet, from women's adoring admiration, from the satisfaction of not having in any way rejected using the worldly sagacity he possessed to such a high degree, from the enjoyment of sophistication's exquisite refinements, from having been a servant of the state Church all his life and finally its head servant, without ever (neither when the state Church stood nor when it fell) having clarified how this kind of Christianity relates to the Christianity of the New Testament— from all this, according to Christianity's doctrine, he has now gone to the accounting, where the judge is the abased one, the one spat upon, the crucified one, whose doctrine ("Follow me,"[120] "My kingdom is not of this world"[121]) Bishop Mynster has proclaimed in Denmark with such wonderful success for more than a generation.

While he lived, he had it in his power with one word to enlighten us others about how he understood the kind of proclamation of Christianity he represented in relation to the Christianity of the New Testament, which teaches asceticism, voluntary renunciation, requires the most unconditional heterogeneity to this world, abhors all use of worldly power, cries woe, woe upon the kind of worship, this show, which, instead of following in suffering, builds the graves of the prophets and decorates the grave plots of the righteous, which the New Testament even labels a crime and just as great as putting prophets to death (Matthew 23:29; Luke 11:47,48)—he had it in his power, and it would have been of the utmost importance. It did not happen and is his affair.

I must, however, to the highest degree understand it as my affair when I see that the Church's new primate from the pulpit portrays Bishop Mynster as a truth-witness, one of the authentic truth-witnesses, one of the holy chain[122] and thereby accordingly authorizes in the strongest expressions this kind of proclamation of Christianity as the Christianity of the New Testament—I must to the highest degree understand it as my duty, with all the power it may have pleased the Omnipotent One to grant me, with all the willingness to suffer that he both by rigorousness and gentleness may have loved forth in my soul, to throw myself against it and raise an objection, to protest that a proclamation of Christianity, which itself to the highest degree needed an explanation in relation to the New Testament, is authorized [*deleted:* and is continued, whereby then in turn, inversely, the continuation is strengthened backward] without any more definite explanation in relation to the Christianity of the New Testament.—*Pap.* XI³ B 95 January, 1855

Just a Few Words about My Relation
to Bishop Mynster

XI³
B 99
156

My relation to Bishop Mynster is so long-standing, on my side so deeply established, so carefully carried through, that it will take time before it can be rightly understood, and no doubt even more explicit explanations on my part if it is to be understood completely. But since, as stated, "Bishop Mynster is a man who fairly correctly can be said to have carried an entire generation,"[123] I can certainly comprehend that my article against Bishop Martensen must have had, as I intended, a fairly strong effect. Therefore without delay a few words here to contribute effectively or preventively so that it does not come to have a strong effect different from what I could wish.

––––––––––

The proclamation of Christianity Bishop Mynster represented: to be a public officeholder, a person of high rank, to receive thousands, many thousands in salary, to parade in silk and velvet, to sit at the head of the table at banquets, to be the secularly powerful man, etc.—this whole proclamation of Christianity has no support in the New Testament.

This is the situation. Then a young man begins to work; I am this young man. His work is many points closer to the Christianity of the New Testament than Bishop Mynster's proclamation of Christianity; he relates himself to the qualifications on which the New Testament lays emphasis. He is precisely a nonentity, has not adulterated his proclamation into a livelihood or official career; at his own expense, putting in money, he works on a scale on which Bishop Mynster has indisputably never worked. Further, when he becomes contemporaneous with a complete moral disintegration, which found its most characteristic expression in *The Corsair*,[124] edited by Goldschmidt and P. L. Møller, with an enormous number of subscribers, he resolves, as is the duty of a proclaimer of true Christianity, he resolves, with Bishop Mynster's sermons beside him (this is literally true), with Bishop Mynster's sermons (which, it cannot be denied Bishop Mynster himself betrayed on Mondays), with these beside him, he resolves to suffer the pain of witnessing against this moral disintegration—and praised, immortalized by rabble-barbarism's press,[125] he requests to be abused[126] and he was— —again properly marked according to what the New Testament understands by proclaiming Christianity.

XI³
B 99
157

When a person has thus in every respect renounced earthly reward for his effort, there can be mention of only one reward, which strictly speaking cannot be called a reward: that it becomes recognizable, seen, that what he is working for is the more true, his effort the more true.

This is the situation. But I said to myself: You cannot gain this recognizability without diminishing Bishop Mynster in one way or another. And that must not happen, "he must live out his life, be buried with full honors."[127] (1) Bishop Mynster is my late father's pastor. (2) He is in many respects an outstanding man. (3) He no doubt has entered with good intentions into the untruth in which he now is, and one cannot insist that an old man change completely. (4) It is fairly correct that he carries a whole generation; thus a conflict between him and me would be the most terrible kind for very many people. (5) It is part of true Christian self-denial to renounce not only all earthly reward but even the recognizability of one's having renounced it.

So what did I do? All the esteem I might have gained as author I collect together, transform it into a present to Bishop Mynster; that happened in the postscript to *Concluding Postscript*.[128] Thereupon I went personally to Bishop Mynster and said (I spoke to him at once, before I would even sit down on the chair he offered me) in the strongest terms: I am in disagreement with you as much as is ever possible.[129]

Then I continued to work. In my books I have truly not changed my view; neither was my life changed. No, I continued year after year to represent the proclamation of the truer Christianity. But recognizability in relation to Bishop Mynster I did not want to have. Here all the old remained—Bishop Mynster's proclamation of Christianity, this with velvet, the Grand Cross, the many thousands a year, the secular power etc.—and was Christian earnestness and wisdom; my proclamation was an eccentricity, a peculiarity, a strange exaggeration, etc. And this I have endured year after year through the best years of my life—all also out of devotion to the old man.

During these years there is much that belongs to the story of my relation to Bishop Mynster that I cannot elaborate here.

Then he dies. And then there steps into the pulpit a man, Prof. Martensen, who is neither Bishop Mynster nor my late father's pastor, and, confusing all the Christian concepts at their deepest foundation, insulting the house of God in which he is speaking, offending the God whose presence he must have secured for himself by supplicating him in prayer before the sermon, he presents, as an example for the congregation to live up to, Bishop Mynster as a truth-witness, one of the authentic truth-witnesses, assigns him a place in the holy chain of witnesses that from the day of the apostles etc.[130]

In order to make it evident that it is not in the remotest manner earthly goods and advantages about which I am contending, I keep silent until the bishopric is occupied—and by Bishop Martensen. In order not to interfere in any way whatever with the subscription to the monument people have contemplated raising to the old bishop,[131] I once again keep silent for a time. Finally I speak and raise an objection.

You who read this—if you have loved Bishop Mynster (and it

XI[3]
B 99
158

XI³
B 99
159

is precisely to you I wish to speak): keep calm for just five minutes and you will see, you will say to yourself, "It is probably true that it is Magister K. who in the relation to Bishop Mynster has displayed a resignation that is unusual in a young man in relation to an old man; it is probably true that we who call ourselves Mynster's friends, followers, admirers, are instead indebted to Magister K." And that is the way, that is just the way it is! Notwithstanding anyone who claims to have loved Bishop Mynster and from that perhaps has had joy or even advantage—I have loved Bishop Mynster, for I have loved him to my own harm. My best years have passed in frightful efforts with renunciation of everything that is called earthly reward—and the only thing I could receive, recognizability, I have renounced as long as the old man lived, because if my view becomes known, Bishop Mynster is diminished. And therefore you women—since it is no doubt mostly you who are making the biggest fuss—be still, be still. Despite all your sincere and genuine devotion, likewise despite all your curtseying before the old man, all your bowing and idolizing, despite all your embroidered New Year's and birthday gifts, I have in devotion served Bishop Mynster quite differently—but the truth must also be heard! If you really do hold his memory dear, then keep calm; in what I have said, not the remotest wrong has been done to him, but to the same degree that an uproar is raised, to the same degree it is made necessary for me to be more emphatic on the issue. Therefore do not fume as if something scandalous has happened because I have said some true words about Bishop Mynster. The scandalous thing happened just about a year ago when someone from the pulpit ventured to present to the congregation for compliance, Bishop Mynster as a Christian prototype, a truth-witness, one of the holy chain.

If someone should finally say: But is it Christianly permissible that you have concealed something in this way?—then let me also clear this up in a few words. Suppose now that my idea had been this. Bishop Mynster is involved in an untruth; it is not the Christianity of the New Testament that he represents. Yet it does not help to want to force him with evil, with power; that only hardens him. But should it not be possible to move him? After

XI³
B 99
160

all, as a psychologist Bishop Mynster is a very clear-sighted man, and he sees very well, that I know, what resignation I am showing in relation to him—should it not be possible to move him? It is indeed moving, is it not, that on Mondays I suffer for his preaching on Sunday (and this I am doing, whereas he betrays it); it is indeed moving, is it not, that I make sacrifices while he takes all the advantages—and that I am not the one who makes a request for any recognizability in relation to him, on the contrary, that I am the one who bows most deeply before him, that I am everywhere present where it is a matter of protecting Bishop Mynster (and if the situation of Danish literature in the last ten years is ever cleared up, something very remarkable in this regard will appear), that I am the one who takes issue with his enemies, that I take on the thankless tasks—to me this seems moving— should I not be able to succeed in moving the old man? He is now an old man, night is drawing on—the accounting awaits; should I not be able to succeed in moving the old man so that it would end with—truly, it may be hard, bitter, but it will make the accounting easier—so it would end with his voluntarily making the declaration that the Christianity he has represented is not the Christianity of the New Testament, but a mitigation veiled in manifold ways in illusion?

You who read this, tell me, can you imagine any more moving kind of awakening (and awakening we *must* have; no jabbering and blather are of any good here; we must have an awakening; we must break the worldly spell in which Bishop Mynster's proclamation of Christianity has enchanted us by its artistic perfection), but can you imagine any more moving awakening than there would have been if this had happened? And would it then have been advisable to make this possibility impossible by changing my relation to him?

But the situation is this: for many years, in sad devotion to the old man and for many other reasons I have renounced the recognizability that is Christianly due me, have caused my contemporaries to see me in an utterly wrong light, and, regretably, the old bishop cannot be said to be free from having contributed to this by misusing my devotion to him and my Christian resignation.

—*Pap.* XI[3] B 99 *n.d.,* 1855

XI[3]
B 99
161

Deleted:

The Atmosphere of My Contemporaneity

with Bishop Mynster

In Three Pictures

By

—*Pap.* XI³ B 108 *n.d.*, 1855

Deleted addition to Pap. XI³ B 108:

II

The Atmosphere of My Contemporaneity with
Bishop Mynster

[*Deleted:* In Three (*changed to:* Two) Pictures]

[*Deleted:* I have no desire in a deeper sense to initiate others into what I have suffered in this relationship. But inasmuch as these sufferings are related to Christianity's cause, they may well have meaning for others. But I shall make the presentation in such a way that it may quite generally be read with interest.]

[*Deleted: First Picture*]

Imagine a very large ship, even larger than the great ships we have today. Let it have room for one thousand passengers and, of course, everything planned as conveniently and comfortably and luxuriously etc. on the largest scale possible.

It is evening. In the lounge there is gaiety, everything is beautifully illuminated, everything glitters, the orchestra is playing; in short, all is merriment, frivolity, enjoyment—and the racket and noise from the happy, hilarious fun rings out into the night.

Up on the deck stands the captain, and with him the second in command. The latter takes the telescope from his eye and hands it to the captain. He replies: I do not need it; I see it all right, the little white speck on the horizon—it will be a frightful night.

Thereupon, with the noble, resolute calmness of the experienced seaman, he issues his orders: The crew will remain on duty tonight; I myself will take command.

He goes into his cabin. He has not taken an especially large library along, but he has a Bible. He opens it and, curiously enough, he opens it up to the passage: In this night your soul will be required of you.[132] Curious!

After his prayers he dresses for night duty, and now he is the full-fledged able-bodied seaman.

But the frivolity goes on in the lounge. There is song and music and conversation and noise, the clatter of plates and dishes; the champagne bottles pop, toasts are drunk to the captain, etc. etc.—"It will be a frightful night"—and perhaps this night your soul will be required of you.

Is this not frightful? And yet I know something still more frightful.

Everything is the same, only the captain is different. The lounge is full of gaiety, and the gayest of them all is the captain.

The white speck on the horizon is there; it will be a frightful night. But no one sees the white speck or suspects what it means. But no (this would not be the most frightful)—no, there is one person who sees it and knows what it means—but he is a passenger. He has, after all, no commission on the ship; he cannot do anything. But in order to do the one single thing he can do, he asks the captain to come up on deck, only for a moment. It takes a while, but finally he comes—but does not wish to hear anything and, passing it off as a joke, hurries down to the noisy, hilarious company in the lounge, where the toasts are being drunk to the captain with the usual enthusiasm, for which he thanks affably.

In his anxiety the poor passenger decides to dare once again to inconvenience the captain, but this time he is even impolite to him. But the white speck is still there on the horizon—"It will be a frightful night."

XI[3]
B 109
179

Is this not even more frightful? It was frightful to have the thousand carefree, noisy passengers, frightful to have the captain be the only one who knows what is imminent—but, ah, still the most important thing is that the captain knows it. Consequently it is more frightful that the only person who sees and knows what it is that is imminent—is a passenger.

*   *

That there is a white speck on the horizon that signifies (from a Christian point of view) that frightful weather is coming and threatens—this I knew, alas, but I am and was only a passenger.

[*Deleted:*

Second Picture

[*Deleted:* Imagine a young woman, not a splendid lady—no, she is, we might indeed think this, really what one would call a capable housewife.]

"We certainly do need a general housecleaning," she says, 'but," she continues, "I say with Magister Kierkegaard Either/ Or, one of two alternatives: either we must nicely manage to get old Auntie away for a few days, or we must let the general house-cleaning go, since to do the housecleaning when she is at home is out of the question."

But this is the situation with this old aunt. She is the sister of the young woman's mother; [*deleted:* incidentally, she is a beauti-ful and lovable old woman] the household dotes on her, espe-cially the young wife, for whom it is a need to honor and almost worship this old woman in every imaginable way—

—"But if there is to be a general housecleaning we must find a nice way to get old Auntie away in the meantime."

XI³
B 109
180 Imagine that time goes by and it is not possible to get old Auntie to go away.

Time goes by, the young woman becomes discouraged. The husband explains to her in vain that the whole thing is not so awful. "Oh," she replies, "you don't understand at all; you have no idea of what I am suffering. Only a woman understands how frightfully I am suffering, what an agony it is to have to look perpetually at all this dirt everywhere and not be able to get at a thorough cleaning." "But, my dear girl, you can certainly go ahead, because Auntie is home, and I can certainly go away for a few days." "That's a fine proposal! What do I care about you; you may certainly stay home and take part in the soaping. No, Auntie is the either/or; if Auntie is home, I understand my task is to see to it that not a breath of air blows on her—and to do a thorough cleaning with that in mind—no, my friend, impossible!"

*   *

That Christianly precisely the opposition is [*changed from:* That Christianly we are] in dire need of a thorough housecleaning and soaping is certain. But as long as the old bishop lives: no, either/ or! What we desperately need, from a Christian point of view, is to get everything *exposed*—and the fact that the late bishop's strength lay in his being able to *conceal*, an art in which he was really a master, is precisely why he has to be followed by a master in the art of being able to expose.]

Second [changed from: *Third*] *Picture*

[*Changed to:* The Atmosphere of My Contemporaneity with Bishop Mynster]

———

Imagine a young officer; we can indeed imagine it, a competent young officer.

There is a battle. Our young officer commands half a battery.   XI³

He sees (and we can suppose that he is correct): [*deleted:* God   B 109
in heaven] my three cannons aimed this second at that spot—and   181
the victory is ours.

But on that very spot (or if not on that spot then situated in such a way that it is impossible to aim the cannons toward that spot) on that spot his own general, the venerable Field Marshal Friedland, is standing with his staff.

Think what this young officer must suffer! "I am young," he says to himself. "My future would be made for me if I could get to use my cannons . . . . . Oh [*deleted:* my God], this is the time to act." A second goes by. "Forget myself," the young officer says to himself, "but the battle could be decided if only I could use my cannons: Oh [*deleted:* my God], it's terrible that it is my own general who is in such a position that I am unable to use my cannons."

* *

That the only way, *Christianly*, to pressure the opposition was to apply the ideals—this I saw; but then not to be able to do it because the old bishop (my general!) did not want the effect of the application of the ideals! Or if I did it nevertheless (for, after all, I was not his subordinate in the way an officer is to his general), so that it perhaps then would be interpreted by him as a traitorous act, perfidy, because he did not want that effect! This I understand; he had his good reasons not to want it. Although I did everything and was willing to do everything to draw attention away from this effect, he nevertheless understood that even if only very few saw it, the effect would have to bring to light that, Christianly, the old bishop's own Christian proclamation was not just what it should be. But the situation is as heartbreaking as possible, just about what one would imagine in the following incident. It is dark, and there is danger. Someone comes hurrying, willingness and devotion personified, and, quite properly, with a light. And now it becomes clear that the people he wants to help do not want a light, because if there is a light they cannot avoid being seen—and that they do not want.—*JP* III 3069 (*Pap.* XI³ B 109) *n.d.*, 1855

Addition to Pap. XI³ B 109:

The Moral

More sagacious than all of us sagacious ones (something even the sagacious frequently are unsagacious enough to forget entirely) is the power that is everywhere with us (something that frequently is also forgotten entirely): Governance.

This Governance has its own thoughts, and seldom are its thoughts the thoughts of human beings.

See the enclosed [*Pap.* XI³ B 111].

[*Deleted:* For many different reasons, and led to it in many

XI³
B 109
182

different ways, I had conceived the idea of wanting to defend the established ecclesiastical order.

Governance no doubt had the idea that I was just the one who should be used to tear down the established order. But in order to prevent such an enterprise from becoming a young man's impatient, perhaps arrogant, audacity, I first had to understand the very opposite as my task and then in much painfulness, inwardly understood, be developed for the task when the moment arrived.

What I will now say it is my duty to say, because it is true; if someone wants to create a terrible hubbub, it cannot, after what I have experienced in Denmark, have much meaning for me. I]
—*Pap.* XI³ B 110 *n.d.*, 1855

Addition to Pap. XI³ B 110:

My agreement with the late bishop was in one sense perfect, in another sense such that the disagreement could be equally as great. The agreement was in wanting to defend the established order and to fight against the opposition. The disagreement involved how the established order should be defended. He wanted to defend it worldly-sagaciously, diplomatically, by veiling, concealing, by optical illusion, in which he was a master, by the sagacious use of small measures *à la* Louis Philippe,[133] by yielding and accommodating and bargaining if necessary. I wanted, religiously, to defend it by the greatest possible honesty in concealing nothing but acknowledging the true situation.

United in wanting to defend the established order and fighting against the opposition, he then pursued his way, I mine. The result of this was that the relation finally must have appeared to him such that regarding me he must have thought, "Would that I only were rid of the man. My sagacity is more than sufficient for me to be able to cope splendidly with such a characterless and such a clumsily served opposition as the one we have in the religious sphere. But to me this man with his defense is extremely calamitous—and I cannot ever say that. Everyone believes that he is defending the established order. Everyone believes that he is to the highest degree personally devoted to me—and he also

XI³
B 111
182

XI³
B 111
183

no doubt is—he himself says that he is defending the established order: and then he exposes the situation to such a degree that his defense is the most dangerous attack, doubly dangerous because, as if things were bewitched, it is for me, who am the only one who has enough sagacity and perspicuity to see the danger, impossible to make it comprehensible to people, so if I hinted at any such thing the end of it would probably be that people would have a suspicion (something that to me is the most repugnant of all) that I have grown old, decrepit, a feeble old man who sees danger where there is no danger."

With regard to myself, the result of this circumstance was that I became ever more deeply aware of the established order's basic wretchedness and, by enduring what was exasperating in the situation, became more and more developed.

But I was not and am not what is called opposition, I who continually have taken sides against the opposition. I was the defense, the—**honest**—defense for the established order. And then it appears (how frightfully ironic!) that this is by far the most dangerous for the established order. I want to defend the established order, yet in such a way that we are completely honest concerning how in truth things stand with us, and the result of that is, since the established order refuses to speak, that I am compelled—for the sake of the defense—to expose more and more the true situation, whereby it then becomes more and more clear that the established ecclesiastical order is an established order for which the greatest danger is to be defended **honestly**. Aha! Thus the established order has the peculiarity that it can be defended only with skulduggery. But an established order such as that is, of course, thereby *eo ipso* shown to be skulduggery. Just do not forget that I have wanted to defend the established order; it is the established order itself that transforms me into the attack [*changed from:* If I become the attack on the established order, then it is the established order itself that transforms me into that] by not being able and not being willing to be served by an—honest defense.

From the point of view of the idea, I was the only one who could defend the established order. Mynster has never had anything to do with the idea; in his innermost heart he was even

XI³
B 111
184

against it. And worldly-sagacious, ambitious, self-indulgent as he was, he therefore loved only and promoted only a drilled mediocrity. But from the point of view of the idea, through the introduction of the honest defense, it is manifest [*changed from:* If I then become the attack upon the established order, it must be because the idea in this way brings it along with itself, because, from the point of view of the idea, it must, through the introduction of the honest defense, be manifest] that the established order is defended only by untruth and optical illusion, namely, is not defended. So the defense does indeed become the attack, yet by being the defense; and then a statement about me that the Judge in *Either/Or* says to the Young Man is fulfilled: You never attack something before you are the one who could best defend it.[134]

Thus the honest defense became the most perilous attack upon the established order. Frightful, frightful demonstration of the extent to which the established order is untruth and mirage and lie! From this, the most profoundly designed attack, by being the defense, the established order will never recover again; for a time it may perhaps, perhaps not, sustain an apparent life, but death has marked it.—*Pap.* XI³ B 111 *n.d.*, 1855

In margin of draft of article in Fædrelandet, *January 12, 1855; see* 18:30:

Postscript

XI³
B 216:8
357

In the same article in *B. T.*,[135] there is a phrase that, properly understood, is so amazing that I will pay attention to it—I almost believe signs and wonders are happening and the *B.T.* is prophesying against its will.

It says that with my two articles in *Fædrelandet* I have annihilated myself as an upbuilding author.

As *B.T.* sees it, it is insolent and nonsense—but, now comes the amazing thing, in an utterly different sense I myself could be tempted to say the same thing. I myself have understood those two articles in the very same way; I have annihilated myself as an upbuilding author, since by the living God I am not destined to build up but to tear down. I only thank Governance again that

XI³
B 216:8
358

the mitigation fell to my share, that I carried out my first, my so precious thought, that it could be postponed as long as the old bishop lived and he was buried with full honors. And when I said to old Grundtvig: Bishop Mynster must live out his life, be buried with full honors, I then added: But the hour people go home from the funeral, I begin to prepare everything for the attack.)

—*Pap.* XI³ B 216:8 January 1855

See 14:4:

XI²
A 411
398

Babbling

or

Kjøbenhavnsposten

May 28

There are various kinds of talk; there is idle talk, flippant talk, stupid talk, wheedling talk, etc. There is also the kind of talk we describe as talking on and on, and perhaps this is the kind that is also called babbling.

When a newspaper, in both prose and poetry, has declared a man lunatic, then this man might venture to expect that, in all fairness, the paper will quit talking about him; and it betrays contempt for its readers when, after declaring a man lunatic, it goes on chatting with them about him as if he were not lunatic. This kind of conduct is talking on and on, is babbling.

This is the relation of *Kjøbenhavnsposten* to me. On the occasion of my first article against Martensen,[136] the paper declared me—in both prose and poetry—lunatic.[137] "Fine," thought I, "so I am in the future free from *Kjøbenhavnsposten*, one fewer pestering triviality."

XI²
A 411
399

But later *Kjøbenhavnsposten* got other notions. Without retracting that statement, it now wants to talk about me as if I were not lunatic. Perhaps that first declaration was a test to see if it could be done, something like a bid a person makes at an auction to see if he might have the good luck of buying what he is bidding on at such a ridiculously low price.

Incidentally, what it is saying about me now[138] is, if not babbling, nevertheless talk that clearly shows (a) that *Kjøbenhavns-*

posten is utterly unqualified to discuss religious matters, (b) that it never reads what it nevertheless discusses of my writing, something that is not important for me to demonstrate. [*Deleted:* It is merely something that ought to be said.] [*In margin:* (c) that its biased articles against me are intended to be vexatious, for which it perhaps is hired by the clergy.]

My suggestion to *Kjøbenhavnsposten* is that it get itself a more reliable contributor, if not, that it include in its paper a special column for religious matters and caption it "Babbling" and that the editorial staff members write in it themselves. Or if it so happens that as far as politics is concerned the paper also babbles (of this I have no idea since I do not understand politics), the whole paper should take the title "Babbling." The old name of *Kjøbenhavnsposten* need not be dropped; unfortunately, there is enough babbling in Copenhagen, so the paper could well be called *Babbling or Kjøbenhavnsposten*.

*   *

It is on religious grounds that I get mixed up in this right now—because it has so pleased the Omnipotent One, who best knows how reluctant I am to do so. They may rage at me as aggressively as they please, but by speaking occasionally I will make sure that I do not avoid whatever hubbub it is my duty to expose myself to [*in margin:* but I shall not shirk by keeping silent], and that anyone who pays attention to me will know my opinion on what happens in connection with this affair and me.

—*JP* VI 6964 (*Pap.* XI² A 411) May 28, 1855

See 39:2–40:13:

Exordium

XI³
B 105
169

O Luther! . . . . . And yet in one sense a happy situation, because at that time there were 95 theses; now, however, there is only one thesis: Christianity does not exist at all.

Christianity does not exist at all; but we—since I am speaking only about us Danes, as far as I can know—by having the **objective** doctrine are more or less tranquilized in an enormous illusion, that we are Christians.

Yet I, who indeed from the beginning have said again and again and continually that I am without authority,[139] I accuse no one, judge no one, not one single person, neither of the laity nor of the clergy, although I think that everyone who claims to be a Christian and everyone who has taken it upon himself to be a teacher in Christianity has a responsibility before God.

But I judge no one. If I should judge anyone, it must be myself: that I perhaps allowed too long a time to pass before I took this step, or that I, now that it is finally happening, perhaps am still not doing it emphatically enough. What is surely the object of many a person's aspiration, the glory of daring to say of oneself: To me much was entrusted—I do before God dare to say that about myself with a good conscience. It no doubt would also be pleasant for me if the other side of the matter did not fall on my troubled conscience more heavily than a leaden weight ". . . . . and of him shall much be required!"[140] It could seem joyous to dare to say of oneself: I have had faith to lift a mountain—and before God I do dare to say this with a good conscience. But it is not so joyful, because the other side of the matter, this other side from which I must see it: this tension unto the anxiety of death; if faith is now insufficient and the mountain that I am lifting topples over me, then I would scarcely have the faith that dares to say to a mountain, "Rise"— —and it rose—— and toppled over me—then it would be infinitely, infinitely better not to have had such a faith.

––––––––––

In order to arrive at the point that has now been reached, up to the present everything has been used by me: time, abilities, means. Moreover, in order to make sure of being duly known, I voluntarily exposed myself to being ridiculed. I have served as a caricature in Copenhagen, had a role in comedy, been known under a nickname, even mentioned in books in that manner,[141] etc. The gain from this is that we can now come to the issue. If I imagined that someone else, an unknown, would begin directly with the thesis: Christianity does not exist at all—he would then have to be prepared to be delayed at least one to three years until all had laughed enough at him, and all had heard again and again everything that can be said by waggery and scurrility etc. This I, as a prudent man, have in time arranged fairly well so that even at this moment there perhaps are not really many who laugh when they hear the thesis: Christianity does not exist at all.

XI³
B 105
171

Bishop M.

"Why must it be pushed to extremes in this way?"

Because it is a religious cause. All politics is a matter of "to a certain degree." The religious cause is: Either/Or. But it is precisely this that in the religious domain has engendered the enormous illusion, namely, that one *piously* (I assume that it is so) has served the cause of Christianity politically, worldly-sagaciously, so that one has still attained "something Christian" and "Something is surely better than nothing"—yes, politically, but Christianly this is an enormous error.

If my contemporaries will have confidence in me and remain calm while I complete my task, then not the slightest inconvenience will be caused, since only a movement of inwardness is to be made—and in that case there may lie before me a joyful life such as I truly have never imagined it. And I dare with a good conscience to receive it, because I have *first* squared my relationship with God; I have set forth my thesis, loudly and clearly, this thesis: Christianity does not exist at all. If, however, my contemporaries want to oppose me, I will by no means conceal this: they are indeed far, far stronger than I, I an individual person, who moreover have not utilized my time to safeguard myself by forming parties, but on the contrary have done everything to diminish myself, have repelled those who would espouse me and thereby have embittered them, have voluntarily exposed myself to becoming ridiculed etc. It is then easy to see that in that case my hitherto not exactly carefree life will become so troublesome that very likely no one will envy me for it. In God's name I have indeed honored my God-relationship; I have set forth my thesis: Christianity does not exist at all.—*Pap.* XI³ B 105 *n.d.*, 1855

Bishop Martensen's Silence
or
a Contribution to a Characterization of the Truth-Witnesses

When in a previous article,[142] I said that Bishop M. has a gift, fateful for the established order especially at this moment, for exposing, by the least little thing he undertakes, one or another of the established order's weak sides, it might seem strange that I, now when Bishop M. seems to want to embark upon what for him is the most sagacious, to maintain silence, it could seem strange that I again object to this silence of his.

But it is not so strange; this silence of his, looked at more closely, is again a confirmation of the truth of what I said, that by the least thing he undertakes—and to remain silent is doing something—he exposes one or another of the established order's weak sides.

Among the many various arts of optical illusion that the late Bishop practiced with masterful dexterity was also this: to use silence, to ignore, where it perhaps was dangerous to speak; and then this silence of cowardly sagacity was prinked up, Christianly, to be gentleness, peace, conciliation, wisdom. But one thing must be said about Bishop Mynster: he always conducted himself sagaciously.

Not so with Bishop Martensen, who therefore also by his clumsy silence manages to expose the several years of, Christianly, altogether indefensibly used silence on the part of the established order.

In other words, if one wants to be silent and then in such a way that this silence should be able to signify superiority, wisdom, etc., then one must be silent from the beginning. But that Bishop Martensen was not; no, he wrote an article[143] against me in which in the most unfortunate way he managed to betray what significance his silence has had and will have in the future.

What significance his silence has had. Well, my differences with Bishop M. are, after all, an old story. But Bishop Martensen has always kept silent, and that could be done splendidly as long as the old master in this forgery lived and maintained the conception of that kind of silence, also as long as I, out of piety's regard for the old bishop, let everything remain in force, honored all his forged bank drafts. But, as stated, Bishop Martensen kept silent. He kept silent in connection with the pseudonym Johannes Climacus; he kept silent in connection with Prof. N.'s use of the pseudonym against him.[144] Yes, he has more than once silently read in print that the pseudonym has annihilated him—but M. has kept silent.

XI³
B 107
174

Then I write an article[145] against Bishop Martensen, an article in which I could not avoid aiming at the late Bishop Mynster. At the same time a hubbub was raised here in the city by women and children and pastors [*deleted:* and God knows who], in short, a hubbub by those best qualified to make a hubbub about breaking the peace of the grave, flogging a dead person, etc. etc. What happens? Eureka, says Bishop M., here is something for me; at the head of this hubbub I can fall upon S. K. That he did, and in the *Berlingske T.*[146] the Hon. Rt. Rev.—the silent—Bishop poured out a mass of abuse.

I for my part have paid no attention to his abuse but made the matter more earnest*—and now again Bishop Martensen wants to maintain silence! Oh dear, what prostitution for the established order, for Christianity here in the land, for the profession, whose visible—indeed, he is its visible head, but more truly one may certainly now call him its invisible head, he, who like the ostrich (of which the newspapers nowadays remind us)—well, just as this bird thinks that by sticking its head in the sand it makes itself invisible, he thinks by keeping silent he makes it impossible to get hold of him.

How this silence characterizes Bishop M. and thereby in turn

XI³
B 107
175

In margin: *Note. The matter has also in this way become more earnest. On the occasion of my first article,[147] all made a noise, almost the whole populace— at that moment what in all events was needed was that Bishop Martensen would speak against me. In the course of a few weeks the opinion changes very remarkably; one becomes aware that something else is amiss than one thought at the very first, likewise aware that Bishop M. has blundered considerably. Furthermore, Bishop M. is prompted in print to express himself—and now, now when there was good reason to break the silence, if he originally had kept silent, now he wants to observe silence after having spoken when he was less called upon.

what he presumably understands by a truth-witness! You who read this, look a little more closely and do not allow yourself to be disturbed by what I say, something that must indeed be said if the elucidation is to be true. Just look at Bishop Martensen's silence! In relation to whom does he want to maintain it? It is in relation to me. Ask yourself if it is immodest of me that I consider myself, literarily, to be at least as fully a legitimate figure as Bishop Martensen. Thus the silence is in relation to—at least an equal—and this silence is supposed to be superiority! Next, this silence is maintained after having, almost as at the head of the street hubbub, in the simplest way made a noise in the tumult! And this silence is in relation to an altogether justified Christian protest that, sharpened, has placed the matter, Christianly, at the peak of decision.

What wretchedness! But never mind. Yet this silence is, Christianly, inadmissible. A Christian bishop—and who wants to be a truth-witness—certainly has to witness, that is, not to declaim on Sunday but to witness on Monday. I diligently call this distinction to mind again, because in the address Bishop Martensen delivered at the most recent consecration of a bishop[148] he asks whether it is proper for shepherds, for the chief shepherd, not to stand firm but to shake like a reed. Charming, it is Sunday's dramatic entertainment—since we now do indeed see how this firm man stands firm on Monday. Yet Bishop Martensen no doubt intends to come to terms with the obligation, according to the apostle's instruction,[149] resting on every Christian, not to mention every bishop, not to mention every truth-witness, not to keep silent before a justified objection; he no doubt thinks he has come to terms with the obligation by, in costume, not merely in velvet but in cloth of gold, having orated on Second Christmas Day in Frue Church.

Therefore this silence must not—silently—be tolerated, but be stamped for what it is: obtuse, cowardly, unchristian. Neither does it help him in the least; on the contrary, this silence shouts to heaven, shouts accusingly against him more loudly than the most raucous obtusity or shamelessness could shout. And it will continue to shout in the same way; indeed, as is proverbially said of the Punic honesty about the Greek calendar etc., in the same way we in the future will speak of "Martensenian silence" if one wishes to designate a silence that is obtuse, cowardly, unchristian, and which—deservedly—has the curious feature that it punishes itself.

*   *

You who read this, allow me to say a few words to you. You have scarcely any idea of the degree to which the whole established ecclesiastical order is, Christianly, an untruth, and, what makes it worse, the degree to which the persons involved are themselves aware of it. Therefore judge slowly if you see me press so hard that I now again object to Bishop Martensen's silence. Let me tell you this [*deleted:* in advance] so that you can be attentive. The conditions are such that the person who in truth is to serve Christianity could come into the situation of even having to request that a court case be brought against him, of even having to request to be arrested, of even having to request to be executed—to that degree is the established order itself aware of how untrue it is, to that degree is concerned only that it can be put off as long as possible. One would perhaps defend oneself as follows: with regard to the most justified Christian objection, one will keep silent, and if the adversary is compelled even to request to be prosecuted, arrested, executed, then one will see to escaping from it by labeling it as a kind of lunacy, which it must indeed seem to be to all the bourgeois and job-holders and all the mediocrity on which pastors live.

Christianity entered into the world as the most excellent of all, as what it is, the divine. If you would see the most wretched of all, then observe the established ecclesiastical order in Denmark under the name of Christianity with Bishop M.—as a truth-witness!—at the head.—*Pap.* XI³ B 107 *n.d.*, 1855

See 50:2–24:

[*Deleted:* On the Occasion of an Anonymous Challenge to Me in This Newspaper, No. [79]

XI³
B 117
191

changed to: Should I Be Attacked Anonymously?
changed to: About Anonymous Attacks on Me]

[*Deleted:* Sophist: "You continually say
the same thing, Socrates."
Socrates: "Yes, and about the same thing."[150]]

April [4 *changed to* 8 *changed to* 7,] 1855

S. K.

XI³
B 117
192

When someone has come forth personally to the degree that I
have, has personally exposed himself to that degree, has made it
obvious to that degree that a personality is embattled here; when
someone has a whole age, indifferent or even indignant, against
him to the degree that I have; when someone is surrounded by
disapproval, misunderstanding, intentional misrepresentation,
slander, etc. to the degree that I am—then to want to attack
someone anonymously is, in my opinion—well, what it is with
regard to character I shall leave undecided—but it is (and this is
my main concern) it is: to judge oneself, that one does not oneself
really believe in the correctness and truth of what one has to say.
[*Deleted:* Whoever is not so passionately opposed to me that his
passion prevents him from judging soundly, whoever—man or
woman—has the heart in the right place will surely also agree
with me in this. In any case I ask everyone who is interested in
me and the cause I (the defamer, who tarnishes the memory of
honorable men and violates the peace of the grave) have—eyes
upward!—have the honor to serve, I ask him to practice this:
when it is an anonymous article, then quite calmly lay it aside
with the words: Under such circumstances, to want to be anonymous is to judge oneself.

My intention is, therefore, as a rule to follow: to give no consideration whatever to anything anonymous, something I in fact
originally had in mind, even if for another reason. That is, one
thing I thought I should in any case be reasonably protected
against] [*In margin:* If one is sagacious, one would avoid attacking me anonymously; if everyone is that, no one would do
it; whereas now the situation is perhaps almost that I, precisely

I, attacked solely and only anonymously, become—a splendid epigram.

Far be it from me to complain about it; to me it is a matter of indifference. I do not even ask so much as to be protected against what fairness seems to demand], that any pastor, who after all is financially interested in the established order, would receive permission to write against me anonymously. Therefore I do not say that what motivates such a man is simply and solely the financial, the livelihood, no, but I say that the fact that he is interested financially belongs to the proper understanding of him, ought to be known alongside; I say that his possibly well-composed, warm, [*deleted:* eloquent,] enthusiastic, convincing defense of the established order is nevertheless understood somewhat differently if this is known alongside, that he is financially interested. Is this not the way it is? If I were to engage in a battle for gaslighting against whale-oil lamps, would not fairness demand that I be protected against someone's receiving permission to write anonymously against me if he was financially interested in whale-oil lamps? Therefore I do not say that it is only the financial that motivates him, but I say that his possibly well-composed, clear, enthusiastic, convincing defense of whale-oil lamps is nevertheless understood somewhat differently when it is also known that he is a whale-oil dealer. [*Deleted:* This was my idea. But when I perceived the impossibility of protecting myself against anonymous writing by pastors, I considered it best to follow as a principle, as a rule: not to give consideration to anything anonymous.

Since, however, I have not said this before, I would like to consider briefly the present anonymous article, which otherwise to a high degree could need even a very considerable name in order to have significance and to prevent the tone of superiority it maintains from producing the impression of someone anonymously putting on airs.

To want, by calling attention to Mynster's observations,[151] to suggest taking the matter back to a perhaps learned discussion of Mynster's observations, *à la* Pastor Paludan Müller,[152] strikes me as childishness or as wanting to set a trap for me, so that I possibly could be lured out into prolixity, forgetting the moment and its

XI³
B 117
193

truly burning question. Yet I myself am sufficiently secure and shall therefore repeatedly warn against (what a no doubt well-intentioned theological graduate in *Nordisk Kirketidende* possibly could have caused) warn against that one, ...]

[*Deleted with pencil:* NB (*in red crayon*)]
The note becomes:
A Postscript
—*Pap.* XI³ B 117 April 7, 1855

From draft of article in Fædrelandet, *83, April 11, 1855; see 53:8–21:*

Just one comment in conclusion. [*Deleted:* May I thank the anonymous author because my reading of his article[153] has definitely convinced me of the necessity of doing what I previously have neglected, of arranging a separate reprinting of my articles in *Fædrelandet.*[154] It has really become necessary to have my articles available in order by reading the separate individual phrases again in their context to get the impression of them, which they certainly do not fail to make even there (*deleted:* but which they naturally must completely fail to make when they are piled up and arbitrarily thrown together). That by heaping up what has arbitrarily been torn out one can produce the impression of something convulsive, hysterical, I readily admit; but I certainly am not the one who is doing it. On the contrary, it is my opinion that to want to characterize the degree of unrest that is the unrest of the New Testament, only approximately, of course, but yet truthfully, it is my opinion that to want to characterize it as convulsive is to idolize mediocrity, as if the tame bird (*changed from:* the tame geese) would call its (*changed from:* their) waddling and meaningless beating of wings the true elevation and the wild bird's flight toward the heavens the convulsive.]

The note from the article: "Should I
Be Attacked Anonymously"[155]
is introduced here as:
A Postscript
—*Pap.* XI³ B 229:10 April 7, 1855

See 56–57; 367–71:

Dean Block Is in Error
Concerning Me

XI³
B 138
220

Dean B. thinks, as he says (in the supplement to the *Berlingske Tidende* for June 2) that he must "take the credit" that I, although I have said that I would pay no attention to "blather and rage,"[156] have even "promptly" paid attention[157] to his article in *Fædrelandet* no.   .[158] It seems to have really excited him, because he is inexhaustible; he goes on and on like a house afire with "results and the result" and "the result of the results" and result and re-sult—such a stream that I am convinced that if I would ask an undertaker, who certainly knows the value of ecclesiastical elo-quence, how high do you evaluate this speech, he would answer: It is definitely at the very least priced at twenty-five rix-dollars.

XI³
B 138
221

Yet we shall disregard this. However, I must—out of interest for my cause—briefly explain that Dean B., when he concludes from my having paid attention to his article that I have involved myself further with him, is in error, which the reader of my arti-cle, even merely from its title, must be able to understand is not the case and which he will better be able to understand if he has read what has come from my hand later.

The situation is this. There was something I should have said—then Dean B.'s article came very opportunely, gave me the occasion of being able to get it said and in exactly the way I wished. The situation with Dean B.'s article is similar to that of Bishop Martensen's discourse on "truth-witnesses, one of the au-thentic truth-witnesses, one of the holy chain."[159] And since, just as something can be so significant that for that reason attention must promptly be paid to it—something can be so insignificant that if it is to be used it must be used promptly—attention was "promptly" paid to Dean B.'s article.

There was something I should have said. What this is the reader now knows, since it is in a printed pamphlet titled *This Must Be Said; So Let It Be Said*: "by ceasing to participate (if you do participate in it) in the public divine service as it now is, you always have one and a great guilt less."[160] This decisive statement

XI³
B 138
222

is dated December 1854. But as certain as it is that the decisive factor must be introduced "suddenly and concentrated in one sortie" (see *The Moment*, no. 1, article 2^{161}), so must one also very carefully see to it that it is not introduced so suddenly that it does not enter the consciousness of people at all.

Consequently there had to be preliminary work. This took place in what became the beginning: the attack on Bishop Martensen, and thereupon the whole series of articles in *Fædrelandet*.

But before the decisive statement was published, I wanted very much to touch more lightly on the point, to turn the thinking of some individuals in the direction of whether the situation of the whole ecclesiastical established order was not such that it became, Christianly, a duty to refrain from participating.

Then a dean in Jutland gets the happy idea to say in print that the church door ought to be shut to me.[162] Splendid dean! It is done just as perfectly, manifests utterly the same view of the situation of the present age, as when Bishop Martensen from the pulpit hailed Bishop Mynster as a truth-witness, one of the authentic truth-witnesses, one of the holy chain! This was advantageous to me; now I could touch more lightly on this point in an article and without arousing offense damaging to the cause, because, after all, it was the dean who wanted to have the church door shut to me.

This is how the matter hangs together. His article in *Fædrelandet* has otherwise not interested me at all; to carry on a discussion with him never occurred to me. I gratefully name him, however, among those who have served my cause. And since I do not dare to be so forward as to desire that Dean B. come yet again just as opportunely for me, I cannot have anything against it [*changed from:* I regard it as the most desirable] that Dean B. does as he says he will: in the future keep silent.—*Pap.* XI³ B 138 *n.d.*, 1855

See 67:5–68:29:

XI³
B 142
224

Dr. Zeuthen

From an earlier reference[163] the reader will recall the following. Intermingled in a few articles (in *Evangelisk Ugeskrift*) that did not have to do with me, Dr. Z. had made some random remarks concerning me.[164] I had disregarded them, partly because they were insignificant, partly because Dr. Z. really is too insignificant for one to make much fuss about his—random remarks. Then it was that an anonymous person in *Kjøbenhavnsposten*, as could be expected, availed himself of my having disregarded them to pass them off as being something.

Well, well, I thought, then let me say a few words on this occasion, which I then did in *Fædrelandet*, no.   .[165] I did it reluctantly. In other words, Dr. Z. impresses me as a kind of thinker who is continually out of work, expecting that someone will address a word to him, or that in another external way there will come an opportunity for him to get something to do. Therefore, I had to fear getting Dr. Z. something to do, so much more so because concerning me there has been a great deal of talk about arrogance, pride, and the like. Just as someone who lives off and for cutting corns spontaneously thinks, as soon as he hears mention of a man who has a bad corn, "Here is something for me to do; here my help could be needed"—in the same way Dr. Z. (who, as is well-known and noted earlier, in the capacity of an independent author has concentrated primarily on the subject of modesty and humility[166]), as soon as he hears mention of pride, arrogance, promptly thinks: Here is something for me to do; here my help will be necessary.

The only thing that made me consider a possibility that Dr. Z. still could not, at least not immediately, manage to get underway was that lately he has been occupied with Grundtvig, whom he naturally has had under treatment for arrogance, but no doubt in such a way that Dr. Z., in order to substantiate his activity with a Bible verse, can choose for that purpose what is said (Mark 5:26) about the woman who had a flow of blood—"she had suffered much under many physicians, but her state became worse"—which I ask my contemporaries to take note of in case it should become apparent that under Dr. Z.'s treatment my state became worse, and that they do not therefore become angry with me or lay the blame on me, but consider that it lies with the physician, Dr. Z., who cures people in such a way that they become worse.

It is manifest, namely, that Dr. Z. is not taken up with treating

XI³
B 142
225

Grundtvig to such a degree that he does not think he is also able
to start on me—and now he has gone into action.

It is no longer random remarks in *Evangelisk Ugeskrift*; it is
what is even more than an ordinary article there in the weekly;
it is a separate work he has begun: a polemic periodical against
Dr. Søren Kierkegaard, no. 1.[167] So seriously is he engaging in
this matter—I may to a high degree be obsessed by arrogance,
but certainly not to the degree that my state could not become
worse, because under Dr. Z.'s treatment it will surely become
worse.

Dr. Z.'s motto is: "We can do nothing against the truth, but
for the truth"[168]—quite as could be expected; indeed, could mediocrity ever write a polemical religious article without this
motto, which very likely is supposed to conceal the truth that
mediocrity can do nothing either for or against the truth.

XI³
B 142
226

And thereupon Dr. Z. takes the field, adapting himself in a
double way. Just as a citizen who on a Sunday afternoon in summer goes to Frederiksberg and, in view of its being, of course, a
pleasure trip, takes a thin cane, a "cool" cane, in hand, but for
safety's sake also takes along an umbrella—Dr. Z. does the same.
If I dare say so, with a thin swagger stick in his hand, Dr. Z. plays
the superior and now sets to on pride, arrogance, dishonesty,
unreliability, foolishness—in short, I become a mere wisp before
this power lord Dr. Z., who expresses his power simply by not
ever needing more than a very thin swagger stick—for Dr. Z. the
polemic against me is a piece of cake, a pleasure trip. But somewhat further on one sees to one's amazement that Dr. Z. has also,
for safety's sake, taken along an umbrella. That is, there one
learns that this wisp of straw Dr. Kierkegaard "still does not lack
the capacity or will to thrust his witty words' sharpest poisoned
dagger of contempt and scorn into his opponent's breast, that
in this regard he is still the master of all in the land."[169] Indeed,
Dr. Z. becomes quite solemn at the thought of what he, as he
believes, "is exposing himself to"; he becomes so solemn it is
almost as if he were approaching death, and he is completely
prepared to have me keep the laughter on my side.[170] What a
desirable opportunity is offered me here to show that I am nevertheless also modest where it is truthful to be that, since I think I

already have the laughter on my side—but I must modestly say that it is not my merit but Dr. Z.'s. Let us assume (for it does not rest with me) that Dr. Z. has greater capacities than I. On my part there is a consistent effort, continued over fourteen years, in the service of one single thought. The daily diligence of this effort Dr. Z. not only does not have, but he can scarcely form a conception of it. This diligence and effort are applied to undermine *the illusion,* and in my earlier writings I have used flammable material at every decisive point. And through my way of life (on which is applied equally as much reflection and purpose as on my work as an author) I have—known by all—rapport everywhere. So I only waited for the moment. It came. I struck a light, lit the fire—now it is burning. And this "conflagration" Dr. Z. wants to extinguish "with a squirt gun."

XI[3]
B 142
227

To draw a conclusion from no. I, it must certainly be said that this whole enterprise, seen in the ideal, is wasted trouble. So a sarcastic person could be tempted to advise Dr. Z. to call no. I no. 0, which does not count, and then let it end with no. I or, if more are to come, not number them at all, inasmuch as 0 does not count. The few, students etc., who have the qualifications on a greater scale to be familiar with the matter, for them Dr. Z. has nothing instructive to communicate, nothing that they certainly will not be able to read and no doubt already know from quite different men. And Dr. Z.'s theologizing cannot engage people; people have an entirely different interest in short statements such as this, that the public worship, as it now is, makes a fool of God. That can engage people; on some it makes the impression that I am right, on others that I am wrong; but it can engage, something that theological scholarship, however, does not do. People, particularly the common man among the people, can understand very well that to reason this way: to have oneself already held a royal appointment for a long time and with family, that is, in the middle of the illusion—and then in relation to a man who for a period of years has made every sacrifice to stay out of the illusion and now declares, "Christianity is Either/Or"— —in relation to him to say: I have already **said** the same thing many years ago—people can understand very well that this, especially if one does not see it oneself—is to reason like the leg of a boot. And although I am not very impressed with Dr. Z., I actually believe, however, that he could not have come with such things if, through Mynster's proclamation of Christianity, he were not (like all of us so-called cultured people) more or less demoralized, Christianly, which people perhaps are not and so will not become either. I hope that heaven will certainly see to it that it does not come to pass, as the truth-witness, Bishop Martensen, was so good to give us to understand in his memorial address, that Mynster will shine like a star up in the heavens.

From the point of view of the idea, Dr. Z.'s undertaking is no doubt wasted trouble. It is something else if the corporation, the 1000 stockholders, of course not in that capacity but in the capacity of spiritual counselors, which they indeed also are, should get the notion (which is not improbable) of recommending Dr. Z.'s polemical paper as something absolutely decisive, something utterly annihilating for me, and then perhaps get some anonymous persons to "witness" in a few papers, perhaps to repeat every day that Dr. Z. has utterly annihilated me—without once being troubled by the self-contradiction that every day it must be said of a person that he is annihilated (the best evidence that it is indeed not true), and without once being aware of the difficulty, which is connected with getting me annihilated by Dr. Z., that according to the anonymous article in the *Berlingske Tidende*[171] Pastor Paludan-Müller and Bishop Martensen with his article have already "annihilated me." What a wonderful role I have come to play, what a heavy fate in which I am tested: I am annihilated; and when I then will put my soul to rest, patiently put up with what has happened to me, my deserved punishment for light-mindedly involving myself with superiority—then I am suddenly roused up by something new that has annihilated me.

There is only one thing I find worth noting in Dr. Z.'s papers, that he has come to the conclusion that more must be written against me than hitherto. In that Dr. Z. may be right—against Bishop Martensen, whose "Christianly indefensible, ridiculous, obtusely sagacious, in more than one sense contemptible silence" will perhaps become a costly story for the clergy. In that Dr. Z. makes sure of continuing to be right in a peculiar way, because what he writes merely causes—so much more to be written

XI[3]
B 142
228

against me. Incidentally, learned discussion is certainly not what
I am inviting anyone to, is much more what I must take care to
prevent. It is a Christian criminal case, and it is in this sense that
I aim at the clergy's and especially Bishop Martensen's silence.

—*Pap.* XI³ B 142 *n.d.*, 1855

XI³
B 142
229

See 3–85:

Why I Have Used This Newspaper[172]

XI³
B 120
194

April 8, 1855

Luther declares in one of his sermons that preaching actually
should not be done inside churches.[173] He says this in a sermon
that presumably was delivered inside a church. So it was nothing
more than talk; he did not carry it out in earnest. But certainly
preaching should not be done inside churches. It is extremely
damaging for and represents a changing (an altering) of Christianity by placing it at an artistic distance from actuality instead of
letting it be heard right in the middle of actuality—and precisely
for the sake of conflict (collision), because all this talk about quiet
and quiet places and quiet hours as the proper element for the
essentially Christian is upside down.

XI³
B 120
195

Therefore preaching should not be done in churches but in
the street, right in the middle of life, the actuality of ordinary,
daily life. Our age might not be ready for this and perhaps must
first be prepared for it, but in any case I cannot do it for the
simple reason that I lack the physical strength. My assignment is
to speak with individuals, to converse, and then to use the pen.

Still I did want to achieve an approximation of preaching in
the streets or of placing Christianity, thinking about Christianity,
right into the middle of life's actuality and in conflict with its
variants, and to that end I decided to use this newspaper. It is a
political paper, has completely different interests, occupies itself
with very many other things—but the essentially Christian is not
its concern.

Having these little articles printed in this daily paper got them
a hearing in what is quite different from what they deal with; this
corresponds somewhat to listening to a sermon on Christianity in

the street. I could not accomplish this effect with a specialized organ.

Another advantage was that I could communicate my thoughts in very small doses. If I had a special organ, I would have to give considerably more at a time, with the result that it would be read in a different way, sometimes perhaps with greater concentration, but never with the stimulation experienced when, unprepared, one unexpectedly encounters the essentially Christian.

Furthermore, I managed in a simple way to maintain an independence, free from the possibility of becoming a party etc. (something most people surely regard as a great misfortune, the very last thing to be desired, but which I view differently). In a daily paper completely unassociated with me and my cause, I live, if you please, as a tenant. It does not take sides with me in any way; in fact it accepts articles, even anonymous articles, against me (which I told the editor I did not object to, although I would not like to see the opposite). Thus I also succeeded in using the daily press without contradicting my own views of the press. Part of my objection to the daily press is its being used in such a way as to become a sensate power itself, also to its being used anonymously.

*   *

I gladly apologize to the readers of this paper, who may have very little or no interest at all in what so greatly concerns me, for taking up with my articles space for what would be of quite different interest to them.—*JP* VI 6957 (*Pap.* XI³ 120) April 8, 1855

See 3–85:

About the Way I Have Used *Fædrelandet* and

How People Have Wanted to Use It against Me

June 9 [1855]

In Denmark, and no doubt in just about all Europe, everything is politics. Politics is all that occupies people, politics is all that people understand; and it is the case not only with the prom-

XI³
B 120
196

XI²
A 413
402

inent political leaders but it is the case with actually every or at least almost every person in our age that he very sagaciously understands how a cause is served *politically*. On the other hand, among all my contemporaries there is perhaps not one single person who is better informed about how a cause is served *religiously* than I am about how one plays *L'Hombre*, except that I do not pass myself off as a *L'Hombre* player; whereas all, of course, are Christians.

Now, it is easy to see that there must appear to be something very strange here when people who are informed only about how a cause is served *politically* want to judge someone who serves a cause religiously. Political service and religious service relate to each other altogether inversely, inasmuch as politically everything turns on getting numbers of people on one's side, but religiously on having God on one's side. Therefore one must make every effort precisely to avoid wanting to strengthen oneself through the numerical, through human help—because then one loses God's help. According to his nature, he does not want to be along where, instead of believingly holding to the improbable, one sagaciously wants only the probable.

This accounts for the strange situation that a person who uses a perhaps even rare sagacity—in order to avoid doing what would be politically sagacious—is judged by people whose ultimate is: political sagacity.

XI²
A 413
403

Thus it will also end with the contemporaries' discovering someday that they missed the mark, that what they smugly judged to be politics and found as such to be unsagacious, what in turn made them very secure, that precisely this was purposeful—so with their great political sagacity they had merely managed to fool themselves in regard to an effort that surely has not lacked sagacity but has only used it in a totally different way.

I began by using [*changed from:* choosing] this paper, a widely read political journal, which occupies itself mainly with politics, and even though it has interested itself also in much else on the side yet has never shown the slightest interest in the religious. At most, then, it could be a question of the paper's having at first a political interest in an attack on Bishop Martensen, which is something entirely different from being able to have or to having an interest in taking on a religious cause—therefore politically how unsagacious. Here I of course could not expect any support; here I must come to be isolated— —yes, but it was just this that I should be and wanted to be; religiously it is precisely a matter of forestalling human help, because otherwise God draws back.

Immediately at the very first, on the occasion of an article ("A Good Deed") by Prof. N.,[174] a discussion began between editor Giødvad[175] and myself [*changed from:* So some time went by; then there began a discussion between editor Giødvad and me on the occasion of the paper's having printed an article by Prof. N.] about what I thought of it, of the paper's having printed the article. My reply was that even if it were so that I had any influence on the paper I could not allow myself to make any use of it; I must leave it entirely up to it to act as it wanted to. I would say only this much, "It would not have made me happy, because I feared to see my cause strengthened because it seemed as if we were quite a few. Therefore I would not like to see the paper print articles for me; I could not, however, have the slightest objection to its printing articles against me; that would simply contribute to keeping me in my isolation, my separateness as an individual." Hear this, you politicians; indeed, everyone easily sees how ill advised this was and certainly therefore looks almost sympathetically, from the politicians' exalted position, down on poor Dr. S. K. Well, you are quite welcome to do so! What I did was exceedingly correct—but it was a religious service.

So time passed. I provided my articles, the paper on occasion a contra-article, and thereby it was expressed that the paper did not take sides, either pro or contra. Whether this, seen from another angle, was defensible on the part of *Fædrelandet*, or whether what motivated the editorial staff was only political sagacity, whether it perhaps had become uneasy because of the alarm here in the city, and yet again uneasy because of the more recent dodge of keeping silent, whether it perhaps thought that it was most sagacious to print a contra-article and thereby make sure, if the cause prevailed, of being the one who brought it up, or if the cause stranded, the one who, after all, printed contra-articles— whether the editorial staff understood it this way and perhaps had no worries at all about doing it because I had indeed said that I

XI²
A 413
404

had nothing against it, yes, that I was even in agreement—of that I know nothing.

From the very beginning, however, I have of course seen that in the long run I could not continue to use this paper as the only organ. However much courtesy and attentiveness have been shown to me from the editorial side, I readily understood that because of me the journal would find itself in the position of being changed into something quite different from what it is, which would be the consequence if I [continued] with a fullness corresponding to the importance of the cause, and especially if polemics also ensued. So I chose, something I had considered for many various reasons, to begin some pamphlets myself and in that way to have an organ solely for myself and as an individual.

This is the progress of the cause. Now suppose that someone who understands only how a cause is served politically had been aware of what happened, suppose that he disregarded that my involvement with *Fædrelandet* was politically unsagacious from the very first, because in a politically sagacious way I ought either to have become associated with a religious party or to have founded such a one myself—suppose that he disregarded this and suppose that he also harbored hostile feelings toward me—in that case he will think that the whole thing could be explained as follows. I wanted to have support in *Fædrelandet*, but *Fædrelandet* dodged by printing contra-articles—and finally I was obliged to pull out of *Fædr.*—in short, a breaking point was reached between *Fædr.* and me, and this will now be used against me.

Indeed, *Kjøbenhavnsposten* did this immediately—was so keen on joining me with *Fædr.* that it [*in margin:* raised an outcry the very instant I had published *This Must Be Said,*] simply could not wait [*deleted:* 24 hours], because then it would have seen that the same morning as its article was distributed an article by me was printed in *Fædrelandet.*[176] So much for *Kjøbhsposten.* Later in *Fyens Avis*[177] an anonymous person (and all who write against me prefer to be that), an anonymous person who quite sagaciously chose to be anonymous since he wanted to say that I am lunatic, informed people that I had been "expelled" from *Fædrelandet*— and as evidence pointed out that I had published a couple of separate papers and had begun *The Moment*—this he gave as evidence for it and naturally has not allowed himself to be

XI²
A 413
405

embarrassed by, as he himself must know, its being a lie, inasmuch as when the article for *Fyens Avis* was written a later article by me appeared in *Fædrelandet.*

I regard it religiously as my duty to give a little information now and then, because I am well aware that people are quite unfamiliar with how a cause is served religiously. I have never for a moment been concerned with whether *Fædrelandet* agrees with me or not. If it were the case that *Fædrelandet* agrees with me, it could no more occur to me to argue from that than it could occur to me to allow myself to be disturbed if it were the case that *Fædrelandet* does not agree with me—to be honest, it is my opinion that that paper has as few qualifications for being able to have an opinion as any other of our journals. It is another matter that I can feel personally obliged to the editorial staff for the attentiveness and courtesy they have shown to me.

XI²
A 413
406

What I am writing here will be misunderstood, that I know very well, and it is of no importance at all to me. On the other hand, I consider it my duty to make it possible that whoever wants to understand will be able to do so. I will be misunderstood; neither will the opportunity be missed to incite people against me, as if it were enormous pride and arrogance to want to stand alone this way. This is a matter of indifference to me; I must serve the religious cause religiously and above all shun politics and political considerations. One must strengthen oneself religiously by the relation to God; from him strength will come, and not by forming parties, by becoming a lot of people etc. Thus it is as if God said to me: My little friend, just remain calm where you are; it is your place, alone in your kayak;[178] where I am along, there, even if it were a nutshell, is nevertheless the flagship. But woe unto you if you become indolent, impatient, worldly sagacious, and think that it still would be best for you to get a larger ship and a little crew for help—because at that very same moment I will disembark.

See, here is the mistake! Meanwhile my contemporaries, politically sagacious, criticize my way of proceeding, foisting on me that I, too, am a politician, and now make out that I am going about it the wrong way, also that what I aim at is a failure. It is completely hidden from their eyes that I, religiously, am going about it absolutely right, and that everything is going just as it should go—something that these good politicians will no doubt begin to sense, these people who, simply because of their politics or because of their not understanding anything else than how a cause is to be served politically, are prevented from seeing the criterion by which I am working and with what progress and consequently are also prevented from taking what steps could possibly be taken, and now it is too late.—*Pap.* XI² A 413 June 9, 1855

See 3–85:

Articles in *Fædrelandet*[179]
from Dec. 18, 1854 to May 26, 1855
By
S. Kierkegaard

Reitzel's Publishing House
—*JP* VI 6960 (*Pap.* XI³ B 128) *n.d.*, 1855

Addition to Pap. XI³ B 128:

Contents

XI³
B 129
206

I.   Was Bishop Mynster a "Truth-Witness," One of "the Authentic Truth-Witnesses"—Is This the Truth?
II. There the Matter Rests!
III. A Challenge to Me from Pastor Paludan-Müller
IV. The Point at Issue with Bishop Martensen, as Christianly Decisive for the, Christianly Viewed, Dubious Previously Established Ecclesiastical Order (Feuilleton)
     Two New Truth-Witnesses
V.   At Bishop Mynster's Death
VI. Is This Christian Worship or Is It Making a Fool of God?
     (A Question of Conscience [in Order to Relieve My Conscience])

[*In margin:*
To Mr. Schou, typesetter:
N.B. This article is not on the first page but in
the feuilleton, columns 4 and 5.]
　　　　—*JP* VI 6961 (*Pap.* XI³ B 129) *n.d.,* 1855

XI³
B 129
207

Addition to Pap. XI³ B 129:

Perhaps you will be so kind as to undertake the publication of a separate edition of my articles in *Fædrelandet,* which are enclosed.

XI³
B 131
207

They are to be printed verbatim.[*] Each article is to have an initial page and number of its own; only in case of a serialized article is the text to be printed directly following the lead article, but with a division line and in smaller type and also with "feuilleton" printed with very small type in parentheses under its title.

XI³
B 131
208

In addition, under the number of each article, *Fædrelandet,* no. , 18 , is to be printed in parentheses and in very small type. For example:

No. I
(*Fædrelandet,* no. 295, Dec. 18, 1854)
Was Bishop Mynster a "Truth-Witness," One of
"the Authentic Truth-Witnesses"—Is This the Truth?
February 1854.

Another example:

No. XV
(*Fædrelandet,* no. , date, year)
A Result

A Monologue
(Feuilleton)

"Feuilleton" is to be set in brevier.
—*JP* VI 6962 (*Pap.* XI³ B 131) *n.d.,* 1855

In margin of Pap. XI³ B 131:

[*]But of course my name, which is under each title, is to be omitted.

[*Deleted:* It is preferred that type like that in *Fædrelandet* be used.]

—*JP* VI 6963 (*Pap.* XI³ B 132) *n.d.,* 1855

Addition to Pap. XI³ B 128:

XI³
B 134
209

Preface

Already long ago I was requested to publish these articles separately. Now I regard it as proper to do it. Formerly I wanted them circulated, thrown out among the people, read in a journal that on the whole deals with everything else, brought into the most casual contacts with the actuality of daily life—now one may read the articles by themselves, collected, oneself perhaps more collected.

As one will see, it ends and begins with Bishop Martensen. Certainly not because I have wanted "to prompt a discussion, thinking that then we would learn something very important and instructive," or because I on the whole ascribe to Bishop Martensen as a thinker some worth apart from being a user of the thoughts of others. No, but he is, of course, the country's leading bishop, the official authority; and it is in this his capacity that I have taken aim at him.

His Honorable Right Reverence has, however, maintained perfect silence, the negatively ranking so-called Martensenian silence (different from a Brutus's and Orange's ranking silence[180]), a kind of silence that a flurried fellow (who by ill luck comes to wear velvet and is supposed to govern) assumes when he unfortunately is all at sea and therefore day after day counts on playing hooky. [*Deleted:* , which certainly will cost the clergy a great deal.] He has no Lord Chancellor to whom he can turn for advice, no Lord Chancellor so that he can say to others, "Ask my Lord Chancellor," because unfortunately for Bishop Martensen the Lord Chancellor died with Bishop Mynster. Thus he knows nothing else than, like a sagacious ruler, to use obtusely what he had heard from the sagacious Bishop Mynster would be the most sagacious—that is, if it is sagaciously used. How comic [*changed from:* compared with Mynster's sagacious silence, how very obtuse-sagacious, low-comic, this Martensenian silence! What incalculable harm for the whole established order, whose only rescue was "The first loss is the best."]! And esthetically, how unfortunate [*changed from:* how personally annihilating] for Bishop Martensen that this silence occurs after he, if not like the

XI³
B 134
210

pawned peasant boy by blowing his nose in his fingers,[181] then nevertheless by the rowdy tone [*changed from:* talking about boxing ears (see his article in the *Berlingske Tidende*[182])] unfortunately has begun to betray which character it is that we, after the esthetically appraised most beautiful and most resplendent representative Denmark has ever seen in velvet, have obtained as a successor in velvet!

But to the more earnest, the ethical point of view! So Bishop Martensen has observed silence; indeed, he is probably even completely ignorant of my whole work! Excellent! It is for this that one is paid thousands by the state, is ranked with councilors of conference—to rule, and then one's ruling means nothing more nor less than that the bishop's farmhand could just as well rule the Church. Bishop Martensen, a man who is himself well aware of my knowledge of his whole career, of all this flattery devoid of the idea, all those petty measures that are used—he is now ignorant of S. Kierkegaard's work in the service of the idea. Bishop Martensen perhaps does not even know that I exist! And he is ignorant of a cause that has decisively taken possession of the moment, a cause that, despite the opposition of an entire contemporary public, and although I am doing absolutely nothing to spread it, yet has managed—indeed, there does exist a Governance!—to press through, one does not comprehend how, a cause that occupies the neighboring countries, is read in Norway, translated in Sweden, then in the end the only one who is ignorant of it is the Church's leading ruler, the man salaried with thousands by the state, the councilor of conference adorned in velvet.

A practical man, an Englishman (and the English are indeed practical people) is supposed to have said that he regarded having a conscience as such a luxurious mode of life that his circumstances by no means permitted him to maintain a conscience.[183] Well, perhaps my ideas about having a conscience are impractical; thus I, a poor impractical man, would be doing harm to apply my ideas about having a conscience—but the Bishop of Sjælland is probably so well remunerated that he could afford to have a conscience. If that is the case, then of course one is justified, according to the judgment of practical folk, to point out to him

XI³
B 134
211

that such a silence, such a Church administration, in that way to allow oneself to be paid for doing nothing under the rubric of ruling, is a lack of conscience—one is justified in doing that, because one is, according to the judgment of practical folk, and considering the size of the income, indeed justified in daring to assume that the Bishop of Sjælland can afford to have a conscience. Or if the income should still be too small, if it should be necessary for him to receive the frequently mentioned 300 bushels of barley in addition if he is to afford to keep a conscience—in that case I ask everyone to do his part to lay it as earnestly as possible on the conscience of the Minister of Culture, Ecclesiastical Affairs, and Education, so that His Reverence might receive the 300 bushels of barley as soon as possible, because there ought to be a man in Sjælland's bishopric who can afford to have a conscience.

Incidentally, it will make no principal difference whether Bishop Martensen now—conscientiously or perhaps cravenly—begins to speak; now it is too late. As a result of Bishop Martensen's wise and conscientious silence, the established order will, if I dare say so, come to buy at the highest possible price.

I have no responsibility. Anyone who has followed along and has only a smidgen of understanding of such things will see that I have proceeded according to a definite method, in that I, as was my duty, have taken into account the silence of the clergy in the face of an objection as justified as mine, and, inasmuch as this silence continued, have intensified the claim.

In three articles[184]—a prelude to what would come—I finished with Bishop Martensen, and in such a way that I, if I wanted to avail myself of such things, would have had it in my power to turn the matter so that everything later was a result of the Martensen blunder of representing, from the pulpit, Bishop Mynster as a truth-witness, one of the authentic, one of the holy chain.

I did not, however, do this; no, the three articles were the prelude—now I began.

The first article ("At Bishop Mynster's Death") had an epigraph that expressed so precisely just what it should that a more deliberately used epigraph will not easily be found. It was

XI³
B 134
212

Christ's words, "Do you see these great buildings? There will not"—.[185] It is the dash it depends upon. The epigraph expresses as precisely as possible: the beginning, *à point* [in the nick of time]. After the dash can follow: if one stone in the established order is moved. This indeed was my incessant proposal: Let us make an admission about ourselves and in that way see to getting some truth into the established order and our consciences lightened. This was my incessant proposal, and it was both for my own sake and for everyone else's sake my wish that it would be resolved to do this "as solemnly as possible." In that case the dash means: there will not be one stone moved in the established order.

If, however, they do not want this, if they want to harden their hearts against the, Christianly, perhaps most justified objection ever made, if the clergy (by oath pledged to the imitation of Christ) want to observe silence, perhaps by their silence (excellent imitation of Christ!) want to give the Church's holy blessing on the anonymous contemptibility in the daily press's seeking to have me made into a lunatic or a villain, if in such a contemptible manner (excellent imitation of Christ!) they want to manage to protect their livelihoods, something I otherwise have not attacked at all—well then! As long as this silence is maintained, it looks to me as if a little of the epigraph's dash is eaten away, until finally it is entirely consumed.

Then the epigraph reads differently, exactly as it stands in the New Testament: There will not be left one stone upon another that will not be pulled down.

No, there will not be left one stone upon another that will not be pulled down! These buildings [*changed from:* pest holes], which no one leaves without being infected, I mean the churches— there will not be left one stone upon another that will not be pulled down! All this trumpery, Satan's work or human work— there will not be left one stone upon another that will not be pulled down! And these disguised males, the truth-witnesses— there will be no hiding places for them, no lurking place, but, abandoned by what has sustained their existence, the lie, which must give way to the truth, they will—the oath, the oath takes revenge!—be brought to despair, either scorned as perjurers or

XI³
B 134
213

laughed at as deceivers, who unfortunately cannot deceive anyone. I shall certainly be on my guard against helping them out of their vestments; on the contrary, I shall do my best to keep them in their vestments, the higher salaried the better, and then in vestments—and then, Christianly, made transparent—no other punishment do I ask for them!—*Pap.* XI³ B 134 *n.d.*, 1855

From draft of Addendum to The Moment, *no. 1; see 101:*

Subscription Plan
—*Pap.* XI³ B 246:1 March 1855

Addition to Pap. XI³ B 246:1:

To that end I intend to begin some papers [*changed from:* a flysheet, *changed from:* a pamphlet] called
[*Deleted:* **At**] **The Moment**
to which subscriptions can be made at the bookstores.
—*Pap.* XI³ B 246:2 March 1855

From draft of The Moment, *1; see 89:*

The Moment
No. 1

Contents: 1. Exordium (it is the article that is addressed to the readers); 2. Addition to This Must Be Said, or How Is Something Decisive to be Introduced (one of the addenda from the original Cry); 3. Is It Defensible for the State, the Christian State, to Make, If Possible, Christianity Impossible; 4. Take an Emetic.
—*Pap.* XI³ B 242 *n.d.*, 1855

Addition to Pap. XI³ B 242:

[*Deleted: The Moment* will have a separate sheet for the title page, and the contents are to be printed there but each article on separate lines.]

Reitzel's Publishing House.
The subscription plan is an addendum
to No. 1 and will not be called a
subscription plan.
—*Pap.* XI³ B 248 *n.d.*, 1855

Deleted from margin of draft; see 122:3–5:

. . . . . the most frightful high treason against God is to make
him and his Word into something ludicrous, not by mockery,
no, but by imputing in the blather of mediocrity that he also is a
blatherer;—*JP* III 2577 (*Pap.* XI³ B 260:8) *n.d.*, 1855

[*Deleted:* I¹⁸⁶]
"Christian": "State"
or
The Union for Mutual Destruction

XI'
B 126
202

This is the way it must be if the union is to be of benefit:
Christianity, that heterogeneity to finitude, *resignation* (since we
will not here consider Christianity in its highest truth as the impatience of martyrdom), should provide the counterweight to
finitude, the state.[187]

XI³
B 126
203

The finite, the finite objectives, living for finite objectives,
easily cause too great and too fast a pendulum swing, either in
craving (for the fortunate), or in despair (for the unfortunate).
Therefore eternity should be continually introduced counter-
actingly.

But inasmuch as Christianity became served in homogeneity
with all finite objectives (which is achieved especially in Protestantism, especially in Denmark), Christianity essentially dropped
out, eternity dropped out; that which was supposed to represent
the eternal became exactly like all other finite things, a living for
finite objectives.

The result was that the pendulum swings of finite objectives
became too powerful, [*deleted:* that human existence was ignited

by spontaneous combustion, so to speak,] which is the significance of the 1848 crisis[188] and explainable by the dropping out of
eternity, inasmuch as its service had become finitized.

The Christian state does indeed fancy that it takes Christianity
along, but this is a misunderstanding. Let me speak metaphori-
cally. Imagine a machine so constituted that there are two wheels
originally designed so that the one wheel turns in the direction
opposite to that of the other and by this turning interlocks in
counteraction with the turning of the other wheel—if then
someone were to claim to have such a machine, demonstrate that
it did indeed have both wheels, but, please note, they did not
turn in opposite directions but turned together: then this certainly is a falsehood; it is not the same machine.

It is the heterogeneity of Christianity as *resignation* that is precisely the saving factor for the state. But then Christianity must
actually be served in heterogeneity. The destruction of the state
is the absorption of Christianity as homogeneity, served by
public officeholders, personages of rank, professionals, in short,
just as all other finite things are served. "The state" is "politics";
what it needs is something else that is not politics. But Christianity served in homogeneity with all other finite things is—also
politics.

XI³
B 126
204 Therefore the union became the destruction of the state, and
of course the destruction also of Christianity, because only in its
heterogeneity is it what it is, the protection of the state (*si placet*
[if you please!]) its ruination.

How then is it possible that this union can come to pass, a
union that both simple Christian honesty and true human wisdom must condemn: it becomes mutual destruction [*changed
from:* ruination]?

Yes, see here what human sagacity leads to—and see here also
its punishment!

The state thought that it was sagacious to get this doctrine of
eternity and instructions about another world introduced in
order to tranquilize people and thus be better able to control
them. The state (perhaps also because of a craving for power) still
did not want to have Christianity in its truth (as resignation in

character) introduced; the state wanted to have it to a certain degree, wanted itself to have it in its power, wanted to determine how it should be introduced—everything is sagacity. But this sagacity was shortsighted, and it was blasphemy against Christianity.

On their part the clergy thought it was very sagacious to accept the protection of the state. The clergy understood, of course, that it is considerably more pleasant to be a hired servant of the state than to serve Christianity according to the understanding of the New Testament. But this sagacity was shortsighted, and it was blasphemy against Christianity.

Therefore the punishment came: the pendulum swings of finitude became too powerful [*changed from:* , finitude's impatience set fire to the whole thing, a kind of spontaneous combustion].

What the craving fortunate ones in their impatience had needed to get to see was that there is an eternity, a goal of eternity to live for: this is tempering. But they did not get to see that; they merely came to see that describing eternity and living for the goal of eternity were made into a finite endeavor just like any other, rewarded by all the things of this earth.

What the despairing ones needed to see was that there is an eternity, a goal of eternity to live for, and that one gladly renounces the things of this earth for the sake of this goal. But they did not see this; however, what they did see was that describing eternity and living for the goal of eternity were made into a finite endeavor just like any other, rewarded by all the things of this earth.

On the whole, the state ought to have learned, certainly from earlier experiences, this much from God's governance, that what the people really need is not to be made fools of, that it is a sin to exploit what unfortunately is true—that people want to be deceived—and that it also is shortsightedness, because when the goal is reached it always ends with frightful revolutions, the punishment for the shortsightedness of sagacity and for the outrage of having wanted in this way to make capital of Christianity for finite ends, and for having wanted with political sagacity to "utilize"—the divine.—*JP* IV 4242 (*Pap.* XI³ B 126) *n.d.*, 1855

XI³
B 126
205

[*Deleted:* II¹⁸⁹]
The Strategy of the "Truth-Witnesses"

June 1, 1855

That, seen in the idea, I have been victorious over the "truth-witnesses" is something anyone who can see must admit if he wants to see. Nor did it at any moment ever occur to me to doubt that, understood in this way, I would be victorious, because what Prof. R. Nielsen said about me in *Fædrelandet*,¹⁹⁰ that I have the idea, is true; I know that on a scale completely different from that on which Prof. Nielsen knows it.

But it is one thing to be victorious in the idea, something else to be victorious in the external world; this is different to such a degree that the very ones who in the very highest sense must be said to have been victorious in the idea have had to succumb in the external world, indeed, have been put to death. Or to take an example (and yet not the very highest even if it is too high for me), must not Socrates, seen in the idea, be said to have been completely victorious over the contemporary public—and yet he had to empty the poison cup.¹⁹¹ It is not as the inexperienced youth probably thinks, that true superiority gives security against having to get the worst of it in the external world; no, true superiority is rather the cause of a person's coming to get the worst of it in the external world, of being persecuted, of being put to death, something an insignificant person never achieves, and something against which half measures and mediocrity are completely secured. [*Deleted:* On the whole, there are very few who have an eye for the idea, and among the few who still have a little eye there is very, very seldom someone who acknowledges that, viewed in the idea, he has lost.]

Although, seen in the idea, it must be said that I have been victorious, it by no means escapes me what a superior external power I am fighting against, nor how fanatic it is—yes, how fanatic, because what is most precisely understood by fanaticism, fanaticism for something ideal, certainly appears more rarely in our day, but the more common fanaticism for something earthly, for example, for livelihood, profit, a fanaticism that is far more malignant than the first, is comparable to that as intoxication on brandy to intoxication on champagne. If this fanaticism then undertakes to fanaticize harmless simple-mindedness, incites the women, then the danger in the external world can become rather great for me, although, from the point of view of the idea, I have been victorious.

Now, to escape dangers does not interest me [*deleted:* , nor do I want any human assistance at all]—there is one to whom I most devotedly relate myself, who has taught me to understand my life in another way and moved me to want to understand it another way. On the other hand, I regard it, religiously, as my duty to elucidate what in all likelihood is the strategy of the "truth-witnesses" so that whoever wants to can see.

The truth-witnesses seem to have the following view: "To become involved publicly with Magister Kierkegaard does not help us.

"But therefore we may very well be victorious. Magister Kierkegaard, as he himself says, is literally only a single person and, what is even better for us, with an unaltered firmness refuses to form a party, does not try to become a power in the external world, which certainly in a very high sense is precisely to his praise, but we—'truth-witnesses'!—are then not so lunatic as to tell that to the people, and by themselves the people cannot understand it. Then we will surely be finished with him.

"Therefore, officially, [*deleted:* absolute] silence; let us all agree on that. Then, on the other hand, we have: the *churches.* Here people are gathered in a more solemn mood; the surroundings exert their power over them—here is the place, here we can speak, 'witness,' and here he cannot attack us [*deleted:* , indeed, there is even an ordinance against reviewing unprinted sermons]. And we have: *confessionals* and *family visits;* here he is even less able to tackle us. Then we are 1000 men with families, and men who through official service are accustomed to being able to deal deftly with what simply is not altogether true. We can calmly wager that we are bound to be victorious; what is more, we are so certain of victory that basically we are already able, prophetically, to call him a sacrifice."

Is that not what I am saying; I am—indeed, O God, cheerfully

XI³
B 136
217

and gratefully!—a sacrifice, sacrificed to a generation for whom
ideals are tomfoolery, a nothing, the earthly and temporal are
earnestness, a generation whom worldly sagacity in the form of
teachers of Christianity has shamefully, in the Christian sense,
demoralized. See *This Must Be Said; So Let It Be Said*, p. 12
[p. 78].

"In open battle we cannot be victorious over him; he must be
disposed of silently, with the help of the masses, in such a way
that it is no one who does it; with the help of the insidiousness
that no one can get hold of [*deleted:* he must be stealthily assassi-
nated]." Ah, stealthily assassinated! Yes, that is indeed something
for pastors and bandits, and best of all for pastors and bandits
together.

But there are various kinds of bandits. There are also literary
bandits. So perhaps the publicly tongue-tied servants, the "truth-
witnesses," for the sake of safety could consider hiring a couple
of literary bandits to work publicly. These could then perhaps be
used to incite the rabble against me. "That the clergy should have
a liking for such a thing—oh, good heavens, how can you think
that, the clergy, those holy [*changed from:* God's] men, who
moreover are as silent as the grave, so one must be struck with the
most profound astonishment at the Christian humility, the
Christian patience, with which they publicly remain silent about
all the embittering things Dr. S. K. writes about them. Moreover, I know that they themselves say—imagine, how beautiful!—they themselves say that it is a disgrace that K. is treated in
this way by certain papers."

*   *

When I decisively commenced—inasmuch as my earlier articles in *Fædrelandet* were preliminary—I took aim at the Minister
of Ecclesiastical Affairs and Education,[192] in case it should be
from this corner that danger threatened: legal persecution etc. I
did it also because I actually felt a need at one time to ease my
mind in this regard; there was something I had to get said. But
[*deleted:* I did not believe that any danger actually threatened
from that corner, although I took aim at the Minister] I in fact
had my eye directed somewhere else.

The danger for me, I thought, could also come from this

XI³
B 136
218

side—all the mediocrity, secretly steered by the pastors, will conspire against me [*deleted:* and by a kind of ostracism try, if possible, even to force me to clear out]. "If he," I more or less imagined the argument against me, "if he is to be along in public life, and not remote in the way he hitherto has kept himself, then he will interfere altogether disturbingly in the whole thing; he knocks down all the relativities in which we are in the habit of complimenting and recognizing each other and applies a criterion that threatens to reduce our existence to a triviality. Just think, our beautiful solemnity of having truth-witnesses, to whom we friends of the truth give presents while they live and raise monuments when they are dead, he makes into tomfoolery, and the same with all relationships. Brief and to the point, he is unbearable! In a certain sense we do not deny that he has unusual gifts or that he is unusually diligent and unselfish; that he really is. But of what help is that to us; he is a too-much that spoils the whole thing for us."

This I have very well foreseen. [*Deleted:* If anyone were to say to me, "But you could, after all, travel abroad," I would, if I felt like joking, reply with Per Degn, "Why should I do that; why should I leave a congregation I love and respect";[193] and if I do not feel like joking, I would reply, "Particularly since I am in the service of Governance, here is my place—here I remain."] "I am a sacrifice to a generation." I have acquiesced to that. I am well aware that on the greatest scale the generation has the superiority in the external world. This is quite in order; otherwise I would not be sacrificed, something to which I "cheerfully and gratefully" have acquiesced [*deleted:* —there the matter rests!].—*Pap.* XI³ B 136 June 1, 1855

XI³
B 136
219

[*Deleted:* III[194]]
Where Does the State Get the Money with
Which It Pays Teachers of Christianity?

XI³
B 115
187

Somewhere else[195] I have pointed out what dreadful confusion has arisen because someone got the disastrous idea of introducing the pecuniary element in relation with Christianity,

XI³
B 115
188

whereby an enormous illusion has been produced that has become the ruination of Christianity and an equivocation was created that has fostered hypocrites or troubled consciences. Oh, if Christianity ever shakes off all this equivocation, it will be like awakening from a hard and heavy sleep of troubled dreams!

I have, however, always thought of the role of the state as being similar to that of, for example, a millionaire who got the idea of paying thousands of teachers of Christianity out of his own pocket and to whom one then must say: For God's sake, stop! Do not risk this blasphemy! Don't you know it is high treason against Christianity! Don't you know it is not Christianity you are serving but Satan, for one can give all one's money to the poor in order to serve Christianity in poverty, but one cannot serve Christianity with contributions of money—this confuses Christianity with what it definitely is not, an ordinary human enterprise. And yet such a private individual, by paying thousands of teachers of Christianity, could not occasion as great a confusion as the state does when it pays them. The private individual, after all, has no authority; he has only money, but the fact that the state pays the teachers has created the additional confusion of abolishing the authority of Christianity and substituting the authority of the state, so that people have thought—infinite confusion!—that one cannot be a proper teacher of Christianity unless one is a public official, that is, unless one is authorized by the state.

Thus I have assumed that the state, which pays the teachers of Christianity, is like a private millionaire. But now I will raise the question: Where does the state get the money with which it pays the teachers of Christianity? Now we see from a new angle how infinitely confusing and corrupting this whole thing is, since the state itself gets the money by falsifying Christianity in one way or

another; the falsifying of what Christianity is brings in the money, and in turn this money buys the falsification of what Christianity is.

Actually it may be said that the state has turned the suffering and death of Christ into money. That Christ by his suffering and death has saved people and gained for them an eternal salvation (which, however, in the New Testament is always proclaimed in such a way that it is just as much, just exactly as much, a responsibility as it is a gift to people, which is why instead of becoming a gift it becomes most demoralizing to all who do not receive it rightly by relating themselves to it in responsibility) has been made simply and solely a gift. If there had been awareness of the other side, of the responsibility, it would never have occurred to any reasonable person to behave as the state has behaved [*changed from:* to force this upon people as a matter of course].

The suffering and death of Christ has been made solely a gift; by leaving out all the responsibilities, all *nota benes* have been disposed of, and thus Christianity becomes plainly and simply a gift, a present. The state then took over or availed itself of this infinite gift, this enormous good, and interposed itself as the middle term between Christ and the individual, which confuses Christianity at the deepest level.

This is how the state has taken over Christianity; it has said something like this: We are going to see to it that people share in this great, priceless good (salvation by Christ); not only is your getting a Tivoli[196] dependent upon us, but an eternal salvation, too, is obtainable only from us. According to the size of the country, it will cost so and so many thousands—and now an estimate is made of how many thousands of teachers and how many thousands of rix-dollars the teachers need—this is how the money is obtained.

But if it is assumed that the value of Christ's suffering and death is measurable (commensurable) in money, then it is actually incumbent upon Christ himself to say: It costs so and so much. On the other hand, it is a dreadful assault for a third party to force himself in between Christ and the individual and say: It costs so and so much.

But this is what the state has done; it has perpetrated what according to the New Testament must be called a robber-assault or a swindle, and on a grand scale, on so grand a scale that the robbers, the swindlers, do not, as is customary, end up in prison, but the person who will not voluntarily let himself be assaulted and swindled ends up in prison. And it is the state that does it, the state from which one usually seeks help against robbers and swindlers! And the state thinks it is doing this in the interest of

XI³
B 115
190

Christianity—yes, of course, if it can be in Christianity's interest to become thoroughly confused.

See again how infinitely confusing and corrupting it is that the state has wanted to help Christianity financially! Truly, no good will ever come of it until the relationship becomes natural again. Let Christianity take care of itself; it can do it so very nicely; [*deleted:* by the living God,] it is not in bad straits. You have a fixed idea, most Honorable State, if you think it needs your help, or is it one of your tricks that in the name of serving [*tjene*] Christianity you have wanted to make use of [*betjene sig af*] Christianity, perhaps in order to govern people all the better, as if the state controlled or had the slightest influence on the decision: an eternal salvation. No, let Christianity shift for itself. And if there are some who want to use Christianity to swindle people, blackmail them, then let us just turn to the state, the police, to get protection against swindlers.—*JP* III 2774 (*Pap.* XI³ B 115) *n.d.*, 1855

From draft of Moment, *4; see 172:28–31:*

. . . . . then I (just as my pseudonym, Johannes Climacus, in his time, when the system was flourishing, said to himself[197]), I have said to myself: You must see to it that you also can think of doing something; you are getting on in years and are becoming an old man, becoming a nobody, while all the others are in beneficial activity.

So then I thought like this: Well, then, I will see to it that . . . . .

—*Pap.* XI³ B 278:8 *n.d.*, 1850

From draft of Moment, *4; see 173:4–8:*

XI³
B 278:10
427   Take a human relationship. A woman will put up with her beloved's many defects; even if he perhaps expresses his love as disastrously clumsily as possible, she will overlook it. But one

XI³
B 278:10
428   thing she never forgives—and even if he were the greatest virtuoso in it, she never forgives him if she has the least little suspicion that his love is official, that what he says is formulas. No, she

never forgives him that, because she understands quite correctly that precisely that is a personal insult, since it is treating her like a thing, which is even much, much worse than personally treating her as nothing.—*Pap.* XI³ B 278:10 *n.d.*, 1855

See 183–184:

> There Are Two Kinds of Christianity (Pastor Fog in the *Berlingske Tidende*[198]) —Are There Perhaps More?

XI³
B 102
164

> > "Do you want to have fine sand, or do you want to have coarse sand?" (Peer Degn)[199]

d.*   [*Deleted:* S. K.]

One day I saw a man walk down the street staggering in such a way that one had to assume that he was drunk. As he passed a cabstand, two cab drivers noticed him, and the one said to the other, "Do you see him; he no doubt has had something of the kind [*Retning*] that leads a person to the gutter"—and Herr Pastor Fog, in the capacity of direction-major, is on the verge of wanting to give the conflict the direction [*Retning*] that leads a conflict into blather. Whoever is a lover of this, just follow this man, because he has the direction.

There are two kinds of Christianity, Herr Pastor Fog has discovered, or he even thinks he ought to thank Prof. Nielsen for the discovery.

XI³
B 102
165

There are two kinds of Christianity! The New Testament is of a somewhat different opinion; it breathes in Either/Or. In the New Testament everything is put at stake, heaven/hell, everything at stake, to the point of hating father, mother, one's own child—either/or. The New Testament is of the opinion that

*Note. The article was written in the days when in the *Berlingske Tidende* one read Herr Pastor's thanks to Prof. R. Nielsen. At the time I did not want to have it printed. But Pastor Fog's conduct had something typical about it; so I find it fitting that he is honored with the recognition of standing as the representative of pastor-blather that under the name of Christianity, in the form of dispassion ("there are two kinds") recites what in its truth is the most passionate of all: Christianity.

whoever does not see that there is only one kind of Christianity, only one that is Christianity, is Christianly just as useless as a needle without an eye is in daily life, all the rest of his zeal and willingness just as ludicrous as if a needle, by all the more willingness, wanted to compensate for the lack of an eye.

But there are two kinds of Christianity—perhaps more? This conception helps to make Christianity popular in the sense of spiritlessness, is preachifying [*præke*] Christianity down into meaninglessness, into—nonsense [*Præk*]. Quite right, in relation to sensate, temporal, earthly things it is almost ludicrous to apply Either/Or. Let us take an example from daily life—for example, butter. If one were to apply Either/Or to butter, quite properly the reply would be, "Come now, not so eager, there are many kinds of butter. There is the absolutely extra prime manor house butter from Fyn and Langeland; there is the good prime manor house butter from Sjælland and Jylland; there is a very good homemade butter and farmer butter; there are also very good drippings that are almost as good as butter." And this is very sensible talk about butter. But just because, as the aphorism (very often only all too true) says of the pastor: He preaches only for his butter tub, Christianity is not therefore actually something of the same kind and nature as butter.

If it could occur to me to take up the matter in this way, I would be perfectly justified if I petitioned the Minister of Ecclesiastical Affairs and Education to have a pastor like that immediately discharged. No one bound by an oath to the New Testament has permission, publicly and quite without embarrassment, to say: There are two kinds of Christianity. Yet it could never occur to me to take up the matter in this way. No, if I had influence in such a matter, I would much prefer to propose an increase in salary for this pastor, or this truth-witness, because if one uses life here on earth to perfect oneself in nonsense, by which one qualifies oneself to flunk in eternity, then it seems reasonable that everything be made as good as possible for such a man in this life.

S. K.

—*Pap.* XI³ B 102 *n.d.*, 1855

XI³
B 102
166

From sketch of Moment, *6; see 211:1:*

Fear [*changed from:* To fear] most of all
    to be in error!
  Deleted from margin: Here could be used:
    The passage from the first draft of a subscrip-
    tion plan[200] [*deleted:* N.B. lies in the desk among
    things in blue paper under the bronze medal-
    lion]: stay with the pastor
            and
    the last of the original and addendum to the
    first "Cry"[201] [*deleted:* , which lies nearest the
    window in the wide compartment of the high
    desk].
            —*Pap.* XI³ B 295:1 May 30, 1855

See 227–28:

The Condition for Salvation. Its Change.

That It Is Unchanged.

XI³
B 124
200

Let me speak figuratively. Think of a fisherman. He owns a splendid net that he has inherited from his father.

Year after year he puts out his net—but gets no fish.

What is the matter? What can it be? "Sure enough, I know," says the fisherman. "The fish have changed; in the course of time they have decreased in size; if I want to catch them, I must get myself a net that is not made for large fish."

The net, however, totally disinterested in whether fish are caught or not, is quietly aware of being a splendid net and therefore could not dream of changing because the fish have changed.

Now think about eternity and the condition for salvation.

From generation to generation, steadily, incessantly, the cost of being a Christian has become cheaper and cheaper; the condition for salvation has become easier and easier. One generation of jubilant millions, served by huckster clergy, has replaced the

XI³
B 124
201

other and is not merely happy over the easy condition gained but is proud of it, because this process of rendering Christianity worthless or of taking Christianity in vain has occurred in the name of perfecting Christianity.

Eternity has quietly looked on and observed: I am catching no one.

But—eternity is not subjective like the fisherman, does not need human beings—that was a bad *nota bene* [note well]. It is human beings who need eternity, to be caught is to be saved— also a bad *nota bene*. In being subjectively objective like the net, eternity is just as objective as it is subjective, or eternity is at one and the same time the fisherman and the net—therefore it does not change, and therefore humanity has succeeded only in fooling itself.—*JP* I 846 (*Pap.* XI^3 B 124) May 8, 1855

Deleted from draft of Pap. XI^3 B 124:

It is not at all eternity's idea with Christianity to want to catch human beings in the egotistical sense in which the fisherman wants to catch fish. Eternity wants to save human beings. So it does not change just because people prefer to fool themselves and to be fooled.

The Moral

The fisherman needs the fish; ergo, he changes the net. If, on the contrary, it is the fish that need to be caught—and this is the Christian way: to be caught is to be saved—then there is nothing else to be done; the fish must change, which is impossible as far as the metaphor is concerned but not in respect to what the metaphor signifies.

By becoming smaller the fish can fool the fisherman if he does not decide to change the net; by changing the condition for salvation humanity succeeds only in fooling itself—because eternity does not change the condition. The fish is right and behaves sensibly in doing everything to avoid being caught; human beings are self-deceived when they try in every way to avoid being caught, are happy over not being caught, or are happy over being caught in a way that is not the right way—they are self-deceived,

because to be caught is to be saved.—*JP* I 847 (*Pap.* XI³ B 125:8)
May 8, 1855

[*Deleted:* So with This Let It Be Settled!]
Something Once and for All
[*Deleted:* By
S. K.]

Contents.
1. Is Grundtvig a Kind of Apostle, Is This the
   Truth?

*   *

2. The Grundtvigians
3. Dr. Zeuthen's Capability
[*Deleted:*   4. The Seriousness of Serious People
5. A Bunch of Pastors (Convention)
6. That Pastors Want To Influence by Numbers!
7. A Pastor: Mr. Andersen]
8. Indeed, Then What Do I Have To Worry
   About!
9. So with This Let It Be Settled!
   N.B.
                              —*Pap.* XI³ B 179 *n.d.*, 1855

Addition to Pap. XI³ B 179:

To the typesetter: All these numbers are to be set in very small
brevier; and only numbers I and II have new pages, and from
number III on the articles are to be printed directly following
each other, with only a rule between.—*Pap.* XI³ B 181 April
1855

Addition to Pap. XI³ B 179:

Is Grundtvig a Kind of Apostle? Is
This the Truth?

XI³
B 182
299

April 55

We have had to hear this often enough; but just in the last days this truth has found an extremely significant expression: stated in *Flyveposten*[202](!) and by an anonymous writer (!!). Just as this is reliable, just so is it true that G. is a kind of apostle.

No more really needs to be said; but since Pastor G. has done such great harm in the religious sphere through his lack of character, it is indeed most proper to place him in a truer light than the one used by the party, which speculates in his renown and by promoting him up to apostle counts on promoting itself. Then, too, I fortunately in this case do not in the slightest way feel bound by devotion to my late father. And the circumstance that I have an older brother, who, by nature superbly gifted, exceptionally well informed, has been botched up by coming in contact with Grundtvig and Grundtvigianism—that circumstance cannot impose on me any consideration of devotion but can instead perhaps prompt someone to understand the attack upon G. as if it were intended to avenge my brother.

Pastor G. is a man from whom at one time one may have received the impression: this seems to be a person who in truth wills only one thing. But in the course of time G., too, has been corrupted by the endemic evil of our age: "also," not to will one thing but to will this and also. Christianly, he is without character—a peculiar kind of apostle! And I think that through his lack of character he has a responsibility in relation to the late Bishop Mynster, because if Bishop M. had had a Christian character opposite him, he perhaps would have become different from what he became. Bishop Mynster disregarded G. not only because he was so infinitely superior to him in sagacity, no, in a far deeper sense. Fine judge that he was, Bishop M. readily perceived that the whole thing with G., even if it originally may have been something more, in the course of years had become bombast— that to sit in an official position of the state Church, with a salary of a couple thousand rix-dollars, Knight of the Dannebrog, and then also to want to be a kind of apostle, that this, to put it mildly, was childish tricks, which did not become more earnest with the aid of raised eyebrows, knitted brows, a Norwegian accent, rolling one's *r*'s, and all the other Grundtvigian affectations, which

XI³
B 182
300

unfortunately will not die out with him, since a retinue of apostolic disciples has successfully learned the art from him. No wonder, therefore, that in the past Bishop Mynster could be so amused that G.'s apostolic manliness, about which so much has been heard but of which nothing has been seen, dissolved into the manliness of becoming engaged to be married anew as an old man.

G.'s claim is that the state Church destroys Christianity—and with this claim, which he rhetorically recites, he has settled down in just about the most pleasant and one of the most advantageous offices in the state Church, since Vartov[203] has no ministerial functions and, as far as I know, Vartov has tithes. This, Christianly, is lack of character.

But just as all lack of character pays well in this world, so also that which is designated here, Grundtvig's Vartov type. According to my way of looking at things, it must be said that Pastor G. makes improvements far beyond what Bishop Mynster ever did. [*Deleted:**] He remains in office, takes all the earthly and temporal gains and security—also recites that it is the state Church that is destroying Christianity: what an improvement! Pastor G. is too superior to want to be a simple, ordinary pastor who keeps his mouth shut and silently takes the earthly—no, G. takes the earthly and also—to use the Martensenian term—"witnesses" loudly that it is the state Church that is destroying Christianity. That was one improvement. But there are more. By remaining in the royal office, yet spouting forth, he causes a staff of theological graduates and pastors, who attach themselves to him, to thank him as for a work of love that by not resigning he did not bring them to the decision of also having to venture out. Thus he terrifies, flirtingly, that staff of pastors and graduates with his fulminations against the state Church, but there the matter rests; yet G. is a kind, a lovable man, whom we now doubly love: he remains in office—what an improvement! And not only those in the party but all the clergy in a way thank G. for remaining in

XI³
B 182
301

Deleted: *Note. Just as I, while Bishop Mynster was living, took polemical aim at G. on occasion, so also I did not forget, despite all the hubbub and shrieking against me here in the city, to have it said directly in my second article about Mynster that I would ask his enemies not to be jubilant.[204]

office, because a withdrawal would indeed be bound to bring the position of the established order closer to a decision. Here again is an improvement: to terrify—and then to be the "good-natured fellow" who does not carry through, remains in office, remains—in Vartov! And not only all the clergy but the entire society in a way feel themselves in a debt of gratitude to G. because he, this threatening figure, does not after all withdraw from the state Church and establish free congregations, but out of love for the weak remains in office, for it is out of love for the weak that he remains in the royal office, receives his tithes and expressions of gratitude (what an improvement; it is more than other pastors receive) because everything still remains the same with the old, all of us—in Vartov.

G. is a genius, but he is as far from being a Christian character as his Christianity is from being the Christianity of the New Testament. Moreover, he has in this way caused incalculable harm in our situation. Because of the inimical position he has taken to the official Christianity, attention has been completely diverted from the fact that his Christianity is not at all the Christianity of the New Testament. G.'s Christianity is: Judaism. The very kind of religion that Christ came to the world to end—precisely that is what G. presents and by contrast to the official Christianity has passed as being the Christianity of the New Testament.

XI³
B 182
302

What circumcision was for the Jews, Baptism, according to G., becomes for the Christians; in the same sense as Jews thought themselves to be the chosen people through circumcision, so also the Christians through Baptism. And so it goes full blast with filling time and life with world-historical visions, hearty and lively "chatter"[205] about the glorious achievements and enterprises of the race—a clinging to the earthly and to the promises for this life, which is also the reason that being prolific and becoming fruitful is something that preoccupies Grundtvigians altogether Jewishly.

But precisely the kind of objective certainty that circumcision was—and when Baptism is used in the same way, there is no essential difference—this was what Christ wants to do away with, that is, he does not want tranquillity, he wants restlessness.[206] And he truly did not come to the world to proclaim a blithe joy of life, but suffering, dying to the world, anguish, misery, to be borne, however, through the expectancy of an eternal salvation. Nor is it the propagation of the race and history that interest the Christianity of the New Testament, which is characterized explicitly by its unworldliness (acosmism) and the spiritual person's being without relatives. Finally, the Christianity of the New Testament is anything but hearty and lively chatter about what others have done, but is: imitation of the prototype in the time of testing on the way to the accounting of eternity.

*   *

The party [*deleted:* (which, incidentally, over the years has undergone a remarkable change, for although during the time when the government wanted forcibly to prevent withdrawal from the state Church it shouted about "the horrible yoke" etc., the talk sounds somewhat different from the moment the government shifted the matter thus, "Please, you are quite free to withdraw," because now it is supposed to be because of fervency that they nevertheless remain—in their livelihoods) the party] will perhaps get busy now; perhaps the whole squadron will vault into the saddle, the whole society or partnership will start shooting off their mouths and not forget to admire and thank each other mutually (Basil and Bartholo[207]). I have nothing more to say about that. [*Deleted:* I do, however, want to comment as follows. At the very moment when I myself attacked the official Christianity here at home, at that very moment (instead of *politically sagaciously* seeking to form a kind of alliance with the old Orthodox) to attack G. and turn the party's assiduous opposition toward me—everyone no doubt regards that as: unsagacious.] It is only this that I want to be understood, that I myself am well aware that what I am doing is not sagacious, but yet I do it, because Christianity most of all scorns political sagacity. [*Deleted:* On the other hand, I want to point out one thing (*changed from:* Yet in order not to come to say anything untrue by what has been said above, as if it were my opinion that the Grundtvigian party is truly a party of importance and power, I must point out one thing)]. What a party can pass for in the eyes of a few and what it in a way can do are one thing; what it truly can do is

XI³
B 182
303

something else. In my opinion, of all the parties here at home the Grundtvigian party most resembles the corruption Scribe has felicitously labeled: a society for mutual admiration,[208] except that this title ought to be lengthened so that, as one speaks of the society for the propagation of music, it will come to be: the society for the propagation of mutual admiration. As far as G. himself is concerned, he, by being waited upon over the years by the party, which converses with him only in interjections, has become what he has an original disposition for: personified self-satisfaction [*changed from:* personal unruliness] for the benefit of—indeed, if it is for anything, it certainly must be for the benefit of—irony.

XI³
B 182
304

Finally, I am assuming that some wailing women and womanish pastors will all together now say the opposite of what they said previously. Then they wailed that Bishop Mynster was dead and that I had waited until after his death to attack him; it must, however, be kept in mind that it was not until after his death that he was canonized as a truth-witness. Now I assume that they will wail about: attacking an old man, not being able to wait the short time he perhaps has to live. In that, however, I have not been able to oblige them, also for the reason that since G., as he himself said in the parliament, has for 40 years been considering withdrawing from the state Church, so it could very well be possible—as I once said to Bishop Mynster in a conversation about that—that he would also have the singularity of becoming two to three hundred years old, an age that would fittingly be in proportion to using a 40-year period for considering.—*Pap.* XI³ B 182 April 1855

Addition to Pap. XI³ B 179:

XI³
B 188
308

The Grundtvigians

When in December of 1854, after almost two years of having kept silence, I broke it and [*deleted:* (instead of as hitherto using a foil tipped with a guard to show where there could be wounding yet without wounding)] with a sharp weapon directed the attack against Bishop Martensen with regard to the late Bishop

Mynster—there was, I was well aware, a party here in the country to whom this was by no means unwelcome, the Grundtvigians. If I had in any way had anything to do with using worldly sagacity, I would certainly at that very moment have sought a rapprochement, or allowed such a thing if it was sought. This I did not do; on the contrary, despite all worldly sagacity, I used that very moment to ask them not to be jubilant (see the article in *Fædrelandet*: "There the matter rests"[209]).

[*Deleted:* No, in my mind the Grundtvigians, of all those with whom I can least become involved, are, Christianly, the most demoralized ones we have; yet I could not begin to attack them, since I would not be at all understood and, moreover, *on the whole* I have nothing at all to do with them.

XI[3]
B 188
309

But it had to come, and I confess that it is with a certain solemnity that I see that the affair, through the cooperation of Governance, is starting to turn the way I could wish it.

There is no one with whom I truly can be said to want to pick a quarrel; on the contrary, in much suffering but also supported in another way, I more and more become, strive more and more to become, a passive instrument in the hand of Governance. But in every instance I have never wished to pick a quarrel with those called the Mynsterians, if with anyone then with the Grundtvigians, who in a far deeper sense are demoralized.

Most likely it would end with their having initiated the attack, something I in turn would rather see.]

[*In margin:* That the Grundtvigians also would themselves have their eyes opened soon and would begin to see me differently, I was well aware; that it could come to the point of their attacking me was what I preferred.] And it was not unlikely, because—while the rest of the clergy, as far as my attack was concerned, may have thought like this: There is something true in what he says, and it can do us no good to become involved with him, there was the probability that those deep, earnest, apostolic Christians, the Grundtvigians, who mutually beguile each other in conceitedness, would believe themselves called to speak up and attack me.

Unfortunately, the truth about the Grundtvigians is that they are as thoroughly secularized as all the rest of the clergy; the only difference is this—and it is this difference that in my eyes places them so low [*changed from:* might make me want to pick a quarrel with them, something I have not wanted with regard to the rest of the clergy]—the difference is this, that at a very cheap price they pretend to be better than others. A pastor ordinarily takes his earthly benefits, sweats his turn in the pulpit every Sunday, keeps his Church records—and in other respects is decent enough to keep his mouth shut. A Grundtvigian is different. He takes the earthly benefits just as the others, is just as greedy for advancement as the others; but he is also the profound, earnest Christian with vision and heart for the affairs of the Church—as oratorical features at the conventions and other places of entertainment.

XI³
B 188
310

The very most serious affair was this question of the separation of Church and state, that the state Church is destroying all Christianity. The Grundtvigians had availed themselves of this in order by its help to become: interesting. Ah, interesting! They were not like ordinary pastors, jobholders without spirit; they talked about these important Christian affairs. Ah, they talked about them! Meanwhile the Messrs. Grundtvigians calmly remained in their royal livings, paid close attention to advancement—yet they talked about these important Christian affairs. Oh, they talked about them! And these important Christian affairs were a matter of vital concern to them—I assure you. Oh, I assure you! In the meantime the Grundtvigians even became Knights just like the others when their turn came. But yet it was a matter of vital concern to them. What? The Cross of the Order of the Dannebrog? No, no, these important Christian affairs, they were a matter of vital concern to them—along with the Cross of the Order of the Dannebrog, which is worn on the breast. How interesting!

That I was bound to come to this party as inopportunely as possible, I knew very well, and likewise that it certainly would be discovered when I went further and the talk was no longer about an attack on Mynster.

Yes, I believe that it is almost impossible that anyone could come more inopportunely than I was bound to come to the Grundtvigians [*deleted:* *²¹⁰]. That by which they had planned to make themselves interesting, no doubt thinking that it would abundantly stretch through their lifetime, perhaps to their children and grandchildren—someone comes along and carries it out! This is just about the most unfortunate thing that can happen, that earnestness is introduced in relation to the very thing by which characterlessness has reckoned to become interesting.

Let me give a few examples. They tell of a man who stood on Langebro[211] and dejectedly gazed down into the deep water. They tell that when a second man came alongside him and had stood silent for some time, the first man said to him, "I intend to throw myself into the sea." "Then I really advise you to do it at once. Such a thing should never be postponed; otherwise it becomes a mess." Believe me, the first man, as they say, blew his top with a vengeance; the most calamitous thing that can happen when one has planned to become interesting by talking about committing suicide is to have someone turn the matter in this way.

I myself was a party to the second example, but despite this I can tell it. It was in my room. We were three persons in all. The one said to the other person and me, "I do, of course, dare to count on your secrecy; if you will promise me perfect secrecy, I will tell you what is being said about that man" (it was of course something bad that would come), "but you must promise me secrecy." Then I spoke up and said, "If you are so very concerned that secrecy be maintained, would not then the simplest way be for you not to tell it to us?" I can testify that the man became, as they say, sore. It is as calamitous as possible when someone wants to make himself honorable by—how interesting!—*running down* the neighbor *in secret*; it is as calamitous as possible that the matter is then turned in such a way that secrecy is taken seriously.

How inopportunely, then, I must come to the Grundtvigians! To this, however, I am not averse; to this, Christianly, radically corrupted party that with the aid of platitudes and heartiness and blather and alliance has shammed a Christian importance it does not in the remotest way have—I cannot be averse to come as inopportunely as possible. The Grundtvigians in particular are the traitors to Christianity. In a little country where unfortunately everything is mediocrity only all too easily, in a little

XI³
B 188
311

country where indifference is really the religion—a party avails
itself of this wretchedness to become at a bargain price "profound, earnest, hearty, true, apostolic Christians." In a certain

sense the Grundtvigians are more advanced than the others, but
now instead of, in honesty to Christianity, paying attention to
what it requires, they avail themselves of the wretchedness of the
others to pass themselves off in great style as being something.
This is the deeper dishonesty; and this is why I continually say
that, Christianly, the Grundtvigians are the most demoralized
ones we have. If there lived in a city (we can, of course, imagine
it) none but robbers, with only a few exceptions who occupied
themselves with less violent and less important thefts—if these
few would then avail themselves of being taken for honest people, in that case I regard their corruptness as far deeper than
that of the others who were robbers but were also regarded as
robbers.

It certainly is not my opinion that it has been Christianly beneficial for Denmark that Bishop Mynster has proclaimed Christianity for a long time, but the influence of the Grundtvigians has
had a far more corrupting effect, except that they have not had
the extensiveness. Among the so-called Mynsterian Christians
there are great numbers of indifferentists, secularists, etc. etc. But
the really deeper decay, that is found among the Grundtvigians.
The majority of the so-called Mynsterian Christians are perhaps
unripe fruit, but the Grundtvigians on the whole are spoiled
fruit, spoiled by making what should be action into chatter.[212]
And in my opinion there is a very great difference between unripe fruit and spoiled fruit. Unripe fruit—well, who knows, perhaps it would still be possible to find a way in which it could be
ripened. But spoiled fruit—that can just as well be thrown away
first as last. Among all the Mynsterians there perhaps is not a
single one who has dabbled in wanting to be salt—who knows,
perhaps something can still be accomplished if salt is added to this
insipidity. But the Grundtvigians are a lump of tasteless salt and,
according to Scripture, are good for nothing but to be cast out.[213]

That I am right, I know very well; that my contemporaries
will eventually realize it, I also know very well; and how it will
turn out, I also know very well. Simply by my having entered in

and having taken their thesis, the Grundtvigians have been forced into an ever greater untruth, after they have not had the courage of truth to denounce their past life and carry out what they have talked about, indeed, after they have even attacked the one who has taken their thesis seriously. Enterprising and active as they are, numbering at least one experienced sophist among them, they want to become more inventive and more inventive in equivocations, stock phrases—but it will not help them. The contemporaries will see through them more and more, will only expose their stock phrases all the more, just as someone who wants to wrap himself up in a cloak that is much too small of course does best to let it hang in one position and not try to conceal by throwing it about him now one way and now another, because every such protective turn provides a new, hitherto unseen exposure.

*   *

Time is a dangerous power; it discloses—just give it time and the truth is sure to come to light and a kind of justice will prevail. Thus what has been happening to the Grundtvigians in recent years I am not disinclined to regard as a kind of justice that is being done to Prof. Clausen and thereby to those who have seen something important in him. During the years '25, '26, '27, the Grundtvigians made a big point of how weak it was of Clausen not to resign his official position.[214] Then—it goes around!— then came the Grundtvigians' turn, and it turned out, yes, it turned out that they also remained in their official positions. But then the Clausen way is indeed much to be preferred, because he had not beaten the big drum about the apostolic, had not allowed himself to be complimented as an apostle.

As a matter of fact, I naturally do not want to involve myself in any way in a more detailed specific discussion with the Grundtvigians; [*deleted:* it does not interest me at all and, what is decisive, it would lead attention away from the main issue. My relationship is to the established order. But the Grundtvigians certainly do not represent the established order, indeed, do not wish to have common cause with the established order, declare themselves to be a party. Understood in this way, the party of

XI³
B 188
313

XI³
B 188
314

course must ask to be treated separately; but, to repeat, this does not interest me at all and would draw attention away from the main issue. Thus far, however,] it is not needed either. The party whose thesis was the separation of Church and state, now when it would become a serious matter with regard to profit, perhaps still wants to make common cause with the established order, even to undertake to defend the established order, that is, the livelihoods—I am, of course, speaking also of them when I speak about the established order, except that their situation is undeniably, deservedly, so precious that one could wish that the late Bishop Mynster had experienced this. People do a lot of strange running around in our day, but there is no one who runs around the way those apostolic men, the Grundtvigians, run around. When the rest of the clergy defend the established order, they must put up with being reminded—since it is true—that they are also financially interested. But the Grundtvigians have also the thesis of separation of Church and state; therefore it is simply and solely the financial that in fervent love holds them to and warmly inspires them for—the established order. For lack of an appropriate Bible verse, which perhaps will be difficult to find, I recommend to you as a motto the words of Niels the drayman (in *Det lykkelige Skibbrud*), "You beloved brandy, do not abandon me; I will never abandon you."[215]

[*Deleted:* In conclusion, there is a comment by a Grundtvigian to which I wish to draw attention. It is by Dr. Pastor Boisen on Lolland. In an article against me (in *Nordisk Kirketidende* [216]),

XI³
B 188
315

he says that he is fully convinced that if one has nothing but the New Testament the established order is untenable even in relation to the Mormons, to say nothing of S. K. More I do not ask for; what he adds is of no value to me. He adds: For that very reason it is so gratifying to have Grundtvig. Excellent! One sees what a role Grundtvig plays; he takes the place of the New Testament. One also sees how a certainly otherwise more conscientious man understands the pastoral oath. He takes an oath upon the New Testament. Then he declares that if one has only the New Testament the established order is untenable. But he does not resign his office, does not try to get out of this oath. No, he lives quite calmly in the service of the established order and consoles himself with—having Grundtvig. Ultimately the victim of the pastors' unconstraint is the Minister of Ecclesiastical Affairs and Education; it becomes almost ludicrous to be Minister. It can already be bitter enough to have to put the best face on a bad business, to have to pretend that this pastoral oath was holy earnestness and truth. But as long as the pastors themselves support it, seek to maintain an appearance, it can go on. But when the pastors themselves say: The established order is untenable if one has only the New Testament—this pastoral oath, on the New Testament, becomes too much. The pastor's existence becomes a laughing stock, but one is perhaps more inclined to reconcile oneself to that in him, because, good heavens, it is his livelihood, it is his means of support; after all, there are many others who must put up with earning a livelihood by being a laughing-stock, so why not also support oneself by being a laughing-stock as a pastor. This helps the pastor. He becomes the object of sympathy; one does not have the heart to laugh at him, and the laughter turns from him to—the state, the other partner in this collusion, that it wants to pass as something rational and then finds itself in a religious situation such as that.]

Postscript

For this the note found in the margin, pp. 4, 5, 6 [*Pap.* XI³ B 189], is to be used.²¹⁷—*Pap.* XI³ B 188 *n.d.* 1855

Marginal addition to Pap. XI³ B 188:

N.B. The note becomes: postscript.

[*Deleted:* **Note.* That I] However true it is that I may come to the Grundtvigians as inopportunely as possible, I quite understand that in another sense it could seem that I come to the party opportunely [*deleted:* I quite understand]. I also see that the soul-concerned, enterprising party is already active along this line: S. Kierkegaard is dealing official Christianity an incurable wound; he penetrates into circles of society we have never succeeded in interesting—but he does it so decisively that he exasperates. He continually repels personally; he in no way wants to form a party—here is something for the party to do: what in this way loses confidence in officialdom must throw itself into the arms of our party. If there should be someone who clings so firmly to the name Kierkegaard that he cannot tear himself away from it, then the party, by fortunate chance, sees itself in a position to be able to satisfy even this strangest accidental circumstance, because the party also has in its midst a Dr. Kierkegaard, who, to the same degree as S. K. has the cold, the heartless, the repelling qualities, has the opposite [*changed from:* the moistly warm, the hearty, the sticky] qualities.

But this whole thing is only something apparent that cannot last very long. Soon the contemporaries will perceive that the advantage the Grundtvigians have over the established order is only a few stock phrases, a lack of character, by means of which they try to pass themselves off as better, which simply makes them less significant than the rest. The transition therefore—within the established order (since the Grundtvigians have certainly not withdrawn) to cross over from the universal to the Grundtvigian—will soon be seen by the contemporaries to be fatuous and preposterous.—*Pap.* XI³ B 189 *n.d.*, 1855

Addition to Pap. XI³ B 179:

Dr. Zeuthen's[218] Capability

_____

July 5, 1855

Polemicist Dr. Zeuthen's motto [*changed from:* watchword] is "We can do nothing against the truth, but for the truth."[219]

Quite true, quite true. Dr. Zeuthen can do nothing—neither for nor against the truth.

If only he does not go ahead and change the motto, then I ask no more. That is, I regard it as appropriate that it be practiced continually, and therefore that "we can do nothing" be printed each time on the title page, to which one can then reply as Frederik VI is supposed to have replied to someone who, kneeling before him, received the ennobling shoulder-stroke and recited the formula, "I am unworthy, your Majesty": "Yes, to be sure, we know that."—*Pap.* XI³ B 192 July 5, 1855

Addition to Pap. XI³ B 179:

Indeed, Then What Is There to Worry About?

XI³
B 193
320

———————

My dear reader, imagine my joy that Pastor Birkedal[220] (in *Dansk Kirketidende*)[221] finds that there is something in what I say!

"Who is Pastor Birkedal?" What, you do not know him! Then you ought to get to know him; he is a very influential man. I truly believed that you knew him inasmuch as just a short time ago he gloriously proved his capability by something I thought could have come to your knowledge.

There is this monthly publication edited by Dr. Steenstrup. It has had many readable articles; this was acknowledged. But people complained that the editor had not procured one single original philosophical article. Then Pastor Birkedal furnishes it and does it so splendidly that the subscribers to that monthly will no doubt have enough for a long time and for a long time will not trouble the editor with requests for more philosophical articles. See, such a man is Pastor Birkedal!

XI³
B 193
321

Imagine my joy, then, that this man did not want to denounce me unconditionally, that he finds that there are elements of truth, something true in what I am saying! That I should have the whole truth—and faced with Pastor Birkedal—no, that would be asking too much. But this alone, that Pastor B., who naturally has the whole truth, nevertheless finds that there is something true in what I say—what joy!

Moreover, Pastor B. is so kind with his authority as to corroborate the justice of what I have said about myself, that I have to do with God, relate myself to him, that Governance uses me. What assurance I thereby obtain in something of such infinite importance to me! Yet only to a certain degree will I be able to trust in and appeal to the fact that Pastor B. with his authority corroborates what I say about myself. According to Pastor B., it is indeed entirely true that Governance uses me—but not in the way I think. What a man Pastor B. is! I have been and am of the opinion that the highest to which a person can advance is to succeed in penetrating his consciousness in such a way that he actually dares to believe that he has to do with God. Over a long period of years under his upbringing, this has cost me the most dreadful conflicts and sufferings, which will continue, because, in my opinion, this is not attained as a result once and for all but is attained only through the same suffering. But to be involved with God in such a way that one knows how it actually is with others in their relation to God, knows (obviously from God) how he uses other people—I become dizzy as I futilely try to think it!

But when one is involved with God in such a way, saying *du*[222] to God, in quite another sense than we others are, no wonder then that one is extremely jealous of his honor—as Pastor B. is. In a tirade, I am taken to task by the pastor, am reminded that I must not fancy myself to be so witty that I can make God ludicrous, that compared with God I am only a canary brain—quite true, if it can occur to anyone to compare God and a human being from the angle of: What a brainy fellow! This is the story. In a number of *The Moment* there is an article that states: If we are Christians, then God is the most ludicrous of all beings.[223] Even a school child can understand the article: God cannot be the most ludicrous being; ergo we are not Christians. But Pastor B. makes out that I have wanted to make God "ludicrous." See, this is zeal for God's honor! I could also say (since after all the question is about brains) that this is reading like "a blockhead," so dense that it could be enough for a person's whole life to have exhibited once such evidence of competence to read. But I prefer to see in Pastor B.'s harangue an evidence of his matchless zeal for God's honor.

And what a man, as influential as we have seen, so zealous for God's honor, he has the kindness to be my patron; indeed, then what is there to worry about?—*Pap.* XI³ B 193 *n.d.*, 1855

XI³
B 193
322

Addition to Pap. XI³ B 179:

So With This Let It Be Settled!

XI³
B 195
323

It is, as I have said, the errors of the centuries that must be taken up, examined, corrected; this is my work, for which I am very particularly assigned by Governance.

But even if this were not so, just my fourteen years of consistent work as an author, that I always have something behind me to point to, makes anyone who does not insist on being stubborn have to admit that it is meaningless for me, beginning all over again on an entirely equal footing, to involve myself with every pastor etc. or with anyone who himself puts the slave-stamp on his article: anonymous.

What the triviality of the contemporary age wants, of course, is to pull me down into a kind of squabbling, whereby in the idea I actually would become ludicrous (because I would have involved myself with people who, from the point of view of the idea, simply do not exist) and (what mainly concerns me) botch up my cause, draw attention away from it.

No, I dare not become involved with such triviality. I must put up with the fact that all those who are so superior to me (the insignificant especially love to pose in the character of superiority) say whatever comes into their heads about me, also about my honesty, accuse me of dishonesty—and demonstrate it. [*changed from:* (suppressing the date of my article in which I say it) demonstrate] [*deleted:* it, for example, on the basis of my saying that the clergy have maintained silence[224]—although individual pastors (N.B. later) have nevertheless expressed themselves; and even if a single individual had expressed himself earlier, should one then not be able to understand that what I am talking about when I say that the clergy have maintained silence is that no official reply has come from the one, the only one, I have to do with? Or let them demonstrate my dishonesty from this, that at the same time as I speak about the clergy's having maintained silence, I do speak about the opposition made to me—quite as if pastors were the only human beings or daily newspapers, for example, did not

XI³
B 195
324

exist and have not been used against me as crudely and vulgarly and bestially as possible. And furthermore, if the clergy maintain silence in print, does it follow that they are otherwise silent, or would there be something dishonest in calling it opposition that is made against me when the churches are used against me, when everything is done on a huge scale to set chatter in motion against me?] [*In margin:* My dear reader, if it concerns you, then for your own sake you could wish to be informed that it is not as those honest people say—you will, by taking a little trouble, easily convince yourself about it—and you must not cause yourself any inconvenience for my sake; nor do I intend to cause myself any inconvenience for the sake of your comfort.]

As was stated, the cause I have the honor to serve bids me observe the strictest regimen with regard to not involving myself further in all such things, continually bearing in mind what the cause demands, that it is definite that I am a sacrifice, destined to be sacrificed (to which I gladly and gratefully consent) to a generation (see *This Must Be Said*), and reminding you, my dear reader, that I am of the kind of person who must require faith. If you are unable to receive such a strong impression of the rightness of my cause, such a strong impression that it is a matter of eternity, so that you use your will to guard yourself against entering into all the triviality that is said and demonstrated about me and my character—then you cannot follow me, and then it is best for you to let go of me, the sooner the better.—*Pap.* XI³ B 195 *n.d.*, 1855

XI³
B 148
235

To Have Religion

Regrettably, people ordinarily live only in the finite and for the finite.

XI³
B 148
236

It is precisely *religion* that should lift them up and out of this kind of life, which is unworthy of a being who is in kinship with the divine, should draw their minds up and away from this downward-turned living, which, also according to the pagan view, is suitable only for animals.

But it is readily apparent that this does not happen, that instead of letting themselves be lifted up by religion, people drag religion down into finitude and the finite, talk and think about it and possess it the way one talks and thinks about and possesses the finite.

With regard to everything finite it is quite right that if one cannot have the very best, one can make do with something less. For example, if one cannot afford to drink the finest Bordeaux wine, one can make do with a lesser wine, and so it goes with everything finite, although there is a limit even here: the wine that is served may be so bad that one may say: No, then it is better to drink water.

But religion has an inverse relation to the finite, simply because religion is to elevate people.

Either/Or holds true of religion: either prime quality or really none at all; either with all your heart, all your mind, and with all your strength[225] or really none at all.

But people do not relate themselves to religion this way; they treat it as if it were something finite, are well satisfied with having religion in blather and mediocrity.

But to have religion in this way is not merely not to have religion; no, it is the most dangerous and culpable kind—it is irreligion. If you look at it more closely, you will see that it really is contempt for religion. Religion insists on being an Either/Or for a person; to treat it as if it were like beer and food etc. is fundamentally to scorn it, which is quite different from decisively willing not to have religion.

The point is really to get this made clear to people. But this is a difficult thing in itself, and doubly difficult when 1000 state-authorized tradesmen and their families live on making people think that this ungodly mediocrity is—true Christianity.

This *ungodly* mediocrity. I have here added to mediocrity an adjective that one may think cannot be used, however disparagingly one may otherwise truthfully talk about mediocrity. Therefore the point is to drill it in that *religion* must brand mediocrity as the most culpable kind of ungodliness, the worst possible insult to religion, a far more serious offense than decisively rejecting religion.

XI³
B 148
237

Oh, what Christ judges of mediocrity! When the Apostle Peter, that intrepid man, when he, well-intentioned, wants to hold Christ back from being willing to be sacrificed (and compared with the mediocrity I am talking about, this cannot be called mediocrity), Christ replies: Get behind me, Satan! You are an offense to me.[226] He declares that he is an offense to him, and he calls him Satan, says that his idea is inspired by Satan!

In the world of mediocrity in which we live, it is assumed—and this is one of the ways used to safeguard mediocrity—that only crackpot boldness etc. should be deplored as offensive, as inspired by Satan, and that the middle way, however, is secure against any such charge. Christ and Christianity are of another mind: precisely mediocrity is the offense, the most dangerous kind of demon possession, furthest removed from the possibility of being cured. To have religion, especially the Christian religion, on the level of mediocrity is the most certain form of perdition and has protected itself best—how frightfully ironic—against the possibility of being saved.—*JP* IV 4494 (*Pap.* XI³ B 148) *n.d.*, 1855

Grundtvig, the Grundtvigians, One of Them

A Decision

By

Contents
  I. Is Grundtvig a Kind of Apostle; Is This the Truth?[227]
 II. The Grundtvigians.[228]
III. Pastor P. Chr. Kierkegaard, Lic. theol.,[229] My Brother.

                        —*Pap.* XI³ B 154 *n.d.*, 1855

Addition to Pap. XI³ B 154:

XI³
B 155
244

Pastor P. Chr. Kierkegaard, B. D., My Brother

_____

So now it is from the Convention [*Convent*][230] that the death-dealing blow will come. First it was Bishop Martensen, then Pastor Paludan-Müller, then Dean Victor Block, then Dr. Zeuthen. Now it is from the Convention, especially from the Grundtvigians, especially from Pastor K., B.D., my brother. And the enterprising party, as I see it and as I expected, is active, presumably together with the many others active against me, in order, before one gets to see the lectures, to utilize the time in spreading, orally or through the press, that this will be something extraordinary.

My opinion is—yet when I say it, it is no doubt a paradox, but ordinarily it is my opinion that one should not take off one's hat before one sees the man. According to what one up until now knows about convention-performances, there is no sound reason to expect anything extraordinary. With regard to convention-performances, I was so fortunate—my precious recollection!—as to be able to agree perfectly with the late Bishop Mynster. He, too, regarded these performances as small beer; and it is really with a certain satisfaction that a short time ago I quite by chance saw in a book something I had not known previously, that small beer is called *Convent Øl* [convent(ion) beer[231]]—if Bishop Mynster were living and did not already know this, it would have pleased him to learn of it.

XI³
B 155
245

Therefore, let us wait until we get to see what it is: I expect neither anything new nor anything instructive, but rather by reading it through to have to endure a reek of heartiness that I find unpleasant. Just as one speaks of not being able to come too close to a drunkard because of the reek of liquor on him, so for me it has always been somewhat unpleasant to approach what the Grundtvigians write, because it is likely to be enveloped in a reek of heartiness, and even among the Grundtvigians Pastor K., B.D., is certainly one of the strongest reekers.

Since, however, he has joined in, it no doubt will be best for me, for the sake of the cause, to prepare a little, to give a little orientation—more will presumably not be at all necessary.

The circumstance that Pastor K., B.D., is my brother will perhaps be used against me in such a way as if he were someone who in a sense quite different from anyone else is informed about me. This is not the case in the remotest sense. Concerning my whole inner religious life, concerning what I want etc., Pastor K., B.D., knows only what he like anyone else can know from my writings; otherwise he knows neither more nor less than anyone else who knows nothing.

Another way in which the circumstance that Pastor K., B.D., is my brother will perhaps be used against me—I shall likewise dissolve in its nothingness. Perhaps the following syllogism will be constructed: S. K. is wrong to such a degree that *even*—just imagine!—*even* his brother and (something I do not doubt will be added) such a brother, such a hearty and loving and hearty man as his brother, that *even* he has taken to speaking against him! Thus on the basis of the heartiness of this brother, Pastor K., B.D., and then on the basis of his having taken to speaking against me, it will be argued: to what a scandalous degree I must be wrong. If only we do not instead become involved here in something that a few others (because I prefer to have no opinion; *mir ist Alles ganz egal* [it is all the same to me]) would call scandalous in another sense.

XI³
B 155
246

For a number of years I have lived as an author in Denmark, certainly not on it but for it, under extremely thankless conditions, continually only making sacrifices, and rewarded with ingratitude. For the sake of the good cause, I have voluntarily exposed myself to raving against me by Goldschmidt and P. L. Møller at the head of the countless public of grinners[232] and have exposed myself to a more select envy that made use of it. Never a word about me is heard from the hearty brother. A few years ago at the Roskilde Convention he finally began to speak,[233] and how? Indeed, in such a way that it was almost like chicanery against me. Yes, he drew a parallel between Martensen and me and made Martensen out to be sobriety. So, I have made sacrifices, renounced earthly reward—and then it is the hearty brother who is so kind, in contrast to this, to represent Martensen, who in every way has profited, as: sobriety. Ah! I, the opposite of sobriety, am depicted as representing ecstasy, presumably a kind of lunacy, whereby the pastor came rather close to agreement with contemptibility's whole attack on me, which continually aims to represent my life as a kind of lunacy. And the majority, who have no idea of what ecstasy is, perhaps have never heard the word before, have no doubt restricted themselves to the following conclusion: it is the opposite of what Martensen is, and what Martensen is—is sobriety. Therefore, what S. K. is must be something like lunacy, but the brother has not had it in his heart to say it directly. The heartiness displayed was of such a singular kind that—since *mir ist Alles ganz egal*, it is entirely clear to me that I am sacrificed; so it makes no difference to me—that even the Grundtvigians' own paper could not agree with Pastor K., B.D., which, if one knows anything about the alliance of the Grundtvigians, is very significant.

XI³
B 155
247

Then came the moment when I attacked Martensen. From that time, on almost the greatest possible scale, rage was vented on me in this little country; everything was set in motion to label me as a villain, someone who disturbs the peace of the grave, or to make me literally into a kind of lunatic man, something that was continually repeated in the press. The hearty brother on that occasion has not had a word to say, which perhaps some (because I myself have neither expected nor wished anything) have expected from such great heartiness, because disagreement with the brother's cause is completely different from the brother's being treated in this way. Yet the hearty brother has not had a word to say. Then, however, he thinks that he has to speak against me. Well now. But he does not choose to do it one to one; no, he chooses: at the Convention to place himself at the head, to become the spokesman for the majority, and thereby in turn also to protect himself. —I assume that the argument from B. D. Pastor K.'s heartiness to—the degree to which I must be wrong—I assume that we can cross out this argument.

No, I am not so easily fooled; I am well aware that this whole fuss that is now being made with this brother is an intrigue. With the exception of the obtusely credulous Grundtvigians, there is scarcely anyone who truly thinks that what Pastor K., B. D., has to say would be able to do anything against me. No, but one reckons that the fact that it is the brother can be used successfully [*deleted:* fits the Danish small-mindedness and thereby could become a little more dangerous for me].

The opposition perhaps thinks that in this way it may be able to use successfully the circumstance that a brother steps forth against me to imbue me with an impression of a kind of life-weariness,[234] which could make me tired of the cause. The cause

I have the honor to serve is the greatest Denmark has ever had; it is the future of Christianity, and it must begin here. This cause, as is fitting, is served on my part in such a way with regard to zeal, exertion, diligence, and unselfishness that Denmark has no other cause that resembles it in this respect—and the only response I receive is that almost the entire daily press abuses me, calls me Søren. This is calculated to produce a life-weariness. But it certainly has not succeeded; if anything has been achieved, it has been only to make the people ludicrous as a nation. Perhaps the opposition thinks that by getting my brother to become spokesman against me I thereby would receive a new impression in the direction of a life-weariness and thus would become tired of the whole thing. A cause that pertains to the entire nation, a cause in which all the clergy are criminally involved, is suddenly supposed to transform itself, while everything else maintained silence, into a private squabble between two brothers, a welcome theme for chatter and gossip, really something for a market town and for a country that is on the way to becoming an out-and-out market town. This seems to be calculated to develop a life-weariness; we shall now see whether it will succeed.

Possibly the opposition also has other ideas in its great eagerness to bring in the brother. Possibly they think: S. K. has peculiarities; who knows, perhaps he does not like quarreling with a brother; so he keeps silent. In that case, the game is won. With the aid of the 1000 and 1000 tongues that are available, with the aid of the press, which is indeed seen as being entirely available for our service, we shall soon have it firmly fixed: the brother has completely annihilated him. This brother, the pastor—see, this is really a stroke of genius, this is thoroughness, this is profundity; the other is only drivel. And then Pastor K., who for a number of years has been sufficiently drilled in that kind of practice, perhaps comes forward, [*deleted:* raises his pastoral gown a trifle,] curtseys, and gives thanks "that the public is much too kind, has far too high an opinion of his little performance, which, moreover, he has not had time to prepare himself for; it was, after all, at the request of the chairman that he was speaking," to which the public then graciously replies to the curtseying pastor, "Once again a new, glorious quality in this excellent, glorious man, a beautiful, genuinely Christian modesty; what a difference from the brother with his conceited arrogance, who merely aspires to make the public look ridiculous."

So it might be if I kept completely silent. But if I express myself, the opposition may perhaps surmise that I for that reason will, as one says, go easy on the punches; thus it is indeed always good that Pastor K. has become the spokesman. If, however, I pay absolutely no heed but tell Pastor K. briefly and to the point [*deleted:* that basically he is a spineless fellow] that by joining this wretched but enterprising Grundtvigian company he actually has underhandedly obtained for himself, with the aid of minor performances and a party alliance, an importance that he does not have at all, whereas, if he had kept himself out of all this rubbish, in the genuine Kierkegaardian way alone with God, he could have attained great importance in Denmark—if I say this, and also that the way he has now taken, perhaps has indeed been lured into, could easily lead him to be completely demoralized—well, then the opposition thinks it would have won the game against me in another way; the shout will be raised, "Scandal, scandal, scandal"—because what the pastor did was glorious and hearty. But I am not at all afraid of creating scandal. The Christianity of the New Testament is simply sheer scandal; the word itself is the Greek σχάνδαλον [*skandalon*, stumbling block], which in the New Testament is continually used about Christianity, that it is: σχάνδαλον.—*Pap.* XI³ B 155 *n.d.*, 1855

XI³
B 155
249

A Little Extra.[235]

Everything is to be printed in the smallest possible brevier and without a new page for each number.

Contents

1. The Seriousness of Serious Men
2. Ditto Ditto
3. A Batch of Pastors (Convention)
4. That Pastors Want to Influence by Numbers!
   —*Pap.* XI³ B 163 *n.d.*, 1855

Addition to Pap. XI³ B 163:

The Seriousness of Serious Men

The pastors, they are indeed serious men.

Forget now for a moment—but also only for a moment—what I usually talk about, the infinitely more important matter, that, *Christianly*, pastors are perjurers, liars, that, *Christianly*, the only thing you have to do, if you in truth desire your eternal well-being, is to avoid any contact with "the pastor," except that you promptly pay him the money due him, and if you want to please me, pay him more richly than before, but otherwise avoid even the least contact with him, since everyone whom we call pastor is guilty, Christianly, of what the apostle speaks about in regard to Holy Communion, *not discerning* the Lord's body, whereby one eats judgment upon oneself;[236] not discerning, thus one has not consulted with one's conscience whether one is mediocrity and whether this is what one aims to become, by an oath—without discerning!—committing oneself on what is as different from mediocrity as good is from evil, white from black: on the New Testament of our Lord Jesus Christ.

As stated, forget this for a moment, but also only for a moment; then I will show you from another side what wretchedness it is with these pastors, how what occupies them is actually in a hypocritical way under the appearance of seriousness a waste of their time and a false ascription of a significance to themselves.

*   *

They get bored around the parsonages: they think it could be splendid once in a while to get together.

Well, why not; after all, it is an honorable thing.

But to go in a group, for example, out to Dyrehaugen, that they do not want to do; it is much too embarrassing if someone comes and asks for "the Pastor" and then of each one it is said: He is not at home; he has gone together with the other pastors to Dyrehaugen. Consequently it is much too embarrassing, and

neither is this going out to Dyrehaugen something of such importance that it can be announced several times in the newspaper far in advance.

No, "conventions," that is better! "The pastor is not at home; he is at the convention." Ah! "On such and such a day the brothers plan to have their summer meeting in Roskilde." Ah! The pastors, the pastors, they are active men; if they are obese, they are not that because of laziness [*changed from:* they are not idle]. You certainly have seen that they are now to be assembled in convention in Roskilde; it will be important for Church and state.

So there is traffic to the gathering. The farmer on the highway is astonished, "That was certainly a pastor who drove by, and now another pastor." "Yes, my good man, it is not for the sake of pleasure that the holy men are on the highway; there is a convention in Roskilde." Ah, it is to the convention!

And in Roskilde itself there is busyness and attention. The citizen looks with respect at the host of pastors; "They are gathered for the convention, a godly affair." Ah, it is for the convention.

It has been announced in the newspaper three times; so the whole country knows about this important matter, that "on such and such a day" (if it was not extraordinary earlier, it will become that!) "the convention is to be held in Roskilde, to which the brothers are invited."

The thrice-printed advertisement has already announced what "the brothers intend to discuss at this time [*deleted:* , matters of importance. It is not for the sake of pleasure that such serious men leave their parsonages and drive perhaps many miles; it is matters of importance], and the effect of this has been to set talk—about the important matters the convention intends to discuss this time—in motion in such a way that the pastors thereby become important. One gets the idea of them that they do not fill out their lives with vanities and tomfoolery, that it is not for the sake of pleasure that they leave the parsonages and drive perhaps many miles—it is indeed important matters they—intend to discuss.

Then there is this matter, for example, of Dr. S. Kierkegaard's conduct. By this conduct the pastors are placed in a certain predicament; the silence they are maintaining—"in contradistinction to the silence of a Brutus and of a William of Orange"—the so-called "Martensenian silence,"[237] becomes more and more dubious, even to the simplest common people, more and more embarrassing to the pastors themselves, who probably are also a little embarrassed because the "vestments" become more and more transparent, and thus for certain people the vestments are really distressing apparel.

But now the matter is something else. Three times it was announced that this time the conference intends to discuss Dr. S. K.'s polemical conduct.

And the circumstance that the announcement is read in every possible newspaper, since this time they are perhaps even more busy than usual to get it publicized, this circumstance has the effect that the talk about what the conference intends to discuss almost gives the impression that the holy serious men had already been assembled and had spoken.

Finally the meeting is held.

Then they drive home, these serious men. The farmer on the highway is astonished, "That certainly was a pastor who drove by, and now another pastor." "Yes, my good man, they are coming from the convention." Oh, from the convention!

Then talk starts going about what was discussed. "It was wonderful; you should have been there; it was extraordinary." The press is also utilized for that purpose; a leading article circulates around the country, is picked up in provincial newspapers. From there one learns that it will become dangerous for this Dr. S. K.

The convention discussions usually are printed—to gain importance again, yet in such a way that one can protect oneself against criticism by saying that, after all, it is only a talk at a conference.

This time, however, there is no hurry with the printing. Perhaps the idea is that one gets on best by living on the talk that what was said at the convention was excellent, profound, true, incisive; "everyone who was present says that."

Finally the addresses are printed.

XI³
B 164
272 *Dansk Kirketidende*[238] prints it; and *Evangelisk Ugeskrift*[239] receives that paper's permission—just think how important!—to have this infinitely important matter be reprinted.

Well, then, read it yourself, whoever you are, read it in *Kirke-*

tidenden or in *Ugeskriftet*, and it is true what Pernille says of the family she visited, where there was rushing around in the kitchen and basement, so she then expected at least a dozen courses of food on the table, and the whole thing ended with a lumpy flour pudding and some hard-boiled eggs![240] Except that at the convention there was even less; there were the table prayers before and after the meals, as if one was to receive something to eat and as if one had had something to eat: an address by Fenger, L.L.B.,[241] in which he says that he does not want to be involved in the matter, and it is only as chairman that he introduces it; and an address by a Pastor Andersen,[242] that now it has been said (namely, by Fenger) and that it is desirable that the matter not be discussed further. So learn to laugh at these pastors and to scorn this whole [*deleted:* miserable] company of windbags! Indeed, I do not deny that this wretchedness, which seeks falsely to ascribe importance to itself, yet compared with the fact that the pastor is a perjurer and liar, his existence the profanation of the holy, is something very unimportant. But it is still demoralizing for the country that the pastors are infected to the highest degree with the very sickness from which the entire age suffers, have it in a far more dangerous degree than others, because with them everything has the appearance of holiness and piety.—*Pap.* XI³ B 164 *n.d.*, 1855

From draft of Pap. XI³ B 166:

> *Deleted:* Quod erat demonstrandum
> *Changed to:* Ditto Ditto.
> > —*Pap.* XI³ B 167 September 17, 1855

Addition to Pap. XI³ B 163:

Ditto Ditto

How it in truth stands with the truth-witnesses, I have to such a degree elucidated and explained that for a long time this certainly has been regarded as established by those who *want* to see—I find it quite in order that the truth-witnesses themselves, for whom

XI³
B 166
274

the matter is a financial question, and their immediate families do not see it this way. But that demonstrates nothing, or it demonstrates what after all needs no demonstration, that the financial is a great power in society.

But when it turns out that the opposition itself undertakes to substantiate my position, I owe it to the matter not to let it go unused.

*   *

In *Evangelisk Ugeskrift* no.   there are the following lines[243]
[*blank space*]
[*In margin:* The lines by the highly esteemed clergyman are to be printed here; the Hiortian[244] lines are, of course, not to be printed.]

With the aid of the above, I shall now further rehearse the truth of what I say, that the truth-witnesses are anything but, are exactly the very opposite, some mediocre fellows who by having taken an oath on the New Testament and by pretending to be truth-witnesses have made themselves exactly the opposite: perjurers, instruments of untruth.

I will, however, first ask the reader for just a moment to pay close attention to what is understood by a truth-witness, that courage is above all required for that, that the courage the bravest warrior displays in battle, the most fearless sailor in peril at sea, is still only an image of the courage of the truth-witness. He does not need to be bound by an oath on the New Testament, nor to be ordained; but if he is that, it does not subtract but adds. Reminding himself of his sacred oath upon the New Testament, bearing in mind that, after all, he has received the assistance of a Holy Spirit, he at every moment is ready to sacrifice, to suffer, he shies away from no danger—no, danger is his element, whatever the danger may be, be it to lose life or to keep life, deprived of everything.

And now to the point.

"From a highly esteemed clergyman." Consequently it is a truth-witness we have before us, and he is—anonymous! To step forward courageously in this manner is just as meaningless as to go courageously into battle by—remaining at home—is mean-

XI³
B 166
275

ingless, is cowardly. And of all cowardliness anonymity is perhaps the most wretched, because, although he himself cowardly remains at home, he nevertheless manages to be able to attack others. A murder in which an air gun is used is generally judged to be cowardly simply because it does not give an alarm. Nevertheless the murdered person was indeed murdered, but we are less aggravated by it when a shot is heard than when in this act of cowardliness not the slightest is heard. We find it cowardly to use poison, and to the same degree more cowardly as a more slowly acting poison is used. We are less aggravated by it when the murder is open, violent, than when it conceals itself in this way, perhaps is completed only years after it was committed. But what is aimed at on a very small scale by the use of an air gun, just as on a greater scale by use of poison—to gain time to escape one's crime—may nevertheless not always succeed. Anonymous, however, you are safe. And this abomination, anonymity, is in my opinion and in that of Christianity the greatest calamity the human race has brought upon itself, because all salvation is related to personality, and Christianity is precisely the personal truth—this abomination, far more corrupt than venereal disease etc., this abomination against which precisely every truth-witness, since even the state guards against it, ought to witness with all one's might, and from which he above all ought to keep himself free, this abomination a truth-witness himself wants to commit, to be impersonal over against personality! So, then, it is a truth-witness who steps forward in such a way that he, despising himself, cowardly sets the slave-stamp of anonymity on what he has to say.

Further. But while this truth-witness by being anonymous in this way cowardly avoids all trouble, there is falsely ascribed to him the significance of having a name, a significant name. "Highly esteemed" is the appellation that is used. This appellation is connected with having a name, a significant name. To say of someone who is a nobody that he is highly esteemed is therefore meaningless, more ludicrous than if it had read: From a blonde, a medium tall, a baldheaded, a pockmarked clergyman, we have received. All such appellations, which by being said about someone who is a nobody certainly become ludicrous,

XI³
B 166
276

nevertheless are not exactly connected with having a name, but "highly esteemed," does this, and thus about someone who has no name the very appellation is used that is most connected with having a name. Consequently the truth-witness has double profit in this way: anonymously one cowardly avoids all trouble, and one "also" (the clergy's category!) has the advantage of even having a significant name. True, the effect is somewhat weakened; the whole scene takes on a vaudeville aspect because the one who introduces this truth-witness this way is theological graduate Hiorth, not to be confused with Professor Hiorth,[245] nor with another theological candidate Hiorth[246]—oddly enough, there are three Hiorths in literature. This is the editor, the one whom the theology professors for a period used to run literary errands, to run around town, until he left off being a good fellow and became, as they say, his own man, something that as far as he is concerned must always be understood figuratively. "A highly esteemed clergyman," that is absolutely certain; theological graduate Hiorth says it.

Further. What is it now that this truth-witness wants? He raises the question whether the best thing would not be to take legal action against me. But the matter is, after all, infinitely simple. When one is a truth-witness, one considers the matter by himself, with God and his conscience. If one then comes to the opinion that a case ought to be brought against me, one then applies to the Minister. It never occurs to the truth-witness to think about the minor danger that it may be turned down by the Minister, also that, if it became known in the city, it might not find favor there; thus one might even be laughed at a little.

XI³
B 166
277 Not so with our truth-witness. He is just like Zerline: I want and I do not want.[247] Let us get it said and then see whether it evokes a response in the city, whether perhaps several others express themselves similarly. If the numbers appear to be for it, well, then one proceeds with it; if it gets no response, well, I have nothing to do with it, I am nobody. What a wretch!

Further, and it is this that especially occupies me: he wants— the Minister must institute legal proceedings against me, consequently judicial power must be used. Splendid, to want to be a truth-witness, to have it entirely at his disposal to use the power of the spirit against me, to be 1000 truth-witnesses against one, literally one single human being—and then to want to have the authorities help defend oneself against—the power of the spirit! What nonsense!—*Pap.* XI³ B 166 *n.d.*, 1855

Continuation of Pap. XI³ B 166:

It is just like wanting to be regarded as a courageous man, and then in the evening, when it is dark, wanting to have someone accompany him because one does not dare to walk alone in the dark. A t.-w. [truth-witness] who has others to defend him! When at one time somewhere in Germany an attempt was made to use the civic guard to keep order on the streets, it turned out that they could not manage to defend themselves with guns. On that occasion a German humorist proposed that they be permitted also to carry canes in order to have something with which to defend themselves. It is ludicrous that a man who has a gun must have a cane to defend himself and the gun, but it would have been still more ludicrous if the proposal was to the effect that each individual civic guard had two from the regiment to defend him. Imagine an army like that, where with every single soldier there walked two other soldiers to defend him. And it is the same with a t.-w.'s wanting to have others to defend him.

With regard to a legal action against me, I am in every way entirely at your service. If it could interest the pastors to have me condemned, I am to the highest degree of willingness and compliance ready to submit to it. I willingly grant them that [*changed from:* It is the least one could grant them] as compensation for their being crushed.

The oddity is only that not until now does something come out about instituting legal proceedings against me. It will be recalled that it was I (in *This Must Be Said*) who began by addressing the Minister of Ecclesiastical Affairs and Education with the question of legal proceedings against me.[248] This again was well-intentioned toward the pastors. But I am more and more convinced that a Governance wants to pick a quarrel with these pastors; so I seek in vain to help them. I was well aware how it stood with the power of the pastors, and only my business occupies me essentially. Now, if at the time when I began and myself directed attention to it legal action had been instituted against me by the Minister, then of course the clergy would keep out of it; setting a great price on appearance, as the clergy do, they would even have it in their power to give the appearance that they did not completely approve the Minister's procedure, that in matters of the spirit only the power of the spirit ought to be used.

It did not happen. And now along comes—how pitiable!—the clergy themselves, and want to have the Minister's help. Think of that man who wants to be regarded as courageous, a hero, and then has to have someone accompany him in the evening. It has now become evening; he is about to walk home. But perhaps it fortunately turns out that there is another man who is going the same way. Then he can of course go along with him without needing to say anything; therefore it does not become evident how it stands with his courage. But imagine that there is no one who is going that way or that perhaps no others have come, so he is there alone—and now he, he, the courageous man, the hero, must ask his host if he does not have someone to accompany him home: how humiliating! The only thing lacking is that the host actually has no one to accompany him except—the servant girl, who accompanies the hero home.

Yes, Governance is against the pastors. If the Minister, at the time when I definitely set forth this question, did not decide to institute legal action against me, if the clergy, promptly, briskly, resolutely had nevertheless said, "It is the only thing there is to do"—it would surely have been better. The contemporary age is certainly not inclined to accept that point of view, the use of judicial power in matters of the spirit, but every age involuntarily responds to resoluteness, and the contemporaries certainly would have been impressed by the clergy if they had been resolute. Now, however, how pitiable! After having for a long time dabbled at using silence, at first feebly defying superiority, as such perhaps diminishing a bit, but continually using silence, they only now come and anonymously feel their way to see whether legal action could not be instituted. Only now, after these t.-w. have presumably made sure what good their silence has been to them, only now, when the whole thing actually has been decided, so a legal proceeding actually is altogether too late.

As stated, Governance wants to pick a quarrel with the pastors. What the clergy have gambled on is, as they say: silence. True enough, my duty is this, on my part to do what I am able to do so that it can become clear to people what this silence means. Now, if I am able even in this regard to do much, if only the clergy had maintained silence, there nevertheless will always be a great number, or more correctly, the majority will still be impressed by the silence of the clergy, if it is maintained. But then along comes Dr. Zeuthen and begins something that looks as if it would become something. He begins a polemical periodical against Dr. S., no. 1.[249] And then as ominously [*changed from:* unfortunately] as possible, he chooses for an epigraph: We are able to do nothing against the truth, but for the truth.[250] "We are able to do nothing!" It is certainly true that Dr. Z. is able to do nothing, either for or against truth; and Dr. Z. is, after all, supposed to be the champion of the established order. When I saw no. 2, I jotted down on a slip of paper [*changed from:* I said to myself]: My only wish is that he, if this periodical continues in the future, does not change the epigraph. I regard it as appropriate to have it continually drilled in and therefore placed on the title page: We are able to do nothing; then the rest of us can say as Frederik VI is supposed to have said to a man who, kneeling, received the ennobling accolade and recited the formula, "I am unworthy"—yes, we know it very well. It came to nothing more than no. 2. This must in all respects weaken the significance of the clergy's silence, insofar as it will make an impression.

XI³
B 168
281

And then finally comes the convention and they want to speak. The conduct of the convention on this occasion exposes t.-w. to such an extent that it now actually is unimportant whether they are silent or speak.

And then finally comes an anonymous "highly esteemed clergyman"[251] and feels his way to see whether or not the Minister could wish to institute legal proceedings.

No, the pastors, as they say, are away. "In agonies such as a human being has rarely experienced, in mental strain that probably in a week would drive another out of his mind, I am a

power" (see *This Must Be Said*[252])—and "the pastor" is in my
power. But what it means to be a power, a spiritual power—
what agony of all the torments but also what power—is completely forgotten; of this no one has an idea in these bestial times,
in which only the human numbers are the power. Therefore
they self-confidently boast of being so superior to me in numbers. But numbers = 0. If the 1,000 pastors get 10,000 for assistance from Germany, let me be sure of just one thing, that no
muddle-head takes it upon himself to want to help me—and I
am assured as a power. As spiritual power these thousands are
utterly impotent face-to-face with me, because I am a bearer of
the idea, in the service of the Almighty; and the only thing that
occupies me is in the moment before eternity to complete the
task especially assigned to me. If these thousands want to work as
animal power, well, then one soldier certainly is enough, for I
am, physically, very weak. If they want to work spiritually as
XI³
B 168
282 opposition against spirit, well now, they of course have it in their
power to embitter my life, to persecute me [*deleted:* if so be it, to
have me condemned], if so be it, to put me to death—but then
I have been just as completely victorious, am just as completely
a power, since the idea that I have the honor especially to serve
mows down the whole population as a nothing. Visualize what
it is to be a spiritual power. Think of death, that withered, dry
skeleton—and then think of the multifariousness of life, all this
fullness and power and burgeoning—it is indeed insane that he,
that withered, dry skeleton, whom one would think a puff of the
fullness of life would be able to blow away, would be able to
cope with all this. Think whether in consideration of this there
would be some who would help him! No, this power needs no
human help; and it is not a puff from the fullness of life that blows
him away but a puff from him who extinguishes the whole
multifariousness of life.

So it is with spiritual power. It is the one and only power. That
I can very well say. It is not my fault if now one or another
conceited pate runs around and wants to be a spiritual power and
perishes. I also say that of all torments the most dreadful is that
any person other than the one chosen and brought up for it—if
he would for merely one single moment endure such a torment,

or if he even would merely see in what torture-screws God the Almighty, yet out of love, holds such a person, because otherwise he would run away from him—will not need more in order to thank God, as for the greatest benefaction, that he is not a spiritual power.

But a spiritual power I am, and a spiritual power I was. And no doubt almost every pastor has been able to see that more or less clearly, and everyone ought to have been able to see that I am that. The guilt of the present age is, in wretched mediocrity, to want to take advantage of my being indeed the only one.

It makes no difference to me, since I am occupied with only one thing: in the moment before eternity to complete the task assigned especially to me. But I will be avenged. Yet it is not I who insist on it. On the contrary, it is Governance that wants it so. It will no longer tolerate that I am treated this way, something I for religious reasons have understood as my task, not only to submit to it, but in such a way that finally the whole contemporary age would fancy that it dealt extremely righteously and honestly with me. But now Governance will no longer tolerate it. Therefore when I, always good-natured as I essentially am, still continue to do it as well as it can be done under the circumstances, Governance thwarts my plan; it does not want leniency, it wants to have this mediocrity exposed for what it is.

Think of Bishop Mynster. For him there had been only one thing to do: to die repenting, to revoke his whole life, his whole proclamation of Christianity. That was my thought. It did not happen. Well, then let his deception remain a secret; let nothing further be said about him. Humanly speaking, it was a most unusual good fortune that it went on as long as he lived, but now let it not be touched upon anymore. In this way I had thought of myself as forming the transition. But Governance did not want it. Then comes Martensen in the pulpit and portrays him as a t.-w., one of the authentic t.-w., one of the holy chain, one who will shine as the stars in heaven. Frightful rigorousness! Now his fate is decided. Now his past will be taken up and under this lighting, and during every month I work it will become clearer that Mynster's whole proclamation was—an optical illusion—that he no doubt was great, but not Christianly great, no, esthetically

XI³
B 168
283

great as a forger. And this will then, as if to fasten it in remembrance, just about coincide with the raising of a monument to him—frightful rigorousness! True enough, it is a great rarity that things work out satisfactorily for a man throughout his whole life, as they did for Bishop Mynster; at times, however much I was devoted to him, it also seemed to me that it was strange that Governance tolerated it. But when I think of the retribution that came afterward, in which I reluctantly had to act—then I shudder!—*Pap.* XI^3 B 168 September 17, 1855

From draft of Pap. XI^3 B 169:

A Batch of Pastors

(Convention.)

[*changed from:* Minor Observations]

———————

August 19, '55.

[*Deleted:* A Batch of Pastors

(*changed from: Convention: the Pastors or: by the Dozen*)

(The Convention)

—————]

—*Pap.* XI^3 B 170 August 19, 1855

Addition to Pap. XI^3 B 163:

A Batch of Pastors

(Convention)

———————

In all possible relations this holds as an expression for and a mark of the entity that has significance: to amount to something as one. To be something, insignificance must make do with—numbers.

Rooted trees are sold individually, kindling by the score; one horse may be purchased, but one shrimp is out of the question; shrimp are sold by the quart, sometimes even (the strongest expression for how little worth their existence has) without any measure, by the batch.

Therefore how appropriate of the pastors (by analogy to shrimp, kindling wood, peat, etc.) that they try to acquire significance by means of numbers.

A batch of pastors, a convention—indeed, how insignificant, how meaningless each one is individually—a batch of them or a lot of them one would think might acquire significance.

Yet this is not so; and it is high time that this, that it is not so, be rehearsed.

In "the external world" it holds that *one can become something by means of numbers.* In "the spiritual world" *numbers subtract.*

What significance you have as one is, *spiritually*, your significance, or your significance *qua* spirit. If you have no significance as one, then in the world of spirit you have no significance, or you are not spirit at all.

To attempt spiritually to acquire significance by becoming a batch *subtracts*, because, just the opposite of spirit, it is *idiocy*; and to attempt to begin to influence *qua* spirit by means of idiocy— no, it cannot be done.—*Pap.* XI^3 B 169 *n.d.*, 1855

Addition to Pap. XI^3 B 163:

That Pastors Want to Influence by Numbers!

XI^3
B 171
285

That this, in view of each individual's insignificance, must be regarded as the most sagacious, also, seen in this way, is sensately the most sagacious, whereas spiritually it is idiocy—I have pointed out elsewhere [*Pap.* XI^3 B 169].

From a totally different side I shall now show that the pastors' wanting to influence by numbers must be regarded as so unsagacious that one would not believe it possible that it could occur to them.

A little country is burdened with a whole crew of pastors.

Does not sagacity admonish these to be sagacious enough to avoid, as far as possible, each other, so that no one, even at the mere sight of 3 pastors together, will begin to think what a damaging luxury it is that a country, to the destruction of all true Christianity, maintains a whole corrosive crew of pastors?

XI³
B 171
286

And so pastors want to influence by numbers, to impress by being many; that of which one is already too many wants to strengthen itself by making known how numerous it is—how unsagacious!—*Pap*. XI³ B 171 August 20, 1855

Deleted from final copy of The Changelessness of God*; see 267:5:*

If a person were permitted to distinguish among biblical texts, I could call this text [James 1:17–21] my first love, to which one usually (*always*) returns at some time; and I could call this text my only love—to which one returns again and again and again and always.—*JP* VI 6965 (*Pap*. XI³ B 291:4) August 1855

XI³
B 175
287

That Christianity has not entered into the world— which "Christendom" in its thieves' slang expresses in this way:
Christianity is perfectible; it progresses.

———————

Think of the beginning: *the apostle*—and it is high time and of great importance, especially in Protestantism, that a word be said about the apostle in order, if possible, to counteract the confusion that Luther has occasioned in his justifiable zeal against malpractice—and yet not justified—by turning the matter in such a way that it becomes the disciple who decides what Christianity is, not the master, not Christ but Paul, something that in the foolish jargon of Christendom has not been called a scaling down of Christianity—there would be some meaning in that—but, meaninglessly, has been called a forward step.

The *apostle* apparently has experienced something human. In his joy and enthusiasm over Christianity he wants to make Christians of as many as possible, the more the better, and therefore perhaps is a little flexible about what it means to be a Christian. Then, struggling with such high seas as Christianity did at the beginning, with the opposition of the whole world, the apostle perhaps has the human experience that he himself feels a need for the strengthening of the Christian cause by the greater number who become Christians—and therefore, as he inflexibly fights against the world, he is a little flexible about what it means to be a Christian.

Thus in a very short time—triumph, triumph, triumph!—perhaps 30 to 40,000 Christians.

With dialectical accuracy it may be said that now Christianity is actually lost. Not even an apostle can control 30 to 40,000. Here is the first germ of Christians-in-name, the ruin of all Christianity.

The result is inevitable. The human numbers of "Christians" get to be a kind of a power directly opposite to the apostle. He who does not fear the whole world, does not retreat a hair's breadth before the opposition of all paganism and Judaism, has created here a force that becomes dangerous to himself and to Christianity; indeed, he himself has agreed that these thousands are Christians.

Now it comes. It soon becomes obvious that these 30 to 40,000 Christians have not exactly intended to comply with Christianity's unconditional demand; it is not so easy to become a Christian as it is to assume the name of Christian, even if there is still mortal danger bound up with this name, but there are also the enthusiasm of risks and perils and an apostle's power to grip people in a mood—and yet they have been allowed to call themselves Christians.

Here it is. The apostle perhaps does not even have the courage of the idea to drop them summarily; in a way they are his own work—and now already here the human numbers exercise their power; already here God's will, his Word, and the prototype are no longer unconditionally decisive for what Christianity is, not for the apostle himself but for the apostle in relation to these human numbers of "Christians," but the human numbers exercise an influence.

Some examples. *The prototype* (who for him is always one) teaches and expresses the single state. If millions x trillions, like

XI³
B 175
289 [Gert] Bundtmager in *The Political Tinker,*[253] "could not take it"
and so do not want to be Christians, he does not alter a jot; for
him millions x trillions do not exist at all, something the society
of the lost, the public, the very honorable cultured public, naturally never gets into its statistics-filled head. The *apostle*, however, who does not retreat before all paganism and Judaism, is
confronted by a power, produced by him, that becomes dangerous to him: 30 to 40,000 "Christians"—who are unable, at least
some of them, to commit themselves to obey unconditionally.
And yet they are, after all, Christians! Here it is. They have been
allowed to call themselves Christians, there has been joy over the
mounting numbers, and now comes the bill for the joy, now the
numbers exercise their power. The apostle cannot make up his
mind to drop them. Thus we already have here the sophistry that
the human numbers of "Christians" presumably do not decide
but do indeed have some influence on what Christianity is, the
sophistry of turning the matter in such a way that if someone who
has obtained permission to assume the name of Christian later
proves not to will entirely as Christianity wills, he still has permission to call himself a Christian, and the dubious character of
the thing comes to light; you see that there are many among the
Christians who are not willing to agree to this or that and who
still are Christians—ergo, it cannot be Christianity. The true relation is: if he will not accept it, then he is not a Christian.

   But the human numbers of "Christians" exercise their power
over the apostle; he gives in: after all, "it is better to marry than
to burn."[254] It is better, because to burn is something unpleasant;
so it is better to marry, in a pinch it is better to marry. It is like the
craving to eat strawberries during a cholera epidemic, to which
the physician may say, "It is not good to eat strawberries." "Yes,
but we would like to. Please, may we not eat strawberries."
"Well, in a pinch eat them, but eat them without cream; it would
XI³
B 175
290 be best not to eat strawberries, but in a pinch it is better to eat
them without cream than with." This is not Christ's proclamation of Christianity. His unconditional proclamation (as in Matthew 5:28, "Everyone who looks at a woman lustfully has already committed adultery with her in his heart") does not really

concede in the remotest way a consultative voice to the immediacy of human nature, does not really change a jot for its sake; on the contrary it is precisely this that he, rescuing (so that human beings may become spirit), wants to slay; he does not tolerate a syllable of hairsplitting such as this: I cannot restrain my lust; ergo, satisfying it in this humanly, most inoffensive manner gets to be Christianity. No, this hairsplitting, containing the seeds of the downfall of Christianity, to him this hairsplitting is scandalous, the impulse of Satan, just as Peter's friendly advice to spare himself and the others was to him scandalous, the impulse of Satan. The apostle's proclamation, however, made a concession to the human numbers. The consequences will appear in the course of centuries, when, in consideration of the millions of Christians who find it most agreeable to marry, the result at last will be that true Christianity, the only thing pleasing to God, is to get married, the more often the better. In time Christianity will have won a total victory: Christians will be produced by the millions, the consumption of clergymen will be enormous, we will have Christian kingdoms, countries, Christian houses of prostitution—in short, all will be Christian, a Christian world, and velvet-clad pork-bearers or, as I was about to say, cross-bearers, to steer Christ's Church as oath-sworn teachers in Christendom.

Another example. "Use a little wine for the sake of your stomach," Paul writes to Timothy (I Timothy 5:23). [*Deleted:* Strictly speaking,] This is not Christ's proclamation of Christianity, comes out of another view of life, does not have the passion of the master's proclamation, is not "Hate yourself; if your right hand tempts you, cut it off" etc. No one, unless he deliberately wants to, can misunderstand me, as if I did not show the apostle the honor due him, something no one does more willingly or promptly than I. No, but the observation is true. To me it is as if I were to imagine a person who, with scarcely a piece of dry bread in his house, sat at the table in a prosperous middle-class home where dinner was being served—and then if the hostess, who once had dined at the royal court, said to him, "Isn't this just like the food and drink at the royal table?" and then he

XI^3
B 175
291

answered, "The food is excellent, and for someone who himself scarcely has a piece of dry bread in the house, it is, of course, a royal banquet, but it is not the same as the food and drink served at the royal court." So it is with my observation (which is so extremely necessary, particularly in Protestantism, because all Christendom's knavish tricks are connected with a continued effort, in the name of progress, in the direction of getting rid of the master and taking one's stand with the follower, and then taking advantage of the apostle—who personally did not scale down but gave in a little—to throw Christianity away completely while perfecting it, to turn it upside down, to get it to be just the opposite of what it is in the Christian proclamation)— my observation that the apostle's proclamation in the cited examples does not have the passion of the unconditional as the master's did.

But examples, incidentally, are not necessary, for nothing is easier to see than that when one hastily gets perhaps 30 to 40,000 "Christians," the human numbers are already so overwhelming that, if one does not immediately resolve to drop almost the whole number again, the result will be that these thousands become a force that restamps Christianity [*deleted:* because the apostle, the teacher, who has plenty of courage over against paganism and Judaism, does not have the courage]. What Christianity is the Christians must surely know; but now it is not maintained rigorously enough to prevent Christians-in-name from slipping in; thus eventually (thanks to the perseverance of the enterprising oath-bound ones!) in the course of centuries the Christians-in-name, the battalions of them, the prodigious human numbers, will decide what Christianity is, and what they call Christianity will be declared to be true Christianity—otherwise the preacher-band (*ad modum* the gypsy-band) will not be able to live by the thousands with families.

XI³
B 175
292   What helped Christianity at first was the enormous opposition from without, having to fight in a life-and-death struggle with a whole world. This, however, also contributed at the outset to giving Christianity a wrong stance by diverting attention from the fact that Christianity intrinsically is a religion of suffering, and it came to seem almost as if it were only the world's opposition

that caused the sufferings, and in this way Christianity came to struggle almost like a political power, which in the course of centuries recurs and becomes the triumphant policy.

*   *

Only when a person immovably holds firm that earnestness is that *he* becomes a Christian, that this is a task for his whole life, that all his activity in relation to others' becoming Christians is only part of his own becoming a Christian—only then can a person relate himself to the unconditional. As soon as he thinks of it in this way: Now I am a Christian and my task is to make Christians of others—Christianity is lost. He insists it is unavoidable, he gets busy, and with human gladness he will rejoice over the thought of having won—think of it!—thousands for Christianity. Here it is again! To catch people for Christianity is not like catching birds or fish—if you have caught them, the matter is finished. But beware of these thousands! If you have allowed them to call themselves Christians, perhaps rejoicing over the thought of their great number, you will see that it becomes the ruination of Christianity. Probably you yourself do not have the courage to drop them when the implications of their being Christians become clear. Then they will take the power away from both you and Christianity and will restamp Christianity.

—*JP* III 3213 (*Pap.* XI³ B 175) August 23, 1855

The Criminal Mediocrity

In one sense, particularly from a Christian point of view, all mediocrity is a crime.

Unfortunately, at the same time it is quite in order and very natural that the majority—mediocrely equipped by nature and not helped by education to anything higher—advance only to mediocrity. Who could think of wanting to pass judgment—that is, if this mediocrity is not inveigled by journalists and agitators, as is the case in our day, into wanting to play the judge of what truth is etc.

Consequently, as stated, this mediocrity cannot be called criminal.

XI³
B 177
294

XI³
B 177
295

No, it is an entirely different kind. There are always individuals (more or fewer, according to the higher or lower criterion) who by nature and by all other conditions are so placed (situated) that they are able to work for something higher. But, sagacious as they are, they soon perceive that greater and greater strenuousness results only in making them conflict (collide) more and more frequently with all the mediocrity, whose selfishness is not served by the introduction of something higher; on the other hand they see that by indolence and minor performances they very easily manage to become admired, loved, esteemed, and rewarded in every way by all the mediocrity, which is the great power in society.

Then these villains commit against the higher the treason of proclaiming mediocrity, in order to become themselves the top in mediocrity's class, instead of being on the receiving end of all mediocrity's racket and opposition and hatred by truly serving something higher.

Oh, it is so villainous! And also so utterly corrupting for the whole; simply because such a traitor to the higher had it in his power to be able to serve the higher, has elements for it (although it certainly is evident that he lacks what is essential: the will), for this very reason his treachery against the higher once more reinforces mediocrity, which boasts that he belongs to their company.

XI³
B 177
296 Within the category "criminal mediocrity," there is in turn a difference of degree, and the culmination point is what is called a Prince of the Church. From the Christian point of view, such a fellow is to the highest degree a qualified criminal. It is not customary to regard him this way, and the majority naturally find it almost deranged to talk this way. This is especially the case with us in our limited context; we do not even have the analogy from civic life that is well-known on the continent: that the very distinguished, decorated Lord Baron, who lives in a splendid palace, surrounded by gallooned servants, turns out to be, when the police come, a runaway galley slave, and thus for a moment it looks as if the detective were a madman, something the gracious Lord Baron, if he is brash and resourceful, perhaps will try to make him out to be. And so it is, *Christianly*, with these princes

of the Church, the vanguard of criminal mediocrity, who, falsifying, give religion a wrong turn; instead of their becoming themselves suffering imitators of a suffering Christ in the New Testament sense, they sell cheap what it means to be a Christian, and
then all this mediocrity fancies itself to be Christian. Then they
utilize the battalions of mediocrity to elevate themselves as the
extraordinary, who are directly admired, praised, and rewarded,
whereas the extraordinary (who, however, is solely the ordinary
or regular) from the Christian point of view is the opposite,
known by: suffering. And then that such a velveted His Grace,
starred, elevated to princely rank, exuding refinement and sanctity, turns out, when the police come, to be in the Christian sense
a galley slave or something much, much worse and more revolting—what wonder, then, that the majority regard the detective
as a deranged man, whereas his detective's eye is recognized
particularly by his ability to see that such a person is a most con-
summate criminal precisely because he, disguised in a fabric of
lies and hypocrisy, is regarded by the majority as being holiness
personified.

Consequently this is the pinnacle of criminal mediocrity. But
with differences in degree it is present wherever a person,
shrewdly or in fear of people, prefers (perhaps even covering up   XI³
his crime against God, the idea, the higher, by calling it love of   B 177
humanity) prefers, in order to have profit (people's money or   297
their friendship, their regard) to scale down the more true, instead of coming to suffer at the hands of people by being loyal to
the more true, to the higher.

Just as there is an eternal enmity between fire and water, between mouse and cat, so is there an eternal enmity between the
idea, the higher, and mediocrity. But it must be said to the
excuse of the battalions of mediocrity that they do not know
what they are doing. It is different with the traitors, the criminal
mediocrity.

How aggravated this crime is can be seen also in the fact that
it actually cannot be punished in this world. He wins people (the
number depends on the degree of the crime) to himself precisely
by betraying the highest, the idea. The battalions of mediocrity
cannot understand it in any other way than that precisely he is the

great one; they have no intimation that the truly great look the very opposite. But eternity is all the better informed about this fellow's true situation.—*JP* III 2686 (*Pap.* XI³ B 177) August 24, 1855

Kierkegaard's last journal entry; see 316–17:

XI²
A 439
439

The Christian Understanding of
the Destiny of This Life[255]

September 25, '55

The destiny of this life is that it be brought to the extremity of life-weariness.[256]

The person who when brought to that point can maintain or the person whom God helps so he is able to maintain that it is God who out of love has brought him to that point—such a person, from the Christian point of view, passes the examination of life and is matured for eternity.

I came into existence through a crime; I came into existence against God's will. The guilt, which in one sense is not mine even though it makes me an offender in God's eyes, is to give life. The punishment corresponds to the guilt: to be deprived of all zest for life, to be led into the most extreme life-weariness. The human being wants to dabble in the Creator's activity, if not by creating human beings, at least by giving life. "You certainly must pay for this, because the destiny of this life is, yet by my grace, for it is only to those who are saved that I show this grace, to lead you to the extremity of life-weariness."

Most people these days are so devoid of spirit and bereft of grace that the punishment cannot be used for them at all. Completely wrapped up in this life, they clutch at this life of nothingness and become nothing, their lives a waste.

The persons in whom there still is some spirit and whom grace still does not disregard are led on to that point where life reaches the extremity of life-weariness. But they cannot reconcile themselves to it; they rebel against God, and so on.

Only those persons who, brought to this point of life-weariness, are able by the help of grace to maintain that it is out of love that God does it and do not conceal in their souls, in the remotest corner, any doubt that God is love—only those persons are matured for eternity.

XI²
A 439
440

God also accepts them into eternity. But what, specifically, does God want? He wants souls who are able to praise, adore, worship, and thank him—the business of angels. Therefore God is surrounded by angels. The sort of beings found in legions in "Christendom," who for 10 rix-dollars are able to shout and trumpet to God's honor and praise, this sort of being does not please him. No, the angels please him, and what pleases him even more than the praise of angels is a human being who in the last lap of this life, when God seemingly changes into sheer cruelty and with the most cruelly devised cruelty does everything to deprive him of all zest for life, nevertheless continues to believe that God is love, that it is out of love that God does it. Such a human being then becomes an angel. In heaven it is easy to praise God, but the period of learning, the time of schooling, is always the most strenuous. Like a person who got the idea of traveling around the whole world in order to hear a male or female singer with a perfect tone, God sits in heaven and listens. And every time he hears praise from a person whom he has brought to the extremity of life-weariness, God says to himself: This is the tone. He says it as if he were making a discovery, but of course he was prepared, for he himself was present with the person and helped him insofar as God can give help for what only freedom can do. Only freedom can do it, but the surprising thing is to be able to express oneself by thanking God for it, as if it were God who did it. And in his joy over being able to do this, he is so happy that he will hear absolutely nothing about his having done it, but he gratefully attributes all to God and prays God that it may stay that way, that it is God who does it, for he has no faith in himself, but he does have faith in God.—*JP* VI 6969 (*Pap.* XI² A 439) September 25, 1855

EDITORIAL APPENDIX

ACKNOWLEDGMENTS

Preparation of manuscripts for *Kierkegaard's Writings* is supported by a genuinely enabling grant from the National Endowment for the Humanities. The grant includes gifts from the Danish Ministry of Cultural Affairs, the General Mills Foundation, Gilmore and Charlotte Schjeldahl, and the Vellux Foundation.

The translators-editors are indebted to Grethe Kjær and Julia Watkin for their knowledgeable observations on crucial concepts and terminology.

Per Lønning, Wim R. Scholtens, and Sophia Scopetéa, members of the International Advisory Board for *Kierkegaard's Writings*, have given valuable criticism of the manuscript on the whole and in detail. Nathaniel Hong and Regine Prenzel-Guthrie, associate editors of *KW*, scrutinized the manuscript and Nathaniel Hong prepared the index.

Acknowledgment is made to Gyldendals Forlag for permission to use the text and to absorb notes in *Søren Kierkegaards samlede Værker* and *Søren Kierkegaards Papirer*.

Inclusion in the Supplement of entries from *Søren Kierkegaard's Journals and Papers* is by arrangement with Indiana University Press.

The book collection and the microfilm collection of the Kierkegaard Library, St. Olaf College, have been used in preparation of the text, notes, Supplement, and Editorial Appendix. Gregor Malantschuk's marked set of *Kierkegaards samlede Værker* has been used in the preparation of the text and notes.

Word processing of the manuscript and electronic preparation of the manuscript were done by Francesca Lane Rasmus and Nathaniel Hong. Gretchen Oberfranc was the compositor. The volume has been guided through the press by Marta Nussbaum Steele.

COLLATION OF *FÆDRELANDET* [NEWSPAPER] ARTICLES AND *THIS MUST BE SAID; SO LET IT BE SAID* IN THE DANISH EDITIONS OF KIERKEGAARD'S COLLECTED WORKS

Vol. XIV Ed. 1 Pg.	*Vol. XIV* Ed. 2 Pg.	*Vol. 19* Ed. 3 Pg.	*Vol. XIV* Ed. 1 Pg.	*Vol. XIV* Ed. 2 Pg.	*Vol. 19* Ed. 3 Pg.
5	11	9	40	43	37
6	11	9	41	44	39
7	12	10	42	45	39
8	13	11	43	46	40
9	15	12	44	47	41
10	16	13	45	48	43
15	17	15	46	48	43
16	18	16	47	50	45
17	18	16	48	50	45
18	20	17	49	51	46
19	21	18	50	53	47
20	22	19	51	54	48
21	23	20	52	55	49
22	25	22	53	55	49
23	25	22	54	57	50
24	26	23	55	58	51
25	27	24	56	59	53
26	28	25	57	59	53
27	28	25	58	60	54
28	30	26	59	60	54
29	31	27	60	61	55
30	32	28	61	63	57
31	34	30	62	63	57
32	34	30	66	65	59
33	36	31	67	65	59
34	37	32	68	67	60
35	38	32	69	68	61
36	39	34	70	69	63
37	40	34	71	69	63
38	41	35	72	71	64
39	42	37	73	72	65

Vol. XIV Ed. 1 Pg.	Vol. XIV Ed. 2 Pg.	Vol. 19 Ed. 3 Pg.	Vol. XIV Ed. 1 Pg.	Vol. XIV Ed. 2 Pg.	Vol. 19 Ed. 3 Pg.
74	73	67	90	89	80
75	73	67	91	90	81
76	75	69	92	91	82
77	75	69	93	92	83
78	76	70	94	92	83
79	77	70	95	93	84
80	78	72	96	94	85
81	79	72	97	95	85
84	82	76	98	96	86
85	83	77	99	97	87
86	84	77	100	98	88
89	89	79			

COLLATION OF *THE MOMENT, WHAT CHRIST JUDGES OF OFFICIAL CHRISTIANITY,* AND *THE CHANGELESSNESS OF GOD* IN THE DANISH EDITIONS OF KIERKEGAARD'S COLLECTED WORKS

Vol. XIV *Ed. 1* *Pg.*	*Vol. XIV* *Ed. 2* *Pg.*	*Vol. 19* *Ed. 3* *Pg.*	*Vol. XIV* *Ed. 1* *Pg.*	*Vol. XIV* *Ed. 2* *Pg.*	*Vol. 19* *Ed. 3* *Pg.*
105	103	91	135	137	123
106	103	91	136	138	123
107	105	93	137	139	125
108	106	93	138	140	125
109	107	95	141	143	129
110	108	95	142	144	129
111	109	96	143	145	130
112	110	97	144	146	131
113	111	99	145	147	132
114	112	99	146	148	133
115	115	101	147	149	134
116	115	101	148	150	135
117	119	105	149	151	136
118	120	105	153	155	139
119	121	107	154	156	139
120	122	107	155	157	140
121	123	109	156	158	140
122	124	109	157	159	143
123	125	110	158	160	143
124	126	112	159	161	145
125	126	112	160	162	145
126	128	113	161	163	147
127	129	115	162	163	147
128	130	115	163	165	148
129	131	117	164	166	149
130	131	117	165	167	149
131	133	119	169	171	153
132	133	119	170	171	153
133	135	121	171	172	154
134	136	121	172	174	156

Vol. XIV *Ed. 1* *Pg.*	*Vol. XIV* *Ed. 2* *Pg.*	*Vol. 19* *Ed. 3* *Pg.*	*Vol. XIV* *Ed. 1* *Pg.*	*Vol. XIV* *Ed. 2* *Pg.*	*Vol. 19* *Ed. 3* *Pg.*
173	174	156	220	226	197
174	176	158	221	227	197
175	177	158	222	228	198
176	178	159	223	229	199
177	179	161	224	230	200
178	180	161	225	232	202
179	181	162	226	233	202
180	182	163	227	234	203
181	182	163	228	236	205
182	184	164	229	237	205
183	185	164	230	238	206
184	186	165	231	239	207
185	188	167	232	240	207
186	188	167	233	241	208
189	193	171	234	242	209
190	194	171	235	243	211
191	195	172	236	244	211
192	196	173	239	247	215
193	197	173	240	248	215
194	198	174	241	249	216
195	200	176	242	250	217
196	200	176	243	251	217
197	201	177	244	252	219
198	203	178	245	253	219
199	204	178	246	254	220
200	205	180	247	255	221
201	205	180	248	256	223
202	207	181	249	256	223
203	208	182	250	257	224
204	208	182	251	259	225
205	210	183	252	260	227
206	211	184	253	260	227
207	211	184	254	262	228
208	213	186	255	263	229
209	214	186	256	264	230
210	215	187	257	266	232
211	216	188	258	267	232
212	217	188	259	268	233
213	218	189	260	269	234
214	219	190	261	270	235
217	223	195	262	271	236
218	223	195	263	272	237
219	224	196	264	274	239

| *Vol. XIV* | *Vol. XIV* | *Vol. 19* | *Vol. XIV* | *Vol. XIV* | *Vol. 19* |
| *Ed. 1* | *Ed. 2* | *Ed. 3* | *Ed. 1* | *Ed. 2* | *Ed. 3* |
Pg.	*Pg.*	*Pg.*	*Pg.*	*Pg.*	*Pg.*
265	275	239	315	328	285
266	276	240	316	329	285
267	278	242	317	330	286
268	279	242	318	331	288
269	280	243	319	332	288
270	281	244	323	337	293
271	282	245	324	337	293
272	283	246	325	339	294
273	284	247	326	340	296
274	285	247	327	341	296
275	286	248	328	342	298
281	291	253	329	343	298
283	293	255	330	344	299
284	294	255	331	345	299
285	295	256	332	346	300
286	296	257	333	347	302
287	297	258	334	348	302
288	298	259	335	349	303
289	299	260	336	351	305
290	301	261	337	352	305
291	302	262	343	357	311
292	303	264	344	357	311
293	304	265	345	359	312
294	305	266	346	360	313
297	309	269	347	361	314
298	310	269	348	362	315
299	311	270	349	363	316
300	312	271	350	364	317
301	313	272	351	365	318
302	314	273	352	366	319
303	316	275	353	367	320
304	317	275	354	368	321
305	318	276	355	369	322
306	319	278	356	371	323
307	319	278	357	372	324
308	321	279	358	373	325
309	322	280	359	374	325
310	323	280	360	375	326
311	324	281	361	376	327
312	325	283	362	377	328
313	326	283	363	378	329
314	327	284	364	379	330

NOTES

FÆDRELANDET [NEWSPAPER] ARTICLES AND *THIS MUST
BE SAID; SO LET IT BE SAID*

1. Bishop Jakob Peter Mynster died January 30, 1854. With reference to the following article, see Supplement, pp. 434–36, 469–70, 473–75, 481–85, 491–96, 505–09, 510–14 (XI¹ A 1; XI² A 312, XI³ B 53, 201, 202, 82, 99, 109).

2. *Fædrelandet*, 295, December 18, 1854. See Supplement, pp. 535–41 (*Pap.* XI³ B 120; XI² A 413).

3. The memorial service for Bishop Mynster was on February 5, 1854. Hans Lassen Martensen's sermon text was Hebrews 13:7–8. Bishop Mynster was buried February 7.

4. "*Prædiken, holdt i Christiansborg Slotskirke paa 5te Søndag efter Hellig Tre Konger, Søndagen før Biskop Dr.* Mynsters *Jordefærd*" (Copenhagen: 1854).The parenthetical page references are to that printed version of Martensen's memorial sermon. See pp. 359–60 for excerpts.

5. Kierkegaard had been devoted all his life to Mynster, but in later years became disappointed in him. See, for example, Supplement, pp. 434–36, 469–70, 473–75 (*Pap.* XI¹ A 1; XI² A 312; XI³ B 53).

6. See, for example, Romans 6:2; Colossians 2:20, 3:3.

7. An expression Bishop Mynster frequently used for the Sunday church services.

8. On this important theme of confession [*Tilstaaelse*] or admission [*Indrømmelse*], see Historical Introduction, p. xxiii and note 53.

9. Since 1818 the *Berlingske Tidende* was the official state newspaper.

10. Since 1845 Martensen was the royal court chaplain.

11. The Copenhagen clergy raised funds for a monument to Bishop Mynster.

12. See I Corinthians 4:9.

13. See I Corinthians 4:13.

14. On April 15, 1854, Martensen was appointed Bishop of Sjælland.

15. Henrik Nicolai Clausen (1793–1877) was also a candidate but was rejected by the government ministry on political grounds. The National-Liberal party, which supported Clausen's candidacy, was critical of Martensen. See, for example, *Dagbladet*, 90, April 19, 1854. Among the criticisms of Martensen was his approval of the retention of German as the language in the churches in Slesvig.

16. For Bishop Martensen's reply to Kierkegaard's article, see Supplement, pp. 360–66.

17. *Fædrelandet*, 304, December 30, 1854.

18. With reference to the following footnote, see Supplement, pp. 491–96 (*Pap.* XI³ B 82).

19. See Supplement, pp. 360–66.

20. See Martensen, *Dogmatiske Oplysninger* (Copenhagen: 1850; *ASKB* 654), p. 13 (ed. tr.): ". . . my acquaintance with this prolix literature is, as stated, only very meager and fragmentary . . .."

21. The source has not been located.

22. A Danish social club founded in 1783. See *Postscript,* p. 248, *KW* XII.1 (*SV* VII 209).

23. Anders Sandøe Ørsted (1778–1860), foremost Danish jurist and in 1853–54 minister of Church affairs and education.

24. Johan Ludvig Heiberg (1791–1860), leading Danish literary critic and dramatist and at the time director of the Royal Theater.

25. Johan Nicolai Madvig (1804–1886), foremost Danish and internationally recognized classical scholar.

26. Olaf Bang (1788–1877), professor of medicine and most prominent Danish physician.

27. Nicolai Peter Nielsen (1795–1860), actor for a generation at the Royal Theater.

28. Christen Niemann Rosenkilde (1786–1861), famous comic actor at the Royal Theater.

29. Ludvig Phister (1807–1896), renowned comic actor at the Royal Theater. See Addendum, *Christian Discourses,* pp. 327–44, *KW* XVII (*Pap.* IX B 68).

30. Chloroform was first used as an anesthetic in 1848 by Sir James Simpson.

31. See Supplement, p. 497 (*Pap.* XI³ B 83).

32. See *Kjøbenhavnsposten,* 300, December 24, 1854, in which Kierkegaard is declared insane. See Supplement, pp. 518–19 (*Pap.* XI² A 411).

33. See J. L. in *Flyveposten,* 301, December 27, 1854.

34. See Anon., "*Søren Kierkegaard,*" *Kjøbenhavnsposten,* 299, December 23, 1854. See also A., "*Hvorledes Pieteten kan byde Taushed,*" *Dagbladet,* 299, December 21, 1854.

35. See Supplement, pp. 408–10 (*Pap.* X³ A 563).

36. See, for example, B, "*Endnu et Ord om Dr. S. Kierkegaards Angreb paa Mynster,*" *Dagbladet,* 300, December 22, 1854.

37. See *Self-Examination,* p. 21, *KW* XXI (*SV* XII 311).

38. *Fædrelandet,* 10, January 12, 1855. Jens Paludan-Müller, "*Søren Kierkegaards Angreb paa Biskop Mynsters Eftermæle*" (Copenhagen: 1855; *ASKB* 2190), p. 7: "I challenge Dr. S. Kierkegaard, with the New Testament alongside, to establish his above-mentioned allegation in any way worth discussing; I shall then take it upon myself to show that the allegation is altogether without warrant."

39. *Berlingske Tidende,* 7, January 9, 1855.

40. See Mozart, *Figaros Givtermaal eller Den gale Dag,* tr. Niels Thoroup Bruun (Copenhagen: 1817), II, 11, pp. 80–83; *Le Nozze di Figaro* (*The Marriage of Figaro*), tr. Ruth and Thomas Martin (New York: Schirmer, 1951), pp. 271–77.

41. See p. 10.

42. W. Hjort in the *Berlingske Tidende*, 5, January 6, 1855: "In the strictest sense of the word, Mynster is not a preacher of repentance; he is more a messenger of peace."

43. See Luke 12:51.

44. See Cicero, *De natura deorum*, I, 20, 52; *M. Tullii Ciceronis opera omnia*, I-IV and index, ed. Johann August Ernesti (Halle: 1756–57; *ASKB* 1224–29), IV, p. 485: "*nisi quietum autem, nihil beatum est*"; *Cicero, De natura deorum, Academica*, tr. H. Rackham (Loeb, Cambridge: Harvard University Press, 1979), pp. 52–53: "but repose is an essential condition of happiness."

45. See Supplement, pp. 517–18 (*Pap.* XI³ B 216:8).

46. See, for example, *JP* VI 6636 (*Pap.* X⁶ B 137).

47. *Fædrelandet*, 24, January 29, 1855. With reference to the following article, see Supplement, pp. 472–73 (*Pap.* XI³ B 49).

48. See Matthew 10:7–10.

49. See *Practice*, p. 7, *KW* XX (*SV* XII xv).

50. Matthew 19:21; John 18:36.

51. See II Corinthians 11:23–27.

52. See, for example, Matthew 24:9.

53. See, for example, Rasmus Nielsen, "*En god Gjerning*," *Fædrelandet*, 8, January 10, 1855: "A matter that unfortunately has aroused such great indignation."

54. See p. 12.

55. *Fædrelandet*, 24, January 29, 1855 (feuilleton).

56. See p. 361.

57. The consecration of Martensen as bishop was celebrated in Vor Frue Church on Second Christmas Day, December 26, 1854. In his address ("*Bispeveielse i Frue Kirke paa anden Juledag, 26de December 1854*" [Copenhagen: 1855]) on the text Acts 1:8, "But you shall receive power when the Holy Spirit has come upon you; and you shall be my witnesses," the concluding phrase is frequently repeated.

58. See John 15:27; Acts 1:8.

59. Martensen, *Bispeveielse*, p. 14.

60. *Fædrelandet*, 67, March 20, 1855.

61. See Supplement, p. 547 (*Pap.* XI³ B 134).

62. *Fædrelandet*, 68, March 21, 1855

63. See Matthew 10:32.

64. See Matthew 19:21.

65. See Matthew 11:28.

66. From a children's rhyme. See Evald Tang Kristensen, *Danske Börnerim, Remser og Lege* (Aarhus: 1896), p. 19 (ed. tr.):

Sko min Hest, / hvem kan bedst?
det kan vor Præst, / nej, det kan han ej,
det kan vor Smed / som boer ved vort Led
og ta'r kun to Skilling for 'et

[Shoe my horse / Who can do it best?
Our pastor can / No, he cannot,
Our blacksmith can do it / Who lives near our gate
And takes only two shillings for it].

67. *Fædrelandet*, 69, March 22, 1855.

68. *Fædrelandet*, 72, Monday, March 26, 1855.

69. Vigilius Haufniensis, *The Concept of Anxiety*, pp. 67–68, *KW* VIII (*SV* IV 337).

70. See Supplement, pp. 394–95, 407–08 (*Pap.* VIII^1 A 673; X^2 A 445).

71. See Supplement, pp. 519–21 (*Pap.* XI^3 B 105).

72. *Fædrelandet*, 74, Wednesday, March 28, 1855.

73. *Fædrelandet*, 76, Friday, March 30, 1855.

74. See, for example, *Self-Examination*, pp. 15–17, *KW* XXI (*SV* XII 306–08).

75. See *Postscript*, p. [630], *KW* XII.1 (*SV* VII [549]).

76. With reference to the following paragraph, see Supplement, pp. 451–52 (*Pap.* XI^1 A 7).

77. See Matthew 5:13; Mark 9:49–50.

78. Christoff's song in Ludvig Holberg, *Jacob von Thyboe Eller Den stortalende Soldat*, IV, 6, *Den Danske Skue-Plads*, I–VII (Copenhagen: 1788; *ASKB* 1566–67), III, no pagination.

79. See Luke 18:8.

80. The bishop's gown was made of silk, and the gown of a doctor of theology had velvet panels in the front.

81. See Matthew 11:5.

82. See Matthew 27:6.

83. See Matthew 26:15.

84. Cf., for example, *Fear and Trembling*, pp. 32–33, 37 ("going beyond," "going further"), *KW* VI (*SV* III 84, 88); *Fragments*, p. 111, *KW* VII (*SV* IV 272).

85. An allusion to *mundus vult decipi* (The world wants to be deceived). Attributed to Pope Paul IV but found earlier in Sebastian Brandt, *Das Narrenschiff*. In Danish the line is part of the title of a frequently performed drama by Augustin E. Scribe, *Puf, eller verden vil bedrages*, tr. Nicolai C. L. Abrahams, *Det Kongelige Theaters Repertoire*, 167 (Copenhagen: 1849; *ASKB U* 101). See for example, *Irony*, pp. 253–54, *KW* II (*SV* XIII 328); *Stages*, p. 340, *KW* XI (*SV* VI 318); *JP* V 5937–38; VI 6680 (*Pap.* VII^1 A 147–48; X^3 A 450).

86. *Fædrelandet*, 77, March 31, 1855.

87. See, for example, Rasmus Nielsen, "En god Gjerning," *Fædrelandet*, 8, January 10, 1855: " . . . since my [Kierkegaard's] more stringent proclamation of Christianity is only a commentary on Mynster's more lenient one."

88. See Luke 9:24, 14:26; John 12:25.

89. A reference to Kierkegaard's intention at one time to seek ordination.

90. *Fædrelandet*, 81, April 7, 1855. See N-n., "Forslag til Hr. Dr. S. Kierke-

gaard," *Fædrelandet,* 79, April 3, 1855. See Supplement, pp. 525–28 (*Pap.* XI³ B 117).

91. The second edition of *Practice* appeared May 8, 1855.

92. *Fædrelandet,* 83, April 11, 1855.

93. See note 90 above.

94. With reference to the remainder of the paragraph, see Supplement, pp. 465–66 (*Pap.* XI² A 41).

95. Luke 12:49.

96. The first line in Johann Martin Usteri, "*Freut euch des Lebens,*" tr. Rasmus Frankenau; *Lommebog for lystige Brødre,* 206 (Copenhagen: 1812).

97. See I Peter 2:11.

98. See Shakespeare, *King Henry the Fourth, Part One,* IV, 2, 12–52; *William Shakspeare's tragiske Værker,* I–IX, tr. Peter Foersom and Peter Frederik Wulff (Copenhagen: 1807–25; *ASKB* 1889–96), III, pp. 136–138; *Shakspeare's dramatische Werke,* I–XII, tr. August Wilhelm v. Schlegel and Ludwig Tieck (Berlin: 1839–41; *ASKB* 1883–88), I, pp. 287–88; *The Complete Works of Shakespeare,* ed. George Lyman Kittredge (Boston: Ginn, 1936), p. 571:

> If I be not ashamed of my soldiers, I am a sous'd gurnet. I have misused the King's press damnably. I have got, in exchange of a hundred and fifty soldiers, three hundred and odd pounds. I press me none but good householders, yeomen's sons; inquire me out contracted bachelors, such as had been ask'd twice on the banes—such a commodity of warm slaves as had as lieve hear the devil as a drum; such as fear the report of a caliver worse than a struck fowl or a hurt wild duck. I press'd me none but such toasts-and-butter, with hearts in their bellies no bigger than pins' heads, and they have bought out their services; and now my whole charge consists of ancients, corporals, lieutenants, gentlemen of companies—slaves as ragged as Lazarus in the painted cloth, where the glutton's dogs licked his sores; and such as indeed were never soldiers, but discarded unjust servingmen, younger sons to younger brothers, revolted tapsters, and ostlers trade-fall'n; the cankers of a calm world and a long peace; ten times more dishonourable ragged than an old fac'd ancient; and such have I to fill up the rooms of them that have bought out their services that you would think that I had a hundred and fifty tattered Prodigals lately come from swine-keeping, from eating draff and husks. A mad fellow met me on the way, and told me I had unloaded all the gibbets and press'd the dead bodies. No eye hath seen such scarecrows. I'll not march through Coventry with them, that's flat. Nay, and the villains march wide betwixt the legs, as if they had gyves on; for indeed I had the most of them out of prison. There's but a shirt and a half in all my company; and the half-shirt is two napkins tack'd together and thrown over the shoulders like a herald's coat without sleeves; and the shirt, to say the truth, stol'n from my host at Saint Alban's, or the red-nose innkeeper of Daventry. But that's all one; they'll find linen enough on every hedge.

99. With reference to the following paragraph, see Supplement, p. 528 (*Pap.* XI³ B 229:10).

100. *Fædrelandet*, 83, April 11, 1855 (feuilleton).

101. Johan Ludvig Heiberg, *Alferne*, 2, *J. L. Heibergs samlede Skrifter. Skuespil*, I-VII (Copenhagen: 1833–41; *ASKB* 1553–59), VI, pp. 25–26 (freely quoted).

102. See Supplement, pp. 360–66.

103. See Supplement, pp. 467–69 (*Pap.* XI³ A 201; XI² A 102, 103).

104. *Fædrelandet*, 97, April 27, 1855.

105. See Supplement, pp. 360–66.

106. See note 90.

107. See note 40 above.

108. A double entendre referring to one of Kierkegaard's pseudonyms, Victor Eremita, editor of *Either/Or*, and to one who is victorious.

109. See John 18:36.

110. In *Adresseavisen*, 94, April 24, 1855, there appeared an advertisement signed by Joseph Perlstein and others. A complaint was directed against Rabbi A. A. Wolff, who as a Knight of the Order of the Dannebrog wore the decoration (a cross) of the royal order. The statutes of the order stipulated that those inducted into the order must be adherents of the evangelical Christian religion.

111. See Luke 18:8.

112. *Fædrelandet*, 107, May 10, 1855

113. See Arthur Schopenhauer, "On Ethics," 114; *Parerga und Paralipomena: kleine philosophische Schriften*, I-II (Berlin: 1851; *ASKB* 774–75), II, p. 178; *Parerga and Paralipomena. Short Philosophical Essays*, I-II, tr. E.F.J. Payne (Oxford University Press; 1974), II, p. 211.

114. A red light, as used by merchants, theaters, and others, signified "sold out," "full house," etc.

115. *Fædrelandet*, 107, May 10, 1855 (feuilleton). With reference to the following article, see Supplement, pp. 466–67 (*Pap.* XI² A 75).

116. See Holberg, *Den Ellefte Junii*, III, 6, *Danske Skue-Plads*, II, no pagination. Studenstrup, who had come from the country to Copenhagen, lost his money to a swindler who pledged the Copenhagen city hall as collateral.

117. *Fædrelandet*, 111, May 15, 1855.

118. The pseudonymous author of *Fragments* and *Postscript*.

119. Dr. Frederik Ludvig Bang Zeuthen (1805–1874), pastor in Sorø, Sjælland, who repeatedly wrote against Kierkegaard and was also an opponent of Grundtvig. See, for example, various articles under the title "*Aand og Bogstav*," in *Ugeskrift for den evangeliske Kirke i Danmark*, V, 1855; *Polemiske Blade imod Dr. Søren Kierkegaard*, I-II (Copenhagen: 1855; *ASKB* 2190). See Supplement, pp. 530–35 (*Pap.* XI³ B 142).

120. See Zeuthen, *Beskedenhed og Ydmyghed* (Copenhagen: 1851).

121. According to a rule in the game *Gnavspil*, "the fool moves and takes one with it."

122. See note 40.

123. See *Kjøbenhavnsposten*, 109, May 12, 1855.

124. *Fædrelandet*, 112, May 16, 1855. See note 91 above.

125. *Practice*, pp. 7, 73, 149, *KW* XX (*SV* XII xv, 71, 139).

126. *Ibid.*, pp. 67–68 (64–65).

127. *Ibid.*, p. 7 (xv).

128. See Supplement, pp. 408–10 (*Pap.* X³ A 563).

129. See Supplement, p. 408 (*Pap.* X³ A 563).

130. See Supplement, pp. 485–86, 491 (*Pap.* XI³ B 78, 59, 77).

131. Carl Christian Hall (1812–1888), Danish jurist and politician.

132. *Fædrelandet*, 120, May 26, 1855. See Supplement, pp. 535–41 (*Pap.* XI³ B 120; XI² A 413).

133. See I Peter 3:15.

134. See pp. 3–8.

135. See Supplement, pp. 360–66 (*SV* XIV 11–14).

136. See note 87 above. In his article Rasmus Nielsen proposed that he, but as on Martensen's behalf, make the admission that Kierkegaard had asked for. Upon receiving no reply from Martensen, Nielsen, in an article titled *"Til Høivelbaarne Høiærværdige Biskop Martensen"* (*Fædrelandet*, 13, January 16, 1855), asked whether, in the absence of a reply from Martensen, his view of Kierkegaard's objection as "a good deed" remained standing. In the *Berlingske Tidende*, 15, January 18, 1855, a short article signed X stated that under the circumstances any reply would only throw oil on the fire, and therefore it could be assumed that no reply would be given.

137. See X, *"I Fædrelandet . . . ,"* *Berlingske Tidende*, 15, January 18, 1855.

138. Cf. Mozart, *Don Juan*, tr. Laurids Kruse (Copenhagen: 1807), II, 8, p. 91; *Don Giovanni*, tr. Ellen H. Bleiler (New York: Dover, 1964), II, 3, p. 172.

139. Johannes Climacus. See *Postscript*, pp. 513–14, *KW* XII.1 (*SV* VII 447).

140. Lessing, *Emilia Galotti*, IV, 5; *Gotthold Ephraim Lessing's sämmtliche Schriften*, I-XXXII (Berlin, Stettin: 1825–28, *ASKB* 1747 62), XXI, p. 273; *The Dramatic Works*, ed. Ernest Bell (London: 1878), p. 201.

141. According to folklore, if one has in one's mouth a twig with the bark removed, one becomes invisible.

142. See p. 84. Presumably a reference to an account, favorable to Kierkegaard, in *Christiania-Posten* [Oslo, Norway], 2317–18, 2320, 2323, 2325, 2333, Feb. 19–20, 22, 25, 27, March 7, 1855. An article opposed to Kierkegaard appeared (2335, March 9) and was reprinted in the Copenhagen paper *Flyveposten*, 63, March 15, 1855.

143. In *Fragments* and *Postscript*, Johannes Climacus's critique of theological speculation and Hegelianism is in part directed against Martensen. See also, for example, *JP* VI 6636 (*Pap.* X⁶ B 137); *Pap.* X⁶ B 133–43. Martensen, in his *Dogmatik* (Copenhagen: 1850), p. iii, deprecatingly discusses Kierkegaard's writings without mentioning his name.

144. See Rasmus Nielsen, *Evangelietroen og den moderne Bevidsthed* (Copenhagen: 1849, *ASKB* 700). Although neither Kierkegaard nor Martensen is named, Nielsen, who had been close to Martensen, now appeared for the first time as an adherent of Kierkegaard.

145. See Peter Michael Stilling, *Om den indbildte Forsoning af Tro og Viden med særligt Hensyn til Prof. Martensens Dogmatik* (Copenhagen: 1850; *ASKB* 802).

Although Climacus is mentioned only once, the work is considered influenced by the writings under his name. Stilling, as well as Nielsen, had been close to Martensen for a long time.

146. Presumably Rasmus Nielsen, *Mag. S. Kierkegaards "Johannes Climacus" og Dr. H. Martensens "Christelige Dogmatik"* (Copenhagen: 1849; *ASKB* 701), and *Dr. H. Martensens dogmatiske Oplysninger* (Copenhagen: 1850; *ASKB* 703).

147. Possibly an allusion to Marcus Junius Brutus (85–42 B.C.), who had a contemporary reputation as a Stoic philosopher.

148. William I, Prince of Orange (1533–1584), known as William the Silent.

149. Cf. *Practice*, p. 49, *KW* XX (*SV* XII 47).

150. See p. 50 and note 91 above.

151. See note 87 above. In his article, Nielsen had used the phrase "Christian self-denial."

152. Martensen was forty-five years old when on April 15, 1854, he became Bishop of Sjælland.

153. See Anon., *"Den Kierkegaardske Strid. (Af et Brev),"* *Dagbladet*, 95, April 25, 1855.

154. See note 142 above.

155. See Supplement, pp. 541–48 (*Pap.* XI³ B 128, 129, 131, 132, 134).

THE MOMENT; WHAT CHRIST JUDGES OF OFFICIAL CHRISTIANITY; AND THE CHANGELESSNESS OF GOD

1. See Supplement, pp. 548–49 (*Pap.* XI³ B 248). For Kierkegaard, "the moment" has two meanings: the moment of decision and newness when time and eternity meet (see, for example, *Fragments*, pp. 14–18, *KW* VII [*SV* IV 184–88]) and the ordinary meaning of actual present time.

2. See *Fear and Trembling*, p. 9, *KW* VI, and note 1.

3. See Plato, *Republic*, 347 b–d, 520 a–e; *Platonis quae exstant opera*, I–XI, ed. Friedrich Ast (Leipzig: 1819–32; *ASKB* 1144–54), IV, pp. 48–49, 390–91; *Udvalgte Dialoger af Platon*, I–VIII, tr. Carl Johan Heise (Copenhagen: 1830–59; *ASKB* 1164–67, 1169 [I–VII]), IV, pp. 49–50, V, pp. 155–57; *The Collected Dialogues of Plato*, ed. Edith Hamilton and Huntington Cairns (Princeton: Princeton University Press, 1963), pp. 596–97, 752–53.

4. See Supplement, pp. 458–59 (*Pap.* XI¹ A 275).

5. See pp. 71–78; with reference to the title and the following three paragraphs, see Supplement, p. 486 (*Pap.* XI³ B 64).

6. Cf. Frater Taciturnus, *Stages on Life's Way*, p. 210, *KW* XI (*SV* VI 198).

7. Adam Oehlenschläger, *Palnatoke* (Copenhagen: 1809), V, 2, p. 175.

8. See Historical Introduction, *Corsair Affair*, p. xxx, *KW* XIII.

9. For continuation of the text, see Supplement, pp. 486–87 (*Pap.* XI³ B 66).

10. An expression frequently used by Bishop Mynster for the Sunday service.

11. For a contemplated heading, see Supplement, p. 548 (*Pap.* XI³ B 246:1).

12. With reference to the remainder of the paragraph and the following paragraph, see Supplement, p. 548 (*Pap.* XI³ B 246:2).

13. See note 1 above.
14. See p. 94 and note 8.
15. See, for example, *Eighteen Upbuilding Discourses*, p. 5, *KW* V (*SV* III 11).
16. Cf. Romans 8:17–18; II Corinthians 4:17.
17. An allusion to Socrates. See Plato, *Apology*, 30 d-e; *Opera*, VIII, pp. 130–31; *Dialogues*, pp. 16–17:

> Neither Meletus nor Anytus can do me any harm at all; they would not have the power, because I do not believe that the law of God permits a better man to be harmed by a worse. No doubt my accuser might put me to death or have me banished or deprived of civic rights, but even if he thinks—as he probably does, and others too, I dare say—that these are great calamities, I do not think so. I believe that it is far worse to do what he is doing now, trying to put an innocent man to death. For this reason, gentlemen, so far from pleading on my own behalf, as might be supposed, I am really pleading on yours, to save you from misusing the gift of God by condemning me. If you put me to death, you will not easily find anyone to take my place. It is literally true, even if it sounds rather comical, that God has specially appointed me to this city, as though it were a large thoroughbred horse which because of its great size is inclined to be lazy and needs the stimulation of some stinging fly. It seems to me that God has attached me to this city to perform the office of such a fly, and all day long I never cease to settle here, there, and everywhere, rousing, persuading, reproving every one of you. You will not easily find another like me, gentlemen, and if you take my advice you will spare my life. I suspect, however, that before long you will awake from your drowsing, and in your annoyance you will take Anytus' advice and finish me off with a single slap, and then you will go on sleeping till the end of your days, unless God in his care for you sends someone to take my place.

See also, for example, *Works of Love*, pp. 128–29, *KW* XVI (*SV* IX 124).
18. See Luke 2:1.
19. See Matthew 7:14.
20. See John 18:36.
21. A French word with a Danish ending.
22. Cf. Mark 14:64.
23. See I Peter 2:17.
24. See John 18:36.
25. See Matthew 7:14.
26. See Genesis 30:31–43.
27. See Luke 18:8.
28. See John 19:30.
29. See Ovid, *Remedia amoris, 91; P. Ovidii Nasonis opera quae supersunt*, I–III, ed. A. Richter (Leipzig: 1828; *ASKB* 1265), I, p. 278; *The Remedies for Love*, *Ovid*, I–VI, tr. J. H. Mozley et al. (Loeb, Cambridge: Harvard University Press, 1984–88), II, pp. 184–85.
30. With reference to the following two pages, see Supplement, pp. 454–55 (*Pap.* XI¹ A 107).

31. See I Peter 2:1.
32. See, for example, Hebrews 13:9.
33. See, for example, Colossians 2:18–23.
34. See Matthew 5:48.
35. See Ephesians 6:12.
36. See Matthew 7:14. Cf. p. 120. Here the text has *Trang* (hard); p. 110 has *snever* (narrow).
37. See Matthew 10:22.
38. See John 16:2.
39. See, for example, Matthew 10:28.
40. See John 4:24.
41. For this recurring metaphor, see, for example, *Sickness unto Death*, p. 93, *KW* XIX (*SV* XI 204).
42. Published June 16.
43. Presumably an allusion to the German writer Ludwig Andreas Feuerbach (1804–1872). See, for example, the preface to *Das Wesen des Christenthums* (Leipzig: 1843; *ASKB* 488), pp. iii–xxiii; *The Essence of Christianity*, tr. George Eliot (New York: Harper, 1957), pp. xxxiii–xliv (pp. iii–viii of the original omitted).
44. Cf. Supplement, pp. 364–65.
45. See pp. 73–74.
46. See, for example, Matthew 10:38.
47. See, for example, I Peter 4:13–19.
48. Cf., for example, Matthew 15:14, 23:16; Mark 6:34; Luke 6:39.
49. See Mark 12:38.
50. See Mark 11:17.
51. See Matthew 23:33.
52. See John 2:15.
53. Probably a reference to a character in a children's book by M. K. Traugott Thieme, *Gutmann oder der dänische Kinderfreund* (1798) (in Danish translation, *Godmand eller den danske Børneven*).
54. See Matthew 27:20, 25.
55. See Matthew 10:26.
56. Cf., for example, I Corinthians 4:9–13.
57. Cf. I John 2:15–16.
58. See John 18:36.
59. See Matthew 5:34.
60. See Ludvig Holberg, *Peder Paars* (Copenhagen: 1772; *ASKB* U 67 [*n.d.*]), I, 2, 48, p. 20; *Peder Paars*, tr. Bergliot Stromsoe (Lincoln: University of Nebraska Press, 1962), p. 15. After a shipwreck, Peder Paars finds himself on an island, where he is told that the inhabitants "live like Christians and sustain themselves on wrecks."
61. See pp. 50–52.
62. See *Postscript*, pp. 478–80, *KW* XII.1 (*SV* VII 415–17).
63. Proposals for a new altar book had been made frequently, and from 1834

to 1839 Bishop Mynster had worked out a new proposal, which after considerable controversy came to naught. The various proposals for a new hymnbook, new altar book, and a musical church service were all discussed by the newly established pastoral convention, which both Kierkegaard and Mynster opposed. See p. 354.

64. See I Corinthians 1:23.

65. See, for example, Matthew 10:16–23, 24:9–10; Mark 13:9–13, 14:27.

66. See, for example, I Corinthians 4:9–13.

67. The first line of a song by Carl Søeborg, *Fader Evans Stambog*, ed. Andreas Peter Liunge (Copenhagen: 1824), p. 220. See also *Discourses in Various Spirits*, p. 77, *KW* XV (*SV* VIII 178).

68. Cf. Johan Ludvig Heiberg, *Kong Salomon og Jørgen Hattemager*, 23; *J. L. Heibergs samlede Skrifter, Skuespil*, I-VII (Copenhagen: 1833–41; *ASKB* 1553–59), II, p. 375.

69. Cf. J. L. Heiberg, *Aprilsnarrene eller Intriguen i Skolen*, 29, *Skuespil*, IV, pp. 111–12.

70. See Holberg, *Ulysses von Ithaca, Eller En Tydsk Comoedie*, II, 1, *Den Danske Skue-Plads*, I-VII (Copenhagen: 1788; *ASKB* 1566–67), III, no pagination; *Jeppe of the Hill and Other Comedies*, tr. Gerald S. Argetsinger and Sven H. Rossel (Carbondale, Edwardsdale: Southern Illinois University Press, 1990), p. 211.

71. See Mozart, *Don Juan*, tr. Laurids Kruse (Copenhagen: 1807), I, 9, p. 31. There are no corresponding lines in *Don Giovanni*, tr. Ellen H. Bleiler (New York: Dover, 1964).

72. See Mark 15:34.

73. See, for example, Romans 6:2; Colossians 2:20, 3:3.

74. See, for example, Luke 14:26.

75. See, for example, Matthew 10:17–22.

76. See Galatians 6:7.

77. Cf. I Corinthians 1:23.

78. A combination of the German word *Seelenverkäuferei* and the Dutch word *Zielverkooperie* for the practice of shanghaiing, the forcible and underhanded impressing of sailors for long journeys. See *Repetition*, p. 200, *KW* VI (*SV* III 234).

79. An allusion to Bishop Martensen's pastoral letter, "*Til Geistligheden i Sjællands Stift*," June 6, 1854, p. 3; *Mindre Skrifter og Taler af Biskop Martensen*, ed. Julius Martensen (Copenhagen: 1885), p. 112.

80. See Matthew 19:21.

81. With reference to the remainder of the sentence, see Supplement, p. 558 (*Pap.* XI³ B 278:8).

82. With reference to the following sentence, see Supplement, pp. 558–59 (*Pap.* XI³ B 278:10).

83. See Matthew 5:44.

84. See Jonah 4:5–7.

85. See p. 42 and note 78.

86. See, for example, John 16:20, 33; 17:14; Ephesians 3:1; 4:1; 4:8; 6:20.

87. See I Thessalonians 2:4.

88. See Matthew 12:36; I Peter 4:5.

89. See *Anxiety*, pp. 107–10, *KW* VIII (*SV* IV 376–78); "The Difference between a Genius and an Apostle," *Two Ethical-Religious Essays*, in *Without Authority*, pp. 91–108, *KW* XVIII (*SV* XI 93–109).

90. See Philippians 2:7. See, for example, *Fragments*, pp. 31–34, 55–56, 63–65, 93, 103–04, *KW* VII (*SV* IV 199–201, 221–22, 228–29, 255–56, 266).

91. With reference to the remainder of the paragraph and the following paragraph, see Supplement, pp. 456–457 (*Pap.* XI¹ A 189).

92. Based on the Gospel according to St. John.

93. See Acts 2:41.

94. See Matthew 10:24; John 13:16.

95. See Horace, *Epistles*, I, 10, 24; Q. *Horatii Flacci opera* (Leipzig: 1828; *ASKB* 1248), p. 239 ("*Naturam expellas furca*"); *Horace Satires, Epistles and Ars Poetica*, tr. H. Rushton Fairclough (Loeb, Cambridge: Harvard University Press, 1978), pp. 316–17 ("*Naturam expelles furca*"): "You may drive out Nature with a pitchfork, yet she will ever hurry back, and, ere you know it, will burst through your foolish contempt in triumph."

96. With reference to the following article, see Supplement, pp. 000–00 (*Pap.* XI³ B 102).

97. See I Timothy 6:11; Galatians 5:22.

98. See Bruun Juul Fog (pastor in Mogenstrup and Nestelsø, later Bishop of Sjælland), "Til Hr. Professor Nielsen," *Berlingske Tidende*, 14, January 17, 1855. See also Supplement, pp. 559–60 (*Pap.* XI³ B 102).

99. See pp. 33–34.

100. See, for example, *Fragments*, p. 76, *KW* VII (*SV* IV 240); *Postscript*, pp. 190, 192, *KW* XII.1 (*SV* VII 158, 160); *JP* III 3660–64 (*Pap.* X² A 116; X³ A 28, 740; XI¹ A 33; XI² A 65).

101. See Luke 14:26.

102. See p. 42 and note 78.

103. See Galatians 5:19.

104. See I Peter 2:1.

105. See Galatians 5:26.

106. See I Corinthians 7:9.

107. See Galatians 5:24.

108. See Luke 14:26.

109. See, for example, II Timothy 1:11–14, 2:1–3, 3:12–15.

110. See John 16:20.

111. See Luke 14:26.

112. See Psalm 22:6.

113. See, for example, Matthew 11:6; John 6:60–61. See also *Practice*, pp. 97–144, *KW* XX (*SV* XII 93–134).

114. A German word with a Danish ending.

115. Cf. *Judge for Yourself!*, pp. 135–37, *KW* XXI, (*SV* XII 412–14).

116. See I Corinthians 7:1, 8.
117. With reference to the following paragraph, see Supplement (*Pap.* X⁴ A 566).
118. Cf. Psalm 56:8; Jakob Peter Mynster, *Betragtninger over de christelige Troeslærdomme,* I–II (Copenhagen: 1837; *ASKB* 254–55), II, p. 19.
119. See Mark 14:36.
120. See John 14:6.
121. See Matthew 7:14.
122. With reference to the following three pages, see Supplement, pp. 415–18 (*Pap.* X⁶ B 253, 254).
123. See I Peter 2:9. The Danish *Præst* is usually translated as "pastor," but in this context the terminology of I Peter is followed: "a royal priesthood."
124. An allusion to Hans Lassen Martensen (1808–1884), who was named Royal Chaplain by King Christian VIII in 1845. On Martensen, see, for example, *JP* VI 6636 (*Pap.* X⁶ B 137).
125. See I Corinthians 1:28.
126. See Philippians 2:7.
127. See, for example, Acts 9:16.
128. See I Corinthians 7:7–8.
129. See p. 203 and note 123.
130. Cf. Cicero, *On Divination,* II, 24, 51–52; *M. Tullii Ciceronis opera omnia,* I–IV and index, ed. Johann August Ernesti (Halle: 1756–57; *ASKB* 1224–29), IV, p. 678; *Cicero De senectute, De amicitia, De divinatione,* tr. William Armistead Falconer (Loeb, Cambridge: Harvard University Press, 1979), pp. 429–31:

> But indeed, that was quite a clever remark which Cato made many years ago: "I wonder," said he, "that a soothsayer doesn't laugh when he sees another soothsayer." For how many things predicted by them really come true? If any do come true, then what reason can be advanced why the agreement of the event with the prophecy was not due to chance?

131. See Mark 10:21.
132. See Luke 14:26; John 12:25.
133. Nicolai Frederik Severin Grundtvig (1783–1872), historian, educator, poet, hymn writer, pastor, and politician, the most influential theologian of the religious awakening in nineteenth-century Denmark.
134. In an article in *Flyveposten,* 87, April 16, 1855, by "a layman," Grundtvig was characterized as "a man with a certain apostolic authority." See Supplement, p. 564 (*Pap.* XI³ B 182).
135. Grundtvig was involved in many controversies and movements. For example, in 1826 Grundtvig resigned his pastorate during a controversy (involving Bishop Mynster) over the introduction of his hymnal in the Church. In his *Kirkens Genmæle* (1825), Grundtvig attacked Henrik Nicolai Clausen (1793–1877) as a rationalist and asked him for a retraction or for withdrawal as university professor. Clausen brought suit for injury, and Grundtvig received lifetime censure. In 1838 the censure was lifted, and Grundtvig became pastor

of a congregation in Vartov in central Copenhagen. For many years Grundtvig had worked for the dissolution of parish bonds (*Om Sognebaandets Løsning og Hr. Professor Clausen*, Copenhagen, 1834), and on April 4, 1855, the bonds were dissolved.

136. See p. 78.

137. See Supplement, p. 561 (*Pap.* XI³ B 295:1). Cf. Diogenes Laertius, *Lives of Eminent Philosophers*, II, 31; *Diogenis Laertii de vitis philosophorum*, I–II (Leipzig: 1833; *ASKB* 1109), I, p. 75; *Diogen Laërtses filosofiske Historie*, I–II, tr. Børge Riisbrigh (Copenhagen: 1812; *ASKB* 1110–11), I, p. 70; *Diogenes Laertius*, I–II, tr. R. D. Hicks (Loeb, Cambridge, Harvard University Press, 1979–80), I, pp. 160–61.

138. See Matthew 10:28.

139. See Mark 15:34.

140. Cf. Luke 17:24.

141. See note 113 above.

142. See Luke 14:26.

143. See Supplement, p. 399 (*Pap.* IX A 424).

144. See John 12:25.

145. See, for example, Romans, 10:11.

146. See Matthew 16:18.

147. See, for example, p. 369.

148. See, for example, *Kjøbenhavnsposten*, May 12, 1855: "In the Danish press there has scarcely ever been anything like the arrogance now expressed by Herr Søren Kierkegaard in a series of aphoristic articles."

149. The motto of the notorious Caesar Borgia (1478–1507), soldier and politician, son of Pope Alexander VI.

150. With reference to the following two paragraphs, see Supplement, pp. 404–05 (*Pap.* X² A 143).

151. On the old Gendarmenmarkt in Berlin, there was a theater flanked on either side by a church. Kierkegaard lived on that market square during his visits to Berlin.

152. With reference to the following two pages, see Supplement, pp. 561–63 (*Pap.* XI³ B 124, 125:8).

153. See Shakespeare, *Hamlet*, IV, 3, 17–26; *William Shakspeare's Tragiske Værker*, I–IX, tr. Peter Foersom and Peter Frederik Wulff (Copenhagen: 1807–25; *ASKB* 1889–96), I, p. 153; *Shakspeare's dramatische Werke*, I–XII, tr. August Wilhelm v. Schlegel and Ludwig Tieck (Berlin: 1839–41; *ASKB* 1883–88), VI, p. 97; *The Complete Works of Shakespeare*, ed. George Lyman Kittredge (Boston: Ginn, 1936), p. 1178:

> *King.* Now, Hamlet, where's Polonius?
> *Ham.* At supper.
> *King.* At supper? Where?
> *Ham.* Not where he eats, but where he is eaten. A certain convocation of politic worms are e'en at him. Your worm is your only emperor for diet.

We fat all creatures else to fat us, and we fat ourselves for maggots. Your fat king and your lean beggar is but variable service—two dishes, but to one table. That's the end.

154. Horace, *The Art of Poetry*, 5, *Opera*, p. 274; Loeb, pp. 450–51:

If a painter chose to join a human head to the neck of a horse, and to spread feathers of many a hue over limbs picked up now here now there, so that what at the top is a lovely woman ends below in a black and ugly fish, could you, my friends, if favoured with a private view, refrain from laughing?

155. See Mark 1:9–11.
156. See Romans 6:3; I Corinthians 10:16.
157. A five rix-dollar banknote, worth about $25.00 in 1973 money.
158. See I Timothy 1:10.
159. See Matthew 6:33. Cf. *Judge for Yourself!*, pp. 110–13, *KW* XXI (*SV* XII 391–93).
160. The Danish *from* means "pious."
161. See *Wunderbare Reisen des Freiherrn v. Münchhausen* (Göttingen: 1813), p. 40; Rudolph Erich Raspe, *The Surprising Adventures of Baron Munchhausen* (New York: Crowell, 1902), p. 24.
162. See Holberg, *Den Stundesløse*, I, 11, *Danske Skue-Plads*, V, no pagination; *The Fussy Man, Four Plays by Holberg*, tr. Henry Alexander (Princeton: Princeton University Press, for the American-Scandinavian Foundation, 1946), p. 22.
163. Matthew 19:27.
164. Matthew 6:24–34 on the Fifteenth Sunday after Trinity.
165. Cf. pp. 73, 74.
166. See Horace, *Epistles*, I, 1, 54; *Opera*, p. 225; Loeb, pp. 254–55.
167. Cf. p. 44 and note 84.
168. See pp. 73, 74, 131.
169. See J. L. Heiberg, *Recensenten og Dyret*, 3, *Skuespil*, III, p. 204.
170. See, for example, I Corinthians 7:1, 7–8.
171. See I Corinthians 7:9.
172. See Luke 19:10.
173. See I Corinthians 6:20.
174. See J. H. Wessel, *Stella*, I, VII, *Johan Herman Wessels samtlige Skrivter*, I–II (Copenhagen: 1787), I, pp. 198, 233.
175. John 20:19–31, the text for the first Sunday after Easter, which at the time was the established confirmation Sunday.
176. See Exodus 20:13.
177. See I Corinthians 7:1,7–8.
178. I Corinthians 7:9.
179. Presumably an allusion to a legendary blacksmith (but actually a tobacconist) in Gretna Green, Scotland, who was allowed to perform weddings. Gretna Green was famous as a place of runaway marriages from 1754 until 1856,

when a law was passed requiring one of the partners to marriage to reside in Scotland for at least twenty-one days before the issuance of a license.

180. Diogenes Laertius, "Bias," I, 86; *Vitis*, I, p. 41; Riisbrigh, I, p. 38; Loeb, I, pp. 88–89:

> He was once on a voyage with some impious men; and, when a storm was encountered, even they began to call upon the gods for help. "Peace!" said he, "lest they hear and become aware that you are here in the ship."

181. See Matthew 12:49.

182. See Luke 14:26.

183. Georg Johan Carstensen (1812–1857), publicist, founder of Tivoli, and arranger of outdoor festivities in the Rosenborg castle gardens.

184. A German word with a Danish ending.

185. See Matthew 10:8.

186. See I Peter 2:11.

187. See Supplement, p. 383 (*Pap.* III A 73).

188. See *Two Upbuilding Discourses* (1843), *Eighteen Upbuilding Discourses*, pp. 31–48, *KW* V (*SV* III 35–52).

189. See II and III of *Four Discourses* (1843), *Eighteen Discourses*, pp. 125–58, *KW* V (*SV* IV 24–53).

190. For continuation of the paragraph, see Supplement, p. 602 (*Pap.* XI³ B 291:4).

191. See Plato, *Theaetetus*, 151 b-d; *Opera*, II, pp. 28–31; *Dialogues*, p. 856:

> And now for the upshot of this long discourse of mine. I suspect that, as you yourself believe, your mind is in labor with some thought it has conceived. Accept, then, the ministration of a midwife's son who himself practices his mother's art, and do the best you can to answer the questions I ask. Perhaps when I examine your statement I may judge one or another of them to be an unreal phantom. If I then take the abortion from you and cast it away, do not be savage with me like a woman robbed of her first child. People have often felt like that toward me and been positively ready to bite me for taking away some foolish notion they have conceived. They do not see that I am doing them a kindness. They have not learned that no divinity is ever ill-disposed toward man, nor is such action on my part due to unkindness; it is only that I am not permitted to acquiesce in falsehood and suppress the truth.

See also *Fragments*, pp. 20–21, *KW* VII (*SV* IV 190); *Works of Love*, p. 277, *KW* XVI (*SV* IX 263).

192. The customary reckoning at that time, based on the Old Testament.

193. See Matthew 7:14.

194. See Luke 9:62.

195. On omnipotence and creation, see Supplement, pp. 390–92 (*Pap.* VII¹ A 181).

196. See Hebrews 1:12.

197. See Matthew 10:29.

198. See Luke 1:52.

199. Cf. James 1:17.

200. See II Peter 3:8.

201. See I John 5:19.

202. See Galatians 6:7.

203. See Matthew 12:36.

204. See Psalm 90:10.

205. *Varietas delectet* (change pleases). See, for example, "Author's Prologue" to Book Two, *Phaedri Augusti Liberti Fabularum Aesopiarum Libri V* (Leipzig: 1828), p. 16; *Babrius and Phædrus*, Loeb, pp. 232–33.

206. See Supplement, pp. 413–14 (*Pap.* X⁴ A 297).

207. See pp. 69–70.

208. See John 9:22.

209. See pp. 3–4.

210. Matthew 23:29–33.

211. *Fear and Trembling*, pp. 63–64, *KW* VI (*SV* III 113).

212. The reference is to St. Lawrence (d. 258), who during a persecution of Christians was ordered by the Roman prefect to turn over the treasure of the Church. He assembled the poor, to whom he had distributed the ecclesiastical possessions, and presented them to the prefect, saying, "Here is the treasure of the Church," whereupon he was with great torture executed by fire.

213. See p. 43 and note 80.

214. See *Tausend und eine Nacht*, I–IV, tr. Gustav Weil (Stuttgart, Pforzheim: 1838–41; *ASKB* 1414–17), IV, *Nacht* 765, p. 121; *Arabian Nights*, ed. Joseph Campbell (New York: Viking, 1962), "The Devout Platter-maker and His Wife," p. 397. See Supplement, p. 394 (*Pap.* VIII¹ A 631).

215. See Matthew 8:20.

216. See Luke 10:20.

217. See I Corinthians 15:19.

218. See Exodus 20:7.

219. With reference to the following two pages, see Supplement, pp. 453–54 (*Pap.* XI¹ A 37).

220. Cf., for example, Supplement, pp. 390–92 (*Pap.* VII¹ A 181).

221. Cf. Babrius, 84; *Babrii fabulae Aesopeae*, ed. Otto Crusius (Leipzig: 1897), p. 74; *Babrius and Phaedrus*, tr. Ben Edwin Perry (Loeb, Cambridge: Harvard University Press, 1965), pp. 102–03:

> A gnat settled on the curved horn of a bull. After lingering there for a moment he said with a buzz: "If I'm weighing down your neck and bending it, I'll go away and sit on that poplar tree yonder by the river." Said the bull: "It doesn't matter to me whether you stay or go; I wasn't aware even of your coming."

222. The familiar form of the second person pronoun, used with family members and close friends and in addressing God as father.

223. See *Kjøbenhavnsposten*, 122, May 30, 1855: "Poor miserable Søren."
224. See *Flyveposten*, 122, May 31, 1855.
225. An euphemistic form of "Satan."
226. See p. 79.
227. See Supplement, p. 552 (*Pap.* XI³ B 136).
228. See p. 78.
229. See pp. 73–74.
230. Galatians 6:7.
231. The Danish *Livslede* means "life-weariness" in the ordinary sense, with an admixture of sadness and disgust with life. With reference to the following two pages, see Supplement, p. 610 (*Pap.* XI² A 439).
232. Cf. Matthew 6:21.
233. See Matthew 26:31.
234. Cf. Acts 17:28.
235. See Psalm 22:6.
236. See Matthew 7:13–14.
237. Under the letter C, illustrated by a picture of a crocodile, the caption in commonly used Danish ABC books reads: When the crocodile most piteously weeps, it is most likely to eat people.
238. The origin of the expression is unclear. It may have been formed from the initial letters of *Hierosaluma est perdita* [Jerusalem is lost].
239. *The Moment*, no. 10, in fair copy ready for the press before Kierkegaard's death, November 11, 1855, was first printed in *Søren Kierkegaards Efterladte Papirer*, I-VIII, ed. Hans Peter Barfod and Hermann Gottsched (Copenhagen: 1869–81), VIII, pp. 567–90.
240. Martensen became professor in 1840 and Royal Chaplain in 1845.
241. A card game, originally Spanish (*hombre*, literally, "man").
242. See p. 4.
243. An expression attributed to Marquise de Pompadour (1721–1764) in conversation with Louis XV (1710–1774), a version of a line by an unknown Greek poet quoted, for example, by Cicero, *De finibus bonorum et malorum*, III, 19, 64; *Opera*, IV, pp. 188–89; *Cicero*, I-XXVIII, tr. H. Rackham (Loeb, Cambridge: Harvard University Press, 1983), *De finibus bonorum et malorum*, XVII, pp. 284–85: "And as we feel it wicked and inhuman for men to declare (the saying is usually expressed in a familiar Greek line) that they care not if, when they themselves are dead, the universal conflagration ensues, it is undoubtedly true that we are bound to study the interest of posterity also for its own sake."
244. Two Latin paradigms that are declined differently.
245. See Supplement, pp. 455–56 (*Pap.* XI¹ A 136).
246. See pp. 181 and 239.
247. See Plato, *Sophist*, 223 b; *Opera*, II, pp. 224–25; *Dialogues*, p. 965:

> *Stranger.* Then now, Theaetetus, his art may be traced as a branch of the appropriative, acquisitive family—which hunts animals, living, land, tame animals—which hunts man, privately, for hire, taking money in exchange,

having the semblance of education—and this is termed Sophistry, and is a hunt after young men of wealth and rank—such is the conclusion.

See also Aristotle, *Sophistical Refutations*, 165 a; *Aristoteles graece*, I-II, ed. Immanuel Bekker (Berlin: 1831; *ASKB* 1074–75), I, p. 165; *The Complete Works of Aristotle*, I-II, ed. Jonathan Barnes (rev. Oxford tr., Princeton: Princeton University Press, 1984), I, p. 279:

> Now for some people it is better worth while to seem to be wise, than to be wise without seeming to be (for the art of the sophist is the semblance of wisdom without the reality, and the sophist is one who makes money from an apparent but unreal wisdom); for them, then, it is clearly necessary to seem to accomplish the task of a wise man rather than to accomplish it without seeming to do so.

248. See Plato, *Apology*, 22 d-23 b; *Opera*, VIII, p. 110–13; *Dialogues*, p. 9:

> So I made myself spokesman for the oracle, and asked myself whether I would rather be as I was—neither wise with their wisdom nor stupid with their stupidity—or possess both qualities as they did. I replied through myself to the oracle that it was best for me to be as I was.
>
> The effect of these investigations of mine, gentlemen, has been to arouse against me a great deal of hostility, and hostility of a particularly bitter and persistent kind, which has resulted in various malicious suggestions, including the description of me as a professor of wisdom. This is due to the fact that whenever I succeed in disproving another person's claim to wisdom in a given subject, the bystanders assume that I know everything about that subject myself. But the truth of the matter, gentlemen, is pretty certainly this, that real wisdom is the property of God, and this oracle is his way of telling us that human wisdom has little or no value. It seems to me that he is not referring literally to Socrates, but has merely taken my name as an example, as if he would say to us, The wisest of you men is he who has realized, like Socrates, that in respect of wisdom he is really worthless.

249. Hans Peter Kofoed-Hansen (1813–1893), pastor and writer and in 1854 named Dean of Maria Church in Haderslev.

250. Rasmus Nielsen (1809–1884), professor of philosophy, University of Copenhagen. On his relations with Kierkegaard, see, for example, *Letters, KW* XXV, Letters 253, 257. Among Nielsen's writings were: *Evangelietroen og den moderne Bevidsthed* (Copenhagen: 1849; *ASKB* 700); *Mag. S. Kierkegaards "Johannes Climacus" og Dr. H. Martensens "Christelige Dogmatik"* (Copenhagen: 1849; *ASKB* 701); and *Evangelietroen og Theologien. Tolv Forelæsninger holdte ved Universitetet i Kjøbenhavn i Vinteren 1849–50* (Copenhagen: 1850; *ASKB* 702). For S. K.'s private opinion of Nielsen and his work, see, for example, *Pap*. X^3 A 2; *JP* VI 6607, 6610 (*Pap*. X^3 A 3, 12).

251. Israel Levin (1810–1883), philologist and writer, and for a considerable time Kierkegaard's amanuensis.

252. Jacob Davidsen (1813–1891), journalist and writer, editor of *Flyveposten* at the time.

253. Gottlieb Siesby (1803–1884), shoemaker, journalist, and poet, and an associate of *Flyveposten* at the time.

254. J.P.M. Grüne (1768–1845), editor of *Kjøbenhavnsposten* 1839–59, a paper much opposed to Kierkegaard. Grüne was noted for his ability to hold contrary positions simultaneously.

255. See Mynster (Kts), "*Kirkelig Polemik,*" *Intelligensblade,* ed. Johan Ludvig Heiberg, 41–42, January 1, 1844, p. 112.

256. Virgil, *Aeneid,* VI, 258; *Virgils Æneide,* tr. Johan Henrik Schønheyder (Copenhagen: 1812), p. 263; *Virgil,* I–II, tr. H. Rushton Fairclough (Loeb, Cambridge: Harvard University Press, 1978), I, pp. 524–25. See *Practice,* title page, *KW* XX (*SV* XII xiii).

257. See Matthew 11:28; *Practice,* pp. 5–68, *KW* XX (*SV* XII xiii-65).

258. Kierkegaard was Copenhagen's "greatest peripatetic," as Villads Christensen has called him in *Peripatetikeren Søren Kierkegaard* (Copenhagen: 1965). Andrew Hamilton, in the earliest English account, *Sixteen Months in the Danish Isles,* I-II (London: 1852), II, pp. 268–70, wrote:

> There is a man whom it is impossible to omit in any account of Denmark, but whose place it might be more difficult to fix; I mean Søren Kierkegaard. But as his works have, at all events for the most part, a religious tendency, he may find a place among the theologians. He is a philosophical Christian writer, ever more dwelling, one might almost say harping, on the theme of the human heart. There is no Danish writer more in earnest than he, yet there is no one in whose way stand more things to prevent his becoming popular. He writes at times with an unearthly beauty, but too often with an exaggerated display of logic that disgusts the public. All very well, if he were not a popular author, but it is for this he intends himself.
>
> I have received the highest delight from some of his books. But no one of them could I read *with pleasure* all through. His "Works of Love" has, I suppose, been the most popular, or, perhaps, his "Either—Or," a very singular book. A little thing published during my stay gave me much pleasure, "Sickness unto Death."
>
> Kierkegaard's habits of life are singular enough to lend a (perhaps false) interest to his proceedings. He goes into no company, and sees nobody in his own house, which answers all the ends of an invisible dwelling; I could never learn that anyone had been inside of it. Yet his one great study is human nature; no one knows more people than he. The fact *is he walks about town all day,* and generally in some person's company; only in the evening does he write and read. When walking he is very communicative, and at the same time manages to draw everything out of his companion that is likely to be profitable to himself.
>
> I do not know him. I saw him almost daily in the streets, and when he was alone I often felt much inclined to accost him, but never put it into execu-

tion. I was told his "talk" was very fine. Could I have enjoyed it, without the feeling that I was myself being mercilessly pumped and sifted, I should have liked [it] very much.

259. Presumably Meïr Goldschmidt and *The Corsair.*

260. A large woods, with many deer, north of Copenhagen. The woods and also Dyrehavsbakken were, and still are, favorite areas for outings by Copenhageners.

261. The rix-dollar (worth about $5.00 in 1973 money) contained six marks of sixteen shillings each.

262. By the royal resolution of June 29, 1854, Bishop Martensen was granted a supplement in money to the value of six hundred bushels of barley.

263. Free pastoral assemblies or conventions were held, particularly by Grundtvigians, during the 1830s and on. Peter C. Kierkegaard was a prominent participant. The Danish *Convent* means both "convention" and "convent" or "monastery." The play on "convention beer" and "monastery beer" (thin) is ineluctably lost. See Supplement, p. 583 and notes 230, 231.

SUPPLEMENT

1. Hans Lassen Martensen, *"Prædiken holdt i Christiansborg Slotskirke paa 5te Søndag efter Hellig-Tre Konger, Søndagen før Biskop Dr. Mynsters Jordefærd"* (Copenhagen: 1854), pp. 5–6, 9–10; also in Martensen, *Leilighedstaler* (Copenhagen: 1884), pp. 17–31, esp. 20, 23–24.

2. Hans Lassen Martensen, *"I Anledning af Dr. S. Kierkegaards Artikel i 'Fædrelandet' Nr. 295,"* *Berlingske Tidende,* 302, December 28, 1854.

With reference to the following article, see Supplement, pp. 491–96 (*Pap.* XI³ B 82).

3. Cf. I Corinthians 12:4.

4. In 1806 the rationalist theologian, Peter Outzen Boisen, Bishop of Lolland-Falster, published a proposal for a revision of the worship service. The government established a commission for the development of a new liturgy. In the same year Mynster, then a virtually unknown rural pastor, published a response, with the result that the revision was left in abeyance.

5. See I Corinthians 2:2.

6. See Matthew 7:24–27.

7. See II Corinthians 6:8.

8. See Homer, *Iliad,* II, 211–23; *Homers Iliade,* I-II, tr. Christian Wilster (Copenhagen: 1836), I, pp. 23–24; *Homer The Iliad,* I-II, tr. A. T. Murray (Loeb, Cambridge: Harvard University Press, 1976–78), I, p. 67:

> Now the others sate them down and were stayed in their places, only there still kept chattering on Thersites of measureless speech, whose mind was full of great store of disorderly words, wherewith to utter revilings against the kings, idly, and in no orderly wise, but whatsoever he deemed would raise a laugh among the Argives. Evil-favoured was he beyond all men that came to

Ilios: he was bandy-legged and lame in the one foot, and his two shoulders were rounded, stooping together over his chest, and above them his head was warper, and a scant stubble grew thereon. Hateful was he to Achilles above all, and to Odysseus, for it was they twain that he was wont to revile; but now again with shrill cries he uttered abuse against goodly Agamemnon. With him were the Aohaeans exceeding wroth, and had indignation in their hearts.

9. An allusion particularly to *Fear and Trembling*, pp. 38–50, *KW* VI (*SV* II 89–100).

10. See Heinrich Jacobi, *Allwills Briefsammlung, Friedrich Heinrich Jacobi's Werke* I–VI (Leipzig, 1812–25; *ASKB* 1722–28), p. 205.

11. Cf. Titus 2:12.

12. *Works of Love*, pp. 345–58, *KW* XVI (*SV* IX 327–39).

13. N-n, *Fædrelandet*, 79, April 3, 1855

14. An anonymous article (see note 13 above) and Kierkegaard's reply (p. 56) elicited the following article by J. Victor Bloch, "*I Anledning af Forslaget til Dr. S. Kierkegaard,*" *Fædrelandet*, 94, April 24, 1855.

15. P. 36.

16. P. 40.

17. P. 35.

18. See Matthew 16:18.

19. Ibid.

20. See John 14:19.

21. See Matthew 22:14.

22. See II Timothy 2:19.

23. See Matthew 25:1–13.

24. See pp. 46–49.

25. See I John 4:19.

26. See Augustine, *De gratia et libero arbitrio*, 15; *Sancti Aurelii Augustini hipponensis episcopi operum*, I–XVIII (Bassani: 1797–1807; *ASKB* 117–34), XIV, col. 891–92; *Grace and Free Will, Basic Writings of Saint Augustine*, I–II, ed. Whitney J. Oates (New York: Random House, 1948), I, pp. 745–46.

27. On July 3, 1840, Kierkegaard took the final examination at the University of Copenhagen and on July 19 began a journey of filial piety to Sæding in Jylland, the birthplace and home of his father, Michael Petersen Kierkegaard, until as a young man he left for Copenhagen. On August 6 Kierkegaard returned to Copenhagen. For journal entries on his visits and reflections during the journey, see *JP* VII, p. 111, a listing of *Pap.* III A 15–84 in *JP*.

28. In Danish "churchyard" or "cemetery" is *Kirkegaard*, a term that was also used to designate the two farms (*Gaard*) belonging to the Sæding parish. The family name, with an "e" added, is based on "church farm," *not* on "churchyard" or "cemetery."

29. The wish that the student Kierkegaard would settle down and finish his university work, which he did after his father's death. This is also the "task" referred to later in the paragraph.

30. Cf. *Adler*, pp. 245–47, *KW* XXIV (*Pap.* VII² B 235, pp. 56–59).

31. See "*Von dem Machandelboom*," *Kinder- und Haus-Märchen. Gesammelt durch die Brüder Grimm*, I–III (2 ed., Berlin, 1819–22; *ASKB* 1425–27), no. 47, I, p. 236; "The Juniper Tree," *The Complete Grimm's Fairy Tales*, tr. Margaret Hunt, rev. James Stern (New York: Pantheon, 1972), p. 226.

32. Presumably a reference to the Copenhagen amusement park Tivoli, which was opened in August 1843.

33. Jacob Rasmus Damkjær (1810–1871), appointed pastor in Kjettrup and Gjøttrup in 1835.

34. Announcement of *Kirke Psalmer* (Copenhagen: 1845), *For Literatur og Kritik. Et Fjerdingaarsskrift udg. af Fyens Stifts literære Selskab*, III, 1845, p. 367.

35. Johann Wolfgang v. Goethe, *Faust*, I, 1479–80; *Goethe's Werke. Vollständige Ausgabe letzter Hand*, I–LX (Stuttgart, Tübingen: 1828–42; *ASKB* 1641–68 [I–LV]), XII, p 169; *Faust*, tr. Bayard Taylor (New York: Random House, 1950), p. 62.

36. A game (*Forundringsstolen*; also, but rarely, named *Beundringsstolen*) sometimes called the "wonder stool" or "wonder game," in which one person sits blindfolded on a stool in the middle of a circle while another goes around quietly asking others what they wonder about the person who is "it." Upon being told what others had wondered about him, he tries to guess the source in each instance. See, for example, *Sickness unto Death*, p. 5, *KW* XIX (*SV* XI 117); "To Mr. Orla Lehmann," *Early Polemical Writings*, p. 24, *KW* I (*SV* XIII 28).

37. See *The Concept of Anxiety*, p. 78, *KW* VIII (*SV* IV 347).

38. Goethe, *Egmont*, II.1; *Werke*. VIII, pp. 199–200; *Goethe's Works*, I–IV, tr. Hjalmar H. Boyesen (Philadelphia: George Barrie, 1885), II, p. 202.

39. Ammen Sire in Holberg, *Barselstuen*, III, 5, *Den Danske Skue-Plads*, I–VII (Copenhagen: 1788; *ASKB* 1566–67), II, no pagination.

40. See Holberg, *Peder Paars* (Copenhagen: 1798; *ASKB* U 67 [n.d.]), IV, 1, pp. 308; *Peder Paars*, tr. Berglivt Stromsoe (Lincoln: University of Nebraska and American-Scandinavian Foiundation, 1962), p. 145.

41. Presumably an allusion to Thorkel B. Madvig (1765–1849), *Kritiske Undersøgelser* (Copenhagen: 1845).

42. See Genesis 30:37–42.

43. René Descartes, *A Discourse on Method*, II; *Renati Descartes opera philosophica. Editio ultima* (Amsterdam: 1685; *ASKB* 473 [1678]), p. 7; *A Discourse on Method and Selected Writings*, tr. John Veitch (New York: Dutton, 1951), p. 9:

> I was then in Germany, attracted thither by the wars in that country, which have not yet been brought to a termination; and as I was returning to the army from the coronation of the emperor, the setting in of winter arrested me in a locality where, as I found no society to interest me, and was besides fortunately undisturbed by any cares or passions, I remained the whole day in seclusion, with full opportunity to occupy my attention with my own thoughts. Of these one of the very first that occurred to me was, that there is seldom so much perfection in works composed of many separate parts,

upon which different hands had been employed, as in those completed by a single master. Thus it is observable that the buildings which a single architect has planned and executed, are generally more elegant and commodious than those which several have attempted to improve, by making old walls serve for purposes for which they were not originally built.

44. See, for example, *Sickness unto Death*, pp. 99, 117, 121, *KW* XIX (*SV* XI 210, 227, 231); *Practice*, p. 140, *KW* XX (*SV* XII 130).

45. During the so-called Spjellerup period (1802–10), after earlier years dominated by a mixture of romantic and rationalistic influences, Mynster came to a personal appropriation of historical biblical Christianity. See *JP* VI 6793 (*Pap.* X⁴ A 474).

46. Kierkegaard saw this possibility and hoped for its realization, and in this connection he intended to dedicate *Christian Discourses* (1848) to Bishop Mynster. See *JP* V 6068, 6069; 6112 (*Pap.* VIII² B 116, 118; VIII¹ A 560).

47. *Tausend und eine Nacht*, I–IV, tr. Gustav Weil (Stuttgart, Pforzheim: 1838–41; *ASKB* 1414–17), IV, pp. 99–105, 113–23.

48. Kierkegaard considered this to be the task of Anti-Climacus in *Sickness unto Death* and *Practice*. See also, for example, *Fear and Trembling*, pp. 121–23, *KW* VI (*SV* III 166–68); *JP* VI 6445 (*Pap.* X¹ A 546). *Postscript* was the "hint."

49. In 1848 there were uprisings in many European countries, notably the February Revolution in Paris. There was also political agitation in Denmark. Then in the context of the old Slesvig-Holsten issue, Prince Frederick of Augustenburg put himself at the head of a provisional government proclaimed at Kiel in March 1848. A Danish army subdued the rebels north of the Eider River. A new national assembly of Germany decided to incorporate Slesvig, and a Prussian army under Wrangel drove the Danes back and entered Jutland. On August 26, 1848, an armistice was signed in Malmø and the government of the two duchies was entrusted to a commission composed of two Prussians, two Danes, and a fifth member by common consent of the four. War was renewed between March and July, 1849, and a second armistice was signed between Prussia and Denmark. Germans in the duchies increased their army under General Willesen. The Danes trapped Willesen's army at Idsted on July 23, 1849. In July 1850, Prussia concluded a treaty with Denmark and gave up claim to the duchies. In London, May 8, 1852, the leading European powers signed a treaty concerning the succession after Frederik VII, and there was no further outbreak until his death in 1863. From 1848 on, the financial situation of the country was precarious and inflation rampant.

On March 21, 1848, as the result of earlier events, movements, and an enormous demonstration at Christiansborg, King Frederik VII (King Christian VIII had died January 28, 1848) agreed to the dissolution of the ministries. Thereupon the March government, the Moltke-Hvidt government, was formed and Frederik VII declared that he now regarded himself as a constitutional monarch.

50. Bishop Jakob Peter Mynster was in the highest rank (Grand Cross) of the Order of the Dannebrog.

51. Hans Lassen Martensen, *Den christelige Dogmatik* (Copenhagen: 1849; *ASKB* 653).

52. Matthew 11:28. See also *Practice*, pp. 3–68, *KW* XX (*SV* XII xi-65).

53. Just Henrik Voltenen Paulli (1809–1865), church leader, writer, and from 1837 pastor of Christiansborg Slotskirke.

54. *Practice*, pp. 233–34, *KW* XX (*SV* XII 213–14).

55. See pp. 263–81.

56. The source is given in *Pap.* X⁴ A 237 as August Petersen, *Die Idee der christlichen Kirke*, I-III (Leipzig: 1839–46; *ASKB* 717–19), III, p. 420 fn.

57. Ludvig Holberg, *Ulysses von Ithaca*, III, 2, *Danske Skue-Plads*, I-VII, III, no pagination.

58. Danish *Mundharpe*, literally, "mouth harp."

59. Cf. Isaiah 3:4; Ecclesiastes 10:16.

60. "A First and Last Explanation," *Postscript*, p. [629], *KW* XII.1 (*SV* VII [548]). The reference there to Kts is to Bishop Jakob Peter Mynster (the initial consonants of the second syllables of his names).

61. "An Occasional Discourse," *Discourses in Various Spirits*, pp. 3–154, *KW* XV (*SV* VIII 115–242).

62. Jakob Peter Mynster, *Yderlige Bidrag til Forhandlingerne om de kirkelige Forhold i Danmark* (Copenhagen: 1851). On p. 44 Mynster places Goldschmidt and Kierkegaard together:

> Among the gratifying *phonomena*—we borrow this word from one of our most talented authors—to appear during these discussions is the resonance accorded a voice recently raised against "a belief etc."

See *JP* 6748 (*Pap.* X⁶ B 171) and note 2967.

63. Michael Pedersen Kierkegaard read Mynster's sermons regularly, and his son Søren appreciatively continued this practice. See, for example, *JP* VI 6749 (*Pap.* X⁶ B 173). Twenty-two volumes of Mynster's sermons and other writings are listed in *ASKB*.

64. See *JP* V 6069 (*Pap.* VIII² B 118).

65. Jakob Peter Mynster, *Betragtninger over de christelige Troeslærdomme*, I-II (Copenhagen: 1837; *ASKB* 254–55), II, 19.

66. See Supplement, pp. 392, 437, 506 (*Pap.* VIII¹ A 332; XI³ B 15, 99, p. 157).

67. Jakob Peter Mynster, Bishop of Sjælland.

68. See *Practice*, pp. 7, 73, 149, *KW* XX (*SV* XII xv, 71, 139).

69. J. P. Mynster, *Yderlige Bidrag*. See *JP* VI 6748, 6749, 6750, 6751 (*Pap.* X⁶ B 171, 173, 188, 194). See note 62 above.

70. Hans Lassen Martensen.

71. See note 173 below.

72. See note 69 above.

73. Second Christmas Day 1853 in Slotskirke.

74. Ernst Wilhelm Kolthoff (1809–1890), associated with Helligaands Church, Copenhagen, 1845 to 1880.

75. Presumably *Practice*, pp. 233–38, *KW* XX (*SV* XII 213–17).
76. See note 49 above.
77. "An Open Letter Prompted by a Reference to Me by Dr. Rudelbach," in Corsair *Affair*, pp. 50–59, *KW* XIII (*SV* XIII 436–44).
78. See note 62 above.
79. *Berlingske Tidende*, 25, January 30, 1854. See *JP* VI 6967 (*Pap.* XI^2 A 437).
80. Kts (Mynster), "*Kirkelige Polemik*," *Intelligensblade*, IV, 41, Jan. 1, 1844, pp. 111–12.
81. Meïr Goldschmidt, editor of *Corsaren*. On Kierkegaard and Goldschmidt, see Corsair *Affair*, pp. xiii–xxi, especially pp. xviii–xx.
82. A play on *Mønster* (model) and the name of Mynster the bishop.
83. Philosopher Poul Martin Møller (1794–1838). Kierkegaard's favorite professor at the University of Copenhagen.
84. Frederik Christian Sibbern (1785–1872), professor of philosophy, University of Copenhagen, 1813 to 1870.
85. Matthew 16:23.
86. See John 8:48.
87. An allusion to Pierre Joseph Proudhon (1809–1865). See Alfred Südre, *Communismens Historie*, tr. Carl Ebeling and Johannes Beyer (Copenhagen: 1851), pp. 349, 373.
88. Mozart, *Don Juan*, tr. Laurids Kruse (Copenhagen: 1807), I, 11, p. 36. The corresponding lines are not found in *Don Giovanni*, tr. Ellen H. Bleiler (New York: Dover, 1964).
89. Jens Baggesen, "*Min Gienganger-Spøg, eller den søde Kniv*," *Jens Baggesens danske Værke*, I-XII (Copenhagen: 1827–32; *ASKB* 1509–20), VI, p. 144.
90. See p. 359.
91. See note 82 above.
92. *Either/Or*, I, pp. 42–43, *KW* III (*SV* I 27).
93. See, for example, *Self-Examination*, p. 21, *KW* XXI (*SV* XII 312).
94. See pp. 3–8.
95. See, for example, *Postscript*, pp. [625–26], *KW* XII.1 (*SV* VII [546]); *Self-Examination*, pp. 3, 17, 18, 21, 22, *KW* XXI (*SV* XII 295, 308, 309, 312); *On My Work as an Author*, in *The Point of View*, *KW* XXII (*SV* XIII 507).
96. See p. 94 and note 8.
97. See note 93 above.
98. See p. 93.
99. *Pap.* XI^3 B 71, essentially the same as p. 212, fn.
100. See pp. 360–66.
101. See p. 9 and note 20.
102. See pp. 3–8.
103. See p. 80 and note 138.
104. See p. 18 and note 44.
105. See, for example, *For Self-Examination*, pp. 17–24, *KW* XXI (*SV* XII 308–14).

106. See *Works of Love*, pp. 345–58, *KW* XVI (*SV* IX 327–39).

107. See note 53 above.

108. See p. 7 and note 15.

109. See pp. 361 62.

110. See pp. 36, 477 and note 95. See also, for example, *Self-Examination*, pp. 21, 24, *KW* XXI (*SV* XII 312, 314).

111. See p. 3 and note 3; *JP* VI 6874 (*Pap.* XI¹ A 142).

112. Petronius, *Satires*, 55, 113; *Satyricon*, tr. Michael Heselfine (Loeb, Cambridge: Harvard University Press, 1969), pp. 114–15.

113. See pp. 3–8.

114. See pp. 360–66.

115. See Ludvig Holberg, *Den Pantsatte Bonde-Dreng*, I, 3; *Danske Skue-Plads*, I–VII, IV, no pagination; *The Peasant in Pawn, Seven One-Act Plays by Holberg*, tr. Henry Alexander (Princeton: Princeton University Press, 1950), p. 141.

116. Cf. p. 366.

117. See p. 362.

118. Ibid.

119. J. H. Wessel, *Kierlighed uden Strømper*, IV, 3; *Johan Herman Wessels samtlige Skrivter*, I–II (Copenhagen: 1787), I, p. 59.

120. See, for example, Matthew 10:38; Mark 2:14.

121. See John 18:36.

122. See p. 359.

123. See p. 7.

124. See Corsair *Affair*, *KW* XIII.

125. See "The Activity of a Traveling Esthetician and How He Still Happened to Pay For the Dinner," Corsair *Affair*, p. 46, *KW* XIII (*SV* XIII 431).

126. Ibid.

127. See p. 8.

128. See *Postscript*, p. 622, *KW* XII.1 (*SV* VII 542).

129. See Supplement, p. 392 (*Pap.* VIII¹ A 332).

130. See pp. 359–60.

131. See p. 4 and note 11.

132. See Luke 12:20.

133. Louis Philippe (1773–1850), king of France 1830 to 1848, whose method was conciliation and appeasement. His method failed, and in 1848 he abdicated and fled to England.

134. *Either/Or*, II, p. 89, *KW* IV (*SV* II 81), freely quoted.

135. See p. 16 and note 39.

136. See pp. 3–8.

137. See p. 14 and note 32.

138. *Kjøbenhavnsposten*, 120, May 26, 1855.

139. See, for example, p. 73; the prefaces to the discourses in *Eighteen Upbuilding Discourses*, pp. 5, 53, 107, 179, 231, 295, *KW* V (*SV* III 11, 271; IV

7, 73, 121; V 79); *On My Work*, in *Point of View*, *KW* XXII (*SV* XIII 501); *For Self-Examination*, p. 3, *KW* XXI (*SV* XII 295).

140. Luke 12.48.

141. See, for example, Historical Introduction, *Corsair Affair*, pp. xxx–xxxi, *KW* XIII; *JP* V 6088 (*Pap.* VIII¹ A 458); *Pap.* X¹ A 254.

142. P. 25.

143. Pp. 360–66.

144. Rasmus Nielsen, *Mag. S. Kierkegaards "Johannes Climacus" og Dr. H. Martensens "Christelige Dogmatik"* (Copenhagen: 1849; *ASKB* 701).

145. Pp. 3–6.

146. See Supplement p. 491 (*Pap.* XI³ B 82).

147. Pp. 3–8.

148. Martensen, *Bispevielse i Frue Kirke paa anden Juledag, den 26de December, 1854* (Copenhagen: 1855), p. 16.

149. I Peter 3:15.

150. See Callicles' complaint in Plato, *Gorgias*, 490 e–491 b; *Platonis quae exstant opera*, I–XI, ed. Friedrich Ast (Leipzig: 1819–32; *ASKB* 1144–54), I, pp. 372–73; *Udvalgte Dialoger af Platon*, I–VIII, tr. Carl Johan Heise (Copenhagen: 1830–59; *ASKB* 1164–67, 1169 [I–VII]), pp. 111–12; *The Collected Dialogues of Plato*, ed. Edith Hamilton and Huntington Cairns (Princeton: Princeton University Press, 1963), p. 273:

> CALLICLES: How you keep saying the same things, Socrates!
>
> SOCRATES: Not only that, Callicles, but about the same matters. . . . You see, my good Callicles, that you do not find the same fault with me as I with you. For you claim that I keep saying the same things, and reproach me with it, but I make the opposite statement of you, that you never say the same things about the same subjects.

151. Mynster, *Betragtninger over de christelige Troeslærdomme*, I–II.

152. See p. 16 and note 38.

153. See p. 51 and note 93.

154. See Supplement, pp. 541–48 (*Pap.* XI³ B 128, 129, 131, 132, 134).

155. See Supplement, pp. 525–28 (*Pap.* XI³ B 117).

156. See p. 46.

157. See pp. 56–59.

158. See Supplement, pp. 367–71.

159. See p. 3.

160. See p. 73.

161. See pp. 93–94.

162. See Supplement, p. 369.

163. See p. 67 and note 119.

164. *Ugeskrift for den evangeliske Kirke i Danmark*, V, 1855, especially pp. 181–82, 351.

165. See pp. 66–68.

166. See p. 67 and note 120.

167. The publication of Frederik L. B. Zeuthen, *Polemiske Blade imod Dr. Søren Kierkegaard*, I, was announced June 14, 1855.

168. Ibid., p. 1. See II Corinthians 13:8.

169. Zeuthen, *Polemiske Blade*, I, p. 9.

170. See *Either/Or*, I, p. 43, *KW* III (*SV* I 27).

171. See pp. 16–17 and note 39.

172. *Fædrelandet.*

173. See Luther, sermon on Acts 6:8–14, Second Christmas Day (St. Stephen's Day), *En christelig Postille, sammendragen af Dr. Morten Luthers Kirke- og Huuspostiller*, I–II, tr. Jørgen Thisted (Copenhagen: 1828; *ASKB* 283), II, p. 66; *Dr. Martin Luther's Church-Postil. Sermons on the Epistles*, I-III, tr. Ambrose Henkel, J. R. Moser, and W. Wetzel (New Market, Va.: New Market Evangelical Lutheran Publishing Co., 1869), I, pp. 102–03. See Supplement, p. 434 (*Pap.* XI² A 289); *For Self-Examination*, p. 19, *KW* XXI (*SV* XII 309); *JP* I 653; VI 6150 (*Pap.* VIII² B 85:18; IX A 39).

174. Professor Rasmus Nielsen. See pp. 46, 80, 81, 82 and notes 87, 136, 144, 151.

175. Jens Finsteen Gi[j]ødvad (1811–1891), editor of *Kjøbenhavnsposten* from April 1, 1837. He had been the middleman between Kierkegaard and the printer and bookseller of the pseudonymous works.

176. See pp. 3–8.

177. *Fyens Avis*, 124, May 30, 1855.

178. See *Either/Or*, II, p. 84, *KW* IV (*SV* II 77); *JP* V 5403 (*Pap.* II A 520); *Kierkegaard: Letters and Documents*, Letter 54, *KW* XXV.

179. The plan for a volume of the articles in *Fædrelandet* was not carried out. In 1857 the articles were included in a comprehensive volume titled *S. Kierkegaard's Bladartikler*, edited by Rasmus Nielsen.

180. See p. 81 and notes 147, 148.

181. See note 115 above.

182. See Supplement, p. 366.

183. See Arthur Schopenhauer, "*Preisschrift über die Grundlage der Moral,*" 13, *Die beiden Grundprobleme der Ethik* (Frankfurt/M: 1841; *ASKB* 772), p. 196.

184. See pp. 3–18.

185. See p. 28; Mark 13:2.

186. For numbers II and III, see Supplement, pp. 552–58 (*Pap.* XI³ B 136, 115).

187. See, for example, *JP* VI 6255–57 (*Pap.* IX B 63:7; X⁶ B 40, 41).

188. See note 49 above.

189. For numbers I and III, see Supplement, pp. 549–51, 555–58 (*Pap.* XI³ B 126, 115).

190. *Fædrelandet*, 8, January 10, 1855. See p. 79 and note 136, and p. 82.

191. See Plato, *Phaedo*, 115 c–118; *Opera*, I, pp. 612–19; Heise, I, pp. 119–25; *Dialogues*, pp. 95–98.

192. See pp. 76–77.

193. Ludvig Holberg, *Erasmus Montanus eller Rasmus Berg*, I, 4; *Den Danske Skue-Plads*, V, no pagination; *Comedies by Holberg*, tr. Oscar James Campbell and Frederic Schenck (New York: American-Scandinavian Foundation, 1935), p. 127.

194. For numbers I and II, see Supplement pp. 549–55 (*Pap.* XI³ B 126, 136).

195. See *JP* III 2773 (*Pap.* XI² A 363).

196. The amusement park in the center of Copenhagen. Founded in 1843 by Georg Carstensen, it gradually became and still is an international attraction.

197. Cf. *Postscript*, pp. 186–87, *KW* XII.1 (*SV* VII 155).

198. See p. 183 and note 98.

199. Holberg, *Erasmus Montanus*, I, 3; *Danske Skue-Plads*, V, no pagination; cf. *Comedies*, p. 124.

200. See p. 211; *Pap.* XI³ B 247, draft of a subscription plan. See also Supplement, pp. 548–49 (*Pap.* XI³ B 246:1–2, 248).

201. See Supplement, p. 490 (*Pap.* XI³ B 70).

202. *Flyveposten*, 87, April 16, 1855.

203. From 1666 an old hospital foundation for the poor and aged, in what is now the center of Copenhagen between Farvegade, Løngangstræde, and Vestervold. It had its own church, of which Nicolai Frederik Severin Grundtvig (1783–1872) was pastor from 1839 to 1872.

204. See p. 12.

205. Danish: *Snak*. Presumably an allusion to Grundtvig, *Brage-Snak om Græske og Nordiske Myther og Oldsagn for Damer og Herrer* (Copenhagen: 1844; *ASKB* 1548). *Brage-Snak* is a version of an Old Norse expression meaning "the conversations of Brage" (in Norse mythology, Brage was the god of rhetoric) and was first used by Grundtvig. Later it came to be a pejorative expression denoting unclear emotional outpourings and particularly the Grundtvigian manner of speaking the jargon of Grundtvig's adherents.

206. See, for example, *Self-Examination*, pp. 17–24, *KW* XXI (*SV* XII 308–14).

207. See p. 16 and note 40.

208. Augustin-Eugène Scribe, *Kammeraterne*, tr. anon., *Det Kongelige Theaters Repertoire* (Copenhagen: 1848), p. 10; *La Camaraderie ou La Courte-Echelle*, I, 8 (Boston: 1920), p. 38.

209. See p. 12.

210. See Supplement, pp. 575–76 (*Pap.* XI³ B 189).

211. A bridge between Copenhagen on Sjælland and Christianshavn on Amager.

212. See note 205 above.

213. See Matthew 5:13.

214. Grundtvig in his *Kirkens Gjenmæle mod Professor Theologiae Dr. H. N. Clausen* (Copenhagen: 1825) made a strong attack on Henrik Nikolai Clausen after the publication of his *Catholicismens og Protestantismens Kirkeforfatning, Lære og Ritus* (Copenhagen: 1825; *ASKB* AI 42). Clausen brought legal action and

won the case. For five years Grundtvig's adherents, especially Jacob Christian Lindberg, continued attacks on Clausen.

215. Holberg, *Det lykkelige Skibbrud*, III, 6, *Danske Skue-Plads*, IV, no pagination.

216. See repr., *Dansk Kirketidende*, 20, May 6, 1855, col. 316–17.

217. See pp. 575–76.

218. See p. 67.

219. See Supplement, p. 532 (*Pap.* XI³ B 142).

220. Schøller Parelius Vilhelm Birkedal (1809–1892), pastor in Ryslinge on Fyn and an adherent of Grundtvig.

221. *Dansk Kirketidende*, 36, August 26, 1855.

222. The familiar singular second person pronoun *du* is used for family members and close friends and in addressing God.

223. Cf. p. 121.

224. See pp. 60–61.

225. See Matthew 22:37; Mark 12:30; Luke 10:27.

226. Matthew 16:23.

227. See Supplement, pp. 563–68 (*Pap.* XI³ B 182).

228. See Supplement, pp. 568–75 (*Pap.* XI³ B 188).

229. Peter Christian Kierkegaard (1805–1888) was pastor in Sorø until, with Bishop Martensen's backing, he was named Bishop of Aalborg. He was one of the most prominent adherents of Grundtvig. The Licentiate degree corresponds approximately to American degrees such as Bachelor of Divinity, Bachelor of Law, etc.

230. The first so-called Roskilde Convention of pastors was held in the cathedral city of Roskilde, October 30, 1849. At this meeting Peter Christian Kierkegaard gave an address. See *JP* VI 6550, 6553, 6554, 6557–60 (*Pap.* X² A 256, 273, 275, 280; X⁶ B 130, 131; Letter 240). Six years later, on July 5, 1855, again in Roskilde, three months before Søren Kierkegaard died, Peter Kierkegaard gave another address, under the title "Remarks on the Famous Pseudonyms of the Day and the Theology of Their Author," in which Peter discussed the "misgivings I, for my part, have long entertained against the theology, or what could better be called the non-theology, that an academy of pseudonyms has developed these last years in the literature of our fatherland." (Otto Holmgaard, *Exstaticus* [Copenhagen: 1867], p. 57.) This second Roskilde Convention address was the occasion of the rift between the brothers during the last days of Kierkegaard's life.

231. See p. 354. Convent-beer was a thin beer for the monastic brothers as distinguished from the stronger beer served to the priests.

232. See Corsair *Affair*, especially pp. xix-xxi, xxx-xxxi, 105–37, *KW* XIII.

233. See note 230 above.

234. See p. 316 and note 231.

235. Drafts of the four parts of the projected publication were written August 20-September 17, 1855, but they were not completed and used in *The Moment* or published as a collection.

236. See I Corinthians 11:28–30.
237. See p. 81.
238. *Dansk Kirketidende*, August 5, 12, 19, 1855, col. 545–47, 561–63, 588–93.
239. *Ugeskrift for den evangeliske Kirke i Danmark*, August 17, 1855, p. 84.
240. Holberg, *Den Stundesløse*, I, 1, *Danske Skue-Plads*, III, no pagination.
241. *Dansk Kirketidende*, August 19, 1855, col. 588.
242. Ibid., col. 591. In col. 592 it is reported that Peter Christian Kierkegaard gave an address that will be printed later.
243. *Ugeskrift for den evangeliske Kirke i Danmark*, September 14, 1855, p. 164.
244. Cand. theol. Jens Mathias Lind Hi(j)ort, cand. theol. 1848.
245. Peder Hjort (1793–1871), Lektor in Københavns Cathedralskole, retired 1849 with title of Professor.
246. Niels Schørring Hi(j)ort, cand. theol. 1821.
247. See Mozart, *Don Juan*, tr. Laurids Kruse, I, 16, p. 52; *Don Giovanni*, tr. Ellen H. Bleiler, I, 3, p. 104. See *JP* IV 3835 (*Pap.* XI¹ A 440).
248. See p. 77
249. See Supplement, p. 532 (*Pap.* XI³ B 142).
250. See Supplement, p. 532 and note 168.
251. See Supplement, p. 592 (*Pap.* XI³ B 166).
252. See p. 78.
253. Holberg, *Den politiske Kandestøber*, II, 3; *Danske Skue-Plads*, I, no pagination; *Jeppe of the Hill and Other Comedies*, tr. Gerald S. Argetsinger and Sven H. Rossel (Carbondale: Southern Illinois University Press, 1990), p. 18.
254. I Corinthians 7:9.
255. This entry of September 25, 1855, written on loose sheets, is Kierkegaard's last piece of writing. On September 3, 1855, the discourse *The Changelessness of God* was published. No. 8 and no. 9 of *The Moment* appeared on September 11 and September 24, 1855. No. 10 was published posthumously.
256. See p. 316 and note 231.

BIBLIOGRAPHICAL NOTE

For general bibliographies of Kierkegaard studies, see:

Jens Himmelstrup, *Søren Kierkegaard International Bibliografi*. Copenhagen: Nyt Nordisk Forlag Arnold Busck, 1962.

International Kierkegaard Newsletter, ed. Julia Watkin. Launceton, Tasmania, Australia, 1979-.

Aage Jørgensen, *Søren Kierkegaard-litteratur 1961–1970*. Aarhus: Akademisk Boghandel, 1971. *Søren Kierkegaard-litteratur 1971–1980*. Aarhus: privately published, 1983.

Kierkegaard: A Collection of Critical Essays, ed. Josiah Thompson. New York: Doubleday (Anchor Books), 1972.

Kierkegaardiana, XII, 1982; XIII, 1984; XIV, 1988; XVI, 1993; XVII, 1994, XVIII, 1996.

Bruce H. Kirmmse, *Kierkegaard in Golden Age Denmark*. Bloomington: Indiana University Press, 1990.

François H. Lapointe, *Sören Kierkegaard and His Critics: An International Bibliography of Criticism*. Westport, Connecticut: Greenwood Press, 1980.

Søren Kierkegaard's Journals and Papers, I, ed. and tr. Howard V. Hong and Edna H. Hong, assisted by Gregor Malantschuk. Bloomington, Indiana: Indiana University Press, 1967.

For topical bibliographies of Kierkegaard studies, see *Søren Kierkegaard's Journals and Papers*, I-IV, 1967–75.

INDEX

abolition: of Christianity, 160–61, 188, 237–42; of imitation, 412
Abraham: and Isaac, xx
accommodation: cultural, ix, xvi, 168; and Martensen, 403
account, unsettled, 81
actor(s), 404–05; and pastor, 349
actuality: and poet-relation, 226
adage, 314
admiration: object of, 301–02
admission, xxiii–xxiv, xxix, 39, 623; and Christendom, xxiii–xxiv; and Mynster, xxv–xxvii, 15, 28, 434–35, 439, 599; need for, 412; and reform, xxiii–xxiv
Adresseavisen, 628
"Æskelup," 14
age: of movement, 384–85
alarm ringing. *See* analogy
all: logic of, 187
"also," 462, 478
altar book: and Mynster, 633; new, 158, 632
Amagerport, 448
analogy: alarm ringing, 51; beast, 93; bow and arrow, 488; boys, 79; building, 183; butter, 560; chest of drawers, 53; cinnamon, 422; civic guard, 595; clock, 458; clothing, 162; coats in running, 476; color, 422; counterfeiting, 165–66, 463; cuckold, 259–60; cuttlefish, 460; Deer Park, 348; dogs on two legs, 182; eagle, 93; eating, 159; emetic, 99; filtering, 219; fire, 51; fire chief, 217–20; fishing, 227–28; fishing with net, 561–63; fruit, 572; garment, 271; guitar, 130; horse, 393; hospital, 157; housecleaning, 512–13; in-

cognito king, 112–13; kayak, 540; kite, 260; knotting of thread, 126; large banknote, 351–52; lemonade, 332; ludicrous threat, 121; merchant, 61; military officer, 513–14; money, 325; mountain, 273; musical composition, 178; nuts, 222; peasant boy, 501, 545; poet and ideal of love, 38; possession of inheritance, 336–37; price of spices, xxi; private and general, 462; royal poets, 153; sale of building, 64–65; sale of courthouse, 466–67; saloon-keeper, 36; sand, 467; seamen, 41; secrecy, 571; servant, 426; ship, 510–12; skunk, 460; smothering, 158; spring, 280; sterling and silver plate, 480; strawberries, 604; suicide, 571; swimming, 468–69; temperance society and clergy, 125; thunderstorm, 204, 416, 418; wine, 581
Andersen, Hans Christian: *Only a Fiddler*, ix
anonymity, 450–51; Kierkegaard on, 526–28, 592–94, 596–97
anonymous author, 50
anonymous writer: *"Den Kierkegaardske Strid. (Af et Brev),"* 630; "Søren Kierkegaard," 624; X, 629
aphorisms, 415–18
apostle: authority of, 407–08; Grundtvig as, 563–68, 582; as prototype, 423–24
Arabian Nights, 639
Archimedean point, xii, xiv, xxx
Aristotle: *Sophistical Refutation*, 641
assurances: religious, 194

ADVISORY BOARD

KIERKEGAARD'S WRITINGS

Howard V. Hong, General Editor, *St. Olaf College*, 1972–
Robert L. Perkins, *University of South Alabama*, 1972–76.
Niels Thulstrup, *University of Copenhagen*, 1972–76.
Gregor Malantschuk, *University of Copenhagen*, 1977–78.
John W. Elrod, *Iowa State University*, 1977–85.
Per Lønning, *Bergen, Norway*, 1977–
Sophia Scopetéa, *University of Copenhagen*, 1978–
Wim R. Scholtens, *Boxmeer, Holland*, 1986–